Legal Aspects of Nursing

We work with leading authors to develop the
strongest educational materials in law, bringing
cutting-edge thinking and best learning practice
to a global market.

Under a range of well-known imprints, including
Longman, we craft high quality print and
electronic publications which help
readers to understand and apply their content,
whether studying or at work.

To find out more about the complete range of our
publishing, please visit us on the World Wide Web at:
www.pearsoneduc.com

Legal Aspects of Nursing

Third edition

Bridgit Dimond MA LLB D.S.A. A.H.S.M.

Barrister-at-Law

Emeritus Professor University of Glamorgan

Longman

An imprint of **Pearson Education**

Harlow, England · London · New York · Reading, Massachusetts · San Francisco · Toronto · Don Mills, Ontario · Sydney
Tokyo · Singapore · Hong Kong · Seoul · Taipei · Cape Town · Madrid · Mexico City · Amsterdam · Munich · Paris · Milan

Pearson Education Limited
Edinburgh Gate
Harlow
Essex CM20 2JE
England

and Associated Companies throughout the world

Visit us on the World Wide Web at:
www.pearsoneduc.com

First published 1990
Third edition published 2002

© Prentice Hall Europe 1990, 1995
© B Dimond 2002

ISBN 0–582–42359–7 PPR

British Library Cataloguing-in-Publication Data
A catalogue record for this book is available from the British Library

Set in 10/12^{1}/$_{2}$pt Sabon Roman by 35
Printed by Ashford Colour Press, Gosport

10 9 8 7 6 5 4 3
06 05 04 03 02

To Clare and Bec

Contents

List of figures and tables

Figures

Tables

Table of cases

Table of statutes

Abbreviations

The health services are awash with abbreviations and jargon. It would, however, be immeasurably tedious and unrealistic to ignore these and always use the full words. Some of the most commonly used abbreviations are therefore set out here. Where there is any possibility of confusion, words are spelt out in full.

ABI	Association of British Insurers
ABPI	Association of the British Pharmaceutical Industry
ACAS	Advisory, Conciliation and Arbitration Service
ACGT	Advisory Committee on Genetic Testing
A & E	Accident and emergency department
AID	Artificial insemination by donor
AIDS	Acquired immune deficiency syndrome
AIH	Artificial insemination by husband
AIP	Artificial insemination by partner
ARC	Aids-related complex
ASW	Approved Social Worker
BID	Brought in dead
BMA	British Medical Association
BMJ	*British Medical Journal*
BNF	British National Formulary
BP	Blood pressure
CAB	Citizens Advice Bureau
CAM	Complementary and Alternative Medicines
CCETSW	Central Council for Education and Training in Social Work
CESDI	Confidential Enquiry into Stillbirths and Deaths in Infancy
CESU	Clinical Effectiveness Support Unit
CHC	Community Health Council
CHI	Commission for Health Improvement
CICA	Criminal Injuries Compensation Authority
CNST	Clinical negligence scheme for trusts
COSHH	Control of Substances Hazardous to Health (Regulations)
CPN	Community psychiatric nurse
CPR	Cardio Pulmonary Resuscitation
CPS	Crown Prosecution Service
CSAG	Clinical Standards Advisory Group
CSSD	Central sterile supply department
D and C	Dilation and curettage

	DHA	District health authority
	DHSS	Department of Health and Social Security, divided in 1989 into
	DH	Department of Health, and
	DSS	Department of Social Security
	DNR	Do Not Resuscitate
or	DNAR	Do Not Attempt Resuscitation
	EC	European Community
	EL	Executive letter (Guidance from DoH)
	ET	Embryo transfer
	EWC	Expected week of confinement
	GIFT	Gamete intrafallopian transfer
	GMC	General Medical Council
	GP	General practitioner
	GUM	Genito-urinary medicine
	GWC	General Whitley Council
	HAI	Hospital Acquired Infection
	HASWA	Health and Safety at Work Act
	HFEA	Human Fertilisation and Embryology Authority
	HGAC	Human Genetics Advisory Commission
	HGC	Human Genetics Commission
	HIV	Human Immunodeficiency Virus
	HSC	Health and Safety Commission or
	HSC	Health Service Commissioner
	IC(T)U	Intensive Care (Treatment) Unit
	IM and T	Information Management and Technology
	IV	Intravenous(ly)
	IVF	*In vitro* fertilisation
	LA	Local Authority
	LBC	Liquid-based Cytology
	LOLER	Lifting Operations and Lifting Equipment Regulations
	LREC	Local research ethical committee
	MDA	Medical Devices Agency
	MDU	Medical Defence Union
	MHAC	Mental Health Act Commission
	MPP	Maternity period pay
	MRSA	Methicillin-resistant Staphylococcus aureus
	NAI	Non-accidental injury
	NAO	National Audit Office
	NFR	Not for resuscitation
	NHS	National Health Service
	NHSLA	National Health Service Litigation Authority
	NICE	National Institute for Clinical Excellence
	NMW	National Minimum Wage
	NSF	National Standard Framework
	ODP	Operating department Practitioner
	PGD	Pre-implantation Genetic Diagnosis
	QC	Queen's Counsel

PCC	Professional Conduct Committee
PCG	Primary Care Group
PCT	Primary Care Trust
PPE	Personal protective equipment
PREP	Post-Registration development
PRN	*pro re nata* (as required, whenever necessary)
PUWER	Provision and Use of Work Equipment Regulations
PVS	Persistent vegetative state
QW	Qualifying week
RCM	Royal College of Midwifery
RCN	Royal College of Nursing
RCP	Royal College of Psychiatrists
RIDDOR	Reporting of Injuries, Diseases and Dangerous Occurrences
RMO	Responsible Medical Officer
RSI	Repetitive Strain Injury
SEN	State Enrolled Nurse
SMP	Statutory maternity pay
SRSC	Safety Representative and Safety Committee
SSP	Statutory sick pay
TB	Tuberculosis
T+P	Temperature and pulse
TUR & ER 93	Trade Union Reform and Employee Rights Act 1993
UKCC	United Kingdom Central Council for Nursing, Midwifery and Health Visiting
ULTRA	Unrelated Live Transplant Regulatory Authority
VD	Venereal disease

Foreword from first edition

The author, Bridgit Dimond, is well known to nurses working in Wales. She has assisted many of us in developing an increased awareness of the need for expert legal advice and knowledge of the law to inform our practice in the interests of our patients, our colleagues and ourselves.

The text of the book illustrates very graphically that she has skilfully drawn her material from frequent contact with nurses, midwives and health visitors working in a variety of settings. The topics are relevant to the work of the practitioner, the educator and the manager and presented in a form which encourages the reader to delve further into the subject. Although this book is seen by the author primarily as a work of reference, the very fact that many of the issues identified are at the centre of the profound changes taking place in the pattern and organisation of services and within the nursing profession itself, ensures that it will have wider interest and will assist nurses considerably with understanding their responsibilities in a period of significant development.

Bridgit Dimond has, through this publication, yet again provided valuable assistance for improving the practice of nursing – by encouraging nurses to acquire a deeper understanding of the relevant legal aspects of the work of nursing.

Miss M. Bull
Chief Nursing Officer
Welsh Office

Foreword to the third edition

With the first edition of *Legal Aspects of Nursing* Bridgit Dimond quite rightly acquired an enviable reputation for having written the foremost text in the field. Her book established a new standard of comprehensiveness and clarity. Accessible to the non-lawyer yet unyielding in its attention to the detail of the law, it provided nurses and others with a superb reference and guide to professional practice.

While many of the principles that inform effective professional practice are enduring, the health and legal landscape have changed significantly in recent years. There can be few areas of modern life that are more dynamic than health care and the law.

In this third edition Bridgit Dimond has maintained the high standards established in the first but she has updated and extended the text to take account of new laws, cases and developments in professional regulation and practice. As before, she very ably draws out the implications for nurses, exposing the important issues and identifying the key points that need to underpin accountable practice.

Patients and client protection should be paramount in professional thinking, but *Legal Aspects of Nursing* does not espouse the defensive practice sometimes associated with a preoccupation with the law. Rather, it encourages a positive approach to nursing based on a firm understanding of the legal implications and potential ramifications for professional practice.

The challenge of making the law both relevant and accessible to nurses should not be underestimated. Bridgit Dimond has achieved it again with this third edition of *Legal Aspects of Nursing*.

Sarah Mullally
Chief Nursing Officer
Department of Health

Preface to first edition

I make no apologies for producing a book on law for nurses. It is apparent to me that nurses are increasingly aware of the need for up-to-date legal knowledge, that they realise that they practise their profession within the constraints and limitations of the law and very occasionally with the powers of the law, and that they are increasingly held responsible. The approach adopted here is, however, a practical one. I attempt to start with the problems and move outwards to the legal significance of the events described. The result is very different from the traditional textbook approach. My aim is not to teach the nurse the academic niceties of contract law, nor of the law of negligence but, rather, to take some everyday situations in which the nurse finds herself and examine the legal consequences of the situations so that she comes to an understanding of the legal principles which arise. In this way her legal understanding will develop and she will then be able to apply those principles to similar situations.

I am aware of the dangers of this approach. Any situation is of course very complex; there are considerable dangers of over-simplification. However, I am not of the persuasion that because a little knowledge is a dangerous thing law must be kept for the lawyers. It is essential that nurses understand the legal implications of their work so that they can protect both themselves and their patients. With a basic understanding of the law they should know when they need to seek expert legal advice and also know what elementary precautions they should be taking to protect themselves. Where possible, actual wording of Acts of Parliament has been placed in Figures, so that it would not break the flow of the text, and so that the nurse can see the actual wording. It is anticipated that the book would be used as a source book to dip into rather than be read from cover to cover. The appendices thus include much reference information and the index has been designed with this purpose in mind. I have not flinched from including some of the technical legal terms and have given the case references so that the nurse who wishes to pursue the subject in more detail can follow the cases.

Many of the problems discussed here are ones cited to me by hundreds of nurses in seminars I have conducted throughout the country and this explains the apparent concentration on issues relating to negligence litigation. This is a field that nurses are considerably anxious about and constantly ask questions on problems relating to the extended role, responsibility for others, and aspects relating to resourcing.

A note of caution: there are many situations which arise where there are no clear legal guidelines; the dilemmas which arise are of an ethical rather than a legal dimension. The law is both narrower and wider than the field of ethics. There are some problems where ethical issues arise and where the law as yet provides no specific guidelines other than the basic legal principles, for example many issues arising from the developments in reproductive technology have still not been covered by legislation although, following the Warnock Report, this situation is about to be changed. In other respects the law is wider than ethical issues: for example the need to register a birth, marriage or death raises no ethical issues other than that of obeying the law. Some of these ethical issues will be covered although, clearly, it is only where there is a breach of the law that specific guidance can be given. This is not to say that ethical issues are not important. It is simply that there is no space for their discussion here. However, reference is made in the extended reading list to books which deal solely with these issues.

Some of the discussion relates to nursing procedure and practice which does not have legal status. However, it is considered essential to include this in a work of this kind.

A word about terminology. I have used the term 'nurse' to cover all categories of nursing staff from auxiliary to nursing officer. When it is significant that the nurse has a particular rank, then I have used the appropriate grade. I have also tended to refer to the nurse as she; this is not meant to be sexist: it simply covers the vast majority of nursing staff and is less clumsy than any contrived alternative such as 'he/she'. To illustrate practical situations two different terms have been applied: **situation** to describe an imaginary series of events which could well occur but in fact the names are fictitious and not intended to refer to any actual persons living or dead; **case** to cover actual cases which were heard before the courts. Not all of these refer to nursing staff; indeed the actual number of cases in which nurses have personally been defendant or accused are comparatively rare. Many of the cases involve medical staff or are not directly concerned with the health professions. However, the principles which arise are significant for nursing practice and on that account have been included. Because law even more than health care is a jargon-dominated profession, a Glossary has been included to explain those legal terms which could cause difficulties.

The aim is to provide some practical guidance to nursing staff on the many problems that they might encounter. Part I of the book deals with those general problems which face all nursing staff covering principles of professional negligence and the rights of the patient, and also those areas where the nurse herself is a victim of an accident or assault, etc. Part II deals with those specialist areas which are more likely to be encountered by nurses working in different fields but they may also be of general interest. Finally, certain areas which seem to require attention in their own right such as property matters, handling complaints, drugs and AIDS are considered separately, in Part III. Appendices provide additional useful information to which the nurse may wish to refer. I have endeavoured to state the law for England and Wales at 31 August 1989.

I am grateful for the support and encouragement of so many in the preparation of this book. I am considerably indebted to Tessa Shellens and Dr Sue Revel who painstakingly read through the draft and offered much advice and guidance and to Mrs Brenda Hall, my indexer, for her patience, tenacity and thoroughness. I also thank Ann Cross for her detective work. In addition, I am grateful to the following who read individual sections: Dawn O'Brien, Val Taylor, Margaret Winter, Anne Ryall-Davies, Sylvia Parker, Sue Bowers, Yvonne Peters, Gillian Davies, Helen Gray, Keith

Weeks, Heather Anderson, Duncan Bloy, Helen Power, Jean Jones, and Jean Whyte. The responsibility, however, for the accuracy and contents of the book remains mine. I also acknowledge the support and encouragement of my publishers, particularly Cathy Peck and Mike Cash.

Finally I am conscious of the great debt I owe to my family whose delight in my work is encouragement in itself. I thank you all.

Preface to third edition

Five years have elapsed since the second edition was published and major changes have taken place in both the NHS and the legal framework within which UKCC (NMC) practitioners work. The internal market has come and gone and the organisations established under the NHS and Community Care Act have been replaced by the new structure set up under the Health Act 1999. Group fundholding practices have been abolished and new Primary Care Groups have been set up with many receiving Primary Care Trust status. Clinical Governance, supported by the statutory duty of quality, is making itself felt at every level within NHS organisations. The Commission for Health Improvement, also established under the Health Act 1999, has started its work as a watchdog for the NHS, with considerable powers of inspection. The National Institute for Clinical Excellence has made recommendations to the NHS on the medications that justify being prescribed from NHS funds and has an extensive programme for evaluations of clinically effective practice. National Standards frameworks have been published for Mental Health and Coronary Care and others are awaited. Major changes are taking place in the organisation of registration bodies, including the UKCC and the GMC and the Council of the Professions Supplementary to Medicine. Professional conduct proceedings are being reformed to improve the protection of the public. In civil proceedings, the Woolf Reforms have been implemented and are taking effect. Litigation is increasing and the cost to the NHS rising dramatically. New Data Protection legislation now applies to both computerised and manually held records. Major changes in the scope of professional practice envisaged by the NHS Plan and by the recommendations in the Crown Report on the supply and administration of medicines are still to have their full impact. New laws, cases and guidance in the health and safety field are increasing demands on managers and employees. Other significant changes in the Mental Health Legislation and decision making on behalf of the mentally incapacitated adult are still on the drawing board. It is possible to say that there is not one area of nursing, midwifery or health visiting practice that has not been changed over the past four years. Amongst the many significant changes that have taken place, the most momentous must be the Human Rights Act 1998 which came into force on 2 October 2000 in England and Wales. Its effect will permeate through every aspect of health service law as courts look at existing legislation in the light of its compatibility with the European Convention on Human Rights and existing case law is reviewed against the Convention. There appears to be no doubt that litigation will increase as claimants attempt to enforce their rights against the public authorities. This third edition seeks to ensure that the registered practitioner understands the changing context within which she works and that she has a knowledge of the law and its implications so that she can the better protect her patient/client and herself.

Acknowledgements

I wish to convey my thanks to the Stationery Office for being able to print sections of the Statutes and the Statutory Instruments and to the various law reports for the quotations from the cases. In the preparation of this third edition, I am grateful once again to so many people – not least the hundreds of nurses who have raised legal concerns at the seminars and conferences I have spoken at – that it is invidious to mention just a few by name. I must give specific thanks to Tessa Shellens, Eleris Rees, Kirsten Tinman, Rachel Burnett, Angela Perrett, Carol Davies and her colleagues. My special thanks are due to Bette Griffiths who prepared the index and tables and provided constant encouragement and support, as did my daughters Clare and Bec to whom this book is dedicated.

Part I | General principles affecting all nurses

1 Introduction: four arenas of accountability, the legal system and human rights

This book is about the accountability of the nurse, which means that it is concerned with how far the nurse can be held in law to account for her actions. No distinction is drawn in this context between responsibility and accountability. Responsibility is seen as being liable to be called to account, answerable for, accountable for. Space does not permit discussion of the moral or ethical dimensions. There may be circumstances where a nurse could be held morally responsible but there is no legal liability. For example, if a nurse fails to volunteer her services at the scene of a road accident the law at present recognises no legal duty to volunteer help and thus any legal action brought against the nurse would fail. The United Kingdom Central Council (UKCC) may however consider that she was guilty of professional misconduct and in its Guidelines for professional practice it states that a nurse owes a professional duty of care at all times. Many would hold that there is a moral duty to use her skills to help a fellow human being. Obviously, the law and ethics overlap, but each is both wider and narrower than the other. The list of extended reading on page 599 promotes further consideration of the moral dilemmas in health care. The topics to be covered in this chapter are shown in Figure 1.1.

Accountability
Criminal liability
Professional liability
Civil liability
Accountability to the employer
Relationship between the four arenas of accountability
Sources of law
Differences between civil and criminal law
Civil actions
Legal personnel and legal complaints
Legal language
Legal aid and conditional fees
Human Rights Act 1998

Figure 1.1 Issues covered in Chapter 1.

Accountability

In this book we are concerned with the legal aspects of the accountability of the nurse. Many problems arise, however. Can a nurse, who does not have control over the resources, be held liable for harm suffered by a patient? Can a nurse be held responsible if she is ignorant, through lack of training, of certain procedures, and as a result the patient is harmed? Issues such as these are of significant concern to the nurse.

In order to be responsible it is necessary to have knowledge and this includes legal knowledge. Ignorance of the law is no defence and the nurse should be aware of the limits which the law imposes upon her, and also of the power it gives her. The increase in litigation over the past ten years and the possibility of the nurse being personally involved in court proceedings is also a major anxiety for nurses.

Four main arenas of accountability in law are identified and discussed in detail. It might be considered that the most important has been omitted, i.e. accountability to oneself. This, however, is the moral dimension. There are no legal means of enforcing this form of accountability, though many would recognise it as being at the heart of the best of professional competence and skill.

Figure 1.2 illustrates the many areas of law which concern the nurse and most of these topics are considered in this first part. Some of the more specialist areas, e.g. the Abortion Act, are considered in the second part of the book which deals with different specialities. In this introductory section, the four fields of accountability which the nurse faces will be considered.

When a patient suffers harm or there is loss of or damage to property, the nurse may be called to account in four different courts and tribunals. Not all actions will

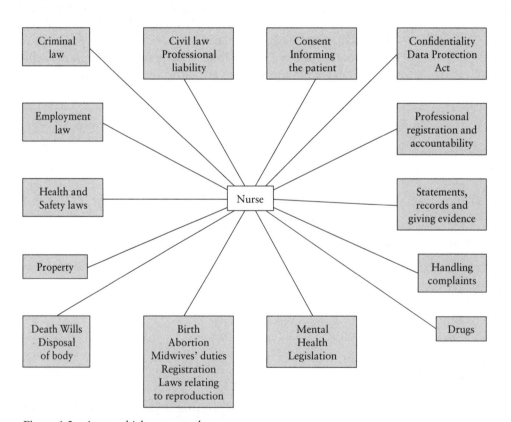

Figure 1.2 Areas which concern the nurse.

be heard in all four but we shall give an example incident to illustrate the different procedures which could involve all four. Figure 1.3 illustrates the four arenas of accountability: accountability in the civil and criminal courts, in disciplinary proceedings and before the professional conduct committee of the UKCC.

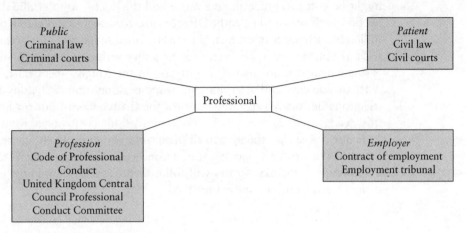

Figure 1.3 Arenas of accountability.

Situation 1.1   The wrong drug

Staff Nurse Greaves was under considerable pressure on the paediatric ward. A spate of very seriously ill patients being admitted and a few absences from 'flu put great strains on the ward. A junior doctor wrote up a 4-year-old child with suspected meningitis for a high dose of antibiotics, and told the staff nurse that he was prescribing a higher dose than was usual because of the severity of the child's condition. Normally, Staff Nurse Greaves would have checked the dose in the *British National Formulary* (*BNF*), but since they were so busy she took the doctor's word for it and gave the child the dose indicated on the sheet. Not long afterwards, the child showed signs of kidney failure and despite efforts to save him, he died. Subsequently, the post mortem investigations revealed that the child had been given a 1,000-fold overdose of the antibiotic.

Criminal liability

Death in circumstances like that described above would have to be reported to the coroner, who would immediately take control of the whole case, would probably order a post mortem, which the relatives would have no right to refuse, and may hold an inquest to establish the cause of death. Details of the coroner's powers and the progress of an inquest are discussed in Chapter 29. The staff nurse is likely to be asked to provide a statement and may well be called to give evidence at the inquest. The Chief Officer of Police or the Director of Public Prosecutions can request the coroner to adjourn the inquest on the grounds that a person may be charged with an offence committed in circumstances connected with the death of the deceased. The coroner also has the power to adjourn the hearing.

In a case like this, it is highly likely that after investigation by the police a decision might be taken to prosecute the nurse and the doctor for a criminal offence in connection with the child's death. Offences are classified as indictable or summary. An indictable offence is one which is heard before a judge and jury in the Crown Court, such as murder, manslaughter, rape and very serious offences. A summary offence is one which is heard by the magistrates in the Magistrates Court, such as driving without due care and attention and some parking offences. Many offences can be tried in either the Magistrates Court or the Crown Court. For further discussion on this, see Chapter 2.

Figure 1.4 shows the system of our criminal courts. Even where a case is to be heard in the Crown Court because it concerns an offence which can be tried only on indictment, the magistrates will still hear the case as examining justices to decide if the case is to be committed for trial.

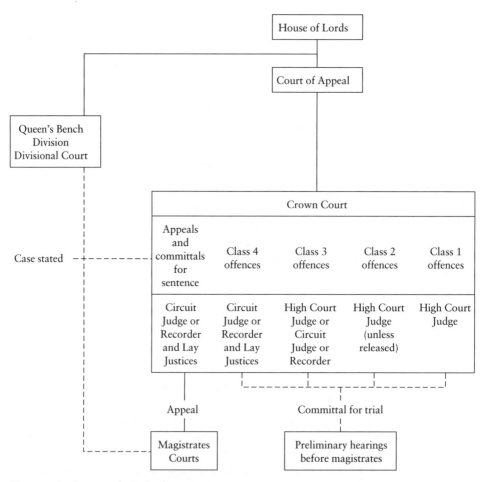

Figure 1.4 System of criminal courts.

In a situation like the above, it is quite likely that the inquest would be adjourned and that criminal proceedings would then take place against the staff. The prosecution have the burden of establishing to the satisfaction of the jury that the accused is guilty beyond all reasonable doubt of the offence.

Once the jury has found the accused guilty, the judge has considerable discretion over sentencing. Only where the accused has been found guilty of murder is the judge compelled to sentence him to life imprisonment. In other cases, the judge has a discretion which ranges from an absolute discharge to imprisonment. There is a right of both the prosecution and the defendant to appeal against sentencing.

Criminal charges in relation to the care of the patient are rare, but when they do arise they attract considerable publicity. The trial of Dr Arthur in connection with the death of a severely handicapped Down's syndrome baby, the committal proceedings of Dr Hamilton on a charge under the Infant Life Preservation Act, the conviction of Dr Nigel Cox (for causing the death of a woman suffering from rheumatoid arthritis by prescribing and administering potassium chloride) and the case of Dr Shipman who was convicted of the murder of 15 women have raised serious issues in relation to the position of the doctor and the criminal law. The nature of criminal proceedings is considered at greater length in Chapter 2.

Professional liability

In the situation described above, Staff Nurse Greaves could be found guilty of causing the death of the child, though this obviously depends on the detailed facts of the case. The result would automatically be reported to the United Kingdom Central Council for Nursing, Midwifery and Health Visiting (UKCC), and it is highly likely that a Professional Conduct Committee (PCC) would hear the case to decide if Staff Nurse Greaves is guilty of misconduct and if so whether she should be removed from the Register. Information goes to the UKCC from a variety of sources about the conduct of a nurse, and in a case like this the police would also report it to the registration body. Non-criminal misconduct may also be reported.

The nurse is entitled to challenge the findings of the criminal court and to argue that she is not guilty of misconduct. Even if she fails in this, she could argue that the special circumstances of the case do not warrant her being removed from the Register. The full details of the powers and procedures of the PCC are discussed in Chapter 11. In contrast to the criminal prosecution in the Crown Court, there is no jury here and the members who make up the constitution of the PCC are concerned with protecting the public from an irresponsible nurse; their intention is not to punish the nurse. The powers of the PCC are set out in Figure 1.5. Following any decision by the PCC, an appeal on a point of law can be made to the High Court which can instigate a judicial review.

Following investigation by the Preliminary Investigation Committee and referral to the Professional Conduct Committee of the UKCC, the Professional Conduct Committee after a finding of misconduct by the nurse can take one of the following courses:

(i)   no action
(ii)   refer respondent to the Health Committee
(iii) postpone decision
(iv)   strike off the Register
(v)   issue a caution
(vi)   suspend from registration.

Figure 1.5   Powers of the Professional Conduct Committee.

Civil liability

The death of the child gives the child's personal representative the right to sue in the civil courts (see Figure 1.6) for the negligence that led to the child's death. The action could be brought against the nurse and the doctor personally, or against the NHS Trust, which could be sued either for its direct responsibility for the death of the child or its vicarious (indirect) liability for the negligence of its staff while acting in the course of employment. If the NHS Trust is found vicariously liable, then it has a right under the contract of employment to seek an indemnity from the negligent employee, although this right is rarely exercised. The vicarious liability of the employer is considered in Chapter 4. The claimant, i.e. the person who is bringing a civil action for negligence, must show fault on the part of the person or organisation he is suing. Figure 1.7 shows the elements which must be established by the plaintiff, and the importance of these elements in a claim for compensation for negligence is considered in Chapter 4.

Because of rising costs and awards of compensation, and owing to the injustice to claimants should they fail to obtain compensation, many associations are now urging the adoption of a system of no-fault liability. The DH is considering such a scheme (Press Release 14 July 2001). If this system is adopted, then a patient who is harmed will be able to obtain compensation without establishing that someone is to blame for the harm. New Zealand is one example of a country that operates a system of no-fault liability. However, even with this system, the patient must show that the harm resulted from an untoward occurrence rather than as the natural course of an illness.

In the situation that Staff Nurse Greaves faces here, it is particularly unlikely that the NHS Trust would defend an action for vicarious liability for her negligence if she had already been found guilty of a criminal offence. They would be more likely to offer a sum in compensation for the death of the child, the only likely dispute being over the appropriate sum of compensation. The problems of quantifying harm and putting a monetary figure on loss suffered are discussed in Chapter 6.

In the civil courts, the claimant has to establish liability of the defendant on a balance of probabilities. This is an easier task than that facing the prosecution in the criminal courts, where proof is required beyond all reasonable doubt.

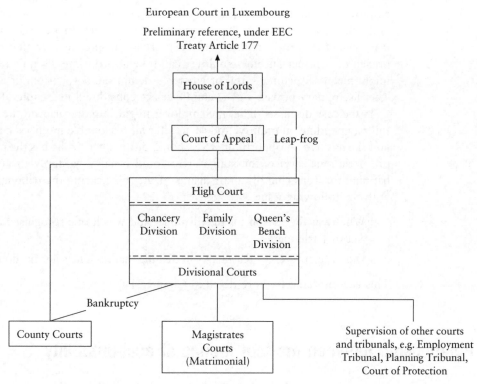

The European Economic Community set up by the First Treaty of Rome in 1957 was joined by the United Kingdom in 1973. Sovereign powers were surrendered and the supremacy of Community law over the national systems of law was accepted. There are four main institutions responsible for discharging the functions of the EEC:

1. The Commission – the executive body
2. The Council of Ministers – one representative from each state
3. The Assembly or European Parliament directly elected by voting in member states
4. The Court of Justice – sits in Luxembourg

Figure 1.6 The civil courts.

---

1. A duty of care is owed by the defendant to the claimant.
2. There is a breach in the standard of the duty of care owed.
3. This breach has caused reasonably foreseeable harm.

Figure 1.7 Elements in an action for negligence.

Accountability to the employer

Finally, the staff nurse has to account to her employer. There is an implied term (i.e. a term that may never even be discussed or written down but which is assumed by the courts to exist unless there is evidence to the contrary) in every contract of employment that the employee will obey the reasonable instructions of the employer and will use all care and skill in carrying out her duties. In a case such as this where it is evident that the employee has been grossly negligent, then that employee is in breach of contract and the employer can take appropriate disciplinary action. This might mean a warning – oral or written – demotion, suspension, or even dismissal. The disciplinary powers of the employer are considered in Chapter 10.

In the case discussed here, the employer might initially suspend the staff nurse on full pay pending an inquiry, and then, after all reasonable inquiries have been made and she has had an opportunity to respond, dismiss her. If she has the requisite length of continuous service, the staff nurse would be able to apply to an employment tribunal for a hearing of unfair dismissal. At this hearing the tribunal is concerned with the following issues:

1. What was the reason for the dismissal and was it one recognised by statute (i.e. Act of Parliament)?

2. Did the employer act reasonably in treating that reason as justification for dismissal?

This is considered in more detail in Chapter 10.

Relationship between the four arenas of accountability

In a situation such as the one described here, if the staff nurse has been grossly negligent, then consistent results for all four hearings are likely: she will be found guilty in the criminal courts; liable in the civil court; removed from the Register by the PCC and dismissed by the employer. However, this is not necessarily so and cases are on record where the employer dismisses the nurse, but the UKCC keeps her on the Register, or where the employer does not dismiss the nurse, but she is removed from the Register (in which case, of course, the nurse would lose her registered post). In addition, a criminal charge may fail where a civil charge succeeds. The reason for the lack of consistency is that the four forums are concerned with different aspects of the situation and have different standards of proof.

Sources of law

A brief word is appropriate on what is meant by the term 'law' and what its origin is. The law derives from two main sources:

1. *Acts of Parliament and Statutory Instruments which are enacted under the powers given by the former*: these are known as statutory sources, include the legislation of the European Community, and take precedence over all other laws. Laws of the European Community automatically become part of the law of the United Kingdom (see Figure 1.5). The Council and the Commission have law-making powers and this can be in the form of Regulations or Directions. The Human Rights Act 1998 is in a special position (see below on page 14).

2. *The common law (also known as case law or judge-made law)*: this is made up of the decisions by judges in individual cases which are often, but not always, interpretations of statute law. The judge, in deciding a particular case, is bound by a previous decision on the law made by judges in an earlier case if it is relevant to the facts before him and if that decision was made by a higher court than the one in which he is sitting. There is a recognised order of precedence so that, for example, a decision by the House of Lords is binding on all other courts except itself, but would be subject to relevant precedents of the European Court of Justice. The decisions are recorded by officially recognised reporters, so that in a case similar to a previous one the earlier decision can be put before the court. If the facts and the situation are comparable and the decision was made by a court whose decisions are binding, then the earlier precedent will be followed. If there are grounds for distinguishing the case then a different decision may follow.

Of vital importance to the system of precedence is a reliable procedure for recording the facts and decisions on any court case. Each court has a recognised system of reporting and the case is quoted by a reference which should enable the full report of the case to be found easily. An example is given in the glossary.

Similarly, Acts of Parliament and Statutory Instruments have chapter numbers for each year, or a serial number.

There are recognised rules for interpreting Acts of Parliament and in relation to the following of precedents. Ultimately, however, if the law is unsatisfactory and fails to provide justice, the courts look to the Houses of Parliament to remedy the situation by new legislation. There is a right of appeal on matters of law to courts of higher jurisdiction. An appeal can be taken to the Court of Appeal and from there to the House of Lords, if permission is granted. Until the House of Lords has pronounced on a particular point of law, there may be considerable uncertainty as to what the law in a given situation is. A considerable number of medical law cases have been referred to the House of Lords in recent years.

Department of Health (DH) circulars, Department of Social Security (DSS) circulars and UKCC codes of practice are not legally binding, but they are recommended practice. Breach of these codes may be evidence of failure to follow the approved practice, but cannot in itself result in successful civil or criminal action. This does not apply to the Midwives Rules which do have statutory force.

Differences between civil and criminal law

What is the difference between the civil law and the criminal law? The only safe answer is that a breach of the criminal law can be followed by prosecution in the criminal courts, whereas liability in civil law is actionable in the civil courts and may or may not be a crime. There is no necessary moral difference between the two. Prior to the Suicide Act of 1961, suicide and attempted suicide, for example, were crimes and as such the latter was subject to criminal proceedings. To many people, however, suicide may still be regarded as morally wrong irrespective of its non-criminal status and it is still a criminal offence to assist someone in a suicide attempt. Some acts may be both criminal and civil wrongs: thus to drive without due care and attention and cause harm can be followed by both criminal and civil proceedings.

How does one know if an act is a civil wrong? One way would be to consider previous cases to find if there is a precedent. The ultimate way would be to establish in the House of Lords whether a particular action gives rise to civil liability. There is, for example, an increasing acceptance by the courts that information given in specific circumstances can give rise to an action for breach of confidence. Liability in civil law is thus a growth area.

Civil actions

A civil action for negligence will be the main one considered here in relation to the liability of the nurse or NHS Trust, but there are other civil actions which will be considered briefly. The various forms of civil action are shown in Figure 1.8. All these, except actions for breach of contract, are known as torts, i.e. civil wrongs.

The action for breach of a statutory duty arises when an Act of Parliament or Statutory Regulations place duties on organisations or individuals. In certain circumstances where an individual suffers harm as a result of the breach of these statutory duties, an action for compensation may ensue in the civil courts. For example, many of the provisions of the Factories Acts give rise to such actions. In contrast, a breach of the general duties under the Health and Safety at Work Act does not give rise to such an action, though breach of the regulations made under the Health and Safety at Work Act may do so. This is considered in Chapter 12.

Defamation is another tort which is considered in Chapter 9. An action for nuisance is not considered and is unlikely to concern the nurse at work. An action for breach of contract will be briefly considered in Chapter 10 in connection with the nurse's contract of employment. An action for trespass to the person exists where a person alleges that they have been touched without their consent, and this is considered further in Chapter 7.

---

1. Torts
   Negligence
   Trespass to property
              to land
              and to the person
   False imprisonment
   Wrongful interference
   Breach of a statutory duty
   Nuisance
   Defamation
   Malicious prosecution
   Deliberate interference with interests in trade or business
2. Breach of Contract

Figure 1.8 Some forms of civil action.

Legal personnel and legal complaints

At present we have a divided legal profession: solicitors and barristers (counsel). There are about 50,000 solicitors and about 5,500 practising barristers. The former are the main link with the client. Thus in the situation quoted above, if the parents of the child decided to take civil action against the NHS Trust, they would consult a solicitor, who would give them advice and possibly prepare an application for legal aid. If the case were to proceed, he would probably instruct counsel (i.e. a barrister) to prepare the pleadings (see Chapter 6) and represent the client in court. Under Part III of the Access to Justice Act 1999, major reforms are made to the law on lawyers' rights of audience before the courts and rights to conduct litigation. It provides that, in principle, all lawyers should have full rights of audience before any court, subject only to meeting reasonable training requirements. There are also reforms to the procedures for authorising further professional bodies to grant rights of audience or rights to conduct litigation to their members; and for approving changes to professional rules of conduct relating to the exercise of these rights. It replaces the Lord Chancellor's Advisory Committee on Legal Education and Conduct with a new Legal Services Consultative Panel. The Act also makes changes relating to complaints against lawyers. It gives additional powers to the Law Society and the Legal Services Ombudsman to strengthen the system for handling complaints against lawyers, and creates a Legal Services Complaints Commissioner to set targets for the handling of complaints by the professional bodies. A recent case has decided that professional work in court is no longer immune from actions for negligence.[1]

These reforms are likely in the long term to lead to a single legal profession. At present the initial training for both solicitors and barristers is the same (a law degree or Part 1 of the Common Professional Examination). Would-be solicitors then undertake practical training with a firm of solicitors, and then take the Law Society's Part 2 examination, called the Legal Practice Course, while would-be barristers study for the Bar to which they are 'called'. They must join one of the Inns of Court and must dine there on a specified number of occasions. The barrister must then undertake pupillage where they are attached to a practising barrister. Barristers usually work together in Chambers managed by a clerk who negotiates and collects the fees from solicitors. Fees are at present negotiated in advance and include a brief fee for accepting a case and a refresher fee which is a daily fee for each day that the case is in court. Senior barristers are eligible 'to take silk', i.e. they become Queen's Counsel (QC) appointed by the Lord Chancellor.

Legal language

Lawyers, like any profession, have their own language which can create barriers. In April 1999, new procedures for civil litigation were introduced together with a simplification of language to assist communication: thus the term plaintiff (used to describe a person bringing a civil action) was replaced by the word claimant; a writ (the document issued by the court which begins the civil case) is replaced by claim form. A glossary is provided to assist the reader with any specialist terms. It is the aim of this book to break down the barriers between the law and the nurse and to facilitate communication.

Legal Aid and conditional fees

Major changes have been made to the legal aid system under the Access to Justice Act 1999.

Part I of the Act provides for two new schemes, replacing the existing legal aid scheme, to secure the provision of publicly-funded legal services for people who need them. It establishes a **Legal Services Commission** to run the two schemes; and enables the Lord Chancellor to give the Commission orders, directions and guidance about how it should exercise its functions. It requires the Commission to establish, maintain and develop a **Community Legal Service**. The Community Legal Service fund will replace the legal aid fund in civil and family cases. The Commission will also be responsible for a **Criminal Defence Service**, which will replace the current legal aid scheme in criminal cases. The new scheme is intended to ensure that people suspected or accused of a crime are properly represented, while securing better value for money than is possible under the legal aid scheme. The Legal Services Commission will be empowered to secure these services through contracts with lawyers in private practice, or by providing them through salaried defenders (employed directly by the Commission or by non-profit-making organisations established for the purpose).

Part II of the Access to Justice Act 1999 makes changes to facilitate the private funding of litigation. Over recent years there has been introduced a scheme known as 'no win, no fee' or conditional fee system. By this system, potential litigants can agree with lawyers terms on which they will be represented. Insurance cover is taken out to meet the expenses of witnesses and other costs arising in case the action is lost. The 1999 Act amends the law on conditional fee agreements between lawyers and their clients, in particular it allows the additional fees payable to a solicitor in a successful case in a no win no fee agreement, to be recovered from the other side.

The Human Rights Act 1998

The United Kingdom was a signatory of the European Convention for the Protection of Human Rights and Fundamental Freedoms in 1953. However, anyone who sought to bring an action for breach of their human rights, as set out in the Convention, was unable to take the case to the courts in this country but had to go to the European Court of Human Rights in Strasbourg. (NB This is not the court of the European Community, the European Court of Justice, which meets in Luxembourg). It was estimated that to take a case to Strasbourg cost over £30,000 and took over five years. The Human Rights Act 1998 came into force on 2 October 2000. It has three main effects: first, it is unlawful for a public authority to breach the rights set out in the Convention; secondly, from 2 October 2000 an allegation of a breach of the rights can be brought in the courts of this country; and thirdly, judges can make a declaration that legislation which is raised in a case before them is in breach of the Convention and the legislation will then be referred back to Parliament for reconsideration. The Act is not in itself retrospective, but any person concerned about an infringement before 2 October 2000 can of course take a case to Strasbourg.

Action can be brought against a public authority or organisation exercising public functions for breach of the Convention articles in the courts of this country. Appendix A sets out Schedule 1 to the Human Rights Act 1998. At the time of writing, it is not possible to predict the likely effect of the Act, and there have been alarmist prophecies of a huge increase in litigation. Some of the more significant articles will be considered below, but articles are also considered in relevant chapters. It is recommended that health care staff should undertake a proactive exercise in identifying possible breaches of the Act and endeavour to take any necessary remedial action. Further information is available from the Home Office website.[2] The Home Office has set up a Human Rights unit that services a Human Rights Task Force.

Right to life

Article 2(1) states:

> Everyone's right to life shall be protected by law. No one shall be deprived of his life intentionally save in the execution of a sentence of a court following his conviction for a crime for which this penalty is provided by law.

Claims have been made that this right to life could be used as the basis for legal action when resources are refused or when decisions are made for a person not to be resuscitated or treatment is withdrawn or withheld. For example, in a case where parents challenged a not for resuscitation decision for their severely disabled baby,[3] the court held that the full palliative care recommended by the doctors, allowing the baby to die with dignity, was not a breach of either article 2 or article 3 (see below) of the European Convention for the Protection of Human Rights and Fundamental Freedoms. The President of the Family Division, Dame Elizabeth Butler-Sloss held that the withdrawal of life-sustaining medical treatment was not contrary to Article 2 of the Human Rights Convention and the right to life, where the patient was in a persistent vegetative state. The ruling was made on 25 October 2000 in cases involving Mrs M, 49 years, who suffered brain damage during an operation abroad in 1997 and was diagnosed as being in a persistent vegetative state (PVS) in October 1998 and Mrs H, 36, who fell ill in America as a result of pancreatitis at Christmas 1999.[4]

Right not to be subjected to inhuman or degrading treatment

Article 3 of the Convention states that:

> No one shall be subjected to torture or to inhuman or degrading treatment or punishment.

It could be argued that patients who spend six hours on a stretcher in a corridor outside the A&E Department whilst a bed is being sought are being subjected to both degrading and inhuman treatment. The physical conditions in some hospitals or nursing or residential care homes may be seen to be an infringement of this right. Other examples could probably be given where patients are not treated with dignity or humanity. In the field of manual handling, there have been suggestions that to require a person to use a hoist is contrary to their human rights. However, it is thought that such an argument will not succeed, since if the alternative to a hoist is manual handling by another person, then that might be contrary to the rights of the other.

Article 5: Right to liberty and security

> Everyone has the right to liberty and security of person. No one shall be deprived of his liberty save in accordance with a procedure prescribed by law.

The use of common law powers (i.e. powers recognised by the courts as in the Re F[5] case) to detain mentally incapacitated adults in psychiatric hospitals could be regarded as a breach of this article, since although the article envisages the lawful detention of persons of unsound mind, it is difficult to see a House of Lords decision as laying down a procedure. This issue was raised in the Bournewood case[6] which is discussed in Chapter 20.

Article 6: Right to a fair trial

> In the determination of his civil rights and obligations or of any criminal charge against him, everyone is entitled to a fair and public hearing within a reasonable time by an independent and impartial tribunal established by law . . .

This will apply to disciplinary hearings as well as courts and tribunals. Hearings must be independent and impartial. In criminal prosecutions, the accused is presumed innocent until proved guilty.

Article 8: Right to respect for private and family life

> Everyone has the right to respect for his private and family life, his home and his correspondence.

It was argued by a father[7] whose wife wished to obtain an abortion that for it to be undertaken against the wishes of the father was contrary to Article 8. This is considered in Chapter 15. Failures to recognise confidential information or support the privacy of patients may lead to court action against hospital and other organisations. In a case heard by the European Court of Human Rights, it was held that the fact that the rights in law of an unmarried father differed from those of a married father were not a breach of Article 8 since there was an objective and reasonable justification for the difference in treatment.[8] The High Court held that restrictions on child visits to patients in high security hospitals who had committed murder, manslaughter or certain sexual offences, unless the child was one of a permitted category, were lawful and not in breach of Article 8 of the European Convention on Human Rights.[9] The onus of establishing family life lay on an applicant.

Other significant articles include article 9, freedom of thought, conscience and religion; article 10, freedom of expression; and article 14, prohibition of discrimination. As cases come before the courts, case law will develop on the interpretation to be given to the various articles and the extent to which the NHS is recognising the rights of its staff and its patients.

Freedom of Information Act 2000

This Act, which gives a right of access to information held by public authorities, is to be brought into force over the next four years. An Information Commissioner has been appointed. There are many exceptions to the right of access including personal information, information provided in confidence and legal professional privilege (see Chapter 8).

Questions and exercises

1 Consider any situation you know of where a patient (almost) suffered harm as a result of a careless act by a professional and analyse the potential consequences as far as the civil and criminal courts, the PCC and the employment tribunal are concerned. Refer to Chapters 2, 3, 10 and 11 for more details.

2 What is the difference between law which derives from a statute and the common law?

3 Try to arrange a visit to one of the four forums described here, or a coroner's court (see Chapter 5) and draw up a plan for the procedure that you witness.

4 What is the difference between a solicitor and a barrister?

5 Look at the Glossary and identify those words with which you are not familiar.

6 With colleagues choose any Article in the Convention of Human Rights (see appendix A) that is relevant to your work and decide on the extent to which there are any infringements of that right. What action could you take?

References

1 *Arthur JS Hall and Co* (a firm) v. *Simons, The Times Law Report* 21 July 2000 HL
2 http://www.homeoffice.gov.uk/hract
3 *National Health Service Trust A* v. *D, and others*, Lloyds Law Rep Med [2000] 411
4 *NHS Trust, A* v. *M; NHS Trust B* v. *H* [2001] 1 All ER 801
5 *In Re F* (Mental Patient: Sterilisation) [1990] 2 AC 1, [1989] 2 WLR 1025, [1989] 2 All ER 545
6 *R.* v. *Bournewood Community and Mental Health NHS Trust ex p L* [1998] 3 All ER 289
7 *Paton* v. *UK* (1980) 3 EHRR 408
8 *B.* v. *UK* [2000] 1 FLR 1 ECHR
9 *R.* v. *Secretary of State for Health ex parte Lally, The Times* 26 October, 2000

2 Actions in the criminal courts and defences to criminal charges

In this chapter, we consider the course followed if criminal proceedings are brought against a nurse, and the ways in which she could defend herself. It must be emphasised that the burden is upon the prosecution to establish the guilt of the accused beyond all reasonable doubt. The accused still has a right of silence at all stages of the prosecution, but failure by the accused to answer questions or mention something she relies on later in court or failure to give evidence may allow adverse inferences to be drawn during the trial.

Situation 2.1   Theft

A discrepancy is found between the ward drug control records and the stock. An investigation is initiated and suspicion falls upon Staff Nurse Jarvis. The police are brought in and after making their enquiries they decide that Staff Nurse Jarvis should be charged with the offence of theft.

A situation such as this involves several kinds of investigation. The NHS Trust will be concerned to determine whether there are grounds to discipline and possibly eventually dismiss the staff nurse. The fact that the police are brought in does not mean that the NHS Trust can abandon its own investigation, but clearly its enquiries should not conflict with those of the police. The NHS Trust must allow the staff nurse to give a full explanation of what has occurred and she should be allowed a representative. Disciplinary proceedings by the employer are discussed in Chapter 10. There is also the possibility of a hearing before the PCC of the UKCC, but this may well be postponed pending the outcome of the police investigations and criminal charges. Here we are concerned only with the criminal proceedings, aspects of which are shown in Figure 2.1.

Initial stages of arrest and prosecution

The staff nurse may well be asked to accompany the police to the station (see Figure 2.2). A Code of Practice (C) prepared under the Police and Criminal Evidence Act 1984, provides guidance on the detention, treatment, and questioning of persons by police officers, and is intended to provide clear and workable guidelines for the

1. Initial stages of arrest and prosecution.
2. Magistrates Court.
3. Committal proceedings.
4. Crown Court proceedings.
5. Elements of a crime.
6. Case of Dr Cox,
    Dr Adomoko,
    Beverley Allitt, and
    Dr Shipman.
7. Defences.
8. Criminal Injuries Compensation Scheme.

Figure 2.1 Issues covered in Chapter 2.

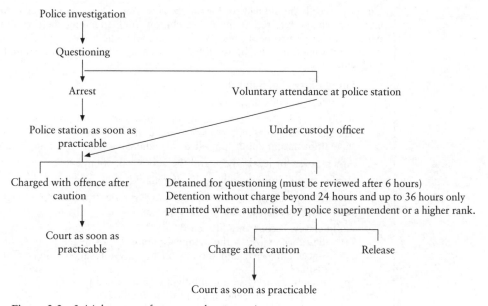

Figure 2.2 Initial stages of arrest and prosecution.

police, while strengthening safeguards for the public at the same time. This Code of Practice must be readily available at all police stations. The Code applies both to those who have been arrested and those who have voluntarily attended the police station. One of the most important safeguards is the right of the detained person to have access to free legal advice at the police station before and during any interview.

The staff nurse may have been arrested before she is taken to the police station, or she may be arrested there. In either case, she should be given a caution as soon as there are grounds to suspect her of the offence and before she is questioned about it for the purpose of obtaining evidence which may be given to a court in a prosecution. The caution should be given in the following terms: 'You do not have to say anything but it may harm your defence if you do not mention when questioned something which you later rely on in court. Anything you do say may be given in evidence.'

Minor deviations do not constitute a breach of this requirement provided that the sense of the caution is preserved. The documentation that the police must retain is shown in Figure 2.3. The Code sets out rules for the police in the interview. The usual procedure now is for the interview to be tape recorded and the guidelines and Code of Practice for tape recording should be followed.

When the officer considers that there is sufficient evidence to prosecute a detained person, he should bring her before the custody officer without delay, who will then be responsible for considering whether or not she should be charged. A further caution must then be given. In addition, a written notice should be given

---

Custody records should be kept for each person who is brought to a police station under arrest or who is arrested at the police station after attending there voluntarily. He is entitled on request to be supplied with a copy when he leaves the police station.

The information must be recorded as soon as practicable and should include the following:

1. Grounds for a person's detention.

2. Detained person's property.

3. Request made for a person to be informed and action taken; any letters or messages sent, calls made or visits received and any refusal on the part of a person to have information about himself or his whereabouts given to an outside enquirer.

4. Any request for legal advice and the action taken on it.

5. Replacement clothing and meals offered.

6. Medical examination by a police surgeon, or request for one and the arrangements made; any medication the detained person is on.

7. An interview record should record
   (a) the times at which the detained person is not in the custody of the custody officer and why, and the reason for any refusal to deliver him out of that custody;
   (b) any intoxicating liquor supplied to a detained person;
   (c) any decision to delay a break in an interview;
   (d) a written record of the interview (unless tape recorded) signed by the detained person as correct.

8. Any action taken to call an interpreter and any agreement to be interviewed in the absence of an interpreter.

9. Grounds for and the extent of any delaying in conducting a review.

10. Anything a detained person says when charged, any questions put after the charge and answers given relating to the offence shall be contemporaneously recorded in full on the forms provided and the record signed by the detained person.

11. Details of any intimate or strip search: which parts were searched, by whom, who was present, reasons and the result.

12. Grounds for any action in delaying the notification of an arrest or allowing access to legal advice.

Figure 2.3 Documentation kept by the police (see Code of Practice C).

showing the particulars of the offence with which she is charged and including the name of the officer in the case, their police station, and a reference number for the case. Questions relating to an offence may not be put to a person after she has been charged with that offence, or after she has been informed that she may be prosecuted for it, unless they are necessary to prevent or minimise harm or loss to some other person or to the public, or to clear up an ambiguity in a previous answer or statement, or where it is in the interests of justice that she should have an opportunity to comment on some fresh information. Before these additional questions are put, the accused must be given another caution. Annex D to the Code of Practice gives rules on written statements given under caution.

Role of the Crown Prosecution Service

Since the introduction of the Crown Prosecution Service, the responsibility for the conduct of most criminal proceedings is on the Director of Public Prosecution and the Crown Prosecution Service. They have the responsibility of instituting criminal proceedings and appearing for the prosecution.

The Magistrates Court

If the staff nurse is charged with the offence of theft, she would probably be given police bail and told to appear at the Magistrates Court. Almost all criminal cases begin in the Magistrates Court and 98 per cent are dealt with completely there. The remaining cases go before the Crown Courts before judge and jury or are dismissed by the magistrates at the committal proceedings.

Indictable-only offences can be heard only before a judge and jury in the Crown Court, summary offences can be heard only by magistrates, but many offences are triable either way. Figure 2.4 shows the classification of the offences.

When the staff nurse is brought before the magistrates on a charge of theft she will be asked to indicate a plea. If she indicates a plea of guilty to the summary offence, she will be sentenced by the magistrates. If she pleads not guilty, she will be tried by the magistrates.

---

1. Offences triable only on indictment (i.e. by judge and jury): murder; genocide; infanticide; causing death by reckless driving; robbery; treason; wounding with intent.
2. Offences triable only summarily (i.e. by magistrates): drunk and disorderly; careless driving; assault on police; and other offences set down by statute, such as the Road Traffic Act 1972 and Schedule 1 of the Criminal Law Act 1977.
3. Offences triable either way (by judge and jury or by magistrates) – case can be heard by magistrates in summary trial if the defendant agrees to be tried by them: theft; handling, obtaining property or pecuniary advantage by deception; assault occasioning actual bodily harm.

Figure 2.4 Classification of offences.

The Magistrates Courts hear:

(a) offences that are triable only as summary offences, e.g. careless driving;

(b) offences that are triable either way (e.g. theft).

Hearing

1. Plea:
    a plea of guilty must be unequivocal;
    a plea of guilty may be made by post, but only to summary non-imprisonable offences.

2. Summary trial where the defendant pleads not guilty
    A. Prosecution:
        1. Opening speech by prosecution lawyer.
        2. Examination in chief of prosecution witnesses.
        3. Cross-examination by defence.
        4. Re-examination by prosecution lawyer.
    B. Submission by defence of no case to answer (if appropriate). Prosecution have the right to reply and magistrates determine the question.
    C. Defence case:
        1. Defendant can remain silent or give evidence. (The court may in certain circumstances draw adverse inferences from silence.)
        2. Defence witnesses are called.
        3. Defence lawyer addresses the magistrates.
    D. The finding: the magistrates determine the guilt or innocence and determine the sentence if a guilty verdict and if they feel their powers are adequate.

Figure 2.5 Course of a hearing in a Magistrates Court.

If she is charged with an offence that is triable either way (i.e. as a summary offence before the magistrates or on indictment by a judge and jury), and she indicates a plea of guilty, then the magistrates will decide whether she should be sentenced by them; if they consider their powers are inadequate, they may then commit her to the Crown Court for sentencing. If she indicates that she intends to plead not guilty or declines to indicate a plea, the magistrate will then decide whether the trial should be before them or whether the defendant should be committed to the Crown Court for trial. If the magistrates decide the case is suitable for trial before them, the defendant will be asked to consent to that procedure. The defendant has the right at that stage to elect trial by judge and jury at the Crown Court.

Proposals have been put forward to decrease the kind of offences that can be heard in the Crown Court, so limiting the choice of the accused to opt for trial by jury.

Committal proceedings

If on the other hand, Staff Nurse Jarvis elects to have the case heard in the Crown Court, she must first face committal proceedings before the magistrates. Here they act as examining justices and decide if there is sufficient evidence for the case to be committed to the Crown Court. The two forms of committal proceedings are shown in Figure 2.6. The full committal proceedings have been curtailed in recent years and are no longer a full hearing of the evidence.

Before the Examining Justices in the Magistrates Court to determine if there is sufficient evidence to put the accused upon trial by jury for any indictable offence.

A. Short form of committal (S.1 of Criminal Justice Act 1967, as amended). The accused, legally represented, may agree that the magistrates should formally commit him to the Crown Court without their considering the evidence against him at all.

   The prosecution must have available all their evidence in statements and must have given copies of those statements to the defence counsel, who must be satisfied that there is a case to answer.

B. Full committal proceedings (This is extremely rare)
   1. Address by prosecution.
   2. Written evidence: written statements taken by the police are read to the court.
   3. Submission by defence: at the conclusion of the prosecution evidence, the defendant can submit that the evidence produced by the prosecution is not of sufficient weight to warrant committing the accused for trial.

      The magistrates decide whether or not to uphold the defence submission. If it is upheld, the accused is discharged. If not, then the committal proceedings continue.
   4. Committal to Crown Court for trial: Court decides on the types of witness, order (full or conditional).

   The defendant may apply for bail.

Figure 2.6 Forms of committal proceedings.

Crown Court proceedings

Let us assume that Staff Nurse Jarvis's case is committed to the Crown Court for trial. The procedure followed is shown in Figure 2.7. Changes have been made regarding the right to challenge the jury (see Figure 2.8 on page 25). Once the jury have been sworn in, the hearing follows the same path as that in the Magistrates Court, but only counsel or solicitor-advocate can represent the accused before the court and a barrister may therefore have been briefed by Staff Nurse Jarvis's solicitor.

The charges on the indictment must be put to Staff Nurse Jarvis. If she pleads not guilty, the trial will then proceed as set out in Figure 2.7. There will be an opening address by the prosecution counsel, setting out the elements that the prosecution have to prove and the standard of proof. This has no evidential value, but can be an important scene-setting for the jury. The prosecution then calls its witnesses who are examined in chief, which means that the witness cannot be asked leading questions. The witness can be cross-examined by the defence, and here leading questions designed to show the irrelevance of this evidence, or in some other way discredit it, can be asked (see Chapter 9 on evidence in court). After the cross-examination has finished, the party calling that witness can re-examine the witness on points arising from the cross-examination. The judge can call a halt to the case on completion of the prosecution evidence if he is not satisfied that there is sufficient evidence to go before the jury, in which case the jury is asked to bring in a not-guilty verdict.

If the case proceeds, the defence calls its witnesses. At present, although the accused does not have to give evidence, the judge may in certain circumstances allow adverse inferences to be drawn by the jury.

1. Attendance of the defendant to appear (or the governor of the prison if the defendant has been remanded in custody).

2. The indictment (the document embodying the charge(s) brought by the Crown against the defendant) is read by the clerk to the accused and he is asked whether he pleads guilty or not guilty. This is known as the arraignment.

    The accused can:
    (a) plead guilty – if accepted, court proceeds to sentencing;
    (b) plead not guilty – see below 3;
    (c) stand silent – if mute of malice (this is determined by the jury) a plea of not guilty entered – if mute by visitation of God, court will decide if accused is fit to plead (see insanity below);
    (d) object on legal grounds – e.g. indictment is invalid and should be quashed; the accused has already been tried for the same offence (i.e. a plea of *autrefois* acquit or convict).

3. Empanelling of the Jury: if the defendant has pleaded not guilty to any count on the indictment, a jury must be empanelled. The jury is not present during the arraignment so that they are kept in ignorance if the accused has pleaded guilty to some offences and not guilty to others.

    The jurors are called in after the arraignment and the names of 12 are called out. They can be challenged by defence or prosecution for cause (see Figure 2.8). They are then sworn and the clerk reads the indictment to them, tells them the defendant has pleaded not guilty and that their charge is to say, having heard the evidence, whether he be 'guilty' or 'not guilty'.

4. The trial
    A. Prosecution:
        1. Opening speech by the prosecution.
        2. Prosecution evidence:
            (a) attendance of witnesses whose statements were tendered at committal proceedings (see Figure 2.6); (The defence must give 14 days notice of the committal proceedings to any prosecution witnesses they wish to attend.)
            (b) if use additional witnesses, defence must be informed and given a statement of evidence.
        3. Examination in chief: prosecution witnesses questioned by the prosecution.
        4. Cross-examination – to discredit witnesses, leading questions can be used and earlier inconsistent statements by the witness can be put to him.
        5. Re-examination – to offset the effects of cross-examination. It cannot be used to produce new evidence which should have been brought out in the examination in chief.
        6. Written statements of witnesses whose evidence the defence does not wish to dispute will be read out.
        7. Challenges to admissibility of evidence: the defence can (in the absence of the jury) challenge the admissibility of evidence. The judge will rule on the admissibility and if he upholds the defence objections to the evidence, all reference to the evidence must be omitted.
    B. Defence
        1. Defence submission: after the conclusion of the prosecution evidence, the defence can ask the trial judge to direct the jury as a matter of law that they should acquit the defendant either:
            (a) because the prosecution have failed to produce any evidence to establish some essential ingredient of the offence; or
            (b) because the evidence produced is so weak or so discredited by cross-examination that no reasonable jury could convict. If the defence submission is upheld, an acquittal is directed.
            If this submission fails then the defence case is put.

Figure 2.7 Procedure in the Crown Court.

> 2. Case for the defence: an opening speech can be made where the defendant and other witnesses are being called to give evidence as to facts (not where only the defendant is called or the other witnesses are only as to character).
>
> Procedure as above.
> Examination in chief.
> Cross-examination.
> Re-examination.
>
> C. Closing Speeches: by prosecution and defence counsel.
>
> D. Summing up by judge.
>
> E. Verdict of jury.
>
> F. Sentencing following finding of guilt.

Figure 2.7 *continued*

> Prosecution: can ask for any would-be juror to 'stand-by' until they have gone right through the panel.
> Can challenge for cause (e.g. ineligibility, disqualification, presumed or actual bias).
> Defence: has lost right to three peremptory challenges (i.e. challenging without having to give any reasons).
> Can challenge for cause (e.g. ineligibility, disqualification, presumed or actual bias).
> The effect of challenging for cause is that if either side can show that a juror is personally concerned in the facts of the particular case or closely connected with a party to the proceedings or with a prospective witness he can be removed. A challenge for cause should not succeed if the only ground for bias is so insubstantial as to be unlikely to affect the jurors' approach to the case.
> The challenging party says 'challenge' immediately before the juror takes the oath. He then has the burden of satisfying the judge on a balance of probabilities that his objection is well founded and produce *prima facie* evidence of this.

Figure 2.8 Challenging the jury.

After all the evidence has been given, the defence and prosecution conclude their cases in final speeches. The judge then sums up the case for the jury. He has the task of explaining to the jury the elements of the crime that the prosecution must prove the accused committed, the nature of the burden of proof that is upon the prosecution; and he analyses the evidence which both sides have put before the jury.

The foreman of the jury is then chosen and the jurors retire to decide their verdict. Initially, the jury is asked to return a unanimous verdict. If it is clear that they can never reach a unanimous verdict, then they can return to court and can be given instructions on returning a majority verdict.

If the jury decide that the staff nurse is guilty, evidence of previous convictions (until this moment usually kept secret from the jury) and the present social and economic circumstances she is in will be given before sentencing. Figure 2.9 sets out the powers of sentencing.

The staff nurse has the right to appeal against the finding of guilt on any matter relating to the way in which the judge directed the jury or in the decisions taken by

Absolute/conditional discharge.
Bindover.
Adults
Fine (and compensation).
Probation.
Probation and attendance at training centre, with condition of intensive training programme.
Probation and attendance at mental hospital as in-patient or out-patient.
Community service.
Combination order (i.e. combination of probation and community service).
Suspended sentence.
Suspended sentence and supervision.
Prison.
Extended sentence.
Guardianship order.
Hospital order Section 37 Mental Health Act 1983.
Hospital order and restriction order Sections 31 and 41 Mental Health Act 1983.

Figure 2.9   Sentencing in the Crown Court.

the judge over the admissibility or inadmissibility of evidence. She also has the right to appeal against the sentence imposed. The prosecution can appeal against sentencing and it has the right to appeal on a point of law.

The elements of a crime

In order to establish guilt, the prosecution must be able to show that each element of the crime charged is proved beyond all reasonable doubt. Each crime thus has its ingredients which make up that particular offence. Examples are given of the elements of some crimes in Figure 2.10.

Mental and physical elements

There is a further breakdown of the elements that have to be established to prove that a crime has taken place, i.e. between the *actus reus* and the *mens rea*. The *mens rea*, or mental element, includes all those elements that relate to the mind of the accused. The *actus reus* is everything else. There are some crimes where there is no requirement to show a mental element. For example, the sale of medicine by a person who was not qualified and while unsupervised by a pharmacist and which was contrary to Section 52 of the Medicines Act 1968 was held to be a strict liability offence.[1] The law has now been changed. As a rule, however, there is a distaste for offences of strict liability, i.e. where there is no requirement for the prosecution to prove *mens rea*.

If there were no requirement for the prosecution to establish a mental element in the crime of theft, Staff Nurse Jarvis could be successfully prosecuted for theft

1. Assault (common law offence)
   actus reus: an act that causes the victim to fear the immediate application of force against him;
   mens rea: an intention to cause the victim to apprehend the immediate application of force or recklessness as to whether the victim might apprehend immediate force.

2. Battery (common law offence)
   actus reus: an act that results in the application of force to the person of another;
   mens rea: an intention to apply force or recklessness as to whether force might be applied.

3. Wounding or causing really serious harm. Section 18 Offences against the Person Act 1861
   actus reus: wound or cause any really serious harm to any person;
   mens rea: maliciously and unlawfully with intent to do really serious harm or an intent to resist or prevent lawful apprehension or detaining of any person.

4. Wounding or inflicting really serious harm. Section 20 Offences against the Person Act 1861
   actus reus: to wound or inflict any really serious harm upon any other person, either with or without any weapon or instrument;
   mens rea: unlawfully and maliciously (intentional or recklessly and without lawful justification).

5. Theft. Section 1(1) Theft Act 1968
   actus reus: appropriate property that belongs to another;
   mens rea: dishonest with the intention of permanently depriving the true owner of that property.

Figure 2.10 Examples of the definition of certain crimes.

in circumstances where someone had accidentally dropped a bottle of tablets in the staff nurse's open bag and she had therefore taken them home inadvertently. In order to secure a conviction, whether the prosecution takes place in the Magistrates Court or in the Crown Court, all the elements, mental and physical, must be shown to have existed at the time it was alleged that the crime was committed.

Several cases where health professionals have been convicted of criminal offences are discussed below.

The case of Dr Nigel Cox[2]

Dr Nigel Cox, a rheumatologist in Winchester, was convicted of causing the death of a patient to whom he had administered potassium chloride. He was given a suspended prison sentence. The patient was in crippling pain, terminally ill and her relatives were concerned at her condition. Dr Cox was also brought before his employers, the Wessex Regional health authority, to face disciplinary proceedings, but retained his post. He was also brought before professional conduct proceedings of the General Medical Council, but stayed on the register.

The case of Dr Adomako

Gross professional negligence can constitute both a criminal offence of manslaughter and also grounds for an action for compensation in the tort of negligence as the case of Dr Adomako shows. Dr Adomako was an anaesthetist who failed to realise during an operation that a tube had become disconnected as a result of which the patient died. He was prosecuted in the criminal courts and convicted of manslaughter.[3]

Box 2.1

R.V. Adomako Manslaughter by an anaesthetist.

At approximately 11.05 a.m. a disconnection occurred at the endotracheal tube connection. The supply of oxygen to the patient ceased and led to a cardiac arrest at 11.14 a.m. During this period, the defendant failed to notice or remedy the disconnection. He first became aware that something was amiss when an alarm sounded on the Dinamap machine, which monitors the patient's blood pressure. From the evidence it appeared that some four and a half minutes had elapsed between the disconnection and the sounding of the alarm. When the alarm sounded, the defendant responded in various ways by checking the equipment and began administering atropine to raise the patient's pulse. But at no stage before the cardiac arrest did he check the integrity of the endotracheal tube connection. The disconnection was not discovered until after resuscitation measures had been commenced.

He accepted at his criminal trial that he had been negligent. The issue was whether his conduct was criminal. He was convicted of involuntary manslaughter, but appealed against conviction. He lost his appeal in the Court of Appeal and then appealed to the House of Lords.

The House of Lords clarified the legal situation.[4]

The stages which the House of Lords suggested should be followed are set out in Box 2.2.

Box 2.2

House of Lords ruling in Adomako case

1. The ordinary principles of the law of negligence should be applied to ascertain whether or not the defendant had been in breach of a duty of care towards the victim who had died.

2. If such a breach of duty was established, the next question was whether that breach caused the death of the victim.

3. If so, the jury had to go on to consider whether that breach of duty should be characterised as gross negligence and therefore as a crime. That would depend on the seriousness of the breach of duty committed by the defendant in all the circumstances in which the defendant was placed when it occurred.

4. The jury would have to consider whether the extent to which the defendant's conduct departed from the proper standard of care incumbent upon him, involving as it must have done a risk of death to the patient, was such that it should be judged criminal.

The judge was required to give the jury a direction on the meaning of gross negligence as had been given in the present case by the Court of Appeal.

The jury might properly find gross negligence on proof of:

(a) indifference to an obvious risk of injury to health or of
(b) actual foresight of the risk coupled either
    (i) with a determination nevertheless to run it or
    (ii) with an intention to avoid it but involving such a high degree of negligence in the attempted avoidance as the jury considered justified conviction or
(c) of inattention or failure to advert to a serious risk going beyond mere inadvertence in respect of an obvious and important matter which the defendant's duty demanded he should address.

(Lettering and numbering are the author's.)

The House of Lords held that the Court of Appeal had applied the correct test and the appeal was dismissed.

There would also be vicarious liability on his employers in the civil courts for his negligence in causing the death of the patient. The Law Commission[5] has recommended that the law should be changed to enable it to be made easier for corporations and statutory bodies to be prosecuted for manslaughter and this may lead to more charges being brought in connection with deaths that arise from gross negligence. The government has accepted the recommendations and is proposing that there should be a new corporate killing offence with the Health and Safety Executive responsible for its enforcement. At the time of writing, legislation is awaited.

The case of Dr Shipman

On 31 January 2000, Dr Shipman, a general practitioner, was found guilty of the murder of 15 patients and was suspected of having killed many more. The atrocious offences raised serious concerns about the inadequacy of professional regulation and control. An inquiry set up by the Secretary of State has not yet made its report.

The case of Beverley Allitt

Following the deaths and injuries to children caused by the nurse Beverley Allitt, an independent inquiry was set up. Its recommendations are considered in Chapter 5.

The case of Kevin Cobb

Kevin Cobb was found guilty of the manslaughter of a nurse and also convicted of drugging three female patients and raping two of them.[6]

Defences

The main defences to a criminal act are shown in Figure 2.11. They are all given here for completeness, but not all of them are relevant to Staff Nurse Jarvis's case.

---

1. Absence of any of the elements making up the offence: *mens rea* or *actus reus*.
2. Infancy:
   below 10 years no crime.
3. Insanity:
   (a) unfit to plead and stand trial;
   (b) not guilty by reason of insanity at the time of the crime.
4. Diminished responsibility and provocation.
5. Mistake.
6. Necessity.
7. Duress and coercion.
8. Superior orders.
9. Self-defence.

Figure 2.11   Main defences to a criminal offence.

Absence of any of the elements making up the offence

It will be apparent from what has been said above that if the accused can show that any of the required elements, either *actus reus* or *mens rea*, as defined in the Act of Parliament or the common law definition of the crime, are missing, then there should be an acquittal. Even though it is usually for the prosecution to show they exist rather than for the defence to prove their absence, it would clearly be an advantage for the defence to show their absence. Thus, for example, in the offence of theft, one of the elements is that the property that has been taken belonged to another. If the defence can show that the property did not belong to anyone but had in fact been abandoned, then that would be a successful defence.

Infancy

Children under 10 years are exempt from criminal responsibility and cannot be found guilty of a crime. The infant is know as *doli incapax*.

Minors over 10 years are presumed to be responsible for their actions but there are considerable procedural differences from the way in which an adult is proceeded against.

Insanity

Insanity can be pleaded before or when the trial takes place so that the accused is held unable by reason of insanity to stand trial. Alternatively, it can be pleaded as a defence to the crime on the basis that at the time the crime was committed the accused was insane. The definition of insanity as a defence is based on the M'Naghten Rules, which were laid down in 1843. The basic propositions are:

every man is presumed to be sane and to possess a sufficient degree of reason to be responsible for his crimes, until the contrary be proved;

and that to establish a defence on ground of insanity, it must be clearly proved that at the time of the committing of the act, the party accused was labouring under such a defect of reason, from disease of mind, as not to know the nature and quality of the act he was doing, or if he did know it, that he did not know he was doing what was wrong.

Since 1843, there have been many interpretations and refinements of this definition, but the substance has survived.

Diminished responsibility and provocation

These statutory defences are provided by the Homicide Act 1957, apply only to murder, and have the effect of enabling the accused charged with murder to be found guilty of manslaughter on grounds of diminished responsibility or provocation.

Mistake

This can be an effective defence where it prevents the accused from being able to form the required mental element (i.e. *mens rea*) to be guilty of the offence charged. Mistake of law is not sufficient, for knowledge that an act is a crime is not usually a necessary ingredient of the *mens rea*.

Necessity

There is considerable debate on the question as to whether there is a defence of necessity to a criminal charge. There are some examples where it has been accepted as a defence to a murder charge, but there is no recognised principle that necessity is a valid defence to any crime.

Duress and coercion

This will be a valid defence where it can be established that the force or compulsion was such that the accused had no choice. It is unlikely to be accepted as a defence to a charge of murder, but has been invoked on other lesser crimes.

Superior orders

It is not a defence for the accused to argue that the crime was committed in obedience to the orders of a superior. However, it might be possible for her to show that as a result of the orders she lacked the required mental element for the crime and that she was acting reasonably in all the circumstances. The issue of obeying orders as a defence in the civil courts is considered in Chapter 4.

Self-defence

Reasonable force can be used to defend oneself or another person against an attack. However, greater force than is reasonable would result in the possibility of the defender being liable to prosecution for assault or, in the event of the assailant dying, murder or manslaughter. This is considered further in Chapter 12.

Criminal injuries compensation

A scheme to compensate those who have suffered personal injuries as the result of criminal action has been in existence since 1964. A new scheme for compensation following injuries or death as a result of a crime was established on 1 April 1996 under the Criminal Injuries Compensation Act 1995 based on a statutory scale of awards known as the 'tariff'. Claims are processed by the Criminal Injury Compensation Authority[7] (CICA) and claims officers and adjudicators on a panel determine whether a claim can be met. Evidence is obtained from applicants, the police medical bodies and others such as witnesses to the incident.

Compensation can be paid to an applicant who has sustained a criminal injury on or after 1 August 1964 or to the family of a person who has died following a criminal injury. The criminal injury must have been sustained in Great Britain (this includes a British aircraft, hovercraft or ship and that part of the Channel tunnel system incorporated into England) and be defined as a crime of violence (including arson, fire-raising or an act of poisoning), or an offence of trespass on a railway, or the apprehension of an offender or giving help to any constable engaged in any such activity. Under the previous scheme, train drivers who witnessed a suicide on the line were not eligible for compensation. Injury includes both physical and mental injury and disease. Where injuries were caused by a motor vehicle, an award of compensation can be made only if the vehicle was used as a weapon. (In injuries resulting from ordinary road traffic offences, compensation is available from the driver's insurance company, or if the driver is uninsured or unknown, from the Motor Insurer's Bureau.[8]) The assailant does not have to have been convicted of a criminal offence, but the police should have been informed of the incident. There is a discretion to refuse to pay awards where the applicant has unduly delayed in making a claim, failed to co-operate with the police in bringing the assailant to justice, or the applicant's conduct before or after the incident makes it inappropriate that a full or any award should be made, or the applicant's character as shown by his criminal convictions make it inappropriate for an award to be made. An application must be made within 2 years of the date of the incident giving rise to the injury, though discretion to extend this limit can be made where it is reasonable and in the interests of justice to do so.

Payments are made according to a tariff set out in the Scheme. There are 25 levels of compensation: the minimum level 1 being £1,000 (e.g. blurred vision of eyes lasting 6 to 13 weeks); level 25 is set at £250,000 (e.g. quadriplegia/tetraplegia or permanent brain damage with no effective control of functions). The death of a viable fetus is set at level 10 £5,000. Compensation is paid for loss of earnings as a direct result of the injury after the first 28 weeks of incapacity.

The fact that the aggressor is a mentally disturbed patient against whom a prosecution may not succeed on the grounds of insanity will be left out of account in deciding whether compensation should be paid.

In 1998–99 £195 million was paid out to 46,000 applicants (6,000 of these received £114 million under the pre-1996 scheme). Nearly 80,000 applied, so almost half failed to receive an award. A report by the Comptroller and Auditor General investigated the functioning of the CICA and reported to the House of Commons.[9] It made significant recommendations to improve the recruitment and selection of staff, to provide more support and information to applicants particularly on eligibility, to monitor the characteristics of applicants, especially their ethnicity to establish if there are differences in application rates between different ethnic groups and to improve quality assurance mechanisms. It also suggested improvements in the processing of applications and suggested that a telephone call centre should be set up.

Information relating to the CICA should be available to all NHS staff, who should ensure that if they are injured at work they can check on their eligibility to receive compensation.

Order that the convicted defendant make a compensation payment to the victim

Judge and magistrates also have the power to order a defendant to make a payment to the victim of the offence of which they have been convicted. Before making the order, the judge has to take into account the defendant's ability to pay the amount ordered.

The future

Recommendations by the Royal Commission on Criminal Justice for changes in criminal procedures are currently being discussed.

Questions and exercises

1   In the case of Staff Nurse Jarvis, trace the course which would be followed if:
    (a)   she was tried in the Magistrates Court;
    (b)   she was tried in the Crown Court;
    (c)   she pleaded guilty in the Magistrates Court;
    (d)   she pleaded guilty in the Crown Court.

2   What do you consider are the advantages and disadvantages of trial before the magistrates compared with a jury trial for an offence which is triable either way?

3   What evidence do you consider that the prosecution would require in a case similar to that of Staff Nurse Jarvis and what evidence would the defence seek?

4   Visit your Magistrates Court and Crown Court and analyse the difference between the two in terms of formality, procedure, and justice to the accused.

References

1. *Pharmaceutical Society of Great Britain* v. *Logan* 1982 Crim. LR 443
2. *R.* v. *Cox, The Times* 22 September 1992
3. *R.* v. *Adomako* [1995] 1 AC 171; [1994] 3 All ER 79
4. *R.* v. *Adomako* [1995] 1 AC 171; [1994] 3 All ER 79
5. Law Commission Report on Criminal Prosecutions March 1996, Stationery Office
6. Robert Munro, Victim's mother's chaperone call, *Nursing Times* 25 May 2000 Vol 96 no 21 p. 8
7. Criminal Injuries Compensation Authority, Tay House, 300 Bath Street, Glasgow G2 4JR
8. Motor Insurer's Bureau 152, Silbury Boulevard, Central Milton Keynes MK9 1NB
9. Home Office Report by the Comptroller and Auditor General Compensating Victims of Violent Crime HC 398 Session 1999–2000 April 2000

3 Liability in a civil court case for negligence

Litigation to obtain compensation in the civil courts is one of the growth areas of recent years. The National Audit Office has estimated that almost £4 billion is required to meet actual and potential claims from events which have occurred. In claims of up to £50,000 more than half the cost is paid to lawyers. There is therefore clear evidence of an increase in litigation and the number of civil claims.[1] If harm has occurred to a patient, then the patient or his/her representatives can seek compensation. However, not all harm is compensatable. Accidents to patients are infinite: they include incidents where the patient falls out of bed, pressure sores develop, the wrong dose of medicine is given, it is given at the wrong time or at the wrong site by the wrong method or the expiry date is passed, the wrong limb is amputated, the treatment is given to the wrong patient, the patient dies as the result of a mistake. Some of these are the result of negligence and the victims may receive compensation. Not all accidents, however, will result in the payment of compensation to the patient or relatives. This chapter looks at the circumstances that must exist for compensation to be payable, the personal liability of the nurse and the liability of her employer, and the type of harm for which compensation will be paid are considered in Chapter 4. The calculation of compensation is considered in Chapter 6.

The elements that must be established by the claimant in a case of negligence before the civil courts are set out in Figure 1.7. In this section we are concerned with four basic questions:

1. What is meant by the term 'duty of care'; when does the nurse owe a duty of care; and to whom is it owed?

2. What is the appropriate standard of care and what criteria determine whether the nurse is in breach of that duty?

3. What is meant by 'reasonably foreseeably caused' and why and how must the claimant prove this in an action for negligence?

4. What type of harm do the courts recognise as capable of being compensated?

This chapter will answer these questions by providing examples where patients have been harmed. The next chapter will consider some specific problems of liability in relation to inexperienced staff, team responsibility, limits on resources, and also the liability of the NHS Trust. The topics covered in this chapter are shown in Figure 3.1.

Duty of care
Does a nurse have a duty to volunteer help?
Standard of care
Deviation from approved practice
Policies, protocols, procedures, guidelines and their effect
Reasonable foreseeability
Keeping up to date
Balancing the risks
Causation
Factual causation
Reasonably foreseeably caused
Taking one's claimant as one finds him
Harm
Post traumatic stress

Figure 3.1   Issues covered in Chapter 3.

Duty of care

Difficulties can arise as to whether a duty of care arises, especially outside the immediate employment situation. A duty of care is not owed universally and the claimant bringing the action has to show that a duty of care was owed to him or her personally.

The legal test of whether a duty of care exists was laid down in the case of *Donoghue* v. *Stevenson*.[2] In this case, manufacturers were held to owe a duty of care to the ultimate consumer. The facts of this case were that a person who was bought a bottle of ginger beer discovered the decomposed remains of a snail when half the beer had been drunk and sued the manufacturer arguing that the manufacturer owed a duty of care to the consumer. In the case, Lord Atkin stated that:

> You must take reasonable care to avoid acts or omissions which you can reasonably foresee would be likely to injure your neighbour. Who then in law is my neighbour? The answer seems to be persons who are so closely and directly affected by my act that I ought reasonably to have them in contemplation as being so affected when I am directing my mind to the acts or omissions which are called in question.

In other words, a duty of care can be said to exist if one can see that one's actions are reasonably likely to cause harm to another person.

In recent years, there have been several cases on whether a duty of care is owed to an individual by different public services: the ambulance service, social services, the police and the fire service. In a recent case,[3] the Court of Appeal held that although the ambulance service owed no duty to the public at large to respond to a telephone call for help, once a 999 call had been accepted, it was arguable that the ambulance service did have an obligation to provide the service for a named individual at a specified address. Subsequently the Court of Appeal dismissed an appeal by the London Ambulance Authority that it should pay the victim £362,377.[4] The facts of the case are below.

Case 3.1   Ambulance slow to arrive

A doctor called an ambulance for a woman who was asthmatic at 4.27 p.m. on 16 February 1991. The standards recommended were that the ambulance should come within 14 minutes. The husband phoned again at 4.39 p.m. and was told they would be there within 7 to 8 minutes. The doctor phoned at 4.55 p.m. and was told it would be a couple of minutes. The ambulance arrived at 5.05 p.m. 38 minutes after the first call. During the journey, the claimant was given oxygen, but on the way suffered a respiratory arrest with tragic consequences, including serious memory impairment, change of personality and miscarriage. The Court of Appeal refused to strike out the case as disclosing no reasonable cause of action for negligence, but held that the case should continue to trial.

The Court of Appeal held that a duty of care could be owed by the ambulance service which was comparable to hospital services rather than to the police or fire services.

In the second appeal, the Court of Appeal held that the acceptance of the call in the present case established the duty of care. It was delay that caused the further injuries. If wrong information had not been given about the arrival of the ambulance, other means of transport could have been used.

Educational psychologist

In the case of *Phelps* v. *Hillingdon London Borough Council*,[5] the Court of Appeal held that an educational psychologist, employed by a local education authority to give advice to it in respect of children in its schools suffering from learning difficulties, did not owe a duty of care to such a child, unless he or she had assumed responsibility for that child. The House of Lords, however, allowed the appeal.[6] It held that a local education authority is liable for the negligent actions of a teacher or educational psychologist and can be sued for a failure to provide an education commensurate with a child's needs. The House of Lords gave a judgment on four cases: the Phelps case against London Borough of Hillingdon; Marcus Jarvis against Hampshire County Council (failing to diagnose dyslexia); G against Bromley (failure to provide him with computer technology and suitable training to help him deal with a muscular problem); and Rhiannon Anderton against Clwyd County Council (she sought pre-action disclosure of educational records: to succeed she had to show that she was suffering from personal injury).

The House of Lords emphasised that liability for negligence by a Council would require exceptional circumstances. It held that a failure to improve a condition from which a child suffered could count as personal injury. It rejected the argument that providing pyschological advice was part of a multi-disciplinary approach which in the past has justified immunity from negligence in care claims.

Placing of foster child

In the case of *W. and others* v. *Essex County Council and another*,[7] the local authority placed a foster child with a couple, having given an assurance that he was not a known sex abuser. In fact, the LA knew that the boy had been cautioned three years previously for indecent assault on his sister. The boy subsequently sexually abused three of the claimants' children. The foster parents' claim for psychiatric shock failed in the High Court and the Court of Appeal on the grounds that the court held no duty of care was owed to them at common law. The children succeeded since they were not subject to any statutory duty by the LA, but were living at home with their parents and express assurances had been given that a sexual abuser would not be placed in that home.

The House of Lords[8] allowed the parents' appeal on the grounds that the parents should not be barred from pursuing their claim: the parents could be seen as victims of the situation, the psychiatric injury they suffered could be seen as within the range of psychiatric injury recognised by law and it could be argued that the local authority owed a duty of care to the parents. They should therefore be allowed to pursue their claim.

In a similar case, the House of Lords[9] allowed the claim by a boy who had been in local authority care all his life to pursue an action against the local authority for psychiatric damage he had suffered as a result of the authority's breach of statutory duty and negligence in failing to place him for adoption or place him in suitable foster homes.

Does a nurse have a duty to volunteer help?

Situation 3.1   Volunteering help

A nurse on her way to work passes a road accident. She sees that a man is still trapped in a vehicle. Does she have an obligation to stop and render first aid? If she does stop and help and something goes wrong, would she be liable?

Unless there is a pre-existing relationship between the parties (for example, if the nurse has caused the accident or if she is employed to assist people in such circumstances), she has no duty in law to stop and render first aid. So if, for example, someone saw her drive past and, knowing that she was a nurse believed that she could have saved the victim, she was consequently sued, the action would fail. Her failure to help is not actionable. There is in law no duty to volunteer help. There must be a pre-existing duty. However, once the nurse undertakes the duty of care, she is then bound to follow the standard of care that would be expected of a reasonable person. So, for example, imagine that she moves the victim and causes spinal injury. If it can be shown that she should have anticipated the dangers of moving a person when a spinal injury was possible, and if there was no immediate danger in leaving the man where he was, then she could be sued for any further injuries she had caused him.

Whilst there is no legal duty, the UKCC has made it clear in its Guidelines for Professional Practice that it expects the nurse to volunteer help in such a situation. It states that the registered practitioner is bound by the Code of Professional Practice at all times. The nurse who failed to volunteer help could therefore not be held legally liable in the civil courts for failing to act; she could, however, face professional conduct proceedings (see Chapter 11). Where the nurse has volunteered help in such a situation, it is unlikely that her employer would accept any responsibility for her actions, (i.e. would not be vicariously liable, see page 62.) and therefore the nurse would have to rely on personal insurance cover in the event of any action being brought against her. This cover, known as cover for samaritan actions, is provided by some professional associations.

Situation 3.2   A fall in the night

Mary Smith is in the post-operative ward following a gall-bladder operation. She becomes very disturbed during the night and Staff Nurse Janice Parker hears a crash and rushes to the ward. She finds Mrs Smith on the floor.

How is the civil liability of the staff nurse determined? The questions to be answered are:

1. Does Staff Nurse Parker owe a duty of care to Mrs Smith?
2. Is she in breach of the duty of care?
3. Has her breach of care led to reasonably foreseeable harm?
4. Has the patient suffered compensatable harm?

To win compensation in a civil case, Mary Smith would have to show that the staff nurse failed to follow the approved accepted practice without good reason in carrying out her duty of care towards her, and that as a reasonably foreseeable result she suffered harm.

Does a duty of care arise?

A nurse, by virtue of the nurse/patient relationship, does owe a duty of care to her patients. Whether a duty of care exists will be decided by established legal principles. There is no doubt that in these circumstances, the nurse does owe a duty of care to the patient.

Once it is decided that a duty of care is owed, the next question is: has there been a breach of this duty? Before this can be answered, the nature of the standard of care owed must be established.

Standard of care

Approved practice

Case 3.2   Birth traumas

Stuart Whitehouse was born on 7 January 1970 with severe brain damage. His mother alleged that the brain damage was caused because the doctor pulled too hard and too long with forceps, as a consequence of which the baby was severely disabled. The doctor denied the allegations.

The House of Lords stated that whether an error of judgement was negligence or not depended on the facts of the situation. The test to be applied to determine if there was negligence was the Bolam Test (from an earlier case in 1957[10]). In applying this test in this case, the House of Lords decided that Mr Jordan had not been negligent. The Bolam Test is as follows:

> When you get a situation that involves the use of some special skill or competence, then the test as to whether there has been negligence or not is . . . the standard of the ordinary skilled man exercising and professing to have that special skill. If a surgeon failed to measure up to that in any respect ('clinical judgement' or otherwise), he had been negligent and should be so adjudged.[11]

In the last sentence, any other professional can be substituted for the word 'surgeon'. Thus the negligence of a nurse is to be determined by the standard of the ordinary skilled nurse.

Let's turn to the situation above of the patient falling out of bed and see how the court would decide whether or not Staff Nurse Janice Parker was in breach of care in relation to the patient Mary Smith.

What would the ordinary skilled nurse be expected to do in those circumstances? Was it reasonably foreseeable that this patient was likely to be restless? If so, what additional precautions should have been taken? Was she in the right location and was she adequately supervised? Had the patient called earlier for help or a bedpan and did that request go unheard or unmet? In the actual court hearing, expert evidence would be given as to what would have been expected of a nurse in that context, and the judge would decide what should be regarded as acceptable practice in that context.

Deviation from approved practice

It does not follow that simply to fail to follow the accepted practice is in itself evidence of negligence since there may well be very strong reasons why the usual properly accepted practice was not followed in a particular case. The following case illustrates this point.

Case 3.3 Biopsy[12]

A consultant physician and a consultant surgeon, while recognising that the most likely diagnosis of the patient's illness was tuberculosis (TB), took the view that Hodgkin's disease, carcinoma and sarcoidosis were also possibilities. Because Hodgkin's disease was fatal unless remedial steps were taken in its early stages, they decided that rather than wait several weeks for the result of a sputum test, the operation of mediastinoscopy should be performed to provide a biopsy. This involved some risk of damage to the left laryngeal recurrent nerve, even if correctly performed. The operation was carried out properly, but that damage did in fact occur. The biopsy proved negative and it was subsequently confirmed that the patient did have TB and not Hodgkin's disease. The patient brought an action against the health authority, claiming that the decision to perform the biopsy rather than wait for the result of the TB test had been negligent.

At the trial, a distinguished body of medical opinion was called approving of the action of the consultants in carrying out the operation, but the judge said that he preferred the evidence of an expert witness called for the claimant, who had stated that the case had almost certainly been one of TB from the outset and should have been so diagnosed, and that it had been wrong and dangerous to undertake the operation. The trial judge gave judgment for the claimant. The defendants succeeded before the Court of Appeal and the claimant therefore appealed to the House of Lords. The House of Lords held that in the medical profession there was room for differences of opinion and practice, and that a court's preference for one body of opinion over another was no basis for a conclusion of negligence. Where it was alleged that a fully considered decision by two consultants in their own special field had been negligent, it was not sufficient to establish negligence for the claimant to show that there was a body of competent professional opinion that considered that the decision had been wrong if there was also a body of equally competent professional opinion that supported the decision as having been reasonable in the circumstances. The claimant therefore lost the appeal and the case.

While this decision might seem very hard for the patient, it is only fair to the professional staff where a decision has been made carefully and with great consideration and is supported by substantial professional opinion, even if not everyone would have followed the same practice. In applying this to nursing staff, it can be said that in most circumstances the nurse will be expected to follow the standards of practice laid down by her profession, or the local policy of her employer, but there may be very exceptional circumstances where it is justifiable not to follow the accepted practice. In a more recent case, the Court of Appeal has suggested that where there was more than one acceptable standard, competence should be gauged by the lowest of them.[13] The Bolam Test applied where there was a conscious choice of available courses made by a trained professional. It was inappropriate where the alleged neglect lay in an oversight.

The wording of the Congenital Disabilities (Civil Liability) Act 1976 (which does allow right of action in cases of pre-natal infliction of harm) puts the point very clearly:

> Section 1(5) The defendant is not answerable to the child, for anything he did or omitted to do when responsible in a professional capacity for treating or advising the parent, if he took reasonable care having due regard to then received professional opinion applicable to the particular class of case; but that does not mean that he is answerable only because he departed from received opinion.

This Act is considered in detail in Chapter 14.

The courts rely upon expert evidence to decide on what is a reasonable standard of care and the House of Lords in the Bolitho case recently emphasised that such expert opinion must flow logically, and reasonably from the specific circumstances:

> The use of the adjectives 'responsible, reasonable and respectable' (in the Bolam case) all showed that the court had to be satisfied that the exponents of the body of opinion relied upon could demonstrate that such opinion had a logical basis.[14]

Following the changes to the civil procedure as a result of the Woolf Reforms, parties to a civil action are required, if possible, to agree upon experts who are to give evidence of the required standards and the extent to which what actually happened measured up to that standard.

The application of the Bolam Test was considered in the work of the laboratory screeners who read the slides for cervical cytology.[15] The High Court and Court of Appeal held that the Bolam Test did not apply where no professional judgment was required by the employee. The full facts of the case are given in Chapter 23.

Policies, protocol, procedures, guidelines and their effect

The questions arise: When must I follow a procedure and when should I not follow it? Is there any difference in law between a policy, a procedure and a guideline and their effect? In the main, guidance issued by an employer, by a professional association or by the registration body should as far as is reasonable be followed. However, there may be specific circumstances that make the following of a particular procedure inappropriate and therefore any reasonable practitioner would modify compliance with the procedure accordingly. Clearly, advice from others would be required to ascertain whether rigid compliance with the procedure would be justified. The courts require a reasonable standard to be followed; a standard that would be supported by competent professional opinion and practice. Where the practitioner decides that circumstances justify a modification of the usual procedure, it is essential that she records exactly why the usual practice was not followed.

Procedures, policies, protocols and guidelines do not have a recognised hierarchy in courts of law. The same principles would apply to them all. In general, they should be followed, if it would be reasonable to do so. If a policy, etc is issued by an NHS Trust that is not acceptable in the light of professional practice, it should be challenged as soon as possible and a revised policy which does accord with reasonable standards of care issued. Reference should be made to the work by Brian Hurwitz where this issue is considered in detail.[16] The significance of protocols will become more important as the work of the National Institute for Clinical Excellence (NICE) expands (see Chapter 5). In its NHS Plan, the government has stated its intention that NICE's work in undertaking appraisals and setting guidelines will increase by 50%.

The situation is thus as follows:

1. There is no breach of the standard of care if the professional has acted in accordance with the practice accepted as proper by a responsible body of professional skill in that particular art, and this was appropriate in the circumstances of the case.

2. There is no breach of the standard of care if there is no acceptable body of opinion covering that situation, but what the professional did was considered reasonable in all the circumstances.

3. There is no breach of the standard of care if the professional did not follow the accepted practice, but his actions were reasonable in all the circumstances and would be supported by competent professional opinion.

Reasonable foreseeability

Other criteria are considered in determining if the professional has been negligent. One of the basic principles of the law of negligence is that precautions can be taken only against reasonably known risks.

Case 3.4   Ampoules in phenol

A local anaesthetic was given by injection in a hospital. The ampoule, which was stored in phenol to sterilise it, contained invisible cracks caused by some mishandling in the hospital, through which the phenol seeped into the ampoule and the injection caused paralysis.

The patient sued the anaesthetist and nurses and their employer. The patient, however, lost the case. The possibility of seepage through invisible cracks was not known at that time and precautions against an unforeseeable possibility are not required of the defendant. However, successful defence may of course mean that the next claimant has a greater chance of winning since such risks are now known. The standard of care thus increases.[17]

The Judge, Lord Denning, said in this case:

> It is so easy to be wise after the event and to condemn as negligence that which was only a misadventure. We ought always to be on our guard against it, especially in cases against hospitals and doctors. Medical science has conferred great benefits on mankind, but these benefits are attended by considerable risks. Every surgical operation is attended by risks. We cannot take the benefits without taking the risks. Every advance in technique is also attended by risks. Doctors like the rest of us have to learn by experience; and experience often teaches in a hard way. Something goes wrong and shows up a weakness, and then it is put right . . . We must not look at the 1947 accident with 1954 spectacles.

Exactly the same could be said of practice today and of nurses as well as doctors. There may be many occasions when one looks back and says, 'I would do things differently if I were to do it again,' but that does not mean the professional has been negligent.

Keeping up to date

When one looks at the many professional journals that exist, the question must arise as to what extent the professional can be expected to master all this knowledge. How up to date is one expected to be?

Case 3.5   Crawford v. Charing Cross Hospital, The Times, 8 December 1953[18]

A patient developed brachial palsy during a blood transfusion. An article had appeared in the Lancet six months previously describing this hazard.

The patient lost the case on the grounds that, provided the professional staff were following the accepted approved practice at that time, then it could not be said that they were negligent in failing to apply or be aware of recent knowledge.

Articles in magazines and journals can be of very different status. Some are pure research articles, the lessons from which have not yet been absorbed into current accepted practice; others are controversial and their conclusions may never become part of the recognised procedure. Other instructions, however, would have immediate effect. Thus, if a directive from the Committee for the Safety of Medicines warned against prescribing a particular drug to a patient, to ignore that instruction might well be evidence of negligence. Nursing staff who had received comparable instructions from their profession or senior nurse management would be expected to be aware of these orders and to comply. The instructions would become part of the accepted practice.

Balancing the risks

As the quotation from Lord Denning above points out, there are hazards in modern medicine and much of professional discretion is concerned with balancing the risks of taking action A compared with action B or compared with taking no action at all.

Situation 3.3   *Meningitis*

A patient was admitted with a provisional diagnosis of meningitis. She was immediately barrier nursed in a single room, even though that meant moving a very sick patient onto a four-bed ward. The patient who was removed died in the night. There was criticism from relatives that the patient should not have been moved and also a suggestion that the death was accelerated. Was the nurse at fault if the next day it is discovered that the suspected meningitis patient was only suffering from a non-fatal virus?

Provided the nurse used her professional judgement in making the decision to give the single room to that particular patient, with the knowledge available to her at that time, then there should be no finding of negligence. In fact, if meningitis had been confirmed, then the nurse may well have been negligent in not taking precautions to prevent any danger of staff or patients being infected. She has to use her judgement in determining the degree of risk to both patients.

Causation

The third element in the plaintiff's case against the NHS Trust or the nurse is to establish that there is a causal link between the breach of the duty of care by the nurse and the harm suffered by the plaintiff. It is possible for the nurse to fail in her duty of care to the patient and for the patient to suffer harm, yet the nurse or her employer not be liable in civil law. This is because one of the essential elements that the claimant must establish in an action for negligence is that there is a causal link between the failure of the defendant to follow the approved practice and the harm suffered by the patient. The possibility that this harm could occur must be reasonably foreseeable and must also take place.

Factual causation

Case 3.6   Causation

A patient attended the casualty department after drinking tea that unknown to him had been contaminated with arsenic and that caused prolonged vomiting. The doctor did not examine him, but sent a message that he should see his own doctor. He died a few hours later.

The widow failed in her action because it was established that the patient would have died even if properly examined and treated. In this case, the pathological evidence on the progress of arsenic poisoning and the projected timetable of events had the patient been examined and admitted was of vital importance.[19]

In such circumstances, although a civil action fails there are likely to be professional and disciplinary proceedings by the professional body and the employer.

Barnett's case was an example of a lack of factual connection between the breach of duty of care and the harm suffered by the patient.

Another example of a case that has been before the House of Lords is the following:

Case 3.7   Blindness, but how caused?

In the Wilsher case considered below (page 56) the House of Lords decided that the case should be reheard by a new High Court judge on the issue of whether it was the defendant's negligence that had caused the harm to the child. In this case, it was agreed that there were several different factors that could have caused the child to become blind and the negligence by the defendant was only one of these. The trial judge had failed to make a relevant finding of fact and could not presume that it was the defendant's negligence that had caused the harm.[20]

Following the House of Lords' ruling, the parties came to a settlement and compensation was paid to the parents for the child.

> ### Case 3.8 *The cause of deafness*
>
> A child suffering from meningitis was given 300,000 units of penicillin instead of 10,000 units. The mistake was discovered and remedial action taken. The health authority admitted liability and made an offer to the parents for the additional pain and suffering that the negligence caused the boy. However, the parents argued that the overdose had caused the boy to become deaf and they rejected the board's offer, claiming instead many thousands of pounds more because they held the health authority liable for the deafness.

The House of Lords decided that the parents had not made out the factual causation between the overdose and the deafness and thus that the boy was not entitled to the larger amount. It is a well-known fact that meningitis itself can cause deafness.[21]

Reasonably foreseeably caused

In a civil case for negligence, the plaintiff also has to establish that the harm that occurred was a reasonably foreseeable consequence of breach of duty by the defendant.

> ### Situation 3.4 *Reasonable foreseeability*
>
> In breach of her duty of care, a nurse failed to dispose properly of contaminated dressings which were left on a stainless steel trolley in the treatment area. By chance, two boys broke into the room looking for syringes and needles. When they heard footsteps approaching, they grabbed as much as they could from the trolley and ran off, taking a dressing with them. Subsequently, an outbreak of disease attributable to the dressing occurred in the neighbourhood. Was the nurse responsible in law for this?

The nurse was certainly at fault in not disposing correctly of the dressings. However, it could be argued that the subsequent events were not reasonably foreseeable and in any event the chain of causation between the nurse's action and the outbreak of the disease was broken by the action of the boys. This is sometimes known as a *novus actus interveniens* (i.e. a new act intervening).

Taking one's claimant as one finds him

There is one important exception to the rule that the harm resulting from the breach of duty is reasonably foreseeable, known as the thin skull rule or 'you take your claimant as you find him'.

Situation 3.5   The thin skull rule

A nurse puts some drops in the wrong eye. They were meant to dilate the pupil in the other eye. They would not normally have caused any harm, but because of an existing defect in that eye the patient became blind.

The nurse in this case is clearly negligent. However, in the majority of patients her error would have caused none, or very little, harm. In this case, however, even though she could not have predicted the outcome she would be liable for the harm that has occurred on the basis of the doctrine 'you take your claimant as you find him'.

Case 3.9   The thin skull rule

An accident occurred at work when a labourer was splashed with a piece of molten metal and his lower lip was burnt. The burn was treated and the labourer thought nothing more about it. However, the place where the burn had been began to ulcerate and get larger. He consulted his general practitioner who sent him to hospital where cancer was diagnosed. Treatment by radium needles enabled the lip to heal and destroy the primary growth. Subsequently, however, secondary growths were observed. He had six operations and died of cancer just over three years after the accident. His widow claimed compensation from the employers.

They admitted liability for the original accident, but denied that they were responsible for the man's death. Lord Parker in the Queen's Bench Division held that the test was not whether the defendants could reasonably have foreseen that a burn would cause cancer and that Mr Smith would die. The test was whether these defendants could reasonably foresee the type of injury that he suffered, namely the burn. The amount of damage that he suffers as a result of that burn depends on the characteristics and constitution of the victim. The widow therefore won her case.[22]

Harm

Not all forms of harm are compensatable by the civil courts. Grief itself is not a ground for a claim, although there is now a statutory right for compensation for bereavement where the death has resulted from negligence. This is considered in Chapter 6 when the basis for the amount of compensation is discussed. The court recognises that harm that involves personal injury or death or loss or damage of property should be compensated if the other elements of negligence can be proved. However, the harm must be a reasonably foreseeable consequence of the breach of duty: it must not be too remote. This is a particularly difficult question when economic loss has occurred and the courts have limited the liability of the defendants to reasonably foreseeable economic loss. Similar difficulties arise over determining the liability for causing nervous shock or post traumatic stress as it is now termed.

Post-traumatic stress

Case 3.10   Post-traumatic stress syndrome (nervous shock)

Mr Thomas McLoughlin and his three children George (aged 17), Kathleen (aged 7) and Gillian (aged 3) were in a motor car driven by George when it was in collision with a lorry. George was not at fault. Mrs McLoughlin, who was not in the vehicle, was told by a friend who was in the car behind (with Michael, another McLoughlin child (aged 11), who was a passenger) that George had probably died and that he was uncertain of the condition of the husband or the other children. She was driven to the hospital and saw Michael who told her that Gillian was dead. She was taken down the corridor and through a window she saw Kathleen, crying with her face cut and begrimed with dirt and oil. She could hear George shouting and screaming. She was taken to her husband who was sitting with his head in his hands. His shirt was hanging off him and he was covered in mud and oil. He saw his wife and started sobbing. She was then taken to see George. The whole of the left face and left side was covered. He appeared to recognise her and then lapsed into unconsciousness. Finally, she was taken to see Kathleen who by now had been cleaned up. The child was too upset to speak and simply clung to her mother. As a result of this experience Mrs McLoughlin suffered from severe shock, organic depression and a change of personality. She was normally a person of reasonable fortitude.[23]

Obviously, in a case like this damages would be payable to the husband and the children for the harm which they had suffered, but in addition to that, compensation was claimed by Mrs McLoughlin for nervous shock. The defendants argued that she was too remote from the defendants' negligence: she was not herself a direct victim of the accident, nor was she a bystander witnessing what happened. The House of Lords decided that she was entitled to receive compensation since she was so closely related to those injured, and the nervous shock that she suffered was close in both space and time.

Lord Wilberforce said:

It is necessary to consider three elements inherent in any claim: The class of persons whose claims should be recognised; the proximity of such persons to the accident; and the means by which the shock is caused. As regards the class of persons the possible range is between the closest possible of family ties, of parent and child or husband and wife, and the ordinary bystander. Existing law recognises the claims of the first; it denies that of the second, either on the basis that such persons must be assumed to be possessed of fortitude sufficient to enable them to endure the calamities of modern life or that defendants cannot be expected to compensate the world at large.

Any persons wishing to claim compensation for nervous shock (now referred to as post-traumatic stress syndrome) would have to show that they were actually suffering from a mental illness and not just grief and that they were sufficiently closely related to the objects of the defendant's negligence and also in time and space.

The law has been further clarified by the House of Lords in the case of *Alcock* v. *Chief Constable South Yorkshire Police*.[24] In this case, people who were present at or watched the disaster at Hillesborough where 95 people died (as a result of overcrowding in the stadium, allegedly due to negligence by the police), brought a claim in respect of post-traumatic stress syndrome. The House of Lords held that in order to establish a claim in respect of psychiatric illness resulting from shock it was necessary to show not only that such injury was reasonably foreseeable, but also that the relationship between the claimant and the defendant was sufficiently proximate. Proximity could include not only blood ties, but also ties of love and affection. The closeness would have to be proved in each individual case. The claimant would also have to show propinquity in time and space to the accident or its immediate aftermath. It was held that those claimants who viewed the disaster on television could not be said to be equivalent to being within sight and hearing of the event or its immediate aftermath.

In *White and others* v. *Chief Constable of the South Yorkshire Police and others*,[25] police officers sued for post-traumatic stress syndrome following the same disaster. The House of Lords decided that merely being an employee of the person/organisation responsible for the negligence did not automatically create sufficient proximity for the claimant to succeed in obtaining compensation for post-traumatic stress syndrome. The employee had to satisfy the usual rules of establishing proximity. To obtain compensation for psychiatric illness, a rescuer would have to show that he had objectively exposed himself to danger or reasonably believed that he was doing so. Rescuers were not entitled to claim compensation when they were not within the range of foreseeable physical injury and their psychiatric injury was caused by witnessing or participating in the aftermath of accidents which caused death or injury to others. The police therefore failed in their claim.

Both the McLoughlin and Alcock's cases were referred to in a case in 1998,[26] where a mother failed in her case to obtain compensation for psychiatric illness following the abduction and death of her daughter by a mentally ill out-patient. The Court of Appeal held that the judge was correct to find that there was no proximity between the mother, the daughter and the Tees Health Authority. It was also relevant to consider how the offences could have been avoided even if sufficient proximity were established having regard to the difficulty in identifying and protecting potential victims and to the limited effectiveness of the health authority's powers under the Mental Health Act 1983.[27]

The High Court[28] applied these House of Lords cases in a situation where a fire officer sued his son, claiming damages for psychiatric harm suffered as a result of attending the scene of an accident in which the son had suffered head injuries. The accident occurred as a result of the son driving a car negligently after drinking. The court held that a victim of self-inflicted injuries owed no duty of care to a secondary party who, after witnessing the event from which the injuries resulted or its aftermath, suffered psychiatric injury. In addition, in the circumstances of the case, to allow one family member to sue another would potentially result in an objectionable form of intra family litigation.

This topic of post-traumatic stress syndrome relates to the nurse in two ways. First, she may herself be the victim of post-traumatic stress arising from another person's negligence, in which case she needs to know whether she is likely to obtain compensation. Secondly, in her own work she should be aware of the dangers of causing stress shock in others, and the possibility of claims for compensation arising out of this.

Questions and exercises

1 Consider the duty of care possibly owed by the nurse of an NHS Trust and discuss whether and upon what grounds you think a duty would be owed in the following circumstances:
   (a) an informal patient who wanders away from the hospital and damages cars in the vicinity of the hospital;
   (b) a detained patient who does likewise;
   (c) a patient in the accident and emergency department who after an attempted suicide insists on taking his own discharge and is shortly afterwards found dead on a railway line;
   (d) a doctor in a cinema who gives a person having a cardiac arrest the wrong treatment;
   (e) a community nurse who is caring for a neighbour, not on her list, and who accidentally leaves the door open and the neighbour is mugged and the house burgled.

2 How would you determine the standard of care that should be adopted in carrying out the following procedures:
   (a) lifting;
   (b) administering medication;
   (c) informing patients of their rights;
   (d) advising relatives on the procedures to be followed in dealing with death?

3 Why do you consider that causation is an important element in an action for negligence? Would it be fairer to the claimant if causation did not need to be proved?

4 If there has been a negligent act but no harm has occurred to the patient, what remedies are available (if any) for the patient to obtain compensation?

5 Some countries (e.g. New Zealand, Finland, and Sweden) have a system of no-fault liability, where fault does not have to be proved in order that the claimant can obtain compensation. Discuss the advantages and disadvantages of this system.

References

[1] National Audit Office. Handling clinical negligence claims in England. Report of the Comptroller and Auditor General. House of Commons Session 2000–2001, 3 May 2001.
[2] *Donoghue* v. *Stevenson* [1932] AC 562
[3] *Kent* v. *Griffiths and Others*, *The Times Law Report* 23 December 1998
[4] *Kent* v. *Griffiths and Others* (no 2), *The Times Law Report* 10 February 2000; [2000] 2 All ER 474

5 *Phelps v. Hillingdon London Borough Council* [1998] 1 All ER 421

6 *Phelps v. Hillingdon Borough Council, Anderton v. Clwyd C C; Jarvis v. Hampshire CC; re G* (a Minor) [2000] 4 All ER 504

7 *W. and others v. Essex County Council and another* [1998] 3 All ER 111

8 *W and others v. Essex County Council and another* [2000] 2 All ER 237 HL; [2000] 2 WLR 601 [2000] 1FLR 657

9 *Barrett v. Enfield LBC* [1999] 2 FLR 426

10 *Bolam v. Friern Barnet HMC* [1957] 2 All ER 118

11 *Whitehouse v. Jordan* [1981] 1 All ER 267

12 *Maynard v. W. Midlands RHA* [1984] 1 WLR 634

13 *Michael Hyde and Associates Ltd v. JD Williams and Co Ltd, The Times Law Report* 4 August 2000

14 *Bolitho v. City and Hackney Health Authority* [1997] 3 WLR 115

15 *Penney, Palmer and Cannon v. East Kent Health Authority* [2000] Lloyds Reports Medical 2000 p. 41 CA

16 Brian Hurwitz, *Clinical Guidelines and the Law*, Radcliffe Medical Press, Abingdon 1998

17 *Roe v. Minister of Health* 1954 2 QB 66

18 *Crawford v. Charing Cross Hospital, The Times* 8 December 1953

19 *Barnett v. Chelsea HMC* 1968 1 All ER 1068

20 *Wilsher v. Essex Area Health Authority* CA 1986 3 All ER 801 HL 1988 1 All ER 871

21 *Kay v. Ayrshire and Arran Health Board* 1987 2 All ER 417

22 *Smith v. Leech Brain & Co. Ltd* QBD 1961 3 All ER 1159

23 *McLoughlin v. O'Brian* 1982 2 All ER 298

24 *Alcock v. Chief Constable S. Yorks. Police* 1992 2 AC 310 HL

25 *White and others v. Chief Constable of the South Yorkshire Police and others* [1999] 1 All ER 1

26 *Palmer v. Tees Health Authority and another, The Times Law Report* 1 June 1998, [1998] Lloyds Rep 447 QBD

27 *Palmer v. Tees HA* (2000) 2 LGLR 69 CA

28 *Greatorex v. Greatorex and another* (Pope, Pr 20 Defendant) [2000] 4 All ER 769

4

Specific problem areas in civil liability: the personal liability of the nurse, the vicarious liability of the employer and managerial issues

In this chapter, we explore some of the particular difficulties that can arise in determining the liability of a professional in some specific situations (see Figure 4.1), beginning with liability for negligence in communicating. In addition, we consider the problems that can arise from inadequate resources; the nurse as a manager; and the liability of the employer. The scope of professional practice and the role of clinical nurse specialist and consultant nurse are considered in Chapter 24.

Negligence in communicating

It is possible to be negligent in failing to communicate with the appropriate person at the correct time and in the proper way.

> *Case 4.1   Crushed fingers*
>
> Mr Coles suffered a crush injury to his finger. He went to the cottage hospital where the nurse cleaned the wound of dust and dirt and told him to go to a proper hospital where he would have an anti-tetanus injection. But neither she nor anyone else impressed upon him the purpose and importance of the visit and so he did not go. He later saw his general practitioner who believed that he had had the injection and so he did not give him one. He subsequently died of tetanus.[1]

In this case, there was negligence by all those professional staff (including the nurse) who had failed to communicate adequately with other professionals and with the patient. Failure to communicate, if it falls short of the required professional standard, can be regarded as negligence and is actionable if it causes reasonably foreseeable harm to the patient.

Failure to communicate rarely causes such devastating harm as in this tetanus case, but there are other well-known examples where it is vital that the patient receives certain information and it cannot be assumed that the patient is aware of the dangers. For example, in head injury cases there may be no detectable sign of head injury when the patient is seen in the accident and emergency department. However, it is essential that the patient is warned to return if certain symptoms appear.

```
Negligence in communication
Inexperience
Team liability and apportioning responsibility
Taking instructions: refusal to obey
Obeying orders in an emergency
Nurse as a manager
Delegation and supervision
Pressure upon manager
Liability of employer
Vicarious liability
In the course of employment
Liability for volunteers
Liability for independent contractors
Direct liability of employer
Indemnity
Pressure from inadequate resources
Public Interest Disclosure Act 1998 and whistle-blowing
```

Figure 4.1 Issues covered in Chapter 4.

Comparable instructions must be given after plastering and in many other situations. In such circumstances, it is advisable for a strict procedure to be implemented to ensure that the correct information is given both by word of mouth and in writing. If there is likely to be any dispute as to whether the information was given and/or where there are considerable dangers if the patient is not informed, it is possible to ask the patient to acknowledge in writing his receipt of that information. This procedure has the added advantage of making the patient aware of the importance of the information or instructions.

Negligence in instructing others is considered in further detail in Chapter 18 which deals with the law and the nurse educator. Liability for a negligent mis-statement was found when a local authority recommended a registered childminder to a mother despite an earlier case of non-accidental injury by the minder.[2]

Inexperience

Does a newly qualified nurse have to follow the same standard of care as an experienced nurse?

In practical terms, it is of course impossible to expect the same standard of care from the junior nurse as from the experienced senior nurse. However, in law that is what the patient is entitled to expect. You cannot say in defence to a patient, 'The reason that you were given the wrong drug is that nurse X administered it and she has only just qualified.' The patient is entitled to receive the accepted standard of care whoever provides it. It is, however, essential that staff work within their field of competence and that work requiring greater experience is performed by those with the appropriate skills, or that those lacking in experience have adequate supervision to ensure the task is safely undertaken. This point is discussed in the Wilsher case which is considered below on page 56.

Case 4.2   A learner driver

Mr Nettleship was teaching Mrs Weston to drive in her husband's car. On the third lesson, he was helping her by moving the gear lever, applying the hand-brake, and occasionally helping with the steering. In the course of the lesson, they made a slow left-hand turn after stopping at a halt sign. However, Mrs Weston did not straighten up the wheel and panicked. Mr Nettleship got hold of the handbrake with one hand and tried to get hold of the steering wheel with the other. The car hit a lamp standard. Mr Nettleship broke his knee-cap. He claimed compensation and succeeded before the Court of Appeal.[3]

The crucial question in the case was: since Mrs Weston was not a qualified driver, was the standard of care that she owed to him lower than would otherwise have been the case? The court decided not. They preferred to have one standard of driving, not a variable standard depending on the characteristics of the individual driver:

'The certainties of a general standard is preferable to the vagaries of a fluctuating standard' (Lord Justice Megaw).

This might seem irrelevant to the standard of the nurse but Lord Justice Megaw, in discussing the issue, used the example of the young surgeon:

Suppose that to the knowledge of the patient, a young surgeon, whom the patient has chosen to operate on him, has only just qualified. If the operation goes wrong because of the surgeon's inexperience, is there a defence on the basis that the standard of care and skill was lower than the standard of a competent and experienced surgeon? In cases such as the present it is preferable that there should be a reasonably certain and reasonably ascertainable standard of care, even if on occasion that may appear to work hardly against an inexperienced driver.

Mr Nettleship obtained his compensation, subject to a reduction for contributory negligence.

Situation 4.1   No experience

Ruth Evans is recently qualified and is a staff nurse at Roger Park Hospital. She is asked to work initially on the orthopaedic ward until a vacancy occurs on the childrens' ward, which is her chosen specialty. The orthopaedic consultant suggests that Fred Timms, who has recently been taken off traction, could start some mobility exercises. Ruth, following this advice, approaches Fred's bed with a nursing auxiliary and with a pair of crutches. She suggests that Fred should manoeuvre himself to the side of the bed and gently put his sound leg on the floor. Then when he feels steady enough, he should take the crutches and start to walk. Fred shifts to the side of the bed, puts his sound leg on the floor, but as he stands up holding onto the crutches, they slide away from him and he falls heavily to the ground. Subsequently, X-rays reveal a further fracture of the injured leg and

Situation 4.1   continued

a fresh fracture in the other leg. Where does Ruth stand as far as liability is concerned? Is the fact that she has only just commenced on the orthopaedic ward and has never specialised in it a good defence for her personally against any potential court action that Fred might bring?

It is quite likely that if this case were investigated it would be established that there was a recognised procedure for mobilisation of orthopaedic patients, which would most likely involve the physiotherapist, and that Ruth had failed to follow this and probably was not even aware of its existence. This would be no defence against Fred. If he can establish the four elements of negligence – (a) a duty of care was owed to him, (b) Ruth was in breach of that duty by failing to follow the accepted approved practice and that (c) as a reasonably foreseeable consequence, he has (d) been caused harm – then he would succeed in his action. Ruth would be held to be negligent. Fred is, however, more likely to sue the NHS Trust as Ruth's employer on the grounds that it is vicariously liable for her negligence and is also directly liable for failing to ensure a system of supervision of inexperienced staff. Other staff may also be held negligent. For example, who should have ensured that Ruth had the requisite training, that she was made aware of ward procedures, and that she had adequate support? Someone else should have ensured that she was aware of the role of the physiotherapist.

In practice, of course, the experience of individual staff varies greatly and, even where staff have had the same experience and training, their level of skill and manual dexterity may also vary greatly. However, the patient should be assured that the recognised approved standard of care will be given. Occasionally, a patient may require a higher standard.

For example, Mr Links may have held himself up as a specialist in a complex ear operation which is not often performed because of its particular hazards and difficulties. A general practitioner might refer a patient to Mr Links because of his particular skill. If Mr Links then fails to perform the operation carefully and the patient suffers harm, it is no defence for Mr Links to claim that he knows he did not perform it correctly, but no other ear surgeon could have done it. He has held himself up as having that particular skill. Of course, it would have to be shown that he had failed to perform the operation with the required level of care and skill. The fact that things go wrong does not in itself mean that there has been negligence.

Team liability and the apportionment of responsibility

Team liability

If harm is caused by another member of the team, is the nurse responsible?

Work in the health service is, above all, team oriented. Very few tasks are performed entirely on one's own. In the community, particular tasks are often allocated not purely on a professional basis, but on a key worker basis, which enables one person to take responsibility for a wide range of tasks.

Situation 4.2   The team

Jane is a third-year student who, together with other members of staff on the ward, is caring for orthopaedic patients. The nursing process is in operation. One day, Jane is asked to work in the plaster unit where it is her task to bind the plaster bandage around the patients' limbs. One of the patients, a young boy called Sam, has a broken wrist and Jane is told to strap it up. She bandages the wrist and then calls the sister to look at it. The sister glances at it, but does not touch it and the boy's mother is asked to bring him back in three weeks' time. No instructions are given about checking the tightness of the bandage or moving the hand. Three weeks later the boy returns with his mother and it is noticed that the bandage has been put on too tightly and it appears that permanent damage has been done to the boy's hand. What is Jane's responsibility?

Jane is, of course, the employee who actually bandaged his wrist and her personal liability will depend on such questions as: Had Jane been trained to plaster? Was such a task entirely within her competence? Should she have refused to undertake an activity for which she was not competent? Was her level of expertise such that the sister should have checked her work? If, for example, it should have been quite clear that Jane was too inexperienced to undertake the task without supervision, the fact that she asked the sister to check over the work might be sufficient to relieve her of personal responsibility. The failure to communicate to the parent the need to check on the plaster is also a breach of duty and liability will depend upon who had the responsibility of ensuring that this was done. As has been noted in the first section of this chapter, failure to communicate can itself be grounds for an allegation of negligence.

The team may be a group of nurses working together – it might be a multidisciplinary group. In the following case, the team was made up of doctors and nurses working under one consultant.

Case 4.3   No team liability

A premature baby was placed in a special care baby unit staffed by a medical team consisting of two consultants, a senior registrar, several junior doctors and trained nurses. A junior doctor, while monitoring the oxygen intake, inadvertently put the catheter in a vein rather than in an artery. He asked the senior registrar to check what he had done. The registrar failed to see the mistake and several hours later made exactly the same mistake himself. As a result, the catheter failed to monitor the oxygen correctly and it was alleged that the child suffered from an incurable condition of the retina resulting in near-blindness.[4]

At the trial, the judge awarded £116,199 to the child. The health authority appealed to the Court of Appeal on the grounds that (1) there had been no breach of care of duty owed to the child because the standard of care required of doctors in the unit was only that reasonably required of doctors having the same formal qualifications and practical experience as the doctors in the unit, and (2) the child had failed to show that the health authority's actions had caused or contributed to his condition since excess oxygen was merely one of several different factors, any one of which could have caused or contributed to the eye condition from which the child suffered. This last point is known as causation and is discussed in Chapter 3.

On the point of the standard of care, the Court of Appeal held that there was no concept of team negligence, in the sense that each individual team member was required to observe standards demanded of the unit as a whole, because it could not be right, for example, to expose a student nurse to an action for negligence for her failure to possess the experience of a consultant. The standard of care required was that of the ordinary skilled person exercising and professing to have that special skill, but that standard was to be determined in the context of the particular posts in the unit rather than according to the general rank or status of the people filling the posts, since the duty ought to be tailored to the acts which the doctor had elected to perform rather than to the doctor himself. It followed that inexperience was no defence to an action for negligence. One judge, however, stated that an inexperienced doctor who was called on to exercise a specialist skill and who made a mistake nevertheless satisfied the necessary standard of care if he had sought the advice and help of his superior when necessary. The court in this case applied the same standard as the court in the White-house and Jordan case (see page 40), i.e. the 'Bolam Test'. The judges held that the junior doctor had not been negligent and had upheld the relevant standard of care by consulting his superior. His superior had, however, been negligent in failing to notice that the catheter had been mistakenly inserted in a vein rather than an artery and, accordingly, the health authority was vicariously liable for the registrar's negligence.

An additional finding was that there was no reason why, in certain circumstances, a health authority could not be directly liable to a claimant if it failed to provide sufficient or properly qualified and competent medical staff for the unit, see page 69 on direct liability. The House of Lords subsequently ordered a new trial on the issue of causation and the parties then settled the case (see Chapter 3).

Apportioning responsibility

Although there is no concept of team negligence in law, each person is individually responsible for his/her negligence; it does not follow that there are no occasions of multiple liability, i.e. in a given situation several different professionals might be individually responsible for their own individual negligence. An example of this is given in Chapter 28 on the prescribing of medicines.[5] Under the Civil Liability (Contribution) Act 1978, if there are several defendants, a successful claimant can recover damages from any one of the defendants. That defendant may then sue the other defendants to recover a sum which represents their responsibility for the harm which has occurred.

Taking instructions: refusal to obey

The general principles

When we look at the scope of professional practice (see Chapter 24), we will consider the possibility that the nurse might have to refuse to undertake a task where, for example, she was not trained to perform it or where she had insufficient time to undertake it safely. In this section, we look at the wider field of obeying orders.

Situation 4.3   Orders are orders

A registrar decides that Margaret Brown should be prescribed a new drug that has only just been released onto the market and writes her up for it. The staff nurse on that ward is not familiar with the drug and says that she would like to check it with the pharmacist before she administers it. The doctor is furious with this insolence and says that if he has written it up then she should administer it without questioning his competence. The nurse says that she needs some understanding of the drug before she gives it to the patient. The doctor insists she gives it. Where does the nurse stand?

This is a simplified version of situations that often confront the nurse. This particular example raises the issue of what the nurse's responsibility is in relation to the administration of drugs, but examples could be given from other fields such as obeying the order 'not for resuscitation', not passing certain information on to a patient, etc.

It is impossible to give an answer that would apply to every situation. In an emergency, for example, certain risks have to be taken which would not be appropriate in non-urgent circumstances. In the above situation, the nurse would be quite correct in obtaining further information about the drug in question. When she administers a drug she must be sure that she is administering the right drug, at the right time, in the right place, at the right dosage, in the right way, to the right patient. She should not administer a drug of which she has no knowledge without taking all reasonable steps to ascertain that it is appropriate for that particular patient. If in the above situation she were to go ahead and administer the drug on the orders of the doctor and the patient were to die or suffer harm as a result, she could be held to be negligent in any civil action (for which her employers would be held vicariously liable) since she failed to follow the reasonable standards of care expected of a nurse. She could also face professional disciplinary proceedings before the PCC and disciplinary proceedings before her own line manager because she failed to use all care and skill in carrying out her contract of employment. If the patient died, the nurse might have to appear in the coroner's court and there might also be criminal proceedings brought against both her and the doctor. (See the UKCC advisory paper, 'Guidelines for Professional Practice' on this issue.)

In all these courts and hearings, the phrase 'but I was only carrying out orders' will not be sufficient defence on its own. In the civil courts, the professional proceedings and the employer's disciplinary proceedings, the nurse would have to show that what she did was reasonable having regard to the approved accepted practice to be expected from any qualified nurse. In the criminal courts, she would have to show that her acts did not constitute the ingredients of the particular charge and/or that she lacked the required mental state.

Obeying orders in an emergency

In certain circumstances, time does not permit the usual practice to be followed, but the risks taken must be balanced against the risk of the patient dying.

Situation 4.4 *Emergency*

A patient has been brought into the accident and emergency department with severe bleeding. A blood sample is taken for cross-matching and he is immediately put on an intravenous infusion of plasma. The doctor places the cannula in the patient's arm for the intravenous infusion and asks the nurse to set up a saline solution for administration straight away. Staff Nurse Bryant takes the bag that the doctor is holding out to her and attaches it to the IV line. She does not check the bag. The patient's condition worsens and he eventually dies. It is then discovered that the doctor inadvertently gave the nurse a bag containing a substance other than saline. What is the nurse's liability?

It is clear that a quick check of the label on the bag would not have delayed the patient's treatment and could have been done by the nurse without any difficulty. It is most likely that she would be found personally negligent (though her employer would have to pay compensation because of its vicarious liability for her negligence) in these circumstances and any defence of 'but that was the bag the doctor gave me' would be unlikely to succeed. There could be other circumstances where emergency life-saving measures are required and the nurse would be unable to make the same checks. Very rarely, however, would the defence of 'obeying orders' succeed, since as a professionally qualified person the nurse would be expected to act responsibly and carefully and to ensure that her own personal actions are safe.

Nurses sometimes complain that the misgivings they express to doctors are ignored. What do they do then? Obviously, it depends upon the circumstances. Where her misgivings concern treatment that could be harmful to the patient and if one doctor ignored her concern, then the nurse should express her misgivings to her own line manager and, if necessary, the advice of a more senior doctor should be sought. Much depends upon the approach made by the nurse and the nature of the relationship and understanding that exists between the nurse and the doctor. Undoubtedly, encouragement of a team approach to patient care could prevent many unnecessary confrontations of this kind. It should, of course, be stressed that a nurse should not disobey the instructions of a doctor lightly; she should have compelling reasons from the patient's point of view. She should ensure that she keeps detailed records indicating the reasons for her actions and that her nurse manager is brought in at the earliest opportunity. If it should happen that the nurse's attitude was unreasonable then she would, of course, face disciplinary action and, if the patient has been harmed as a result of the nurse's action, civil proceedings and professional misconduct proceedings.

In a case heard by the Court of Appeal in 1942,[6] Lord Goddard said:

> If a doctor in a moment of carelessness, perhaps by the use of a wrong symbol in a prescription, ordered a dose which to an experienced ward sister was obviously incorrect and dangerous, I think it might well be held to be negligence if she administered it without obtaining confirmation from the doctor or higher authority. In the stress of an operation, however, I should suppose that the first thing required of a nurse would be an unhesitating obedience to the orders of the surgeon.

Since 1942, as the recognition of the nurse's personal professional accountability has strengthened, the number of occasions on which a nurse would be expected to obey orders without question has clearly diminished.

The nurse as manager

Delegation and supervision

As the scope of professional practice develops (see Chapter 24), more and more work that is currently undertaken by registered staff will have to be delegated to health care support workers under the supervision of registered practitioners. Delegation may take place to other trained staff, learners, and nursing assistants, and also volunteers. On some occasions, these volunteers may be very unwilling helpers as, for example, where youth training schemes include an attachment to a hospital. If such persons are assigned to work on a ward or department and the nurse manager is responsible for them, then she would have to ensure that their training and the tasks delegated to them are appropriate, and that adequate supervision is provided.

As a manager, the nurse would be responsible for ensuring that the resources were effectively used and were sufficient for treating patients according to the approved standard of care. If harm is caused by inadequate resources and it is established that she failed to take the appropriate measures to prevent unreasonable risks arising, then she may well be liable (see above).

Pressure upon the manager

Situation 4.5   *Manager's nightmare*

Nursing Officer Janice Clarke is on duty and is informed by the staff in the surgical ward that although they are on intake and have three empty beds, owing to illness and the failure to fill vacancies they are so far below their establishment that the situation is dangerous and the present staff cannot cope with any more patients.

Obviously, the nursing officer would ensure that the facts are correct and that the nurses on that ward are using their time appropriately and not undertaking tasks that could safely be left, in order to give priority to the work that is most important. Having assured herself that the situation is critical, she would then look internally at other wards and decide whether staff could be transferred. She might also have to consider bringing in agency nurses. If necessary, she would consider the situation on a district basis which might mean that she would have to discuss the possibility of another hospital taking over the intake at the present. Ultimately, she might have to bring in other districts or at least refer the problems to a more senior manager. The decision might be made that waiting list admissions are cancelled for the time being. Clearly, at all stages in this decision the evidence of the individual ward staff on the dangers and hazards is vital for informed decisions to be made. Like the ward sister or staff nurse, the nursing officer herself should keep records of the reasons behind the actions she has taken since this information may well be relevant to a court or PCC hearing. (Whistle-blowing is considered below.)

Covering several wards

Another difficulty that can arise in this context is where a ward sister is in charge of her own ward and also holds the drug cupboard keys for another ward because there is no trained nurse on that ward. In such a situation, the ward sister would have the same responsibilities for both wards. Her tasks of delegation and supervision become extremely difficult and if something goes wrong on one ward in her absence, she may well be liable if that task required her personal supervision. If such problems were likely, then she would obviously have to ensure that this was made known to the senior nurse management and ultimately the NHS Trust whose duty it is to take reasonable steps to provide the appropriate facilities.

Situation 4.6   On holiday

Marion is ward sister of an acute surgical ward of 30 patients. When she is on holiday, a patient is given a premedication prior to the form of consent for his operation being signed. The mistake is discovered and because it was felt that there was no doubt that the patient wanted to have the operation he was still asked to sign the form. He was then taken to theatre. Subsequently, he disputed the extent of his operation as he had understood that the operation was only exploratory, but he received radical surgery including the provision of a colostomy. He argued that had he known that this was a possibility he would not have agreed to have the operation and he could not remember signing any form of consent. The circumstances of his signature then were discovered. Since the ward sister was on holiday at the time, is there any possibility of her being liable?

It would be cheering for ward sisters and managers if the question could be answered with a definite 'No'. However, this is not possible. A manager has a continuing responsibility to ensure that procedures and policies are designed and implemented to prevent any likelihood of harm to the patient. A vital question to be answered would be: had a procedure been established to ensure that the nursing staff checked that the consent form had been signed before administration of premedication? It would be the ward sister's responsibility to ensure that those procedures that come under the responsibility of the nursing staff are carried out competently and diligently, even when she is not there. In this example, the doctor would be liable for failing to obtain consent. In addition, as far as the immediate responsibility is concerned, the manager in charge of the ward at the time would also share liability for the events, but if, for example, it were established that there was no clear system for ensuring a correct procedure in relation to the checking of consent forms prior to the premedication being given, then the ward sister who should have implemented and supervised such a procedure would share some responsibility for the events. It is likely, too, that evidence of similar events in the past would be used to show the deficiencies in overall ward management in this particular context. In this context, the ward sister's liability is not vicarious (see next section), i.e. it does not concern taking responsibility for the fault of others. It is direct, her own personal liability for failing in her management role. If, of course, it can be shown that a sound practice had been implemented and was not followed on that occasion owing to the negligence of the staff on duty at that time, then there is less likelihood that the ward sister would be held liable.

Her failings in her responsibilities as manager could result in her being sued in the civil courts and, in addition, it could result in her facing a hearing for professional misconduct before the PCC of the UKCC. The definition of misconduct which may justify removal from the Register is sufficiently wide to cover mismanagement by a nurse. It is thus an increasing feature of the PCC hearings that as well as hearing a case against an individual nurse who has been at fault in the care of patients, that nurse's manager or managers may also appear before the PCC to answer the charge of misconduct in failing to take responsibility for the situation and having shown a failure in management. Similar principles would apply if, for example, a nurse was known to be on drugs or under the influence of drink at work. If this was known or should have reasonably been known to the managers (they cannot simply turn a blind eye and pretend to be ignorant) and they failed to take appropriate action, then they may well face a hearing for professional misconduct.

The Royal College of Nursing has provided guidance on the principles of good management practice[7] covering the topics of: vision and strategy, leadership, managing people, managing financial resources, management of care, and quality and risk management. Its aim is to provide a template for managers to develop their own performance standards. It emphasises the importance of regular updating. The implications of clinical governance are considered in Chapter 5.

The liability of the employer

Vicarious liability

The NHS Trust or employer has two forms of liability in negligence: one is known as direct liability, i.e. the Trust itself is at fault; the other is known as vicarious liability or indirect liability, i.e. the Trust is responsible for the faults of others, mainly its employees. In this first section, we look at the vicarious liability of the employer, which could be a health authority, an NHS Trust, a private hospital, a company, or even a general practitioner who employs his own staff.

Situation 4.7 *Assault on behalf of the employer*

Kate was a staff nurse in casualty where at weekends there tended to be a problem with drunks. The hospital was close to the town centre and to several pubs and not infrequently people needing some assistance were accompanied by friends who were incoherent and abusive. One evening, Kate was very busy and therefore extremely annoyed to find some very obstreperous men accompanying a man with a cut head. She asked them to leave him and wait outside. They refused to go. She said she would have to summon the police if they did not leave quietly. One particularly aggressive visitor moved towards the treatment trolley and Kate, fearing that he would knock it over, raised her arm to prevent him. He was taken by surprise at her actions and fell heavily to the ground, catching his head on the side of the trolley. Kate has subsequently learnt that he intends to sue her and her employer.

In a personal action against her for assault, Kate would have to prove that she took reasonable action in self-defence or in protecting her employer's property or in evicting on behalf of the occupier a trespasser who refused to go. In such cases, it is more likely that the claimant would sue the NHS Trust responsible for the wrongs of its employees. The claimant does not have to choose whether to sue the employer or the employee. He can sue both. The obvious advantage of suing the employer is that funds will be available to pay him should he win the case. To win against the employer, he has to establish the following:

1. Kate was negligent or was liable for a civil wrong (see below).
2. Kate was an employee (see below).
3. Kate was acting in course of her employment (see below).

There is no problem with the second element in this case. Kate was an employee, but there may be cases where this is not so clear, for example, if Kate were an agency nurse it might not always be obvious whether Kate is considered to be an employee of the authority to which she is sent or whether she continues to be an employee of the agency.

In practice, the first element could cause some considerable difficulty. Much would depend on the circumstances of the assault: whether she had lost her temper, the level of provocation she was subjected to, etc. Let's assume, for the purpose of this discussion, that it was established as a matter of fact that Kate had acted unlawfully and that personal action against her would therefore succeed.

In the course of employment

In the employer's interests

The third element now needs to be considered. Was the nurse acting in course of her employment when she assaulted the visitor? The test used to answer this question is as follows: what was she employed to do, and when she carried out that act was she acting for the benefit of her employer? In this case, she was clearly not employed as a bouncer, but she was trying to prevent a trolley from being upset by an obstreperous visitor (or even trespasser). This could certainly be seen as being in the interests of the employer's business. Even if there were a clear policy that nursing staff should not attempt to deal with aggressive visitors on their own, this should not necessarily prevent the act from being in course of employment. The performance of a prohibited act does not on its own mean that the employee has ceased to be acting in course of employment. All the facts have to be considered. If it can be shown that all three elements were present, the NHS Trust could be held vicariously liable for the harm caused by the nurse.

The difficulties in establishing whether an act is in course of employment are shown in the following cases. See Figure 4.2 for an example of criteria used by the courts to decide if an act is in course of employment.

When is an assault considered to be in course of employment, and when is it not?

Case 4.4   A bag of sugar

Hall, a carter, employed by the defendants, honestly and reasonably believed that the plaintiff, a boy of 12, was pilfering or about to pilfer from a bag of sugar on the defendant's wagon. He hit him on the back of the neck, causing him to fall under one of the wheels of the wagon, which injured his foot.

The term may cover:

1. Acts authorised by employer;
2. Acts not authorised by employer, but
   (a)   performed for the purpose of the employer's business;
   (b)   prohibited acts, but the prohibition does not take the conduct outside the sphere of employment (*Rose* v. *Plenty* 1976 1 All ER 97);
   (c)   acts incidental to the employment, undertaken for the employee's benefit whilst the employee is working on the employer's business (e.g. smoking on duty) (*Century Insurance Co. Ltd* v. *Northern Ireland Road Transport Board* 1942 1 All ER 491);
   (d)   acts for the protection of the employer's property and business (*Poland* v. *Parr and Sons* CA 1926 All ER 177);
   (e)   dishonest or fraudulent acts of the employee, if the employer is under a duty to the person suffering the loss (*Lloyd* v. *Grace Smith & Co.* 1912 AC 716; *Morris* v. *C. W. Martin & Sons Ltd* 1965 2 All ER 725).

Figure 4.2   Definition of 'in the course of employment'.

The court held that Mr Hall was acting within the class of acts that the servant (i.e. employee) is authorised to do in an emergency. In this case, he was protecting his masters' property, which was, or which he reasonably thought was, being pillaged. His mode of acting was not such as to take it out of the class. The masters were therefore held vicariously liable for the act of Mr Hall.[8]

Case 4.5   Petrol problems

Beaumont was employed as a petrol pump attendant by the defendants. He wrongly accused the plaintiff, in violent language, of having tried to drive away without paying for petrol that had been put into the tank of his car. The plaintiff paid his bill, called the police and told the pump attendant that he would be reported to his employers. The attendant assaulted and then injured the plaintiff, who then sued the employers for their vicarious liability for the actions of their employee.

The court held that the act of the attendant was not of the class of acts that he was authorised to perform. It was performed entirely on his own account. The employers were therefore not liable for it.[9]

The differences between these two cases are clear. Had the attendant used reasonable force on the basis of a reasonable belief that the car driver did not intend to pay, then there may well have been a different result. He was hardly acting in the employer's interests. Similarly, in Kate's case, both the timing of her assault and also the reasonableness of what she did would be taken into account in determining if the act was in course of employment.

Outside the job description

Situation 4.8   Helping others

Ann Barrett was a staff nurse on a medical ward and was concerned that the kitchen had not sent up the diets. She telephoned for them and was told that she would have to wait since there were no porters available. Rather than wait, she decided to fetch them herself. She went to the kitchen, passing the notice saying 'No admission, kitchen staff only'. She went across to the diet bay and as she did so she knocked into a cook who was removing a pan of gravy from the stove. The gravy splashed over the cook and also over Ann. What remedies do the cook and Ann have in this situation and is the employer vicariously liable for Ann's negligence?

The cook could, of course, sue Ann personally. Ann owed a duty of care to the cook, and by her carelessness she caused reasonably foreseeable harm to the cook. However, is the employer vicariously liable for Ann's actions? There is no doubt that she is an employee. There is also no doubt that she was negligent in knocking into the cook. However, is the third element satisfied, i.e. was she acting in course of employment when she went to the kitchens and when she knocked into the cook? She was employed as a nurse, not as a kitchen porter, but she was acting in the care of the patients (her employer's business) when she went to the kitchens. Even if there was a clear prohibition on non-kitchen staff entering the kitchens, this would not in itself remove the act from the course of employment. The crucial point would be whether she was acting on the employer's business when she entered the kitchen, and the answer to that in this case is yes. It would be very different if she entered the kitchen to have a chat on non-hospital business with a friend of hers who worked there.

It is not, of course, uncommon for staff in the health service to step outside the strict confines of their job descriptions. If the employer is aware of this and turns a blind eye to it, then it could be said that he condones it and accepts that the employee's duties have been expanded to include the additional tasks. In such cases, if the employee acts negligently while carrying out these duties, it could be argued that he or she is acting within the course of his or her employment. In addition, particularly during times of industrial action, employers specifically authorise staff to cover for the strikers or those working to rule. In such cases, the employees are acting in the course of their employment: they have the express authorisation of the employer.

Activities incidental to the work

Situation 4.9 Smoking on duty

There was a clear and enforced policy at Roger Park Hospital that there was no smoking except in authorised areas. One of the nurses ignored these instructions and regularly smoked with the patients in the ward area. On one such occasion, she accidentally dropped the cigarette and burned a patient's foot. He threatened to sue the NHS Trust. Was the nurse acting in course of employment?

The answer is probably yes, based on the following case.

Case 4.6 Lighting up

A tanker driver ignored his instructions not to light matches when loading or unloading his vehicle and as a result the tanker, a vehicle belonging to the garage, and several nearby houses were destroyed.

In this case, the court held that even though the act of lighting a cigarette is for the employee's own comfort and even though it is prohibited, the act could not be separated from the circumstances of his employment. The driver was held to be negligent in the course of performing his authorised work and the employers (and therefore their insurers) were liable.[10]

In our example of the smoking nurse, it is highly likely that she will face disciplinary proceedings and possibly even dismissal, yet she may still be held to be acting in course of employment and therefore the employer is liable.

In a recent case the House of Lords held that school owners were vicoriously liable for acts of sexual abuse committed by the school warden against pupils – the abusive acts were sufficiently connected with his work as to be in the course of employment (*Lister & Others* v. *Helsey Hall Ltd*) *The Times Law Report* 10 May 2001 [2001] 2 WLR 1311.

What if a nurse is off duty?

There can be no easy answer. It depends entirely on what she is doing and in what way she has been negligent. In a recent case, the Court of Appeal allowed an appeal with costs against the decision of the PCC who found that a nurse was guilty of misconduct when she refused to answer a heart patient's call for help because she was having her tea-break. The decision was based on the fact that it had not been established that the nurse knew it was an emergency. However, this case was before the PCC and different principles might apply in a civil case.

In one case, for example, some employees in their employer's van left the authorised route and went to a café to have a snack. On the way back, they had an accident and the court held that they were not acting in course of employment.[11] It might have been different if they had deviated from their route to collect goods for the employer.

Non-employees

It will be recalled that in order to establish vicarious liability it must be established that the negligent person is an employee of the defendant. Figure 4.3 (overleaf) shows some of the criteria used by the courts to decide if an individual is an employee. The following case illustrates this principle.

> ### Case 4.7 *Classroom chaos*
>
> A deputy headmistress was injured when she fell over a tricycle that had been negligently placed near a classroom door by a 10-year-old boy in the course of carrying out his assigned task of distributing milk in the classrooms. There was a strict rule that tricycles were not to be removed from their safe position in the middle of the assembly hall.

The Court of Appeal held that the boy was not an employee of the authority, that he was doing those duties as part of his education, and that the authority was therefore not vicariously liable.[12]

In a recent case,[13] the Court of Appeal held that it was necessary for a contract of employment to contain an obligation on the part of the employee to provide services personally. A contract that allowed services to be provided by another person was a contract for services and not a contract of service.

> 1. The employee agrees that in consideration of a wage or other remuneration he will provide his own work and skill in performance of some service for the employer.
> 2. He agrees, expressly or impliedly, that in the performance of that service he will be subject to the other's control in a sufficient degree to make that other the employer.
> 3. The other provisions of the contract are consistent with its being a contract of service. 'Control in itself is not always conclusive'. *Ready-Mixed Concrete (South-East) Ltd* v. *Ministry of Pensions and National Insurance* 1968 1 All ER 433.

Figure 4.3   Criteria used to define an employee.

Liability for the negligence of volunteers

What about volunteers? Do the same principles apply? Is the NHS Trust liable for the negligent acts of the volunteer? If we follow the basic principles of vicarious liability, it could be argued that since the volunteer is not an employee, then the NHS Trust should not be liable. However, the philosophy that underlies the concept of vicarious liability is one of public policy, i.e. the person or organisation that has set in motion a particular activity that has caused harm should bear the loss rather than an innocent victim. In addition, one of the essential elements in the principle of vicarious liability is that the master is in control of the servant's activity. Unfortunately, there is no decided case on whether the NHS Trust would be liable to a third person for the negligence of a volunteer. Much would, of course, depend on the circumstances of the volunteer's negligence. It may be that the NHS Trust or its staff are themselves at fault in failing to provide adequate training or supervision, or have delegated an entirely inappropriate task to the volunteer. Circular HSG (92)15 advises providers to define clearly the scope or limits of volunteers' activities and accept liability for the results of such activities.

Liability for independent contractors, i.e. self-employed persons or company employees

Situation 4.10   Agency liability

Mary Downs is employed by a nursing agency and is often sent to work in National Health Service hospitals who call on the agency for additional staff to cover any crises. While she is assisting on the ITU, she fails to notice that one of the monitoring machines has ceased to function and she then discovers that the patient has died. The relatives wish to bring a complaint or even take the NHS Trust or the agency to court.

In a case like this, there may well be direct responsibility of the NHS Trust for failing to provide a machine that had an effective alarm system or had been satisfactorily maintained. If there is also negligence on the part of the agency nurse, does it make any difference that she is not an employee of the NHS Trust, but is employed by the agency? Could the NHS Trust still be liable for her negligence? The answer would depend to a considerable extent on the agreement between the NHS Trust and the agency on the terms of employment of their staff. In the unlikely event that this has not been predetermined, the control test would be applied. The general or permanent employer has to shift the presumption of responsibility for the negligence of the employee on to the hirer. He can do this by showing that the control of the employee has passed to the hirer. In a health service context, this should be relatively easy since an agency staff nurse sent to help out at an NHS hospital would automatically become part of the ward/department, would be under the control of the ward sister or departmental head, and would be subject to their supervision. In most cases, unless there is a clear agreement to the contrary, the NHS Trust would probably be vicariously liable for the negligence of the agency staff.

Direct liability of employer

The Secretary of State has a statutory duty (i.e. one laid down by Act of Parliament) under the NHS Act 1977 to provide medical services throughout England and Wales and to direct the regional health (in England) and the district health authorities to exercise his functions. It has been argued that if any employee or independent contractor or agency person is negligent, then there is a breach of the duty under the Act and the NHS Trust is primarily liable, without having to establish all the elements of vicarious liability. This was the opinion of Lord Denning in the case described below.

> ### Case 4.8   A hand operation[14]
>
> The patient lost the use of his left hand and had severe pain and suffering as a result of negligent treatment following an operation on his hand. The evidence showed a *prima facie* case of negligence on the part of the persons in whose care the plaintiff was, although it was not clear whether this was to be imputed to Dr Fahrni, the full time assistant medical officer, or to the house surgeon, or to one of the nurses.

The Court of Appeal held that the hospital authority was liable. Lord Denning said:

Whenever (hospital authorities) accept a patient for treatment, they must use reasonable care and skill to cure him of his ailment. The hospital authorities cannot, of course, do it by themselves. They have no ears to listen through the stethoscope, and no hands to hold the knife. They must to it by the staff which they employ, and, if their staff are negligent in giving the treatment, they are just as liable for that negligence as is anyone else who employs others to do his duties for him . . . I decline to enter into the question whether any of the surgeons were employed only under a contract for services, as distinct from a contract of service. The evidence is meagre enough in all conscience on that point, but the liability of the hospital authorities should not, and does not, depend on nice considerations of that sort. The plaintiff knew nothing of the terms on which they employed their staff. All he knew was that he was treated in the hospital by people whom the hospital authorities appointed, and the hospital authorities must be answerable for the way in which he was treated.

This suggests that the NHS Trust cannot delegate its duty by providing competent trained staff. It will always be primarily responsible for any negligence to the patients whether the negligent person is an employee, a volunteer, an independent contractor or an agency employee.

A recent case on this point is that of *Wilsher* v. *Essex Area Health Authority*,[15] discussed above. In this case, it was held that there was no reason why, in certain circumstances, a health authority could not be directly liable to a plaintiff (claimant) if it failed to provide sufficient or properly qualified and competent medical staff for the unit.

It must be pointed out, however, that even where it is possible to hold the NHS Trust directly liable for the harm caused to the patient under the principle set out by Lord Denning above, those individuals who were negligent could still face an action for their personal liability. In addition, if the NHS Trust pays out compensation as a result of its negligence, it would be possible for it to seek an indemnity from the negligent person. At present, this indemnity is rarely sought.

Indemnity from the employee at fault

This indemnity arises as a result of an implied term in the contract of employment, that the employee will indemnify the employer as a result of any losses caused by a breach of contract by the employee. In these circumstances, this would be a breach of the term to use all reasonable care and skill.

Case 4.9 *Family trouble*

Lister was employed as a lorry driver who worked with his father. He negligently ran down his father while backing the lorry in a yard. The father recovered damages from the employers on the grounds of their vicarious liability for the negligence of their employee. The employers' insurers then brought an action against the son for damages for breach of an implied term in his contract of employment that he would exercise reasonable care and skill in his driving. The son in his defence claimed that he was entitled to the benefit of any insurance that his employer either had or should have taken out. Therefore they could not claim an indemnity from him.

The House of Lords held by a majority decision that they could claim an indemnity from the employee and they refused to imply a term in the contract of employment that the employer would not seek to claim an indemnity from the negligent employee.[16]

> Case 4.10   Anaesthetic
>
> The widow of a patient who died as a result of negligent hospital treatment sued for damages. The hospital board claimed an indemnity from Dr Wilkes, an inexperienced physician, who had administered the fatal anaesthetic under the instructions of Dr Sejrup, a house surgeon.

The Court of Appeal rejected this claim for an indemnity partly because the hospital itself was at fault.[17]

A new scheme was introduced for claims lodged on or after 1 January 1990 (see HC (89)34). Health authorities became formally responsible for handling and financing claims of negligence against their medical and dental staff. Arrangements were introduced at regional level to share the legal costs and damages of large settlements between districts. Guidance in relation to NHS Trusts is contained in EL (90) 195, EL (91) 19 and EL (92) 8. (Previously, claims against doctors and dentists were met by their defence association and liability with other health professionals divided on an agreed basis with the health authority. If agreement could not be reached, then it was divided 50:50.) Whilst there is a theoretical legal right to recover costs from the negligent employee, the Department of Health advises against this in practice.

Claims brought against the NHS organisations are handled by the NHS Litigation Authority (NHSLA). Trusts have joined in a clinical negligence scheme (CNST) whereby resources are pooled and claims over a certain amount are met from the pool. This is discussed further in Chapter 6.

Pressure from inadequate resources

Unfortunately, harm to the patient can occur due to shortage of staff, inadequate equipment and unsafe premises. This section deals with the liability of those concerned. Refer to the UKCC advisory paper, 'Guidelines for Professional Practice' and, in particular, paragraphs relating to the environment of care.

General principles

> Situation 4.11   Resources
>
> Pauline Cross is working on a busy geriatric ward with only two staff. The patients are severely confused and can do little for themselves. As she is transferring a patient from a wheelchair into bed, the patient falls to the floor and breaks her hip bone. Is Pauline likely to be held responsible in law for the patient's injuries?

It could be argued that this incident took place because there was inadequate staffing. However, there are many factors to be considered. Were they so short-staffed that even when priorities were set it would have been impossible for another member of the staff to help Pauline? Had the staff been trained in manual handling and was a risk assessment carried out? Was such an incident reasonably foreseeable such that additional precautions should have been taken, or was it an inevitable accident and therefore unavoidable? If the conclusion is that the accident was avoidable and another nurse should have been assigned to assist Pauline, then this will not automatically relieve Pauline of responsibility, especially if she was in charge of the ward. The question arises whether it would not have been possible to have transferred the patient to bed later when more help would have been available. Alternatively, could the tasks that were occupying the other nurses have been given a lower priority?

Even if all the questions could be answered negatively, i.e. they were so short-staffed that they could not take the necessary foreseeable precautions to ensure the patient was put to bed safely, Pauline may still be responsible. If she was in charge of the ward, had she warned her senior nurse management of the staffing difficulties and suggested remedial action such as discharging patients to other wards or home, or suggesting the use of agency nurses if nurses could not be transferred from other wards? Failure to take such action where her management role requires it would mean that Pauline would have to share some measure of responsibility for the occurrence (see the section on the nurse as manager above on page 60).

Employer's responsibility

If a patient is harmed because of an accident that would not have occurred had reasonable resources been available, then the patient would have a valid action to recover compensation in the civil courts. It is no defence to say to a patient, 'We are sorry we amputated the wrong leg, but Wednesday is our busiest day and we had a lot of staff off with influenza.' A patient is entitled to the approved standard of care. Even in an emergency situation, staff would be expected to take additional precautions to prevent further harm arising on the basis of a clear order of priorities. In such circumstances, the patient would be able to sue the NHS Trust for its vicarious liability for the negligence of the staff. However, it is probable, too, that an action of direct liability also might succeed against the Trust because harm was caused to the patient as a result of inadequate resources.

> Case 4.11   Inadequate resources 1
>
> A casualty officer, through pressure of work, made only a brief examination and treated a major head injury on the assumption that it was a minor one.

Both he and the health authority were held liable. The judge held that pressure of work was no defence to the patient's claim.[18]

> ### Case 4.12   Inadequate resources 2
>
> In one case,[19] several allegations were made by a patient that she was not treated with proper professional care and skill during the delivery of her first child. A Shirodkar suture had been fitted at an earlier stage because of an incompetent cervix. It was important that the suture should be removed promptly once labour had commenced, otherwise there was a danger that the cervix could be damaged. The patient claimed that the staff had failed to act speedily and as a consequence her cervix was damaged. The defendants claimed that the ward was very busy that night and the patient received appropriate care.

At the defendants' request, the judge directed that the notes of the other patients should be made available to show what was going on in the labour ward that evening. He did so with reluctance because he did not wish a breach of the duty of confidentiality owed to the patients and the defendants had not pleaded any special emergency that prevented speedier attention to the patient. These patients were referred to by code names. Their notes were exhaustively examined in the course of the evidence. 'In summary they showed that the doctors were busy and that the patient bringing the action was not the only patient who presented problems. But they did not show there was anything to prevent the doctors performing a vaginal examination or removing the suture sooner than they did.'

One of the criticisms was that the doctors had failed to give the patient sufficient priority. The doctor in his defence said that on a busy labour ward the doctors do not sit down and work out a list of priorities. The judge, however, had to decide if the patient had been kept waiting too long. He said: 'I appreciate that one must not be too critical of what goes on in a busy ward but it is difficult to understand why the patient did not have a vaginal examination until two hours after admission. Other ladies were admitted at about the same time as she was and whose cases were of no greater urgency had their examinations far sooner.'

The judge commented on the statement of one of the experts for the defence who had said, 'I think the time scale is within the pattern of what occurs in a busy ward.'

> That may well be, but it does not resolve the question whether this particular patient was given proper care . . . I do not pinpoint any particular moment when a particular doctor did something wrong. It was rather a case where there was a lack of sufficient sense of urgency on all sides. In these circumstances I hold that the second defendants (Leicester Health Authority) did not treat the patient with proper professional care and skill.

The patient was awarded £1,500.

Several important points emerge from this case.

1. The assessment of priorities can be carried out negligently or not at all and can itself form the basis of a claim for compensation.

2. To ascertain the work load and other demands, it is possible with the approval of the judge for the records of other patients to be made available. It is essential that comprehensive records are always kept.

Coping under pressure

One question often asked by nursing staff in relation to shortage of resources is, 'What happens if we are dangerously short of staff and yet we cope? What is the situation then?' This is a frequent situation. Yet if no person suffers harm as a result of the inadequate levels, then there can be no action for negligence, since harm must be established. However, it would be part of the duties of the nurse, both in her professional duties and as a manager, to ensure that senior levels are notified of any dangers or hazards so that harm does not eventually occur. An inadequate number of trained staff in proportion to the demands of patients could lead to inexperienced people administering drugs, using specialised equipment or assisting doctors in complex treatments and patients could therefore suffer overdoses or other forms of harm. In extreme situations, where it is impossible to obtain sufficient numbers of staff to run a service safely or to run a service with the correct skill-mix, then the provision of that service may have to be transferred to other providers.

Legal requirements on staffing

Another question that is raised is, 'What are the legal staffing levels or of what legal significance is a particular staffing ratio that has been recommended by different researchers?' Minimum staffing levels or ratios are unlikely to be laid down by Act of Parliament or by the courts. Under the principles relating to liability in negligence, sufficient resources must be provided to ensure that the patients being cared for are provided with the approved accepted standard of care. All circumstances must be taken into account in determining whether this has been provided in respect of a given patient who has suffered harm. Obviously, evidence could be given of the extent to which the staffing levels had fallen below the levels considered by experts in the field to be the minimum consistent with good practice, but this is evidence, not law.

Failures by management

What does the nurse do if she has drawn the attention of management to a situation that she considers dangerous and nothing is done about it? Whatever the situation, whether it is concerned with inadequate resources or incompetent staff, the nurse should not give up if she feels her concern about a dangerous situation is being ignored. She has a duty to ensure that the patients are cared for appropriately. She should therefore put her concerns in writing with evidence of hazards that have occurred. Her report would need to be a detailed account that is meaningful to management of the levels of staffing and the needs of the patients. If nothing is done, she should then be prepared to refer the matter to a higher level of management. Eventually, if she is still concerned that the dangers are being ignored, she should take the matter to her NHS Trust or national board or the UKCC and utilise the procedure set up under the Public Interest Disclosure Act 1998. This is preferable to bringing the local or national press into a field that should be sorted out internally.

Public Interest Disclosure Act 1998 and whistle-blowing

Nurses are required under the Code of Professional Practice to bring hazards and dangers to the attention of management. Unfit practitioners must also be reported to the UKCC.[20] Many nurses have feared victimisation (see report on Rodney Ledward, Chapter 5). To allay such fears and prevent victimisation, the NHS Management Executive issued 'Guidelines for Staff on Relations with the Public and the Media' (1993). This emphasised that under no circumstances are employees who express their views about health service issues in accordance with this guidance to be penalised in any way for doing so (paragraph 6). Each NHS employer has a duty to establish a procedure for employees to raise concerns. Statutory provision was made in the Public Interest Disclosure Act 1998 to ensure that a procedure is set up to ensure that staff who raise justifiable concerns are protected from victimisation. Justifiable concerns are shown in Box 4.1 Guidance has been issued by the Department of Health (HSC(99)198.)

Box 4.1

Protected Disclosures under the Public Interest Disclosure Act 1998

1. that a criminal offence has been, is being or likely to be committed;

2. that a person has failed, is failing or is likely to fail to comply with any legal obligation to which he is subject;

3. that a miscarriage of justice has occurred, is occurring or is likely to occur;

4. that the health or safety of any individual has been, is being or is likely to be endangered;

5. that the environment has been, is being or is likely to be damaged; or

6. that information tending to show any matter falling within any of the above paragraphs has been, is being or is likely to be deliberately concealed.

The protected disclosures in Box 4.1 are extensive and would cover most of the situations in which a registered practitioner would have a professional duty to inform an appropriate person or authority under the Professional Code of Conduct.

Under the Act, the disclosure is only protected if certain conditions are satisfied. The employee must have made the disclosure in good faith to his employer; or where the employee reasonably believes that a person other than the employer is to blame, then the disclosure can be made to that other person. Disclosure is also protected if it is made in the course of obtaining legal advice; or if the employer is a body any of whose members are appointed by a minister of the Crown, then the disclosure can be made to a minister of the Crown. This would cover disclosures by employees working within the NHS. Other disclosures are protected if the conditions set out in Box 4.2 are satisfied.

> **Box 4.2**
>
> ### Conditions for other protected disclosures
>
> 1. the employee makes the disclosure in good faith;
> 2. he reasonably believes that the information disclosed, and any allegations contained in it, are substantially true;
> 3. he does not make the disclosure for personal gain;
> 4. any of the conditions in subsection 2 is met (see below); and
> 5. in all the circumstances of the case, it is reasonable for him to make the disclosure.

The subsection 2 conditions referred to in Box 4.2 include the reasonable belief that the employee would be subjected to detriment by his employer if he makes the disclosure. Factors determining the reasonableness of the disclosure include the identity of the person to whom it is made; the seriousness of the failure; whether it is continuing or likely to occur in future; whether the disclosure is made in breach of a duty of confidentiality; previous disclosures to the employer or to another person prescribed by the Secretary of State; and compliance with any procedure specified for making disclosures.

Disclosures relating to exceptionally serious failures

Special provisions apply to a disclosure of an exceptionally serious failure. Such a disclosure is protected if the employee makes the disclosure in good faith, reasonably believing the allegations to be true, not making the disclosure for personal gain, and in all the circumstances it is reasonable to make the disclosure and to that particular person.

Gagging of an employee

The Act states that any provision in an agreement is void in so far as it purports to preclude an employee from making a protected disclosure. Thus, if a Trust attempts to introduce a term into a contract of employment that prevents an employee making a disclosure that comes under the protection of the Act, that term is void.

Before the Public Interest Disclosure Act, a student nurse reported a Rampton Hospital nurse for ill-treating and assaulting patients.[21] The abuser was subsequently convicted in the criminal courts and struck off the UKCC register. The student nurse, however, suffered considerable abuse after blowing the whistle. Such victimisation should now lead to compensation for the whistle blower. In one of the first cases to be reported after the coming into force of the Act, an accountant who was dismissed after blowing the whistle on his managing director's expense claims was awarded compensation of £293,441 by an employment tribunal. The Tribunal held that he was victimised for raising genuine concerns.[22]

Conclusions

This chapter has covered a wide range of topics relating to the role of the nurse in communicating, delegating, managing, and dealing with inadequate resources. It has also considered the direct and vicarious liability of the employer. Nurses and employers, however, work within the wider scope of the NHS and it is to the structure and management of the NHS to which we now turn.

Questions and exercises

1 There can be liability for failure to communicate. Apply this principle to your particular post and consider how and to what extent communication with the patient could be improved.

2 Consider any work you undertake as a member of a team and assess the extent to which it is clear where the boundaries of individual responsibility lie.

3 There are times when it is essential that a nurse obeys the orders of a doctor without question, and others where it is imperative that she checks that the instructions are appropriate. What distinguishing features would decide whether an order falls in the first category or in the second?

4 What is the difference between direct and vicarious liability?

5 Obtain a copy of your NHS Trust's policy on the use of volunteers and study in particular those parts that relate to liability for the negligence of volunteers.

6 In what way do you think that the liability of the NHS Trust for the safety of the volunteer differs from its liability for the safety of staff (see, in addition, Chapter 12)?

7 An employee can be liable for the negligent actions of another person if the employee should not have delegated a task to him or, having correctly delegated it, has failed to provide the appropriate level of supervision. Apply this principle to the role of the nurse manager in relation to junior trained staff, learners, volunteers and untrained assistants.

8 Obtain a copy of your employer's policy on whistle-blowing and familiarise yourself with its contents. Do you understand how the procedure would work in practice?

References

[1] *Coles* v. *Reading* HMC 1963 107 SJ 115

[2] *Harrison* v. *Surrey County Council and others*, TLR 27 January 1994

[3] *Nettleship* v. *Weston* 1971 3 All ER 581

[4] *Wilsher* v. *Essex Area Health Authority* CA 1986 3 All ER 801 HL 1988 1 All ER 871

[5] *Dwyer* v. *Roderick* 20 June 1984 QBD

[6] *Gold* v. *Essex County Council* [1942] 2 All ER 237

[7] The Royal College of Nursing Guidance on Good Management Practice, Order No. 001001 RCN March 1999

[8] *Poland* v. *Parr and Sons* CA 1926 All ER 177

9   *Warren* v. *Henley's Ltd KBD* 1948 2 All ER 935
10 *Century Insurance Co. Ltd* v. *Northern Ireland Road Transport Board* 1942 1 All ER 491
11 *Hilton* v. *Thomas Burton (Rhodes) Ltd* 1961 1 WLR 705
12 *Watkins* v. *Birmingham City Council, The Times* 1 August 1975
13 *Express and Echo Publications Ltd* v. *Tanton, The Times* 7 April 1999
14 *Cassidy* v. *Ministry of Health* 1939 2 KB 14
15 *Wilsher* v. *Essex Area Health Authority CA* 1986 3 All ER 801
16 *Lister* v. *Romford Ice and Cold Storage Co. Ltd HL* 1957 1 All ER 125
17 *Jones* v. *Manchester Corporation CA* 1952 2 All ER 125
18 *McCormack* v. *Redpath Brown, The Times* 24 March 1961
19 *Deacon* v. *McVicar and another* 7 January 1984 QBD
20 UKCC Reporting unfitness to practise – information for employers and managers, UKCC August 1996
21 News Item, *Nursing Times* June 8 2000 Vol 96 No 23 p. 4
22 Jenny Booth, Man who shopped boss wins £290,000, *The Times* 11 July 2000

5 Statutory functions and management of the NHS

This chapter considers the statutory background to the NHS and the functions of the Secretary of State. It also looks at recent changes in the NHS following the Health Act 1999, including the duty of quality, the Commission for Health Improvement and the National Institute for Clinical Excellence. Issues of resource management and the Public Interest Disclosure Act 1998 are also considered in relation to whistleblowing.

The areas to be covered in this chapter are shown in Figure 5.1.

National Health Service
Enforcement of statutory duties
NHS and Community Care Act 1990
Abolition of the internal market
White Paper on the NHS
Primary Care Groups and Trusts
Standard Setting
Clinical Governance
Duty of Quality
Commission for Health Improvement
National Institute of Clinical Excellence
National Standard Frameworks
NHS Direct and walk-in clinics
Early warning scheme
National Health Service Plan

Figure 5.1   Issues covered in Chapter 5.

The National Health Service

The National Health Service (NHS) was set up 5 July 1948 as a result of the National Health Service Act 1946. It was based on the principle that services should be provided free at the point of delivery unless there was clear statutory authorisation for any charges. Charges for prescriptions were the first to be introduced. The duty to provide services was placed upon the Secretary of State who delegated these functions to regional hospital boards, hospital management committees and other statutory organisations. Family practitioner services were administered by the Executive Councils, later superseded by the Family Practitioner Committees. A major reorganisation of health care provision took place in 1973 and the statutory duties were re-enacted in the National Health Service Act 1977. The duties placed upon the Secretary of State are shown in Box 5.1.

Box 5.1

Duties of the Secretary of State under the National Health Service Act 1977

Secretary of State's duty as to health service

Section 1(1) It is the Secretary of State's duty to continue the promotion in England and Wales of a comprehensive health service designed to secure improvement:
In the physical and mental health of the people in those countries; and
In the prevention, diagnosis and treatment of illness
And for that purpose to provide and secure the effective provision of services in accordance with this Act.

(2) The services so provided shall be free of charge except in so far as the making and recovery of charges is expressly provided for by or under any enactment, whenever passed.

Secretary of State's general power as to services

2. Without prejudice to the Secretary of State's powers apart from this section, he has power –

To provide such services as he considers appropriate for the purpose of discharging any duty imposed on him by this Act; and
To do any other thing whatsoever which is calculated to facilitate, or is conducive or incidental to, the discharge of such a duty.

This section is subject to Section 3(3) below.

Services generally

3(1) It is the Secretary of State's duty to provide throughout England and Wales, to such extent as he considers necessary to meet all reasonable requirements –

Hospital accommodation;
Other accommodation for the purpose of any service provided under this Act;
Medical, dental, nursing and ambulance services;
Such other facilities for the care of expectant and nursing mothers and young children as he considers are appropriate as part of the health service;
Such facilities for the prevention of illness, the care of persons suffering from illness and the after-care of persons who have suffered from illness as he considers are appropriate as part of the health service;
Such other services as are required for the diagnosis and treatment of illness.

3(2) . . .

3(3) Nothing in Section 2 above or in this section affects the provisions of Part II of this Act (which relates to arrangements with practitioners for the provision of medical, dental, ophthalmic and pharmaceutical services).

Other services which the Secretary of State has a duty to provide are set out in Section 5 and include: medical inspection of school children; contraceptive advice and treatment; dental inspection; treatment and education of school children; invalid carriages; accommodation and treatment for TB; microbiological services; and research activities. Part II covers the provision of services by general practitioners, dental practitioners, pharmacists and others who provide services under a contract for services with the Health Authorities (which took over responsibilities from the Family Health Service Authorities in 1996).

Enforcement of statutory duties

There have been several cases where patients who have waited a considerable time for operations or for other treatments have brought legal action to enforce the provision for them of health services. By and large, the courts have taken the view that it is not for the court to become involved in issues relating to resource allocation, unless there are clear failures in public duty.

Where a patient is kept waiting for treatment, there is an interesting distinction in the following two situations.

1. Where the treatment has commenced, it must be carried out according to the accepted approved standard. If a negligent act occurs that causes harm to the patient, then this is actionable by the patient.

2. Where treatment has not commenced and the patient has to wait on a waiting list, then even though the patient's condition might deteriorate this is not actionable provided the health authority has carried out its provision of health services rationally. It may, of course, be the subject of a complaint since the provider has failed to comply with the standards set in the Patient's Charter, but these standards do not have any legal effect unless they are already incorporated in an Act of Parliament or a decided case or unless they infringe the European Convention on Human Rights.

Case 5.1   Inadequate resources

Orthopaedic patients at a hospital in Birmingham who had waited for treatment for periods longer than was medically advisable, brought an action against the Secretary of State, the regional health authority and the area health authority. They were seeking a declaration that the defendants were in breach of their duty under Section 1 of the National Health Service Act 1977 to continue to promote a comprehensive health service designed to secure improvement in health and the prevention of illness, and under Section 3 to provide accommodation, facilities and services for those purposes.

The judge held that it was not the function of the court to direct Parliament as to what funds to make available to the health service and how to allocate them. The Secretary of State's duty under Section 3 to provide services 'to such extent as he considers necessary', gave him discretion as to the disposition of financial resources.

The court could interfere only if the Secretary of State acted so as to frustrate the policy of the Act or as no reasonable minister could have acted. No such breach had been shown in the present case. The court could not grant mandamus or a declaration against area or regional authorities since specific remedies against them were available by Section 85 and Part V of the 1977 Act. Nor if a breach were proved did the Act admit of relief by way of damages. The application was therefore dismissed.[1]

The reasoning behind the above ruling was confirmed in the following case.

Case 5.2   Postponed operation

Mrs Walker's baby son required a heart operation and was on the waiting list. A date was fixed for the operation to be performed but was postponed by the Birmingham Health Authority. She applied to the court for a judicial review of the decision of the health authority. The High Court judge refused her application. She appealed to the Court of Appeal who upheld the earlier decision.

The Health Authority had accepted that the regional district health authorities could be subject to judicial review where there was reason to believe that they might be in breach of their public duties. There would always be individuals who believed that treatment was not provided quickly enough, but the financial resources were finite and always would be. The court held that it was not for the court to substitute its own judgement for that of those responsible for the allocation of resources. It would interfere only if there had been a failure to allocate funds in a way that was unreasonable or where there had been breaches of public duties. Mrs Walker's application was refused.[2]

Case 5.3   Bone marrow transplant postponed operation[3]

A 10-year-old girl was suffering from acute myloid leukaemia and required a further session of chemotherapy and a second bone marrow transplant to survive. It was estimated that the chance of success was between 10% and 20%. Costs of the drug and transplant were estimated as £15,000 and £60,000 respectively. The Health Authority refused to resource this and the father challenged its decision. The High Court upheld his application for judicial review. The Health Authority appealed to the Court of Appeal and the case was heard that same day. The Court of Appeal held that the four criticisms made by the trial judge of the health authority's decision were not acceptable. The Court should confine itself to the lawfulness of the decision. It held that it was not in the best interests of the child to undergo further treatment and that resources had to be taken into account.

The principles set in this case were followed in a South African case[4] where a diabetic suffered from irreversible chronic renal failure and required renal dialysis. Because of a lack of resources, he was not admitted to the programme. He failed in his application for breach of his right to life, since it was for the political and medical authorities to determine rationing policy and where those decisions were rational and in good faith, the court would be slow to interfere.

Whilst the general principle that the courts will not intervene in resourcing issues of the NHS appears to continue to be accepted by the courts, there have been two recent cases where health authorities have been held liable for failure to provide services.

In one case,[5] the health authority decided that it would not enable Beta Interferon to be prescribed for patients in its catchment area, since it was not yet proved to be clinically effective for the treatment of multiple sclerosis. A sufferer from multiple sclerosis challenged this refusal of the Health Authority and succeeded on the grounds that the health authority had failed to follow the guidance issued by the Department of Health.[6] A declaration was granted that the policy adopted by the health authority was unlawful and an order of mandamus was made requiring the defendants to formulate and implement a policy that took full and proper account of national policy as stated in the circular.

The second case concerned three transsexuals who wished to undergo gender reassignment.[7] The Health Authority refused to fund such treatment on the grounds that it had been assigned a low priority in its lists of procedures considered to be clinically ineffective in terms of health gain. Under this policy, gender reassignment surgery was, amongst other procedures, listed as a procedure for which no treatment, apart from that provided by the Authority's general psychiatric and psychology services, would be commissioned, save in the event of overriding clinical need or exceptional circumstances. The transsexuals sought judicial review of the health authority's refusal and the judge granted an order quashing the authority's decision and the policy on which it was based. The health authority then took the case to the Court of Appeal, but lost its appeal. The Court of Appeal held that:

1. Whilst the precise allocation and weighting of priorities is a matter for the judgment of the Authority and not for the court, it is vital for an Authority:
    (a) to accurately assess the nature and seriousness of each type of illness, and
    (b) to determine the effectiveness of various forms of treatment for it, and
    (c) to give proper effect to that assessment and that determination in the formulation and individual application of its policy.

2. The Authority's policy was flawed in two respects:
    (a) it did not treat transsexualism as an illness, but as an attitude of mind which did not warrant medical treatment, and
    (b) the ostensible provision that it made for exceptions in individual cases and its manner of considering them amounted to the operation of a 'blanket policy' against funding treatment for the condition because it did not believe in such treatment.

3. The authority were not genuinely applying the policy to the individual exceptions.

4. Article 3 and Article 8 of the European Convention on Human Rights (see Chapter 1) did not give a right to free healthcare and did not apply to this situation, where the challenge is to a health authority's allocation of finite funds. Nor were the patients victims of discrimination on the grounds of sex.

It is inevitable that there will always be a gap between the demands that are made for health care and the resources to meet those demands. Decisions will therefore have to be made on priorities and who is refused treatment. New developments in technology, such as the identification of the human genome and the treatment possibilities for identified genetical diseases, are just one example of increasing pressures. The impact of the implementation of the Human Rights Act 1998 on the pressures on resources is not at present known.

Distinction between statutory duties and guidance from the Department of Health

In fulfilling its statutory duties, the government issues circulars providing guidance to NHS organisations on how they should function. These are now available from the DoH website. Whilst in general the advice in these circulars is not the law as such, there is a clear responsibility on organisations to follow the recommendations. The failure by a health authority to follow DoH guidelines on the prescribing of Beta Interferon led to a successful action being brought by a patient suffering from multiple sclerosis[8] (see above). In a contrasting case,[9] a court held that a government circular 1998/158, which limited the powers of GPs to prescribe Viagra, was unlawful in that by preventing the issue of a prescription, where the GP considered it to be justified, the clinical judgment of the GP was usurped.

The National Health Service and Community Care Act 1990

This legislation saw the introduction of the internal market in the NHS. NHS trusts were established that provided services under a non-legally enforceable contract or agreement with the health authorities. In addition, group fund-holding practices of general practitioners were established which were allocated the funds to purchase services for the patients on their lists from the providers. Competition was expected to take place between providers of health services to obtain the agreements for the purchase of their services. However, this organisation was radically changed following the White Paper on the NHS and the Health Act 1999 (see below).

The 1990 Act also changed the basis of community care implementing the recommendations of the Griffiths Report.[10] Instead of places in nursing homes and residential care homes being funded on a means tested basis by social security, funds were given to the local authority social services departments to become the purchasers of places, on a means tested basis, for those residents in its catchment area who required nursing or residential care.

The abolition of the internal market

The White Paper on the NHS[11] envisaged major initiatives in the management of the NHS, which were brought into force following the passing of the Health Act 1999.

These developments included a statutory duty of quality set out in Section 18 of the Health Act 1999 (which is the statutory basis for the concept of clinical governance); the establishment of the Commission for Health Improvement with considerable powers of inspection and audit; the setting up of the National Institute of Clinical Excellence and the development of National Standard Frameworks for specific specialties.

The White Paper on the new NHS

The main features of the White Paper on the NHS are shown in Box 5.2.

Box 5.2

Main features of the White Paper

1. abolition of the internal market and GP Fundholding;
2. establishment of Primary Care Groups leading to Primary Care Trusts;
3. establishment of the National Council of Clinical Excellence;
4. establishment of the Commission for Health Improvement;
5. setting up of National Service Frameworks;
6. introduction of NHS Direct;
7. introduction of Clinical Governance.

Establishment of Primary Care Groups leading to Primary Care Trusts

In Chapter 5 of the White Paper, proposals were set out for Primary Care Groups. They were to bring together GPs and community nurses in each area to work together to improve the health of local people and would grow out of the range of commissioning models that have developed in recent years. They would have strong support from their health authority and the freedom to use NHS resources wisely, including savings. Their intended functions are shown in Box 5.3.

Box 5.3

Functions of Primary Care Groups

1. contribute to the health authority's Health Improvement Plan (HIP) to ensure it reflected the perspective of the local community and the experience of patients;
2. promote the health of the local population;
3. commission health services for their populations;
4. monitor performance;
5. develop primary care by joint working across practices;
6. better integrate primary care and community health services and work more closely with social services on both planning and delivery.

Primary Care Trusts

The White Paper envisaged that some Primary Care Groups could become Primary Care Trusts, i.e. free-standing organisations. Such trusts could include community health services from existing trusts. All or part of an existing community NHS trust could combine with a Primary Care Trust in order to better integrate services and management support. The White Paper specifically stated that these new trusts would not be expected to take responsibility for specialised mental health or learning disability services. It considered that 'on mental health, where health and social care boundaries are not fixed and where joint work is particularly important, and where an integrated range of services from community to hospital care is required, specialist mental health NHS trusts are likely to be the best mechanism for co-ordinating service delivery.'

More than 40 PCGs have said that they wish to apply for PCT status in October 2000 and there are possibly a further 100 or more applications for trust status in 2001.[12] These are major organisational developments which are still in the process of being reviewed. It is likely that there will be many different models followed and considerable flexibility across the country.

The powers recognised in Schedule 1 Part 111 of the Health Act 1999 are shown in Box 5.4.

Box 5.4

Powers of the Primary Care Trust

'A Primary Care Trust may do anything which appears to it to be necessary or expedient for the purpose of or in connection with the exercise of its functions.'
   This includes:

1.   acquiring and disposing of land and other property;

2.   entering into contracts;

3.   accepting gifts of money, land and other property.

Specific powers and duties are also outlined in Schedule 1 Part 111 paragraphs 14, 15 and 16 of the Health Act 1999. These include the power to conduct, commission or assist the conduct of research, together with making officers available or providing facilities for research. It is a specific requirement of the PCT that as soon as practicable after the end of each financial year every PCT shall prepare a report of the Trust's activities during that year and shall send a copy of the report to the Health Authority within whose area the trust's area falls and to the Secretary of State.

Official guidance has been provided by the Department of Health covering the financial framework,[13] the arrangements for staff transfer[14] and arrangements for estates and facilities management.[15] All these documents are available from the website.[16] The Department of Health has recently announced the establishment of 4 more Primary Care Trusts, bringing the total to 17 Trusts.[17] These Primary Care Trusts were to be evaluated at the end of the year 2000.

The NHS Confederation provided a briefing note on the Primary Care Trusts[18] and expressed concerns about the lack of clarity of accountability within the Primary

Care Trusts and the internal governance arrangements outlined in the Department of Health Guidance. It is likely that when the review of the pilot Primary Care Trusts takes place, this will lead to more robust arrangements.

Employment issues

Part V of Schedule 1 of the Health Act 1999 sets rules on the transfer of staff and empowers the Secretary of State to order transfer to a Primary Care Trust of any employees of a Health Authority, an NHS Trust or a Primary Care Trust. The contract of employment of an employee is not terminated by the transfer. An employee is enabled to object to the transfer. It is important for employees to obtain advice about their transfer to a Primary Care Trust, especially where they are likely to suffer a detriment as a result of the transfer. However, for the vast majority of employees, whilst in theory they could argue that they do not want to be transferred, in practice, if they fail to agree, they will be without a job. The NHS Plan[19] envisages that by 2004 all Primary Care Groups will have become Primary Care Trusts and, in addition, Care Trusts will have been established to commission and provide social services as well as community healthcare (see Chapter 23). Further provisions to regulate Care Trusts are contained in the Health and Social Care Act 2001.

Standard setting

Following the White Paper, there has been greater emphasis on standard setting in the light of research findings on clinical effectiveness and excellence. Standard setting and monitoring will become an even more significant part of the practitioner's professional responsibilities. Standards in relation to the law are discussed in Chapter 3 on the law of negligence. The extent to which clinical guidelines, protocols, procedures and practices are enforceable through the courts is considered in a fascinating work by Brian Hurwitz[20] (see Chapter 3).

Clinical Governance

One of the most significant changes envisaged by the government in its White Paper is the concept of clinical governance. It is defined as:

> A framework through which NHS organisations are accountable for continuously improving the quality of their services.[21]

The idea of clinical governance is basically simple. In the past, the Trust board and its chief executive has been responsible for the financial probity of the organisation; there has been no statutory responsibility of the Trust for the overall quality of the organisation. Under the concept of clinical governance, the board and its chief executive are responsible for the quality of clinical services provided by the organisation. In theory, this could mean that a board is removed or a chief executive dismissed if a baby suffers brain damage at birth as a result of negligence or a mother dies in childbirth.

The concept of clinical governance is based on the statutory duty of quality under Section 18 of the Health Act 1999.

The duty of quality

For the first time in its history, there is a statutory duty on the NHS to promote quality. Section 18 of the Health Act 1999 is shown in Box 5.5.

Box 5.5

Section 18 Health Act 1999

It is the duty of each Health Authority, Primary Care Trust and NHS Trust to put and keep in place arrangements for the purpose of monitoring and improving the quality of health care which it provides to individuals.

The duty falls primarily upon the chief executive of each health authority and NHS trust to implement. In practice, each chief executive designates officers to be responsible for quality or clinical governance in specified areas of clinical practice. Government guidance was published in March 1999.[22] This follows from the original consultation document A First Class Service: Quality in the new NHS.[23] The aim to develop quality within the NHS is to be secured in three ways:

1. setting clear national quality standards;
2. ensuring local delivery of high quality clinical services; and
3. effective systems for monitoring the quality of services.

The Clinical Effectiveness Support Unit (CESU) is a sister organisation to the NHS clinical governance Support Team in Wales.

Guidance for nurses on clinical governance has been provided by the RCN.[24] It defines clinical governance as 'an umbrella term for everything that helps to maintain and improve high standards of patient care' and in a series of case studies, shows the implications for nurses.

Commission for Health Improvement (CHI)

CHI's forerunner, the Clinical Standards Advisory Group (CSAG), was set up under the NHS and Community Care Act 1990 as a statutory body to advise UK Health Ministers on standards of clinical care. It was abolished on 1 November 1999 under the Health Act 1999, its duties being taken over by the Commission for Health Improvement. The last four reports of CSAG were published in March 2000 on Outpatients, Depression, Pain and Epilepsy.[25] These reports highlighted variations in care and health services across the country.

The Commission for Health Improvement has much wider functions and powers than CSAG. Sections 19 to 24 of the Health Act 1999 establish the Commission for Health Improvement and set out its functions and powers. It is a body corporate, i.e. it can sue and be sued on its own account. The functions are listed in Box 5.6.

Section 19(2) of the Health Act 1999 gives powers to the Secretary of State to make regulations covering:

1. the times at which, the cases in which, the manner in which the persons in relation to which or matters with respect to which any functions of the Commission are to be exercised;

2. the matters to be considered or taken into account in connection with the exercise of any functions of the Commission;

3. the persons to whom any advice, information or reports are to be given or made;

4. the publication of reports and summaries of reports;

5. the recovery from prescribed persons of amounts in respect of expenditure incurred by the Commission in the exercise of any of its functions; and

6. the exercise of functions of the Commission in conjunction with the exercise of statutory functions of other persons.

Box 5.6

Functions of the Commission for Health Improvement

1. provide advice or information with respect to arrangements by primary care trusts or NHS trusts for the purpose of monitoring and improving the quality of health care for which they have responsibility;

2. conducting reviews of, and making reports on, arrangements by Primary Care Trusts or NHS trusts for the purpose of monitoring and improving the quality of health care for which they have responsibility;

3. carrying out investigations into and making reports on, the management, provision or quality of health care for which Health Authorities, Primary Care Trusts or NHS trusts have responsibility;

4. conducting reviews of and making reports on, the management, provision or quality of, or access to or availability of, particular types of health care for which NHS bodies or service providers have responsibility; and

5. other functions as may be prescribed relating to the management, provision or quality of, or access to or availability of, health care for which prescribed NHS bodies or prescribed service providers have responsibility.

Under Section 19(3), the Secretary of State may give directions with respect to the exercise of any functions of the Commission and it is the legal duty of the Commission to comply with any such directions (S.19(4)).

The Commission for Health Improvement can suggest to the Audit Commission that it joins with it in exercising its functions. For certain functions, this can include conducting and making reports on studies designed to improve economy, efficiency and effectiveness in the performance of NHS functions. Before the Audit Commission acts with the Commission for Health Improvement, the latter must agree to pay the Audit Commission the full costs incurred by the Audit Commission in so acting.

Section 24(1) makes it a criminal offence to disclose confidential information obtained by the Commission without lawful authority, knowingly or recklessly.

Activities of CHI

One of the earliest tasks undertaken by CHI on the day it was established was to visit Garlands Hospital in Carlisle run by the North Lakeland Healthcare NHS Trust in Cumbria. An independent investigation[26] had found that staff had physically and mentally abused patients. The chairman of the NHS trust was dismissed by the Secretary of State. The Secretary of State ordered the CHI to visit the hospital and the Department of Health issued guidance for health and social service workers in the form of a national framework for all professionals caring for vulnerable people.[27] Subsequently, CHI published its report on 15 November 2000.[28] It contained evidence of appalling lack of professional standards and cruelty and abuse and made significant recommendations for reform. On the same day, a report on Prince Philip Hospital Llanelly (where the wrong kidney was removed from a patient) was published, which made major recommendations for improvement. A spokesman for the Commission has stated that its programme for scrutinising NHS Trusts could include questions about the resuscitation of older people, following complaints that some hospital doctors are ignoring guidelines.[29]

National Institute for Clinical Excellence (NICE)

This statutory body was established on 1 April 1999 to promote clinical and cost effectiveness. The then Secretary of State stated that its task would be to abolish postcode variation in the country, so that there would be national standards for the provision of health care such as medicines. There had been a lack of uniformity in the decisions of health authorities over the provision of services, particularly of medicines. One of the functions of NICE is to issue clinical guidelines and clinical audit methodologies and information on good practice. The National Institute for Clinical Excellence has a major role to play in the setting of standards of practice, by disseminating the results of research of what is proved to be clinically effective, research-based practice.

One of NICE's first activities was to recommend to the Secretary of State that the expense of Relenza (a drug developed by Glaxo Welcome for mitigating the severity of flu) did not justify funding through the NHS, since it appeared to have little benefit for those groups most at risk: the elderly and asthma sufferers. NICE's recommendations were accepted by the Secretary of State. However, subsequently, in the light of further research, NICE has recommended that Relenza could be used for at-risk adults who present within 36 hours of the onset of influenza-like illness. The Department of Health has issued implementation guidance on the use of Relenza.[30] NICE has also recommended that there should be no routine extraction of wisdom teeth. (It is estimated that the NHS should save up to £5 million per year if this is implemented.) NICE has also recommended that the NHS should use replacement hips for first-time surgery that last for 10 years or more. If this is clinically not possible, the chosen hip should last at least 3 years. It also suggested that the NHS should set up a hip registry.

In May 2000, NICE issued guidance on the use of Taxanes in the treatment of ovarian cancer. It recommended that the drug paclitaxel (Taxol) should be used to treat women who have previously received it and whose cancer has recurred or been resistant to other forms of treatment.[31] On 21 June 2000, it was reported that NICE was about to announce that the drug Beta Interferon does not justify the cost of £10,000 per year for patients suffering from multiple sclerosis. The Association of British Neurologists recommended that the drug should be used for about 10% of the country's 85,000 sufferers.[32]

It was announced in April 2000[33] by the Department of Health that NICE is to prepare guidelines advising GPs on when to refer patients with acute lower back pain to specialists. The NHS Plan announced that the work programme of NICE will be increased and it would carry out 50% more appraisals and produce 50% more guidelines (compared with 23 appraisals and 10 sets of guidelines it was to produce in 2000). An additional £2 million was given to NICE to meet the increased workload. Its work programme for 2001 was published on 16 November and includes the investigation of: anti-smoking treatments Zyban and Nicotine Replacement Therapy; drugs for rheumatoid arthritis and schizophrenia; guidelines for infection control and treatment of people with heart failure. In addition, NICE is to follow up a survey carried out by the National Sentinel Audit on the reasons behind caesarean sections to produce evidence-based guidelines for when a caesarean is necessary.

Effects of national guidelines

A memorandum of understanding on appraisal of health interventions was published by the Department of Health in August 1999. This set out the ground-rules under which NICE would carry out the appraisal of individual health interventions.[34] In discussing the legal status of guidance, the memorandum states that:

> All guidance must be fully reasoned and written in terms which makes clear that it **is** guidance. Guidance for clinicians does not override their professional responsibility to make the appropriate decision in the circumstances of the individual patient, in consultation with the patient or guardian/carer and in the light of locally agreed policies. Similarly guidance to NHS trusts and commissioners must make clear that it does not take away their discretion under administrative law to take account of individual circumstances.

In practice, in the determination of reasonable professional practice (the Bolam Test,[35] see Chapter 3), the fact that a specific treatment has been endorsed as clinically effective by NICE will carry weight in deciding what is reasonable practice, and a clinician may have to show what the individual circumstances were that justified a different treatment for a particular patient. Patients who claim that they have suffered as a result of a failure to provide a reasonable standard of care, could use evidence of clinical effectiveness and research-based practice to illustrate failings in the care provided to them. It could be argued therefore that failure to follow the recommendations of NICE will be prima facie evidence of a failure to follow a reasonable standard of care according to the Bolam Test.

In addition, since the aim of NICE recommendations is to end the postcode lottery, health authorities that decide that they do not have the funds to make available within their catchment area, medicines and treatments, which NICE has recommended as clinically effective, may find that their decisions are subject to judicial review.

Setting up of National Service Frameworks

The White Paper envisaged that there would be evidence-based National Service Frameworks that set out what patients can expect to receive from the NHS in major care areas or disease groups. National Service Frameworks have been published in the fields of mental health and coronary heart disease. A National cancer plan is to be published in the autumn of 2000 and diabetes in 2001. The work of NICE contributes to the development of National Service Frameworks. For example, NICE has undertaken investigations into type 1 diabetes to develop clinical guidelines and these will contribute to the implementation of the Diabetes National Service Framework, which is to be published in 2001 for implementation in the NHS from 2002.

NHS Direct

The pilot scheme whereby patients could phone direct to a 24-hour phone line and get immediate advice from a registered nurse was followed by the implementation of NHS Direct across the country. The government's aim is that by the end of the year 2000 the whole country will be covered by a 24-hour telephone advice line staffed by nurses. A director has been appointed for NHS Direct in Wales and this became operational in 2000. The service aims to provide both clinical advice to support self-care and appropriate self-referral to NHS services as well as access to more general advice and information.

Evaluation of NHS Direct

The Medical Research Unit at Sheffield University is undertaking an evaluation of NHS Direct and is expected to report at the end of 1999. In its interim report, published in March 1999,[36] it stated that 97% of callers surveyed said that they were satisfied or very satisfied with the service and the service appears to have been of great benefit to parents since about 1 in 4 calls is about a child of five or under.

However, there are some concerns: there was a small number of callers who expressed some dissatisfaction, including the length of time taken to speak to a nurse, and some callers were not happy with the large number of questions asked during the call.

The NHS Direct report stated that over the 1998 Christmas period NHS Direct pilot schemes handled 2700 calls.[37] Overall, 40% of callers who spoke to a nurse were advised that they could look after themselves. In general, around 25–30% of triaged calls over this period were about flu-type symptoms and in half of these cases nurses were able to give advice on how patients could look after themselves. Three million calls had been taken by NHS Direct by September 2000.

A Report by the Consumers' Association[38] stated that in its survey emergency situations were not recognised and inconsistent advice was given, depending upon the computer guide used by that particular area. Over half of those using the service then contacted their GP. Doctors at the BMA conference in 2000 suggested that it should be closed down and the funds transferred to primary care.

In September 2000, the Department of Health[39] announced a new seven-year partnership with Axa Assistance to provide a £22 million national computer system for NHS Direct. It would ensure that there is consistency of advice for patients wherever they are phoning from and would play a key part in developing plans for NHS Direct to work closely with other services such as out-of-hours doctors' services and ambulance services. It is estimated that the new system will be operating across the entire country by April 2001.

In a press release in November 2000,[40] the Department of Health stated that the helpline has received over 3.5 million calls and takes an average of 60,000 calls a week, expected to rise to 100,000 by the end of the year. It is the largest telephone-based healthcare provider in the world. It provides a nurse-led telephone advice line; a website;[41] an NHS Direct Healthcare Guide which is available in Safeways and in high street pharmacies; and NHS Direct information kiosks.

Guidance for nurses has been provided by the RCN on nurse telephone consultation services.[42] It states on the topic of professional and legal issues that 'there is no reason why a properly trained and experienced nurse providing telephone consultation should be at any greater risk of being held liable for negligence than nurses operating in other clinical settings.' As in any other clinical setting, it is essential that a nurse works within her competence.

Walk-in Clinics

A press announcement[43] publicised the setting up of more Direct Access Clinics run by nurses, to which any person can go for assistance and advice on health care. Seventeen new clinics were announced on 30 September 1999, bringing the number up to 36 in total. They aim, in the words of the press release:

> to offer quick access to a range of NHS services including free consultations, minor treatments, health information and advice on self-treatment. They are based in convenient locations that allow the public easy access and have opening hours

tailored to suit modern lifestyles, including early mornings, late evenings, and weekends. The centres will have close links with local GPs ensuring continuity of care for their patients.

The advantages to the public are clearly apparent: fast service, no wait, close to work, easy access, immediate advice, and speedy prescriptions. Many of the clinics are planned to be linked with GP surgeries through information technology. However, perhaps one of the advantages for some people is the anonymity that such clinics may provide: pregnancy testing, and other immediate tests without any receptionist recognising the patient.

On 11 April 2000, a new Walk-in Centre was opened by the Prime Minister in Peterborough.[44]

Nurses and expanded role practice in NHS Direct and Walk-in Clinics

NHS Direct and the Walk-in Clinics depend heavily upon nursing staff who are the main group employed in these areas. Nurses have to be sure that they work within the scope of their professional competence. This is considered in Chapter 24. In February 2000, nurses who work in Walk-in Centres were added to the list of the nurses who were able to have limited prescribing powers.[45] (see Chapter 28)

Early warning on negligence and failures in the NHS

In June 2000,[46] the Government published a press release on the setting up of a national system for the NHS to learn from experience. A report 'An Organisation with A Memory' (Department of Health (4) 2000),[47,48] written by an expert group chaired by Professor Liam Donaldson, Chief Medical Officer, Department of Health had recommended setting up a national reporting system. The Expert Committee was established in February 1999 with the brief to 'examine the extent to which the National Health Service and its constituent organisations have the capability to learn from untoward incidents and service failures so that similar occurrences are avoided in the future. To draw conclusions and make recommendations.'

The new NHS mandatory reporting system would log all failures, mistakes, errors and near-misses in health care. The new system was to be in place before the end of 2000.

The recommendations of the report include:

1. the introduction of a mandatory reporting scheme for adverse health care events and 'near-misses' based on sound, standardised reporting systems and clear definitions;

2. the introduction of a single overall database for analysing and sharing lessons from incidents and near misses, as well as for litigation and complaints data that will identify common factors and consider specific action necessary to reduce risks to patients in the future;

3. the encouragement of a reporting and questioning culture in the NHS which moves away from 'blame' and encourages a proper understanding of the underlying causes of failures;

4. improving NHS investigations and inquiries and ensuring that their results are fed into the national database so the whole NHS can learn lessons.

Specific targets are set to reduce levels of litigation. In April 2001 the Department of Health set out its proposals for a National Patient Safety Agency which will run a mandatory national reporting system of all adverse incidents. (*Building a Safer NHS for Patients*, D of H April 2001)

The need for a national system of the reporting of untoward incidents is apparent from some of the Reports and evidence of professional misconduct described below.

Beverly Allitt

Beverly Allitt, a state-enrolled nurse, was convicted of murdering four children, of attempting to murder three others and of causing grievous bodily harm to six others. She was sentenced to life imprisonment on every count. An independent inquiry,[49] chaired by Sir Cecil Clothier, made significant and substantial recommendations on the selection procedures for nurses, including the prohibition of employment of those with a personality disorder and that there should be formal health screening; that postmortem reports should be sent by the coroner to doctors involved in the patient's care; that there should be a review of paediatric pathology services; that there should be a review of sickness information being referred to Occupational Health and of the criteria for management referrals to Occupational Health; that there should be untoward incident reports if there is a failure of an alarm on monitoring equipment; and that reports of serious untoward incidents should be made in writing to district and regional health authorities. The Department of Health drew the attention of NHS managers to the report's recommendations.[50] The report accepted that no measures can afford complete protection against a determined miscreant and emphasised that:

> Our principal recommendation is that the Grantham disaster should serve to heighten awareness in all those caring for children of the possibility of malevolent intervention as a cause of unexplained clinical events.

Shipman Inquiry

It was apparent from the prosecution of a general practitioner, Dr Shipman, for the murder of 15 patients, that the principal recommendation of the Allitt Inquiry applies as much to the care of adults as to children. An inquiry was set up after his conviction and at the time of writing, its report is still awaited.

Dr Ledward

An inquiry into the conduct of Rodney Ledward[51] found that there had been a climate of fear and intimidation preventing nurses and junior doctors from telling tales in case they lost their jobs. The inquiry recommended that: each trust should develop a list of untoward non-clinical events that should trigger an incident report; each Royal College should identify a minimum list of untoward clinical events that should trigger the completion of an incident report; the person completing the form should generally identify themselves to encourage a culture of openness in the NHS; the earlier that concerns about a doctor's practice are noted the sooner they can be rectified. Further, Clinical Governance should apply to the private sector as well as the NHS.

The National Health Service Plan[52]

In July 2000 the NHS Plan was published. It describes itself as 'A Plan for investment in the NHS with sustained increases in funding. This is a Plan for reform with far reaching changes across the NHS.'

The Executive summary states that the investment in the NHS 'has to be accompanied by reform'. The reforms envisaged are set out in Box 5.7.

Box 5.7   **Major reforms of the NHS Plan**

1. principles of subsidiarity;
2. national standards;
3. regular inspections by CHI;
4. NICE will ensure cost effective drugs are not dependent upon where one lives;
5. a Modernisation Agency will be set up;
6. £500 million performance fund;
7. linking of NHS and Social Services with new agreements to pool resources: new care Trusts to commission health and social care in a single organisation;
8. new contracts for GPs and hospital doctors to reflect quality and productivity; limitation on newly qualified consultants to do private work;
9. expansion of roles for nurses and other health professionals;
10. individual learning accounts for support staff worth £150 million;
11. increase in number of nurse consultants to 1000;
12. leadership centre to be set up for developing managerial and clinical leaders;
13. patients to have more powers and influence in the NHS:
    (a) will receive copies of letters about care;
    (b) will have better information to choose GP;
    (c) patient advocates and advisers in each hospital;
    (d) proper redress when operations are cancelled;
    (e) patients' surveys and forums to help services become more patient centred;
14. Concordat with private providers of healthcare to enable NHS to make better use of facilities in private hospitals.

In addition to the reforms set out in Box 5.7, specific targets and dates are set in the NHS Plan. These include:

1. By 2004 all patients should be able to have a GP appointment within 48 hours;
2. By the end of 2005, the maximum wait for an out-patient appointment will be three months and for in-patients, six months.

Specific targets were also set for cancer care, heart disease, mental illness services and services for the elderly. The implications of the NHS Plan for the care of the elderly are considered in Chapter 19 and for community and primary care in Chapter 23.

In order to ensure implementation of the NHS Plan, the government has set up a new NHS Modernisation Agency. Its first task was allocated in August 2000 when it was required to visit the 7 hospitals with the longest waiting times. The action teams of the NHS Modernisation Agency would then decide how the additional money to be made available under the NHS Plan would be spent at these hospitals in order to bring down the waiting lists within 6 months.

Improving the NHS

The Chief Nursing Officer invited *Nursing Times* readers to give their views on how the NHS should be changed.[53] They were asked to provide their views on the following areas:

1. Patient access: How can the NHS treat patients faster and more conveniently?
2. Patient empowerment: How can the NHS enable people to take more control of the management of their care and enable them to inform the way we shape our services?
3. Professions and the wider workforce: How can the NHS get the right number of staff with the right skills to deliver modern, flexible care to patients?
4. Partnership: How can the NHS, social services and other local organisations work together better?
5. Performance: How can the NHS organisations improve their performance and how can we improve clinical care?
6. Prevention: What more can the NHS do to help people avoid getting ill?

Conclusions

This chapter has considered the statutory duties placed upon the Secretary of State and the new organisations that have been introduced in recent years to ensure that there are accountability and high standards of care provided in the NHS. It has also considered the National Plan and the changes that are envisaged over the next ten years within the NHS. It is clear that there will be considerable developments in the scope of professional practice of the nurse, who will have a major role to play in the implementation of the Plan. The legal implications of the expanded role of the nurse are considered in Chapter 24. In addition, practitioners must keep up to date with the publications of NICE and CHI and with the National Service Frameworks, since these are likely to have a significant effect on the standards of care to be provided and also on public expectations.

Perhaps the most significant set of recommendations for the NHS are those contained in the Report of the Bristol Inquiry.[54] So profound are their implications for the NHS in terms of respect for patients, the emphasis on professional openness and the standards of safety that, if implemented, the Report will be a watershed in the history of the NHS – BB or AB – Before Bristol or After Bristol.

Questions and exercises

1 Assess the likely contribution of NICE, CHI and the statutory duty of quality to the standards of care within your own sphere of professional practice.

2 Discuss the national scheme for the reporting of adverse healthcare incidents. How does it operate within your particular field of work?

3 Analyse the NHS Plan and consider specifically the effects that it could have in the area in which you work. To what extent do you consider that it will affect your own working practices?

4 Obtain a copy of the Bristol Inquiry Report and consider the extent to which its recommendations are in place in your department.

References

1 R. v. *Secretary of State for Social Services ex parte Hincks and others, Solicitors' Journal* 29 June 1979 436

2 *In re Walker*'s application, *The Times* 26 November 1987

3 R. v. *Cambridge Health Authority ex parte B* (a minor) (1995) 23 BMLR 1 CA; [1995] 2 All ER 129

4 *Soobramoney* v. *Minister of Health* (Kwazulu-Natal) 4 BHRC 308

5 R. v. *North Derbyshire Health Authority* [1997] 8 Med L R 327

6 NHS Executive Letter: EL (95)97

7 *North West Lancashire Health Authority* v. *A, D, and G* [1999] Lloyds Law Reports Medical p. 399, (1999) 2 CCL Rep 419

8 R. v. *North Derbyshire Health Authority* [1997] 8 Med L R 327

9 R. v. *Secretary of State for Health ex p Pfizer Ltd* [1999] 3 CMLR 875

10 Sir Roy Griffiths, Community Care: Agenda for Action, HMSO 1988 followed by Command Paper 849 Caring for People: Community Care in the next decade and beyond, HMSO November 1989

11 White Paper on the NHS: The New NHS – Modern Dependable, Stationery Office 1997

12 Department of Health press announcement 2000/0041 20 January 2000

13 NHS Executive, Primary Care Trusts: Financial Framework December 1999 Catalogue No 10389

14 NHS Executive, Working Together: Human resources guidance and requirements for Primary Care Trusts December 1999 Catalogue No. 10390

15 NHS Executive, Primary Care Trusts: A Guide to estate and facilities matters December 1999 Catalogue No 10393

16 http://www.doh.gov.uk/coin.htm or they can be viewed on the internet at http://tap.ccta.gov.uk/doh/coin4.nsf.

17 Department of Health press announcement 2000/0041 20 January 2000

18 NHS Confederation, Briefing Primary Care Trusts – new guidance, Issue No 39 February 2000;

19 Department of Health, The NHS Plan: a plan for investment a plan for reform, Cm 4818-1 July 2000 Stationery Office

20 Brian Hurwitz, *Clinical Guidelines and the Law*, Radcliffe Medical Press, Oxford 1998

21 A First Class Service Quality in the new NHS Department of Health 1998

22 HSC 1999/065 Clinical Governance: Quality in the new NHS, NHS Executive, London 1999

23 HSC 1998/113 A First Class Service: Quality in the new NHS, NHS Executive, 1998

24 Royal College of Nursing Clinical Governance: how nurses can get involved RCN 001 171 March 2000

25 Healthcare Parliamentary Monitor Issue No 250 24 April 2000 p. 18

26 North Lakeland Healthcare NHS Trust, Report of Independent Inquiry into Garlands Hospital March 2000 North Lakeland Healthcare NHS Trust and North Cumbria Health Authority

27 Department of Health, No Secrets: Guidance on Developing Multi-agency Policies and Procedures to Protect Vulnerable Adults from Abuse DoH 2000 (Available free from DoH PO Box 777 SE1 6XH www.doh.gov.uk/scg/nosecrets.htm)

28 Commission for Health Improvement Investigation into the North Lakeland NHS Trust Report to the Secretary of State for Health Department of Health November 2000

29 Healthcare Parliamentary Monitor Issue No 250 24 April 2000 p. 3

30 Department of Health, NICE Guidance on the Use of Zanamivir (Relenza): Implementation Guidance for NHS 21 November 2000 DoH and Welsh Assembly

31 Healthcare Parliamentary Monitor Issue No 251 p. 5 May 15 2000, www.nice.org.uk/appraisals/taxguide.htm

32 Helen Rumbelow, Secrecy exposed by MS drug ban leak, *The Times* 22 June 2000 p. 11

33 Healthcare Parliamentary Monitor Issue no 250 24 April 2000

34 Department of Health Memorandum of Understanding on appraisal of health interventions August 1999 DoH

35 *Bolam* v. *Friern Barnet Hospital Management Committee* [1957] 1 WLR 582

36 Evaluation of NHS Direct first wave sites, University of Sheffield's interim report March 1999

37 Information leaflet published by NHS Direct 7 October 1999 NHS Direct 0845 4647

38 Consumers' Association, Health Which August 2000 Consumers' Association London

39 Department of Health Press notice 11 September 2000

40 Department of Health Press release 2000/0679 20 November 2000

41 http://www. nhsdirect.nhs.uk

42 Royal College of Nursing, Nurse telephone consultation services: information and good practice RCN 000 995 (no date)

43 Department of Health Press Release, Frank Dobson announces more NHS walk-in clinics 30 September 1999 London DoH

44 Healthcare Parliamentary Monitor Issue No 250 24 April 2000 p. 10

45 Statutory Instrument 2000 No 121 The National Health Service (Pharmaceutical Services) Amendment Regulations 2000

46 Department of Health (3) National System for NHS to learn from Experience 2000/349 13 June 2000

[47] Department of Health (4) An Organisation with A Memory: report of an expert group chaired by Professor Liam Donaldson, Chief Medical Officer, Department of Health

[48] Copies are available from the Stationery Office, PO Box 29, Norwich NR3 1GN or from the Department of Health website http://www.doh.gov.uk.

[49] Clothier Report, The Allitt Inquiry An independent inquiry relating to deaths and injuries on the children's ward at Grantham and Kesteven General Hospital during the period February to April 1991, HMSO 1994

[50] DGM (95) 71 The Allitt Inquiry

[51] Jean Richie, Inquiry into Quality and Practice within the NHS arising from the actions of Rodney Ledward DoH 2000 (available free from DoH 0541 555455 reference number 601FR9217411)

[52] Department of Health, The NHS Plan: a plan for investment a plan for reform Cm 4818-1 July 2000 Stationery Office

[53] Sarah Mullally, How would you change the NHS? *Nursing Times* June 1 Vol 96 No 22 2000 p. 27

[54] Bristol Royal Infirmary Inquiry: Learning from Bristol. The Report of the public inquiry into children's heart surgery at the Bristol Royal Infirmary 1984–1995. Common Paper CM 5207, www.bristol-inquiry.org.uk

6   Progress of a civil claim: defences and compensation

This chapter considers the likely course that any civil case against a nurse and/or NHS Trust might follow, the ways in which compensation in the civil courts is assessed, and the defences that may be available (see Figure 6.1). It takes into account the major reforms in civil procedure which came into effect in April 2000 following the Report on Access to Justice by Lord Woolf.[1]

Civil proceedings
Mediation
Case management
Res ipsa loquitur
Compensation

    1.   Special damages.

    2.   General damages.

Defences

    1.   Denial of facts.

    2.   A missing element.

    3.   Contributory negligence.

    4.   Willing assumption of risk.

    5.   Exemption from liability.

    6.   Limitation of time.

Clinical Negligence Scheme for trusts
NHS Litigation Authority

Figure 6.1   Issues covered in Chapter 6.

Civil proceedings: stages, hearing and outcome

Two issues

In any civil case there are two separate issues:

1.   Is the defendant liable?

2.   How much compensation is payable?

It is sometimes possible that one of these issues has been agreed, e.g. the defendant accepts liability, but disagrees with the amount of compensation claimed by the victim, or that the amount of compensation that would be payable is agreed, but the defendant refuses to accept liability for that sum. Sometimes both issues are disputed. Evidence will therefore be required on both issues. The elements to establish liability and the kinds of harm for which compensation is payable are discussed in Chapter 3.

A nurse is first likely to be asked by management to provide a statement on the events. Care should be taken in the completion of this and guidelines are given in Chapter 9. If the victim has sought advice and has decided to commence an action, the next stages are set out below. These are stages in the High Court. The County Court, which deals with claims up to £50,000, is less formal and speedier, but the stages are similar (see Chapter 1 for civil courts).

Mediation

One of the results of the Woolf Reforms in civil justice is that the parties are encouraged to resolve the dispute before going to court using mediation or other forms of resolution such as Alternative Dispute Resolution. Often such processes can be linked with the complaints procedure (see Chapter 26) to avoid litigation. In mediation, an independent mediator attempts to assist the parties to reach an agreement to resolve the dispute. Unlike arbitration, the parties are under no compulsion to accept any ruling by the independent person.

Case management

The overriding principle enshrined in the new Civil Procedure Rules[2] (see Figure 6.2) is that all cases should be dealt with justly. The court must seek to give effect to this overriding principle when it exercises any powers under the rules and when it interprets any rule. The parties also have a duty to help the court to further this

---

The Rules are a new procedural code with the overriding objective of enabling the court to deal with cases justly.

Dealing with a case justly includes, so far as is practicable:

1. Ensuring that the parties are on an equal footing;

2. Saving expense;

3. Dealing with the case in ways which are proportionate:
   (a) to the amount of money involved;
   (b) to the importance of the case;
   (c) to the complexity of the issues; and
   (d) to the financial position of each party.

4. Ensuring that it is dealt with expeditiously and fairly; and

5. Allotting to it an appropriate share of the court's resources, while taking into account the need to allot resources to other cases.

Figure 6.2   Overriding objective in civil proceedings.

overriding objective. The court in furthering this principle of dealing with cases justly must actively manage the cases. Active management includes:

1. Encouraging the parties to co-operate with each other in the conduct of the proceedings.
2. Identifying the issues at an early stage.
3. Deciding promptly which issues need full investigation and trial and accordingly disposing summarily of the others.
4. Deciding the order in which the issues are to be resolved.
5. Encouraging the parties to use an alternative dispute resolution procedure if the court considers that appropriate and facilitating the use of such procedure.
6. Helping the parties to settle the whole or part of the case.
7. Fixing timetables or otherwise controlling the progress of the case.
8. Considering whether the likely benefits of taking a particular step justify the cost of taking it.
9. Dealing with as many aspects of the case as it can on the same occasion.
10. Dealing with the case without the parties needing to attend court.
11. Making use of technology.
12. Giving directions to ensure that the trial of a case proceeds quickly and efficiently.

A prime mechanism for judicially-led case management is the introduction of three tracks:

1. Small claims track.
2. Fast track.
3. Multi-track.

The court allocates each case to one of these three tracks on the basis of information provided by the claimant on the statement of case. If it does not have enough information to allocate the claim, then it will make an order requiring one or more parties to provide further information within 14 days.

Small claims track
This provides a procedure for straightforward claims that do not exceed £5,000, without the need for substantial pre-hearing preparation and the formalities of a traditional trial and where costs are kept low.

Fast track
Factors deciding whether a case is allocated to the fast track include: the limits likely to be placed on disclosure; the extent to which expert evidence may be necessary; and whether the trial will last longer than a day. Case management directions will be given at the allocation stage or at the listing stage.

Multi-track
Other cases may be allocated to be dealt with on a multi-track basis and dealt with at a Civil Trial Centre.

Pre-action protocol

Lord Woolf found that one of the major sources of increased costs and delay in clinical negligence litigation is at the pre-litigation stage and he therefore recommended the development and introduction of a pre-action protocol. A draft protocol was drawn up in 1997 by the Clinical Disputes Forum and was formally launched on 23 July 1998.[3] The protocol sets a standard of good practice with emphasis on better handling of potential disputes and more effective and efficient management of information and investigation and also sets out the steps to be followed where litigation is in prospect.

Summary judgment or other early termination

Part of the court's duty of active case management is the summary disposal of issues that do not need full investigation and trial. The court can strike out a statement of case or give a summary judgment where either claimant or defendant has no reasonable prospect of success.

Disclosure and Inspection of documents

A party discloses a document by stating that the document exists or has existed. Rules relating to the Disclosure and Inspection of documents are to be found in Part 31 of the Civil Procedure Rules. There are rules relating to standard disclosure that list the documents that are to be disclosed. These include:

1. The documents on which the party relies.
2. The documents that adversely affect his own case; or another party's case or support another party's case.
3. The documents that he is required to disclose by a relevant practice direction.

A party is required to make a reasonable search for any relevant documents. Some documents are obtainable before a case begins under the Supreme Court Act 1981, Section 33. The nurse may well not be aware of this activity unless she is being personally sued or unless good communication ensures that she is kept in the picture. In *Harris* v. *Newcastle HA* 1989 2 All ER 273, the court allowed pre-trial disclosure of records relating to events 26 years before, even though the Health Authority intended to plead that the case was out of time. The emphasis now is on full disclosure by each party to ensure that the case can be dealt with as promptly as possible.

Claim form is issued

This marks the beginning of the case. There are important time limits (discussed below) within which the claim form (originally known as a writ) is issued. The claim form indicates that action is now being commenced. It is preceded by what is known as a letter before action, i.e. a warning by the claimant (usually the claimant's solicitor) that if there is no acceptance of the claim, then the legal action will commence. The claim form usually names the NHS Trust as the defendant, but it is possible for an individual employee to be named as a party and more than one defendant can be named.

Service of the claim form

This must be sent to the defendant within four months of its issue. (In the past there was a requirement for personal service, i.e. the claim form had to be handed to the defendant personally. Now, however, the claim form is sent to a known address.) The defendant must then respond by filing a defence or an admission, or file an acknowledgement of service. If the defendant fails to respond, then the claimant may be able to obtain judgment in default.

The drafting of the documents or statements of case (these were once known as pleadings) is arranged by the respective parties' solicitors, who often instruct counsel (i.e. barristers). A litigant may, however, represent himself personally. Strict time limits are laid down for the service and response to the documents. Under the Woolf reforms, the documents exchanged between the parties should be simpler and be verified by the parties. If there are uncertainties, the court can require the parties to clarify any matter in dispute.

Pre-trial review

Eventually there will be an assessment of the situation by the parties, together with a registrar or judge, account taken of the number of witnesses to attend, exchange of any experts' medical reports and, finally, the case will be set down for hearing.

Payment into court

Rules about offers to settle and payments into court are set out in Parts 36 and 37 of the Civil Procedure Rules. In some cases where there is dispute over the amount of compensation, but liability is accepted, the defendant will probably be advised to pay a sum in settlement of the case into court. If the claimant accepts this payment in, then the defendant will be liable for the claimant's costs up to that point. The court will be notified that there has been a settlement of the case. A payment in may also be made where the defendant does not accept liability, but he is not confident of winning the case and rather than risk losing and having to pay the costs of both sides he offers a sum in full and final settlement.

If the claimant decides that the payment in is not acceptable, the case will continue. In these circumstances, the judge is not told that there has been a payment in. He will not therefore be influenced by that in determining the case and deciding what compensation to award. If he awards less than the payment in or if he decides there is no liability by the defendant, then the claimant will have to pay both the defendant's costs from the time of the payment in as well as his own, since, of course, had the claimant accepted that sum deemed reasonable in comparison with the judge's award, there would have been no time-consuming and costly court hearing. These costs may well exceed the amount of the award. The judge has a discretion over whether to award the defendant the costs in these circumstances.

The hearing

Claimant's case

Examination in chief

This is when questions are put to the witness by the party that has called him to give evidence.

The claimant has the burden of establishing to the satisfaction of the judge, on a balance of probabilities, that there has been negligence or some other alleged civil wrong. The claimant will therefore be asked to give evidence first.

His witnesses will be sworn in, in turn, and will then give evidence under examination of the claimant's legal representative. This has in the past usually been a barrister (counsel), instructed by the solicitor; but increasingly solicitors are taking on an advocacy role. Sometimes the claimant appears personally. This initial questioning is known as examination in chief. The witness cannot be asked leading questions when being examined in chief. Counsel will have before him the proof of the witness's statement to the solicitor and will take him through this to bring his evidence to the court.

Expert evidence

Expert evidence from witnesses may be required on the nature of the standard of care that should have been provided or on the amount of compensation payable. The new civil procedure rules have led to major changes in the giving of expert evidence and these are discussed in Chapter 9.

Cross-examination

Counsel for the defence is then able to question the witness, i.e. cross-examine. Here the task is to discredit the evidence by showing that it is irrelevant, or that it is unreliable, or for some other reason is of no weight against the defendant. Alternatively, the witness can be used to support the case of the other side. Leading questions are allowed when the witness is under cross-examination. The judge will, however, intervene to protect the witness from harassment (see Chapter 9 on giving evidence in court). At this stage, the judge may wish to question the witness to clarify points on which he is not certain.

Re-examination

Finally, the side calling that witness has the chance of repairing any damage that the cross-examination has inflicted, but the re-examination is confined to points that have arisen during cross-examination or under questioning by the judge. All the claimant's witnesses give evidence in this way.

When the case for the claimant has ended the judge has the opportunity of ending the case at this point and of finding against the claimant on the grounds that he has not established a *prima facie* case and therefore the defence is not required to give evidence. He cannot, of course, decide at this point against the defendant because the defence has not as yet given evidence.

Defendant's case

If the case proceeds, the defence must put forward its witnesses who are examined in chief, cross-examined and then re-examined as previously described. If it is alleged that the nurse has been negligent, she will be called as a witness for the defence. Several years may have elapsed since the events and her recall may be limited or even nil. She is able to refresh her memory by referring to contemporaneous records and therefore she should refer to the case notes. In this situation, she will appreciate the value of detailed, accurate, clear information on those events. Counsel who examines her in chief will have a copy of statements she has previously given. She should ensure that she had help in making this statement and prior to the court hearing she should be instructed on the procedure to be followed and some of the pitfalls she may encounter. Most of those who have appeared in court describe the event as particularly harrowing, and preparation is essential. Giving evidence in court is discussed further in Chapter 9.

Judge's summing up

After summaries by counsel, the judge then has the task of making his judgment. This may be reserved, i.e. the parties are notified that they will be informed of the outcome, or it might be given immediately. The judge will determine both liability and damages (whichever are in dispute). The party having to pay costs will usually depend upon the outcome, i.e. the loser pays the costs of both sides. There is no jury in a civil case (except in defamation cases).

Res ipsa loquitur

In certain cases, inferences can be made from the facts about the existence of negligence. If the plaintiff can establish that it is a *res ipsa loquitur* situation ('the matter speaks for itself'), then the defendant can be asked to show how the incident occurred without negligence on his part. The claimant would have to show the following factors to raise a presumption of *res ipsa loquitur*:

1. What has occurred would not normally occur if reasonable care were taken.
2. The events were under the control or management of the defendants.
3. The defendant has not offered any reasonable explanation for what occurred.

The most obvious example is leaving a swab inside a patient, or amputating the wrong limb. This procedure gives the claimant a technical advantage that is very necessary when he is ignorant of the actual events that caused harm. If the defendant fails to give a reasonable explanation of the events, then the court can draw the inference that there was negligence.

Compensation in civil proceedings for negligence

Nurses sometimes meet patients who are hesitant to undertake all the necessary physiotherapy and other rehabilitative work lest the compensation will be reduced because they are seen to have made a full recovery. However, the powers of the court to make provisional awards or award interim amounts of compensation should make it easier for a claimant to focus on rehabilitation.

Situation 6.1   Leslie's leg

Leslie was travelling on his motorbike when a car started to overtake him. Unfortunately, a lorry was coming in the opposite direction and the vehicle pulled in to the side, knocking Leslie off. Leslie was admitted to the orthopaedic ward from accident and emergency. He suffered a serious compound fracture. The prognosis was that he was unlikely to make a complete recovery, but could anticipate further problems with the leg, a slight limp and a vulnerability to arthritis later on. He had been advised not to expect to return to his existing job (a PE instructor) for at least nine months. How will his likely compensation be calculated?

Special damages

Leslie will first be entitled to receive special damages. These are amounts to cover specific losses that have already been suffered and where the amount can therefore be accurately stated. For example, the loss and damage to his motorbike, damage to his clothing, loss of wages up to the present day. Interest is allowed on the items.

General damages

The headings under which such damages are calculated are shown in Figure 6.3.

---

1. Special damages: expenses and losses to the date of judgment.
2. General damages
    (a)   non-pecuniary loss:
          pain and suffering;
          loss of amenity;
    (b)   pecuniary loss:
          loss of earnings;
          loss of earning capacity;
          cost of future care and expenses;
          interest.

Figure 6.3   Headings of compensation.

Non-pecuniary loss (i.e. non-financial loss)

1. *Pain and suffering*: this is to cover the pain from the injury itself, as well as from any consequential medical treatment and worry about the effects of the injury on the patient's lifestyle. It could also include damages for the mental suffering resulting from the fact that the person's life has been shortened. (Administration of Justice Act 1982, Section 1(1)(a) introduced this form of compensation since there is no longer any compensation for the actual shortening of life itself. This used to be known as 'loss of expectation of life' and was abolished by this Act.)

2. *Loss of amenity*: Leslie will be able to recover additional compensation if it is established that his activities will be restricted because of the injuries to his leg. Clearly, if his leg had to be amputated, then he would recover an additional sum for that loss.

These non-pecuniary losses are notoriously difficult to calculate. How can money ever be an adequate compensation for blindness or loss of the ability to have children or to enjoy normal activities? The answer is that it cannot be. However, since there is no other form of compensation, the non-pecuniary loss has to be converted into pecuniary form. Judges follow precedents in calculating the awards. They examine decisions in preceding cases, taking into account any relevant differences between the present case and the earlier cases and allowing for inflation. A judge's award is subject to appeal.

Pecuniary loss

1. *Loss of earnings*: Leslie's loss of future earnings would be calculated by determining his net annual loss multiplied by a figure to cover the number of years the disability will last. The figure takes into account the fact that the compensation will be paid out all at once rather than each week or month over the next few years.

2. *Loss of earning capacity*: because of his injury Leslie may never be able to work as a PE instructor again. Alternatively, he may retain his job initially, but with the risk that if he loses it he might never get similar paid work again because of his disability. He is entitled to be compensated for this risk.

3. *Expenses*: Leslie would also be entitled to recover reasonable expenses in getting to and from hospital, medical and similar expenses (e.g. physiotherapy) and, in some circumstances, domestic help.

4. *Interest*: interest is payable on the pecuniary loss already suffered and on the non-pecuniary loss.

5. *Deductions*: deductions are made in respect of the value of certain social security benefits which are paid to the compensation recovery unit.

Interim payments can be made by the court under the Rules of the Supreme Court. The plaintiff can apply for an interim payment at any time after the claim form has been served on the defendant. Thus, where the defendant has admitted liability, but disputes the amount of damages payable, the court could make an order for an interim payment to be made. Because of the uncertainty of prognosis, there is the power for an order of provisional damages for personal injuries to be made if there is a chance that at some time in the future the injured person will, as a result of the act or omission, develop some serious disease or suffer some serious deterioration in his physical or mental condition (Supreme Court Act 1981, Section 32A and Rules of Supreme Court 0.37, pp. 7–10). Provisional damages in relation to exposure to asbestos were awarded in one case.[4] Where large settlements are to be paid, parties often agree a structured settlement whereby an annuity is purchased with part of the lump sum, thus providing an income to the claimant for life.

> ### Case 6.1 *A living nightmare*
>
> Sally Kralj was admitted to hospital for the expected birth of twins. In the course of delivery without the use of anaesthetic, the consultant obstetrician put his arm inside Mrs Kralj in an effort to turn the second twin, who was lying in a transverse position, by manual manipulation of its head. There was expert opinion that such treatment was horrific and wholly unacceptable and must have caused the patient excruciating pain. The obstetrician's efforts were unsuccessful and the baby was later delivered by caesarian section. The child was born with severe disabilities that resulted from the obstetrician's attempt to turn it and it died eight weeks later. Liability was admitted and the only issue was how much compensation should be paid.

The court held that the concept of aggravated damages was not appropriate to claims arising out of medical negligence. Nevertheless, the compensatory damages could be increased if the impact of what had happened to the patient was such that it would be more difficult for the patient to recover. She was also entitled to damages for nervous shock as the result of learning what happened to the child and of seeing it, and was further entitled to have those damages increased if, because of her grief at the loss of the child, it would be more difficult for her to recover from her own injuries. If medical negligence resulted in the death of a child during pregnancy, the financial loss suffered by the mother in replacing the dead child was not too remote

---

Spastic quadriplegic cerebral palsy sustained at birth.

The claimant was aged nine when the settlement was approved. As a result of a late delivery, he was severely acidotic at birth and had suffered bilateral cerebral cortical damage resulting in quadriplegic cerebral palsy. The defendants admitted negligence by the midwife in failing to summon an obstetrician, but they denied causation. Damages were eventually agreed as follows:

	£
General damages	125,000
Interest	12,500
Past care	58,500
Accommodation	50,000
Other past expenses	139,000
Future care	600,000
Claimant's loss of earnings	115,000
Accommodation (future)	40,000
Other future expenses	225,000
Education	50,000
Total	£1,300,000

A structured settlement was eventually agreed after some dispute and approved by the judge. A sum of £689,000 was returned to the defendants to provide £20,000 per year to the claimant to the age of 19 and thereafter £35,000.

Figure 6.4 Example of an assessment of compensation *Inman* v. *Cambridge Health Authority* January 1998 (taken from Kemp and Kemp[5]).

to be recoverable as damages. General damages of £10,500 were awarded (*Kralj* v. *McGrath* 1986 1 All ER 54).

An example of the assessment of compensation is shown in Figure 6.4.

Calculating the amount of compensation

In a recent case, the House of Lords has ruled that in awarding compensation, victims should not be expected to speculate on the stock market and therefore lower levels of return based on index-linked government securities can be used as the basis of calculation.[6] The effect of this ruling will be to increase the capital amount awarded to victims. In the case itself, James Thomas, a cerebral palsy victim as a result of negligence at birth, was awarded £1,285,000 by the High Court judge, but this was reduced by the Court of Appeal by £300,000 on the basis that the capital could be invested in the higher returns (but more risky) equities. The House of Lords restored the original amount.

The Law Commission recommended changes to the present system relating to the quantifying of damages for personal injury[7] in 1996 and suggested, amongst other recommendations, that the NHS should be able to recover the costs arising from the treatment of road traffic and other accident victims. It is estimated that this might bring in £120 million to the NHS. A later report by the Law Commission[8] in 1999 recommended that compensation for non-pecuniary loss (e.g. pain suffering and loss of amenity) should be increased and this could be implemented through the courts' decisions on damages. The Court of Appeal gave judgment in March 2000[9] and decided that a modest increase was required to bring some awards up to a figure that was fair, reasonable and just. It recommended that damages for claims above £10,000 should be raised by a maximum of about 35% with increases tapering downwards. The Court of Appeal acknowledged that the life expectancy for many seriously injured claimants has increased and they can now survive for many years. The Judicial Studies Board has been asked to provide new guidelines. There is likely to be a significant impact upon the NHS as a result of this judgment, though not perhaps as much as if the Law Commission recommendations had been supported in full.

Defences to a civil action

A considerable number of claims that are brought against NHS trusts and health authorities are dropped before they reach a final outcome and many of those that survive to the end are unsuccessful. They may fail because on investigation there are no grounds for negligence or some of the other defences succeed. This section looks at the defences open to a nurse or her employer in civil actions for negligence.

Denial of facts

It often happens that when things go wrong it is one person's word against another. The patient might complain that the nurse has been negligent, but the nurse might be able to show that the events were not as the patient describes. Many court cases are simply disputes over facts. Where only two people are involved, with no other witnesses and no other circumstantial evidence, then if such a case comes before the courts, the judge will have to decide on the basis of the evidence in court and the way the parties stand up to cross-examination which account of the events is acceptable.

In civil cases, the burden is on the claimant to establish, on a balance of probabilities, that the defendant has been negligent.

A missing element

Even where the facts are not disputed, it might still be possible for an action for negligence to be defended on the grounds that one of the essential elements is missing. From Chapter 3 it will be recalled that to succeed in a negligence case it is necessary for the claimant to establish that a duty of care was owed by the defendant, that the defendant was in breach of this duty, and that this breach caused reasonably foreseeable harm to the claimant. If one of these elements has not been established on a balance of probabilities, then the defendant will win the case.

Contributory negligence

Situation 6.2   Walking aids

Fred, who has recently had an operation for a fractured leg, has been receiving help from the physiotherapist in walking with crutches. Fred asks a nursing auxiliary, who has only just come onto the ward, for help in going to the toilet. She is not aware that Fred has been told not to try to walk yet unless he is accompanied by a qualified person. She assists him out of bed and onto the crutches. As she does so, the crutches slip from under Fred and he falls to the ground, sustaining another fracture.

In this situation, the nursing auxiliary or the ward management are clearly at fault in allowing Fred out of bed in these circumstances. However, Fred is also at fault. He should have followed instructions. Fred's responsibility for the harm that has occurred depends to a large extent on his level of understanding, how clear the instructions were to him, and how reasonable it was to expect him to have waited for experienced help in using the crutches. If he were to sue the NHS Trust and its staff, they may well defend themselves on the grounds that he was partly at fault in not taking care of himself. This defence is known as a defence of contributory negligence. The defendant is saying to the claimant: you failed to take care of yourself and that has led to or increased the harm that you have suffered. If the judge is satisfied that the defendant has succeeded in this defence, he is able to reduce the compensation by the extent to which he considers the claimant's fault has contributed to the harm. The wording of Section 1 of the Law Reform (Contributory Negligence) Act 1945 is shown in Figure 6.5.

Section 1(i) Where any person suffers damage as the result partly of his own fault and partly of any other person or persons a claim in respect of that damage shall not be defeated by reason of the fault of the person suffering the damage, but the damages recoverable in respect thereof shall be reduced to such an extent as the court thinks just and equitable having regard to the claimant's share in responsibility for the damage.

Figure 6.5 Law Reform (Contributory Negligence) Act 1945 Section 1.

Case 6.2   No seat belt

Mr Froom was driving his car carefully at a speed of 30–35 mph with his wife sitting beside him and his daughter in the back seat. The front seats were fitted with seat belts, but neither Mr nor Mrs Froom was wearing them. Unfortunately, Mr Froom's car was struck head on by a car travelling at speed in the opposite direction and on the wrong side of the road as it had pulled out to overtake a line of traffic.

The trial judge decided that failure to wear a seat belt was not contributory negligence. The defendant appealed to the Court of Appeal and won his appeal. Lord Denning emphasised that where the damage to the claimant would not have been reduced by failure to wear the seat belt, then there should be no reduction of compensation, but where, as here, the injuries would have been reduced by wearing a seat belt, there should be a reduction of compensation. In Mr Froom's case, the injuries to the head and chest would have been prevented by wearing a seat belt. His finger would have been broken anyway and therefore there was no reduction on that account. The overall deduction of compensation for Mr Froom's contributory negligence was held to be 20 per cent.[10] (This case was heard before the wearing of front seat belts was compulsory.)

Reductions of compensation on grounds of contributory negligence can vary from 95 per cent to 5 per cent. When it is larger, then there is held to be no liability on the part of the defendant; when it is smaller it is considered to be too insignificant to count. To succeed, the defendant has to establish that the plaintiff failed to take reasonable care of himself and that this failure contributed to the harm he suffered, or increased it.

Contributory negligence and children

Lord Denning has said:

A very young child cannot be guilty of contributory negligence. An older child may be; but it depends on the circumstances. A judge should only find a child guilty of contributory negligence if he or she is of such an age as reasonably to be expected to take precautions for his or her own safety: and then he or she is only to be found guilty if blame should be attached to him or her.

In the same case Lord Justice Salmon said:

> The question as to whether the plaintiff can be said to have been guilty of contributory negligence depends on whether any ordinary child of 13½ years could be expected to have done any more than this child did. I say 'any ordinary child'. I do not mean a paragon of prudence; nor do I mean a scatter-brain child; but the ordinary girl of 13½ [the age of the child in that case].[11]

Willing assumption of risk *(volenti non fit injuria)*

Sometimes, where there is a known risk, the possibility of this taking place is accepted and the defendant is not liable. The most obvious example is dangerous sports where both players and spectators are at some risk. If that risk occurs, it is assumed that there will be no court action, but that the risk has been willingly accepted. For example, in a rugby match it is possible that a player may be seriously injured, even though no rules have been broken and there is no criminal act. This is a risk of the game and is accepted by the players. If, of course, the rules have been broken and thus resulted in injuries, then the injured player may well have an action for assault.

In the health service context, the agreement by the patient that treatment can proceed counts not only as consent to what would otherwise count as a trespass to the person, but it is also an acceptance of the possibility that those hazards that are an inextricable risk of that particular treatment could occur. Consent, however, does not imply consent to the risk that the professional will be negligent (see Chapter 7 on consent).

Situation 6.3   Blood donor

Rachel had been giving blood for many years. She was summoned on one occasion to the session. As the needle was inserted and the canula put in place, she felt an appalling pain. She shrieked and the needle was quickly withdrawn and a new painless site was found. After the session, Rachel found that it was very difficult to move her hand, arm and fingers. She was examined by a doctor who sent her for tests and eventually she was told that a very rare damage to the nerve had occurred. However, she was assured that with physiotherapy she would soon recover full function. Unfortunately, this did not prove to be true. She was eventually forced to take early retirement on the grounds of ill health, and did not recover full arm or hand movement. She sought advice about suing the doctor and was given an expert's report that such a rare event could occur without any negligence on the part of the doctor, so that there was no point in suing either the doctor or the health authority. However, Rachel argued that if she had known of the risk she would not have agreed to give blood unless she had been given an assurance that in the event of the risk taking place she would have received compensation.

As the law stands at present, unless Rachel can show negligence by the professional staff or the employer, she would be unable to recover compensation in court. We do not have a system of no-fault liability. As a volunteer, she can be assumed to have accepted the possibility of those risks occurring, although she may well be able to show that there was a breach of the duty owed to her as a volunteer if certain risks were not pointed out to her. The Pearson Report on compensation for personal injuries recommended that there should be an acceptance of no-fault liability for volunteers in medical research. These recommendations have not yet been implemented in law (though pharmaceutical companies offer compensation on a no-fault liability basis to those who take part in drug trials) and it could be argued that if they ever are they should be extended to cover such situations as donation of blood. In such situations, many NHS Trusts would make an *ex gratia* payment, i.e. a payment without any acceptance or implication of liability on its part.

To establish a defence of willing assumption of risk, the defendant has to show that the plaintiff knew of the risk, willingly consented to run it, and waived any right to sue for compensation. If it is successfully pleaded, it operates as a total defence.

Sometimes employers have tried to rely on this defence when sued by an employee for injuries at work. For example, it has been said that back injuries are an occupational hazard for nurses; all psychiatric nurses accept the risk of physical violence; CSSD assistants are likely to suffer from 'sharp' injuries as an occupational hazard. However, it is quite clear that where there is a failure of the employer in his duty to care for the employee's safety, then the defence of willing assumption of risk will not prevail. (See Chapter 12 on health and safety law.)

Exemption from liability

NHS Trust premises are a blaze of exemption notices: 'no responsibility is taken for cars parked in this area'; 'the "X" NHS Trust accepts no liability for patients' property'. How effective are these notices if the NHS Trust or its employees are negligent? Can a patient be persuaded to sign a form saying that he will not hold the 'X' NHS Trust liable in any respect? Sometimes an NHS Trust responds to a complaint by asking for a declaration that if the complaint is to be pursued and an investigation conducted, then the NHS Trust requires an assurance that there will be no civil action. Can such a declaration be held against the person who signed? The answer to these questions is to a considerable extent given by reference to the Unfair Contract Terms Act 1977. This Act prevents anyone in the course of any business activity (and this covers professional, local, and public authority activity) from exempting himself from negligence if that negligence gives rise to personal injury or death. Any agreement, notice or clause to that effect is void (see Figure 6.6).

Situation 6.4   *No liability*

A surgeon said, 'I am prepared to carry out upon you a very risky operation and I want you to sign that you will exempt me from all blame if anything goes wrong.' The patient, in his desire to have the operation, signed the form, but unfortunately the surgeon made a very careless error that no competent surgeon would have made, leaving the patient severely crippled.

1. *Scope of Part I*

1. For the purposes of this part of this Act, 'negligence' means the breach:
   (a) of any obligation, arising from the express or implied terms of a contract, to take reasonable care or exercise skill in the performance of the contract;
   (b) of any common law duty to take reasonable care or exercise reasonable skill (but not stricter duty);
   (c) of the common duty of care imposed by the Occupiers' Liability Act 1957 or the Occupiers' Liability Act (Northern Ireland) 1957.

2. This part of this Act is subject to Part III; and in relation to contracts, the operation of Sections 2 to 4 and 7 is subject to the exceptions made by Schedule 1.

3. In the case of both contract and tort, Sections 2 to 7 apply (except where the contrary is stated in Section 6(4)) only to business liability, that is liability for breach of obligations or duties arising
   (a) from things done or to be done by a person in the course of a business (whether his own business or another's); or
   (b) from the occupation of premises used for business purposes of the occupier; and references to liability are to be read accordingly.

4. In relation to any breach of duty or obligation, it is immaterial for any purpose of this part of this Act whether the breach was inadvertent or intentional, or whether liability for it arises directly or vicariously.

2. *Negligence liability*

1. A person cannot by reference to any contract term or to a notice given to persons generally or to particular persons exclude or restrict his liability for death or personal injury resulting from negligence.

2. In the case of other loss or damage, a person cannot so exclude or restrict his liability for negligence except in so far as the term or notice satisfies the requirement of reasonableness.

3. Where a contract term or notice purports to exclude or restrict liability for negligence a person's agreement to or awareness of it is not of itself to be taken as indicating his voluntary acceptance of any risk.

11. *The 'reasonableness' test*

3. In relation to a notice (not being a notice having contractual effect), the requirement of reasonableness under this Act is that it should be fair and reasonable to allow reliance on it, having regard to all the circumstances obtaining when the liability arose or (but for the notice) would have arisen.

4. Where by reference to a contract term or notice a person seeks to restrict liability to a specified sum of money, and the question arises (under this or any other Act) whether the term or notice satisfies the requirement of reasonableness, regard shall be had in particular (but without prejudice to subsection (2) above in the case of contract terms) to:
   (a) the resources which he could expect to be available to him for the purpose of meeting the liability should it arise; and
   (b) how far it was open to him to cover himself by insurance.

5. It is for those claiming that a contract term or notice satisfies the requirements of reasonableness to show that it does.

14. *Interpretation of Part I*
In this part of this Act:
'business' includes a profession and the activities of any government department or local or public authority; . . .

Figure 6.6 Unfair Contract Terms Act 1977 (summarised by author).

Is the patient bound by that form? The answer is no. The Act prevents the surgeon relying upon that form as a defence against the patient. He cannot exclude or restrict his liability for death or personal injury resulting from his negligence. The same principles do not apply to loss of or damage to property. Under the Unfair Contract Terms Act 1977, an exemption for damage to or loss of property is valid if it is reasonable (see Figure 6.6). For further discussion upon this, see Chapter 25.

Limitation of time

Most civil court actions must be brought within a certain length of time. The time limit for actions concerning personal injury and death is three years from the cause of action arising or the date of the knowledge of the cause of action arising. The issue of the claim form marks the beginning of the court action and it is the time that elapses from the cause arising to the day the claim form is issued that is critical.

Knowledge of the harm

If a patient did not realise that he was suffering from the effects of someone's negligence in that time, then the time limit does not apply till he has that knowledge. It used to be law that if the claimant was out of time for whatever reason then he was barred from proceeding with the case. The injustice of this rule is very easy to see from cases involving such long-term diseases as pneumoconiosis, asbestosis, and similar conditions. The law was therefore amended so that the period did not start to run until the claimant had knowledge of the facts shown in Figure 6.7 overleaf.

The potential claimant cannot, however, simply turn a blind eye to knowledge which any reasonable person would acquire from the facts around him. If, however, he had no knowledge of the facts, then he is not barred from proceeding.

Situation 6.5   Delay

Claire French was admitted for an appendectomy. The operation was performed successfully and she was discharged. From time to time, however, she complained of violent stomach pain for which she took very strong pain killers. Some six years after the first operation, she was admitted to hospital in intense agony and no pain killer could relieve it. The consultant was reluctant to operate since he could not identify any possible cause for which surgery was the solution. However, a laparoscopy was performed and it was then discovered that a swab had been left behind in the previous operation. The consultant was completely open with Claire about his findings and assured her that from now on she should not get any pain. She felt that she should be compensated for the fact that she had already suffered much pain and had had to endure the risks, pain and suffering of a second operation. Is she entitled to obtain compensaiton?

As a result of the changes to the Limitation Act 1980, she would not be barred on the grounds of exceeding the time limit, which would run from the time she was informed of the cause of her suffering.

> (a) that the injury in question was significant;
> (b) that the injury was attributable in whole or in part to the act or omission which is alleged to constitute negligence;
> (c) the identity of the defendant; and
> (d) the identity of any other defendant.
>
> The term 'significant' is further defined as where 'the person whose date of knowledge is in question would reasonably have considered it sufficiently serious to justify instituting proceeding against a defendant who did not dispute liability . . .' Limitation Act 1980.

Figure 6.7 Limitation Act 1980: definition of 'knowledge'.

Judge's discretion to extend time limit

In addition, the judge has the discretion to allow a case to proceed which would otherwise be outside the time limit where it would be just to the plaintiff to permit him to continue. A judge refused to extend the time limit in the following case.

Case 6.3   No extension of time[12]

On 5 July 1960, the claimant gave birth to her first child. Afterwards the doctor suturing her episiotomy informed her that the needle that he had been using had broken. In fact, a two inch piece of the needle had been left inside the wound. The claimant experienced pain in the area of the episiotomy, but was too embarrassed to discuss her symptoms with her general practitioner. She gave birth to five more children. In 1983, she came under the care of a female gynaecologist and underwent a number of negative investigations and operations over a period of 11 years. The fragment of the needle was identified on a hip X-ray when she was being reviewed by orthopaedic surgeons in 1991, but it was not till a repeat X-ray in 1994 that she was informed of the needle's presence. She issued proceedings in January 1997 and the issue of limitation was tried as a preliminary point. At the County Court, her claim was held to be statute barred: although she had not attained actual knowledge till 1994, she had had constructive knowledge 'long before 1994'. She appealed to the Court of Appeal on the grounds that the judge had erred in refusing to take into account her embarrassment when considering when she ought reasonably to have sought medical advice and the defendant could not prove that such earlier advice would have led to an earlier detection of the needle fragment.

The Court of Appeal dismissed the appeal on the grounds that she should have sought medical advice earlier, she failed to give the gynaecologist sufficient information about her symptoms and whilst the 1991 X-ray had revealed the fragment of the needle, its significance and relationship to her gynaecological problems were not realised by the orthopaedic specialists who were reviewing her for a hip replacement.

Extension of the time limit on other grounds

Where minors under 18 years of age have suffered personal injury, there is no time barrier to bringing an action until they reach the age of 18 years at which time the time limit comes into operation. (See Chapter 13 on children.) The same principle applies to the mentally disordered whose disorder prevents them from bringing an action within the appropriate time limits. The time limits do not commence until the disorder ceases, which in most cases will be at death.

Legal aid and conditional fees

One of the recent changes in civil justice is the withdrawal of legal aid in personal injury claims. This is further discussed in Chapter 1.

Role of the Clinical Negligence Scheme for Trusts (CNST) and the NHS Litigation Authority (NHSLA)

Trusts may take part in a voluntary scheme whereby compensation is met from a pooling system. The payment into the pool is dependent upon an assessment of the risk presented by that particular trust and amounts over a specified minimum will be met from the pool. The CNST visits organisations that belong or wish to belong to the scheme in order to assess their risk: they examine in particular, the standard of risk assessment and management in the organisation; and the standards of record keeping. In the light of their assessment, premiums payable into the scheme are assessed. Over 95% of NHS Trusts are members of CNST. Liabilities prior to April 1995 are covered by the Existing Liabilities Scheme (ELS), which is centrally funded.

The NHS Litigation Authority (NHSLA) is a special health authority, i.e. a statutory body set up in 1995 to oversee the clinical negligence scheme for trusts in the handling of claims. The NHSLA uses an approved list of solicitors to handle litigation. In one case discussed above,[13] when the parties disputed the details for the setting up of a structured settlement, the claimant gave notice that they would ask the judge to summon the NHSLA's Chief Executive to explain why the defendants were attempting to charge the claimant for setting up the structured settlement. The defendants then reached agreement with the claimant. The NHSLA is subject to an annual performance review.

The future

At the time of writing, it is too soon to know if the Woolf Reforms are effective and have reduced the time and cost of bringing civil action. One of the greatest concerns is the ever-growing cost of litigation within the NHS. The Woolf Reforms may lead to earlier settlement of cases, and therefore reduced legal costs. There is clear concern from Parliament: the Public Accounts Committee has investigated the handling of clinical negligence cases[14] and the Health Service Committee of the House of Commons has recommended a review of the possibility of no fault compensation being introduced.[15] Increase in mediation and alternative systems of dispute resolution may also considerably reduce costs. In addition, reforms to the Complaints system may also mean that fewer complaints lead to litigation. (See Chapter 27.) In July 2001 the Secretary of State announced the setting up of a Committee chaired by the Chief Medical Officer to consider a new system for clinical negligence claims in the NHS, including a no-fault liability and a fixed tariff for compensation. A White Paper is to be published early in 2002. (D of H Press Release 2001/0313 10 July 2001)

Questions and exercises

1   Look at the aspects of case management as set out on pages 102–3 and consider the extent to which this should ensure that cases are dealt with faster and more justly to the parties.

2   What is meant by *res ipsa loquitur*? In what situations in health care do you think it could apply?

3   What is the difference between pecuniary loss and non-pecuniary loss as a result of a civil wrong? How is compensation for the latter calculated?

4   What is meant by contributory negligence? What are the principles upon which the judge works in deciding the level of deduction of compensation? (See Figure 6.5.)

5   Are there any tasks that you perform that are likely to cause harm to you? Do you consider the principle of *volenti non fit injuria* applies to any of them and if so why?

6   Examine the notices in your hospital that disclaim any responsibility for loss or damage. Consider any ways in which they might not be completely effective in the light of the Unfair Contract Terms Act 1977.

7   What action do you consider could be taken to reduce the level and therefore the cost of litigation within the NHS?

References

[1] Lord Woolf, Access to Justice. Full details of the Civil Procedure Rules are available on the website at http://www.open.gov.uk/lcd/civil/procrules_fin/crules.htm

[2] Ian Grainger and Michael Fealy, Introduction to the new civil procedure rules, Cavendish Publications Ltd, London 1999

[3] NHS Executive, Handling Clinical Negligence Claims HSC 1998/183

[4] *Hurditch* v. *Sheffield* HA 1989 2 All ER 869

[5] *Inman* v. *Cambridge Health Authority* January 1998 (Taken from *Quantum of Damages* Vol 2 by Kemp and Kemp, Sweet and Maxwell 1998 edition.)

[6] *Wells* v. *Wells* [1998] AC 345

[7] Law Commission Damages for Personal Injury: medical, nursing and other expenses, Stationery Office 1996

[8] Law Commission Report No 257 Personal Injury Compensation for non-pecuniary loss 19 April 1999

[9] *Heil* v. *Rankin, The Times* 24 March 2000; (2000) 2 WLR 1173

[10] *Froom* v. *Butcher* 1975 3 All ER 520

[11] *Gough* v. *Thorne* CA 1966 3 All ER 398

[12] *Alice Maud Fenech* v. *East London and City Health Authority* [2000] Lloyds' Reports Medical p. 35 CA

[13] *Inman* v. *Cambridge Health Authority* January 1998 (Taken from *Quantum of Damages* Vol 2 by Kemp and Kemp, Sweet and Maxwell 1998 edition.)

[14] Committee of Public Accounts HC 619-1(1998–9) Hansard

[15] Health Select Committee HC 549(1998–99) Hansard October 1999

7 Consent to treatment and informing the patient

This chapter covers the principles relating to consent to treatment and giving information to the patient. The topics covered are shown in Figure 7.1.

Basic principles
Requirements of a valid consent
How should consent be given
Right to refuse treatment
Taking one's own discharge
Mentally incompetent persons
Unconscious patients
Hunger strikes
Amputation of healthy limbs
Defences to trespass to the person
Necessity
Mental Health Act 1983
Giving information to patient
Sidaway Case
Non-therapeutic procedures
Giving information to the terminally ill
Patients' rights
Notifying the patient of negligence by a colleague

Figure 7.1   Issues covered in Chapter 7.

The basic principles

Any adult, mentally competent person has the right in law to consent to any touching of his person. If he is touched without consent or other lawful justification, then the person has the right of action in the civil courts of suing for trespass to the person – battery where the person is actually touched, assault where he fears that he will be touched. The fact that consent has been given will normally prevent a successful action for trespass. However, it may not prevent an action for negligence arising on the ground that there was a breach of the duty of care to inform the patient. This chapter explores both these aspects of consent and looks at the information that must be legally given to the patient and other questions that arise on informing the patient. Reference should be made to Chapter 13 on consent in relation to children – those under 18 years; to Chapter 20 on consent in relation to the mentally disordered; to Chapter 19 on consent in relation to the elderly; and to Chapter 17 in relation to consent to operations. The situation relating to AIDS and HIV is considered in Chapter 26.

Requirements of a valid consent

To be valid, consent must be given voluntarily by a mentally competent person without any duress or fraud. In the case of *Freeman* v. *Home Office*,[1] a prisoner challenged the legality of his being injected with drugs for his personality disorder on the basis that he had not given his consent and that being given medicine by a doctor in a custodial situation precluded consent being voluntarily given. The Court of Appeal refused to accept this proposition and agreed with the High Court judge that: 'where, in a prison setting, a doctor has the power to influence a prisoner's situation and prospects, a court must be alive to the risk that what may appear, on the face of it, to be real consent is not in fact so.' There is a presumption that the patient is mentally competent. However, this can be rebutted if there is evidence to the contrary. The criteria to be used in assessing competence are discussed in Case 7.3 (see below).

How should consent be given?

Figure 7.2 illustrates the different forms of giving consent. As far as the law is concerned, there is no specific requirement that consent for treatment should be given in any particular way. They are all equally valid. However, they vary considerably in their value as evidence in proving that consent was given. Consent in writing is by far the best form of evidence and is therefore the preferred method of obtaining the consent of the patient when any procedure involving some risk is contemplated. The Department of Health (HG (90) 20 as amended by HSG (92) 32 D.H.) provides advice and model forms. Reference should also be made to the NHS Management Executive's 'Guide to Consent for Examination and Treatment'. In April 2001 the Department of Health published a Reference Guide to Consent to Treatment and Examination, which will be regularly updated on its website.

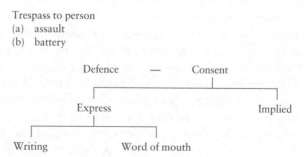

Figure 7.2 Various forms of consent.

Consent, it should be noted, is not a defence to an offence of causing actual bodily harm under the Offences Against the Person Act 1861.[2]

Consent in writing

Some specimen forms of consent to an operation, currently used in the health service, are shown on pp. 125–31. They give the surgeon the right to undertake other procedures that are deemed necessary. However, unless these additional procedures are related to the operation for which consent has been expressly given, or can be justified out of necessity, they will not be covered by this consent. For example, liability has been accepted for a surgeon who, while operating on the patient's abdomen, saw that the patient had an ingrowing toenail and remedied that. The surgeon had not received the patient's consent for this and it was thus a trespass to the person. If, on the other hand, the surgeon had noticed a life-threatening tumour while performing an operation for a hernia, to remove that might have been justifiable, if it was of urgent necessity to save the patient's life.

Nurses are often aware that the patient who has put his signature to a consent form has very little idea of what he has given consent to. Often the ward round where the doctor obtains the signature of the patients to operations is followed by the nurse's round explaining to what the patient has agreed. Where does the nurse stand if she is aware that the patient has signed a form without realising what is involved?

Situation 7.1   *Ignorance is bliss*

Susan Smith had signed the form to consent to an operation for the investigation of a lump in her breast. She was very distressed to be undergoing surgery and ever since she had come into hospital had been able to understand and take in very little of what was said to her. The doctor had explained that a biopsy would be carried out and if that were positive further surgery would be undertaken. It was apparent to Staff Nurse Rachel Bryant that Susan had very little awareness that a radical mastectomy could be performed.

Where does Staff Nurse Bryant stand in relation to the proposed operation? The staff nurse has a legal duty to the patient and if she knows that the patient did not understand what she signed or failed to take in the information given by the doctor, she should arrange for the doctor to return and give the patient more information. From the court's point of view, the fact that the patient has signed the form and expressly agreed that the 'nature and extent of the operation has been explained to me' would be very strong evidence to defend any action for trespass to the person. There is a possibility, however, of a successful action in negligence if the patient has not been given relevant information (see below). There is a clear duty on the doctor to take reasonable care that a patient receives the appropriate information before any consent form is signed and treatment proceeds. The nurse should, as far as possible, take appropriate steps to inform the doctor if she discovers that this duty has not been carried out.

CONSENT FORM

For medical or dental investigation, treatment or operation

Health Authority ....

Hospital ....

Unit Number ....

Patient's Surname ....

Other Names ....

Date of Birth ....

Sex: *(please tick)* Male ☐ Female ☐

DOCTORS OR DENTISTS *(This part to be completed by doctor or dentist. See notes on the reverse)*

TYPE OF OPERATION INVESTIGATION OR TREATMENT

I confirm that I have explained the operation investigation or treatment, and such appropriate options as are available and the type of anaesthetic, if any (general/regional/sedation) proposed, to the patient in terms which in my judgement are suited to the understanding of the patient and/or to one of the parents or guardians of the patient

Signature ....   Date ..../........./.........

Name of doctor or dentist ....

PATIENT/PARENT/GUARDIAN

1. Please read this form and the notes overleaf very carefully.

2. If there is anything that you don't understand about the explanation, or if you want more information, you should ask the doctor or dentist.

3. Please check that all the information on the form is correct. If it is, and you understand the explanation, then sign the form.

I am the patient/parent/guardian *(delete as necessary)*

I agree
- to what is proposed which has been explained to me by the doctor/dentist named on this form.

- to the use of the type of anaesthetic that I have been told about.

I understand
- that the procedure may not be done by the doctor/dentist who has been treating me so far.

- that any procedure in addition to the investigation or treatment described on this form will only be carried out if it is necessary and in my best interests and can be justified for medical reasons.

I have told
- the doctor or dentist about any additional procedures I would not wish to be carried out straightaway without my having the opportunity to consider them first.

Signature ....

Name ....

Address ....

(if not the patient) ....

....

Figure 7.3 Specimen forms of consent. Appendix A(1) medical or dental investigation, treatment or operation.

NOTES TO:

Doctors, Dentists

A patient has a legal right to grant or withhold consent prior to examination or treatment. Patients should be given sufficient information, in a way they can understand, about the proposed treatment and the possible alternatives. Patients must be allowed to decide whether they will agree to the treatment and they may refuse or withdraw consent to treatment at any time. The patient's consent to treatment should be recorded on this form (further guidance is given in HC(90)22 *A Guide to Consent for Examination or Treatment*).

Patients

■ The doctor or dentist is here to help you. He or she will explain the proposed treatment and what the alternatives are. You can ask any questions and seek further information. You can refuse the treatment.

■ You may ask for a relative, or friend, or a nurse to be present.

■ Training health professionals is essential to the continuation of the health service and improving the quality of care. Your treatment may provide an important opportunity for such training, where necessary under the careful supervision of a senior doctor or dentist. You may refuse any involvement in a formal training programme without this adversely affecting your care and treatment.

Figure 7.3 *continued*

CONSENT FORM

For sterilisation or vasectomy

Health Authority .... Patient's Surname ....

Hospital .... Other Names ....

Unit Number .... Date of Birth ....

Sex: *(please tick)* Male ☐ Female ☐

DOCTORS *(This part to be completed by doctor. See notes on the reverse)*

TYPE OF OPERATION: STERILISATION OR VASECTOMY

Complete this part of the form
I confirm that I have explained the procedure and any anaesthetic (general/regional) required, to the patient in terms which in my judgement are suited to his/her understanding.

Signature .... Date ..../........./........

Name of doctor ....

PATIENT

1. Please read this form very carefully.

2. If there is anything that you don't understand about the explanation, or if you want more information, you should ask the doctor.

3. Please check that all the information on the form is correct. If it is, and you understand the explanation, then sign the form.

I am the patient

I agree	▪ to have this operation, which has been explained to me by the doctor named on this form.
	▪ to have the type of anaesthetic that I have been told about.
I understand	▪ that the operation may not be done by the doctor who has been treating me so far.
	▪ that the aim of the operation is to stop me having any children and it might not be possible to reverse the effects of the operation.
	▪ that sterilisation/vasectomy can sometimes fail, and that there is a very small chance that I may become fertile again after some time.
	▪ that any procedure in addition to the investigation or treatment described on this form will only be carried out if it is necessary and in my best interests and can be justified for medical reasons.
I have told	▪ the doctor about any additional procedures I would not wish to be carried out straightaway without my having the opportunity to consider them first.
For vasectomy I understand	▪ that I may remain fertile or become fertile again after some time.
	▪ that I will have to use some other contraceptive method until 2 tests in a row show that I am not producing sperm, if I do not want to father any children.

Signature ....

Figure 7.4 Specimen forms of consent. Appendix A(2) sterilisation or vasectomy.

NOTES TO:

Doctors

A patient has a legal right to grant or withhold consent prior to examination or treatment. Patients should be given sufficient information, in a way they can understand, about the proposed treatment and the possible alternatives. Patients must be allowed to decide whether they will agree to the treatment and they may refuse or withdraw consent to treatment at any time. The patient's consent to treatment should be recorded on this form (further guidance is given in HC(90)22 *A Guide to Consent for Examination or Treatment*).

Patients

- The doctor is here to help you. He or she will explain the proposed procedure, which you are entitled to refuse. You can ask any questions and seek further information.

- You may ask for a relative, or friend, or a nurse to be present.

- Training health professionals is essential to the continuation of the health service and improving the quality of care. Your treatment may provide an important opportunity for such training, where necessary under the careful supervision of a senior doctor. You may refuse any involvement in a formal training programme without this adversely affecting your care and treatment.

Figure 7.4 *continued*

CONSENT FORM

For treatment by a health professional other than doctors or dentists

Health Authority .... Patient's Surname ....

Hospital .... Other Names ....

Unit Number .... Date of Birth ....

Sex: *(please tick)* Male ☐ Female ☐

HEALTH PROFESSIONAL *(This part to be completed by health professional. See notes on the reverse)*

TYPE OF TREATMENT PROPOSED

Complete this part of the form
I confirm that I have explained the treatment proposed and such appropriate options as are available to the patient in terms which in my judgement are suited to the understanding of the patient and/or to one of the parents or guardians of the patient.

Signature .... Date ..../........./........

Name of health professional ....

Job title of health professional ....

PATIENT/PARENT/GUARDIAN

1. Please read this form and the notes overleaf very carefully.

2. If there is anything that you don't understand about the explanation, or if you want more information, you should ask the health professional who has explained the treatment proposed.

3. Please check that all the information on the form is correct. If it is, and you understand the treatment proposed, then sign the form.

I am the patient/parent/guardian *(delete as necessary)*

I agree ■ to what is proposed which has been explained to me by the health professional named on this form.

Signature ....

Name ....

Address ....

(if not the patient) ....

Figure 7.5 Specimen forms of consent. Appendix A(3) treatment by health professional other than doctors or dentists.

NOTES TO:

Health Professionals, other than doctors or dentists

A patient has a legal right to grant or withhold consent prior to examination or treatment. Patients should be given sufficient information, in a way they can understand, about the proposed treatment and the possible alternatives. Patients must be allowed to decide whether they will agree to the treatment and they may refuse or withdraw consent to treatment at any time. The patient's consent to treatment should be recorded on this form (further guidance is given in HC(90)22 *A Guide to Consent for Examination or Treatment).*

Patients

- The health professional named on this form is here to help you. He or she will explain the proposed treatment and what the alternatives are. You can ask any questions and seek further information. You can refuse the treatment.

- You may ask for a relative, or friend, or another member of staff to be present.

- Training health professionals is essential to the continuation of the health service and improving the quality of care. Your treatment may provide an important opportunity for such training, where necessary under the careful supervision of a fully qualified health professional. You may refuse any involvement in a formal training programme without this adversely affecting your care and treatment.

Figure 7.5   *continued*

Medical or dental treatment of a patient who is unable to consent because of mental disorder

Health Authority .... Patient's Surname ....

Hospital .... Other Names ....

Unit Number .... Date of Birth ....

Sex: *(please tick)*   Male ☐   Female ☐

NOTE   If there is any doubt about the ability of a mentally disordered patient to give
consent to treatment, the Registered Medical Practitioner in charge of the
patient should be asked to interview the patient. If, in his or her opinion, the
patient is able to give valid consent to medical, dental or surgical treatment,
he or she should be asked to do so and no-one further need
be involved.

If the patient is considered unable to give valid consent it is considered good
practice to discuss any proposed treatment with the next of kin.

For surgical or dental operations the form should also be signed by the
Registered Medical or Dental Practitioner who carries out the treatment.

DOCTORS/DENTISTS

Describe investigation, operation or treatment proposed.

(Complete this part of the form)

In my opinion .... is not capable of giving consent to treatment. In my opinion the
treatment proposed is in his/her best interests and should be given.

The patient's next of kin have/have not been so informed. *(delete as necessary)*

Date: ....

Signature   Signature

....

Name of Registered Medical Practitioner   Name of Second Registered Medical/Dental
in charge of the patient: Practitioner who is providing treatment:

....

Figure 7.6   Specimen forms of consent. Appendix B medical or dental treatment of a patient who is unable to consent because of a medical disorder.

Consent by word of mouth

Many of the less risky treatments are carried out without any formal signature of the patient. Consent by word of mouth is valid, but it may be far more difficult to establish in court, since it might be one person's word against another. Many of the day-to-day treatments and tests are, however, carried out on this basis.

Case 7.1   Consent to Anaesthesia[3]

The claimant signed a consent form giving consent to a general anaesthetic. She was subsequently given a caudal block and unfortunately suffered some harm as a result. She claimed that she had not given consent to this block, which therefore amounted to a trespass to her person, i.e. battery. The High Court judge held that separate consent was not required for each part of the treatment.

Implied consent

It is sometimes said that the fact that a patient comes into hospital means that he or she is giving his consent to anything that the consultant deems appropriate. That, however, is not supported in law. There are many choices of available treatment and when care is provided there must be evidence that the patient has agreed to that particular course. Similarly, it is said that when an unconscious patient is treated in the accident and emergency department, then he implies consent to being treated. This, however, is not so. An unconscious patient implies nothing. The professionals care for him in the absence of consent as part of their duty to care for the patient out of necessity in an emergency,[4] and could defend any subsequent action for trespass to the person on that basis.

Implied consent is better reserved for situations where non-verbal communication by the patient makes it clear that he is giving consent. Nurses are familiar with the signs: the patient rolls up his sleeve for an injection; the patient opens his mouth as the nurse waves the thermometer in the air. Such actions indicate to the nurse that the patient agrees to the treatment/care proceeding. No words are spoken, there is no signature, but it is clear that the patient is in agreement. In an Australian case of 1891, a passenger on a ship who held out his hand to be vaccinated lost his action for battery.[5]

The weakness of implied consent is, however, that it is not always clear that the patient is agreeing to what the nurse intends to do. Thus the patient who rolls up his sleeve for blood pressure to be taken would get a nasty shock when the nurse gave him an injection, yet that is how the nurse has interpreted his non-verbal actions. To avoid such misunderstandings, it is preferable if the nurse tells the patient what she wishes to do and obtains a spoken consent from the patient. The problems in giving day-to-day care to the confused elderly are considered in Chapter 19.

Once a mentally competent patient has given a valid consent to treatment, then he/she cannot succeed in an action for trespass to the person,[6] but if it is claimed insufficient information on the risks of the treatment was given to them they would have to bring an action in negligence alleging a breach of the duty of care in failing to provide sufficient information (see page 138 below).

The right to refuse treatment

It is a basic principle of law in this country that an adult, mentally competent person has the right to refuse treatment and take his own discharge contrary to medical advice. The Court of Appeal has emphasised that provided the patient has the necessary mental capacity, which is assessed in relation to the decision to be made, then he or she can refuse to give consent for a good reason, a bad reason or no reason at all. This was the principle set out in the case of *Re MB*.[7]

Case 7.2   Consent to a caesarean section (Re MB)

A pregnant woman suffered from needle phobia as a result of which she was unable to agree to have an injection that would precede a caesarean section. The High Court judge held that her needle phobia rendered her mentally incapacitated to take the decision not to have a caesarean operation. The Court of Appeal confirmed that decision, but emphasised that had she been competent, then she could have refused the operation. The Court of Appeal in *Re MB* laid down the steps and rules that should be followed when a health professional is faced with a patient who appears to be mentally incompetent. This advice is set out in Chapter 14 on page 308, Box 14.2.

The ruling in *Re MB* was followed by the Court of Appeal in a case brought against St George's Hospital[8] which is considered in chapter 14.

The fact that patients can refuse life-saving treatment can be upsetting for staff as the following case shows.

Case 7.3   The patient's autonomy Re C. (an adult)
(refusal of medical treatment) Family Division 1994 1 All ER 819

The patient was a 68-year-old man, who suffered from paranoid schizophrenia and was detained at Broadmoor Hospital. He developed gangrene in one foot and doctors believed an amputation to be a life-saving necessity. He refused to give consent and sought an injunction restraining the hospital from carrying out an amputation without his express written consent. He succeeded on the grounds that the evidence failed to establish that he lacked sufficient understanding of the nature, purpose and effects of the proposed treatment. Instead, the evidence showed that:

1. he had understood and retained the relevant treatment information;

2. believed it; and

3. had arrived at a clear choice.

The sole issue in this case was whether the patient had the mental capacity to give a valid refusal. It should be noted that the presence of a mental disorder does not automatically mean that a person is incapable of making a valid decision in relation to treatment. The patient therefore has a right to refuse treatment, but it must be clear that he is mentally competent. The case clearly brings out the clash between the patient's autonomy and the professional duty of care. Clearly, it would be essential for those in charge of the patient to take all reasonable precautions to ensure that the patient has appropriate counselling and all the necessary information and help in facing the future, but if this fails, it is the competent patient's right to refuse. Similarly, an adult Jehovah's Witness is able to refuse a blood transfusion. Different principles apply in relation to children and these are discussed in Chapter 13.

The Court of Appeal in the case of *Re T* emphasised the importance of ensuring that, when a patient refuses treatment, the patient has the mental capacity to make a valid decision and has not been subjected to the undue influences of another.

Case 7.4   Refusal of blood transfusion. (Re T)[9]

A young pregnant woman was injured in a car accident and told the staff nurse that she did not want a blood transfusion. Her mother was a Jehovah's Witness. At the time, it was unlikely to be necessary. However, subsequently she went into labour and a Caesarean was necessary. She told medical staff that she would not want a transfusion and had signed a form to that effect. She was not told that it might be necessary to save her life. After the operation, she required blood as a life-saving measure and her father and co-habitee applied to court. The judge authorised the administration of blood on the ground that the evidence showed that she was not in a fit condition to make a valid decision.

(See the case of *In Re S.* (an adult) (refusal of medical treatment) 1992 4 All ER 671,[10] discussed on page 304. For a case on refusal of treatment by a 16-year-old, see *In Re W.* on page 284.)

Taking one's own discharge

It follows from what has been said above that the adult, mentally competent patient is able to take his own discharge. However, this principle causes concern for staff in practice.

Situation 7.2   Self-discharge

Don Pritchard was admitted from the accident and emergency department with a suspected head injury. Before X-rays had been taken, he insisted on leaving the hospital, contrary to medical advice. The nursing staff knew that he was still very confused and it seemed likely that his aggression was a result of a brain injury.

This is a difficult situation because it could be argued here that as a result of the brain injury the patient was not mentally competent and therefore his decision to discharge himself was an irrational one. If the patient is mentally incapacitated and there is clear danger to the patient's life if he is allowed to leave, then it could be argued that these are circumstances in which the staff would be justified in acting in an emergency to save the patient's life. If this does not apply, then the patient has the right to go. An assessment should be carried out of his mental competence. If he is deemed mentally competent, he cannot be compelled to stay, unless he presents a danger to other people. If possible, he should be persuaded to sign a form that he took his own discharge contrary to medical advice. However, it is not always possible to get this signature and therefore it is necessary to ensure that another member of the staff can act as a witness to what occurred. In either case, it is essential that full records are made of the circumstances leading to the patient's discharge and the efforts made to persuade him to stay. If harm eventually befalls the patient as a result of his taking his own discharge contrary to medical advice, if there is evidence that the staff did all they could to persuade him to stay, and if there was clear evidence that the patient was mentally competent, there is unlikely to be a successful action for negligence against the staff.

The mentally incompetent patient

This issue is considered below under the defence of necessity and also in Chapter 20 in relation to mentally disordered persons. There are two possible courses: detention under the Mental Health Act 1983, or use of common-law powers to act in an emergency to save life. The latter could be used only if temporary restraint is justified in the interests of the patient.

The unconscious patient

It has been mentioned above that the doctors and nurses in their duty of care for the patient may take life-saving action. This is on the basis of their common law powers (recognised in the *Re F* case[11]) to act out of necessity in the best interests of a mentally incapacitated adult. If there is no consent by the patient, relatives are sometimes asked to give their consent. However, if the patient is an adult, the relatives do not at present have the right to give or withhold consent, unless the patient is a child under 18 years. However, there are under consideration legislative proposals for decisions to be made on behalf of mentally incapacitated adults.[12] This topic is also considered in relation to the care of the elderly in Chapter 19.

The legal situation relating to a patient in a persistent vegetative state is considered in Chapter 16.

> ### Case 7.5   Do not give me blood[13]
>
> In a Canadian case, an unconscious patient was given a life-saving blood transfusion in spite of the fact that she was carrying a card refusing such treatment. She was awarded C$20,000. The doctor had ignored her written request not to give her blood and this constituted a trespass to her person.

In this case, the card setting out the wishes of the patient acted as a living will or advanced directive. (These are discussed in chapter 16.)

Hunger strikes

In an old case,[14] a suffragette went on hunger strike and was force-fed in prison. She lost her claim for trespass to the person. The court held that the prison doctor was justified in feeding her on the grounds that it was the duty of the officials to preserve the health and lives of prisoners. However, in a more recent case,[15] a prisoner went on hunger strike and the application was made to court to decide whether it was lawful for his doctors and nurses to abstain from force-feeding him. The judge held that there were 4 grounds for intervening against the prisoner's right of self-determination:

1.   The interest that the State holds in preserving life.
2.   The interest of the State in preventing suicide.
3.   The maintaining the integrity of the medical profession.
4.   The protection of the rights of innocent third parties.

He concluded that these did not overrule the right of self-determination of a mentally competent person and the prisoner could be permitted to starve himself to death, provided that he has the legal capacity.

In a more recent case,[16] the Moors murderer Ian Brady, who is in Ashworth Special Hospital, applied to court to be allowed to starve himself to death. The court held that he did not have the mental competence to make that decision. The decision to commence force-feeding was in all respects lawful, rational and fair. Brady was incapacitated by his mental illness.

Amputation of healthy limbs

Media attention has been given to the condition of body dysmorphic disorder, where the patient wishes to have his healthy limbs removed. A surgeon in Falkirk and District Royal Infirmary, in a private operation, removed one lower limb from each of two patients who suffered from this disorder.[17] The hospital has subsequently banned such operations. In the absence of any doctor prepared to amputate, patients are known to have shot their limbs off or committed suicide. The General Medical Council has offered ethical guidance and the Medical Defence Union has emphasised that the utmost caution should be taken by doctors considering such an operation. They must be certain that the operation is right and that the patient has had full counselling as to the consequences. Everything must be carefully documented.

Defences to an action for trespass to the person

Consent is the main form of defence to an action for trespass to the person. However it is not the only one and Figure 7.7 shows the main defences.

---

1. Consent.
2. Necessity.
3. Making a lawful arrest.
4. Acting under a statutory power, e.g. Mental Health Act 1983. (See Chapter 20.)
5. Parental powers. (See Chapter 13.)

Figure 7.7   Defences to an action for trespass to the person.

Necessity

Where a practitioner takes measures to save the life of an unconscious patient, that is not a situation of implied consent, but a situation of necessity. In such circumstances, the common law recognises the power of a professional to take action out of necessity in the best interests of the patient following the accepted standard of care of the reasonable professional. The House of Lords established this principle in the case of *Re F*,[18] which concerned the sterilisation of a woman who suffered from severe learning disabilities and was incapable of giving consent. However, the principle of acting out of necessity where an adult was incapable of giving consent also applies to day-to-day care. In the case of a girl of 18 with an intellectual age of 5 to 8, the Court of Appeal held that the court had the power under its inherent jurisdiction and in the best interests of that person, to hear the issues involving her future and to grant the necessary declarations.[19] The House of Lords (in the Bournewood[20] case) has also held that the common law powers can be used to detain a mentally incapable adult if that is in the person's best interests.

Recommendations have been made by the Law Commission No. 231[21] for a statutory duty to replace this common-law power, with specific requirements depending on the seriousness of the treatment to be undertaken. Following further consultation by the Lord Chancellor,[22] the government published its proposals for decision making on behalf of mentally incapacitated adults.[23] Legislation is awaited at the time of writing.

Mental Health Act 1983

Justification for acting without the consent of a patient may also be provided by the Mental Health Act 1983 and this is considered in Chapter 20.

Giving information to a patient prior to consent being obtained

As has been mentioned, there are two main actions in relation to consent:

1. An action for trespass to the person.
2. An action in negligence for a breach of the duty of care to inform the patient.

We now turn to the action for negligence. The courts have made it clear that if a competent patient has given a willing consent for a procedure, then an action for trespass to the person cannot proceed. If the patient alleges that he was not given significant information about possible side effects, then the action will be one of negligence. This raises the question of how much information must be given to the patient. The leading case on this question is the following.

Case 7.6   The Sidaway case

Amy Sidaway suffered from persistent pain in her neck and shoulder and was advised by a surgeon to have an operation on her spinal column to relieve the pain. The surgeon warned her of the possibility of disturbing a nerve root and the possible consequences of doing so, but did not mention the possibility of damage to the spinal cord, even though he would be operating within 3 millimetres of it. The risk of damage to the spinal cord was very small (less than 1 per cent), but if the risk materialised, the resulting injury could range from mild to very severe. Amy consented to the operation, which was performed with due care and skill. However, in the course of the operation, she suffered an injury to her spinal cord that resulted in her being severely disabled. She sued the surgeon and the hospital governors, alleging that the surgeon had been in breach of a duty owed to her to warn her of all possible risks inherent in the operation, with the result that she had not been in a position to give an informed consent to the operation. Amy lost the case before the trial judge and her appeal to the Court of Appeal. She then appealed to the House of Lords.[24]

The House of Lords held that her appeal should fail. Three of the judges held that the test of liability in respect of a doctor's duty to warn his patient of risks inherent in treatment recommended by him was the same as the test applicable to diagnosis of treatment, i.e. the doctor was required to act in accordance with a practice accepted as proper by a responsible body of medical opinion. (This is known as the 'Bolam Test' and is discussed on page 40.) Since the surgeon's non-disclosure of risk of damage to the plaintiff's spinal cord accorded with a practice accepted as proper by a responsible body of neuro-surgical opinion, the defendants were not liable to the plaintiff.

The other two judges (Lord Scarman and Lord Templeman) were also of the opinion that Amy's appeal must fail since she had not proved on the evidence that the surgeon (who had died since the operation) had been in breach of duty by failing to warn her of the risks. Lord Scarman alone of all the judges held that a patient had a right to give informed consent and he followed an American case,[25] where the 'prudent patient' test was applied to decide on the information a patient should be given prior to any consent, i.e. 'What would a reasonable prudent patient think significant if in the situation of this patient?' He concluded that:

> English law must recognise a duty of the doctor to warn his patient of risk inherent in the treatment which he is proposing, and especially so if the treatment be surgery. The critical limitation is that the duty is confined to material risk. The test of materiality is whether in the circumstances of the particular case the court is satisfied that a reasonable person in the patient's position would be likely to attach significance to the risk. Even if the risk be material, the doctor will not be liable if on a reasonable assessment of his patient's condition he takes the view that a warning would be detrimental to his patient's health.

(Lord Scarman)

Comment on the Sidaway case

While the case was concerned with treatment by a doctor, the same principles would apply to treatment by any other professional. Although the judges turned down Amy's appeal, their reasons for doing so were extremely varied. The majority applied the Bolam Test of the accepted approved professional practice.

Even Lord Scarman, who used the 'prudent patient' test, still agreed that there may well be exceptions where the doctor is entitled to use 'therapeutic privilege' in deciding what to tell or what not to tell the patient prior to any procedure. This exception means that in the end the professional must follow the accepted approved practice in so far as it is applicable to the particular needs of that specific patient.

The Sidaway case was cited and followed in the case of *Blyth* v. *Bloomsbury Health Authority*.[26]

Case 7.7 *Blyth* v. *Bloomsbury HA*

In this case, a patient had been given an injection of depo-provera and claimed that she had suffered harm as a result of it and that knowledge which was possessed by hospital researchers about some of the side-effects of the drug was not made known to her at the time that she was prescribed it. The Court of Appeal applied the Bolam Test and the Sidaway case to the facts and decided that there was no negligence by the doctors who cared for her in the information they gave to her. They emphasised that the extent of the duty to give information is to be judged in the light of the state of medical knowledge

---

Case 7.7 *continued*

at the time and one must avoid the danger of being wise after the event. In addition, they refused to interpret the Sidaway judgments as implying that where the patient asked specific rather than just general questions this meant that the doctor is under an obligation to tell the patient all he knows about the subject. 'The amount of information to be given must depend on all the circumstances, and as a general proposition it is governed by what is called the Bolam Test' (Lord Justice Neill).

Another important point is that in subsequent cases (see below), the courts have held that the professional's duty is not divisible. Diagnosis, treatment, carrying out that treatment and informing the patient are all part of the doctor's duty of care and cannot be separated into different boxes. Informing the patient of risks is as much a part of the clinical judgement of the doctor as all his other tasks.

The general proposition therefore is that a person giving information to the patient must follow the reasonable standard of approved practice, i.e. the Bolam Test. However, in one recent case, a judge held that what was purported to be the approved practice was not acceptable.

Case 7.8 *Smith v. Tunbridge Wells HA*[27]

Evidence given by experts to the court suggested that a body of experienced competent surgeons would not have warned the patient of a risk of impotence from the operation. The judge disagreed with this and held that the failure to warn of the risk of impotence was neither reasonable nor responsible and the surgeon was therefore in breach of his duty to warn the patient.

In the following case, the court had to decide if the doctors had followed the reasonable standard of care when they gave advice that the baby should not be induced.

Case 7.9 *Pearce v. United Bristol Healthcare NHS Trust*[28]

Mrs Pearce was expecting her sixth child. The expected date of delivery was 13 November 1991, but it had still not arrived on 27 November. She begged the consultant to give her an induced labour or a caesarian section. He suggested that she should have a normal birth and let nature take its course. He pointed out that it would be very risky to induce the birth and she would take longer to recover from a caesarian. He did not tell her that there was an increased risk of a stillbirth as a result of the delay in delivery between 13 and 27 November. She accepted his advice. The baby died in utero sometime between 2 and 3 December.

The trial judge dismissed the claim. The Court of Appeal dismissed the appeal. It applied the reasoning in the Sidaway case and held that this was a case 'where it would not be proper for the courts to interfere with the clinical opinion of the expert medical man responsible for treating Mrs Pearce.'

Non-therapeutic procedures

It was suggested in a recent case that the principles set out in the Sidaway case did not apply where non-therapeutic care was being provided.

> ### Case 7.10   Gold v. Haringey Health Authority[29]
>
> The claimant had two children and when she became pregnant agreed with her husband that they would have no further children after that pregnancy. She was seen by a consultant who suggested sterilisation following the birth of the child, but made no mention of the possibility of her husband having a vasectomy. Nor did he give her any warning of the risk of the sterilisation failing. The sterilisation operation was performed the day after the birth, but she subsequently became pregnant with her fourth child. She brought an action against the health authority alleging that there was negligence in failing to warn her of the risk of the operation failing and that the statement to her that the operation was irreversible amounted to a negligent misrepresentation.

The trial judge held that there was a distinction in the information that should be given in a non-therapeutic context compared with a decision on therapeutic treatment and that a sterilisation operation was non-therapeutic. He awarded her damages of £19,000. On appeal, the Court of Appeal held that the principles set out in the Sidaway case should apply in both contexts and it did not accept the validity of a distinction between therapeutic and non-therapeutic.

> The (Bolam) principle does not depend on the context in which any act is performed, or any advice given. It depends on a man professing skill or competence in a field beyond that possessed by the man on the Clapham omnibus. If the giving of contraceptive advice required no special skill, then I could see an argument that the Bolam Test should not apply. But that was not, and could not have been suggested. The fact (if it be a fact) that giving contraceptive advice involves a different sort of skill and competence from carrying out a surgical operation does not mean that the Bolam Test ceases to be applicable. It is clear from Lord Diplock's speech in Sidaway that a doctor's duty of care in relation to diagnosis, treatment and advice, whether the doctor be a specialist or general practitioner is not to be dissected into its component parts. To dissect a doctor's advice into that given in a therapeutic context and that given in a contraceptive context would be to go against the whole thrust of (the decision in Sidaway).

The judge should have accepted the body of responsible medical opinion on the standard that should have been followed in giving her information.

Giving information to the terminally ill patient

If a patient is terminally ill, should the nurse tell the patient contrary to medical advice? What is the position if the relatives do not wish the patient to be told?

Situation 7.3   Silence or lies?

Paul George has been operated on for 'ulcers'. Unknown to him, the surgeons actually found an inoperable tumour with wide spreading of the malignancy throughout the body. It is estimated that death is likely to occur in a few months. The consultant, who normally is in favour of a very open approach to patients, believes that Paul, who is 54, would not be able to cope with this news yet and he discusses this with Paul's wife, who agrees. The nursing staff are advised accordingly.

This kind of situation is in substance not unfamiliar to nursing staff and is repeated in different guises on many occasions. Unfortunately, however, it is the nursing staff who are most frequently with the patients and who are most likely to be asked: 'I don't have cancer, do I nurse?' or 'When am I likely to get out of here?' or 'Is it worth my while booking for this holiday next year?' and other direct or indirect questions designed to obtain a little more information for the patient as to where he stands. The questions that then arise in the nurse's mind are: Where does the patient stand in law? Does the patient have a legal enforceable right to obtain this information? What is the nurse's position in regard to the patient, the doctor, and the relative?

The patient's rights

As has been seen in the discussion above, there is a duty on professional staff when advising certain forms of treatment to ensure that the patient is notified of any significant risks of substantial side-effects. However, this duty on the professional is qualified by the power to withhold information if it is deemed to be in the patient's interest not to know. This is known as therapeutic privilege. Informing the patient that he is terminally ill may well come under this heading. Thus, if in the opinion of the doctor it would be harmful to tell a patient such disturbing news, then the doctor can withhold such information on the grounds that he is acting in the patient's best interest. A doctor cannot withhold information about risks because he believes the patient would refuse consent if he was aware of them. There must be other reasons to justify withholding this information. There is no clear right in law for the patient to insist on being told and even where the patient is exercising his right under the Data Protection Act 1998 (see Figure 8.1), there is the power to withhold such data from him (see chapter 8).

The consultant or general practitioner has clinical responsibility for the patient. If in the doctor's opinion the patient would be harmed by any disclosure and he has exercised his judgement on this in accordance with the approved professional practice, then that decision must be accepted and implemented by the rest of the team of professionals. The nurses might disagree with the decision and of course they may well have the opportunity of persuading the doctor to change his mind, based on their own personal knowledge of the patient, his needs and his own understanding. Ultimately, however, they would be obliged to defer to the clinical decision of the doctor. Any nurse who flagrantly went against the doctor's view on this might well face disciplinary proceedings. What is clear at the present is that in the absence of any absolute statutory right, patients do not have a clear right to obtain this information.

The court has yet to deal directly with the question as to whether the patient has a right to be told and whether the doctor has a duty to tell. It is quite likely that if this is put before the courts, the court will apply the Bolam Test and leave it to the approved professional practice in relation to that particular patient.

Even if the patient is ultimately held to have such a right it does not follow that the nurse can ignore the instructions of the doctor. (This issue is considered in Chapter 4.)

The relatives' rights

It is not uncommon for relatives, on hearing of a particularly upsetting diagnosis, to ask for the patient not to be informed of that 'because he could not cope with that yet'. Often, perhaps, it is not the patient's inability to deal with the information, but the relatives' inability to cope with the patient's knowledge of it. The conspiracy of silence thus begins. As far as the law is concerned, unless the patient is mentally incompetent, this should not arise. The patient is entitled to have information about him kept confidential (see Chapter 8). It is a breach of this duty to the patient when the relative is told first. It is always open to the patient to say to the doctor, 'I would rather that my wife was not told about my diagnosis yet.' That is his right. Yet, when terminal illness or chronic sickness are concerned, the rules of confidentiality are broken and the relative is informed first. Obviously, there are exceptions to this duty of confidentiality when the patient is too ill to be told and decisions have to be made that therefore involve the relative. However, that should be the exception.

Let's return to the situation of Paul George above. If the nurse has received clear instructions that Paul should not be told that he is terminally ill, then the nurse should not act contrary to these instructions. Nor, however, should she lie to Paul. If Paul makes it clear that he is seeking more information, then the nurse should arrange for Paul to speak with the doctor concerned and express to the doctor her own views of Paul's needs. Ultimately, the wife has no right to insist that information is withheld from Paul. Obviously, because of her knowledge of Paul, she should be involved in any discussions on the correct approach.

Notifying the patient of negligence by a colleague

If a colleague has been negligent or even acts criminally, should the nurse inform the patient? This is not a hypothetical question as the cases of Beverly Allitt and Dr Shipman (see Chapters 1 and 5) show and it sometimes happens that a nurse is aware that a mistake has been made, and that neither patient nor relatives have been made aware of this, although they may realise that all has not gone according to plan. What is the nurse to do in these circumstances? Does she have a duty to inform the patient?

The nurse's duty to the patient is to ensure that the patient receives all the appropriate care and treatment. If a mistake has been made, for example, a colleague administers eye drops to the wrong eye, it is essential for the nurse to ensure that this is made known so that the patient can be given any necessary antidote. She should also ensure that steps are taken to prevent such an error occurring again and should therefore check that a report has been made to senior nurse management. Hopefully, if a nurse is at fault, she herself will have reported it, as part of her duties under the Code of Professional Conduct. Good practice should ensure that a full disclosure is given to the patient and it would be the consultant's responsibility to see that this was done and to reassure the patient about any future effects.

The nurse should take every action that she reasonably can to ensure that the patient is fully informed. Reference must also be made to the Code of Professional Conduct and the practitioner's duty to ensure that any untoward occurrences are brought to the attention of the appropriate officer. NHS Trusts and health authorities are required to establish procedures to implement the Public Interest Disclosure Act 1998, known as the Whistle-blower's Charter. Guidance is given in HSC 1999/198 by the Department of Health on the implementation of this Act. Its aim is to protect any employee who brings a protected disclosure (e.g. a criminal offence, health and safety danger, failure to fulfil legal duty) to the attention of the appropriate person in the organisation from any victimisation. This legislation is further discussed in Chapter 4.

Questions and exercises

1 What is meant by implied consent to treatment? Consider examples of implied consent from your own practice.

2 Obtain a copy of the standard consent-to-treatment form. How appropriate do you think it is to cover the wide range of treatments for which it is used?

3 Refer to the specialist subject areas in Part II and consider the principles that apply to consent by minors under 16, consent by minors of 17 and 18, consent by the mentally disordered and by the unconscious patient.

4 Relatives have at present no legal right to give consent or withhold consent on behalf of an adult. Do you think the law should be changed to give them this right and how should the interests of the patient be protected from unscrupulous relatives?

5 What is the difference between the 'Bolam Test' and the 'prudent patient' test so far as consent to treatment is concerned?

6 Consider the first Schedule to the Human Rights Act 1998 (see Appendix A to this book) and consider any other rights in relation to health care which you consider should be included.

References

1 *Freeman v. Home Office* [1984] 1 All ER 1036
2 *R. v. Brown and others* House of Lords TLR 12 March 1993
3 *Davis v. Barking, Havering and Brentwood HA* [1993] 4 Med LR 85
4 *F. v. West Berkshire Health Authority* [1989] 2 All ER 545; [1990] 2 AC 1
5 *O'Brien v. Cunard Steamship Co.* (1891) 28 NE 266
6 *Chatterton v. Gerson* [1981] 1 All ER 257
7 *Re MB* (Adult Medical Treatment) [1997] 2 FLR 426
8 *St George's Healthcare NHS Trust v. S* [1998] 3 All ER 673
9 *In re T.* (an adult) (refusal of medical treatment) 1992 4 All ER 649
10 *In re S.* (an adult) (refusal of medical treatment) 1992 4 All ER 671
11 *Re F; F. v. West Berkshire Health Authority* 1989 2 All ER 545
12 Lord Chancellor's Office, Making Decisions: The Government's proposals for decision making on behalf of mentally incapacitated adults, Stationery Office 1999
13 *Malette v. Shulman* 1991 2 Med LR 162
14 *Leigh v. Gladstone* (1909) 26 TLR 139
15 *Secretary of State for the Home Department v. Robb* [1995] 1 All ER 677
16 Russell Jenkins, Judge dashes killer Brady's hopes of starving himself into an early grave, *The Times* 11 March 2000
17 Gillian Harris, Surgeon happy he removed healthy limbs, *The Times* 1 February 2000 p. 7
18 *F. v. West Berkshire Health Authority* 1989 2 All ER 545
19 *In re F* (Adult: Court's Jurisdiction) *The Times Law Report* 25 July 2000; [2000] 2 FLR 512
20 *R. v. Bournewood Community and Mental Health NHS Trust ex parte L* [1999] AC 458
21 Law Commission, Mental Incapacity, HMSO 1995
22 Lord Chancellor, Who Decides? Lord Chancellor's Office, Stationery Office 1997
23 Lord Chancellor, Making Decisions, Lord Chancellor's Office, Stationery Office 1999
24 *Sidaway v. Bethlem Royal Hospital Governors and others* 1985 1 All ER 643
25 *Canterbury v. Spence* 1972 464 F 2d 772
26 *Blyth v. Bloomsbury Health Authority, The Times* 11 February 1987; [1993] 4 Med LR 151
27 *Smith v. Tunbridge Wells Health Authority* [1994] 5 Med LR 334
28 *Pearce v. United Bristol Healthcare NHS Trust* (1998) 48 BMLR 118 CA
29 *Gold v. Haringey Health Authority* [1987] 2 All ER 888

8 Data Protection: confidentiality and access

The topics to be covered in this chapter are shown in Figure 8.1

Data Protection Act 1998
Terminology
Human Rights
Data Protection principles
First Data Protection principle
Duty of confidentiality
Consent of the patient
Disclosure to the press
Disclosure in the interests of the patient
Court orders
Privilege from disclosure
Disclosure in personal injury cases
Disclosure before trial
Disclosure to patient
Statutory duty to disclose
Public interest
Disclosure to police
Disclosure on anonymous basis
Caldicott Guardians
Access to medical records
Withholding of information
Access to medical reports

Figure 8.1 Issues covered in Chapter 8.

Data Protection Act 1998

The European Directive on Data Protection[1] was implemented in this country by the Data Protection Act 1998. Member states were required to comply with its provisions by 24 October 1998, though the UK did not meet this target. Under the legislation, members have to establish a set of principles with which users of personal information must comply. The legislation also gives individuals the right to gain access to information held about them and provides for a supervisory authority to oversee and enforce the law. NHS guidance on the Act was provided by a circular in March 2000[2] and the NHS Information Authority action plan for the NHS is available on its website to ensure the processing of personal data within the organisation is in compliance with the Act.[3] An introduction to the Data Protection Act 1998 is also available from the Data Protection Commissioner.[4]

There are some significant differences between the Data Protection Act 1998 and its predecessor, the Data Protection Act 1984, as follows:

1. The 1998 Act applies to certain manual records (if they form part of a relevant filing system) as well as to computerised records (the 1984 Act applied only to records in automated form).

2. Some terms are defined differently, such as personal data and processing (see below).

3. There are tighter provisions on the processing of sensitive personal data.

4. The fundamental rights are amended.

5. There are new rules for the transfer of personal data outside the European Community.

6. There are changes to the system for registration.

7. The person in charge is now known as the Data Protection Commissioner (rather than Registrar).

Terminology

'Personal data' is data that relates to a living person, who can be identified from that data or from that data together with other information in the possession of the data controller.

'Sensitive personal data' is personal data consisting of information as specified in Section 2 of the 1998 Act. Section 2 includes: racial or ethnic origins, political opinions and his physical or mental health or condition or sexual life.

'Data Subject' is the individual who is the subject of the personal data.

'Data Controller' means a person who either alone or with others determines the purposes for which and the manner in which any personal data are or are to be processed.

'Processing' includes obtaining, recording or holding information or carrying out any operation including retrieval or consultation or use of the information, and disclosure (definition abbreviated by author).

Human Rights

The Data Protection Act 1998 must be read in conjunction with the Human Rights Act 1998 (see Chapter 1), since Article 8 recognises an individual's right to privacy (see Appendix A of this book). The Freedom of Information Act 2000 gives a right to access to information held by public authorities, but this is subject to many exceptions including personal information where the Data Protection Act 1998 applies (S.40 Freedom of Information Act).

Data Protection Principles

The Data Protection Act sets out eight principles which apply to the keeping of computerised data (see Figure 8.2). These principles are designed to ensure that personal data shall be accurate, relevant, held only for specific defined purposes for which the user has been registered, not kept for longer than is necessary, and not disclosed to unauthorised persons. In addition, a right of subject access is given (see below), i.e. the individual should be able, on payment of a small fee, to see what is contained about him and have a right to rectify that if it is not correct. The Commissioner has the power to enforce the duties under the Act and offenders can be prosecuted. The individual data subject has the right to apply to the courts for compensation for damage and any associated distress caused by a breach of these principles by the data user. (The provisions in relation to access to health records are considered below.)

---

1. Personal data shall be processed fairly and lawfully and, in particular, shall not be processed unless:
   a. at least one of the conditions in Schedule 2 is met; and
   b. in the case of sensitive personal data, at least one of the conditions in Schedule 3 is also met.
2. Personal data shall be obtained only for one or more specified and lawful purposes, and shall not be further processed in any manner incompatible with that purpose or those purposes.
3. Personal data shall be adequate, relevant and not excessive in relation to the purpose or purposes for which they are processed.
4. Personal data shall be accurate and, where necessary, kept up to date.
5. Personal data processed for any purpose or purposes shall not be kept for longer than is necessary for that purpose(s).
6. Personal data shall be processed in accordance with the rights of data subjects under this Act.
7. Appropriate technical and organisational measures shall be taken against unauthorised or unlawful processing of personal data and against accidental loss or destruction of, or damage to, personal data.
8. Personal data shall not be transferred to a country or territory outside the European Economic Area unless that country or territory ensures an adequate level of protection for the rights and freedoms of data subjects in relation to the processing of personal data.

Figure 8.2 Principles of the Data Protection Act 1998 Schedule 1.

First Data Protection Principle

This principle, which requires that personal data shall be processed fairly and lawfully, prevents the processing unless at least one of the conditions in Schedule 2 is met, and in the case of sensitive personal data, at least one of the conditions in Schedule 3 is also met. Schedules 2 and 3 are set out in the Department of Health

Guidance.[5] Schedule 2 includes the consent of the patient, contractual purposes, and compliance with legal obligations necessary to protect the vital interests of the data subject or necessary for the administration of justice, or for the legitimate purposes of the data controller. Schedule 3 includes the explicit consent of the patient, rights and obligations in connection with employment, where the processing is necessary to protect the vital interests of the data subject or another person, where the consent cannot be given by or on behalf of the data subject or where the data controller cannot reasonably be expected to obtain the consent. Schedules 2 and 3 can be seen in Appendix C.

The duty of confidentiality

The patient is entitled to confidentiality of the information about him. There is therefore a duty on every professional and indeed every employee of the authority to ensure confidentiality of information. The duty arises:

1. from the duty of care in negligence discussed in Chapter 1;
2. from the implied duties under the contract of employment (see Chapter 10);
3. from the duty to keep information that has been passed on in confidence, confidential, even when there is no pre-existing relationship or legally enforceable contract between the parties. (This is a duty based on equity and only recently recognised by the courts, and was discussed in the case of *Stephens* v. *Avery and others*, 1988 2 All ER 477.)[6]
4. from requirements by professional registration bodies as part of the professional conduct;
5. from statutory duties such as the Data Protection Act 1998 and Article 8 of the European Convention of Human Rights (Schedule 1 of the Human Rights Act 1998, see Appendix A of this book).

Under the duties implied in the contract of employment, the employee has a responsibility to the employer to keep information acquired from work confidential. For the nurse, too, that duty is also spelled out by the Code of Professional Conduct (see Figure 8.3).

While this code is not enforceable in a court of law, it reflects what the law upholds and is used by the PCC as a guideline in determining whether the nurse is guilty of professional misconduct.

Difficulties arise not in understanding the duty of confidentiality, but in knowing when the exceptions arise and in what circumstances breaking the duty is permissible.

Respect confidential information obtained in the course of professional practice and refrain from disclosing such information without the consent of the patient/client, or a person entitled to act on his/her behalf, except where disclosure is required by law or by the order of a court or is necessary in the public interest.

Figure 8.3 Paragraph 9 of the Code of Professional Conduct.

Because of these problems, the UKCC has issued Guidelines on Professional Practice, which expands upon the duty of confidentiality set out in the Code of Professional Practice (UKCC Guidelines for Professional Practice 1996). In a case brought by Ashworth Hospital against Mirror Group Newspapers, the judge made an order requiring the newspaper group to disclose to the hospital the identity of the source of their information about a convicted murderer who was a patient at Ashworth. The Court of Appeal upheld this judgment, holding that the protection of patient information was of vital concern to the NHS.[7] The High Court has also recognised that in exceptional circumstances the court has the jurisdiction to extend the protection of confidentiality of information even to the extent of imposing restrictions on the press where a failure to do so would probably lead to serious physical injury or the death of the person seeking that confidentiality. Thus it granted an injunction to prohibit the publication of the details of the boys who killed James Bulger.[8]

The DoH has also issued advice on the protection and use of patient information.[9] Powers are given to the Secretary of State under Sections 60 and 61 of the Health and Social Care Act 2001 to make regulations on the disclosure of patient information.

Exceptions to the duty of confidentiality

See Figure 8.4.

1. Consent of a patient.
2. Interests of patient.
3. Court orders:
    subpoena;
    civil procedure rules.
4. Statutory Duty to disclose:
    Road Traffic Act 1972;
    Prevention of Terrorism Act;
    Public Health Acts;
    Misuse of Drugs Acts.
5. Public interest.
6. Police.
7. Data Protection Act 1998 provisions.

Figure 8.4 Exceptions to the duty of confidentiality.

The consent of the patient

The duty is owed to the patient and it is therefore in the patient's power to authorise disclosures to be made. Thus announcements to the press, notification of relatives and spouses, and provision of information to a solicitor or to an insurance company are all legitimate disclosures with the consent of the patient. If the patient is unconscious and an adult, the consent of the relatives is often used to justify disclosure on behalf of the patient, but there may well be little justification for this in law, unless the patient has appointed that relative as his agent and given him that authority.

Situation 8.1   *Spouse's confidence*

Annabel was involved in a serious road accident and admitted to hospital. While on the orthopaedic ward, a telephone request came in asking for information on her progress. The nurse taking the call asked who the caller was. The answer was 'her husband'. The nurse then gave the caller full details of Annabel's progress. She then told Annabel that her husband had phoned asking for information about her; the nurse was surprised at Annabel's fury. It appeared that she had recently separated from him, she had not notified him of where she was now living, and did not want any communication with him because of his violence.

The difficulties of the nurse's position in a situation like the above are easily understood. In 99 out of 100 cases, Annabel would be delighted to receive a message of concern and interest. However, it is the hundredth case that causes concern and procedures have to be established to prevent any unauthorised information being disclosed. Annabel is entitled to withhold information of her condition from her relatives and friends. In some cases, even an acknowledgement that a patient is on a particular ward, e.g. psychiatric or gynaecology (abortion), might be an unwarranted disclosure. In the above situation, the nurse was at fault in not checking with Annabel first, and it is now standard practice not to disclose information over the phone unless checks on the caller have been made and the patient is agreeable to the information being given.

There can often be a problem in caring for elderly patients where the patient has made a special request to the nurses that the relatives should not be told about his condition. However, it can give rise to additional problems for staff. 'Where do I stand if I do not contact the relatives regarding the condition of the elderly patient because the elderly patient has asked me not to do so?' is a not infrequent question. Applying the principles discussed here, the patient does have the right to refuse to allow this information to be passed on. However, if the relatives are to care for the patient eventually, there may well be information that they need to know for the patient's own safety and thus disclosure is justified in the interests of the patient (see below).

Disclosure refused by the patient
In the following case the patient refused to permit disclosure of her records to her employer.

Case 8.1   *Waiver of patient's right to confidentiality*[10]

The claimant issued proceedings against her employer alleging that she had sustained radial tunnel syndrome in her right wrist as a result of his negligence in requiring her to perform repetitive movements at work. She had undergone a remedial operation and the employer wished to have details of the reasons for the operation and the nature of the condition. She refused to give permission

> *Case 8.1   continued*
>
> for the employer's legal and medical advisers to discuss the operation with her consultant. The employer sought an 'unless' order from the court, that unless she provided the necessary consent, the proceedings would be stayed. Her consultant also stated that he would not become involved unless instructed by the court. The judge refused the 'unless' order.

The Court of Appeal upheld the appeal and granted the 'unless' order. It stated that the Court could not order a claimant to waive her right of confidentiality, but could stay proceedings until the claimant waived the right of confidentiality. Information requested from a claimant in a case of this kind should be confined to that which was relevant to the issues between the parties and a claimant could not restrict the information requested to a written rather than an oral form.

Disclosure to the press

Exactly the same principles apply when the press are asking for information about a patient. If the patient consents, the information can be given. If the patient refuses, then no information should be given and this includes a condition check, where the press phone up to find out the latest condition of the patient. Where the patient is unconscious, confidentiality should be respected.

Disclosure in the interests of the patient

Disclosure between professionals caring for the patient is justified on the basis that if information obtained by the doctor and relevant to the care of the patient is not passed on to the appropriate professional, then the patient might suffer. An obvious example is the patient's history of allergy to certain medication: if the pharmacist and the nurse were not told of a known allergy or allowed to see the records, they would be unable to ensure that the patient was given appropriate medication. Traditionally, nurses have not usually had difficulties over access to the patient's records. Other professional groups have encountered difficulties: occupational therapists, physiotherapists, social workers and other groups have sometimes been refused access to the patient's records on the grounds that it is unnecessary and also a breach of confidentiality. This is a difficult problem. On the one hand, the wider the range of people who have access to the medical records of the patient, the more difficult it is to maintain the duty of confidentiality. On the other hand, there are many situations where a professional caring for the patient, in ignorance of certain facts known to the doctor, could do the patient considerable harm.

The problem becomes even more complex when we consider the question of how much confidential information should be given to a volunteer who is taking the patient out. For example, if the volunteer is taking a patient with learning disabilities out for the day, it might be vital in the interests of the safety of the patient to advise the volunteer that the patient is epileptic and to ensure that the volunteer would know how to cope should the patient have an attack. On the other hand, the fact that the patient had an abortion five years ago would be irrelevant and thus would be a disclosure that would not be justified in the interests of the patient.

In conclusion, it could be said that disclosure of confidential information to others is justified if it is necessary in the interests of the health and/or safety of the patient or the professional. AIDS has raised many significant problems in this field and these are discussed further in Chapter 26.

Court orders

Subpoena

This is an order made by the court, which must be obeyed under threat of punishment for contempt of court.

The court has the power to subpoena any relevant evidence or witnesses in a case in the interests of justice. There are only two exceptions to this power and these are known as being privileged from disclosure.

Privilege on grounds of public interest   An example of public interest protected from an order for disclosure is national security. It would usually be claimed by a Minister of the Crown when a certificate is signed to the effect that disclosure of a particular document or information would be contrary to the public interest. Following the Scott Inquiry into the Matrix Churchill case, it was recommended that privilege on the grounds of the public interest should not be claimed when a criminal offence was being brought.

Legal professional privilege   This second exception to the power of the court to order disclosure covers communications between client and legal adviser where litigation is envisaged or is taking place. In the interests of total disclosure between client and lawyer, and in the advancement of justice, these communications are free from an order of discovery or disclosure. Difficulties have arisen over the disclosure of statements taken from witnesses to an accident that might be used later in any court proceedings. Are such statements protected from disclosure on the grounds of legal professional privilege?

In the case of *Waugh* v. *British Railway Board*,[11] it was held that where a document comes into being after an accident and where there are two purposes for its use (e.g. management purposes to ensure that the accident does not happen again, and legal purposes to defend any potential action), then if the dominant purpose is for management purposes, the document is not privileged from disclosure under the rules of professional legal privilege. This ruling by the House of Lords was upheld in the following case:

Case 8.2   Disclosure

Marlon Lee, a young boy, was severely scalded and was initially treated in a hospital run by one health authority, then subsequently transferred to a burns hospital run by another district authority. Shortly afterwards, he developed breathing problems and was transferred to the first hospital by the ambulance that came under the South West Thames Regional Health Authority. He suffered brain damage, which was considered to be due to lack of oxygen. The mother

> ### Case 8.2   continued
>
> asked for disclosure of the ambulance report produced by the Regional Health Authority for the first hospital, but was refused it. Her application to the court for disclosure failed on the basis that the report was prepared in contemplation of litigation and to assist the legal advisers, and disclosure could not be ordered even though it had been initiated as a result of the request by the first hospital authority, not by the authority responsible for the ambulance service.[12]

This case shows the disadvantages faced by potential litigants since the health authority or NHS Trust is, of course, both custodian of the records and also a potential defendant, and can use its first function to enable it to have immediate access to all the relevant records. (If the report can be defined as part of the personal health records of the patient, then access may be obtained under the Data Protection subject access provisions (see below) unless the exceptions apply.)

The test to decide whether communication between a solicitor and his client was privileged from disclosure was to consider whether it was made confidentially for the purposes of legal advice, constructing such purposes broadly.[13] Section 42 of the Freedom of Information Act recognises the exception of legal professional privilege.

Apart from these exceptions, the judge has the power to order the production of any evidence relevant to the case. There is no recognition of the privilege of confidential medical information, nor do the courts recognise the secrecy of the confessional or press informants. In the case of *Deacon* v. *McVicar*[14] (see page 73, Case 4.12), the judge ordered the production of the records of other maternity patients.

Health visitors are more likely than any other group of nurses to be summoned by subpoena to appear in court. They had adopted a procedure whereby they would normally require service of a subpoena before giving evidence in court. In this way, they were able to make it clear to their clients that they had no option but to attend court and were obliged to disclose confidential information. The Children Act 1989 has led to health visitors giving evidence in the interest of the child without waiting for a subpoena.

Disclosure in personal injury cases

Disclosure can be made of relevant records under the Supreme Court Act 1981, Sections 33 and 34: Section 33 enables disclosure to be made between parties to a case before litigation commences; Section 34 enables an order for disclosure to be made against a third party. In addition, as a result of pressure from the Health Service Commissioner and also from judges in several cases where there has been evidence of unnecessary delay in the production of medical records, NHS Trusts nowadays rarely wait to be issued with an order for disclosure, but are more likely to produce the relevant documents when the solicitor requests them. Access by the claimant can be sought under the statutory provisions of the Data Protection legislation (see below). In addition, the Woolf reforms in civil justice (see Chapter 6) have led to earlier disclosure of relevant information.

Disclosure before trial

In addition to the rules under the Supreme Court Act 1981, the rules of the High Court enable an order for relevant information to be made once the claim form has been issued and the case commenced. This order for the production of documents is part of the exchange of information that takes place between the parties before the hearing takes place in the court. The aim is to ensure that the parties understand the main points in dispute and are not surprised when the oral hearing takes place. The days in court should thus be kept to a minimum and should take place only when there really is an outstanding issue between the parties. Changes to the civil law procedure have taken place following Lord Woolf's Report on Access to Justice. The emphasis is on openness between the partners and early disclosure between them of all relevant information, including the reports of experts. Under the new system of case management by the courts introduced under the new Civil Procedure Rules, directions will be given to facilitate the exchange of information and the progress of the case (see Chapter 6).

In exceptional circumstances, the court could order disclosure to a person who was neither a party to the case nor a lawyer. Thus, in the case over the alleged harm caused by the drug Opren, the Court of Appeal allowed disclosure to the medical and scientific journalist and writer who was assisting the many claimants in their case against Eli Lilly.[15]

Disclosure to the patient and the right of subject access

The Data Protection Act 1998 gives the right of subject access to health records, subject to several exceptions. This is considered on page 167.

Statutory duty to disclose

Whatever the views of the patient, there are certain circumstances in which disclosure of otherwise confidential information must be made by law. The following are the main provisions.

1. Road Traffic Act 1988 S 170 as amended by the Traffic Act 1991. This requires any person to give information to the police relating to a road traffic accident involving personal injuries. A doctor was prosecuted under its predecessor for failing to disclose the relevant information and was fined £5.[16] His claim that he should not be required to give information that would be a breach of the patient's confidence was not accepted either by the trial judge or by the Divisional Court (see also Chapter 21). In a recent case,[17] it was held that there was a statutory duty to report a road accident, even when the driver was not actually driving at the time.

2. The Prevention of Terrorism Act (Temporary Provisions Act 1988), Section 11 (Continuous Order SI 1993/747), makes it an offence for any person having information, which he believes may be of material assistance in preventing terrorism or apprehending terrorists, to fail without reasonable cause to give that information to the police. This therefore places a burden on staff, for example, in accident and emergency departments, to disclose the existence of wounds that may have resulted from terrorist acts.

3. The Public Health (Control of Disease) Act 1984 requires a medical practitioner attending a patient who appears to be suffering from a notifiable disease to

notify the medical officer of the district of the name and whereabouts of the patient and the disease. Notifiable diseases include cholera, plague, smallpox, and typhus.

4. The Abortion Act 1967 requires doctors to inform the Chief Medical Officer of the DH of detailed information relating to the termination of pregnancy (see Chapter 15).

The Misuse of Drugs (Supply to Addicts) Regulations 1997 have abolished the requirement for a doctor to notify the Home Office of any patient who appears to be drug dependent, but a doctor is expected to notify the local Drug Misuse Database (see Chapter 28).

Public interest

Unfortunately, many of the difficulties relating to the exceptions to the duty of confidentiality come under the broad heading of 'public interest' where there is little guidance from the courts.

Situation 8.2 *An epileptic lorry driver*

Bill, a long-distance lorry driver, is diagnosed as having epilepsy which is not yet under control through medication. The doctor has advised him to notify his employers and cease driving until the epilepsy is under control. Bill does not wish to do this since he has just been interviewed for the job of coach driver on the continent and he has been hoping for this chance for years. April, a nurse in the neurology ward, recognises Bill as her neighbour and is horrified when she hears from Bill's wife that Bill has been given the job of driving a coachload of school children to France. She knows several children who will be on that trip.

Many would argue that in these circumstances a breach of the duty of confidentiality owed to Bill is justified on grounds of the public interest. Obviously, there are advantages in Bill himself being persuaded of the dangers of driving on the trip, but if he fails to disclose this and continues with his plans, then many would justify the doctor making the disclosure. If the doctor is adamant that he will not breach that confidence, does the nurse have any right to do so? The General Medical Council states specifically that it would defend any practitioner who disclosed confidential information in such circumstances. However, it is for each specific practitioner to decide personally if the particular circumstances justify disclosure in the public interest. There is no statutory definition of the public interest. Failure to notify the Vehicle Licensing Authority that a particular driver was not medically fit to drive could even be seen as a breach of a duty of care towards those persons who may be harmed as a result of that person driving. The success of such a hypothetical case would depend upon establishing the following:

1. The doctor (or the nurse or other professional) owed a duty of care to the person who was eventually injured.

2. There was a breach of this duty in that the relevant information was not passed to the appropriate authority.

3. The personal injuries or death were a reasonably foreseeable result of that failure and were caused by that failure.

Until such a case is heard, or a law is enacted, a firm decision cannot be made, but some guidance is provided by the Tarasoff case heard in America and considered below. In addition, it should be pointed out that any person who drives a vehicle contrary to medical advice would himself be committing a criminal offence.

Case 8.3   Tarasoff case[18]

A psychologist in California was told by a patient that he intended to kill a girl. The psychologist informed the campus police, who detained the man, but soon after released him. They did not inform the girl's parents of the danger to her. The patient subsequently killed the girl. The parents sued the university for breach of its duty of care to the girl in failing to warn them. They succeed in a majority verdict. The court held that the therapist owes a legal duty of care not only to his patient, but also to his patient's would-be victim. This duty of care is subject to scrutiny by judge and jury.

A dissenting judge, Judge Clark, was concerned that the very practice of psychiatry vitally depended upon the reputation in the community that the psychiatrist would not tell. He considered that assurance of confidentiality was important to ensure patients were not deterred from seeking treatment; to ensure that they made a full disclosure to the doctor and to ensure that the patient maintains his trust in his doctor which is vital for successful treatment.

The UKCC recognises that the public interest may be a justification for disclosing confidential information. This is defined in its Guidelines for Professional Practice Paragraph 56:

> The public interest means the interest of an individual, groups of individuals or of society as a whole, and would, for example, cover matters such as serious crimes, child abuse, drug trafficking or other activities which place others at serious risk.

Paragraph 59 states:

> In all cases where you deliberately release information in what you believe to be the best interests of the public, your decision must be justified. In some circumstances, such as accident and emergency admission where the police are involved, it may be appropriate to involve senior staff if you do not feel that you are able to deal with the situation alone.

The Guidelines also emphasise the importance of documenting the reasons for the action that has been taken.

The Court of Appeal has given guidance on the public duty of confidence.

Case 8.4   Disclosure in the public interest[19]

W, a psychiatric patient, brought an action against an independent psychiatrist, the health authority, the mental health review tribunal and the Secretary of State for breach of confidentiality. The psychiatrist had sent a copy of his report on W's mental condition to the hospital on grounds of public interest on the basis of W's particular circumstances. The High Court judge held that no distinction should be drawn between a psychiatrist who was independent and one employed by the health authority. The report did not come under the heading of legal professional privilege (see page 153). The judge relied on the General Medical Council's Advice on Standards of Professional Conduct and Medical Ethics and refused an injunction against the use or disclosure of the report and dismissed his claims for damage.

The Court of Appeal dismissed W's appeal and held that the balance came down in favour of the public interest in the disclosure of the report and against the public interest in the duty of confidentiality owed to the patient. Unlike the trial judge, the Court of Appeal considered the General Medical Council's rules as inappropriately relied upon by the judge, since Dr Egdell did not have clinical responsibility for W. The Court of Appeal quoted Article 8(2) of the European Convention on Human Rights which permits intervention by a public authority in the duty of professional secrecy (see Article 8(1) on the interests of public safety and the prevention of crime.) (See Appendix A of this book.)

The same considerations justified Dr Egdell's actions.

Situation 8.3   Occupational health

Brenda works as a nurse in the occupational health department and is horrified to discover that a paediatric nurse, Karen, has an unusual bacterial infection which makes it very dangerous for her to work in the unit, particularly with the premature babies. However, she knows that Karen has exhausted all her sick pay allowance from the authority and would be dependent on DSS benefits. She is bringing up two children on her own and would have great difficulty managing without her NHS pay. Karen herself is not ill: she appears to be a carrier rather than a sufferer of this particular germ and is anxious to continue to work and does not want her nursing officer to be notified.

An occupational health department is sometimes caught in the clash between its duty to keep information acquired from its clients/patients confidential and the interest of the employer in being aware of that information, especially where there is danger to the health or safety of other employees as a result of the person's medical condition. (AIDS is considered separately in Chapter 26.) Exactly the same principles apply as in the situation described above, with the additional dimension of the employers' duty to other employees in the workplace. There is a clear duty owed by the employer to his employees under an implied term in the contract of employment (see Chapter 10), whereas the duty owed in the law of negligence in the situation of the epileptic lorry driver described above is not at all clear.

In Brenda's case, there is clear justification for advising Karen that the information cannot be withheld. The dangers to the patients and to other staff are such that she cannot continue to work until she is free of the germ. Karen may have the right to claim the statutory right of payment on the grounds of medical suspension (see Chapter 10). This breach of confidentiality can be justified by reference to a preceding agreement, namely the contract of employment and the implied terms in it (see Chapter 10). Some authorities may well have an express term in their contract of employment authorising the occupational health department to notify the employer of any condition that would be dangerous to patients or other employees.

The Clothier Report following the conviction of Beverley Allitt[20] made recommendations for Occupational Health Departments. It recommended that they should be involved in the selection of prospective employees and should monitor on-going health problems of employees, alerting the employers when there were any serious risks to others. (See Chapter 5 for a consideration of a National Reporting scheme and Chapter 4 for whistle-blowing.) The recommendations of the Clothier Report were reinforced by the report of an inquiry chaired by Richard Bullock following the case of Amanda Jenkinson, a Nottinghamshire nurse who was imprisoned for harming a patient. Similar recommendations were made to Occupational Health Departments on risks from employees.

Disclosure to a Registration body
In some cases, disclosure to a state registration body may be justified in the public interest as the following case shows.

Case 8.5   Disclosure to a registration body in the public interest[21]

In care proceedings about a pre-school child, expert psychiatric evidence concluded that the mother was suffering from a severe personality disorder. The mother was a paediatric nurse and the three doctors involved in the case were agreed that there would be concern for any child in the mother's care. The court went on to consider whether the matter should be reported to the UKCC for the protection of any children who might be put at risk by contact with the mother in her professional capacity. The court decided that the court's judgment, the expert medical reports, and the minutes of the experts' two meetings should be given to the UKCC. The court had to decide on the balance of the rights of the mother and the child against the public interest in demanding protection from nurses who were, or who were potentially, unfit to practise.

Disclosures to the police
There are very few occasions on which the citizen is obliged as a duty by Act of Parliament to provide the police with information. The main statutes requiring disclosure are cited above. Many quandaries arise outside those areas and concern the powers of the police to require a professional to disclose confidential information during police investigations. Another difficulty is the position where, by chance,

Police and Criminal Evidence Act 1984 Section 9. A constable may obtain access to excluded material or special procedure material by making an application under Schedule 1 Section 11. Excluded material means

(a) personal records which a person has acquired or created in course of any trade, business, profession . . . and which he holds in confidence;
(b) human tissue or tissue fluid which has been taken for the purposes of diagnosis or medical treatment and which a person holds in confidence;
(c) . . .

Section 12. Personal records means documentary or records concerning an individual (whether living or dead) who can be identified from them and relating

(a) to his physical or mental health;
(b) to spiritual counselling or assistance given or to be given to him.

Section 14. Special procedure material means material other than items subject to legal privilege and excluded material in the possession of a person who

(a) acquired or created it in course of any trade, business, profession or other occupation . . . ; and
(b) holds it subject to an express or implied undertaking to hold it in confidence.

A circuit judge can make an order that the person who appears to be in possession of the specified material should produce it to a constable for him to take it away or give a constable access to it, not later than the end of the period of 7 days from the date of the order. The judge must be satisfied that specific access conditions are fulfilled before making the order.

Figure 8.5 Police and Criminal Evidence Act 1984.

particularly through work in the community, the professional obtains evidence that a crime has been committed or is being committed: for example, stolen goods are seen in a client's home; there is evidence of drug abuse; there is evidence that a child is being physically or mentally ill-treated, or sexually abused; there is evidence that a patient has had an illegal abortion; there has been an attempt to conceal the birth of a stillborn child; a wife has suffered a severe battering by the husband.

The police powers are contained in the Police and Criminal Evidence Act 1984. Medical records and human tissue or tissue fluid that has been taken for the purposes of diagnosis or medical treatment and which a person holds in confidence are subject to special procedures (see Figure 8.5).

Disclosure where a criminal offence is believed to have taken place

Situation 8.4   *Rape?*

The police arrive at the accident and emergency department one night inquiring about the possibility of a young man in his twenties having been admitted with severe lacerations to his face and neck. About two hours earlier, a girl of 15 years had been found in a serious condition having suffered an attack. She had tried to defend herself by hitting the assailant in the face with a mirror. There was blood on the mirror and she believed she had cut him severely. The police arrive in the department and ask the duty nurse if they can go through the admissions during the last two hours.

The information required by the police is related to the medical records and thus comes under the special procedure. The police can make an application to a circuit judge for an order for the production of special procedure material. He will do so only if he is satisfied that certain conditions are present. However, these are the ultimate powers. It is unlikely that the police would be obliged to go to this length against an NHS Trust. If it is known that the police can ultimately seek an order for disclosure, then the NHS Trust policy is likely to be one of co-operation with them. In a case such as the rape case above, the nurse would be advised to call the medical officer in charge of the accident and emergency department who would identify any patients who come within a fairly detailed description of the likely assailant. Giving the police the admission book would be beyond this duty.

In a recent case,[22] an order for disclosure to the police of the social security records giving dates of admission and discharge to the hospital was held not to come within the provisions of Schedule 1 of the Police and Criminal Evidence Act 1984.

Drugs offences

Whilst there would appear to be no statutory duty to disclose drug offences, the lessons from a case in Cambridge would suggest that there are advantages in informing the police if one is aware that drug offences are taking place. Two charity workers were jailed for allowing the supply of class A and B drugs. Ruth Wyner, who was director of a Cambridge charity, and her colleague John Brock, manager of the Wintercomfort day centre for homeless people, were convicted of knowingly permitting or suffering the supply of a Class A drug on the premises. They were concerned that handing over the names of suspected drug dealers to the police would put staff at risk of reprisals and undermine the principle of confidentiality that is fundamental to helping homeless people come off the streets.[23] Their appeal to the Court of Appeal was successful. It is clear that there must be clarification of the laws here, since many community psychiatric nurses and those working in hostels and other forms of residential care may be aware that drugs offences are taking place and may be uncertain about their legal position.

Department of Health Advice

The NHS Executive has provided guidance on the Protection and Use of Patient Information,[24] Annex D of which covers the passing on of information in connection with serious crime. It quotes those offences in the Police and Criminal Evidence Act 1984 that are identified as 'serious' as including: treason, murder, manslaughter, rape, kidnapping, certain sexual offences, causing an explosion, certain firearms offences, taking of hostages, hijacking, causing death by reckless driving, and making a threat which if carried out would be likely to lead to:

1. Serious threat to the security of the state or to public order.
2. Serious interference with the administration of justice or with the investigation of an offence.
3. Death or serious injury.
4. Substantial financial gain or serious financial loss to any person.

Situation 8.5   Let me know!

The police are investigating a burglary in which the householder came back early and surprised the burglar, who fell from a first floor window, but still managed to escape. The police have enquired at the various accident and emergency departments in the vicinity. At one hospital, they heard of an admission following a road accident where a man said he fell from a motorcycle when it crashed against a tree. There were no witnesses. They believe that the injuries are comparable to those the burglar might have sustained. Since the patient is not yet fit for interrogation as he has just come from the operating theatre, the police ask the ward sister:

1. to let them know when he can be questioned; and

2. not to let him go until the police arrive.

What is the ward sister's position? Must she obey this order?

1. *Notifying the police of the patient's fitness for questioning*: there is no clear legal right for the police to insist that this is done. For example, if the ward sister decides that her duty is to the patient, not to the police and thus fails to notify the police, could she then be prosecuted for obstructing the police in the execution of their duty? The answer is probably not, unless it can be shown that they had express legal powers to demand the information from her. In practice, of course, staff often rely on the help of the police when they have aggressive visitors, or even aggressive patients, and are therefore prepared to reciprocate. What we are concerned with here is the legal duty on the ward sister to provide this information, and it is unlikely that this power exists.

2. *Keeping the patient until the police arrive*: the citizen does have wide powers of arrest, though they are of course more limited than police powers. The sister would have no statutory power of keeping the patient (which would, in fact, be arresting him) until the arrival of the police unless either she knows that an arrestable offence has been committed and the patient is guilty of this, or she has reasonable grounds for suspecting that he is guilty. In the circumstances described above, it would not appear likely that the ward sister has those grounds since, as far as she knows, the patient could well have fallen from his motorcycle. She would therefore be on very weak ground if she refused to allow him to take his own discharge other than on the basis that she was acting out of her duty of care to save his life. In this situation, the police would have to provide a policeman to wait until such time as the patient could be questioned or taken to the police station under arrest.

Reporting crime to the police

Situation 8.6   Discovery in the community

Jane, a health visitor, goes to inquire at a house where there is a young child of 18 months, since she has not seen her in the clinic and the child is due for several vaccinations and tests. While in the house, she notices the following: small burn marks on the child who looks very undernourished; four brand new video recorders in the corner of the room; and a pipe from the gas supply which by-passes the meter. One might question her imagination over the last item, but if this is in fact what she spotted, does she have any duty in respect of them?

---

1. *Non-accidental injury*: Jane's duty is to the child, so there can be no doubt that if she has reasonable grounds for suspecting that there is any abuse, then she must take the appropriate action to safeguard the child. There is a clear procedure for action if such a situation exists and Jane would have the responsibility to set it in motion. Even if Jane were a district nurse and visiting the mother rather than the child, she would still have a duty to ensure that the appropriate care was taken.

2. *Suspected stolen goods*: there is no duty upon Jane to act as police informer in such circumstances. If, of course, the goods were subsequently found to be stolen and Jane were summoned to court as a witness, she would have to give evidence of what she had seen. What, however, if the goods were NHS Trust property? Does she have a duty to inform her employer that goods are being stolen? The answer depends upon whether a term can be implied into the contract of employment that any employee must inform the employer of any thefts from the workplace. There is no case that has decided the point, but it would appear to make business sense of the contract of employment if such a duty could be seen to be implied (see Chapter 10 on implying terms into a contract of employment).

3. *Gas*: it could be argued that the system for by-passing the meter is simply another case of stolen goods and theft. However, there are additional problems here, since there is a considerable public danger risking fire or an explosion. It could therefore be argued that Jane did have a public duty to notify the police, since her client and others could be in considerable danger.

Disclosure by the police to employers and the UKCC

Where a registered practitioner is charged or convicted of an offence, the police would ensure that both the employers and the UKCC or other registration body are informed.

Case 8.6   Disclosure to the UKCC[25]

Junia Woolgar, a registered nurse and matron of a nursing home, was arrested and interviewed by the police following the death of a patient in her care. The police concluded the investigation without bringing any charges and they referred the matter to the UKCC who asked for further information. It was the practice of the police to seek the consent of those who had given statements. Ms W refused to give consent and sought an injunction to restrain the police from disclosing to the UKCC the contents of an interview they had taped. She appealed against the High Court judge's refusal to grant the injunction. The Court of Appeal held that the police were entitled to release the information to a regulatory body, if they were reasonably persuaded that it was relevant to an inquiry being conducted by the regulatory body. She lost her appeal.

Disclosure under the Data Protection Act 1998

The disclosure of personal information should now be checked against the provisions of the Data Protection Act 1998. All personal health records, whether computerised or manually held, come within the definition of sensitive personal data and therefore at least one of the conditions in Schedule 2 and at least one of the conditions in Schedule 3 must be met. Schedules 2 and 3 of the Data Protection Act 1998 can be seen in Appendix C to this book.

Disclosure on an anonymous basis

The laws of confidentiality usually apply to the disclosure of information when the identity of the patient is made known. However, the Department of Health challenged a data collecting company that was using information provided by GPs and pharmacists about prescribing habits.[26] The company believed the information would be useful to drug companies and would provide useful data for those interested in monitoring prescribing patterns. Even though the information would be anonymous, the Department of Health challenged the use of this information as a breach of the guidelines put forward by the Department of Health[27] in 1996. The Department of Health letter to the company stated that:

> Anonymisation (with or without aggregation) does not, in our view, remove the duty of confidence between the patients who are the subject of the data. . . . Anonymisation (with or without aggregation) would not obviate a breach of confidence.

The Company challenged the policy guidance, maintaining that provided anonymity could be guaranteed, what was proposed would not amount to a breach of confidence. The High Court judge held that:

1. The information in the prescription handed to the pharmacist had the necessary quality of confidence about it to render it confidential, and in receiving that information, the pharmacist was under a duty of confidence in relation to it. In the absence of express or implied consent from the patient, the proposal involved the unauthorised use by the pharmacist of confidential information.

2. There is a public interest in ensuring that confidences are kept. It is important that those who require medical advice should not be inhibited in any way from seeking or obtaining it. Accordingly, breach of confidence may in itself carry with it sufficient detriment to justify the grant of a remedy.

3. There was no breach of the company's rights under Article 10 of the European Convention on Human Rights because the Department of Health's guidance was a correct statement of the law relating to the disclosure of information received in confidence and the rights of the patient were capable of justifying interference with the company's rights.

The Court of Appeal[28] reversed this decision. It held that GPs and pharmacists providing prescription information that did not identify the patient was not a breach of confidence. Anonymous data did not involve a risk to the patient's privacy, even if, with effort, the patient could be identified.

At the time of writing, there is an appeal pending to the House of Lords.

Caldicott Guardians

Concern about the need to improve the way in which the NHS managed patient confidentiality led to the appointment of a committee chaired by Dame Fiona Caldicott. It reported in December 1997 and included in its recommendations the need to raise awareness of confidentiality requirements, and specifically recommended the establishment of a network of Caldicott Guardians of patient information throughout the NHS. Subsequently, a steering group was set up to oversee the implementation of the Report's recommendations.

Following a consultation period, the NHS executive issued a circular on the establishment of Caldicott Guardians.[29] The circular gives advice on the appointment of the Guardians, the programme of work for the first year for improving the way each organisation handles confidential patient information and identifies the resources, training and other support for the Guardians.

The Guardian

Each health authority, special health authority, NHS trust and Primary Care Group was required to appoint a Caldicott Guardian by no later than 31 March 1999. Ideally, the Guardian should be at board level, be a senior health professional and have responsibility for promoting clinical governance within the organisation. The name and address of the Guardian is to be notified to the NHS Executive.[30] Action to be undertaken by each NHS organisation in support of the Guardian is shown in Box 8.1. The Guardian is expected to liaise closely with others involved in patient information, such as IM and T security officers and Data Protection Officers. In making the appointment and defining the role of the Guardian, the duties that are not to be delegated should be clarified. Guardians are responsible for agreeing and reviewing internal protocols governing the protection and use of patient-identifiable information by the staff of their organisation and must be satisfied that these proposals address the requirements for national guidance/policy and law. The operation of these policies must also be monitored. Policies for inter-agency disclosure of patient information must also be agreed and reviewed, to facilitate cross boundary working.

Box 8.1

Action to be taken to support the Guardian

1. develop local protocols governing the disclosure of patient information to other organisations;

2. restrict access to patient information within each organisation by enforcing strict need to know principles;

3. regularly review and justify the uses of patient information;

4. improve organisational performance across a range of related areas; database design, staff induction, training, compliance with guidance etc.

Resources

The preservation of the confidentiality of patient information is seen as a cornerstone of the NHS information strategy. Therefore the NHS executive advised that the modernisation funds which were made available to support local implementation of the information strategy could be used to support Caldicott Guardians.

Training

Seminars have been and are being organised within each region of the NHS and persons interested are advised to make contact with the NHS Executive.[31]

Action taken in the first year

The NHS circular outlined the action that each organisation was required to take in the first year. The main activities included:

1. A management audit of existing procedures for protection and using patient-identifiable information leading to a report for the Guardian to present to the senior management team as a 'stock-take'.

2. The development of an improvement plan that will address any identified deficiencies.

In 2000, the Department of Health issued guidance to Caldicott guardians on the method by which information flows should be reviewed in NHS organisations.[32] It provided a manual that covers the mapping of information flows; the prioritising of mapped flows for review purposes and a rolling programme of review. The specific areas that are considered include: commissioning flows, clinical audit and coding, medical records and patient care services.

Conclusion on confidentiality

It is obvious that the present law on disclosure of confidential information, especially disclosure in the public interest, is unsatisfactory. Much is left to the discretion of the individual nurse in walking the tightrope between keeping the patient/client's information confidential and ensuring the public is not harmed. The Data Protection Act 1998 has tightened up access to and disclosure of personal information, putting more pressure on the decisions of the individual practitioner. Nurses should ensure that they make use of the existence of the Caldicott Guardian in their organisations to advise on issues relating to confidentiality and to assist in protecting the interests of the patient. If necessary, the protection of the Public Interest Disclosure Act 1998 could be sought if concerns on confidentiality need to be made known at a senior level within the organisation (see Chapter 4 and whistle-blowing.) The powers given to the Secretary of State under S.60 of the Health and Social Care Act 2001 to draw up regulations on the processing and disclosure of patient information are yet to be exercised. Their exercise should be consistent with Human Rights. The Human Rights Act, in enabling persons to bring actions against public authorities who have failed to uphold a person's right to respect for privacy set out in Article 8, is likely to lead to more litigation where patients claim that confidentiality has not been respected. Section 61 of the Health and Social Act 2001 enables the Secretary of State to appoint a Patient Information Advisory Group.

Access to personal health records

The Data Protection Act 1998 gives a statutory right for data subjects to access personal information held upon them (subject to exceptions discussed below). The Act applies to both computer records and records held in manual form. The 1998 Act replaces the Access to Health Records Act 1990 which gave access to manual records kept after 1 November 1991. The 1990 Act has been repealed except in respect of records of deceased patients. The definition of 'health record' would include nursing records, physiotherapy records, pathology laboratory records and all other records relating to the patient's health.

The Act enables data subjects to:

1. be informed whether personal data is processed;
2. to be given a description of the data held, the purposes for which it is processed and to whom the data may be disclosed;
3. to be given a copy of the information constituting the data; and
4. to be given information on the source of the data.

The data subject also has a right of rectification if the data recorded appears to be inaccurate. He/she can apply to the court for an order or to the Data Protection Commissioner for an enforcement notice. The data controller would be required to rectify the data, block it, erase it or destroy it. Alternatively, the court or commissioner could require that the record should be supplemented by a statement of the true facts.

Procedure for Access

A request for access to personal health records must be made in writing to the holder of these records or the data controller, most likely the NHS Trust or general practitioner, or possibly the Health Authority. Under the Regulations, a maximum fee of £50 can be charged together with copying charges. The data controller should verify that the applicant is either the data subject or his authorised proxy acting on behalf of the data subject. A response must be given within 40 days of the full information being given, together with the fee, or the applicant informed that there are grounds for withholding the information. The information can be withheld only on the grounds listed below. Failure to provide the fee or the necessary information required by the data controller would justify non-access. It may be that informal access would be permitted outside the legislation. If the Data Protection Act principles are applied, the data subject would pay the required fee, and within 40 days he should be given the required information.

Withholding information

The right of access to health records under the Data Protection Act 1998, like its predecessor, is not absolute and restrictions have been made by statutory instrument. The Data Protection (Subject Access Modifications) (Health) Order[33] modifies the right of access to health records in certain circumstances.

1. Where the access 'would be likely to cause serious harm to the physical or mental health or condition of the data subject or any other person (which may include a health professional).'

    A data controller who is not a health professional shall not withhold information on these grounds unless he has first consulted the person who appears to be the appropriate health professional on whether this exception applies. The obligation to consult does not apply where the data subject has already seen or knows about the information that is the subject of the request.

2. Where the request for access is made by another person on behalf of the data subject, such as a parent for a child, access can be refused if the data subject had provided the information in the expectation that it would not be disclosed.

3. If giving access would reveal the identity of another person, unless that person has given consent to the disclosure or it is reasonable to comply with the access request without that consent. This does not apply if the third party is a health professional who has been involved in the care of the patient, unless serious harm to that health professional's physical or mental health or condition is likely to be caused by giving access.

Certain information can be withheld if it is supplied in a report or other evidence given to the court by a local authority, Health or Social Services Board, Health and

Social Services Trust, probation officer or other person in the course of any proceedings to which various statutes apply, including the Family Proceedings Courts, if under the rules, the information may be withheld. Much needs to be interpreted on the Data Protection Act. What, for example, is meant by 'serious harm to the physical or mental health or condition of the data subject or any other person'? It is not defined in the order. How will the courts define what is appropriate for compensation and how will that be measured?

Correction of records

If a patient uses his right of access under the Data Protection Act to the health records and discovers that they are inaccurate, he can ask for them to be rectified. He also has the right to seek compensation for any harm that he has suffered as a result of the inaccuracy. Some say that the modifications to the right of access have taken much of the power out of the data access provisions. In addition, the data need not necessarily be supplied as a printout. The data user may choose to write or type the information to be supplied with any accompanying explanation.

Access to Medical Reports Act 1988

This Act came into force on 1 January 1989. It gives an individual a right of access to any medical report relating to him that has been supplied by a medical practitioner for employment purposes or insurance purposes. Before any such medical report can be supplied, the individual must be notified that it is being requested and the individual must give his consent to that request. The medical practitioner must not supply the report unless he has the consent of the individual. He is also required to give the individual the opportunity of access to it and to be allowed to correct any errors. These provisions apply unless 21 days have elapsed since the practitioner notified him of his intention to provide a report. The medical report must be retained by the medical practitioner for at least six months from the date on which it was supplied.

There is an exemption from individual access where the medical practitioner is of the opinion that disclosure would be likely to cause serious harm to the physical or mental health of the individual or would indicate the intentions of the practitioner in respect of the individual or where the identity of another person would be made known.

Conclusions

Clarification of the provisions of the Data Protection Act 1998 Section 60 of the Health and Social Care Act and the Human Rights Act 1998 is likely to take place as cases are brought before the courts. There will always be room for the exercise of professional discretion in determining whether disclosure is justified in the public interest or if access should be withheld. The practitioner is personally and professionally accountable for her actions and the burden will be upon her to justify her decisions. As in so many areas, the standard of documentation of the action taken will be of considerable importance. The Freedom of Information Act 2000 is to be brought into force over the next four years and there are likely to be disputes over rights of access in conflict with rights of confidentiality.

Questions and exercises

1   Prepare guidelines for a new employee on the duty of confidentiality.

2   Do you consider that there is a breach of confidentiality if a nurse returns home and tells her husband that they are treating a patient with AIDS on the ward? She does not mention the patient's name.

3   Consider the exception to the duty of confidentiality entitled 'public interest' and consider examples from your own experience that may come under that heading. What justifications could you give for and against disclosure?

4   Do you consider that the patient should have an absolute right of access in law to health records? Justify your answer.

5   Hospitals are often seen as the most difficult institutions in which to keep personal matters secret. What action do you think could be taken to enforce the duty of confidentiality in practice?

6   Identify who the Caldicott Guardian is in your organisation and establish the role that he/she plays in maintaining standards of confidentiality.

7   Obtain information of the function of the Patient Information Advisory Group set up under Section 61 of the Health and Social Care Act 2001.

References

[1] European Directive on Data Protection Adopted by the Council of the European Union in October 1995

[2] NHS Executive, Data Protection Act 1998 HSC 2000/009 and supporting information: DoH and NHS Executive, Data Protection Act 1998 Protection and Use of Patient Information http://www.doh.gov.uk/dpa98/

[3] http://www.standards.nhsia.nhs.uk/sdp

[4] Data Protection Commissioner, Data Protection Act 1998 An introduction, Office of DPC 1998; http://www.dpr.gov.uk

[5] NHS Executive, Data Protection Act 1998 HSC 2000/009 and supporting information: DoH and NHS Executive, Data Protection Act 1998 Protection and Use of Patient Information http://www.doh.gov.uk/dpa98/

[6] *Stephens* v. *Avery and others*, 1988 2 All ER 477

[7] *Ashworth Hospital Authority* v. *MGN Ltd* [2001] 1 All ER 991

[8] *Venables and another* v. *News Group Newspapers Ltd and others* [2001] 1 All ER Family Division

[9] HSG(96) 18 LASSL (96)5.

[10] *Nicholson v. Halton General Hospital NHS Trust, Current Law* November 46 1999

[11] *Waugh v. British Railway Board* 1980 AC 521

[12] *Lee v. South West Thames Regional Health Authority* 1985 2 All ER 385

[13] *Balabel and another v. Air India, The Times* 19 March 1988

[14] *Deacon v. McVicar and another* 7 January 1984 QBD

[15] *Davies v. Eli Lilly and Co.* 1987 1 All ER 801

[16] *Hunter v. Mann* 1974 1 QB 767

[17] *Cawthorne v. Director of Public Prosecutions, The Times* 31 August 1999

[18] *Tarasoff v. Regents of the University of California* 17 Cal 3d 425 (1976) (USA)

[19] *W. v. Egdell* 1989 1 All ER 1089 HC, 1990 1 All ER 835 CA

[20] Clothier Report, The Allitt Inquiry: An independent inquiry relating to deaths and injuries on the children's ward at Grantham and Kesteven General Hospital during the period February to April 1991, HMSO 1994

[21] *Re L* (Care Proceedings: Disclosure to third parties) [2000] 1 FLR 913

[22] *R. v. Cardiff Crown Court ex parte Kellam, The Times* 3 May 1993

[23] Alan Simpson, What price confidentiality, *Nursing Times* March 2 2000 Vol 96 No 9 p. 35

[24] The NHS Executive, The Protection and Use of Patient Information HSG (96)18 LASSL(96)5

[25] *Woolgar v. Chief Constable of Sussex Police and another* [1999] 3 All ER 604 CA

[26] *R. v. Department of Health ex p Source Informatics Ltd.* [1999] Lloyds Rep Medical 264; [1999] 4 All ER 185

[27] Department of Health HSG (1996)18 Protection and Use of Patient Information DoH circular March 1996

[28] *R. v. Department of Health ex p Source Informatics Ltd* [2000] T L R 17

[29] NHS Executive, HSC 1999/012, Caldicott Guardians 31 January 1999

[30] *Raj Kaur NHS Executive* 3E58 Quarry House Leeds LS2 7UE Fax 0113 254 6114

[31] Helen Williams Security and Data Protection Programme, NHS Information Management Centre 15 Frederick Road, Edgbaston Birmingham, B15 1JD Tel 0121 625 1997

[32] Department of Health, Protection and using patient information: A Manual for Caldicott Guardians DoH 2000

[33] 2000 SI No 413

9 Record-keeping, statements and evidence in court

The topics to be covered in this chapter are set out in Figure 9.1.

Record-keeping
  General principles
  Use in court
  Computerised records
Statements
  Status
  Principles to be followed
Evidence in court
  Fears;
  Preparation;
  Cross-examination.
Defamation
References

Figure 9.1 Issues covered in Chapter 9.

Record-keeping

General principles

Record-keeping is part of the professional duty of care owed by the nurse to the patient. As the UKCC says in its Guidelines for records and record keeping (UKCC 1998):[1]

> (Record-keeping) is a tool of professional practice and one which should help the care process. It is not separate from this process and it is not an optional extra to be fitted in if circumstances allow.

Failure therefore to maintain reasonable standards of record-keeping could be evidence of professional misconduct and subject to professional conduct proceedings. The UKCC has set out guidelines for good practice to assist the practitioner in fulfilling this professional duty.

UKCC: Guidelines for records and record-keeping
This document was issued in 1998 and is an invaluable guide to all practitioners. It provides guidelines for recording patient information and sets out the principles underpinning records and record-keeping. Guidance is also provided in the former

NHS Training Directorate booklets and by the NHS Executive.[2] The Audit Commission made recommendations to improve the standard of record-keeping in hospitals in 1995.[3] It reviewed the situation in 1999 and concluded that although progress had been made there was still scope for further improvements.[4]

Common errors noted in record-keeping

These are listed in Figure 9.2 and are the most common errors noted by a group of health visitors in record-keeping.

---

times omitted;
illegible handwriting;
lack of entry in the record when an abortive call has been made;
abbreviations that were ambiguous;
record of phone call (e.g. to social services) that omitted the name of the recipient (e.g. social worker);
use of Tippex and covering of errors;
no signature;
absence of information about the child;
inaccuracies, especially of the date;
omission of date of medical check up and hearing test and records for immunisation;
delay in completing the record; sometimes more than 24 hours elapsed before the records were completed;
record completed by someone who did not make visit;
inaccuracies of name, date of birth, and address;
unprofessional terminology, e.g. 'dull as a door step';
meaningless phrases, e.g. 'lovely child';
opinion mixed up with facts;
reliance on information from neighbours without identifying the source;
subjective not objective comments, e.g. 'normal development'.

Figure 9.2 Common errors in record-keeping.

Clarity

Records should be meaningful, clear accounts of the patients' care. 'Had a good day', which is one of the most unhelpful statements, should not feature in the records. Why did she have a good day? Had her appetite returned? Had she spent most of the time sleeping? Alternatively, had she spent most of the day awake? Had she been of minimal trouble to the nursing staff? Had she in contrast been lively and interacted with the nursing staff? All these situations, many of them incompatible, are within the meaning of those words.

Comprehensive

Some nurses might see this paperwork as a distraction from the real task of nursing, i.e. caring for the patient. However, records are an integral part of nursing care. Failure to record an important item, e.g. administration of a drug, may mislead other professionals such as those on a later nursing shift, and the patient could consequently be given an overdose. Accurate, comprehensive information relating to the care and the condition of the patient is a vital part of the professional role of the nurse. In addition, the information could be used for many other purposes of which the nurse may not be aware at the time.

Use of Abbreviations

The UKCC makes it clear in its Guidelines for Records and Record-keeping that abbreviations should not be used. However, this advice is probably not very realistic in view of the number of everyday abbreviations that are used automatically and reasonably safely, such as BP (blood pressure), T (temperature) . . . If these words were to be written out in full every time, then they would add considerably to the time taken to complete records. There are dangers in the use of abbreviations, e.g.

1. PID Pelvic Inflammatory Disease or Prolapsed Intervertebral Disc?
2. Pt. Patient or Physiotherapist or Part Time?
3. CP cerebral palsy or chartered physiotherapist?
4. BID Brought in Dead or Twice?
5. MS Multiple Sclerosis or Mitral Stenosis?
6. NFR Not For Resuscitation or Neurophysiological Facilitation of Respiration?
7. NAD Nothing Abnormal Discovered or Not A Drop!

What is essential is that there should be an agreed list set up by each Directorate or Trust and it should be a disciplinary matter for anyone to use an abbreviation that is on that list but for another meaning or to use an abbreviation that is not on that list. The approved list should be reviewed at regular intervals. A list of the approved abbreviations could be attached to the front of the patient's records. Eventually there may be a recognised list of nationally agreed abbreviations, but this may be some time away. All that has been said about abbreviations also applies to the use of symbols and signs and other hieroglyphics. Their use can certainly assist record-keeping, especially in spinal care, but there must be a clearly approved list available for both patients and health professionals to access.

Who should sign or write the records?

Any individual, and this would include unregistered staff or learners who have first-hand knowledge of any events regarding the care of the patient, should write up the relevant record and initial or sign it. Countersigning might be required by trained staff in certain circumstances and the procedure for this would be laid down locally. Any member of staff, registered or not, could be summoned to court to give evidence of what took place.

What about errors and mistakes?

If it is necessary to change what has been written, it is good practice for a line to be put through the incorrect statement and the correct statement made underneath rather than heavily scoring out the incorrect sentence or using correction fluid. Tippex and other such deletions should not be used on records. It should always be clear what was originally written and any corrections should be signed and dated. If the records are used in evidence, it should be clear what was originally written and why it was changed. It must be emphasised that these records are not proof of the truth of what they contain, but the writer of the records could be summoned to court to give direct evidence as to their accuracy and reliability.

Audit

Maintaining high standards in record-keeping requires constant vigilance. Regular audit is necessary to identify errors and ensure that standards are met. The UKCC states (page 9):

> Audit is one component of the risk management process and the ultimate aim of risk management is the promotion of quality . . .
>
> Audit can play a vital part in ensuring the quality of care that is delivered and this applies equally to the process of record keeping. By auditing your records, you can assess the standard of the record and identify areas for improvement and staff development. Audit tools should therefore be devised at a local level to monitor the standards of the records produced and to form a basis both for discussion and measurement.

The Clinical Negligence Scheme for Trusts carries out regular monitoring of the standards of record-keeping for those participants in the scheme. Their recommendations should assist in establishing and maintaining high standards. In addition, practitioners can learn from colleagues who have had to face questioning on their records before court or similar hearings.

Use in court

What constitutes a legal document?

There is sometimes confusion over what is a legal document. For example, are the nursing care plans legal documents? The answer is that any document requested by the court becomes a legal document. The court could subpoena the disclosure of Kardex or the nursing process documents, medical records, X-rays, pathology laboratory reports, social workers' records, any document in fact that may be relevant to the case. If they are missing, the writer of the records could be cross-examined as to the circumstances of their disappearance.

Whilst the main purpose of record-keeping is the care of the patient, considerable reliance will be placed upon the records in any court hearing. Any weaknesses in record-keeping will hamper the professional when it comes to giving evidence in court and will render her vulnerable in cross-examination, especially when there has been a considerable delay between the events recorded and the court hearing.

On some occasions, records may be looked at in a matter unconnected with the treatment of that particular patient. For example, in the case of *Deacon* v. *McVicar*[5] (see page 73, Case 4.12), there was a dispute as to the priority that a particular patient should have been given and the judge ordered the records of the other patients on the ward at the time to be disclosed in order to assess whether or not they would have been making demands upon medical and nursing time at a particular point in time.

The preceding chapter considers the rules relating to the disclosure of medical records in cases of personal injury litigation, and the powers of the court to order the discovery of any relevant documents with only privileged records being exempt from disclosure. Health records are not proof of the truth of the facts stated in them, but the maker of the record must be called to give evidence as to the truth of what is contained in them. There are exceptions under civil evidence legislation that permit the records to be used in evidence without the presence of the maker (where, for example, the maker is dead, or overseas), but due warning of the intent to use the records in evidence must be given to the other side.

Maintaining high standards of record keeping

The pressures of work and the lack of adequate time for record-keeping make it extremely difficult to ensure that standards of record-keeping are kept high. Constant vigilance is required. There are, however, examples where a department in an individual hospital discusses on a multi-disciplinary basis ways of ensuring that the existing record-keeping system is satisfactory: that the correct pre-printed material is in place and this is relevant to the information that is recorded and that this prevents any unnecessary writing or duplication. Here are some examples of good practice.

Standards in record-keeping improved following a multi-disciplinary conference in West Cumbria Health Care Trust in respect of the documentation for the Younger Disabled Unit including records that would be patient held.[6] A useful article by Catherine Kerr describes how staff in a coronary care unit were asked to assess their care plan and the model on which it was based. Sue Cockbill-Black[7] describes how, as a result of a study by nurses in an intensive care unit and an audit of pressure area management and documentation, modifications were made to the record-keeping. Factors influencing the documentation of care are considered in *Professional Nurse*.[8] Helpful advice is given in a series of articles on record-keeping in the *Nursing Times*.[9] Deborah Glover provides a check-list for standards of record-keeping and other articles consider the documentation of care plans, record-keeping in mental health and documenting out-patients.

Computerised records

The White Paper on the NHS[10] envisaged a vast investment in information technology within the NHS that would ultimately link GP surgeries and hospitals to an NHS-wide information network. The government published an information strategy[11] on 24 September 1998 with a commitment to invest at least £1billion over the lifetime of the strategy. By June 2000, £139 million from the Modernisation Fund had been provided for Information Technology Investment in 2000/01. Investment is also being made in IT access by patients to the NHS. In October 2000, the terms of service for GPs were changed to enable their records to be kept on computers with no requirement for a manual back-up. GPs, however, have a choice. Electronic patient records will increasingly become the norm. Good Practice Guidelines have been drawn up by the Joint Computing Group of the General Practitioners' Committee and the Royal College of General Practitioners.[12] These guidelines will also be of use to other areas within healthcare as they cover such topics as: the purposes of patient records, the legal issues, hardware, electronic record requirements, maintaining security, confidentiality, training and regulatory requirements. Whilst computerisation will resolve some of the problems arising from manually held records, e.g. illegible spelling, the principles of good record-keeping in terms of the content, clarity, and accuracy of the information put onto the computer will still apply. Data Protection requirements on security and access to the data are enforced through the criminal law (see Chapter 8).

Statements

Figure 9.3 illustrates some of the many occasions on which staff may be required to produce a statement. The statements produced on different occasions have very different purposes and effects. For example, where a statement is taken by the police, it can be used as formal evidence in criminal proceedings and the person who made the statement can be questioned on it. Where it has been made under caution, it can be used in evidence against an accused. In civil proceedings, the statement is not regarded as formal evidence, though the civil court now has the power to order disclosure of witnesses' statements.

The purpose of this section is to explore the principles of statement-making and highlight some of the dangers.

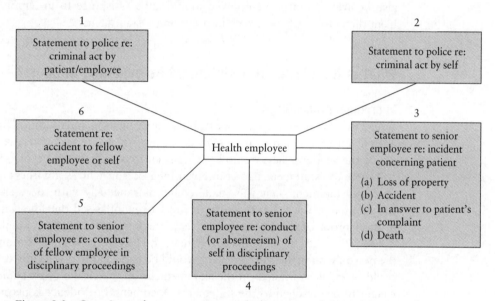

Figure 9.3 Occasions when a statement might be requested: [1 and 2 criminal proceedings; 3(a–c) and 6 civil proceedings; 4 and 5 tribunal proceedings; 3d coroner's proceedings].

Does one have to make a statement?

The one occasion on which one can refuse to make a statement is if it criminally implicates one. No one can be forced to answer a question if the effect of the answer is to incriminate her. There is a right to remain silent when questioned by the police about an alleged offence, but failure to reply can result in an adverse conclusion being drawn about this failure in an address to the jury.

There are considerable advantages in setting out exactly what took place as a record, though help and guidance are clearly essential. In general, a statement is required, not for self-defence, but as evidence of the events to which one was a witness. There have been examples where hospital staff have refused to participate in an inquiry set up by the health authority. For example, in the Shewin case, where a patient went into hospital for a gall-bladder operation and suffered irreversible brain damage, the doctors initially refused to take part in the health authority inquiry. They eventually did so and were exonerated.[13]

In general, it could be argued that provided a member of staff is given appropriate guidance in making a statement, then the statement should be a valuable reminder at a later date of the details of what took place. It has not been tested out in court as to whether the employer could insist upon a statement being made by an employee as a result of an implied term in the contract of employment. However, it could be argued that the National Health Service employee would be expected to co-operate with the police and the coroner's court, and in addition that the employee would give a statement and information relevant to civil claims. It could also be argued that the employee should have assistance from senior managers or from the employer's solicitors in preparing a statement.

What is the status of a statement as evidence in court?

In criminal proceedings

Where the statement forms part of a police investigation and a caution has been given as to its effect, it could be used in evidence against the person who gave it, especially where the account they are now giving is entirely different from the statement.

Where the statement has been given by a person who is a witness of the events, then the statement, if it was made contemporaneously with the events described, can be used as an aid to memory. It must be emphasised that the statement is not in itself proof of the truth of the events therein described. Any number of lies or exaggerations can be recorded in a statement. However, except for certain exceptions, the person who made the statement would be expected to give evidence in court and could be cross-examined on the statement, from which the court could deduce the weight to be attached to the statement. Documentary evidence is permissible under Criminal Justice Act 1988 Ss. 23–28.

In civil proceedings

The statement can be used by its maker to refresh his memory. The court now has access to the statement; it can order disclosure of the witnesses' statements. Written documents can now be entered as evidence under the provisions of the Civil Evidence Act 1968.

Can the court always insist on the statement being produced?

In Chapter 8, the occasions on which documents are regarded as privileged were discussed. Where the statement, document, letter, etc., have come into existence as a result of and for the purposes of proposed or existing litigation, then they are covered by professional legal privilege and the courts cannot enforce disclosure.

Should one make a statement?

A distinction must again be made between the criminal and the civil courts. Where the police are investigating a crime and seeking information from witnesses, then it could be an offence to refuse to co-operate with them. There is, however, no duty to incriminate oneself.

In potential civil cases, there is no duty to make a statement, except possibly under the contract of employment (see above).

However, if one considers the time it takes for a case to come to court – in the civil courts sometimes as long as five or six years – it is highly unlikely that anyone would have a detailed recollection of the facts when they finally come under cross-examination or are giving evidence in chief. A detailed comprehensive statement of the events is essential to refresh one's memory. In addition, a detailed sensibly prepared statement may eliminate the chance of a nurse being called as a witness and thus save a needless attendance in court.

What points should be followed in making a statement?

Purpose?

Before a statement is made, it is always advisable for its maker to have an idea of the purposes for which it is being made. Is it going to the coroner's office? Is it for internal information only? Is it to be used in a criminal prosecution? The purpose will affect the detail, style and content of the statement. The maker should there-fore find out from the person who has asked for the statement who will read it and to what varied purposes it will be put. If there is any danger that the maker would incriminate herself, she should ask for legal advice before making the statement. It is not necessary to wait for a request before writing a statement about a certain occurrence. In some situations, it may be wise for a witness or participant to write down a brief account of the events immediately.

Guidance?

Even in circumstances where there is no question of self-incrimination, it is always advisable to seek advice in making the statement. An objective reader can see gaps, ambiguities and confusion in a statement and give much valuable assistance.

Who should provide the guidance?

Normally a senior nurse manager or the solicitor to the employer should pro-vide this assistance. There will be occasions, however, where advice from a union officer is sought. In disciplinary proceedings, this depends on how far the pro-ceedings have been taken. It would, for example, be contrary to the guidelines for good practice for management to refuse to allow an employee to receive the advice of the union representative prior to any formal disciplinary action being taken.

The essential elements in a statement are shown in Figure 9.4.

(a)   date and time of incident;

(b)   full name of maker, position, grade and location;

(c)   full name of any person involved, e.g. patient, visitor, other staff;

(d)   date and time the statement was made;

(e)   a full and detailed description of the events that occurred;

(f)   signature;

(g)   any supporting statement or document attached.

Figure 9.4   Essential elements in a statement.

Principles to be followed (see Figure 9.5)

1.   Accuracy.

2.   Factual.

3.   Avoid hearsay.

4.   Conciseness.

5.   Relevance.

6.   Clarity.

7.   Legibility.

8.   Overall impact.

9.   Keep copy.

Figure 9.5   Principles to be followed in preparing a statement.

Accuracy

It is essential that the statement should set out clearly the facts that took place. There should be no exaggeration or minimisation. The statement should be read through carefully to ensure that there are no inconsistencies, mistakes or other faults. There should be access to the relevant records so that the statement maker does not rely on memory in preparing the statement. If the record-keeping has been of a high standard, then this will facilitate the writing of the statement.

Factual

The maker should, if at all possible, avoid value judgements and should keep to the facts. For example, a health visitor might have formed the opinion that one of her clients was lazy. If this is relevant to the statement, it is of far more value if she were to write down a description of the facts that led her to that opinion than to make value judgements. Thus 'there were 12 dirty milk bottles on the living room floor and piles of papers on every seat, etc.' is more useful than expressing an opinion that may or may not be acceptable and is not on its own very meaningful. The facts on which those opinions are based are more useful. There are occasions where it is necessary to express opinions, especially where they led one to act in a particular way. Even here, however, it is still necessary to record the facts that led to those opinions. For example: 'Because I felt she was a danger to herself I put the cot sides up.' This statement needs to be amplified in order to expand on what has caused the nurse to believe that the patient was a danger to herself. For example, had she fallen out of bed? Had she tried to leave the ward? Was she in a confused state and if so, how did she show it?

Where it is possible to check facts before making the statement, this should be done. For example, a statement that a patient had a high temperature should be checked against the patient's record; similarly, a description that the patient had been written up for a particular form of medication should be checked against the drug card. Sometimes it is helpful to draw a sketch of the ward layout or where the patient was found or where there is a need to identify the exact location, but only if the plan is a help rather than a further source of confusion.

Avoid hearsay

Hearsay is the recording or repetition of what someone else has seen or heard. If possible, it is best to avoid this as the person making the statement is only repeating what someone else has said and cannot give first-hand evidence of what was heard or seen. Imagine a situation where a nurse hears a fall in the night and runs in to the ward to find a patient on the floor. It is better for her statement to cover what she herself saw and heard rather than to repeat what another employee heard and saw. This other person should be asked to provide a statement of what she witnessed at first hand. Where the only witness to the events may have been another patient, it may be possible to obtain a statement from that patient, but that does depend upon his physical and mental condition.

Concise

The statement must not ramble. It must be to the point in a logical sequence. Padding, waffle, meaningless generalisations should all be avoided. However, essential detail should not be sacrificed on the altar of brevity. The amount of detail required will, of course, depend on the facts described.

Relevance

It is a useful exercise to question oneself on the events to establish what detail a stranger to the situation would require. This questioning would have to take place in the context of the purpose for which the statement is required. In some circumstances, it may be important to describe the colour, material, and style of the patient's clothes – in other circumstances, this may be entirely irrelevant. If there is any doubt as to what is relevant or not, one should err on the side of inclusion. What is in can always be omitted on the grounds of relevance at a later stage; what is left out is left out for good, because such details would soon be forgotten if not recorded.

Clarity

It is essential that the maker should read through the statement to ensure that it is clear and meaningful. If there are any doubts as to what is meant, it should be rewritten until one is sure that it is an exact clear record of what happened. Substitutes for any misleading or ambiguous words or phrases should be found. The use of clichés should be avoided. Abbreviations should be used only after the full terms are set out in full, with the abbreviation set out in brackets after the words. They should not be used for any other meaning. The level of technical language used should relate to the likely readership. In some circumstances, it will be necessary to explain technical procedures in full. In others, there will be no need. Emphasis should be on simplicity rather than complexity. The writer should make sure that he or she understands.

Legibility

If the statement is handwritten, it should be legible. If it is typed at a later date, then the typed copy must be checked for errors.

Overall impact

The statement should be read through and its overall impact assessed. Does it give sufficient detail? Is it clear exactly what happened? Is it accurate? Is there any further information that should be included? Is it internally consistent? Have any facts been checked?

Any necessary changes should be made and the maker should not sign the statement unless he or she is entirely satisfied with it. The maker must be satisfied with every aspect of the statement. The maker must not allow herself to be browbeaten into including information that is not within her knowledge or that she knows is not entirely accurate. Personal accountability must be accepted for the statement. Putting a signature to a statement implies that the maker is satisfied that it is accurate in every detail and she takes personal responsibility for it. A copy should always be kept. The confidentiality of the statement should be protected in accordance with the principles considered in Chapter 8.

Situation 9.1 *Scope of professional practice*

The facts: The Roger Park NHS Trust had agreed with various nursing professional organisations that registered general nurses employed by the Trust would be able to carry out, as part of their expanded scope of professional practice, certain clinical tasks formerly considered to be the sole responsibility of the medical staff. One of these tasks was the setting up of intravenous transfusions. Margery Broome, who had been employed by the NHS Trust for three years as a staff nurse on a surgical ward was off sick when the appropriate course was held (on which she had been selected to go). She thus missed the intense tuition for this skill. No alternative course was suggested to her.

One weekend in December, when Margery was on duty and in charge of the ward, the consultant surgeon, Mr Browne, was on intake and the ward was under heavy pressure. The difficulties were aggravated by the fact that Mr Browne had had a long list on Saturday in an effort to reduce the waiting list (increased as a result of recent industrial action) and to prevent any further build-up before Christmas. Extra beds had been put up in the centre of the ward and the nursing team were particularly harassed because their numbers were reduced by a 'flu epidemic.

Mr Browne's registrar decided that Peter Price, a young man who had been operated on earlier in the week, should receive antibiotics by intravenous transfusion. He recommended that it should be set up immediately. He did not ask Margery if she was eligible to undertake the procedure, nor did she attempt to tell him that she had not yet been on the training course.

Margery collected the IV set and the intravenous antibiotics from the treatment room. She inserted a cannula into a vein in the arm and then set up a saline drip to which she added the antibiotics. Whilst she was finishing this, another staff nurse came to ask if another extra bed could be put up for another emergency admission patient. As Margery Broome indicated where she wished the bed to be placed, she heard a call from another patient and saw that Peter Price had collapsed. She immediately requested that a doctor be called and initiated resuscitative measures. Despite emergency action being taken, Peter Price died. Peter's widow brought an action under the Fatal Accidents Acts and the Law Reform (Miscellaneous Provisions) Act 1934 against Margery Broome, Mr Browne, the registrar and the NHS Trust alleging that their negligence caused the death of her husband. Damages were agreed as being over £100,000. Liability is denied.

Margery Browne's statement: (How many errors can you spot based on the principles already discussed?)

The Death of Peter Price

I certainly remember the day it happened. The morning began with a row with Mr Browne's registrar, Danladi Singh – I'm not racially prejudiced, but I knew from the moment he started that he would be difficult. He never understood the nursing difficulties. He was always admitting patients, never minding how the nursing staff would cope, and since Mr Browne's illness, Singh had made all the decisions. Well, that morning we were on intake, Mr Browne was doing an additional list and Singh wanted me to ask Medical Records to send a telegram to ask the patient to come in the afternoon. Sister was off. I was in charge and I really blew my top. I told him of the difficulties we were in with the flu outbreak and the union dispute. I told him it wasn't fair on the patient – to call her in on a Saturday afternoon. He said it did not matter if it was Christmas Day or Saturday. That's partly the trouble with these foreigners. They don't make any attempt to understand the patients and their ways. Anyway, Singh agreed that he would not call her. I'm sure that it was because of this he then asked me to set up the IV. I knew I had missed the course, but I had seen it done many times by Sister and the doctors. Singh was too bad-tempered to stay and help me, so I started to set it up on my own. I knew that we would soon be having patients back from theatre, so I wanted to get started.

Peter Price was making very good progress. He had had carcinoma of the stomach and I don't think they left much stomach after the operation. Singh always regarded Peter as an aggressive patient, but I never had much trouble with him.

I did not have any difficulty getting the cannula in and I was not aware that he had any allergies to any antibiotics. I still do not know why he collapsed. Just as I was setting the rate of the IV, Janet Pritchard called me about an extra bed that Singh wanted for another emergency patient. I was really incensed. We were too overworked to have extra beds. A patient called out and I saw that Peter Price had collapsed. Pritchard and I rushed to him. I took out the cannula and Pritchard went to get Singh. It seemed as though he had a cardiac arrest or a fit of some sort. He was very blue and I started to do mouth-to-mouth resuscitation. Singh then came and took over. I am sure that the IV had nothing to do with his death.

There can seldom be a statement as bad as this, not only for the irrelevancies that it contains, but also the lack of essential information. The time and date of the events, as well as the time and date of the statement being made, are all missing. The staff on the ward who are potential witnesses should also be named with their appropriate grade. Far more information is required as to what exactly she did with the IV when her attention was diverted as well as more information about patient numbers and more specific information about the pressures: 'too overworked' is meaningless. Specific facts relating to the work pressure should be given along with any information relating to formal or informal complaints to senior nursing staff or medical staff about the pressures. In addition, it is clear that the whole style of the statement is wrong and unprofessional.

Evidence in court

Reference should be made to Chapters 2 and 6 for procedures followed in criminal and civil courts, respectively.

Fears of giving evidence in court

There are few health professionals who relish the possibility of being required to give evidence in court. Preparation and guidance in facing the ordeal are essential, whether it is a criminal court, coroner's court, civil court, professional conduct hearing, or industrial tribunal. Of equal importance, however, are comprehensive, clear and accurate records. Figure 9.6 sets out some of the fears expressed by health visitors (probably the most likely of the nursing profession to face a court appearance).

---

fear of the unknown;
hearing the client call one a liar;
publicity;
waiting and the build-up in tension which can arise;
remembering the detail of what took place;
fear of being made to look a fool;
being unable to express oneself concisely;
contradicting oneself;
omissions in one's statement upon which one could be cross-examined;
being made to feel guilty;
downright rudeness and offensiveness of the others in court, especially the barristers;
tension and nerves;
being turned into the betrayer of the client;
waste of time;
being cross-examined by the client when he is not represented but is conducting his case personally;
failure to understand the legal jargon, the procedure and the gestures;
manipulation under cross-examination and being forced to change one's evidence.

Figure 9.6 Fears over a court appearance.

Preparation for a court appearance

Experience in giving evidence in court will undoubtedly clear some of the anxieties illustrated in Figure 9.6. Many can be solved by a private visit to a court hearing (they are all open to the public except for the few cases such as children's and matrimonial proceedings which are heard in private), and going on one's own or in a group without any personal involvement gives a sense of the procedure and language used and provides a chance of familiarising oneself with the process.

Witnesses are of two kinds: a witness of fact and an expert witness. The witness of fact is required to describe what she saw and did and give direct evidence of the facts in dispute. Her opinion is not usually required. An expert witness, in contrast, provides evidence of opinion of professional practice and approved standards of care, or of causation or the appropriate level of compensation. The expert will be chosen because of her personal standing within a particular specialty.

If a nurse is asked to attend court as a witness of fact, a solicitor would normally assist in explaining the procedure and in preparing the nurse for giving evidence. Considerable expertise can often be built up within a department and the lessons learnt passed from one to another.

Confidence in the records that have been kept and the statements made should ensure that nerves are kept under control. The nurse should know the contents of the original records and where the entries appear so that there is no fumbling through the original records in the course of giving evidence.

Advice on court procedure and giving evidence in court is available from the County Courts or High Court and also from the net at the Lord Chancellor's site.[14] For example, leaflet Ex 341 – w3 is entitled, 'I have been asked to be a witness – What do I do?' It then explains the different court proceedings, the role of a witness of fact, and explains that if the person does not wish to be a witness, then a party to the case can secure a witness summons. Failure to respond to a witness summons can lead to the person being in contempt of court and a fine of up to £1,000. A witness could apply to have the summons withdrawn.

The role of the expert witness is also explained as well as what the report should contain. The advice emphasises that:

> You have a duty to the court to help the court with all matters within your expertise. Your duty to the court overrides any obligations you have to the party instructing you or paying for your reports.

Practical issues such as 'What do I call the judge?' often worry potential witnesses.

- A High Court judge is called 'My Lord' or 'My Lady'.
- A Circuit judge is called 'Your Honour'.
- A District judge is called 'Sir' or 'Madam'.

Advice is also provided by the Royal College of Nursing for nurses asked to give evidence as expert witnesses.[15] The Guidance includes in an appendix a copy of the Civil Procedure Rules 1999 on experts and assessors.

Cross-examination

As far as the cross-examination is concerned, it should be remembered that following a few guidelines should limit the damage to one's evidence in chief.

Go prepared to the court hearing with the relevant records and documentation; read through the contemporaneous notes beforehand; go through the evidence with a senior nurse manager.

In court, be honest; do not exaggerate; do not be drawn into saying something that is not true; do not rush the answers; take time to think.

Be aware of the 'Catch 22' type question:

Q. You are a nurse?
A. Yes.
Q. You are therefore observant?

How do you answer this? If you say, 'Yes', the next questions could be:

Q. How fast was the car going?
A. Er . . . I'm not sure.
Q. But I thought you said you were observant.

If you say, 'No', the next question could be:

Q. Then your observations in this case are entirely useless?
A. Er.

If you answer the original question, 'Sometimes it depends on what I am observing', it is likely to lead to a question or comment such as, 'Then we cannot rely on your evidence in this case'.

Such tactics are unlikely to have any effect on the judge's view, but they can sometimes influence the jury's thinking. (It must be remembered, however, that there is usually no jury in the Civil Court and the nurse's involvement in a jury trial in the Crown Court is likely to be rare.) What is more likely, however, is that the tactics used unnerve the person being cross-examined and cause difficulties for the future. The witness feels discredited. One way of avoiding the Catch-22 question is to expand on the answer so that one is answering fully and accurately.

Q. You are therefore observant?
A. My training has taught me to observe a patient's condition.

It is important under such pressure to avoid becoming angry or upset.

It is important to avoid commenting on the relevance of the question. 'Do I have to answer that question, my Lord?' is fine on a TV drama, but unnecessarily dramatic in court. In most circumstances, one can rely upon one's own lawyer or the judge to protect one from unnecessary harassment.

It must be remembered that in cross-examination there are two purposes. One is to discredit the witness's potentially hostile evidence against a client by showing the witness to be unreliable, dishonest, exaggerated, given to imagination, inconsistent (either internally, i.e. within her own evidence, or externally, i.e. in contrast to what another witness has said or what other evidence shows), unclear, confused, suffering from amnesia, or (and this may be the most effective) irrelevant.

The other purpose of cross-examination is to build up the strength of the side undertaking the cross-examination. Thus, the witness being cross-examined can be used to bolster the good character and reputation of the defendant. 'What were his good qualities?' 'Was she a good mother?' 'Did you see her show any kindness to the child?' 'Did you like her?' is another Catch-22 question since once again to answer negatively implies that the witness being cross-examined is prejudiced; to answer affirmatively shows that the client has likeable qualities.

It is important in this context for the professionals to remember that in cases where they are giving evidence as witnesses as a result of their professional work, they are not on a particular side. They are called to give evidence of facts that they themselves witnessed. Their reputation does not hang upon getting a particular outcome in a negligence case or in a non-accidental injury case. Where the client is personally cross-examining the professional, there should be no sense of betrayal since the professional would have been subpoenaed to attend court and is not there voluntarily.

Defamation

One concern of anyone asked to provide a statement or give evidence is that he or she could face an action for defamation. The main principles of such an action will be discussed very briefly here.

Defamation is either libel or slander. Libel is usually in writing, or at least in a permanent form. Thus broadcasting or a record would be considered to be libel. Slander is the spoken word. The main difference is that to succeed in an action for slander it is necessary to show that harm has occurred as a result of the slander, whereas in an action for libel it is not necessary to establish harm. There are four main exceptions to having to show harm resulting from a slander: imputation of a criminal offence; imputation that the individual suffers from a contagious or infectious disease; accusation of unchastity in a woman; imputations in respect of profession, business or office.

To be defamatory, the statement must tend to injure the reputation of the person to whom it refers, i.e. it tends to lower him in the estimation of right-thinking members of society generally. The statement must be untrue. Truth is a complete defence to an action for defamation. In addition, it must be 'published', i.e. spoken or made to an individual other than the plaintiff. Thus if when we were alone together, I accused you incorrectly of having AIDS, this would not be defamatory since there is no publication. On the other hand, if I said this to someone else about you, it could be actionable.

There are certain occasions that are said to be privileged, i.e. even though the statement is untrue and defamatory, it is not actionable since it is made in privileged circumstances. Some occasions are regarded as absolute privilege, for example, statements made in the Houses of Parliament or in judicial proceedings. Other occasions are considered to have qualified privilege. These include statements made in the performance of duty, in the protection of an interest, professional communications between solicitor and client, or reports of parliamentary, judicial and certain other public proceedings. A statement that is subject to absolute privilege is not actionable, even though the speaker knows that what he is saying is untrue or he is acting out of malice. In contrast, an untrue statement made on a qualified occasion that is actuated by malice is actionable. Malice means the presence of an improper motive, or even gross and unreasoned prejudice. The effect of malice is to destroy the privilege and if the statement is untrue and defamatory, then it is actionable.

References

Situation 9.2   *References*

A ward sister is asked to provide a reference for a staff nurse who has been working on her ward. The staff nurse came under suspicion of theft shortly before this request and the ward sister felt that she would not be honest or accurate if she omitted this fact. The staff nurse failed to get the job she was applying for and subsequently learnt of the contents of the reference. In the meantime, a cleaner was charged and found guilty of the theft. The staff nurse is threatening to sue the ward sister for defamation. Would she succeed?

There is no doubt that to say someone is guilty of theft would be a defamatory statement if it were untrue. However, writing a reference would probably be regarded as an occasion of qualified privilege. If the ward sister wrote the reference without any improper motive, she should have a good defence in an action for defamation. If, on the other hand, she made that statement for some other purpose, then the privilege is destroyed by malice. What if she merely stated that the nurse was under suspicion for theft which would be true? If the words conveyed the impression that there were grounds for considering the nurse to be guilty of theft, then they could be regarded as defamatory and therefore actionable, unless protected by qualified privilege. The Defamation Act 1952 provides defences where an innocent defamation is made.

Liability for references

Any person asked to provide a reference owes a duty of care to both the subject of the reference and also to the recipient of the reference. In the case of *Hedley Byrne v. Heller*, the House of Lords[16] held that a duty of care was owed where a person gave advice that he knew would be relied upon by the person seeking that advice. If the person suffered harm as a result of reliance upon advice that was given negligently, then an action for compensation could be brought against the person who gave the advice. An employer who suffered harm from relying upon a reference, which had been given negligently, could sue for compensation. Alternatively, if the reference contained inaccuracies and had been prepared negligently, the subject of the reference could sue the person providing the reference for harm, including financial loss, arising from the breach of the duty of care owed to him or her.[17]

Conclusions

It is inevitable that given the increase in litigation and complaints greater and greater emphasis is placed upon records and record-keeping in the context of the nurse giving evidence and the nurse is increasingly likely to have to appear in court. However, it must not be forgotten that the most important aspect of record-keeping is the fulfilment of the duty of care to the patient and ensuring that others who care for the patient are fully informed through the records of the action that has been taken or that still needs to be done. If the standard of record-keeping meets the needs for patient care, then they will be of sufficient quality to protect the practitioner should she have to defend her practice in any forum or court of law. Regular audit and monitoring are essential for standards to be set and maintained. If records are maintained at a high standard, then the making of statements and giving evidence in court are greatly facilitated.

Questions and exercises

1   What errors have you noticed in record-keeping? In what ways do you consider that standards of record-keeping could be raised?

2   Prepare a statement concerning an incident that has recently occurred. Read it through and consider if there are any errors.

3   What is meant by hearsay? Give several examples of it.

4   Arrange a visit to court. Write up the points that any potential witness should be aware of in relation to the procedure, formality and language used. If you have the chance to visit more than one court (e.g. Crown or magistrates or County or High Court), draw up a list of the differences between them.

5   What most concerns you about the possibility of giving evidence in court? Prepare a list of your concerns, then consider ways of meeting some of these anxieties.

6   In defamation, information given on a privileged occasion without malice is not actionable, even though it is untrue and defamatory, provided that there is no malice What is meant by this statement? What occasions do you consider could be privileged in this way?

References

[1] UKCC Guidelines for records and record-keeping UKCC 1998

[2] NHS Training Directorate, Just for the Record 1995 NHS Training Division; HSC 1998/217 Preservation, Retention and Destruction of GP Medical Services Records Relating to Patients; HSC 1999/053 For the Record: managing records in NHS Trusts and Health Authorities

[3] Audit Commission, Setting the Records Straight: A study of Hospital Medical Records, Audit Commission, Abingdon 1995

4   Audit Commission, Update Setting the Records Straight, Audit Commission 1999
5   *Deacon* v. *McVicar and another* 7 January 1984 QBD
6   Pat Armstrong, Record Breakers, *Nursing Times* September 8 Vol 95 No 36 p. 34–5 1999
7   Sue Cockbill-Black, Audit describes pressure area care and documentation, *Professional Nurse* December 1999 Vol 15 No 3 pp. 173–6
8   *Professional Nurse*, May 2000 vol 15 No 8 pp. 516–9
9   Deborah Glover, Keep your Record clean, *Nursing Times* December 1 Volume 95 No 48 1999 pp. 26–29
10 DoH White Paper on the NHS, The New NHS – Modern Dependable, Stationery Office 1997
11 NHSE Information for Health 1998 Leeds NHSE
12 Department of Health Electronic Patients Records 3 October 2000 http://www.doh.gov.uk/gpepr
13 1979 BMJ 1232
14 Lord Chancellor's website: www.open.gov.uk/ld
15 Royal College of Nursing, Guidance for Nurse Expert Witnesses RCN 001 084 Jan 2000
16 *Hedley Byrne* v. *Heller* [1963] 2 All ER 575 House of Lords
17 *Spring* v. *Guardian Assurance Co PLC and others*, *The Times Law Report* 8 July 1994

10 The nurse and employment law

The complexities of employment law can be bewildering, yet the nurse needs to know her way through the maze for two basic reasons: on the one hand, she is an employee and therefore should be acquainted with the rights of an employee; on the other hand, she may be or become a manager in which case she will need to be able to advise her staff on their rights and also to understand the relevant employment law covering her role as manager. The areas discussed in this chapter are set out in Figure 10.1. No attempt is made to give the full detail of all the employment statutes but instead the basic principles are set out together with the statutory framework. References are provided so that more detailed information can be obtained.

---

1. The contract:
   A. Formation and contents:
      (a) formation;
      (b) failure to declare a particular medical condition or criminal record;
      (c) are terms agreed at interview binding?
      (d) content of the contract.
   B. Can an employee see or have a copy of the contract?
   C. Changes in the contract.
   D. Breach of contract.

2. Statutory rights:
   A. Rights of the pregnant employee.
   B. Employment Rights Act 1999.
   C. Time-off provisions.
   D. Unfair dismissal:
      (i) general principles;
      (ii) constructive dismissal;
      (iii) the procedure;
      (iv) the hearing.
   E. Statutory sick pay.
   F. Redundancy.
   G. Working Time Directive.
   H. National Minimum Wage.
   I. Part time employees.

3. Trade union rights.

4. Public and private employees.

5. Discrimination by sex or race or disability.

Figure 10.1   Issues covered in Chapter 10

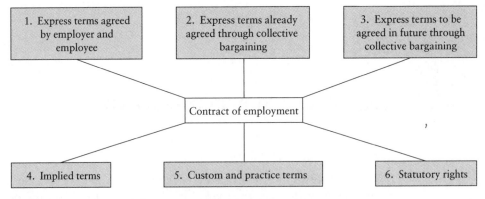

Figure 10.2 Sources of a contract of employment

The legal relationship of employee/employer is composed of many terms drawn from a variety of sources. These are shown in Figure 10.2. First we look at how the contract of employment comes into existence.

The contract of employment

Formation and content

Stages leading to the formation of a contract of employment

When a nurse accepts the offer of a post, a contract then comes into existence and the nurse will be bound by its terms. In this sense the contract is an abstract concept; there may be nothing in writing but the relationship of the parties is radically altered by that agreement.

In any negotiation leading up to a contract of employment there may be many documents circulated: an advertisement, an application form, perhaps a job description, and certainly an interview.

All these stages are known as 'an invitation to treat'. Neither party is bound by them and can usually pull out of the negotiations at any stage. Thus an employer is not bound to appoint after advertising a post. Similarly, someone who has sent in an application form can withdraw at any stage from the field prior to acceptance of an offer. A contract only comes into being once an offer has been accepted. The offer is usually made by the employer. This could be in writing (for example, after holding interviews the applicants could be sent away without knowing the results and be told that they will be notified) or it could be at the actual interview when the applicants wait until the successful one is summoned and offered the post. Sometimes this might be a conditional offer: it might, for example, be an offer dependent on a satisfactory medical examination or references, or the selection panel might not have the power to offer the post but can only recommend to the authority that X be appointed. The candidate should be absolutely clear as to the nature of the offer since if it was subject to approval by a higher authority who did not agree to that appointment, or indeed to any appointment, then the candidate would have no remedy if she has undergone expenses believing that she had a contract, or has even terminated her existing job. If the candidate accepts an unconditional offer then and there she is bound by that contract.

Situation 10.1   Better prospects

A ward sister applies for, is offered and accepts a post in a neighbouring NHS Trust. She then sees a nursing officer post advertised in her own Trust, applies and is accepted before she has commenced work in the new post. What is her position in law?

Technically she is in breach of contract with the neighbouring NHS Trust. She is bound by the contract she has agreed with that Trust. In practice, the Trust is unlikely to take action against her; certainly the publicity that would arise would do little to enhance the reputation of that Trust and the courts are unlikely to order the ward sister to commence work with the new Trust, preferring to compensate by an order for damages to be paid rather than make what is known as an order for specific performance of the contract. The amount payable would be minimal, simply the loss incurred by the Trust as a result of her breach of contract, taking into account the fact that she would have been entitled to give notice immediately.

Failure to declare a particular medical condition or criminal record

Pre employment checks

It is for the prospective employer to ascertain the good and bad about any prospective employee. There is no obligation upon the candidate to present her inadequacies. However, if the applicant is questioned about medical history or criminal record and lies or fails to disclose relevant information, and if this information is later discovered after the applicant has been offered the post and accepted, then the employer is entitled to terminate the contract on the grounds of the misrepresentation provided that he would not have offered the post had he known of the facts. In addition a lie can also be a criminal offence.

The Rehabilitation of Offenders Act 1974 protects those who have a past criminal record from being compelled to disclose it (for example, someone who has been imprisoned for between 6 and 30 months can regard this record as spent after a rehabilitation period of 10 years). However, this Act does not apply to most health service posts and thus the applicant would have to disclose a criminal record when asked. Where the appointment involves working with children, then the employer would be required to check with the Department of Health to ensure that person's name is not contained on lists of those considered unsuitable for such work. In addition, the police should be contacted to ensure that the individual is not on the Sex Offenders' Register. (See below on page 200.)

Situation 10.2   Undisclosed epilepsy

An applicant for a post of nursing auxiliary is not asked and fails to disclose that she suffers from epilepsy. This is discovered subsequently when she has a fit at work. The employers sent her a letter dismissing her. What are her legal rights?

The employers can either give her the requisite notice or they could dismiss her instantly on the grounds that she is not capable of performing the job safely. However, this is subject to the Disability Discrimination Act 1995, which is considered below. If the applicant had lied about her health, this would be taken into account in determining whether a dismissal would be fair. (For her rights to apply for unfair dismissal see page 205.)

Are terms agreed at an interview binding?

It sometimes happens that an applicant at an interview is given certain assurances about the conditions of work: shifts, hours, days off, holiday dates, location of the work place, etc. These terms can be made conditions of the contract. Thus an applicant who had already booked a holiday can obtain an agreement that one of the terms of the contract is that these dates can be retained. Failure to keep to this agreement would constitute a breach of contract by the employer. However, it is a question of fact as to whether the discussion leads to an agreed term or is merely a working arrangement that can be changed by the employer at a later date. In order to safeguard her position, the nurse, in accepting the post in writing, could confirm that certain terms have been agreed as part of the contract. A job description is not regarded in law as setting out terms of the contract. The list of duties contained therein can be changed unilaterally by the employer (within the overall contractual title), and the job description will usually end with a final requirement of 'and any other reasonable instructions of the employer'. This is perfectly lawful since it is an implied obligation on the part of the employee to obey the reasonable instructions of the employer. (See below for implied terms.)

Content of the contract

Figure 10.2 shows sources of the various terms that comprise a contract of employment.

Express terms agreed between employer and applicant

These would include the starting date, the grade and title of post, the point on the salary scale at which the employee would start and many others. It is a matter of interpretation as to how many of the details in the advertisement become terms of the contract.

Express terms already agreed for the post

The bulk of the terms and conditions of posts in the National Health Service are nationally agreed and contained in the Whitley Council Agreements, and the health authority was bound by these. They comprise the General Council Conditions and conditions relating to particular staff groups. The employee's contract should make it clear that it is subject to these nationally negotiated conditions. They should be available for inspection by any employee or applicant. NHS Trusts have power to negotiate terms locally.

Future terms agreed by Whitley Council or set by the Review Body

Even though an employee is not a member of a trade union and not represented on the Whitley Council, the changes and modifications to these terms will be binding on all employees and will usually be incorporated into the individual's contract of employment. At present, the Nurse Pay Review Body recommends revisions to the nurses' pay. NHS Trusts can negotiate terms locally with their employees.

Statutory terms

Additional terms are added by Act of Parliament and are discussed below. These are binding on the employer.

Implied terms

Additional terms are also implied in a contract of employment which place obligations upon the employer or employee. Past court rulings by judges have decided whether certain specific terms should be implied and also what tests should be used to decide if a particular term is implied.

Figure 10.3 sets out implied terms placing obligations on the employer. Figure 10.4 sets out implied terms placing obligations on the employee.

(a)   a duty to take reasonable care for the health and safety of the employee;
(b)   a duty to pay and provide work;
(c)   a duty to treat the employee with consideration and support him.

Figure 10.3   Implied terms binding on the employer.

(a)   a duty to obey the reasonable orders of the employer;
(b)   a duty to act with reasonable care and skill;
(c)   a duty not to compete with the employer's enterprise;
(d)   a duty to keep secrets and confidential information.

Figure 10.4   Implied terms binding on the employee.

Situation 10.3   Implied terms

An emergency arises in Y Hospital following a multiple pile-up on the nearby motorway. A call is put out to those off duty in the nurses' home, which is on site, that help is urgently required. Mavis, a staff nurse who has just come off duty after an eight-hour shift, is asked to return. She refuses, saying she is too tired. She has actually arranged to go out with her boyfriend. Her absence is noted and she is subsequently disciplined. She argued that her off duty was her own time and she had no obligations to the employer during it. Also she was far too tired to be of any assistance and in fact would have been positively dangerous to the patients. The employers, in contrast, might argue that there is an implied term in the contract that even when the employee is off duty, she can still be summoned to assist in an emergency. The outcome of such a case will hinge on whether such a term should be implied and also whether a nurse is correct in refusing to help when she is tired and therefore a potential hazard to the patient.

What tests are used to determine if a term will be implied? The courts have decided that the following tests are appropriate in determining whether a term will be implied. One is known as the Officious Bystander Test. Imagine the following situation: nurse and NHS Trust are discussing the possibility of establishing a contract between them. They are outlining the terms: hours, pay, holidays, etc., and someone over-hearing them asks what happens in an emergency. Does the employer have the right to summon any nurse to return to work? If the negotiating couple were to turn to the questioner and say, 'Of course that goes without saying', then the term would be implied.

Another test used is whether the term is necessary to make business sense of the contract. There is no decided case on the question here, but most nurses would probably agree that such a term would be implied subject to the question of the physical and mental fitness of the nurse to continue to work. In addition, of course, the UKCC states in its Guidelines for Professional Practice that the registered practitioner has a professional duty under the Code of Professional Conduct at all times.

What about Mavis's fitness to work? It is true that an employee who is unfit to work and is likely to be a danger to fellow employees and patients should stay away. However, in an emergency situation, risks might have to be taken and the risk of potential harm to the patient balanced against the value of that additional pair of hands. It would be a question of fact as to where the balance lay.

Terms resulting from custom and practice

This overworked phrase has been used by trade unionists to give contractual force to certain work practices and privileges that were not original terms of the contract. However, the judicial meaning is much narrower and is confined to special trades and works where the nature of the work has led to special terms being implied. To be legally recognised by the courts, a custom must be 'reasonable, certain and notorious'.

Can an employee see or have a copy of her contract?

A statutory right is given to employees to receive a written statement of particulars of employment. Previously, NHS employees, as Crown employees, were excluded from these provisions. However, by Section 60 of the NHS and Community Care Act, health service bodies lost the status of being Crown bodies and all NHS employees now have this statutory right. Employers are required within two months of the commencement of employment, and as soon as possible after any change in the contract, to give written particulars of the terms set out in Figure 10.5. This statement is not the contract itself, but provides *prima facie* evidence of the contractual terms.

(a) Name of employer and employee.

(b) Date when employment (and the period of continuous employment) began.

(c) Remuneration and the intervals at which it is to be paid.

(d) Hours of work.

(e) Holiday entitlement.

(f) Sickness entitlement.

(g) Pensions and pension schemes.

(h) Notice entitlement.

(i) Job title or brief job description.

(j) Period of employment, or date of ending fixed term, if post not permanent.

(k) Place of work or locations if more than one, and the employer's address.

(l) Details of collective agreements affecting employment.

(m) Additional detail if employee is expected to work abroad.

(n) Details of disciplinary and grievance procedures.

Figure 10.5 Written statement of employment particulars.

Changing the contract

Situation 10.4 Job title

A staff nurse was appointed on the basis that she worked on the surgical ward at Roger Park Hospital. After two years, she was asked to work on the medical wards at Green Down Hospital. She was unwilling either to change her specialty or to move from the present hospital. Could she refuse to move?

The answer depends upon whether the location and the specialty are terms of the contract. If they were, then it would be a breach of contract for the employer to change the contract unilaterally. This is because one of the basic principles of contract law is that one party cannot change the terms without the agreement of the other party to the contract. Thus, if these issues are seen to be contractual conditions, then the nurse is entitled to retain them. However, care must be taken in insisting on legal rights since it may be that a redundancy situation exists in which case a nurse who refused unreasonably to accept suitable alternative work would lose both her job and the right to obtain compensation. In addition, if someone has been unfairly dismissed, she has a duty to mitigate the loss (see section on unfair dismissal, page 205).

Often, however, the location and ward are not contractual terms, but simply a working arrangement, in which case they can be reasonably altered by the employer without the consent or the right of refusal of the employee. How does one know if the issue in dispute is a contractual term or not? This would depend upon the nature of the agreement between them, on the letter (if any) offering the post, and on other evidence of the understanding between the parties as to the nature of the contract.

The employer: NHS Trust and Primary Care Trust

Most NHS nurses now work in NHS Trusts. These were set up under the NHS and Community Care Act 1990 and contracts were transferred from health authorities and their directly managed units. Protection is given by Sections 6 and 7 of the 1990 Act to staff who are transferred to NHS Trusts. In addition, Section 33 of the Trade Union Reform and Employee Rights Act 1993, in implementing the Transfer of Undertakings (Protection of Employment) Regulations 1981, makes it clear that protection is provided to the employee whatever the nature of the business or undertaking, and there is a duty to consult with the employees. Section 218(8) of the Employment Rights Act 1996 states:

> that if a person employed in relevant employment by a health service employer is taken into relevant employment by another such employer, his period of employment at the time of the change of employer counts as a period of employment with the second employer and the change does not break the continuity of the period of employment.

Relevant employment includes where persons are engaged by a number of different health service employers whilst undergoing professional training.

Under Section 38 of the Employment Relations Act 1999, the Secretary of State has the power to extend the provisions of the EC transfer of undertakings rules to other employees not covered by the EC regulations.

Under the Health Act 1999, special provisions apply to protection of staff who are transferred from existing employers to work for Primary Care Trusts.

Contracts cannot be changed unilaterally. Where, however, the employee seeks to obtain promotion or change her post she may be asked to accept new contractual provisions which may not be based on Whitley Council Terms and Conditions of Service.

Privity of Contract

There used to be a rule of contract law known as privity of contract whereby only the parties to a contract could enforce it, even though the contract was agreed for the benefit of a third party. However, recent legislation, the Contracts (Rights of Third Parties) Act 1999, enables a third party to enforce the contract in either one of two situations: where the contract expressly provides that he may or where the contract purports to benefit him (unless there is clear provision to the contrary in the contract).

Breach of contract

By employee

The employee, as has been seen, has an implied duty to take reasonable care and skill in his work and to obey the reasonable orders of the employer. If he is in breach of these terms, he can be disciplined. In extreme cases, the employee's actions may justify summary dismissal by the employer. Other rights of the employer include suspension, demotion, warnings, etc.

By employer

The duty to abide by the contractual agreement is reciprocal and the employee is therefore entitled to expect that he will be treated with consideration and that there will be no unilateral change of contract conditions. If it is apparent that the employer is in fundamental breach of contract, then the employee may be able to consider himself constructively dismissed. This is considered below.

Statutory provisions covering employment

The Protection of Children Act 1999 and the Sexual Offenders Act 1997 enable employers to establish if there are grounds for not employing prospective employees.

Protection of Children Act 1999

This legislation has four purposes.

1. It makes statutory the Department of Health's Consultancy Service Index list and it requires child care organisations to refer the names of individuals considered unsuitable to work with children for inclusion on the list.

2. It provides rights of appeal against inclusion.

3. It requires regulated childcare organisations to check the names of anyone they propose to employ in posts involving regular contact with children with the list and not to employ them if listed.

4. It amends Part V of the Police Act 1997 to allow the Criminal Records Bureau to act as a central access point for criminal records information, List 99[1] and the new Department of Health list. In other words, the Criminal Records Bureau will act as a one stop shop in the carrying out of checks.

The effect of the legislation is that organisations working with children, such as local authorities and health trusts, have a statutory duty from 2 October 2000 to vet prospective employees, paid or unpaid, for work involving contact with children. From 9 October 2000, organisations who have registered with the DoH will be able to check names from their own computers via the internet. In October 2000, there were about 1000 names on the DoH Consultancy Service Index,[2] who had been notified to the DoH because they had been dismissed from child care posts or who had left such a post in circumstances where the employer considered that a child would be at risk of harm from them.

Challenging the legal validity of the list

In a recent case,[3] a person challenged the inclusion of his name on the Consultancy Service Index held by the Department of Health to assist prospective employers in child care to decide on a person's suitability to work with children. He had been employed as a child care assistant, but was dismissed after allegations of sexually abusing a foster child and his own children. He lost his claim for unfair dismissal and his appeal. He claimed that the index was ultra vires (i.e. beyond the powers of the organisation), that the inclusion of his name was unreasonable since he had not been convicted and it was a breach of the Convention of Human Rights. The High Court held against him on all three points.

The Sexual Offenders Act 1997

The Sexual Offenders Act 1997 was passed in order to ensure that once a sex offender had served his sentence and was about to be released, he would still be subject to some form of supervision to protect persons against the risk of his reoffending. Part One of the Act requires the notification of information to the police by persons who have committed certain sexual offences.

Statutory rights for employees

Certain Acts of Parliament provide additional rights to employees.[4] The most significant Acts are the Employment Rights Act 1996 and Employment Relations Act 1999. Table 10.1 sets out some of the statutory rights and the minimum time of continuous service that the employee must have in order to claim these rights. They include medical suspension payments, guaranteed pay, rights for the pregnant employee, time off work provisions, rights in relation to trade unions, and many others. In addition, after 2 October 2000, those employees working for a public organisation or an organisation that exercises public functions may have grounds for claiming a breach of their human rights if the employer does not respect the rights set out in the European Convention of Human Rights. (See chapter 1 and appendix A.)

The Employment Rights Act 1996 was aimed at consolidating the laws relating to employment rights and its provisions are shown in Box 10.1

Table 10.1 Statutory rights

Right	Period of continuous employment
Guarantee payment	4 weeks
Not to be dismissed because of medical suspension	4 weeks
Written statement of terms and conditions of employment	4 weeks
Written reasons for dismissal	1 year
Not to be unfairly dismissed	1 year
Maternity rights	
1. Paid time off work to receive ante-natal care	No minimum period
2. Right to return to work after pregnancy	No minimum period
3. Not to be unfairly dismissed on grounds of pregnancy	No minimum period
Redundancy pay	2 years
Not to be dismissed because of trade union activities	No minimum period
Time off for trade union duties, trade union activities and public duties	No minimum period

Box 10.1

Statutory rights set out in the Employment Rights Act 1996

1. Employment particulars

2. Protection of wages

3. Guarantee payments

4. Sunday working for shop and betting workers

5. Protection from suffering detriment in employment

6. Time off work

7. Suspension from work

8. Maternity rights

9. Termination of employment

10. Unfair dismissal

11. Redundancy payments etc

12. Insolvency of employers

Rights of the pregnant employee

These rights have been strengthened by the implementation of the EC Pregnant Workers Directive and recent implementation of rights for parents and those with dependents. No continuous service is required to obtain these rights. These include:

1. the right not to be dismissed on grounds of pregnancy;

2. the right to receive maternity pay;

3. the right to return to work after confinement;

4. the right to attend ante-natal classes;

5. the right to be offered suitable alternative work or be paid during suspension from work on maternity grounds.

Further details of the Statutory Maternity pay scheme are available.[5] In addition to the statutory rights, Whitley Council conditions covering the same field often exist. The employee usually has the right to choose whichever benefits are more favourable to her.

Right not to be unfairly dismissed on grounds of pregnancy

Situation 10.5 Morning Sickness

Barbara is two months' pregnant and suffering very badly from morning sickness and hypertension. Her absence from the ward is causing considerable difficulties and she is not popular with the other staff. She has worked with the authority for three years. It has been agreed that she should be dismissed because of the continual absences. What are her rights?

She is pregnant, a full-time employee for three years and is therefore able to claim the right of not being unfairly dismissed on the grounds of pregnancy. The authority might argue that her pregnancy is making it impossible for her to do her job adequately, there is no suitable alternative work and therefore they are justified in dismissing her. This is, however, no longer an acceptable defence to an application for unfair dismissal on grounds of pregnancy and the employee would probably succeed in her application. No continuous service is required. Furthermore, the employee is entitled to receive pay during a time of suspension from work on maternity grounds, if suspension results from a health ground specified by statute (i.e. pregnancy, birth or breast feeding) or to be offered suitable alternative work. If suitable alternative work is not available, the employee can claim pay during the time of suspension from work. Claims in relation to dismissal on grounds of pregnancy can also be brought under the Sex Discrimination Act (see pages 214).

Maternity right to return to work

In *Halfpenny* v. *IGE Medical System Ltd* 1999,[6] a woman who had left work to have a child, exercised her statutory right to return to work after her maternity leave by giving the appropriate notice. She then sought to delay her return to work on grounds of sickness. The employers allowed a first extension, but then notified her that her job was no longer available. She lost her application for unfair dismissal, wrongful dismissal, and unlawful sex discrimination before the industrial tribunal, and her appeal before the employment appeal tribunal. Her appeal to the Court of Appeal, however, succeeded on the grounds that the exercise of her statutory right to return to work was made complete and effective by the giving of the appropriate notice at the appropriate time. The employers were guilty of unfair dismissal, wrongful dismissal and unlawful sex discrimination.

Dismissal of maternity leave replacement

The European Court in Luxembourg has ruled[7] that, where an employee who was taken on to replace an employee during maternity leave, herself became pregnant and was dismissed, it was an unfair dismissal on the grounds of pregnancy. The facts were that Mrs Webb was recruited with a view initially to replace Mrs Stewart who was to take maternity leave, but following a probationary period would probably continue when Mrs Stewart returned to work. Mrs Webb had not known that she was pregnant when the employment contract was entered into. When the pregnancy was confirmed, she was dismissed.

Her application on the grounds of direct or indirect discrimination on the grounds of sex failed before the industrial tribunal. Her appeals to the employment appeal tribunal and the Court of Appeal also failed. She then appealed to the House of Lords, which referred her case to the European Court of Justice for a preliminary ruling on the effect of Council Directive 76/207/EEC of 9 February 1976 on the implementation of the principle of equal treatment for men and women as to access to employment, vocational training, promotion and working conditions.

The European Court took into account the general context of the measures taken under Council Directive 92/85/EEC of 19 October 1992 to encourage improvements in the safety and health at work of pregnant workers and workers who had recently given birth and were breast feeding, and for special protection to be given to women, by prohibiting dismissal during the period from the beginning of their pregnancy to the end of their maternity leave. The European Court held that this protection of women could not be dependent on whether her presence at work during maternity was essential to the proper functioning of the undertaking in which she was employed. Any contrary interpretation would render ineffective the provisions of the directive. Its decision was therefore that EEC Directive 76/207 precluded dismissal of an employee who had been recruited for an unlimited term with a view initially to replacing another employee during maternity leave, and could not do so because, shortly after her recruitment, she was herself found to be pregnant.

Ante-natal visits

There is a statutory right to attend ante-natal examinations with paid leave. For the first visit, there is no requirement to show the certificate for the expected date of confinement or the appointment card, but for subsequent visits the employer can insist on seeing both. The right is not absolute, however. It depends on the reasonableness of the request and it may be reasonable to refuse such time off if an employee can reasonably make arrangements for an appointment outside normal working hours.

Employment Relations Act 1999

Maternity leave, parental leave and time off for dependants came into force on 15 December 1999. Sections 7–9 and Schedule 4 provide new regulations on parental and maternity leave – a simplified framework of maternity rights and new rights to parental leave and to time off to deal with emergencies affecting dependants. Qualifying employees can exercise the right to parental leave subject to giving notice. Pregnant employees whose expected week of childbirth is 30 April 2000 or later will benefit in full from the changes in maternity leave regulations.

In August 2000, the government announced that it would introduce a scheme whereby parents could obtain paid leave from the state of up to £150 per week to care for newborn babies for the first two weeks of the baby's life.

Leave for family emergencies

This includes unpaid time off if a dependant falls ill, is injured, or assaulted or gives birth; if funeral arrangements need to be made or an employee wants to attend a funeral; if a child is involved in a serious incident at school or during school holidays; or if childcare arrangements break down.

Maternity pay

Statutory Maternity Pay Scheme (SMP): this came into force on 6 April 1987. This is in addition to any rights that the woman has from her employer, but payment under the state scheme will be regarded as part payment by the employer. An employee who has been continuously employed by the same employer for at least 26 weeks continuing into the 15th week before her baby is due (i.e. the qualifying week) and whose average earnings are not less than the lower earnings limit for the payment of National Insurance contributions and who is still pregnant or has had the baby and has stopped working by that time is eligible to receive SMP.

Time-off provisions

Paid or unpaid time off (depending on the benefit) is also a statutory right and can be seen in Figure 10.6 Again, there are comparable Whitley Council rights and the employee is entitled to choose whichever is more advantageous.

In Situation 10.6 rearranging a timetable, Mary took the case to an industrial tribunal and won since it was held that rearranging a timetable was not giving time off. However, Mary was still receiving her full pay and the time-off provisions were only for unpaid time off. (The school could have reduced her work load, reduced her salary accordingly, and then employed a locum to teach in Mary's place with the money saved. Mary might have preferred the existing arrangements!)

Time off for:

1. Trade union duties (officer): reasonable paid time off to carry out duties in connection with industrial relations and for training relevant to carrying out those duties (reasonable defined in ACAS Code of Practice No 3).

2. Trade union activities (member): reasonable unpaid time off during working hours to take part in TU activities (see ACAS Code of Practice No 3).

3. Public duties – local authority member, school governor, JP: reasonable unpaid time off (take into account time off given in relation to 1 or 2 above and other public duties).

4. To seek job in redundancy situation: reasonable paid time off to seek work or seek retraining.

5. Jury service: unpaid time off.

6. Health and safety representative: reasonable paid time off to perform function and train for it.

Figure 10.6 Time-off provisions.

Situation 10.6 *Rearranging a timetable*

Mary Briggs was a nurse tutor. She was also very involved in local government and had recently been elected as leader of the opposition on the County Council. She was appointed to several sub-committees. She applied for time off to attend the meetings. The principal was extremely helpful and rearranged her timetable so that she would not have to teach in the afternoons when the council meetings took place. Mary complained that her work load had not decreased and she now found that she was having to spend several evenings doing work which normally she would have done during her free periods which had now been lost.

Unfair dismissal

General principles

One of the most important of the statutory rights is the right not to be unfairly dismissed. Every employee has a right by virtue of his contract, statute or the common law (see below) to receive notice unless the employee is himself in breach of contract and is summarily dismissed. Thus a nursing officer who has worked for 20 years with that employer could lawfully be given her requisite notice under the contract with no particular reasons for the notice being specified and be lawfully dismissed. This would be contractually acceptable, but highly unjust. The right not to be unfairly dismissed protects employees who meet certain conditions against this unjust treatment. The Sections 94 to 132 of the Employment Rights Act 1996 set out the provisions relating to unfair dismissal. There is also a right not to suffer a detriment or dismissal in health and safety cases. It is unfair to dismiss an employee in circumstances arising out of health and safety matters, e.g. carrying out health and safety activities at the request of the employer, being a safety representative or a member of a safety committee, bringing the employer's attention to harmful circumstances, refusing to work in dangerous conditions, or taking appropriate steps to protect himself or others from damage. The Public Interest Disclosure Act 1998 extends these provisions and protects an employee from victimisation where the employee has made a protective disclosure in accordance with the provisions of this Act (see Chapter 4).

The conditions that the employee must satisfy to bring an action for unfair dismissal are set out in Figure 10.7. If these conditions are met, the employee can then, within three months of the dismissal, apply to the industrial tribunal for an unfair

---

(a) 1 years' continuous service with that employer (except in cases of trade union activity or discrimination) and dismissal on grounds of pregnancy or childbirth;

(b) be eligible under the legislation;

(c) be below retirement age;

(d) be dismissed (i.e. termination by employer, expiry of fixed-term contract or constructive dismissal).

Figure 10.7 Conditions for bringing an unfair dismissal action.

dismissal hearing. The three months' time limit can be extended if the tribunal considers that it was not reasonably practicable for the employee to comply with it.

Unfair dismissal and long hours

Case 10.1   Long hours[8]

Annette Cowley claimed unfair dismissal from her job as a cargo officer following her complaint of excessively long hours: she was required to work 16-hour shifts and claimed that she was unable to care for her baby properly. She said that working back-to-back shifts meant getting up at 5 a.m. to prepare her baby's food for the day, arriving for work at 7.45 a.m., finishing at 10 or 11 p.m., getting to bed at 1.00 a.m. and rising again at 5.00 a.m.

The employment tribunal found that she had been unfairly dismissed because the long hours discriminated against her on grounds of her sex. The airline was ordered to pay her three years' pay and was criticised over the wholly unreasonable demands over hours.

Refer to the working time directive discussed below on page 209.

Unfair dismissal and length of continuous service and compensation
The qualifying period for bringing unfair dismissal claims was reduced in 1999 from two years' continuous service to one year's continuous service. The maximum compensation was raised from £12,000 to £50,000. Larger amounts can be paid following awards under sex discrimination, equal pay and whistle blowing victimisation claims.

Constructive dismissal

Situation 10.7   Dangerous conditions

Kay was a nursing officer in charge of the acute wards of Roger Park Hospital. She had warned the senior managers that the situation was dangerous since, due to an acute shortage of nurses which coincided with a vigorous attempt to reduce the waiting lists, with extra beds being put up on all the wards, there was a danger that accidents could happen. No notice was taken of her warnings and in fact more patients were admitted. She advised the consultants that nurses would not be able to carry out certain tasks normally undertaken by doctors and that the junior doctors would be expected to add the drugs to intravenous transfusions. Her senior nurse manager was advised by the consultants that this was unacceptable and Kay was asked to withdraw that instruction and notify the nurses that they must continue to undertake such tasks. She pointed out that they did not have the time to do these. She was warned that she would face disciplinary proceedings if she continued to defy the managers. She said she would prefer to leave than endanger the lives of patients and stated that the managers were in breach of contract in failing to support her attempt to maintain professional standards. She left and subsequently brought an action for unfair dismissal.

Assuming that Kay qualifies as far as the conditions set out in Figure 10.7 are concerned, she needs to establish as a preliminary point that she was dismissed and did not resign. The employers are likely to argue that they did not dismiss her, that she left work of her own free will, and that she is therefore ineligible to bring an unfair dismissal action.

The question is: have the managers acted in such a way that she is entitled to see the contract as at an end? It will be remembered that one of the implied terms in a contract of employment is that the employer will act reasonably towards the employee and support him. It could be argued here that in failing to support Kay's endeavours in this situation, the employers are in fundamental breach of contract. If this can be established, then Kay can argue that there is a constructive dismissal, she is entitled to bring her action before the tribunal and it is then for the managers to establish that the dismissal was fair. On the other hand, the employers will be arguing that Kay was not dismissed, that she had failed to do all she could to work with them, and that she had defied reasonable orders from them. Kay should also refer to the Public Interest Disclosure Act 1998 to show that her concerns about health and safety come under the disclosures protected by that Act and that she followed the procedure required by the Act (see Chapter 4 on whistle-blowing). Ultimately, the outcome will depend upon the evidence from both sides: Kay would have to show evidence, both documentary and through witnesses, of earlier attempts to persuade management that the situation was dangerous and that the managers were acting in fundamental breach of contract.

Case 10.2   Fair dismissal

The Court of Appeal heard a case where a senior nurse had been dismissed for failure to wear the appropriate uniform. They held that the dismissal was fair.[9]

Procedure in an application for unfair dismissal

The employee is normally expected to exhaust the internal appeal machinery set up by her employer before an application to an employment tribunal is heard. But owing to time limits (an application for unfair dismissal should be brought within three months of the date of dismissal, if reasonably practicable), the employee should instigate the application in any case and ask for an adjournment pending the outcome of the internal appeal. In this way, she will not be out of time. Following the application to the employment tribunal, there will be attempts by the Advisory, Conciliation and Arbitration Service (ACAS) to resolve the dispute. ACAS has published a new Code of Practice on the disciplinary practice and procedures in employment (revised 1998).[10] From September 2000, employers must comply with the new Code. This requires that disciplinary rules and procedures are clearly set out and accessible to the employees. Failure by any employer to follow the ACAS guidelines will not make the employer liable to proceedings in itself, but evidence of this failure could be used against the employer in evidence before an employment tribunal. Since September 2000, employees have had a statutory right to be accompanied at any

> (a) capability or qualifications;
> (b) conduct;
> (c) some other substantial reason;
> (d) redundancy;
> (e) statutory prohibition;
> (f) lock out or participation in strike or industrial action;
> (g) national security.

Figure 10.8 Statutory reasons to dismiss.

disciplinary or grievance hearing. Failure by the employer to permit the employee to be accompanied or to postpone (for up to five days) a hearing to enable the person to attend can lead to up to two weeks' compensation payable to the employee.

Unfair Dismissal – time limit for applications   There is a time limit of 3 months from the dismissal within which an application must be made to the tribunal. However, the tribunal can dispense with this limit if to keep to the time limit was not 'reasonably practicable or feasible'. In one case,[11] the Court of Appeal held that reasonably practicable required that the full circumstances of the applicant's failure to apply within the time limit had to be taken into account, including the aim to be achieved. In the facts of this case, the applicant was suffering from depression and had been trying to avoid litigation by pursuing alternative remedies. New procedures that came into force in November 2000 enable employees seeking to bring applications before an employment tribunal to brief a barrister direct without having to hire a solicitor first. It is estimated that the costs of bringing an action will be reduced by a third to a half. In 1999, 104,000 claims were lodged with tribunals, although only 26,000 came to a hearing, the rest being settled or disposed of.

The hearing   If the employee is able to show that she satisfies the conditions set out in Figure 10.7, the burden will be on the employer to show that the dismissal was based on a statutory reason. These are set out in Figure 10.8. The tribunal must then decide if the employer has acted reasonably in treating this reason as sufficient to justify dismissal. The criteria that have been considered by the tribunals in determining the reasonableness of employers' actions are set out in Figure 10.9. Every circumstance must be taken into account, and the fact that the tribunal might not have acted in the way in which the particular employer acted is not relevant. The crucial question is: was *that* employer acting reasonably? One important point is whether the disciplinary code of practice and the guidelines prepared by ACAS were followed (see above).

The outcome   If the employee's application for unfair dismissal is upheld, the following remedies are available to the tribunal:

1. Reinstatement/re-engagement.
2. Compensation – basic award; compensatory award; special award.

In assessing compensation, the tribunal will take into account any fault on the part of the employee.

(a) code of practice (a recent case has emphasised the importance of following the code of practice, even if following it would make no difference to the outcome);

(b) nature of employment situation, e.g. size and resources of organisation, type of work;

(c) consistency of employer;

(d) timing of dismissal;

(e) length of service of employee;

(f) in cases of dishonesty and other misconduct:
   (i) the employer must show that he genuinely believes the employee to be guilty of the misconduct in question;
   (ii) he must have reasonable grounds on which to establish that belief;
   (iii) he must have carried out such investigation into the matter as was reasonable in all the circumstances;
   British Home Stores v. *Birchell* 1980 I RLR 379;

(g) principles of natural justice.

Figure 10.9 Criteria for the reasonableness of the employer.

Statutory sick pay scheme (SSP)

Most NHS employees enjoy six months' full pay and six months' half-pay while absent on grounds of sickness. The employer is able to recover some of this from the statutory sick pay scheme. Details of the operation of the scheme are available from the Department of Trade and Industry.

All employers can offset any contractual liability to pay sick pay against their payments under SSP.

Redundancy

The NHS has its own redundancy scheme set out in the Whitley Council general conditions of service. It broadly follows the statutory scheme from the point of view of consultation when redundancies are envisaged. However, the NHS has a much wider definition of suitable alternative work.

Surveillance by employers

The European Court of Human Rights, in the case brought before it by Alison Halford, held that her rights of privacy had been invaded when her employers, the Merseyside Police Authority, intercepted the private telephone calls she made from the office. The court held, however, that provided that the employer warned the employees that their calls could be tapped, there would be no breach of the right to privacy as guaranteed by the European Convention. Similar cases are likely to arise under Article 8 of the Convention and the right to respect for privacy and family life (see Chapter 1).

Working Time Directives

A directive had been adopted by the member states of the European Community on 23 November 1996, but implementation in the UK was delayed until 1 October 1998, when the Working Time Regulations[12] came into force.[13]

The main principles

The fundamental provision is that a worker's working time, including overtime, should not exceed an average of 48 hours for each seven days over a specified period of 17 weeks. Regulations also specify provisions for rest breaks and annual leave. Night work should not normally exceed an average of 8 hours for each 24 hours. The employer has a duty to ensure that no night worker, whose work involves special hazards or heavy physical or mental strain, works for more than 8 hours in any 24 hour period. Before assigning a worker to night work, the employer has to ensure that the worker has the opportunity of a free health assessment before he takes up the assignment. There should be a weekly rest period of not less than 24 hours in each 7 day period, or alternatively 2 rest periods each of not less than 24 hours in each 14 day period, or one rest period of not less than 48 hours in each 14 day period.

Employers are required to keep records relating to the hours of work which can be inspected by enforcement agencies. The Health and Safety Executive and Local Authority Environmental Health Officers are responsible for enforcing the working time limits. Individual employees can, if internal appeals mechanisms fail, apply to the Employment Tribunals for alleged infringements of their statutory rights. The application must be made within 3 months of the infringement and the Advisory, Conciliation and Arbitration Service (ACAS) will provide conciliation services. The European Court of Justice has held the UK requirement of 13 weeks work before being eligible to have annual leave illegal. (*R v. S..S for Trade and Industry, The Times Law Report* 28 June 2001.)

UKCC Practitioners

Doctors in training and civil protection services (ambulance) are specifically excluded from the regulations. UKCC practitioners are not specifically excluded. However, they come within the definition of the group:

> where the worker's activities involve the need for continuity of service or production, as the case may be, in relation to:
>
> i.   services relating to the reception, treatment or care provided by hospitals or similar establishments, residential institutions and prisons.

The effect of this is that the regulations on night work, daily rest, weekly rest period, and rest breaks do not apply to UKCC practitioners where there is a need for continuity of service. However, Regulation 24 requires that where a worker is required to work during a period that would otherwise be a rest period or rest break, the employer shall wherever possible allow her to take an equivalent period of compensatory rest and, in exceptional cases, where this is not possible, the employer shall afford her such protection as may be appropriate in order to safeguard the worker's health and safety.

Working hours

The General Whitley Council (GWC) has agreed the implementation of the regulations for non-medical staff.[14] Section 44 of the GWC Handbook sets out the new provisions that apply to all non-medical staff. A UKCC practitioner will normally not be expected to work more than 48 hours per seven day period calculated over an averaging period of 17 weeks. Locally recognised unions could agree that the period of 17 weeks could be extended up to a maximum of 25 weeks.

Definition of working time
Working time means:

1. any period during which the employee is working at the employer's disposal and carrying out her activity or duties;
2. any period during which she is receiving relevant training; and
3. any additional period that is to be treated as working time for the purpose of these regulations under a relevant agreement.

Working longer than 48 hours a week
Individual employees can, if they wish, agree to work more than the average of 48 hours a week. However, this must be an individual decision. It cannot be negotiated as part of the collective agreement and it must be agreed in writing by the employee. The employee should not be placed under pressure to agree to a longer time. The employee can end the agreement by giving notice to the employer, as specified in the agreement, or if no notice time is specified, then seven days' notice must be given. The employer is required to keep records of this agreement, and the term of notice and the number of hours worked since the agreement came into effect.

Helplines are available for those applying the regulations.[15] The Welsh Assembly has issued a circular on the most frequently asked questions.[16] Doctors in training were initially excluded, but are gradually being brought within its scope.[17]

National Minimum Wage (NMW) Act 1998
From 1 April 1999, employers have been obliged to pay a minimum wage to employees. At the time of writing, this is fixed at £4.00 per hour for those over 21 years and £3.00 per hour for those between 18 and 21 years. Employees can appeal to an employment tribunal without any continuous service requirement if they are dismissed because they qualify for the NMW or because they have attempted to enforce the NMW right.[18]

Part-time employees
On 1 July 2000, regulations came into force to prevent part-time workers being treated less favourably than full-time workers,[19] implementing the European Directive.[20] Paragraph 5 of these regulations gives the part-time worker:

> the right not to be treated by his employer less favourably than the employer treats a comparable full-time worker as regards the terms of his contract, or by being subjected to any other detriment by any act, or deliberate failure to act of his employer.

The right applies only if the treatment is on the ground that the worker is a part-time worker and the treatment is not justified on objective grounds. The part-time worker has to compare himself with full-time workers working for the same employer. The right also applies to workers who become part time or, having been full time, return part time after absence, to be treated not less favourably than they were before going part time. It does not give an employee the right to insist on having part-time work.

The regulations (para. 6) also entitle a worker, who considers that he has been treated in a manner that infringes this right, to request from his employer a written statement giving particulars of the reasons for the treatment. The worker must be provided with a statement within twenty-one days of his request. Failure to provide a statement at all or only in an evasive or equivocal way will enable the tribunal to draw any inference that it considers just and equitable to draw, including an inference that the employer has infringed the right in question. The regulations also protect the part-time worker from unfair dismissal and give a right not to be subjected to any detriment (para. 7).

Any worker who considers that his rights have been infringed can present a complaint to an employment tribunal within three months of the day of less favourable treatment or detriment taking place. This is subject to the right of the tribunal to consider out-of-time cases, if in all the circumstances it is just and equitable to do so.

Trade union rights

It is impossible in a work of this nature to be other than superficial in relation to the status and powers of trade unions. Reference should be made to the bibliography on special books in this field. Figure 10.10 illustrates some of the present rights of the independent trade union. The principal Acts are the Employment Relations Act 1999, and the Trade Union and Labour Relations (Consolidation) Act 1992 as amended by the Trade Union Reforms and Employment Rights Act 1993.

Schedule 1 of the Employment Relations Act 1999 sets out details for the recognition of trade unions for collective bargaining purposes, including voluntary recognition, changes affecting the bargaining unit and derecognition. Part VII of the Schedule provides details of the right of a worker not to be subjected to any detriment by any specified act in relation to bargaining. Schedule 3 regulates the holding of ballots for union membership.

Over the last ten years, the power of the unions and employers to enforce a closed shop situation has decreased so that since the Employment Act 1988, the dismissal of a non-unionist in a closed shop situation is now automatically unfair. The 1992 Act gives protection to employees against exclusion or expulsion. The employer cannot prevent anyone from joining an independent trade union. The unions have the right to obtain information relevant to collective bargaining and also to receive notice of any redundancies. A union member should be allowed the presence of a union officer at any disciplinary proceedings. Under health and safety legislation, safety representatives appointed by trade unions have the right to visit the workplace and to inspect the site of any accident. Officials of trade unions have the right to reasonable paid time off for the purposes of their activities in relation to collective bargaining or representing their members, and for training for such purposes. The members, however, only have the right of reasonable unpaid time off work for union activities. Employees have the right not to be dismissed for being, or refusing to be, union members or for taking part in union activities.[21]

1. A union is independent if it is not under the domination or control of an employer, and not liable to interference by an employer. Its independence can be certified by the certification officer, and his certificate is conclusive evidence that the union is independent.

2. Independence is an essential feature if the union is to enjoy the following statutory rights:
   (a) to take part in trade union activities;
   (b) to be given information and be consulted over 'Transfers of Undertaking';
   (c) to gain information for collective bargaining;
   (d) to secure consultation over redundancies;
   (e) to insist on time off for trade union duties and activities;
   (f) to appoint health/safety representatives.

3. A trade union is fully liable for any of its acts which constitute a tort (civil wrong) EXCEPT where it acts in contemplation or furtherance of a trade dispute. The meaning of these words has been narrowed since 1980 so that in general secondary action (e.g. where employees of A go on strike to support the employees of B) is not covered, and therefore the union would be liable for the damage that results from the unlawful action.

4. Safety representatives appointed by a recognised trade union from among the employees.
   Names to be notified to the employer in writing shall represent employees in consultation with the employer under Section 2(4) and (6) of the Health and Safety at Work Act 1974. Functions set out in Regulation 4 of Section 1. 1977 No. 500.
   (a) Investigate potential hazards and dangerous occurrences at workplace and examine cause of accidents at work.
   (b) Investigate complaints of employees relating to health, safety or welfare at work.
   (c) Make representations to employer under (a) and (b).
   (d) Make representations to employer on general matters affecting health, safety or welfare.
   (e) Carry out inspections under Reg. 5, 6 and 7.
   (f) Represent employees in consultation with Health and Safety Inspectorate.
   (g) Receive information from inspectors under Section 28(8).
   (h) Attend meetings of safety committees.

   No function given to a safety representative by this paragraph shall be construed as imposing any duty on him.

Figure 10.10   Trade union rights and the role of safety representatives.

The trade union officers do not have any management rights: they have no power as part of their function as union officials to give orders to the employees. Obviously, they might advise their members to follow a particular course, but it is up to the members' own judgement whether they follow the advice or not. The Employment Act 1988 gave additional protection to the employee: he has the right not to be denied access to the courts by union rules; the right not to be unjustifiably disciplined by a union; the right to complain to an industrial tribunal and obtain compensation if this latter right is infringed.

Public and private employees

Those nurses who work as employees in the private sector enjoy much the same rights as those who work in the NHS. There are, however, some major differences. If the nurse is only one of a few employees, then she may not enjoy all those statutory rights enjoyed by those working for employers of large concerns. This also applies to those NHS nurses who work for single-handed general practitioners or group practices.

In addition, they may not be subject to Whitley Council conditions of service. In this case, there will be other provisions relating to holidays, pay, sick pay, pensions, time off, etc., which will either have been laid down in advance or which will have to be agreed with the employer. The nurse should make sure that she is aware of these provisions before she accepts the post.

Discrimination by sex or race

The Race Relations Act 1976 and the Sex Discrimination Acts 1975 and 1986 outlaw discrimination in employment, education, housing or the provision of goods, facilities, and services on grounds of race, colour, nationality, or ethnic or national origins, sex, and marital status. Referral can be made to the European Court of Justice if there is doubt over the application of its directives on equal pay and equal treatment to domestic law. (See the unfair dismissal and sex discrimination case of Seymour-Smith.[22])

Direct discrimination

This is where one person treats another less favourably on the grounds of sex, race or marital status than he would treat another person of another sex, race or marital status. The two questions that the tribunal would have to determine under the Act are: has the person been discriminated against? And is the cause of that discrimination one of the forbidden grounds?

Indirect discrimination

This is where a condition is applied to persons so that the following prevail:

1. The proportion of people of one race or sex who can comply with it is considerably smaller than the proportion of another.
2. The employer cannot show the condition is justifiable on other than racial or sexual grounds.
3. The condition is to the detriment of the complainant because he cannot comply with it.

Victimisation

This indirect form of discrimination is also prohibited under the legislation and covers the situation where a person is treated less favourably because he brings proceedings, gives evidence or information, alleges a contravention or otherwise under the Acts, or intends to do any of these things.

Segregation

It is unlawful to maintain separate facilities for members of different races. There is no such law in relation to different sexes.

The areas covered by the laws against discrimination are shown in Figure 10.11.

The discrimination laws are wider than much of the employment legislation. For example, they cover an applicant for a post, as well as independent contractors and the self-employed. Along with employers, the following are subject to the laws: trade unions, partnerships, qualification bodies for trades and professions and vocational training, employment agencies, the Manpower Services Commission, and the Crown.

Greater Manchester Police agreed to pay £30,000 to a black musician who said that he was twice beaten up by officers.[23] It has been held[24] that the words 'in the course of employment' in Section 32(1) of the Race Relations Act 1976 were not to be construed restrictively by reference to case law on the law governing vicarious liability. So an employee's racially abusive acts did not have to be connected with acts authorised to be done as part of his work so as to make the employer liable.

Arrangements for recruitment.
Advertisements.
Refusal or deliberate omission to offer employment.
Terms and conditions of service.
Access to transfer or promotion.
Access to training.
Fringe benefits.
Dismissal.
Any other detriment, e.g., full-time working is made a requirement.

Figure 10.11 Areas covered by discrimination.

Exceptions to laws on discrimination

These are listed in Figure 10.12 for discrimination on grounds of sex and Figure 10.13 for discrimination on grounds of race. One of the most important is 'the genuine occupational qualification', i.e. that the employer can justify discrimination because of the particular characteristics of the post. For example, the employment of Chinese people in a Chinese restaurant may be justifiable.

Applications for compensation for discrimination on grounds of sex or race can be made to the employment tribunal. In the case of discrimination on grounds of sex, the European Court held in the case of *Marshall* v. *Southampton AHA* (No. 2)[25] that the upper limit fixed by statute on the payment of compensation infringed the European Equal Treatment Directive which, since November 1993, applies to both public and private sector employees.

Subsequently, substantial sums have been awarded to women who have lost their jobs through dismissal on grounds of pregnancy. On 29 July 1994, the Employment Appeal Tribunal held, in the case of the Ministry of Defence's appeal against the decision in *Cannock* (awarded £172,000 by a tribunal)[26] and other similar awards,

Sex

1. Sex of a person is a genuine occupational qualification for the job:
   (a) The essential nature of the job calls for a man because of his physiology.
   (b) A man is required for authenticity in entertainment.
   (c) The job needs to be held by a man or woman in order to preserve decency or privacy because
      (i) it is likely to involve physical contact with a person in circumstances where that person may reasonably object to it being carried out by a person of the opposite sex;
      (ii) persons of one sex might reasonably object to the presence of the other sex because they are in a state of undress or using sanitary facilities (e.g. lavatory attendants).
   (d) Job is at a single-sex establishment – hospital, prison, etc.
   (e) Holder of post provides individuals with personal services promoting their welfare or education which can most effectively be provided by one sex.
   (f) Job needs to be held by a man because of restriction imposed by laws regulating the employment of women.
   (g) Job likely to involve work abroad which can only be done by men (e.g. Middle East).
   (h) Job is one of two which are to be held by a married couple.
   (i) Employee is required to live on premises.
2. Other exceptions
   (a) Acts done to safeguard national security.
   (b) Undertakings with less than five employees.
   (c) Ministers of religion.
   (d) Sports and sports facilities.
   (e) Special treatment afforded to women in connection with pregnancy or childbirth.
   (f) Provisions in relation to death or retirement (subject to 1986 Act).

Figure 10.12 Exceptions to unlawful discrimination on grounds of sex.

A genuine occupational qualification requires a particular race, e.g.:

(a) authenticity in entertainment;

(b) employee provides personal services towards the welfare or education of others;

(c) a member of a particular race is required for reasons of authenticity in art or photography;

(d) a bar or restaurant has a particular setting (e.g. Chinese restaurant) for which a person of that racial group is required for reasons of authenticity;

(e) immigration rules, civil service regulations which restrict those eligible for Crown employment;

(f) acts done to safeguard national security.

Figure 10.13 Exceptions to unlawful discrimination on grounds of race.

that the assessment of awards in the future by industrial tribunals should assess the chances of a woman returning to work and make a percentage award on that basis.

However, the European Commission has not made comparable directives in relation to discrimination on race-related grounds and the upper ceiling on compensation still applies to those claims.

Discrimination in the NHS

A new action plan called 'Tackling racial harassment' in the NHS was launched in February 1999 by Alan Milburn, Health Minister. He described it as 'the most concerted drive the NHS has ever seen on the issue'. The Plan envisaged that by April 2000 every NHS employer will need to be in position to tackle racial harassment whether committed by staff or by patients.

The NHS Executive has established an Equal Opportunities Unit. It holds regional seminars and is available to assist on equal opportunities policies and current practice.[27]

Male midwives

Originally midwifery was one of the exemptions to the Sex Discrimination Act 1975 and the employment and training of men as midwives was restricted. However, under Order 1983 SI No. 1202, the exemptions were brought to an end. The health authorities were notified that when implementing these legislative changes they must make appropriate arrangements to ensure that:

1. women have the freedom of choice to be attended by a female midwife;
2. where male midwives are employed, provision is made for them to be chaperoned as necessary.

Equal pay

The Equal Pay Act 1970, as amended by subsequent legislation, aims at preventing discrimination as regards terms and conditions of employment between men and women. Central to its provisions is the concept of an equality clause which is to be implied into the contract of a woman who can show she is either employed in like work with a man at the same establishment, or at an establishment where similar terms and conditions are applied, or has been the subject of a Job Appraisal scheme or performs work of equal value.

The Act and Article 119 of the Treaty of Rome enable an employee to claim equal pay in comparison with a person of the opposite sex who is employed by the same employer at the same establishment if she or he is doing the same job or a job of equal value. Thus men as well as women can bring a claim under these provisions.

Domestics, cleaners, ward assistants and cooks, who did not receive bonuses paid to men who did comparable work at the Hartlepool and East Durham NHS Trust, won their case for lack of equal pay in April 1999.[28] They were to receive up to £3000 each in an out of court settlement.

Speech Therapist case[29]

Speech therapists had complained that their lower salaries in comparison with other health professionals, e.g. pharmacists, was a breach of the equal pay legislation. The Court of Justice of the European Communities held that it was for the employer to prove that the difference was based upon objectively justified grounds unrelated to any discrimination on grounds of sex. The fact that the rate was arrived at by collective bargaining did not mean that it was not discriminatory. It was for the national court to determine, if necessary by applying the principle of proportionality, whether and to what extent the shortage of candidates for a job and the need to attract them by higher pay constituted an objectively justified economic ground for the difference in pay between the jobs in question.

The European Court of Justice can review the compatibility of the law in member states with EC Directives. For example, in the Boyle case it reviewed the validity of the maternity leave and pay conditions in the employment contracts of six women who were employed by the Equal Opportunities Commission.[30] The European Court of Justice held that the maternity scheme did not infringe the principles of equal pay or equal treatment, except in respect of the pension provision. The clause that limited the accrual of pension rights during maternity leave to those periods of paid leave was unacceptable. It should have covered unpaid leave.

Disability Discrimination Act 1995

The Disability Discrimination Act 1995 provides disabled people with protection from discrimination in the areas of:

1. access to goods, facilities and services;
2. buying or renting land and property; and
3. employment.

The main sections of the Act are shown in Figure 10.14.

It has been illegal for businesses and organisations since 2 December 1996 to treat disabled people less favourably than other people for a reason related to their disability. From 1 October 1999, service providers have to take reasonable steps to change practices and procedures that make it unreasonably difficult for disabled persons to use a service. From 2004, service providers must take reasonable steps to remove, alter, or provide reasonable means of avoiding physical features that make it impossible for disabled people to use that service. Schools, colleges and universities must provide information to disabled people.

---

1. Definitions of disability and disabled person;
2. Employment: discrimination by employers, enforcement provisions, discrimination by other persons, occupational pension schemes and insurance services;
3. Discrimination in other areas: goods, facilities and services, premises, enforcement;
4. Education;
5. Public transport: taxis, public services vehicles, rail vehicles;
6. National Disability Council;
7. Supplemental: Codes of Practice, victimisation, help;
8. Miscellaneous.

Figure 10.14 Disability Discrimination Act 1995.

Definition of disabled person

A person is disabled if they have a physical or mental impairment that has a substantial and long-term adverse effect on their ability to carry out normal day-to-day activities. Long term means 'lasting' or likely to last at least 12 months. There must be an effect on at least one of the following aspects:

1. Mobility.
2. Manual dexterity.
3. Physical co-ordination.
4. Continence.
5. Ability to lift.
6. Carry or otherwise move everyday objects.
7. Speech.
8. Hearing or eyesight.
9. Memory or ability to concentrate, learn or understand.
10. Perception of the risk of physical danger.

Definition of discrimination

Discrimination occurs if a disabled person is treated less favourably.
Codes of practice have been published by the government covering:

1. Rights of access – goods, facilities, services and premises.
2. Elimination of discrimination in the field of employment against disabled persons or persons who have had a disability.
3. Duties of trade organisations to their disabled members and applicants.
4. Guidance on matters to be taken into account in determining questions relating to the definition of disability.

In addition there are many guides issued by the Department of Education and Employment on various parts of the legislation.

Any allegation of discrimination in employment can be taken to an Employment Tribunal. The Advisory, Conciliation and Arbitration Service provides conciliation services.

A National Disability Council

Part VI of the Act establishes the National Disability Council. This Council, following consultation, advises the Secretary of State on relevant matters as requested, and prepares Codes of Practice. Unlike the Equal Opportunity Commission, it will not have the power to take cases to an industrial tribunal. However this role is taken by the Disability Rights Commission (see below).

In August 1998, it was stated that more than 1,700 claims had been lodged with tribunals since the implementation of the Act in December 1996[31] and large awards are being made. Thus, a shift chemist with poor eyesight, who qualified as disabled and argued that when made redundant he had been discriminated against because of his disability, was awarded £103,146 including £3,500 for injury to feeling.

Disability Rights Commission

In April 2000, the Disability Rights Commission was established, funded by the government. The Commission can sue any company that denied equal treatment to disabled people. The Commission employs 20 lawyers to assist those who claim that they have been discriminated against on account of their disabilities. The aim of the Commission is to attempt to resolve disputes through mediation, but it will bring cases to the courts and thus there will be established a body of case law on the rights of disabled people. The Commission will also provide information and advice to employers about how to meet their responsibilities under the Disability Discrimination Act 1995. It estimated that there are about 8.5 million disabled people in Britain, of whom about 2.6 million are unemployed or on benefits.[32]

Conclusions

Employment law is an area of law that is constantly changing with each government legislating to amend the rights of employer and employees, trade unions and the laws on discrimination. In addition, case law leads to better understanding on the interpretation of statutory provisions. The European Community is increasingly requiring its member states to strengthen the protection that they provide for employees and those subject to discrimination.

Questions and exercises

1 If you have a letter which purports to be your contract of appointment, compare it with particulars set out in Figure 10.5.

2 Obtain a copy of your employer's disciplinary procedure and apply the procedure to any of the situations of alleged negligence by a nurse set out in this book.

3 Take any statutory right and contrast it with the comparable rights given in your contract of employment by national NHS conditions. Which right would be of most benefit to the employee?

4 Visit an employment tribunal and prepare a brief guide for a potential applicant on the procedure and formalities.

5 A manager is both an employee and the representative of the employer. In what way, if any, is there likely to be a conflict between these two roles?

6 If you were preparing to interview prospective employees, what questions do you consider would be unlawful under the sex, race and disability discrimination legislation?

References

1. List 99 is a list held by the Department for Education and Employment of those considered unsuitable to work with children. It has always been a statutory list.

2. Department of Health Press Notice 2 October 2000

3. Case of R. v. *Secretary of State for Health ex parte C* [1999] 1 FLR 1073

4. Further details of statutory rights are available from the Department of Trade and Industry 020 7215 5000; http://www.dti.gov.uk

5. Department of Trade and Industry (see above) and also from the Inland Revenue, National Insurance Contributions Office: www.inlandrevenue.gov.uk

6. *Halfpenny* v. *IGE Medical System Ltd* 1999 1 FLR 944 Court of Appeal

7. *Webb* v. *EMO Air Cargo (UK)* TLR 15 July 1994

8. (*Annette Cowley* v. *South African Airways*); Francis Gibb, Single mother wins fight over 16-hour shifts, *The Times*, news report 3 August 1999

9. *Atkin* v. *Enfield Group Hospital Management Committee* 1975 I RLR 217

10. Employment Protection Code of Practice (Disciplinary Practice and Procedures Order 1998 SI 1998/44

11. *Schultz* v. *Esso Petroleum Co Ltd* [1999] 3 All ER 338

12. Working Time Regulations 1998 SI 1998 No 1833

13. NHS Executive, Working Time Regulations: Implementation in the NHS HSC 1988/204; DTI A Guide to the Working Time Regulations URN 1998/894

14. NHS Advance letter (GC) 3/98 18 November 1998

15. For enquiries on the GWC agreement: Patricia Saunders or Bernard Klose, NHS Executive, Quarry House, Leeds 0113 254 5919 or 0113 254 5761; For general enquiries: Godfrey Perera 0113 254 5757

16. WHC(199)180 Working Time Regulations The 50 most frequently asked questions

17. Charles Bremner and Mark Henderson, NHS may face £1bn bill for 48-hour week, *The Times* p. 8, 19 November 1998

18. Further information is available on 0845 8450 360

19. The Part-time workers (Prevention of Less Favourable Treatment) Regulations 2000 SI 1551

20. Directive 97/81/EC Part-time Work Directive as extended to the UK by Directive 98/23/EC

21. See DTI booklet: PL871 for details of Union membership and non-membership rights

22. R. v. *Secretary of State for Employment ex parte Seymour-Smith and another*, *The Times* 25 February 1999 European Law Report

23. Russell Jenkins, Police pay singer £30,000 to settle race abuse claim, *The Times* 14 April 1999

24. *Jones* v. *Tower Boot Co. Ltd*, *Times Law Report* 16 December 1996

25. *Marshall* v. *Southampton AHA* (No. 2) 1993 4 All ER 586

26. *Minister of Defence* v. *Cannock* TLR 2 August 1994

27. NHS Confederation, Equal Opportunities Update Issue No 4 September 1998

28. News item, Equal Pay deal for NHS, *The Times* 1 April 1999

29. *Enderby* v. *Frenchay HA and the Secretary of State for Health* [1994] 1 All ER 495

30. *Boyle* v. *Equal Opportunities Commission* [1999] 1 FLR 119 European Court of Justice (Case 411/96)

31. Frances Gibb, Putting the pain into being fired, *The Times* 11 August 1998

32. Alexandra Frean, Disabled rights group launched, *The Times* 20 April 2000

11 The nurse as a registered professional

It will be recalled from Chapter 1 that there were four fields of accountability to be faced by the nurse: the civil and criminal courts; the disciplinary proceedings of the employer; and the Professional Conduct Committee (PCC) of the United Kingdom Central Council for Nursing, Midwifery, and Health Visiting (UKCC). This chapter considers the procedure for a hearing before the PCC. First, however, the constitution of the UKCC and the National Boards will be considered. Figure 11.1 sets out the topics to be discussed. Significant changes are due to come into force in April 2002. At the end of this chapter, there is a discussion of the proposed changes to the UKCC and the National Boards and in Appendix D can be found the draft order for the new Nursing and Midwifery Council.

1. United Kingdom Central Council
   (a) constitution;
   (b) functions;
   (c) standing committees.
2. National Boards.
3. Registration
   (a) false representation;
   (b) removal from Register.
      (i) On grounds of misconduct
         1. The hearing:
            is there misconduct?
         2. The outcome:
            postponement of judgement;
            no action;
            striking off Register;
            refer to Health Committee.
         3. Criminal misconduct.
      (ii) Removal on grounds of health
         1. Constitution of Health Committee.
         2. Procedures:
            professional screeners;
            action following reports;
            notice of referral.
         3. Restoration to Register.
4. Professional standards and codes of practice.
5. Education and training.

Figure 11.1 Issues covered in Chapter 11.

The Nurses, Midwives and Health Visitors Act 1979 sets up the framework for the Central Council, the National Boards and the Professional Register. Statutory instruments passed in the exercise of powers conferred by the principal Act fill in the flesh. Rules are laid down in the principal Act on the practice of midwifery, local supervision of midwifery practice, and on re-enacting the offence of an unqualified person attending a woman in childbirth. These are considered in the section dealing with midwifery. The 1979 Act was amended by the Nurses, Midwives and Health Visitors Act 1992 and reenacted in the 1997 Act. By this Act, the UKCC became a mainly elected body and the National Boards became appointed executive bodies with changed functions.

The United Kingdom Central Council

The constitution of the UKCC is given in Figure 11.2 and its functions can be seen in Figure 11.3. The regulations require the UKCC to have specific standing committees and these can be seen in Figure 11.4.

The United Kingdom Central Council for Nursing, Midwifery and Health Visiting: consists of not more than 60 members, two-thirds elected by the profession and the others appointed by the Secretary of State from amongst nurses, midwives, health visitors or registered medical practitioners who have such qualifications and experience in education or other fields as in the Secretary of State's opinion will be of value to the Council in the performance of its functions. He must especially have in mind the need to secure that members of council include registered nurses, midwives and health visitors living or working in each part of the United Kingdom and that qualifications and experience in the teaching of nurses, midwives and health visitors are adequately represented on the Council.

Figure 11.2 Constitution of the UKCC.

(a) to establish and improve the standards of training and professional conduct for nurses, midwives and health visitors;

(b) to ensure that the standards of training meet any Community obligation in the United Kingdom;

(c) to determine by means of rules, the conditions of a person's being admitted to training, and the kind and standard of training to be undertaken with a view to registration;

(d) the rules may also make provision with respect to the kind and standard of further training available to persons who are already registered;

(e) the powers of the Council shall include that of providing, in such manner as it thinks fit, advice for nurses, midwives, and health visitors on standards of professional conduct;

(f) the Council, in the discharge of its functions, shall have proper regard for the interests of all groups within the professions, including those with minority representation.

Figure 11.3 Functions of the UKCC.

A Midwifery Committee and Finance Committee shall be constituted by the Secretary of State as standing committees. The Council shall consult the Finance Committee on all financial matters. If the Council (having regard to the duty to have proper regard for the interests of all groups within the profession) requests the Secretary of State to constitute standing committees then he may by order constitute other standing committees and require the Council to consult them on or empower them to discharge functions of the Council.

The Midwifery Committee must have a majority of practising midwives and the Council has a duty to consult the Committee on all matters relating to midwifery. In addition, the Committee must discharge such functions of the Council as are assigned to them either by the Council or by the Secretary of State by order. The Midwifery Committee also has the function of considering any proposal to make, amend, or revoke rules relating to the practice of midwifery and reporting back to the Council. The Secretary of State will not approve rules relating to midwifery practice unless satisfied that they are framed in accordance with recommendations of the Council's Midwifery Committee.

Figure 11.4   Standing Committees of the UKCC.

The National Boards

These corporate bodies are appointed for England, Scotland, Wales and Northern Ireland. The original constitution under Section 5 of the Nurses, Midwives and Health Visitors Act 1979 has been amended by the 1992 Act and incorporated in S.5 of the 1997 Act. Originally, each Board consisted of a majority of elected members: about two-thirds. The remainder were appointed by the Secretary of State. The maximum in total for each Board was 45 (35 for Northern Ireland). The Secretary of State had a statutory duty to ensure that the qualifications and experience in the teaching of nurses were adequately represented.

Following the changes effected by the 1992 Act, the new Boards were appointed by and accountable to the Secretary of State and must be made from among persons who:

1.   are registered nurses, midwives and health visitors; or

2.   have such qualifications and experience in education or other fields, as in the opinion of the Secretary of State, will be of value to the Board in the performance of its functions.

1.   To approve institutions in relation to the provision of:
     (a)   courses of training with a view to enabling persons to qualify for registration as nurses, midwives or health visitors or for the recording of additional qualifications in the register; and
     (b)   courses of further training for those already registered;
2.   To ensure that such courses meet the requirements of the Central Council as to their content and standard;
3.   To hold or arrange to hold such examinations as are necessary to enable persons to satisfy requirements for registration or to obtain additional qualifications;
4.   To collaborate with the Council in the promotion of improved training methods; and
5.   To perform such other functions relating to nurses, midwives or health visitors as the Secretary of State may by order prescribe.

Figure 11.5   Functions of the National Boards.

He has a duty in exercising these powers to ensure that a majority of the members of the Boards are registered nurses, midwives or health visitors. The functions of the National Boards are shown in Figure 11.5. In addition, they have a statutory duty in Section 6 of the 1997 Act to 'discharge their functions subject to and in accordance with any applicable rules of the council and shall take account of any difference in the consideration applying to the different professions'. The National Boards no longer have a duty to conduct preliminary investigations into misconduct allegations. This function has been taken over by the UKCC.

Registration and removal

The Central Council has the duty of preparing and maintaining a register of qualified nurses, midwives, and health visitors and setting out rules in relation to the entry on to, removal from, and restoration to the Register. These rules are set out in a Statutory Instrument (1993 No. 893).

False representation

Situation 11.1   False qualifications

Brenda had always wanted to be a nurse, but lacked the educational background. When she left school, she worked as a nursing auxiliary for many years and was given much responsibility. She then left the district when her husband moved jobs. She applied for the job of a night nurse in a private nursing home. At the interview, she was asked where she trained and she gave false information about her background. Because of her great experience, they were very impressed with her and failed to take up her references. After she had worked there for two years, a former colleague from her previous hospital came to visit a relative in the home and was surprised to discover that Brenda was referred to as 'Sister'. The colleague made some enquiries and realised that Brenda was being treated as a registered nurse when in fact she was not one. She felt that it was her duty to point this out to the owners of the home because of the possibility that a patient could suffer harm. When the owners discovered the truth, Brenda was dismissed on the spot.

In a situation like this, as well as a loss of job, Brenda could face a criminal charge of falsely representing that she was on the Register or falsely representing that she possessed qualifications in nursing, midwifery or health visiting. These are offences under Section 13 of the Nurses, Midwives, and Health Visitors Act 1997. The matter would not be one for the Central Council or National Boards since she is not registered, but would be a matter for the criminal courts.

However, the Council would be required to provide evidence of the fact that she was not on the Register. Of course, if she was on the Register for one purpose, e.g. a general nurse, it would be an offence under the Act for her to pretend that she was a midwife. This would then be a matter that could be heard before the PCC since, as she is already registered, the Committee could decide if she should remain on the Register or if any other action should be taken against her.

The Statutory Instrument also sets out rules relating to nurse training: the age of entry, educational requirements, interruption of training, admission to parts 1–8 of the Register, the examinations, and student index and health visitor training rules (see section on the midwifery rules).

Removal from the Register

Under Section 10, the Council has the responsibility of determining the circumstances and the means by which a person may, for misconduct or otherwise, be removed from the Register or part of it. These rules are set out in a Statutory Instrument (1993 No. 893).

The circumstances in which a person can be removed from the Register are:

1. that she has been guilty of misconduct; or
2. that her fitness to practise is seriously impaired by reason of her physical or mental condition.

Suspension from the Register

This power was introduced in 1993 and can be exercised where a person's fitness to practise is seriously impaired by reason of her physical or mental condition; or where it appears necessary to suspend as an interim measure:

1. for the protection of the public; or
2. in the practitioner's interests.

Removal on grounds of misconduct

Situation 11.2   Missing ampoule

Janice Lane was a ward sister on a busy surgical ward. One day she was preparing the midday medications on her own and while preparing a morphine injection for a patient dropped the ampoule which broke. Ashamed of what had happened, she locked up the cupboard and pretended that it had not happened instead of following the correct procedure and writing the loss in the correct book and getting a witness. Subsequently, the loss of the ampoule was noticed by the following shift, and a search and an inquiry commenced which revealed nothing. The police were brought in and eventually Janice confessed.

The Vice-Chairman shall be chairman of the Preliminary Proceedings Committee.

The Council shall appoint two of its members to be deputy chairmen of the Preliminary Proceedings Committee and each may act as chairman at the Vice-President's request or in her absence.

The Committee is quorate if at least three members of the Council constitute a majority of those considering a particular case. Members must be selected with due regard to the professional field in which the practitioner under consideration works or has worked.

It shall meet in private.

It shall not be necessary for the Preliminary Proceedings Committee when meeting to consider a particular case to be composed of the same members who considered that case on any previous occasion.

Figure 11.6   Composition of Preliminary Proceedings Committee.

The 1992 Act transferred the function of carrying out a preliminary investigation into any misconduct from the National Boards to the UKCC. Professional Conduct Rules now provide for a Preliminary Proceedings Committee to be constituted by the UKCC. Its constitution is shown in Figure 11.6. It has the function of:

1.   carrying out investigations of cases of alleged misconduct;

2.   determining whether or not to refer a case of alleged misconduct to:
     (a)   the Conduct Committee with a view to removal of a practitioner from the Register; or
     (b)   the professional screeners with a view to consideration of a practitioner's fitness to practise;

3.   determining whether a practitioner is guilty of misconduct and, if so, whether it is appropriate to issue a caution as to her future conduct.

After an allegation of misconduct that the council officer considers may lead to removal from the Register, the Registrar shall send the following, in writing, to the practitioner concerned:

1.   a summary of the allegation;

2.   notice that the preliminary proceedings will in due course consider the matter; and

3.   confirmation that if a Notice of Proceedings is issued by the Preliminary Proceedings Committee, the practitioner will be invited to respond in writing to the Notice, but that if the practitioner wishes to submit a preliminary response to the summary of allegations, such response will be made available to the Preliminary Proceedings Committee, provided that it is in time.

Council can conduct, through the solicitor or otherwise, an investigation before the matter is first considered by the Preliminary Proceedings Committee and if such an investigation indicates that the practitioner may be removed from the Register, the Registrar should send copies of the statements and other documents to the practitioner and notify her that she is entitled to submit a preliminary response for consideration by the Preliminary Proceedings Committee.

The Preliminary Proceedings Committee may:

1. decline to proceed with the matter;
2. require further investigation to be conducted;
3. adjourn consideration of the matter;
4. refer the matter to the professional screeners;
5. take the advice of the solicitor and may instruct him to obtain such documents, proofs of evidence and other evidence in respect of the allegations as he considers necessary;
6. require the complaint to be verified by statutory declaration.

Rules relating to the procedure of the Preliminary Proceedings Committee require a Notice of Proceedings to be sent to the practitioner together with statements and a request that the practitioner respond in writing.

After receipt of any written response by the practitioner, the Preliminary Proceedings Committee can, in addition to the powers outlined above:

1. refer the case to the Conduct Committee (where removal from the Register might be justified);
2. refer the case to professional screeners (where the physical or mental condition of the practitioner may seriously impair her fitness to practise);
3. determine if the practitioner has been guilty of misconduct and, if so, whether it is appropriate to issue a caution.

Professional Conduct Committee

It may be that, after scrutiny of the evidence in Janice's case, the Preliminary Proceedings Committee decides that the case should be referred to the Professional Conduct Committee. The composition of the Professional Conduct Committee is shown in Figure 11.7.

After referral of the case to the Conduct Committee, the Registrar must send to the practitioner a Notice of Inquiry in writing in the form set out in the First Schedule to the Statutory Instrument. This notice must be sent by recorded delivery to the registered address or to any later address known to the Registrar. Twenty-eight days must elapse between the day on which the Notice is posted and the date fixed for

All members of the Council are eligible and may be required to serve on the Conduct Committee. The quorum is three. The composition for any particular case must be chosen with due regard to the professional fields in which the respondent works or has worked. The President of the Council is the Chairman of the Committee but the Council shall appoint a panel of not more than nine persons from whom a deputy chairman may be chosen who shall then take the chair in the absence of the Chairman. Any person who has participated in the preliminary consideration of a case as a member of the Preliminary Proceedings Committee or as a professional screener shall not be permitted to be a member of the Conduct Committee dealing with that case.

Figure 11.7 Composition of the Professional Conduct Committee.

the hearing unless the practitioner agrees otherwise. If there is a complainant, that person, too, must be sent a copy of the rules and the Notice of Inquiry. The Notice of Inquiry must not include any charge inconsistent with the substance of allegations set out in the Notice of Proceedings.

The hearing

The charge(s) shall be read in public and in the presence of the parties to the proceedings by an officer of the Council. If Janice failed to turn up, the hearing could still take place, but the solicitor would be called upon to satisfy the PCC that Janice had received the Notice of Inquiry. Even if there were no evidence that it had been received, the inquiry can still proceed if the PCC is satisfied that all reasonable efforts in accordance with the rules have been made to serve the Notice of Inquiry on her.

Procedure differs initially if a conviction is alleged. The procedure to be followed in such circumstances is considered below.

Is there misconduct?

This is the first issue to be considered. Two different issues arise: first, are the facts upon which the charge of misconduct is based to be accepted by the PCC; and, secondly, if they are admitted by the respondent or accepted as true after a hearing by the PCC, do these facts constitute misconduct? Misconduct is defined in the rules as 'conduct unworthy of a registered nurse, midwife or health visitor as the case may be and includes obtaining registration by fraud'.

The chairman would ask Janice if she admits the facts alleged in the charges. If she does not or if she has failed to attend the proceedings, the solicitor or the complainant will open the case and adduce evidence of the facts alleged. Witnesses would be summoned to give evidence before the Committee and the defendant (or her representatives) is able to cross-examine any witnesses. At the close of the case against her, she may if she wishes make either or both of the following submissions:

1. that no sufficient evidence has been adduced upon which the PCC could find the facts alleged on the charge to have been proved;
2. that the facts alleged in the charge are not such as to constitute misconduct.

The Committee retire and discuss in camera whether either or both of these submissions should be upheld. If they decide that the submissions are not upheld, Janice herself can give evidence to contradict the allegation that her conduct was misconduct.

Janice can address the Committee whether or not she calls witnesses. After she has finished, the solicitor for the complainant may, with the leave of the PCC, adduce evidence to rebut (contradict) any evidence that Janice has put forward. She would then be entitled to address the Committee further to contradict this evidence. The PCC would then consider in camera what allegations have been proved in relation to each charge.

Different procedures apply if the respondent does not appear and if the respondent admits the facts on which the charges are based.

In Janice's case, it is likely, depending upon the evidence of the witnesses and the establishment of the facts upon which the charge of misconduct is based, that they would find Janice guilty of misconduct; more for her failure to confess her mistake and her attempt to cover up than for the actual breaking of the ampoule.

If, however, they decided that either there were no facts from which they could deduce there had been misconduct or that the alleged facts did not constitute misconduct, the chairman would announce the finding that the respondent is not guilty of misconduct in respect of the matters to which the charge relates. This decision must be announced by the chairman in public and he must also declare the respondent not guilty of misconduct.

Where, however, the PCC has found the alleged facts proved to their satisfaction, the respondent is able to put further argument forward as to why these facts do not constitute misconduct. Where the Council has found the respondent guilty of misconduct, the solicitor or complainant can give evidence as to the respondent's previous history. Janice could also give evidence in mitigation and as to her character.

The outcome

Once there has been a decision that the nurse is guilty of misconduct, the Committee then has to decide what sanction to adopt. There are several choices (see Figure 11.8).

1. *Postponement of judgment*: if the PCC decides to postpone judgment, it will decide on the month and year when the hearing will resume and the chairman will announce, in public, the decision and the recommendations that the PCC has decided upon.

2. *No action*: if it is decided not to remove the respondent from the Register, this will also be announced in public.

3. *Striking off the Register*: this is announced in public and the Registrar will remove the respondent's name from the relevant part of the Register either for a specified period or not. The respondent will be required to send to the Registrar within 21 days any document or insignia issued by the Council or its predecessor which indicates registration status and the Registrar's letter will warn her of her liability to proceedings if she holds herself out as being a practitioner in a part of the Register from which her name has been removed.

4. *Refer to the professional screeners* (see below).

5. *Suspension for a specified period from the Register*: on expiry of this time, she shall be restored to the Register.

6. *Caution as to the practitioner's future conduct*: the letter must record the caution. The Council shall keep a record for five years of each caution and the existence of a caution must be taken into consideration by the Preliminary Proceedings Committee and the Conduct Committee.

(a)   postponement of judgement;

(b)   no action;

(c)   striking off the Register;

(d)   referral to the Health Committee;

(e)   suspension (added by 1992 Act);

(f)   caution (added by 1992 Act).

Figure 11.8   Outcomes available to the Professional Conduct Committee.

The professional screeners, the President or the Health Committee can refer a case back to the Conduct Committee.

In all cases the respondent must be notified by recorded delivery of the decision of the PCC.

Criminal misconduct

If the charge relates to criminal misconduct, then slightly different rules apply. Evidence as to a conviction on a criminal charge can be put before the PCC and the respondent can adduce evidence to prove beyond all reasonable doubt that she is not the person referred to in the certificate of conviction or that the offence referred to in the certificate of conviction was not that of which she was convicted (this prevents a second trial on the actual charge that was before the criminal courts).

The PCC will determine whether any conviction has been proved and after that the validity of the conviction will not be questioned. Proof of a conviction alone will not be determined to be misconduct. However, proof of the conviction is evidence of the commission of the offence. It then has to be decided whether that offence constitutes misconduct.

In the case of Balamoody against the UKCC,[1] the court held that the terms of the professional conduct rules covered all criminal convictions regardless of either the seriousness of the offence or whether it was committed in the course of nursing. Whilst a criminal conviction did not of itself constitute misconduct, some offences would almost certainly amount to misconduct and therefore, where a professional had failed to adhere to important statutory requirements whilst discharging functions of a senior and supervisory nature, resulting in a criminal conviction, the relevant professional body and the court would be forced to regard that person's actions as a cause for serious concern.

Situation 11.3   Breach of the peace

A district nurse was very angry to discover that a traffic warden was standing by her car as she returned from visiting a patient. She pointed out her nurse's sticker and explained that she was visiting only for a few minutes to give an injection. The traffic warden was unimpressed by her pleading and took no notice of what she was saying. The nurse became very heated and an argument broke out during which the traffic warden said, 'You nurses are all the same. You all think the law does not apply to you.' The nurse lost her temper and pushed the warden. She was subsequently charged with conduct likely to cause a breach of the peace. She was found guilty and fined. She eventually found herself facing PCC proceedings.

A case like this would be conducted under the procedure to be followed where a conviction is alleged. Once evidence of a conviction was produced, the nurse could adduce evidence to show that she was not the person convicted or that she was convicted of a different crime. If the PCC determined that the conviction had been proved, it is then open to the nurse to submit that the charges are not in themselves evidence of misconduct.

Obviously, the outcome would depend upon the circumstantial evidence and the attitude of the Committee to such conduct. The statutory definition of misconduct given above does not offer much help in this respect and gives considerable discretion to the PCC to define conduct unworthy of a registered nurse, etc., in terms of current conventions of behaviour.

Removal on grounds of health

At any time, the Preliminary Proceedings Committee, when investigating a case of apparent misconduct or a complaint against a nurse, can refer the case to the Health Committee of the UKCC.

The Health Committee is constituted to determine whether or not:

1. a practitioner will be removed from the Register or part of it;
2. a person who has been removed from the Register or part of it may be restored;
3. a practitioner's registration shall be suspended;
4. the suspension of a person's registration shall be terminated.

The constitution of the Health Committee can be seen in Figure 11.9.

No case can be considered by the Health Committee unless it has been referred by professional screeners. These professional screeners are appointed from a panel of Council members. A group of three is to be selected to consider any matters referred to it. Regard must be had to the professional field in which the professional is working.

Procedure

Information, in writing and received by the Registrar, that raises any question of the practitioner's fitness to practise being seriously impaired by reason of her physical or mental condition, shall be submitted to the professional screeners. Anyone wishing to lay information before the Registrar may make a statutory declaration.

1. If the professional screeners decide there is no reasonable evidence to support the allegations, they shall direct the Registrar to inform the complainant and, if they consider it necessary or desirable, the practitioner. The professional screeners may obtain the opinion of a selected medical examiner on the information and evidence that they have received.

Twenty-five members are to be appointed by the Council from among its members who shall be eligible and required to serve on the Health Committee. The members are to be chosen with regard to the need to represent a wide range of fields of professional work. Any ten members constitute the Health Committee. The President of the Council will be the Chairman of the Health Committee and there is a panel of Deputy Chairmen. The quorum is three.

Figure 11.9 Constitution of the Health Committee.

2. If they feel that the matter should proceed further, they shall direct the Registrar to write to the practitioner by recorded delivery:

(a) notifying her that information has been received that appears to raise a question as to whether her fitness to practise has become seriously impaired by reason of her physical or mental condition, and indicating the symptomatic behaviour that gives rise to that question;

(b) inviting the practitioner to agree within 14 days to submit to examination at the Council's expense by two medical examiners to be chosen by the professional screeners and to agree that such examiners should furnish reports to the Registrar on the practitioner's fitness to practise;

(c) informing the practitioner that it is open to her to nominate other medical practitioners to examine her at her own expense and to report to the Registrar on the practitioner's fitness to practise; and

(d) inviting the practitioner to submit to the Registrar any observations or other evidence that she may wish to offer as to her own fitness to practise.

If the two medical practitioners are not able to agree, a third can be appointed at the Council's expense.

The professional screeners can make their own enquiries before giving any of the above directions.

Action following reports received from the medical examiners

1. If the medical examiners are unanimously agreed that she is not fit to practise, then the Registrar shall refer the information, together with the medical examiners' reports, to the Health Committee. The solicitor may be directed to take all necessary steps for verifying the evidence to be submitted to the Health Committee and for obtaining any necessary documents and the attendance of witnesses.

2. If there is considered to be no sufficient evidence of illness, the practitioner and the complainant shall be informed.

Referral of case to professional screeners by Preliminary Proceedings Committee, President or Conduct Committee

The practitioner is invited:

1. to submit to examination by at least two medical examiners to be chosen by the professional screeners;

2. to agree that such examiners should furnish to the Health Committee reports on the practitioner's fitness to practise; and

3. the Registrar informs the practitioner that it is also open to her to nominate another medical practitioner at her own expense to examine her and report to the Health Committee.

If she refuses to submit to such an examination or nominate her own medical examiner, the professional screeners shall decide whether or not to refer the information received to the Health Committee, indicating the reason why no medical report is available.

Notice of referral

Sent by the Registrar to the practitioner which shall:

1. indicate the grounds for the belief that her fitness to practise is seriously impaired; and

2. state the day, time and place at which the Health Committee will meet to consider the matter.

Twenty-eight days must elapse between the date of posting the notice and the day of the hearing, unless the practitioner agrees otherwise. The notice must be sent by registered post or recorded delivery. She must be notified that she can be represented at the hearing and can also be accompanied by her medical adviser.

The Health Committee

The Committee sits in private. At least one of the medical examiners selected by the Preliminary Proceedings Committee to examine her shall be in attendance. The practitioner may be present while her case is heard and may also be represented.

Witnesses may be called and at least one of the medical examiners who has examined the practitioner should be present throughout the inquiry, except where the Health Committee decide to meet in camera. The practitioner shall be entitled to representation while her case is heard and may be represented by a friend or by counsel or by a solicitor or officer of a representative organisation or by any other person of her choice and may be accompanied by her medical adviser.

The chairman opens the proceedings by drawing attention to the grounds for the belief that the practitioner's fitness to practise is seriously impaired as set out in the Notice of Referral and the documentation that has been circulated. If the practitioner has requested that oral evidence be given, the relevant persons are called as witnesses. Even if the requisite notice has not been given, the Health Committee can consult the legal assessor to decide if, in the interests of justice, there should be an adjournment to allow for witnesses to be called. At the conclusion of the practitioner's case, the chairman shall invite the practitioner or her representative to address the Health Committee and to adduce evidence of her fitness to practise.

The Committee can:

1. adjourn for further medical reports;
2. find that the fitness to practise is not seriously impaired by reason of the practitioner's physical or mental condition;
3. postpone judgment;
4. find that the fitness to practise is seriously impaired by the practitioner's physical or mental condition (it can direct the Registrar to remove the practitioner from the Register and can specify a period or not).

In the event of a finding under point 2 above, the Committee must refer the matter back to the committee from which the case was referred or to the President (if she referred it) who shall refer it to the Conduct Committee.

Restoration to the Register

This is governed by Rule 22 which does not set any minimum time before which an application to be restored to the Register is not possible. If suspension from the Register has been for a specified time, then on the expiry of that time the practitioner is restored to the Register. The applicant for restoration must apply in writing to the Registrar detailing the grounds for the application. The Registrar will then send details of the procedure, the recommendations of the Committee at the time of removal from the Register, an application form requiring the applicant to cite two persons who can give evidence for her, require her to state that she has not been convicted of a criminal offence since removal from the Register, require her to testify that she has not held herself out as registered, and request the fee for restoration. Procedure for the hearing is laid down in Rules 15, 16, and 17 and is otherwise as determined by the Committee.

The proceedings of the PCC and the Health Committee are subject to review by the High Court. For example, in *Slater* v. *United Kingdom Central Council for Nursing, Midwifery and Health Visitors, The Times* 10 June 1987, the Queen's Bench Division quashed the decision of the PCC in removing Mr Stephen Slater's name from the Register of nurses and remitted the case to a freshly constituted Committee for a rehearing on the grounds that the practitioner's case had not been fully considered by the Committee and an injustice might therefore have been done. In a later case, *Hefferon* v. *Committee of the UKCC, Current Law* May 1988 221, the High Court quashed the decisions of the Committee on the grounds that there had been a breach of natural justice.

Professional standards and codes of practice

The Chairman of the UKCC emphasised in an opening address at a conference in May 1983 that:

> the professional conduct function should be seen in positive terms – as one of the means through which a regulatory body, acting on behalf of the profession, honours the contract between the profession and society by ensuring that any member of the profession who has failed to meet the trust which society has placed in him or her is not permitted to continue to practise, or if the failure has not been a serious one, is reminded of the standard which professional practitioners are expected to meet.

The functions of the UKCC set out in Figure 11.3 include that of establishing and improving standards of training and professional practice, and also providing, in such manner as it thinks fit, advice for nurses, midwives and health visitors on standards of professional conduct. In fulfilment of this duty, the UKCC has issued and revised a code of professional conduct and many guidelines on different aspects of professional practice, many of which are included here in the appendices. In addition, the Council has decided that, in the future, all nurses (and not just midwives, who have had this requirement since 1936) will be required to maintain their professional competence to enable them to practise. Many of the codes and advisory papers produced by the UKCC are to be found in the appendices here and are frequently referred to in the text.

Education and training

The statutory duty to establish and improve standards of training falls on the UKCC and the National Boards. A team of professional officers works with members through specialist committees, including the Educational Policy Advisory Committee, the Midwifery Committee and a Committee on Research. New rules for the education of students, known as Project 2000, are now in place. The 1992 Act ended the duty of National Boards to provide pre-registration training courses. It is now their function to approve institutions in relation to the provision of training, etc.

Post-registration development (PREP)

The UKCC has set standards for the Future of Professional Practice (UKCC March 1994). This requires the following:

1. a minimum of five study days every three years;
2. a Notification of Practice Form;
3. a Return to Practice programme if practitioners have been out of practice for five years or more; and
4. a personal professional profile.

New standards have been set for specialist post-registration education. Rule 37 of the Midwives' Rules is being superseded, so that midwives will have to comply with the PREP requirements.

Professional Conduct annual report 1999–2000

In October 2000, the UKCC published its report on professional conduct from 1999 to 2000. It noted a steady increase in the number of allegations of misconduct, which totalled 1142 in 1999–2000. 47% of the complaints came from employers, 22% from the police and 22% from the public. Of the 1213 decisions made on cases in 1999–2000, only 164 were referred to the Professional Conduct Committee. 30 cautions were issued. A caution can be issued only where three criteria are satisfied:

1. where the offence was serious enough to warrant removal and a note of proceedings has been issued;

2. in response to the notice, the practitioner has admitted the facts of the charges and has admitted that the facts constitute misconduct; and

3. the practitioner has provided mitigation which has persuaded the committee that removal (and therefore referral to the PCC) would not be appropriate in the circumstances.

132 cases of alleged misconduct were considered by the PCC. The largest category of offences was the physical or verbal abuse of patients and clients, which accounted for 30.7% of the charges. Unsafe clinical practice accounted for 11.59% of the cases considered. 96 practitioners were removed from the Register, 27 cautioned, in 2 cases no action was taken, 1 judgment was postponed, in 8 cases the facts or misconduct were not proven and 1 case was part heard. The Health Committee considered 119 cases and 58 practitioners were considered to have their fitness impaired and 51 of these were suspended from the Register, and 7 were removed. Judgment was postponed in 28 cases.

The annual report also considered some case studies of cases heard by the PCC that relate to the theme of dishonesty. In one case, a practitioner who was the proprietor of three nursing homes had continued cashing money from benefit books after residents had left or died. Another nurse had claimed for hours as a bank nurse that she had not worked. In another case, a nurse had failed to declare previous criminal convictions. In all these cases, the decision was made to remove the nurse from the Register.

Future changes

At the request of the Department of Health, a review of the statutory regulation of nurses, midwives and health visitors was undertaken by JM Consulting. It reported in 1999[2] and made significant recommendations for a major reorganisation of the work, functions and organisation of the statutory regulation machinery. Its main recommendations were accepted by the government and the necessary legislative beginning was made in the Health Act 1999. In August 2000, the Government issued a consultation paper[3] giving three months for feedback. The amending regulations would be passed by Order under Section 60 of the Health Act 1999. A new Nursing and Midwifery Council would replace the UKCC and the four National Boards, maintaining a professional register with some 640,000 entries. Contrary to initial suggestions, health visitors will continue to have separate registration and representation within the new Council. The Health Act 1999 defines four fundamental functions of the new Council, which cannot be transferred by Order to another body. These are:

1. keeping the Register of members admitted to practice;

2. determining the standards of education and training for admission to practice;

3. giving guidance about standards of conduct and performance; and

4. administering procedures (including making rules) relating to misconduct, unfitness to practice and similar matters.

The covering letter to the consultation paper states that the key objectives of the reorganisation are:

1. to reform ways of working, by requiring the Council to:
   (a) treat the health and welfare of patients as paramount;
   (b) collaborate and consult with key stakeholders;
   (c) be open and pro-active in accounting to the public and the profession for its work.
2. to reform structure and functions by:
   (a) giving wider powers to deal effectively with individuals who present unacceptable risks to patients;
   (b) creating a smaller Council, comprising directly elected practitioners and a strong lay input, charged with strategic responsibility for setting and monitoring standards of professional training, performance and conduct;
   (c) streamlining the professional register;
   (d) providing explicit powers to link registration with evidence of continuing professional development.

Three statutory committees are suggested:

1. The Investigating Committee, dealing with initial complaints about individuals.
2. The Professional Conduct Committee, dealing with standards of conduct and disciplinary hearings.
3. The Health Committee, dealing with practitioners with health problems.

A draft contents of the Order in Council are set out in an appendix to the Consultation paper and can be seen in Appendix D of this book.

At the time of writing, the government's draft proposals for the detailed regulations have been published and its response to the feedback is awaited. There are likely to be some significant changes because of criticisms, especially by the UKCC. In its response to the consultation paper, the UKCC criticised the fact that nurses who have been found guilty of professional misconduct would still be able to continue practising for several months because of a new appeals process. In addition, the UKCC has questioned the timetable for setting up the new Council in September 2001 as unrealistic and the proposed timetable for implementation is now April 2002.

Preparation for the establishment of the Nursing and Midwifery Council

One of the main features of the new registration system is that public involvement should increase. In fulfilment of its statutory duties and in preparation for the new Council, the UKCC issued in October 2000 a Strategy for Public Involvement.[4] It has developed an action plan identifying work to be completed by December 2000 and by September 2001 in ensuring that the public are fully involved. ('Public' is defined as patients, clients and their carers; organisations that support the interests of these groups; individuals with an interest in the delivery of health care and the registered practitioners, many professionals, employers, government and statutory organisations and professional and trade union organisations.) The strategy also identifies the current public involvement in the work of the UKCC, including information leaflets, its website, press statements, exhibitions, conferences and seminars, UKCC membership of patient/voluntary groups and public sessions of the UKCC, public meetings, written public consultations, lay membership of the UKCC and regular meetings with consumer panel members for professional conduct.

Questions and exercises

1 The PCC sits in different parts of the country and is open to the public and members of the profession. Next time it meets in your vicinity, try to attend and write up the hearing from the point of view of the formality, the procedure followed, justice to the nurse defendant, and justice to the general public.

2 In what ways does a hearing before the PCC differ from a hearing before a civil court? To what extent do you consider that the hearing and its procedure complies with Article 6 of the European Convention on Human Rights? (See Appendix A.)

3 How would you define misconduct by a nurse? Would any of the following count as misconduct by your definition?
    (a) A nurse has an illegitimate child.
    (b) A nurse is convicted of shop-lifting.
    (c) A nurse is found guilty of a breach of the peace after being involved in an argument with a traffic warden.
    (d) A nurse is fined for speeding.
    (e) A nurse borrows money from a junior member of staff on her ward.
    (f) A nurse is discovered to be drunk when off duty, but still in her uniform.

4 Since the decision as to whether there is misconduct or not depends upon the detailed circumstances, what additional information would you need to answer question 3 above and how would that information affect your answer?

5 Do you consider that there should be a time limit within which the nurse who has been struck off cannot apply to be reinstated?

6 Examine the proposals for the new Nursing and Midwifery Council and consider the extent to which it improves the scheme of self-regulation of practitioners.

References

[1] *Balamoody v. UKCC, The Independent* June 15 1998
[2] J M Consulting Ltd, The Regulation of Nurses, Midwives and Health Visitors; Report on a review of the Nurses, Midwives and Health Visitors Act 1997, J M Consulting Ltd, February 1999
[3] NHS Executive, Modernising Regulation The New Nursing and Midwifery Council: A consultation document August 2000 DoH
[4] UKCC Strategy for Public Involvement 2000

12 Health and safety and the nurse

This chapter covers the basic principles of law relating to health and safety at work, taking examples from nursing practice. It covers both the statutes (Acts of Parliament and Regulations) and the common law (i.e. decided cases or judge made law) that set out the legal requirements on health and safety. Statute law and common law work in parallel and cover similar duties (though statute law is more specific). The topics covered are shown in Figure 12.1.

---

1. Statutory provision:
    Health and Safety at Work Act 1974 (HASAW);
    Regulations under HASAW;
    Reporting of Injuries, Diseases and Dangerous Occurrences 1995 (RIDDOR 95);
    Occupier's Liability Acts 1957 and 1984;
    Consumer Protection Act 1987;
    Medical Devices Agency;
    Control of Substances Hazardous to Health 1988.
2. Common law duties: employer's duty and employee's duty.
3. Remedies available to an injured employee.
4. Special areas:
    (a) Violence;
    (b) Stress;
    (c) Manual handling and back injuries;
    (d) Sexual and other harassment;
    (e) Repetitive Strain Injury;
    (f) Smoking.

Figure 12.1   Issues covered in Chapter 12.

Statutory Provisions

Health and Safety at Work Act 1974 (HASAW)

General principles
The Health and Safety at Work Act 1974 is enforced through the criminal courts by the Health and Safety Inspectorate who have the power to prosecute for offences under the Act and under the regulations and who have also powers of inspection and can issue enforcement or prohibition notices.

The employer has two parallel duties – one under the civil law and enforced through the civil courts (see below), the other under the criminal law and enforced through the criminal courts. The Health and Safety at Work Act is an Act that is enforceable through the criminal courts and places upon both employer and employee considerable duties in relation to health and safety. Some regulations made under the Health and Safety at Work Act 1974 (such as the manual handling regulations) can also be used as the basis for a claim for compensation in the civil courts. Figure 12.2 sets

General duties of employers to their employees

(1) It shall be the duty of every employer to ensure, so far as is reasonably practicable, the health, safety and welfare at work of all his employees.

(2) Without prejudice to the generality of an employer's duty under the preceding subsection, the matters to which that duty extends include in particular:

(a) The provision and maintenance of plant and systems of work that are, so far as is reasonably practicable, safe and without risks to health;

(b) arrangements for ensuring, so far as is reasonably practicable, safety and absence of risks to health in connection with the use, handling, storage and transport of articles and substances;

(c) the provision of such information, instruction, training and supervision as is necessary to ensure, so far as is reasonably practicable, the health and safety at work of his employees;

(d) so far as is reasonably practicable as regards any place of work under the employer's control, the maintenance of it in a condition that is safe and without risks to health and the provision and maintenance of means of access to and egress from it that are safe and without such risks;

(e) the provision and maintenance of a working environment for his employees that is, so far as is reasonably practicable, safe, without risks to health, and adequate as regards facilities and arrangements for their welfare at work.

(3) Except in such cases as may be prescribed, it shall be the duty of every employer to prepare and as often as may be appropriate revise a written statement of his general policy with respect to the health and safety at work of his employees and the organisation and arrangements for the time being in force for carrying out that policy, and to bring the statement and any revision of it to the notice of all of his employees.

(4) Regulations made by the Secretary of State may provide for the appointment in prescribed cases by recognised trade unions (within the meaning of the regulations) of safety representatives from amongst the employees, and those representatives shall represent the employees in consultations with the employers under subsection (6) below and shall have such other functions as may be prescribed.

(5) (Repealed).

(6) It shall be the duty of every employer to consult any such representatives with a view to the making and maintenance of arrangements which will enable him and his employees to co-operate effectively in promoting and developing measures to ensure the health and safety at work of the employees, and in checking the effectiveness of such measures.

(7) In such cases as may be prescribed it shall be the duty of every employer, if requested to do so by the safety representatives mentioned in subsections (4) and (5) above, to establish, in accordance with regulations made by the Secretary of State, a safety committee having the function of keeping under review the measures taken to ensure the health and safety at work of his employees and such other functions as may be prescribed.

Figure 12.2 Health and Safety at Work Act 1974 Section 2. Duty of Employer.

> Section 7(a) to take reasonable care for the health and safety of himself and of others who may be affected by his acts or omissions at work.
>
> (b) as regards any duty or requirement imposed on his employer or other person by or under any of the relevant statutory provisions to co-operate with him in so far as is necessary to enable that duty or requirement to be performed or complied with.

Figure 12.3   Health and Safety at Work Act 1974 Section 7. Duty of Employee.

out the general duties under Section 2 of the Act. Figure 12.3 sets out the duties of the individual employee. A glance will show how comprehensive they are.

Abolition of Crown immunity

Health authorities used to enjoy protection from the enforcement provisions of much legislation on the grounds that, as Crown bodies, they were immune from prosecution. However, this immunity was removed by the National Health Service (Amendment) Act 1986 Sections 1 and 2 in respect of the food legislation and Health and Safety at Work Act 1974. Some immunities were, however, retained under Schedule 8 of the Act, including Employer's Liability (Compulsory Insurance) Act 1969 (see below).

Powers of the health and safety inspector

Health and Safety inspectors employed by the Health and Safety Executive have extensive powers to ensure that health and safety duties are implemented. These powers are set out in Section 20 of the HASAW Act (see Figure 12.4). The inspector is able to issue improvement or prohibition notices that order the recipient to make equipment or premises safe or to cease a particular activity until the danger is removed. He also has the power to prosecute the authority in the Magistrates or Crown Court for a breach of the duties or regulations or to comply with the notice.

Could an individual nurse be prosecuted?

Yes, under the Health and Safety at Work Act 1974 Section 7 (see Figure 12.3), which places a duty on all employees in respect of health and safety. First, a nurse who, for example, failed to follow the correct practice in disposing of pressurised cans as a result of which an incinerator blew up, injuring a porter, could be prosecuted for breach of her duty under Section 7 of the Act. Secondly, the nurse as manager will have responsibilities in advising on and implementing the health authority's duties under the Act and if she neglects these she could also be prosecuted personally.

Situation 12.1   Ward boiler

A ward kitchen has a water heater that is not fixed according to the regulations. The boiler is moved to a more convenient location. A lead from the boiler runs to a point a few feet away. A domestic trips over the lead, the boiler falls on her, and she is severely scalded. The health and safety inspectorate investigate and consider prosecuting the ward sister and others responsible.

An inspector may, for the purpose of carrying into effect any of the relevant statutory provisions within the field of responsibility of the enforcing authority which appointed him, exercise the powers set out in subsection (2) below.

(2) The powers of an inspector referred to in the preceding subsection are the following, namely:

(a) at any reasonable time (or, in a situation which in his opinion is or may be dangerous, at any time) to enter any premises which he has reason to believe it is necessary for him to enter for the purpose mentioned in subsection (1) above;

(b) to take with him a constable if he has reasonable cause to apprehend any serious obstruction in the execution of his duty;

(c) without prejudice to the preceding paragraph, on entering any premises by virtue of paragraph (a) above to take with him:

(i) any other person duly authorised by his (the inspector's) enforcing authority; and

(ii) any equipment or materials required for any purpose for which the power of entry is being exercised;

(d) to make such examination and investigation as may in any circumstances be necessary for the purpose mentioned in subsection (1) above;

(e) as regards any premises which he has power to enter to direct that those premises or any part of them, or anything therein, shall be left undisturbed (whether generally or in particular respects) for so long as is reasonably necessary for the purpose of any examination or investigation under paragraph (d) above;

(f) to take such measurements and photographs and make such recordings as he considers necessary for the purpose of any examination or investigation under paragraph (d) above;

(g) to take samples of any articles or substances found in any premises which he has power to enter, and of the atmosphere in or in the vicinity of any such premises;

(h) in the case of any article or substance found in any premises which he has power to enter, being an article or substance which appears to him to have caused or to be likely to cause danger to health or safety, to cause it to be dismantled or subjected to any process or test (but not so as to damage or destroy it unless this is in the circumstances necessary for the purpose mentioned in subsection (1) above);

(i) in the case of any such article or substance as is mentioned in the preceding paragraph, to take possession of it and detain it for so long as is necessary for all or any of the following purposes, namely:

(i) to examine it and do to it anything which he has power to do under that paragraph;

(ii) to ensure that it is not tampered with before his examination of it is completed;

(iii) to ensure that it is available for use as evidence in any proceedings for an offence under any of the relevant statutory provisions or any proceedings relating to a notice under Section 21 or 22;

(j) if he is conducting an examination or investigation under (d) to require any person . . . to answer any questions as the inspector thinks fit and to sign a declaration of the truth of his answers . . .

(k) to require production of, inspect and take copies of any entry in any books or documents . . .

(l) to require any person to afford himself such facilities and assistance within that person's control or responsibilities as are necessary for him to exercise his powers;

(m) any other power which is necessary for the purpose of exercising any of the above powers.

Figure 12.4 Health and Safety at Work Act 1974 Section 20.

> No person shall intentionally or recklessly interfere with or misuse anything provided in the interest of health, safety or welfare in pursuance of any relevant statutory provisions.

Figure 12.5 Health and Safety at Work Act 1974 Section 8.

It is also a criminal offence for any person to interfere with health and safety measures. (See Figure 12.5.)

General health and safety duty of employer to non-employees

Under Section 3 of the 1974 Act, the employer has a general duty of care to persons not in his employment. The employer has a duty to conduct his undertaking in such a way as to ensure, so far as is reasonably practicable, that persons not in his employment who may be affected thereby are not thereby exposed to risks to their health and safety. This duty would therefore cover patients, visitors and the general public.

The Court of Appeal has recently held[1] that, provided the employer has taken all reasonable care in laying down safe systems of work and ensuring that the employees had the necessary skill and instruction and were subject to proper supervision, with safe premises, plant and equipment, the employer was not guilty of an offence under Section 3 of the 1974 Act, if the employee was negligent and caused harm to others.

Safety Representatives and Safety Committees Regulations 1977 (SRSC)

These regulations brought into force the requirement in the HASAW Act 1974 that employers should permit the safety representative appointed by the recognised trade union to inspect the work place, get information held by the employer relating to health, safety or welfare and have paid time off for training and carrying out their functions. Each employer is required to set up a health and safety committee to consider matters relating to health and safety.

Health and Safety (Consultation with Employees) Regulations 1996

These apply to those workplaces that are not covered by SRSC and require employers to consult with workers or their representatives, on all matters relating to employees' health and safety.

Health and Safety at Work Regulations 1992

Regulations came into force on 1 January 1993 as a result of European Directives. These are shown in Box 12.4.

The regulations shown in Box 12.1 are enforceable against all employers and employees (whether NHS or not). Codes of Practice have been issued by the Health and Safety Commission. Failure to comply with the Code is not in itself an offence, but can be used in evidence in criminal proceedings.

For protection of the employee against dismissal in health and safety cases, see Chapter 10. The Environmental Protection Act 1990 creates duties in relation to waste management.

> **Box 12.1**
>
> **Health and Safety Regulations which came into force on 1 January 1993.**
>
> 1. Management of Health and Safety at Work Regulations 1992 (updated 1999).
> 2. Provision and Use of Work Equipment Regulations 1992 (updated 1998).
> 3. Manual handling operations regulations 1992 (considered in detail on pages 270–4 below)
> 4. Workplace (Health, Safety and Welfare regulations) 1992 (updated 1999).
> 5. Personal Protective Equipment at Work Regulations 1992 (updated 1999).
> 6. Health and Safety (Display Screen Equipment) Regulations 1992 (updated 1999).

Many of these have nowbeen updated and reissued.

Management of health and safety at work regulations 1992

These regulations require each employer to undertake a suitable and sufficient assessment of the risks to the health and safety of his employees. A Code of Practice has been approved in conjunction with these regulations.[2] This Code does not have legal force, but has special legal status.

If an employer is prosecuted for a breach of health or safety law and it is proved that he did not follow the relevant provisions of the Code, he will need to show that he has complied with the law in some other way, or a court will find him at fault.

The Guidance

The guidance emphasises that risk assessment must be a systematic general examination of work activity with a recording of significant findings rather than a de facto activity.

The definition of risk includes both the likelihood that harm will occur and its severity. The aim of risk assessment is to guide the judgement of the employer or self-employed person, as to the measures they ought to take to fulfil their statutory obligations laid down under the Health and Safety at Work Act 1974 and its regulations.

Suitable and sufficient is defined in the guidance as being able to:

1. 'identify the significant risks arising out of work';
2. 'identify useful information and examples of good practice';
3. and as being 'appropriate to the nature of the work and should identify the period of time for which it is likely to remain valid'.

Recording

The record should represent an effective statement of hazards and risks which then leads management to take the relevant actions to protect health and safety. It should be in writing, unless in computerised form, and should be easily retrievable. It should include:

1. a record of the preventative and protective measures in place to control risks;
2. further action required;
3. proof that a suitable and sufficient assessment has been made.

Principles that apply in risk assessment

The following principles apply in risk assessment:

1. If possible avoid the risk altogether.

2. Combat risks at source rather than by palliative measures.

3. Whenever possible, adapt work to the individual.

4. Take advantage of technological and technical progress.

5. Risk prevention measures need to form part of a coherent policy and approach having the effect of progressively reducing those risks that cannot be prevented or avoided altogether.

6. Give priority to those measures that protect the whole workplace and all those who work there, and so yield the greatest benefit.

7. Workers, whether employees or self-employed, need to understand what they need to do.

8. The avoidance, prevention and reduction of risk at work needs to be an accepted part of the approach and attitudes at all levels of the organisation and to apply to all its activities, i.e. the existence of an active health and safety culture affecting the organisation as a whole needs to be assured.

Risk Management and the nurse

For the most part, the nurse would share common health and safety hazards with other hospital, community or social services employees and thus models of risk assessment and management that applied to other health professionals would also apply to nursing. Thus hazards relating to the safety of equipment, cross-infection risks, safe working practices or to violence at work would all apply to nurses who should be involved in the system of the assessment of risk.

Each nurse should therefore be able to carry out a risk assessment of health and safety hazards in relation to colleagues, clients, carers and the general public. Manual handling and risk assessment is considered below.

Reporting of Injuries, Diseases and Dangerous Occurrences 1995 (RIDDOR 95)

The regulations govern the reporting of injuries, diseases and dangerous occurrences. The 1985 regulations were replaced by new regulations, which came into force on 1 April 1996.[3] There is now one set of regulations in place of the four sets under the 1985 regulations. The list of reportable diseases has been updated as has the list of dangerous occurrences. It is legally possible for reports to be made by telephone. A pilot scheme was tested out in Scotland.[4]

Schedule 1 to the regulations lists the major injuries and Schedule 2 lists the dangerous occurrences that are reportable.

Regulation 7 of RIDDOR lays down the requirements in relation to record keeping of reportable events or diseases. These records must be kept for at least three years from the date on which they were made. The records must contain the details set out in Schedule 4 (see Box 12.2).

Records kept under RIDDOR Schedule 4 must contain:

1. date and time of the accident or dangerous occurrence;

2. where accident by person at work: full name, occupation and nature of injury;

3. where accident suffered by a person not at work: full name of person, status, nature of injury;

4. place where the accident or dangerous occurrence happened;

5. a brief description of the circumstances in which the accident or dangerous occurrence happened;

6. date on which the event was first reported to the enforcement authority;

7. the method by which the event was reported.

Schedule 4 also sets out the records required in the event of a reportable disease.

(Chapter 5 discusses a new national reporting scheme for adverse incidents which is to be set up by the government and is to be in place by the end of 2001. This would be in addition to reporting under RIDDOR. The National Patient Safety Agency will link in with the RIDDOR reporting scheme.)

Protection of employees who report health and safety hazards

Additional protection has been given by the Trade Union Reform and Employment Rights Act 1993 against dismissal in health and safety cases and was consolidated in the Employment Rights Act 1996 (see Chapter 10). The Public Interest Disclosure Act 1998 is intended to strengthen protection given to employees who report health and safety hazards. This is considered in Chapter 4 under whistle-blowing.

Occupiers' Liability Acts 1957 and 1984

General principles

If a nurse is injured as a result of the state of the premises, she may be able to bring an action against the occupier who has a duty under the Occupiers' Liability Act 1957 to ensure that the premises are safe. The statutory duty is set out in Figure 12.6. The occupier's duty to trespassers comes under the Occupiers' Liability Act 1984 which is considered below.

The duty under the Occupiers' Liability Act is owed to the visitor. This term 'visitor' includes the person who has express permission to be on the premises as

Section 2(1) An occupier of premises owes the same duty, the 'common duty of care', to all his visitors, except in so far as he is free to and does extend, restrict, modify or exclude his duty to any visitor or visitors by agreement or otherwise.
Section 2(2) The common duty of care is a duty to take such care as in all the circumstances of the case is reasonable to see that the visitor will be reasonably safe in using the premises for the purposes for which he is invited or permitted by the occupier to be there.

Figure 12.6 Occupiers' Liability Act 1957 Sections 2(1) and (2).

well as the person who has implied permission to be there. Thus in the hospital context, the term 'visitors' will include employees, patients, friends and relatives visiting patients, contractors and suppliers, and others who have a genuine interest in being there. If any of these persons were to be injured, for example, when plaster fell off the wall, they could claim compensation from the occupier.

Who is the occupier?

The occupier is the person who has control over the premises. This will usually be the owner of the premises, but not necessarily. There could be several occupiers, each having control over the premises and responsibilities for the safety of the building. For example, contractors might be working on hospital premises and both the NHS Trust and the contractor could be regarded as occupiers for the purpose of the Act. A private house visited by a community nurse may be owner-occupied, in which case that person will be the occupier for the purposes of the Act. Alternatively, it could be under a tenancy agreement, in which case the landlord and the tenant will have different duties under this agreement regarding the upkeep and maintenance of the premises and could therefore be regarded as occupiers under the statutory provisions. Which occupier is liable for harm to a visitor will therefore depend upon the cause of the injury.

Case 12.1   Slippery floor[5]

A visitor slipped on polish, which had been put on the floor but not wiped off, that left the floor excessively slippery.

The visitor succeeded in obtaining compensation for the harm. The occupier had failed to take reasonable care for the safety of the visitor. (This was a case decided before the 1957 Act, but the result would be the same after 1957). In a more recent case,[6] a woman sustained personal injuries when, late at night, she fell down a flight of stairs leading to a public lavatory for which the LA was responsible. The premises were locked and the stairway was unlit. She admitted that she had drunk a relatively small amount of alcohol. She sued the LA on the grounds that they were occupiers of the premises and owed a duty of care to her. She lost the case on the grounds that she had voluntarily accepted the risk of injury by using the stairs in the darkness (*volenti non fit injuria* – see Chapter 6) and without taking proper care for her own safety. Further, the evidence from the A and E department showed that she had consumed a greater amount of alcohol than she had admitted in evidence. Even if the court was wrong on the voluntary assumption of risk, she would be contributorily negligent to a high degree.

What is the effect of a warning notice?

Section 2(4) (a) of the Occupiers' Liability Act 1957 is set out in Figure 12.7. The warning is not conclusive: if compliance with it is sufficient to prevent any harm to the visitor, then it will be effective as a defence in an action under the 1957 Act.

Section 2(4)(a) in determining whether the occupier of premises has discharged the common duty of care to a visitor, regard is to be had to all these circumstances, so that (for example): where damage is caused to a visitor by a danger of which he had been warned by the occupier, the warning is not to be treated without more as absolving the occupier from liability, unless in all the circumstances it was enough to enable the visitor to be reasonably safe.

Figure 12.7 Occupiers' Liability Act 1957 Section 2(4)(a).

Situation 12.2   Warning

An NHS Trust is undertaking major renovation work to a corridor and puts up a warning notice saying 'Danger'. As a nurse walks along, she is struck by a piece of plaster falling from the ceiling.

If there were other precautions that the NHS Trust could reasonably have taken, e.g. a safety net cordoning off the work area, then the NHS Trust would probably be seen to have been in breach of its duty of care to the visitor subject to the possibility of contributory negligence by her. If on the other hand, the notice said 'corridor closed – diversion' and indicated a different route which was practicable, then the occupier would have satisfied the duty under the Act. If, of course, the nurse ignored the notice, continued along the dangerous corridor, and was injured, then it is probable that there would be no breach of duty by the NHS Trust, since the notice was in all the circumstances enough to enable the nurse to be reasonably safe.

Independent contractors

Where independent contractors are brought onto site, the usual occupier or owner of the premises will not normally be liable for their safety (see Figure 12.8).

Privatisation of cleaning and catering services

What is the effect of the privatisation of services upon the occupier's liability? Privatisation may lead to some complications, since where services are contracted out, there is likely to be dual occupation of premises, i.e. by the NHS Trust and by the private company. Thus in the case of a contract for cleaning services, if an injury is caused to a visitor by the conditions of the premises, e.g. an uneven surface or falling plaster, and the NHS Trust has retained responsibility for such conditions,

Section 2(4)(b) when damage is caused to a visitor due to the faulty execution of any work of construction, maintenance or repair by an independent contractor employed by the occupier. The occupier is not to be treated without more as answerable for the danger, if in all the circumstances he had acted reasonably in entrusting the work to an independent contractor and had taken such steps (if any) as he reasonably ought in order to satisfy himself that the contractor was competent and that the work had been properly done.

Figure 12.8 Liability for independent contractor.

> Section 2(3) the circumstances relevant for the present purpose include the degree of care, and of want of care, which would ordinarily be looked for in such a visitor, so that (for example) in proper cases: an occupier must be prepared for children to be less careful than adults.

Figure 12.9 Liability for children.

then the NHS Trust would be responsible for the visitor's injuries. If, on the other hand, the injuries are caused by the carelessness of any of the contractor's employees, then the contractor would be responsible for compensating the person injured as a result of the negligence under the principles of vicarious liability previously discussed in Chapter 4. If, therefore, the employee of the cleaning firm has left the floor in a dangerous state and there are no warning notices and a nurse is injured as a consequence, she would sue the cleaning company because its employee had been negligent in the course of employment and had caused her foreseeable harm.

Liability for children under the Occupiers' Liability Act 1957

It is expressly provided that all the circumstances must be taken into account in deciding whether the occupier is in breach of his duty of care under the Act (see Figure 12.9). The occupier can expect a lower standard of care from children and therefore additional precautions have to be taken where the presence of children can be foreseen.

Case 12.2   Playing about on a boat[7]

Sutton Borough Council were the owners and occupiers of the common parts of a block of council flats. A boat with trailer was brought onto the land and abandoned on a grass area where children played. The boat became derelict and rotten. The Council put a notice on the boat that said, 'Do not touch this vehicle unless you are the owner.' Some boys planned to repair it in the hope that they could take it to Cornwall. They swivelled it round and lifted the bows on to the trailer so as to be able to get under the boat to repair the hull. They jacked the bows of the boat up. The boat fell onto the claimant, a boy of 14 years, as he lay underneath it attempting to repair and paint it. He sustained serious spinal injuries and became paraplegic.

The High Court judge awarded the claimant £633,770, taking into account contributory negligence of 25% for the injuries he sustained. However, the Court of Appeal found in favour of the defendant since, although it was reasonably foreseeable that injuries could have occurred from playing on the boat, the injuries sustained were not reasonably foreseeable and therefore the defendants were not liable for them. The Council had not disputed that it was negligent, but argued that it was not liable because the accident was of a different kind from anything that it could have reasonably foreseen. The claimant appealed to the House of Lords which upheld the appeal. The House of Lords held that ingenuity of children in finding unexpected ways of doing mischief to themselves and others should not be underestimated. Reasonable foreseeability was not a fixed point on the scale of probability. The Council was liable under the Occupiers' Liability Act 1957 and under Section 2(3) had to take into account the fact that children would be less careful than adults. The Council had admitted that it should have removed the boat and the risk that it should have taken into account was that children would meddle with the boat and injuries would thereby occur.

Clearly, following this judgment, liability depends upon how the risk is framed.

Trespassers and The Occupiers' Liability Act 1984

The Occupiers' Liability Act 1957 does not cover any duty towards trespassers. The courts recognised a limited duty of the occupier towards trespassers, particularly children, but subsequently statutory provision was made in the Occupiers' Liability Act 1984. Whether or not a duty is owed by the occupier to trespassers, in relation to risks on the premises, depends upon the following factors:

S.1 (3) a. if the occupier is aware of the danger or has reasonable grounds to believe that it exists;

b. if the occupier knows or has reasonable grounds to believe that the other is in the vicinity of the danger concerned or that he may come into the vicinity of the danger (in either case, whether the other has lawful authority for being in that vicinity or not); and

c. the risk is one against which, in all the circumstances of the case, he may reasonably be expected to offer the other some protection.

In applying these factors to decide if a duty is owed to a trespasser, it would be rare for a duty to be owed to an adult. There is, however, more likely to be a duty owed to a child trespasser. For example, on hospital premises, if a child is expressly told that he cannot go through a particular door or into another section of the hospital and he disobeys those instructions, then he becomes a trespasser for the purposes of the Occupiers' Liability Acts. It is likely that a duty would then arise under the 1984 Act.

The nature of the duty owed to trespassers.

Once it is held that a duty of care is owed to a trespasser, Section 1(4) of the 1984 Act defines the duty as shown in Box 12.3.

Box 12.3

Duty of care to a trespasser 1(4) 1984 Act

'The duty is to take such care as is reasonable in all the circumstances of the case to see that he does not suffer injury on the premises by reason of the danger concerned'.

The duty can be discharged by giving warnings, but in the case of children, these may have limited effect and depend upon the age of the child.

The nurse and premises in the community

Where a nurse is visiting private homes, the occupier may be the owner of the house who is also in occupation, or the occupier may be a tenant. If the nurse is injured on the premises, it will depend upon how the injury occurred as to who would be liable: thus, if she is injured as the result of a frayed rug, the person in occupation, whether tenant or owner, would be liable; if she were injured as a result of a structural defect, then the owner or landlord would be liable depending upon the nature of the tenancy agreement.

The occupier has the right to ask any visitor to leave the premises. Should the visitor fail to leave, then she becomes a trespasser and the occupier can use reasonable force to evict the trespasser. If, therefore, the nurse should be asked by a client or carer to leave, she should go. Should she be concerned for the well being of the client, she should ensure that social services are notified so that appropriate action can be taken under the National Assistance Act 1948 or the Mental Health Act 1983. Where there is a clash between carer and client and the former asks her to leave and the latter for her to stay, the nurse has to decide on the basis of the specific circumstances: the rights of the client to occupation as compared with those of the carer and the specific needs of the client. Where she considers it prudent to leave the premises, she must discuss with her manager how best the client's needs can be met.

Consumer Protection Act 1987

Product liability

The Consumer Protection Act 1987 enables a claim to be brought where harm has occurred as a result of a defect in a product. It is a form of strict liability in that negligence by the defendant does not have to be proved. The Consumer Protection Act 1987 (Part 1), which came into force on 1 March 1988, gives a right of compensation against the producers and suppliers of products if a defect in the product has caused personal injury, death, loss or damage to property, without the requirement of showing that the defendant was at fault. This was introduced into this country following an EEC directive dated 25 July 1985 (No. 85/3741/EEC). The Act applies to the Crown. The NHS Trust itself could be a defendant in a product liability action since it is a producer of many products; it could also be liable as a supplier.

A product is defined as meaning any goods or electricity and includes a product that is comprised in another product, whether by virtue of being a component part or raw material or otherwise.

Defect

The definition of defect is shown in Figure 12.10. The defendant can rely on the fact that the state of scientific knowledge at the time was such that the defect could not have been discovered (i.e. 'the state of the art' defence or that the state of scientific and technical knowledge at the time the goods were supplied was not such that the producer of products of that kind might be expected to have discovered the defect).

How does product liability affect the nurse?

Situation 12.3   Needle injury

A nurse is giving an injection to a patient when the needle snaps and she is injured.

3. (1) Subject to the following provisions of this section, there is a defect in a product for the purposes of this part if the safety of the product is not such as persons generally are entitled to expect; and for those purposes 'safety', in relation to a product, shall include safety with respect to products comprised in that product and safety in the context of risks of damage to property, as well as in the context of risks of death or personal injury.

(2) In determining for the purposes of subsection (1) above what persons generally are entitled to expect in relation to a product all the circumstances shall be taken into account, including:

(a) the manner in which, and purposes for which, the product has been marketed, its get-up, the use of any mark in relation to the product and any instructions for, or warnings with respect to, doing or refraining from doing anything with or in relation to the product;

(b) what might reasonably be expected to be done with or in relation to the product; and

(c) the time when the product was supplied by its producer to another;

and nothing in this section shall require a defect to be inferred from the fact alone that the safety of a product which is supplied after that time is greater than the safety of the product in question.

4. (1) In any civil proceedings by virtue of this part against any person ('the person proceeded against') in respect of a defect in a product it shall be a defence for him to show:

(a) that the defect is attributable to compliance with any requirement imposed by or under any enactment or with any Community obligation; or

(b) that the person proceeded against did not at any time supply the product to another; or

(c) that the following conditions are satisfied, that is to say:

    (i) that the only supply of the product to another by the person proceeded against was otherwise than in the course of a business of that person's; and

    (ii) that Section 2(2) above does not apply to that person or applies to him by virtue only of things done otherwise than with a view to profit; or

(d) that the defect did not exist in the product at the relevant time; or

(e) that the state of scientific and technical knowledge at the relevant time was not such that a producer of products of the same description as the product in question might be expected to have discovered the defect if it had existed in his products while they were under his control; or

(f) that the defect

    (i) constituted a defect in a product ('the subsequent product') in which the product in question has been comprised; and

    (ii) was wholly attributable to the design of the subsequent product or to compliance by the producer of the product in question with instructions given by the producer of the subsequent product.

Figure 12.10 Definition of defect and defences in product liability.

Under the Consumer Protection Act 1987, the nurse would need to discover from the supplier of the needle in the NHS Trust (probably the CSSD) the producer of that particular needle. The supplier has a duty under Section 2(3) to inform her of the name of the producer who will then be strictly liable to the nurse for causing her harm. If the CSSD is unable to provide her with that information, the CSSD could itself be liable to her. The nurse herself would have to show that there was a defect in the needle, i.e. that the safety was not such as persons generally are entitled to expect. This is defined in Section (2) as including the manner in which and purpose for which the product has been marketed, the instructions and warnings accompanying it, and what might reasonably be expected to be done with or in relation to it at the time it was supplied (see Figure 12.9). In addition, the nurse has a remedy under the Employer's Liability (Defective Equipment) Act 1969 (see below).

Timing
There is a ten-year time limit from the date of the supply of the product. The individual plaintiff must bring the action within three years of suffering the harm or having knowledge of the relevant circumstances.

Naming the producer
What if the NHS Trust department that supplied the goods cannot name the producer? The person who suffered the harm must ask the supplier to identify the producer or importer of the product in the EU and must make that request within a reasonable period after the damage has occurred and at a time when it is not reasonably practicable for the person making the request to identify those persons. If the health department supplying the goods fails to comply within a reasonable period after receiving the request, then the claimant is entitled to recover damages from the supplying department. All departments in a NHS Trust that supply products to persons who suffer damage from them could thus become liable: the supplies department, pharmacy, cleaning, catering, CSSD, office equipment, works and buildings.

The implications of this are that department records must be sufficiently comprehensive and clear to provide the appropriate information to the person injured by the defect, in order that the claim can be made against the actual producer of the product rather than the supplier.

The nurse as supplier
Could the nurse ever be a supplier? In the course of her duty, a nurse certainly supplies many products to patients, other staff, visitors, and contractors: drugs, food/drink, equipment, syringes, etc. Could she be a supplier for the purposes of this Act?

Situation 12.4   Supplying defective products

The nurse gives a patient a high protein food to take home with him, which is defective, e.g. it has glass in it and the patient is injured.

In most similar circumstances, it will be clear to the person suffering harm who the producers or trademark user are and it will therefore be reasonably practicable for the person suffering harm to identify the potential defendant. In other cases, the nurse will have obtained the goods from another department in the hospital, which would become the supplier for the purposes of the Act.

Product liability and the Employer's Liability (Defective Equipment) Act 1969

The relationship between these two Acts is shown in Figure 12.11. The right of the employee to claim from the employer under the 1969 Act is unaffected by the provisions of the 1987 Act. Clearly, any person who has been injured by a defective product can use whichever remedy is likely to be most successful and in fact can bring an action using several different causes of action.

---

1. The injured employee can obtain compensation from the employer under the 1969 Act only if there has been negligence by a third party.
2. The injured employee can obtain compensation from the employer as supplier only if he has not identified the producer under the 1987 Act.
3. The 1987 Act covers all persons suffering damage, i.e. patients, employees, visitors etc. The 1969 Act only relates to employees.
4. The 1987 Act covers damages in the form of personal injury, death, loss or damage to property, the 1969 Act only covers loss of life, impairment of a person's physical or mental condition and any disease, not loss or damage to property.
5. Fault need not be established under the 1987 Act – only a defect in the product. However, the defence of what is known at the time is available.

Figure 12.11 Product and defective equipment liability.

Defences

Certain defences are available under Section 4 and are shown in Box 12.4.

Box 12.4

Defences under the Consumer Protection Act 1987 Section 4.

a. that the defect is attributable to compliance with any requirement imposed by or under any enactment or with any Community obligation; or

b. that the person proceeded against did not at any time supply the product to another; or

c. that the following conditions are satisfied, i.e.:
   i. that the only supply of the product to another by the person proceeded against was otherwise than in the course of a business of that person's; and
   ii. that Section 2(2) above does not apply to that person or applies to him by virtue only of things done otherwise than with a view to profit; or

d. that the defect did not exist in the product at the relevant time; or

e. that the state of scientific and technical knowledge at the relevant time was not such that a producer of products of the same description as the product in question might be expected to have discovered the defect if it had existed in his products while they were under his control; or

f. that the defect
   i. constituted a defect in a product (the subsequent product) in which the product in question had been comprised; and
   ii. was wholly attributable to the design of the subsequent product or to compliance by the producer of the product in question with instructions given by the producer of the subsequent product.

What damage must the plaintiff establish?

Compensation is payable for death, personal injury or any loss of or damage to any property (including land) (Section 5(1)). The loss or damage shall be regarded as having occurred at the earliest time at which a person with an interest in the property had knowledge of the material facts about the loss or damage (Section 5(5)). Knowledge is further defined in Section 5(6) and (7).

There have been few examples of actions being brought under the Consumer Protection Act 1987 in health care cases and only a handful of cases brought under it have been reported. One reported in March 1993[8] led to Simon Garratt being awarded £1,400 against the manufacturers of a pair of surgical scissors that broke during an operation on his knee, with the blade being left embedded. A second operation was required to remove it. Had he relied upon the law of negligence to obtain compensation, he would have had to show that the manufacturers were in breach of the duty of care that they owed to him. Under the Consumer Protection Act 1987, he had to show the harm, the defect and the fact that it was produced by the defendant.

A report by the National Consumer Council[9] in November 1995 recommended that consumers should be assisted in using their rights under this Act.

In a recent case (*A and Others* v. *National Blood Authority and Another*, *The Times Law Report*, 4 April 2001), it was held that a claim brought under the Consumer Protection Act 1987 in respect of the infection by patients with hepatitis C contracted from blood and blood products used in blood transfusions could succeed. This decision may well lead to greater use of the Consumer Protection Act 1987 if personal injuries are caused, since negligence does not have to be established under the Act, only that there was a defect in the product that has caused the harm.

Medical Devices Agency and warnings

The Medical Devices Agency (MDA) was established to promote the safe and effective use of devices. In particular its role is to ensure that whenever a medical device is used, it is:

1. suitable for its intended purpose;
2. properly understood by the professional user; and
3. maintained in a safe and reliable condition.

Guidance has been issued by the CPS on the role of the Medical Devices Agency.[10] What is a medical device? Annex B to safety notice 9801 gives examples of medical devices.[11] It covers the following:

1. Equipment used in the diagnosis or treatment of disease, and the monitoring of patients: e.g. syringes and needles, dressings, catheters, beds, mattresses and covers, physiotherapy equipment.
2. Equipment used in life support, e.g. ventilators, defibrilators.
3. In vitro diagnostic medical devices and their accessories, e.g. blood gas analysers. (Regulations are to come into force in 2000 on in vitro diagnostic devices.)

4. Equipment used in the care of disabled people, e.g. orthotic and prosthetic appliances, wheelchairs and special support seating, patient hoists, walking aids, pressure care prevention equipment.

5. Aids to daily living, e.g. commodes, hearing aids, urine drainage systems, domiciliary oxygen therapy systems, incontinence pads, prescribable footwear.

6. Equipment used by ambulance services (but not the vehicles themselves), e.g. stretchers and trolleys, resuscitators.

7. Other examples of medical devices, including: condoms, contact lenses and care products, intrauterine devices.

Regulations[12] require that from 14 June 1998:

> all medical devices placed on the market (made available for use or distribution even if no charge is made) must conform to 'the essential requirements' including safety required by law, and bear a CE marking as a sign of that conformity. Although most of the obligations contained in the Regulations fall on manufacturers, purchasers who are positioned further down the supply chain may also be liable – for example, for supplying equipment which does not bear a CE marking or which carries a marking liable to mislead people.[13]

This is the requirement of the EC Directive on medical devices.[14] The manufacturer who can demonstrate conformity with the regulations is entitled to apply the CE marking to a medical device.

The essential requirements include the general principle that:

> A device must not harm patients or users, and any risks must be outweighed by benefits. Design and construction must be inherently safe, and if there are residual risks, users must be informed about them. Devices must perform as claimed, and not fail due to the stresses of normal use. Transport and storage must not have adverse effects. Essential requirements also include prerequisites in relation to the design and construction, infection and microbial contamination, mechanical construction, measuring devices, exposure to radiation, built-in computer systems, electrical and electronic design, mechanical design, devices which deliver fluids to a patient, function of controls and indicators.

Exceptions to these regulations include the following:

1. In-vitro diagnostic devices to be covered by a separate directive (still being prepared).

2. Active implants (covered by the Active Implantable Medical Devices Regulations[15]).

3. Devices made specially for the individual patient ('custom made').

4. Devices undergoing clinical investigation.

5. Devices made by the organisation ('legal entity') using them.

In January 1998, the MDA issued a device bulletin[16] giving guidance to organisations on implementing the regulations. The bulletin covers the sections shown in Box 12.5.

Box 12.5

Bulletin of the MDA January 1998

Strategies for deploying, monitoring, and controlling devices;
Purchasing medical products;
When a device is delivered;
Prescription of devices;
Record-keeping;
Maintenance and repair;
Training;
Community issues.

The MDA has powers under the Consumer Protection Act 1987 to issue warnings or remove devices from the market.

Devices are divided into three classes according to possible hazards, class 2 being further subdivided. Thus class 1 has a low risk, e.g. a bandage; class 2a has a medium risk, e.g. simple breast pump; class 2b has a medium risk, e.g. ventilator; class 3 has a high risk, e.g. intraaortic balloon.

Any warning about equipment issued by the Medical Devices Agency should be acted upon immediately. Notices from the Agency are sent to Regional General Managers, chief executives of HAs and NHS Trusts, directors of social services, managers of independent health care units and rehabilitation service managers. Failure to ensure that these notices are obtained and acted upon could be used as evidence of failure to provide a reasonable standard of care. The Medical Devices Agency issued further guidance on repair and maintenance of equipment in 2000.[17] It sets out good practice for the organisation responsible for carrying out repairs and maintenance.

Adverse Incident Reporting procedures

In 1998, the MDA issued a safety notice[18] requiring health care managers, health care and social care professionals and other users of medical devices to establish a system to encourage the prompt reporting of adverse incidents relating to medical devices to the MDA. The procedures should be regularly reviewed, updated as necessary, and should ensure that adverse incident reports are submitted to MDA in accordance with the notice.

What is an adverse incident? The safety notice defines this as:

> an event which gives rise to, or has the potential to produce, unexpected or unwanted effects involving the safety of patients, users or other persons.

Such an event may be caused by shortcomings in:

> the device itself, instructions for use, servicing and maintenance, locally initiated modifications or adjustments, user practices including training, management procedures, the environment in which it is used or stored or incorrect prescription.

Where the incident has led to or could have led to the following:

Death; life threatening illness or injury; deterioration in health; temporary or permanent impairment of a body function or damage to a body structure; the necessity for medical or surgical intervention to prevent permanent impairment of a body function or permanent damage to a body structure; unreliable test results leading to inappropriate diagnosis or therapy.

Minor faults or discrepancies should also be reported to the MDA.

Liaison officer

The safety notice suggests that organisations should appoint a liaison officer who would have the necessary authority to:

1. ensure that procedures are in place for the reporting of adverse incidents involving medical devices to the MDA;
2. act as the point of receipt for MDA publications;
3. ensure dissemination within their own organisation of MDA publications; and
4. act as the contact point between the MDA and their organisation.

Single use items

Where a supplier has labelled its products 'single use', then the Medical Devices Agency has advised that it should not be reprocessed and reused unless the reprocessor is able to ensure the integrity and safety in use of each reprocessed item and there is clear evidence of the effectiveness of the reprocessing operation.[19]

Medical devices and the community

The MDA bulletin published in January 1998 gives specific guidance on equipment used in the community. It suggests that the delivery and collection of equipment procedures should include checks that:

1. the correct equipment has been delivered in good order;
2. the end-user has received training; or
3. the end-user has been told not to use the device until trained;
4. the delivery and collection process does not risk cross-contamination.

The guidance emphasises that good device management is the same for hospitals and the community. It covers in particular: the delivery and commissioning of loan equipment; collection of equipment when no longer needed; checking and testing of returned equipment; adaptation of equipment; insurance; and device safety for medical and dental surgeries. Specific guidance on sterilisers, dental X-ray equipment and resuscitators is also provided. For the latter, it suggests that the best practice is for the equipment to be checked daily, including the pressure in the oxygen cylinder, and that the bag is working, any drugs are still in date, any sterile materials are in date and packaging is undamaged.

Control of Substances Hazardous to Health 1988 and 1996

The Control of Substances Hazardous to Health (COSHH) Regulations 1988 came into effect in 1989 and were replaced by amended regulations in 1996. The regulations aim to control activities where exposure to substances could lead to disease or ill health, i.e. substances that are toxic, harmful, corrosive or irritant; the regulations also cover those that have delayed effects or are hazardous in conjunction with other substances. The employer must assess the risks and take appropriate action, e.g. providing protective clothing, information and training of staff. All health workers have responsibilities under the Regulations Relating to the Control of Substances Hazardous to Health. The nurse who uses different substances in her work should be specifically alert to the need to ensure that the regulations are implemented. New Maximum Exposure Limits have been introduced. Further details of the proposals can be obtained from the HSC.

The five stages of a COSHH assessment as set out in the guide issued by the Health and Safety Executive[20] are shown in Box 12.6.

Box 12.6

Stages in COSHH assessment

1. Gather information about the substances, the work and the working practices.
2. Evaluate the risks to health.
3. Decide what needs to be done.
4. Record the assessment.
5. Review the assessment.

There must be clarity over who has the responsibility of carrying out the assessment. The guidance emphasises the importance of involving all employees in the assessment.

All potentially hazardous substances must be identified: these will include domestic materials such as bleach, toilet cleaner, window cleaner, and polishes; office materials such as correction fluids as well as the medicinal products in the treatment room and materials and substances used in nursing.

An assessment has to be made as to whether each substance could be inhaled, swallowed, absorbed or introduced through the skin, or injected into the body (such as needles).

The effects of each route of entry or contact and the potential harm must then be identified.

There must then be an identification of the persons who could be exposed and how.

Once this assessment is complete, decisions must be made on the necessary measures to be taken to comply with the regulations and who should undertake the different tasks. In certain cases, health surveillance is required if there is a reasonable likelihood that the disease or ill-effect associated with exposure will occur in the workplace concerned. Nurses should be particularly vigilant about any substances used in their activities, including cleaning fluids, and ensure that a risk assessment is undertaken and its results implemented.

Mangers should ensure that the employees are given information, instruction and training.

Records should show the results of the assessment, what action has been taken and by whom, and regular monitoring and review of the situation.

Common law duties: employer's duty and employee's duty

The direct duty of care for the safety of the employee

Duty of the employer as an implied term of the contract of employment

As was seen in Chapter 10, some of the terms in the contract of employment are implied by the law. These include the obligation of the employer to safeguard the health and safety of the employee by employing competent staff, setting up a safe system of work and maintaining safe premises, equipment and plant. The employee must obey the reasonable instructions of the employer and take reasonable care in carrying out the work. Thus the employee may have a claim for breach of contract by the employer if her back has been injured as a result of failures on the employer's part in not providing the appropriate training or equipment. The employer's duty at common law is set out in Figure 12.12.

The employer's duty at common law to take reasonable care to safeguard the employees against the reasonable foreseeable possibility of harm arising from work related disorders is paralleled by the duties laid down in the Health and Safety at Work Act 1974 and under the regulations relating to Manual Handling, the Management of Health and Safety at Work, Display Screen Equipment and the other regulations discussed above.

At common law, the employer has an implied term in the contract of employment to look after the safety of the employee:

1. To ensure the premises, plant and equipment are safe.
2. To provide competent staff.
3. To establish a safe system of work.

Figure 12.12   Employer's direct duty of care.

Effect of failures by the employer

Failure by the employer to take reasonable care of the health, safety or welfare of the employee could result in the following actions by the employee:

1. Action for breach of contract of employment.
2. Action for negligence, where the employee has suffered harm. The employee could also use as evidence breach of specific health and safety regulations.
3. Application in the employment tribunal for constructive dismissal, if it can be shown that the employer is in fundamental breach of the contract of employment.

Examples of a case brought in relation to the employer's duty of care at common law are the manual handling case and the stress case outlined below.

There is an overlap between the direct duty of care of the employer for the safety of the employee and the duty of the employer as occupier under the Occupiers' Liability Act 1957 (see above). Thus in a case where a nurse is injured as a result of defects in the NHS Trust's premises, she may have a cause of action under the Occupiers' Liability Act, and also because of breach of the employer's common law duty to care for the employee.

Insurance by the employer

The Employer's Liability (Compulsory Insurance) Act 1969 (see Figure 12.13) obliges all non-Crown employers to be covered by an approved policy of insurance against liability for bodily injury or disease sustained by an employee and arising out of and in course of employment. By Section 60 of the NHS and Community Care Act 1990, health authorities ceased to enjoy Crown immunity. However, Schedule 8 of the Act preserves immunity from this Act for health authorities and NHS Trusts. The employers of a nurse working in the private sector or a practice nurse working for general practitioners are, however, bound by the Act.

Every employer carrying on any business in Great Britain shall insure against liability for bodily injury or disease sustained by his employees and arising out of and in course of their employment.

Business includes a trade or profession, and includes any activity carried out by a body of persons, whether corporate or unincorporate. Penalty for failure to insure.

Figure 12.13 Employer's Liability (Compulsory Insurance) Act 1969.

Defective equipment

If an employee has been injured as the result of defective equipment, an additional remedy may be available under the Employer's Liability (Defective Equipment) Act 1969. This is set out in Figure 12.14. The Act is binding upon the Crown and enables the employee to obtain compensation from the employer if the injury has been caused by defective equipment supplied by the employer where a third party is to blame. Instead of the employee having the cost and hassle of obtaining compensation from the third party, that burden falls upon the employer from whom the employee can obtain direct compensation.

Situation 12.5   Faulty bed

A nurse is injured when a recently supplied bed, which she is raising by the foot pedal, breaks and falls on to her leg. It is discovered that there was a defect in the bed mounting which should have been spotted by the manufacturers before it left the factory.

Factors which must be present

1. Personal injury by employee in course of employment.
2. As a consequence of a defect in equipment.
3. Equipment provided by his employer for purposes of his business.
4. Defect attributable wholly or partly to the fault of a third party (whether identified or not).

Action

1. Injury deemed to be also attributable to negligence on part of employer, i.e. employee can recover compensation from employer.
2. Contributory negligence by employee may be raised as a defence (either full or partial).
3. Employer can recover contribution from third party (in contract or negligence).

Applies to the Crown.

Figure 12.14   Employer's Liability (Defective Equipment) Act 1969.

The nurse could claim compensation from the NHS Trust under the provisions of the Employer's Liability (Defective Equipment) Act 1969. The costs, problems and time associated with suing the manufacturers would then fall upon the shoulders of the NHS Trust. She also has an additional remedy under the Consumer Protection Act 1987 (see above).

Remedies available to an injured employee

The laws relating to health and safety are significant to nursing practice. The nurse herself may suffer from injuries at work and also she has a significant responsibility to protect the health and safety of others, including colleagues, patients and visitors. Back injuries are seen as almost an occupational hazard for nurses and midwives; publicity has recently been given to the number of staff who are injured by violence at work, including work in the community; the hazards that a nurse faces in administering carcinogenic substances such as cytotoxic drugs are only now being appreciated and precautions (such as protective clothing and masks) are being laid down. The nurse has always faced the problem of contamination from infectious diseases and the particular problems relating to AIDS and infectious diseases are considered in Chapter 26. In this section, the remedies available to the nurse for injuries at work will be considered. The remedies can be seen in Figure 12.15 overleaf.

If the nurse has been injured at work, she may be able to bring several of the actions set out in Figure 12.15 and can sue several different defendants.

Injuries caused by another employee

Where a nurse has been injured as a result of the negligence of another employee, she can either sue the employee for compensation or she could bring an action against the NHS Trust under the principles of vicarious liability.

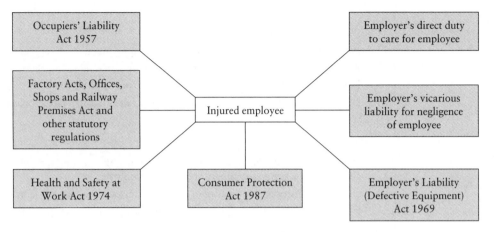

Figure 12.15 Remedies available to an injured employee.

Situation 12.6 Wheelchair chaos

Two nurses, Mary and Jean, are working together in a ward for elderly mentally infirm patients. They are moving a patient from a chair into a wheelchair. As they do so, the wheelchair moves and Mary, in her endeavour to save the patient, takes the full weight and falls to the floor. She suffers a severe injury to her back and shoulder. An investigation reveals that Jean was responsible for ensuring that the wheelchair brake was safely on and her carelessness was responsible for Mary's injuries.

Mary can take one of the following paths.

1. She could sue Jean personally, since Jean is probably in breach of the duty of care she owes to Mary to ensure that reasonable steps are taken to prevent foreseeable harm to Mary. However, such an action is likely to be pointless unless Jean is insured for such liability or has sufficient funds to pay compensation to Mary.

2. She could sue the NHS Trust for its vicarious liability for harm caused by the negligence of an employee. Jean is an employee, has been negligent, and is acting in the course of employment. Mary would still have to establish that Jean was personally negligent, but this action has the advantage over suing Jean personally since the NHS Trust should have the funds to pay compensation.

3. In addition, Mary could sue the NHS Trust for breach of its duty of care to look after her safety as an employee. In this action, Mary would have to establish that the NHS Trust itself was at fault, e.g. if it had failed to provide Jean with adequate training in carrying out such a manoeuvre (see below).

In all three actions, it will, of course, be a defence, complete or partial, that Mary was herself contributorily negligent (see Chapter 6).

Liability of the employer for work outside the premises

In the following case, a health authority was held liable for failing to give adequate instruction to a young resident support worker.

> *Case 12.3   Employer's liability for failing to give adequate instructions*[21]
>
> A resident support worker at a home for mentally and physically disabled residents was sent on a week's camping holiday with a patient without supervision or assistance. She had no training or instruction in the use of camping equipment. She suffered burns to her face and hands when, needing to cook an evening meal for the patient, she changed a cylinder on a gas cooker at the entrance to the tent and near to a lit candle. There was an explosion and the tent caught fire. The Court of Appeal agreed with the High Court finding that she should have been given instruction and better equipment, but held her one third to blame because she realised the risk in what she did.

Special areas

Violence

Violence against health service employees is increasing, not just from strangers in the streets, but also from carers and clients. The rules relating to the terms of service of general practitioners have recently been changed to enable them to arrange for the removal from their list of any patient who threatens them with violence. In 1983,[22] a voluntary patient at a mental hospital was charged with assault occasioning actual bodily harm to an occupational therapist employed at the hospital. An occupational therapist was killed by a mentally ill patient in the Edith Morgan Unit at Torbay. An inquiry was set up following this death.[23] A health care assistant was attacked in the grounds of a Bristol hospital.[24] The incident occurred in spite of the fact that there were security guards and improved lighting and closed circuit television as a result of a review four and a half years before.

If a nurse is involved in violence or witnesses a violent incident, she should make sure that a report and statement are completed.

The employer has a duty to take reasonable care of the nurse in relation to reasonably foreseeable violence. A risk assessment would therefore be required of this possibility and as a result any reasonable means to protect the employee should be adopted.

1. Is it possible to remove the risk altogether?

    If the answer to this is 'yes' but, for example, only by stopping all home visits by nurses, this would not be reasonably practicable.

2. What preventive action or protective measures can be taken?

    The answer to this might include the provision of two way radios, personal alarms or, in very dangerous areas or on visits to clients who present a threat, nurses going in pairs or accompanied by another person. In the institutional setting, protective measures may include more staffing, higher levels of supervision of difficult to manage patients and special security measures.

3. Review the situation to ascertain if the nature of the risk has changed (e.g. Is the district more violent than it was formerly assessed to be? Has the nature and condition of patients in a hospital ward deteriorated?) and to assess the extent of the success of the measures taken to prevent harm to nurses. Are any further measures necessary?

This type of analysis will relate not only to the nurses, but could be part of a wider assessment of all health professionals into which the nurse could have an input.

Reference should be made to the guidance prepared by the Health and Safety Commission.[25] This gives practical advice for reducing the risk of violence in a variety of settings and emphasises the importance of commitment from the highest levels of management. It was reported in October 1998[26] that North West Durham Health Care Trust is to meet the full legal costs and provide emotional and professional support for all health care staff who take court action against an assailant in cases where the Crown Prosecution Service (CPS) fails to pursue the offender. It might be questioned, however, why the CPS is failing to prosecute; if the reason is the unlikelihood of securing a conviction, it may be therefore that the health care professional would not succeed. Perhaps more emphasis should be placed on encouraging the CPS to fulfil its function. In October 2000, the DoH announced new guidelines to tackle violence against NHS staff who are most at risk.[27] The guidelines cover risk assessment, crime prevention, protection of NHS staff in the community, techniques for dealing with abusive and potentially violent situations, training, reporting of incidents, the criminal justice system and support for victims.

Monitoring of potentially violent situations is essential and the nurse should play her full part to bring any concerns to the attention of the management and ensure that action is taken. Steve McHale,[28] an aggression management co-ordinator, emphasises that nurses themselves must develop the skills to defuse rather than build up aggression. He states that, 'The main causes of aggression against nurses are the patient's loss of control or autonomy over a situation, a feeling of depersonalisation and a lack of communication.'

Situation 12.7 Fear of violence

A nurse visited a patient in his home following a stroke. She felt threatened by his attitude, but found difficulty in defining exactly the reason for her fears. Should she record her concerns?

This is a situation with which many nurses could identify. There is almost an intuitive feeling of fear. However, the nurse would have a duty to ensure that her colleagues were warned of potential dangers and she might therefore record in her notes that it might be advisable for a second person to accompany the nurse for the next house call. The duty of confidentiality owed to the patient (see Chapter 8) would be subject to an exception in the public interest where a nurse needed to warn colleagues about a fear of violence from a particular patient.

Suing the NHS Trust

The employer's duty extends to protecting the employee against reasonably foreseeable attacks from violent patients or even from violent visitors and trespassers.

Situation 12.8   Mixed ward

A psychiatric nurse is on an acute mixed ward. Complaints have been made that although this is a mixed ward, there are insufficient numbers of male nurses and thus the female nurses are often dealing with male patients on their own. A known aggressive male patient, without any warning or provocation, suddenly produces a razor and cuts a nurse badly on the face.

To obtain compensation from the NHS Trust, the nurse must establish that another employee has been negligent in course of employment and therefore the NHS Trust is vicariously liable, or that the NHS Trust was itself directly at fault. To establish this, she would need to show that inadequate precautions were taken for her safety: that there were reasonable precautions that the authority could have taken and failed to take, e.g. male staffing; training in the handling of violent patients; special facilities for dealing with known aggressive patients; a special wing; an alarm system; a safe system for control of dangerous items. The injured nurse would also have to show a causal connection between the injuries she suffered and these failures on the authority's part, i.e. if she would still have been injured even had these precautions been taken, then the NHS Trust would not be liable.

In its defence, the NHS Trust would have to establish either that such reasonable precautions had been provided – a dispute on the facts – or that even if such precautions had been taken the injury would still have occurred. In addition, it might be able to show that the nurse was contributorily negligent. Some employers have argued that being injured by aggressive mentally disturbed patients is an occupational hazard for the nurse working with the mentally ill or handicapped and that there is a voluntary assumption of the risk of injury by the staff concerned (see Chapter 6). However, it is not thought that this would provide a successful defence for an employer who was clearly at fault in respect of reasonable precautions in protecting the nurse from harm.

Suing the patient

Could the nurse sue the patient if she has been injured by an assault? Yes, the nurse would have a right of action against anyone who assaults her, but there are difficulties where the defendant is mentally disordered. The Magistrates Courts have thrown out such cases as being inappropriate. If the defendant is prosecuted, then the magistrate or judge can make an order for compensation to be paid by the defendant to the injured person. If the nurse decides to bring civil proceedings for trespass to the person, the defendant may not have the resources to pay any

1. Obtain compensation from the criminal courts following a successful prosecution of the assailant.
2. Sue the aggressor personally for trespass to the person (there is little point if they have no assets or income to pay the damages awarded).
3. Sue the employer if she can establish that there has been a breach of the employer's duty of care to her.
4. Claim compensation from the Criminal Injuries Compensation Authority (see Figure 12.17).
5. She could receive, if eligible, statutory sick pay, Whitley Council sickness pay and DSS benefits.

Figure 12.16 Remedies following violence.

1. Scheme came into force on 1 April 1994.
2. Applies to all applications on or after that date irrespective of when the incident took place.
3. The applicant must have been:
   (a) a victim of a crime of violence or injured in some way covered by the scheme;
   (b) physically and/or mentally injured as a result;
   (c) injured seriously enough to qualify for at least the minimum award.
4. The tariff scheme is from £1,000 (Bond 1), e.g. multiple minor injuries/fractured tooth, to £250,000 (Bond 25), e.g. quadriplegic/permanent serious brain damage.
5. The applicant must have reported the matter to the police.
6. The applicant must apply within one year to the CICA.

Figure 12.17 Compensation from the Criminal Injuries Compensation Authority.

compensation awarded by the civil courts. Alternatively (and probably preferably), the nurse could seek compensation from the Criminal Injuries Compensation Authority (see Chapter 2, page 32 and Figure 12.17).

Violence by a visitor or employee

Situation 12.9   Injuries in the accident and emergency department

A patient with lacerations to the face and severe bruising is brought into the department by two friends. All three have been drinking heavily. Two nurses take the injured man into the treatment room and ask the others to stay in the waiting room or leave the hospital. They insist on following the patient and in the ensuing fracas a nurse is injured. The various possible remedies are set out in Figure 12.16 and compensation from the Criminal Injuries Compensation Authority is set out in Figure 12.17.

Self-defence

Can the nurse defend herself if attacked by a patient, visitor, trespasser or employee?

Every citizen has the right of self-defence. In the above example, therefore, the nurse could use reasonable means to defend herself against an aggressor. What is meant by reasonable?

Situation 12.10   Reasonable means

A nurse is faced by a patient who is approaching her with a knife. He is a 6 feet tall, stockily built man of 35 years. There are no other staff or competent patients in the room and there is no call system available. As he comes forward, she picks up a chair and hits him over the head with it. He is severely concussed and requires stitches. Could she successfully defend an action for assault brought by the patient? Has she acted reasonably in defending herself?

Reasonableness means, first, that the force used should be no more than is necessary to accomplish the object for which it is allowed (so retaliation, revenge and punishment are not permitted) and, secondly, the reaction must be in proportion to the harm that is threatened. Thus all the circumstances must be taken into account: the contrast between the strength, size and expertise of the assailant and the defendant, and the type of harm with which the person is being threatened. Obviously, the greater the severity of the threatened danger, the more reasonable it is to take tougher measures. In assessing the reasonableness of the defence, account is taken of the fact that the defendant may have only a brief period to make up his mind what to do. Turning back to the above situation, if the nurse in question is tiny with no training in self-defence, the odds do seem to be stacked against her, and may justify her use of the chair. All the circumstances must be taken into account, including the possibility of her retreating from the assault. Should the nurse be prosecuted and a trial take place in the Crown Court, it is for the jury to decide if the measures used in self-defence were reasonable in all the circumstances. In a case in May 2000, a householder was found guilty of murder when he shot dead one of two men who were burglars in his house.

Stress

Concern with stress at work is now recognised as part of the employer's duty in taking reasonable care of the health and safety of the employee.

Case 12.4   Stress at work Walker v. *Northumberland County Council*[29]

A social worker obtained compensation when his employer failed to provide the necessary support in a stressful work situation when he returned to work following an earlier absence due to stress. The employer was not liable for the initial absence, but that put the employer on notice that the employee was vulnerable and its failure to provide the assistance he needed was a breach of its duty to provide reasonable care for his health and safety as required to do under the contract of employment

In order to establish grounds for compensation for stress induced by work, an employee would have to show:

1. that she was under an unacceptable level of stress at work;
2. that the employer was aware of this situation;
3. that there was reasonable action that the employer could have taken to relieve this pressure;
4. that the employer failed to take that action;
5. that as a result the employee has suffered a serious mental condition.

Advice on handling stress is given from experience in a Bristol hospital. Paul Bennett and colleagues emphasise the importance of looking at the work environment and personal skills as part of any stress management strategy.[30]

There are reports of more payments for compensation for stress across a wide range of employment. For example, in August 2000, it was reported that a bank manager was paid £100,000 in an out-of-court settlement by Lloyds TSB after suffering intolerable stress at work.[31]

Manual handling and back injuries

Where a nurse has injured her back at work, she may have a claim against her employer for breach of the duty of care owed to her at common law or failure to implement the Manual Handling Regulations. In addition, the employer may be vicariously liable for harm caused by another employee. Alternatively, if her back has been injured as a result of a defect in a product (e.g. a hoist or bed), she may be able to bring a case against the supplier under the Consumer Protection Act 1987.

Case 12.5   Back injury[32]

On 24 July 1994, a nurse was awarded £205,000 for a back injury. The circumstances were that in November 1988, she and a colleague were trying to lift an elderly woman from a commode to a chair, when the patient's legs gave way. Owing to the lack of space, Mrs Boag was forced to twist her back to place the woman in the chair. The Health Authority, which admitted liability, agreed the out-of-court settlement shortly before the case was due to be heard. She was forced to give up her job and is regularly confined to bed. She attended a pain relief clinic and would probably never work again. Her husband had had to take time off work to help with the two children.

Manual handling regulations

Regulations were introduced in 1992 as a result of an EC directive. The Royal College of Nursing and the National Back Pain Association in their 'Guide to the Handling of Patients'[33] point out that there are discrepancies between the EC Framework Directive[34] and the UK regulations and that the former imposes a higher duty on employers closer to that of 'practicality' rather than 'reasonable practicability'.

Guidance on manual handling is given by the Health and Safety Executive.[35] The guidelines are not themselves the law and the booklet advises that the guidelines set out in Appendix 1 'should not be regarded as precise recommendations. They should be applied with caution. Where doubt remains a more detailed assessment should be made.'

A working group set up by the Health and Safety Commission has produced a booklet on 'Guidance on Manual Handling of Loads in the Health Services'.[36] This document is described as 'an authoritative document which will be used by health and safety inspectors in describing reliable and fully acceptable methods of achieving health and safety in the workplace.' Part of this health services specific guidance material relates to staff working in the community. The RCN and NHS Executive have also published guidance on reducing the risks from violence and aggression in the community.[37]

Summary of the manual handling regulations:
The duty under the regulations can be summed up as follows:

1. If reasonably practicable, avoid the hazardous manual handling.
2. Make a suitable and sufficient assessment of any hazardous manual handling that cannot be reasonably avoided.
3. Reduce the risk of injury from this handling so far as is reasonably practicable.
4. Give general indications of risk and precise information on the weight of each load; and the heaviest side of any load, where the centre of gravity is not positioned centrally.
5. Review the assessment if there are any changes in the circumstances.

It is in the interests of all nurses to ensure that the employer is reminded when a review becomes necessary under the above provisions.

The duty that is owed by the employer is owed not only to employees, but also to temporary staff such as agency or bank staff who are called in to assist. All such employees are entitled to be included in the risk assessment process, since, as has been seen, the assessment must take into account the individual characteristics of each employee. Nurses who are unusually small in height or not so strong as the average might require special provisions in relation to manual handling.

Provision and Use of Work Equipment Regulations 1998 (PUWER)

PUWER replaces the earlier Provision and Use of Work Equipment Regulations 1992 and applies to all equipment, including lifting equipment, used at work. There is a new requirement to inspect work equipment where significant risk could result from incorrect installation or relocation, deterioration or as a result of exceptional circumstances, and to record the results of those inspections (reg.6). PUWER places requirements on duty holders to provide suitable work equipment for the task (reg.4), information and instructions (reg.8), and training to people who use it (reg.9). It also requires measures to be taken concerning dangerous parts of machinery (reg.11), controls and control systems (reg.14–8), stability (reg.20) and mobility (reg.25–29).

Lifting Operations and Lifting Equipment Regulations 1998 (LOLER)

These regulations came into force on 5 December 1998 and apply in all premises and work situations subject to the Health and Safety at Work Act 1974 and build on the requirements of the Provision and Use of Work Equipment Regulations 1998.

In its guidance on the application of the LOLER regulations, the Health and Safety Commission note that (para.47), 'As hoists are used to lift patients, e.g. from beds and baths, in hospitals and residential homes, are provided for use at work and are lifting equipment to which LOLER applies, the duty holder, e.g. the NHS Trust running the hospital or the owner of the residential home must satisfy their duties under LOLER.'

Enforcement of regulations on manual handling

What action can be taken if the employer ignores these regulations? The regulations are part of the health and safety provisions that form part of the criminal law. Infringement of the regulations can lead to prosecution by the health and safety inspectorate. The inspectorate has the power to issue enforcement or prohibition notices against any corporate body or individual.

What if the carer or client refuses to use a hoist?

If a risk management assessment for manual handling in a patient's home indicates that a hoist is necessary to prevent harm to any carer/professional, then the professional can insist that when she visits the home, she will use a hoist. If the patient refuses to be placed in a hoist, she can advise the patient that the only way of safely moving her/him is by a hoist, and if the patient continues to refuse, then the patient can be told that support and assistance will not be provided if it endangers the health and safety of the professionals. She can also advise the carer of the reasons why a hoist is necessary, but, of course, she cannot enforce the use of the hoist by the carer. If the carer ignores the instructions, fails to use the hoist and injures her back, then there should be no liability on the staff who gave her the correct guidance.

What remedies exist for compensation?

Section 47 of the Health and Safety at Work Act 1974 prevents breach of a duty under Sections 2–8 of the Act being used as the basis for a claim in the civil courts. Breach of the regulations can, however, be the basis of a civil claim for compensation unless the regulations provide to the contrary. Even where what is alleged is a breach of the basic duties, a nurse who suffered harm as a result of the failure of the employer to take reasonable steps to safeguard her health and safety, could sue in the civil courts on the basis of the employer's duty at common law (see above page 261). The statutory duty to ensure the Act is implemented is paralleled by a duty at common law placed upon the employer to take reasonable steps to ensure the employee's health and safety. Contracts of employment should state clearly the duty upon the employer to take reasonable care of the employee's safety and also the employee's duty to co-operate with the employer in carrying out health and safety duties under the Act and at common law. It is, of course, in the long term interest of the employer to prevent back injuries, thereby avoiding payment of substantial compensation to his injured employees and also reducing the incidence of sickness and absenteeism.

Training

This is essential to ensure that staff have the understanding to carry out the assessments and to advise on lifting and the appropriate equipment. Regular monitoring should take place to ensure that the training is effective and the policies for review are in place. There is also a duty on the employer to ensure that staff who are not expected to be regularly involved in manual handling are aware of the risks of so doing.

This was the decision in the case of *Colclough* v. *Staffordshire County Council*[38] where a social worker obtained compensation following a back injury caused by moving a client to safety. The Council was liable because it failed to provide any training on risk awareness of the dangers of that situation. The implication of this decision is that even staff who are not expected to be involved in manual handling as part of their work, must be trained in risk awareness to protect them, should they ever be in the situation where they could be endangered through manual handling.

Lifting and instructing others

Nurses may be asked to instruct others such as carers, clients or other health or social service employees in the carrying out of the regulations in manual handling. Before they instruct others, they should be sure that they receive the necessary additional training to undertake the task of instruction, since failure to instruct competently could in itself give rise to an action in negligence if harm should occur as a result of negligent instructions.

Failures to instruct by agencies

Sometimes nurses become aware that agency staff have not been instructed in manual handling techniques. It would be reasonable practice in this situation for the nurses to ensure that senior management or the agency were informed so that steps could be taking to provide formal training for agency staff.

Therapeutic handling

It is sometimes argued that therapeutic lifting, e.g. in orthopaedic wards, to facilitate early mobilisation does not come under the manual handling regulations. There are, however, no grounds for this assertion. The definition of manual handling is:

> any transporting or supporting of a load (including the lifting, putting down, pushing, pulling, carrying or moving thereof) by hand or by bodily force.

This would therefore include therapeutic situations.

No lifting policy and therapeutic handling

The first requirement of any manual handling policy is to avoid any manual handling that could reasonably practically be avoided. Clearly, if this were to be implemented in the therapeutic regime, patients would never get mobilised following strokes and orthopaedic and other trauma. The nurse should ensure that a risk assessment is carried out that takes into account both the needs of the patient to become mobile and also dangers that staff face in promoting this mobilisation.

Lifting extremely heavy persons

This is of considerable concern to nurses. An extremely heavy person is defined by E Fazel[39] as 25 stone (130 kg) or over. In a case study of the problems encountered following an emergency admission, the author analyses the possible action that could be taken, including reviewing the equipment that is available. The implications for other services such as the Fire Brigade and funeral directors, and a protocol for the safe handling of extremely heavy patients is supplied. The legal issues arising are considerable. Staff cannot cease to provide services for such persons, but the consequences in terms of costs and effort in minimising the risk of harm are considerable.

Sexual and other harassment

It is essential that nurses are sensitive to the dangers of sexual harassment and make every effort to avoid potentially difficult situations. On the one hand, they must be aware of the sex discrimination laws (see Chapter 10) and must ensure that they do not discriminate either directly or indirectly. On the other hand, they must ensure that they are chaperoned in any situation that could lead to accusations of harassment by the nurse or where the nurse is herself (or himself) at risk.

The Prevention of Harassment Act 1997

The Prevention of Harassment Act 1997 can also provide some protection in the workplace, if an individual considers that they are subject to unreasonable unwanted attention.

The Act creates:

1. a criminal offence of harassment (Section 1), which is defined as a person pursuing a course of conduct that amounts to harassment of another and that he knows or ought to know amounts to harassment of the other (the reasonable person test is applied);
2. a civil wrong whereby a person who fears an actual or future breach of Section 1, may claim compensation including damages for anxiety and financial loss;
3. the right to claim an injunction to restrain the defendant from pursuing any conduct that amounts to harassment;
4. the right to apply for a warrant for the arrest of the defendant, if the injunction has not been obeyed;
5. it creates an offence of putting people in fear of violence, where a person causes by his conduct another person to fear on at least two occasions that violence will be used against him;
6. restraining orders can be made by the court for the purpose of protecting the victim of the offence or any other person from further conduct amounting to harassment or to fear of violence.

Certain defences are permitted in the Act including that an individual is preventing or detecting crime.

Bullying at work

Research into bullying in an NHS Community Trust found that, of the 70% of staff who responded to a questionnaire on bullying, 38% reported being bullied in the previous year and 42% reported witnessing the bullying of others. It was concluded that bullying was a serious problem.[40]

In a recent case, £100,000 was accepted in an out-of-court settlement by a teacher who alleged that he had been bullied by the head teacher and other staff, when he was teaching in a school in Pembrokeshire.[41] Dyfed County Council denied negligence. He suffered a minor breakdown in October 1996 and was returned to the same school, although he had asked for a transfer. He claimed that he was isolated, ignored and subjected to a series of practical jokes. He then suffered a second nervous breakdown. It was claimed that a support plan worked out for him by the council was not properly implemented.

The lessons for managers from this case are obvious. Advice is given by Claire Walker on how to deal with bullying,[42] and Jacqueline Grove gives some practical advice on how to recognise the signs of stress from bullying and provides a survival guide.[43] In August 2000, a teacher was paid £15,000 compensation for unfair dismissal after an education authority had ignored medical reports that the teacher was being bullied into a breakdown, and then dismissed whilst on long-term sick leave. The teacher stated that he is planning to seek civil compensation for personal injuries.[44] An RCN guide on harassment and bullying at work[45] emphasises that nurses should not tolerate harassment, but challenge it by reporting it and keeping records.

Repetitive Strain Injury (RSI)

This condition is also known as Occupational Overuse Syndrome (OOS). Nurses should be aware, both for themselves and their patients, of the legal implications of RSI.

Even though, in an early case, a judge was quoted out of context as declaring that repetitive strain injury has no place in medical books,[46] RSI has been recognised for the purpose of compensation in health and safety cases. A recent House of Lords decision, however, may make it more difficult to obtain compensation for RSI.

On 25 June 1998, the House of Lords[47] rejected claims that a secretary, who was sacked after she developed a form of repetitive strain injury, should be able to sue her employers. It overruled the Court of Appeal decision that Ann Pickford should be allowed to make a claim against Imperial Chemical Industries. The Court of Appeal had found that ICI was negligent in failing to warn her of the need to take breaks during her work using a word processor and gave her the right to take her case back to the High Court for an assessment of damages, which she estimated at £175,000. In a majority judgment (4 to 1), the House of Lords decided that ICI did not need to warn her about the dangers of repetitive strain injury because typing took up only a maximum 75% of her workload. To impose a warning that might cause more harm than good would be undesirable, since it might be counter-productive. The House of Lords questioned whether she had proved that the pain was organic in origin. She had been sacked in 1990 after taking long periods off work because of pain in both hands. She claimed that the injury had been caused by the very large amount of typing at speed for long periods without breaks or rest periods. The House of Lords said that it could reasonably have been expected that a person of her intelligence and experience would take rest pauses without being told.

It also held that RSI as a medical term was unhelpful. It covered so many conditions that it was of no diagnostic value as a disease. PDA4 (Prescribed Disease A4) had, however, a recognised place in the Department of Health and Social Security's list for the purposes of industrial injury, meaning a cramp of the hand or forearm due to repetitive movements such as those used in any occupation involving prolonged periods of handwriting or typing. The House of Lords held that the Court of Appeal should not have overruled the findings of the High Court Judge, since he had ample evidence before him to justify his decision that in the plaintiff's case the giving of warnings was unnecessary, even though typists in another department had been given warnings.

Smoking

The dangers of smoking both to the smoker and those passive smokers in the vicinity have led to an increase in the number of workplaces and public areas where smoking is prohibited. In 2000, the Health and Safety Commission published guidance to employers on smoking in the workplace.

Most hospitals now prohibit smoking generally, but may permit smoking in allocated areas for patients. The RCN publication 'Clearing the air'[48] points out that smoking remains the single biggest avoidable cause of death in the UK and aims to increase nurses' knowledge of the impact of smoking on public health and support their role as providers of smoking cessation advice. In November 2000, the results of a joint *Nursing Times*, Department of Health and Royal College of Nursing survey showed that 90% of nurses who smoke wished to quit. The joint initiative of these organisations, called 'No Butts', aims to give nurses the practical information and support they need to give up. A self-help booklet has been issued by the RCN.[49] The government announced that Nicotine Replacement Therapy will be made available on prescription, subject to consultation.

Conclusions

A risk management strategy is at the heart of any policy relating to health and safety, not just for employees, but also for the clients and general public. Regular monitoring of the implementation of a risk management policy should ensure that harm is avoided and that a quality service is maintained for the public. This should be accompanied by clear, comprehensive documentation. The Health and Safety Executive in 1998 launched a discussion document[50] to reduce the numbers of employees suffering from work-related ill-health. The aim is to produce a strategy that is shared with other organisations to make recommendations to the Health and Safety Commission for Great Britain. The consultation paper is being accompanied by meetings across the country. The government is also targeting those involved in occupational health services to promote health at work. For example, in 2000, the

Department of Health supported an initiative to ensure that GPs, practice nurses and practice managers receive more training to treat and advise patients about health at work and occupational health in general.[51] The Confederation of British Industry estimated that temporary sickness costs business over £10 billion annually. The burden is borne by employers and the NHS as well as the working people who are ill. There are clear incentives to improve both health and safety of the working environment as well as the health of the workforce.

Questions and exercises

1. Ask to see (if you have not already received one) a copy of your NHS Trust's or employer's health and safety policy. How is this policy reflected in your working conditions?

2. The Health and Safety at Work Act 1974 is enforced through the criminal courts. The employer's duty to care for the safety of his employee exists at common law. What is meant by these two statements and what is the difference in the enforcement provisions of each?

3. Who is the occupier of premises owned by the NHS Trust and used by a Primary Care Trust and general practitioners?

4. All the circumstances must be taken into account in deciding whether the occupier is in breach of his common duty of care. What does this mean? Explain the statement in relation to an accident caused to an infant patient who slipped on a pool of water on the floor in the ward.

5. A nurse is injured while lifting a patient because the nurse assisting her suddenly let go and the injured nurse was left supporting the whole weight. What remedies, if any, does the injured nurse have and how could she claim compensation?

6. If a nurse is injured as the result of defective equipment, in what ways could she obtain compensation and what action should be taken?

7. What records should be kept in relation to any health and safety incident or in connection with claims under Part 1 of the Consumer Protection Act 1987?

References

1. *R. v. Nelson Group Services (Maintenance) Ltd, The Times Law Report* 17 September 1998 Court of Appeal
2. Management of health and safety at work, Approved Code of Practice and Guidance, Health and Safety Commission, HMSO 2000
3. Health and Safety Executive, A Guide to the Reporting of Injuries, Diseases and Dangerous Occurrences Regulations 1995, HSE Books 1999
4. Enquiries can be made to Health and Safety Executive Information Centre, Sheffield, Tel 0114 2892345, Fax 0114 2892333
5. *Slade* v. *Battersea* HMC 1955 1 WLR 207
6. *Dobell* v. *Thanet* DC 22 March 1999 *Current Law* August 2000 no 527

[7] *Jolley* v. *Sutton London Borough Council, The Times Law Report* 24 May 2000

[8] Dimond BC, Protecting the consumer, *Nursing Standard* vol.7 No 24 3 March 1993 pp. 18–19

[9] National Consumer Council, Unsafe Products How the Consumer Protection Act Works for Consumers, National Consumer Council November 1995

[10] CSP Professional Affairs Department Information paper No 33 Medical Devices Agency PA 33 July 1997

[11] MDA SN 9801 Reporting Adverse Incidents Relating to Medical Devices January 1998

[12] SI 1994/3017 Medical Devices Regulations 1994 came into force 1 January 1995, mandatory from 14 June 1998. Directive 93/42/EEC

[13] Medical Devices Agency Bulletin, Medical Device and Equipment Management for Hospital and Community-based Organisations MDA DB 9801 January 1998

[14] 93/42/EEC Directive concerning medical devices

[15] Directive 90/385/EEC came into force 1 January 1993 and is mandatory from 1 January 1995.

[16] Medical Devices Agency Bulletin, Medical Device and Equipment Management for Hospital and Community-based Organisations MDA DB 9801 January 1998

[17] MDA, Medical Devices and Equipment Management: Guidance on Repair and Maintenance Provision MDA DB 2000(02)

[18] MDA SN 9801 Reporting Adverse Incidents Relating to Medical Devices January 1998

[19] MDA, The Reuse of Medical Devices Supplied for Single-Use Only MDA London 1995

[20] A step-by-step guide to COSHH assessment, Health and Safety Executive 1993 HMSO

[21] *Fraser* v. *Winchester Health Authority, The Times Law Report* 12 July 1999 Court of Appeal

[22] *R.* v. *Lincolnshire (Kesteven) Justices, ex parte Connor* [1983] 1 All ER 901 QBD

[23] Blom-Cooper L., Hally, H. and Murphy E., *The Falling Shadow – One patient's mental health care 1978–1993*, London 1995 (Report of an Inquiry into the death of an occupational therapist at Edith Morgan Unit, Torbay 1995)

[24] Chris Mahoney, Scene of HCA attack was secure, *Nursing Times February* 10 2000 Vol 96 no 6 page 5

[25] Health and Safety Commission, Violence and Aggression to staff in health services 1997 HSE Books

[26] Alexandra Frean, Funds for Nurses who prosecute violent patients, *The Times* 1 October 1998

[27] Department of Health, Guidance on tackling violence NHS Response line 0541 555455 October 2000

[28] Steve McHale, From Insult to Injury, *Nursing Times* December 8 1999 Vol 95 Number 49 page 30

[29] *Walker* v. *Northumberland County Council, Times Law Report* 24 November 1994 Queens Bench Division

[30] Paul Bennett, Lindsey Scott and Kit Harling, Stress Busters, *Nursing Times* December 15/22/29 1999 Vol 95 No 50 Pages 28–29

[31] Elizabeth Judge, Banker wins £100,000 stress payout, *The Times* 10 August 2000

[32] *Boag* v. *Hounslow and Spelthorne Health Authority, The Times* 25 July 1994

[33] The Royal College of Nursing and the National Back Pain Association Guide to the Handling of Patients 4th edition NBPA with the RCN 1997

[34] EC Directive 90/269/EEC on the minimum health and safety requirements for the manual handling of loads (fourth individual directive within the meaning of Article 16(1) of Directive 89/391/EEC

[35] Health and Safety Executive, Manual Handling Guidance Regulations HMSO 1992

[36] Health and Safety Commission, Guidance on Manual Handling of Loads in the Health Services HMSO 1992

[37] Royal College of Nursing and NHS Executive, Safer Working in the Community, RCN and NHS Executive 000 920 September 1998

[38] *Colclough* v. *Staffordshire County Council* June 30 1994 *Current Law* No 208 October 1994

[39] E Fazel, Handling of Extremely Heavy Patients, *National Back Exchange Journal* Issue 9.2 April 1997 page 13–6

[40] Lyn Quine, Workplace bullying in NHS community trust: staff questionnaire survey, *British Medical Journal* Vol 318 25 January 1999 pp. 228–232

[41] Victoria Fletcher, Teacher 'bullied by staff' wins £100,000, *The Times* news report 17 July 1998

[42] Claire Walker, Bullied to Death, *Nursing Times* May 4 2000 Vol 96 no 18 pp. 26–8

[43] Jacqueline Grove, Survival and Resistance, *Nursing Times* May 4 2000 Vol 96 no 18 pp. 26–8

[44] Paul Wilkinson, Teacher wins payout over school clash, *The Times* 9 August 2000

[45] Royal College of Nursing, Nursing a Grievance? RCN 000 763 May 1997

[46] *Mughal* v. *Reuters Ltd* [1993] IRLR 571

[47] *Pickford* v. *Imperial Chemical Industries Plc*, *The Times Law Report* 30 June 1998 HL

[48] Royal College of Nursing, 'Clearing the air' a nurse guide to smoking and tobacco control RCN 001 159 October 1999

[49] Royal College of Nursing, How to Stop Smoking RCN 2000

[50] Developing an Occupational Health Strategy for Britain, HSE Books 1998

[51] Department of Health Press release 30 October 2000 GPs to give patients specialist advice on health at work

Part II Specialist areas

13 Children's nursing

In addition to the basic principles of law discussed in the first part of this book, children's nurses must also be aware of several special legal provisions that apply to those under 18 years. (In some hospitals, children over 16 years are cared for in adult wards.) These are shown in Figure 13.1 and are the subject of this chapter. The Children Act 1989 has provided a framework for the provision of services for children in need and sets out the basic principles to be followed in determining the welfare of the child. The Department of Health has provided guidance on the welfare of children and young people in hospital[1] and the Audit Commission investigated the care of children in hospitals in 1993.[2] More recently the RCN has published the results of a study into children's nursing and acute health care service provision which found a high level of non-adherence to national recommendations.[3] The British Medical Association has provided guidance on consent and the child (*BMA Consent, Rights and Choices in the Healthcare for Children and Young People* BMA 2001).

---

1. Consent to treatment
   (a) 16- and 17-year-old: (b) Children under 16:
       (i)   treatment;   (i)   parental rights;
       (ii) consent to research;   (ii) children's rights;
       (iii) refusal;   (iii) overruling the parent;
       (iv) emergencies;   (iv) transplants;
       (v)   parallel consent.   (v)   withholding consent by parents;
                                       (vi) letting die.

2. Non-accidental injury.
3. Parental care and the nurse.
4. Disciplining a child.
5. Education of children in hospitals.

Figure 13.1 Issues covered in Chapter 13.

Consent to treatment

At age 18 and over, adults, if mentally competent, are able to make all decisions in relation to their medical care. They can also consent to being participants in research programmes and this applies whether the research is seen as being in their therapeutic interests or not. Prior to 18 years, several different provisions apply.

283

1. the consent of a minor who has attained the age of 16 years to any surgical, medical, or dental treatment, which in the absence of consent would constitute a trespass to his person will be as effective as it would be if he were of full age; and where a minor has by virtue of this section given an effective consent to any treatment, it shall not be necessary to obtain any consent for it from his parent or guardian.

Treatment is defined very widely, Section 8(2). In this section, 'surgical, medical, or dental treatment' includes any procedure undertaken for the purposes of diagnosis and this section applies to any procedure (including in particular the administration of an anaesthetic) which is ancillary to any treatment as it applies to that treatment.

Figure 13.2 Family Law Reform Act 1969 Section 8.

The 16- and 17-year-old

Treatment

Under Section 8 of the Family Law Reform Act 1969, the child of 16 or 17 can give a valid consent to treatment. The provisions of this section are set out in Figure 13.2.

These two sub-sections cover most eventualities as far as consent to treatment is concerned for the 16- and 17-year-old. Treatment is defined widely and would cover all nursing care.

Consent to research

It should be noted, however, that the above does not cover consent to take part in research unless it can genuinely be considered to be part of the treatment. Thus a 16-year-old suffering from a disorder where there is no clearly proven successful method of treatment might well be asked to consent to a new untried form of treatment as part of a research project. If this is clearly in the patient's therapeutic interests and if there are no undue risks, then such a proposal would be covered by the words of the section. If, however, there was at hand a proven successful method of treatment, but the child was approached to see if he would agree to take part in a research programme where there were considerable risks that may or may not be of benefit to him, it is likely that such a treatment would not be covered by the Act.

Refusal to have treatment

Case 13.1 Re W[4]

A 16-year-old girl under local authority care suffered from anorexia nervosa. She refused to move to a specialist hospital. The Court of Appeal held that the Family Law Reform Act 1969 Section 8 did not prevent consent being given by parents or the court. Whilst she had a right to give consent under the Act, she could not refuse treatment that was necessary to save her life.

Emergencies

The Act does not prevent any emergency action being taken to save the life of a child who is unconscious or unable to give consent. Thus a 16-year-old who is wheeled into the accident and emergency department in an unconscious state can be given emergency treatment in the same way that a patient of any age could be treated. The professional providing this emergency treatment would be protected against any allegation of trespass to the person by the defence that he or she was acting in an emergency out of necessity to save life.

Parallel consent

Section 8 of the Family Law Reform Act can also be interpreted as giving power to parents to give a valid consent on behalf of their child of 16 or 17. This is because a third subsection of this section states:

> Section 8(3): Nothing in this section shall be construed as making ineffective any consent which would have been effective if the section had not been enacted.

One interpretation of this is that the fact that the child of 16 or 17 can now give a valid consent to treatment does not mean that consent by the parents on behalf of the child ceases to be effective. Prior to the 1969 Act, a parent could give a valid consent on behalf of his child up to adulthood and this right is not affected by the Act. Thus there exists a parallel right to consent: both the parents and the child of 16 or 17 could give consent. This is unlikely to cause difficulties except in those rare occasions where there is a dispute between the child and the parent. Whose views does the doctor or nurse take?

Situation 13.1   Clash between parent and child

A girl of 17 who had recently become a Jehovah's Witness was involved in a car crash. She was just conscious as she was wheeled into the accident and emergency department and made it clear that she did not wish to be given a blood transfusion. Her parents were notified of the crash and told of her statement. However, not sharing her religious views, they said they would give their consent if blood was necessary to save her life. The consultant wishes to know the legal situation.

The fact that Section 8(3) preserves the right of the parent to give consent means that, legally, the doctor could rely on that consent as a defence against any action for trespass to the person subsequently brought by the girl. Prior to Section 8 of the Family Law Reform being passed, parents had the right to give consent and this right continues.

What, however, if the doctor took notice of the girl's refusal, did not give blood and as a consequence the girl died? Could the parents then sue the doctor for negligence? The answer is that probably such a case would be unsuccessful, but much would depend on the circumstances, for example, the mental competence of the daughter in refusing blood; whether she understood the full implications; her general and specific capacity to give a valid consent.

Where there is a clash, the doctor has the choice of following the wishes of the child or the parents: if the position were reversed and the parents were Jehovah's Witnesses and the daughter consented to having blood, there would be no difficulties; he could rely on her consent under Section 8 (1) and if the girl were unconscious he could act in an emergency to save her life, whatever the views of the parents. However, where it is the child of 16 or 17 who is withholding consent and the parents wish to give it, many would argue that it is the doctor's duty to save life and he should rely on the parents' consent under Section 8(3). The point was considered by the courts in *Re W*[5] where the court overruled the child's refusal (see above, Case 13.1 on page 284). Were such a dispute to arise and where time permits, the best procedure to follow would be a reference to the court under the Children Act 1989.

Children under 16 years

The Children Act 1989 requires the court to have regard to 'the ascertainable wishes and feelings of the child concerned considered in the light of their age and understanding' (Section 1(3)(a)) in deciding whether to make specific orders under the Act. Certain sections require, if the child has sufficient understanding, the child's consent to be given, before the child can be asked to submit to a medical or physical examination.

Case 13.2   Re E[6]

A youth of 15 years 9 months was suffering from leukaemia and required a blood transfusion as part of his treatment. Both he and his parents were devout Jehovah's Witnesses and refused to give consent. The health authority applied for him to be made a ward of court and for a declaration that the treatment could proceed. The judge held that the lad was intelligent enough to take decisions about his own well-being, but that he did not have a full understanding of what the blood transfusions would involve. The welfare of the child was the first and paramount consideration. Although the court should be very slow to interfere in a decision the child had taken, the welfare of the child led to only one conclusion: that the hospital should be at liberty to treat him with blood transfusions. The judge therefore gave leave to the hospital authority to give treatment, including blood transfusion, and the consent of the patient and his parents was dispensed with.

In a case similar to *Re E*, a girl of 15½ years suffered from thalassaemia and had been kept alive by monthly blood transfusions and injections. She and her mother began to attend meetings of Jehovah's Witnesses and subsequently refused to accept blood transfusions. The judge decided that the treatment could be authorised on the grounds that it was in her best interests and the court had the power to overrule a competent child's refusal of treatment. He did, however, find that the girl was not Gillick competent because she lacked emotional maturity.[7]

Non-Parents

The Children Act 1989 Section 3(5) provides that a person who (a) does not have parental responsibility for a particular child, but (b) has care of the child, may (subject to the provision of this Act) do what is reasonable in all the circumstances of the case for the purpose of safeguarding or promoting the child's welfare. It is suggested that this would include giving consent to necessary emergency treatment in the absence of the parents. In addition, professional staff would have a duty of care to take action to save life in such circumstances.

Case 13.3   Re R 1991[8]

The court gave permission for psychiatric medication to be given to a girl aged 15 against her will. Her mental health had deteriorated and she was placed in an adolescent psychiatric unit. Her condition fluctuated between periods of lucidity. The Court of Appeal held that she was not mentally competent due to the fluctuating nature of her mental illness.

Kennedy and Grubb[9] have suggested in discussing the reasoning of the Court of Appeal that 'it is more respectful of patients' autonomy to interpret incompetence so as to include the manic depressive and the anorexic (where appropriate) rather than regard them as apparently competent and then do wholesale violence to the law's commitment to the rights of decision-making of the competent.'

Children's rights: can children give consent themselves?

If the child is mature and capable of understanding the situation and it is not possible to contact the parents, the child can give a valid consent and this principle is emphasised in the Children Act 1989. This issue was considered in the Gillick case on the narrow issue of advice and treatment for family planning. However, the principles established by the House of Lords cover a much wider area.

Case 13.4   The Gillick case

Mrs Gillick questioned the lawfulness of a DHSS circular HN (80) 46, which was a revised version of part of a comprehensive *Memorandum of Guidance* on family planning services issued to health authorities in May 1974 under cover of circular HSC(IS)32. The circular stated that in certain circumstances a doctor could lawfully prescribe contraception for a girl under 16 without the consent of the parents. Mrs Gillick wrote to the acting administrator formally forbidding any medical staff employed by the Norfolk AHA to give 'any contraceptive or abortion advice or treatment whatever to my . . . daughters whilst they are under 16 years without my consent'. The administrator replied that the treatment prescribed by a doctor is a matter for the doctor's clinical judgement, taking into account all the factors of the case. Mrs Gillick, who had five daughters, then brought an action against the AHA and the DHSS

---

seeking a declaration that the notice gave advice that was unlawful and wrong and that did or might adversely affect the welfare of her children, her right as a parent and her ability properly to discharge her duties as a parent. She sought a declaration that no doctor or other professional person employed by the Health Authority might give any contraceptive or abortion advice or treatment to any of her children below the age of 16 without her prior knowledge and consent.[10]

She failed before the High Court judge, succeeded in her appeal before the Court of Appeal and the DHSS and Health Authority, and appealed to the House of Lords. The Lords decided by a majority of three to two against Mrs Gillick. The majority held that in exceptional circumstances a doctor could provide contraceptive advice and treatment to a girl under 16 without the parents' consent. The circular was therefore upheld.

Lord Fraser stated the exceptional circumstances which are set out in Figure 13.3. Many questions still remain uncertain. Can it be assumed that a mature child under 16 can give a valid consent to any form of treatment and research or only when his life is in danger? What efforts must be made to obtain the parents' consent? For what can a child give consent: a few stitches; an anaesthetic; an abortion?

What is the position where the child is a mother? If she has the mental capacity, does she have the legal capability of giving consent for her child to be treated or is it necessary to obtain the consent of her own parents, i.e. the baby's grandparents? As an example, many health visitors treating a child's child protect themselves by obtaining both the consent of the underage mother and also of a grandparent. From the cautious words of the majority judges sitting on the Gillick case in the House of Lords, it would appear that, provided the underage mother had the requisite mental capacity to consent to treatment on the child's behalf, this would be a valid consent.

Another interpretation of Section 8(3) of the Family Law Reform Act 1969 is that statutory powers given to a child of 16 or 17 to give a valid consent, do not remove the ability of the mature child below 16 years to give a legally valid consent to treatment.

Where a child is refusing life saving treatment, the test of Gillick competence will not be the only factor in determining the case, as case 13.5 shows. In this case, the ruling in *Re W* (see case 13.1) was followed.

---

1. The girl would, although under 16, understand the doctor's advice.
2. He could not persuade her to inform her parents or allow him to inform the parents that she was seeking contraceptive advice.
3. She was very likely to have sexual intercourse with or without contraceptive treatment.
4. Unless she received contraceptive advice or treatment her physical or mental health or both were likely to suffer.
5. Her best interests required him to give her contraceptive advice, treatment or both without parental consent.

Figure 13.3 Exceptional circumstances set out in the Gillick case.

Case 13.5   Re L[11]

A 14-year-old girl had sustained extensive and severe burns. Her life was considered to be at risk unless she underwent surgical treatment which involved the possibility of a blood transfusion, although as a practising Jehovah's Witness, she felt unable to consent to this. Her clearly expressed refusal was consistent with two earlier Advanced Directive/ Release forms that she had completed, the last being only two months before her injuries. The hospital applied for leave to administer blood and blood products in the course of essential treatment without her consent.

The court granted the application on the grounds that:

1. She could not be said to be Gillick competent. (Information had been withheld from her about the horrible death brought on by the onset and spread of gangrene, if blood was not transfused; and she had led a sheltered life, very much under the influence of the family.)

2. Even if she had been found to be Gillick competent, the extreme gravity of the case, would, nevertheless, be sufficient basis for the order to be made.

Clash between parents and child under 16

A case is considered in Chapter 17 where a fifteen-year-old child's refusal to have a transplant was overruled by the court.[12]

Overruling the parent

While parents have the power in law to give consent to the treatment of the child, this is not an absolute power. If their consent or their refusal to give consent is considered to be against the interests of the child, then the court can intervene.

Case 13.6   Sterilisation of a mentally handicapped girl

A girl of 11 years suffered from Sotos syndrome, the symptoms of which included accelerated growth during infancy, epilepsy, general clumsiness, an unusual facial appearance and behaviour problems, including emotional instability, certain aggressive tendencies and some impairment of mental function. The mother, taking the advice of the consultant paediatrician that her daughter would remain substantially handicapped and that she would always be unable to care for herself or look after any children, discussed with the obstetrician the possibility of her daughter being sterilised. An operation was arranged. However, before it was performed, the educational psychologist applied for the girl to be made a ward of court. Mrs Justice Heilbron, who heard the case, was not convinced that the operation was in the best interests of the girl and so ordered that the operation should not proceed.[13]

It can be seen from this case how fortuitous it was that the case ever came before the courts. Had it not been for the strongly held views of the educational psychologist, the operation could well have gone ahead. This should not be so in the future. In a House of Lords case,[14] where the judges agreed to a sterilisation proceeding upon 'Jeanette', they made it clear that, in future, every such case of a sterilisation upon a mentally handicapped child should receive the approval of the court before it proceeded. In that case, they did not make the distinction between therapeutic and non-therapeutic sterilisation, which Mrs Justice Heilbron had made *In re D*. In theory, every case of sterilisation on a child should come before the courts, even though the operation is performed because of the presence of a malignancy. This is further discussed in Chapter 15.

The important point for children's nurses is that if they feel that a particular procedure or treatment agreed between the parents and the medical staff is not in the best interests of the child, then the nurse should raise it with her senior management who could, if necessary, arrange for the matter to be brought before the courts.

In a recent dispute between a family and the doctors, violence errupted on the wards as the family fought to prevent morphine, which would depress the respiratory functions, being administered to their child.

Case 13.7   Dispute over treatment[15]

A boy of 13 was severely disabled with only a limited lifespan. The mother wished him to receive whatever medical treatment was necessary to prolong his life. Following an incident in which the hospital gave the child morphine against the mother's wishes, family members resuscitated the child and prevented him from dying. There was a complete breakdown of trust between the family and the hospital. The mother sought a declaration as to the course doctors in the hospital should take if the boy were admitted for emergency treatment and disagreements arose as to the treatment to be given to or withheld from the child. The judge refused the mother's application for judicial review and she appealed to the Court of Appeal.

The Court of Appeal held that it would be inappropriate to grant a declaration in anticipation and indicate to doctors at a hospital what treatment they should or should not give in circumstances that had not yet arisen. The best course was for the parents of a child and the medical staff to agree on the approach to be taken for the treatment of that child, but if that was not possible and a grave conflict arose, then the actual circumstances must be brought before the court so that the court could resolve what was in the best interests of the child in the light of the facts existing at that time. The principles recognized by the Court of Appeal were as follows.

1. the sanctity of life;

2. the non-interference by the courts in areas of clinical judgment in the treatment of patients where that could be avoided;

3. the refusal of the courts to dictate appropriate treatment to a medical practitioner, subject to the court's power to take decisions in the child's best interests;

4. treatment without consent save in an emergency was a trespass to the person;

5. the court would interfere to protect the interests of a minor or a person under a disability.

The Court of Appeal dismissed the appeal.

Members of the family were prosecuted for their violence in the hospital.

Transplants and the interests of the child

Situation 13.2   *Sisterly transplants*

Mary, aged 7 years, had an incurable blood disease and was found to be compatible only with her younger sister Janet who was 4 years old. The parents therefore agreed that Janet would provide a bone marrow transplant for Mary. Staff Nurse Bryant was concerned by the legalities of the proposed transplant.

The parents have the right to consent to any treatment that is in the interests of the child. However, in this case, there is a clash between the interests of Mary and the interests of Janet. Any operation, no matter how small, involves some risk to the patient and Janet would be put at risk for the benefit of Mary. In the case of a bone marrow transplant, it could be argued that the risk is so small and the psychological benefit for Janet when she becomes older so immense that it would be inhuman not to allow Janet to be a donor. If she were asked, she would probably agree herself, though her capacity to understand would be very limited. It would probably be lawful for the transplant to proceed, though there are no statutory or common law guidelines on the question in this country. However, as the risks to the donor increase, so do the problems. Imagine that in the last example Mary requires a kidney and tests show that Janet is an ideal match: do the parents have the power to give consent on Janet's behalf to such a donation? Again, there is no legal precedent, but it could be argued that there is no way in which such an operation can be considered to be in Janet's interests. The situation that would arise if Janet were mentally handicapped and in an institution is discussed in Chapter 20.

A further extreme example of using one child for the benefit of another arose in October 2000 when it was reported that in the USA parents had had a baby selected by IVF who would provide compatible bone marrow for treating their daughter who suffered from a serious blood disorder.[16] As the law stands in this country, IVF for such purposes would not be approved, but the law is being challenged by parents who wish to have a daughter and therefore wish to select the embryo on the grounds of sex. (They have four sons, but a daughter has recently died.) At present, sex selection would be justifiable only if it were on grounds of a genetically inherited disorder (see Chapter 22). A British couple are applying to have IVF in similar circumstances to the USA case since they have a child with Fanconi anaemia and wish to have a child who would be a compatible donor.[17] The Leukaemia Research Fund has stated that it is setting up a bank of stem cells taken from umbilical cords, which should be able to provide an appropriate match for almost every transplant patient.

In 1993, the court held that a blood transfusion should be given to a premature baby girl who suffered from respiratory distress syndrome and whose parents were Jehovah's Witnesses. The order authorising medical treatment was to be made under the court's inherent jurisdiction rather than pursuant to the Children Act 1989.[18]

In 2000, the future of twin Siamese girls came before the Court of Appeal.[19] The Court of Appeal decided that the operation could proceed. The case is discussed in Chapter 14.

Withholding consent by parents

Where the parents refuse to consent to treatment, which the doctors determine is in the interests of the child, then there is a well-tried procedure for taking the appropriate action. No child should die because the parents have unreasonably refused their consent to a necessary treatment.

Situation 13.3   Blood transfusion

Eric, aged 3 years, is admitted with an operable tumour. The neurologist reassures the parents and says that Eric can be saved. The parents say that on religious grounds they could not agree to Eric having a blood transfusion. Mr Sharpe, the neurosurgeon, replies that he would not be prepared to carry out such an operation with such a restriction, as it is highly likely that blood would be required in the operating theatre. The parents therefore refuse their consent to the operation. The neurosurgeon cannot let the child die so he has two options. He can either proceed and justify his action on the basis that he is acting in the best interests of the child in an emergency; or he can arrange for an application to be made to the court for Eric to be made a ward of court, and for the operation to be ordered to proceed.

In the case of an emergency, when there is insufficient time to obtain a declaration from the court, essential action must be taken to save the life of the child, if that is clinically in the best interests of the child.

Case 13.8   Down's syndrome

A child who was born suffering from Down's syndrome and an intestinal blockage, required an operation to relieve the obstruction if she was to live for more than a few days. If the operation were performed, the child might die within a few months, but it was probable that her life expectancy would be 20–30 years. Her parents, having decided that it would be kinder to allow her to die rather than live as a physically and mentally handicapped person, refused consent to the operation. The local authority made the child a ward of court and, when a surgeon decided that the wishes of the parents should be respected, they sought an order authorising the operation to be performed by other named surgeons. The judge in the High Court decided that the wishes of the parents should be respected and refused to make the order. The local authority took the case to the Court of Appeal which said that the operation should proceed.[20]

The court decided that the question before it was whether it was in the best interests of the child that she should have the operation and not whether the parents' wishes should be respected. Since the effect of the operation might be that the child would have the normal life span of a person with Down's syndrome, and since it had not been demonstrated that the life of such a person was of such a nature that the child should be condemned to die, the court would make an order that the operation be performed.

The court will review any decision where parents are withholding consent or giving consent and decide whether the treatment should be given in the light of the best interests of the child. It is open to any interested party to ask the court to determine this question when he or she is concerned at what is proposed or not proposed.

Parents have a legal duty to care for their children. Where they fail to obtain medical treatment, they could be guilty of a criminal offence. A father was convicted of manslaughter and imprisoned and the mother given a suspended sentence for failing to give their diabetic daughter insulin.[21] The couple refused to allow their diabetic daughter to receive modern medicine because of their religious beliefs.

Letting die

The Down's syndrome case above raises the issue of whether it is permissible in law to allow a severely handicapped child to die or even assist him to die. In what circumstances does the doctor cease to have a duty to keep the child alive? Certainly, as the case of *In re B* above shows, the views of the parents are not the deciding factor. The point was raised in the case of Dr Arthur, who was prosecuted for murder (later changed to attempted murder), since he prescribed, with the consent of the parents, the substance DF 118 for a Down's syndrome baby who also suffered from severe abdominal abnormalities. A jury acquitted him.[22]

The law does not recognise any form of euthanasia, but in practice it is left to the discretion of the medical staff to determine the extent of heroic medicine that is justified for severely handicapped babies. This discretion is reviewable in the courts. It is not an easy situation for medical staff, and the Royal College of Paediatrics and Childhealth has published guidelines to assist practitioners[23] as has the British Medical Association.[24] This issue is discussed further in Chapter 14 in the section on special care baby units.

Non-accidental injury

The children's nurse needs to be aware of the possibility that injuries or illness in a child may have been caused by another person. This applies not just to bruising or lacerations, but also to undernourishment and other ailments, including psychological damage. The possibility of sexual abuse must also be borne in mind if the relevant symptoms are present. The parents have a legal duty to provide care for their dependent children under Section 1(1) of the Children and Young Persons Act 1933.

In this situation, the nurse is confronted by the following problems. What action should she take if she suspects a child of being the object of abuse of any kind? What are the potential consequences for her if she is mistaken? What powers does she have to prevent a parent removing a child from the ward when the child has been placed on the Non-Accidental Injury Register? What would her position be in relation to a court hearing? Does she have to make a statement to the police?

Situation 13.4   Cot death or abuse?

Jane, a girl of six months, was admitted to the children's ward with a suspected chest infection. She was immediately placed on antibiotics and sputum samples taken. While the nurse was changing her, she noticed some bruising to the upper legs and a possible burnmark on her back. The nurse pointed these marks out to the senior house officer who suggested that the registrar should be called in, as it was possible that these marks were the result of abuse.

A procedure for dealing with suspected child abuse should be available on every ward. If child abuse is suspected, the nurse should be particularly vigilant in not leaving the child unattended with the parents. In addition, it is quite likely that she could be called upon to give evidence to the court as to the nature of the relationship and interaction between the parents and the child in hospital and also as to the physical and mental state of the child on admission. It is essential, therefore, that her record-keeping should be detailed and clear to enable her to answer questions at some later time.

The social service department of the local authority could apply for a child assessment order or an order for the emergency protection of the child under Part V of the Children Act 1989 to care for the child initially, pending the outcome of the full proceedings for the care of the child.

The orders which can be made in respect of a child suspected of being abused, are contained in the Children Act 1989, set out in Figure 13.4.

A Part IV	Care and supervision order, Sections 31–42	
B Part V	Protection of children, Sections 43–52	
C Part XII	Miscellaneous and general, Section 100 Restriction of wardship; jurisdiction of High Court still exists in emergency situations	
Section 43	Child assessment order	
Section 44	Orders for emergency protection of children	
Section 45	Duration of emergency protection orders	
Section 46	Removal and accommodation of children by police in cases of emergency	
Section 47	Local authority's duty to investigate	
Section 48	Powers to assist in discovery of children who may be in need of emergency protection	
Section 49	Abduction of children in care	
Section 50	Recovery of abducted children	
Section 51	Refuges for children at risk	
Section 52	Risk and regulation relating to emergency protection order	

Figure 13.4   Children Act 1989: protection of children.

Any nurse must also be alert to the possibility of a colleague causing harm to a patient. This is considered in the section on Whistle Blowing in Chapter 4.

Other issues which arise in relation to non-accidental injury include disclosure of confidential information (this is covered in Chapter 8) and giving evidence before the court (covered in Chapter 9).

Working together to safeguard children[25]

This publication is a guide to inter-agency working to safeguard and promote the welfare of children. It replaces the publication 'Working Together under the Children Act 1989' published in 1991. It highlights the duties in the Children Act 1989 that require inter-agency co-operation.

Section 27 enables a local authority to request help from: any local authority; any local education authority; any local housing authority; any health authority and any person authorised by the Secretary of State or in Wales, the National Assembly. The request must be responded to.

Under Section 47, a duty is placed upon such organisations or persons to help a local authority with its enquiries in cases where there is reasonable cause to suspect that a child is suffering or is likely to suffer significant harm. The guidance covers those topics shown in Box 13.1

Box 13.1

Contents of inter-agency guidance

Working together to support children and families
Some lessons from research and experience
Roles and responsibilities
Area Child Protection Committees
Handling individual cases
Child protection in specific circumstances
Some key principles
Case reviews
Inter-agency training and development

The Protection of Children Act 1999

This Act requires organisations to refer persons considered unsuitable to work with children to the Department of Health for inclusion on their list. It is discussed in Chapter 10.

Parental care and the nurse

Situation 13.5   *Mum knows best*

The children's ward at Roger Park Hospital introduced a scheme for mothers and other relatives to undertake some of the tasks in caring for the children. This had many advantages: it put the child at ease, since the person most familiar to him was taking care of him as usual, albeit in a strange place; at the same time, there were savings in staff time. Originally, the scheme covered only the day-to-day routine care of dressing, feeding, bathing and amusing the child. Subsequently, however, it was extended to nursing and extended-role tasks, including the care of nasal-gastric feeding and intravenous medication. The reason for this extension was that several of the mothers of long-term chronically ill children undertook all these tasks in the community. The nurse or doctor had the task of ensuring that the mother had the appropriate training and the necessary equipment.

Mrs Tait agreed to give her 4-year-old child, Robin, who had a chronic lung condition, the appropriate drugs intravenously every six hours. She had undertaken several such treatments on her own before and was familiar with the routine and procedure. On the ward, she was given the keys to help herself to the necessary drugs. This was contrary to the accepted practice, but was permitted because it was felt that she could be trusted. She gave Robin the 8.00 a.m. treatment without problems. She had to leave the hospital in the afternoon, but told another parent that she would be back for the afternoon treatment. Unfortunately, she did not return until 3.30 p.m. because of an unexpected traffic holdup. Robin was with some other children watching Play School. She immediately went to the staff nurse to get the keys to draw up the drugs for the next treatment. She took the boxes from the cupboard and started to make up the syringes. She then took Robin into the single room to give him his treatment. As she was giving the medication, Robin became very ill and she called for help. It was then discovered that the afternoon dose had already been given to Robin and although this had been written up into his notes, the nurse who did so was at tea when Mrs Tait returned and she herself did not check Robin's notes as it was never her practice to do so. Robin suffered severe renal failure as a result of an overdose of an antibiotic. Is the accident entirely the mother's fault or does the nurse carry some responsibility?

What is the situation where responsibilities like this are divided between several people? In legal terms, it is probably true to say that the care of the child in hospital is primarily the responsibility of the nurse under the clinical supervision of the medical staff. In a sense, the nurse is delegating to the mother those duties that she is capable of performing and probably performs on her own at home. The nurse should only delegate those tasks that she feels the mother is competent to perform, and, in addition, she should ensure that the mother (or, of course, any other relative, friend or volunteer) has the correct amount of training and supervision to undertake the task safely. The nurse would be responsible in negligence if she delegated an unsuitable task to the mother or failed to provide her with the appropriate instructions or gave her inadequate supervision. If, however, the nurse has satisfied all those requirements and something still goes wrong because the mother makes a mistake, then it would be the mother's responsibility for any harm caused to the child as a result of the mistake.

In the above situation, there is clearly a failure in communication between nurse and mother. It would have been preferable to set up a procedure whereby the mother was told to look at the drug chart, to fill it in when she gave the drugs to the child and also to check that the drugs had not already been given. She should also be supervised in her administration of the drugs. It is questionable whether the mother should have been allowed direct access to the medicines. Clearly, the nurse would be at fault in failing to set up this procedure and the supervision, and the mother would bear some responsibility for failing to check that they had been given, though in mitigation it could be said that the person responsible for the ward at the time she returned should have known the child had already had his medication and informed the mother accordingly. The problems relating to supervision and instructing others are dealt with more fully in Chapter 4.

Disciplining a child

Situation 13.6   *The nurse* in loco parentis

Adam was a bright 7-year-old who appeared totally undaunted by his stay in hospital for a hernia operation. Unfortunately, his mother could spend very little time with him as she had two younger children and her husband was overseas. Once Adam had recovered from the immediate effects of his operation, he was uncontrollable. He wandered around the wards into the single-bed wards, ignoring all the nurses' instructions and delighting in disobeying them. In one of the single rooms, a child was being barrier nursed with suspected meningitis. Staff Nurse James saw Adam about to enter this room and in her anxiety and her impatience with him, she hit him hard on the leg. Adam screamed and other nurses came running. Staff Nurse James was disciplined by the nursing officer and Adam's mother said that she was going to make a formal complaint against the nurse and the hospital. Staff Nurse James argued that in the circumstances there was little else she could have done to prevent Adam entering that room, and, in any case, she had the powers of a parent to discipline a child who needed to be controlled.

A recent case at the European Court of Human Rights has ruled that severe corporal punishment to discipline children was a breach of Article 3 of the European Convention on Human Rights.[26] In the case, a step-father had beaten a 9-year-old boy on several occasions with a garden cane. The step-father had been prosecuted for assault occasioning actual bodily harm, but had been acquitted by the jury who accepted his defence that the caning had been necessary and reasonable to discipline the boy. The European Court of Human Rights held that ill-treatment must attain a minimum level of severity if it is to fall within the scope of Article 3. It depended on all the circumstances of the case, such as the nature and context of the treatment, its duration, its physical and mental effects and, in some instances, the sex, age and state of health of the victim. In finding that there had been a breach of Article 3, it awarded the boy £10,000 against the UK government and costs. The UK government acknowledged that the UK law failed to provide adequate protection to children and should be amended. Subsequently, guidance was issued by the government on the use of corporal punishment against children. Guidance for good practice in restraining, holding still and containing children has been issued by the RCN.[27]

It therefore follows that corporal punishment should not be used when acting in the place of the parents. In the above example, Staff Nurse James has acted illegally and other methods of control would have been preferable. There were other ways of stopping him entering the room other than hitting him and, in the circumstances, it seems more likely that she lost her temper and was unreasonable.

A respect for the rights of the child and good nursing practice would advocate no use of physical force against a patient. A nurse faces both criminal and civil proceedings against her personally if she uses corporal punishment on a patient. She would, however, be entitled to use reasonable force to protect herself or other people by restraining the child if she or others were threatened with violence. The implications of this for staffing levels are clear and the degree of unruliness in children and the extent of parental help could affect the level of staffing required. Guidance on skill-mix and staffing in children's wards and departments is provided by the RCN.[28] Training for staff in coping with unruly children is essential. Guidelines issued by the Department for Education and Employment[29] in 2000 prohibit physical punishment and smoking in day nurseries, playgroups, children's centres, and creches, but allow smacking and smoking by childminders where parents have given their permission.

Education of children in hospital

The special education of children in hospitals was provided for in the National Health Service Act 1946. Section 62 empowered regional hospital boards and teaching hospitals to arrange with a local education authority or voluntary body to use as a special school any premises forming part of the hospital. By 1955, there were 120 hospital special schools providing teaching for 8,476 pupils in addition to 1,425 children receiving individual or group tuition. In 1971, responsibility for the education of children in hospitals for the mentally handicapped was transferred to the education service (1975 Scotland). Home tuition is an important part of the education service for ill or handicapped children and there are signs that demand is growing. The nurse should be aware that every child has a right to education, even when in hospital, and that, provided his medical condition permits it, every effort should be made to ensure that the child is receiving schooling, preferably off the ward area. The nurse has a positive role to play in encouraging the child to take part.

Questions and exercises

1 Examine the UN Charter of the rights of the child. What impact does this have on the care of the child in hospital?

2 What is the difference between a child of 15 and one of 16 years as far as consent to treatment is concerned? What is the effect of the Family Law Reform Act 1969 Section 8?

3 Obtain a copy of your NHS Trust's procedure on the care of suspected non-accidental injury cases and familiarise yourself with it.

4 The occupier's duty of care for the safety of the visitor should take into account the possibility that children require greater care (see Chapter 12, Figure 12.9). What is meant by this and how does it affect the work of the children's nurse?

5 Consider the extent to which your department allows parents to take part in the care of children in hospital. What additional responsibilities does this place on the nurse?

6 If you were faced with a very disobedient child, how would you control him?

7 Does the law require that every effort must be made to save every child no matter how handicapped? (See also Chapter 14 on special care.)

References

1 Department of Health, Welfare of Children and Young People in Hospital HMSO 1991

2 Audit Commission, Children First: a study of hospital services HMSO 1993

3 Royal College of Nursing, Children's Services: Acute Health Care Provision RCN 001055 June 1999

4 *In re* W (a minor) (medical treatment) 1992 4 All ER 627

5 *In re* W (a minor) (medical treatment) 1992 4 All ER 627

6 *Re E* (a minor) (Wardship: Medical treatment) [1993] 1 FLR 386 Family Division

7 *Re S* (a minor) (Consent to medical treatment) [1994] 2 FLR 1065

8 *In re R* (a minor) (Wardship: Consent to Medical Treatment (1991) 4 All ER 177 CA

9 Ian Kennedy and Andrew Grubb, *Medical Law*, Butterworths, London 2000

10 *Gillick* v. *West Norfolk and Wisbech AHA and the DHSS* 1985 3 All ER 402

11 *Re L* (Medical Treatment: Gillick Competency) [1999] 1 Med L Review 58; [1998] 2 FLR 810

12 *Re M* (Medical Treatment Consent) [1999] 2 FLR 1097

13 *In re D* (a minor) (wardship, sterilisation) 1976 1 All ER 327

14 *In re B* (a minor) (wardship, sterilisation) 1987 2 All ER 206

15 *R. v. Portsmouth Hospitals NHS Trust ex p. Glass* [1999] 2 FLR 905; [1999] Lloyds Law Report Medical 367

16 Damian Whitworth, Joy of the family in front line of science, *The Times* 5 October 2000

17 Mark Henderson, British girl may get cord transplant, *The Times* 6 October 2000

18 *In re O* (a minor) (medical treatment) [1993] 4 Med LR 272

19 *In re A* (minors) (Conjoined twins: Medical Treatment), *The Times Law Report* 10 October 2000

20 *In re B* (a minor) [1981] 1 WLR 1421

21 *The Times* (29 October 1993)

22 *R. v. Arthur* (1981) 12 BMLR 1

23 Royal College of Paediatrics and Child Health, Withholding or Withdrawing Life Saving Treatment in Children A Framework for Practice. RCPCH September 1997

24 British Medical Association, Withholding and Withdrawing Life-prolonging Medical Treatment BMA 1999

25 Department of Health, Home Office, Department for Education and Employment, the National Assembly for Wales, Working together to safeguard children, Department of Health 1999

26 Case of *A* v. *The United Kingdom* (100/1997/884/1096) judgment on 23 September 1998

27 Royal College of Nursing, Restraining, holding still and containing children RCN 000 999 March 1999

28 Royal College of Nursing, Skill-mix and staffing in children's wards and departments RCN 001054 July 1999

29 Department for Education and Employment, Regulations on Childcare August 2000 DEE

14 Midwifery

The midwife has always been in a special position compared with the general nurse in relation to her powers and duties. She is recognised as an independent practitioner with considerable powers in the prescribing and administration of certain drugs which in the past were not possessed by the general nurse. (There have been recent extensions to the prescribing powers of the nurse and other professionals (see Chapter 28).) This section considers the special position of the midwife in law and the effects of some recent cases on midwifery practice.

The areas to be covered are set out in Figure 14.1.

---

1. Midwives Rules and Code of Practice.
2. Law relating to consent:
   (a) opposition to the midwife;
   (b) criminal offence;
   (c) admission and treatment;
   (d) choice of treatment by mother;
   (e) consent to caesarian section.
3. Liability of mother for harm caused to baby:
   (a) civil liability;
   (b) criminal liability.
4. Taking into care.
5. Midwifery practice and standard of care:
   (a) midwife and doctor;
   (b) community midwife.
6. Congenital Disabilities Act:
   (a) liability of midwife to unborn child;
   (b) professional standards;
   (c) child's action is derivative;
   (d) mother's liability under Act;
   (e) action for wrongful life.
7. Nurseries.
8. Special care baby units.
9. Registration of births and stillbirths.
10. Use of foetal tissue.
11. National Guidelines.
12. Record keeping.
13. AIDS and the midwife.

Figure 14.1 Issues covered in Chapter 14.

Midwives rules and code of practice

Under the Nurses, Midwives and Health Visitors Act 1997, the UKCC must make rules regulating the practice of midwives. Figure 14.2 indicates the purpose of these rules. The rules are set out under Statutory Instruments 1986 No. 786, 1990 No. 1624, 1993 No. 1901 and 1993 No. 2106, and the Nurses, Midwives and Health Visitors (Midwives Amendment) Rules Approval Order 1998 SI No. 2649.

In addition, the Central Council has produced a Midwife's Code of Practice.[1] This is complementary to the practice rules but, unlike the practice rules, it does not have the force of law. Of course, the midwives would also be expected to comply with the UKCC Code of Professional Conduct and other guidance from the UKCC. It is not the intention to consider every one of these rules and codes in detail, but rather to consider some of the more common problems concerning the midwife. Every midwife should ensure that they have copies of all the relevant UKCC guidance.

(a) determine the circumstances in which and the procedure by means of which midwives may be suspended from practice;

(b) require midwives to give notice of their intention to practise to the local supervising authority in the area in which they intend to practise (in addition if the midwife practises in an emergency outside her normal authority she has to notify the new health authority within 48 hours); and

(c) require registered midwives to attend courses of instruction in accordance with the rules.

Figure 14.2 Aims of the Midwives Rules.

---

1. A practising midwife is responsible for providing midwifery care to a mother and baby during the antenatal, intranatal and postnatal periods.

2. Except in an emergency, a practising midwife shall not provide any midwifery care, or undertake any treatment which she has not, either before or after registration as a midwife, been trained to give or which is outside her current sphere of practice.

3. In an emergency, or where a deviation from the norm which is outside her current sphere of practice becomes apparent in the mother or baby during the antenatal, intranatal or postnatal periods, a practising midwife shall call a registered medical practitioner or such other qualified health professional who may reasonably be expected to have the requisite skills and experience to assist her.

Figure 14.3 Rule 40: responsibility and sphere of practice.

Law relating to consent in midwifery care

Opposition to the midwife

Situation 14.1   Refusal to have a midwife

Sharon Keene made it clear when her pregnancy was diagnosed that she wanted a natural birth and would not wish the midwife to attend. Sheila Armstrong, a community midwife, visited her and found her aggressive and hostile. She made it clear to Sheila that she did not want to be confined in hospital, but wanted her cohabitee, Jason, to deliver the baby. Sheila told her that if that were to occur, Jason would be acting illegally and Sheila attempted to explain to Sharon the help and assistance that could be made available from the midwifery services. As the pregnancy progressed, Sharon refused all ante-natal care and failed to attend clinic appointments. Where does Sheila stand if she discovers that Sharon intends to proceed with Jason delivering the baby?

Midwives occasionally meet women who are keen to 'go it alone' and not receive help during the pregnancy and also wish to have the baby delivered at home. There is no legal action that could be taken to prevent this if the woman is a mentally competent adult. She can refuse treatment and help for a good reason, a bad reason or for no reason at all (see *Re MB* below page 305). In practice, however, Sheila cannot compel Sharon to receive help. Nor could Sharon be prevented from having a home birth. Even if this is not clinically desirable, there is no legal power to compel a mentally capacitated woman to come into hospital for the confinement.

Criminal offence

It is, however, a criminal offence for a person, other than a midwife or doctor, to attend at a confinement except in an emergency. Section 16 of the 1997 Act makes it a criminal offence for a person other than a registered midwife or a registered medical practitioner (or student of either) to attend a woman in childbirth except in an emergency or while undergoing professional training as doctor or midwife. Thus if Jason (in the above situation) delivered the baby himself, he would be committing a crime. The only exception would be if there were an emergency and the baby arrived before they were aware of it. It is, of course, very difficult to prove that it was not an emergency and that there was no intention to call the midwife. Sheila would be able to warn the couple of the law and she would, of course, record this warning in her notes and also inform her supervisor of midwives. There have been some prosecutions under this section and its predecessor. For example, Rupert Baines from Bristol was found guilty of delivering a baby without assistance and Brian Radley from Wolverhampton was charged with attending a woman in childbirth otherwise than under the direction and personal supervision of a duly qualified practitioner and was fined £100 (August 1983). The difficulty confronting the midwife is in ensuring that she is aware of when the baby is imminent, since the aim is to protect the mother and child rather than take proceedings after the birth.

If she is obstructed by an aggressive partner during a home confinement, the midwife would be able to call upon police powers to assist her.

Admission and treatment

Choice of treatment by mother

Situation 14.2 Consent

Glenys Brown was expecting her first child. From the first moment the pregnancy was diagnosed, she was totally absorbed in her condition and the forthcoming event. She joined the local childbirth group and was very soon the local secretary. She attended psychoprophylactic and yoga classes and avidly read books, journals, leaflets and all available information. She had clear ideas on how her own baby was to be born and while she would have preferred total immersion in water, she accepted the fact that this would not be available in her local hospital. She was, however, adamant that she would not agree to an epidural, gas, an episiotomy or any other unnatural procedures. She was admitted to the delivery ward and after 12 hours of contractions the doctor set up a drip to speed the delivery as it was feared that the fetus was in danger. Glenys was eventually given an episiotomy despite her protests. She is now threatening to sue the midwife and doctor. Where do the midwife and doctor stand in law?

The basic principles relating to consent to treatment (set out in Chapter 7) apply to midwifery. There are no separate statutory laws covering the situation. The general principle is that the mentally competent patient has the right to refuse treatment, and any touching or treatment without her consent is a trespass to her person. If the mother were to sue the midwife for assault , the only defence of the midwife would be that either the woman gave consent or the woman was mentally incompetent and that action was taken without her consent in her best interests. There is no statutory right to compel a mentally capacitated mother to go into hospital for the birth of a child whatever the clinical indications. If the mentally capacitated mother refuses admission, then the midwife has to do all that is reasonable to support her at home. Evidence suggests that many mothers, who would have wished to have had a home birth, are being discouraged from that in spite of the principles set out in the Cumberlege Report 'Changing Childbirth'. It is hoped that the UKCC's new position statement[2] 'Supporting women who wish to have a home birth' will lead to more women being able to opt for home birth. The position statement clarifies the professional position of the midwife in respect of the provision of midwifery care for women who wish to have a home birth.

Consent to caesarian section

There are no statutory powers to compel a mentally competent woman to receive treatment or admission against her will. In an early case of *In Re S*,[3] a woman was compelled to have a caesarean section against her will, but the basis for this decision is no longer acceptable. Subsequently, the High Court agreed that a caesarean could be carried out without the consent of a woman who was suffering from mental disorder.[4] Section 63 permitted treatment to be given to a detained patient for mental disorder, and the caesarean was considered to come within the definition of treatment for mental disorder. In a second case,[5] a compulsory caesarean was declared lawful where a woman with a history of psychiatric treatment denied that she was pregnant. The judge held that there was evidence that the woman was mentally incapacitated and that there was power to act at common law in an emergency out of necessity to use reasonable force in her best interests. In a third case,[6] a woman was declared mentally incompetent and a caesarean authorised against her will. These cases (2 heard by the same judge) led to considerable concern amongst midwives and women over the protection of the rights of the women.

Two decisions by the Court of Appeal have clarified the law on compulsion.

Case 14.1 Capacity and compulsory caesarean[7]

Miss MB required a caesarean section in order to save her fetus. However, whilst she gave consent to the operation, she suffered from a needle phobia which caused her to panic and refuse the preliminary anaesthetic. The Trust applied for a declaration that the caesarean could take place. The judge held that the woman was mentally incapacitated as a result of the phobia and the operation could therefore proceed in her best interests. The same day the Court of Appeal upheld that decision. In a reserved judgment it set out how capacity was to be determined (see Box 14.1) and the general principles that apply to the refusal of treatment and which are shown in Box 14.2

The Court of Appeal emphasised that every person is presumed to have the capacity to consent to or to refuse medical treatment unless and until that presumption is rebutted. A competent woman who has the capacity to decide may, for religious reasons, other reasons, for rational or irrational reasons or for no reason at all, choose not to have medical intervention, even though the consequence may be the death or serious handicap of the child she bears, or her own death. In that event, the courts do not have the jurisdiction to declare medical intervention lawful and the question of her own best interests, objectively considered, does not arise.

Box 14.1

Determining Capacity: *Re MB*

A person lacks the capacity if some impairment or disturbance of mental functioning renders the person unable to make a decision whether to consent to or to refuse treatment. That inability to make a decision will occur when:

(a) The patient is unable to comprehend and retain the information which is material to the decision, especially as to the likely consequences of having or not having the treatment in question;

(b) The patient is unable to use the information and weigh it in the balance as part of the process of arriving at the decision.

> **Box 14.2**
>
> **Principles laid down in *Re MB* and incorporated in guidance issued by the Department of Health[8]**
>
> 1. The court is unlikely to entertain an application for a declaration unless the capacity of the patient to consent to or refuse the medical treatment is in issue.
> 2. For the time being, at least, the doctors ought to seek a ruling from the High Court on the issue of competence.
> 3. Those in charge should identify a potential problem as early as possible so that both the hospital and the patient can obtain legal advice.
> 4. It is highly desirable that, in any case where it is not an emergency, steps are taken to bring it before the court, before it becomes an emergency, to remove the extra pressure from the parties and the court and to enable proper instructions to be taken, particularly from the patient, and where possible give the opportunity for the court to hear oral evidence, if appropriate.
> 5. The hearing should be *inter partes*.
> 6. The mother should be represented in all cases, unless, exceptionally, she does not wish to be. If she is unconscious she should have a guardian *ad litem*.
> 7. The Official Solicitor should be notified of all applications to the High Court . . .
> 8. There should in general be some evidence, preferably but not necessarily from a psychiatrist, as to the competence of the patient, if competence is in issue.
> 9. Where time permits, the person identified to give the evidence as to capacity to consent to or refuse treatment should be made aware of the observations made by the Court of Appeal in this judgment.
> 10. In order to be in a position to assess a patient's best interests the judge should be provided, where possible and if time allows, with information about the circumstances of any relevant background material about the patient.

The ruling in *Re MB* was followed by the Court of Appeal in a case brought against St George's Hospital.[9] In this case, the pregnant woman had refused treatment for pre-eclampsia. She was detained under Section 2 of the Mental Health Act 1983 and a declaration sought from the High Court that a caesarean section could proceed. The declaration was given and the operation carried out. The patient subsequently appealed to the Court of Appeal and won on the grounds that she was wrongly detained under the Mental Health Act 1983 and the caesarean section should not have been ordered. Guidelines were subsequently issued by the court where there were serious doubts about a patient's capacity to accept or refuse treatment.[10]

In *Re T* 1992[11] which is discussed in chapter 7 on page 134, Case 7.4, the Court of Appeal emphasised that professionals had a duty to check on the validity of a patient's refusal to have treatment to ensure that the patient is mentally capacitated and is not under an undue influence.

The liability of the mother for harm caused to the baby

Civil liability

If a mother refuses treatment that is necessary in the interests of the child (for example, an episiotomy), does the child have a right of action for compensation against the mother because of the harm that she or he suffered? The only right of action for a child who was injured prenatally is under the Congenital Disabilities (Civil Liability) Act 1976 (see page 313 below). This Act enables a child who is born injured as a result of negligence, which led to his or her suffering harm whilst a fetus, to sue the person responsible. However, under the Act, the mother can be sued only by the child's representative if she was driving a motor vehicle when she knew or ought reasonably to have known that she was pregnant and failed to take care for the safety of the unborn child. (In practice, the child would be suing the company that insured the mother as driver). The Act, therefore, excludes the right of a child to sue for any harm that the mother may have caused the fetus, for example, by smoking, drinking, taking drugs or refusing treatment that is necessary in the best interests of the fetus.

Criminal liability of the mother

The mother could be liable in the criminal law under the Infant Life Preservation Act 1929. This makes it a criminal offence for any person who, with intent to destroy the life of a child capable of being born alive, by any wilful act causes a child to die before it has an existence independent of its mother (Section 11). There is a defence if the act that caused the death of the child was done in good faith for the purposes only of preserving the life of the mother. There are also criminal provisions relating to attempting to procure an abortion by administering drugs or using an instrument or supplying the same under the Offences Against the Person Act 1861 Sections 58 and 59. For further discussion on this, see Chapter 15.

However, in the context we are considering here, i.e. where a pregnant woman is smoking or addicted to drugs or drink or is refusing a caesarean, it is not thought that she would have the necessary intent to be found guilty of a criminal act under these provisions. Similarly, a pregnant woman who refused to consent to an episiotomy in the circumstances outlined above would not be committing a criminal offence unless this refusal was made with the intention of causing the death of the child and unless this refusal to give consent could be defined as an offence under the 1929 Act.

Planning for the baby of a young teenage mother

Where the mother is very young, then both she and her baby may be the subject of proceedings under the Children Act 1989 (see Chapter 13 on children). In a recent case,[12] the Family Division held that while there were no general principles that the babies of young teenagers should be adopted, it was not appropriate to concentrate on the welfare of the mother to the exclusion of the needs of the unborn baby. It was essential that the local authorities began planning for the baby as well as the mother as soon as possible. In this case, the mother, of 13 years, and her baby were both living with a foster family where the foster mother was caring for the mother who had returned to full-time schooling. Mrs Justice Bracewell held that there was no general principle that the babies of young teenagers should be adopted, but each case had to be considered on its own facts. She laid down the following principles:

1. Planning for the baby as well as the mother should begin immediately. It was not appropriate to concentrate on the welfare of the mother to the exclusion of the needs of the child to be born.

2. There was a need to complete social work and expert assessments well before the birth to ensure that effective and timely planning could be undertaken.

3. If care proceedings under Section 31 of the Children Act 1989 were necessary, they should be issued on the day of birth, and where the mother was very young should be transferred to the High Court and a separate guardian *ad litem* appointed for the mother and the child.

4. The baby's interim placement should be determined on the evidence before the court at an early hearing as a matter of urgency.

5. Early final determination of the case was vital.

6. Twin-track planning and/or concurrent planning was essential where one of the possible outcomes was adoption.

7. It was a misconception for social workers to consider that there was a prohibition on identifying suitable adopters before the final decision of the court, provided that decision was not pre-empted.

The advice of the Family Division will be extremely helpful, but one of the usual difficulties in such pregnancies is that the pregnancy comes to light only at a very late stage, requiring very speedy action to be taken by health and social services professionals.

Taking the newly born into care

A child can be taken into care as soon as it is born, if the requirements of the Children Act 1989 are satisfied. This may be so if there is evidence of the woman's conduct in relation to other children in the family. In one case, an order was obtained where a woman was pregnant and where her two previous children had died in early infancy. The parents' appeal against the decision was halted when the child, the subject of the order, was stillborn.

Case 14.2   Pre-birth conduct

At birth (12 March 1985), the child was suffering from symptoms caused by withdrawal from narcotics. The mother had been a registered drug addict since 1982, had continued to take drugs in excess of those prescribed during her pregnancy and had known that by taking drugs while pregnant she could be causing damage to the child. The child was kept in intensive care in hospital for several weeks immediately following the birth. A place of safety order was obtained on 23 April 1985, followed by successive interim orders.

The House of Lords, in a unanimous judgment, stated that the provisions of Section 1.2 (a) of the Children and Young Persons Act 1969 (which stated that if the court is satisfied that the child's 'proper development is being avoidably prevented or neglected or he is being ill-treated . . . and also that he is in need of care and control then . . . the court may if it thinks fit, make such an order') should be given a broad and liberal construction that gives full effect to their legislative purpose. They saw no reason why the courts should not look back to the time before the child had been born. However, in this case, the mother was still a drug addict and there was thus a continuum between the pre-natal and post-natal period. The decision of the House of Lords against the mother cannot be used as a precedent for arguing that if the mother has failed to take care of herself and the fetus during pregnancy, this will constitute grounds for a care order irrespective of her post-natal care of the child. There is no recognition in law of a child's right to receive, pre-natally, a responsible standard of care from its mother.[13] In a recent case, the Court of Appeal has said that a care order is not available in respect of an unborn child (see page 315, Case 14.5 below).

Midwifery practice and the standard of care

Midwives Rule 40 (2) (see Figure 14.3) states that, except in an emergency, the midwife shall not provide midwifery care or undertake any treatment that she has not, either before or after registration, been trained to give or that is outside her current sphere of practice. This general rule embraces a principle that applies to all UKCC practitioners.

Midwife and doctor

The principles relating to the duty and standard of care discussed in Chapter 3 apply to the role of the midwife, but specific concerns can arise over the respective role of midwife and doctor. The midwife would be expected to follow the standard of care as defined by applying the Bolam Test. Research findings and publications by the National Institute for Clinical Excellence (see Chapter 5) and recommendations from professional bodies such as the Royal College of Obstetricians and Gynaecologists and Royal College of Midwives also provide evidence for deducing what would be a reasonable standard of care. Rule 40 has been the subject of considerable debate and is set out in Figure 14.3. It is at the heart of the debate of the respective roles and relationship of midwife and doctor.

In Case 14.3 overleaf although the time of gastric aspiration was uncertain, it was felt that the nursing staff had not adequately appraised the doctor of the patient's deteriorating condition, and on this basis the hospital's solicitors accepted a proportion of liability. The inadequate attention paid to the patient by the general practitioner in the early post-operative period was thought to be of major significance. The MDU paid two-thirds of the agreed damages.[14] The acceptance of the nurse's partial liability in this case shows how important communication between the practitioners is in the care of the patient and the degree of responsibility that falls on the nurse's shoulders in ensuring that the doctor is adequately informed of the patient's progress or deterioration. The case also shows the importance of detailed and accurate records. In other circumstances, it could well be that the nurse appreciated the severity of the patient's condition, but that the doctor failed to respond to the entreaties to come. Accurate recordings of the times that phone calls were made, together with their content, will be partial evidence of the nurse's understanding of the situation. In serious cases, it may not be sufficient to rely on the judgement of one doctor and it may be necessary to take alternative action, which is a difficult dilemma for junior nursing and midwifery staff.

Case 14.3   Midwife and doctor mix-up

A 25-year-old woman was delivered of a normal baby by caesarian section in a small district hospital. The general practitioner who gave the anaesthetic had no specialist anaesthetic qualifications. The procedure lasted for two hours and was technically difficult because of adhesions from a previous caesarian section. In the immediate post-operative period, the patient developed peripheral cyanosis with a drop in blood pressure (88/60) and was treated with intravenous fluids and oxygen. When she seemed to have improved, the doctor left the hospital.

An hour later, the patient developed a cough and tachycardia and the nurses gave linctus pholcodine. Ninety minutes later, the doctor was informed by telephone that the patient had a persistent cough and he ordered oral aminophylline. After another ninety minutes, he was summoned urgently because the patient had severe progressive respiratory distress and cyanosis. An X-ray confirmed Mendelssohn's syndrome and the patient was transferred to the main hospital where she required intensive resuscitation; she had sustained brain stem infarction with pseudobulbular palsy, spastic quadriparesis and cortical blindness. The Medical Defence Union (MDU) considered the claim for damages to be indefensible.

Litigation, time limits and record keeping

Litigation in obstetrics and midwifery is increasing more than in any other specialty and the levels of compensation are, because of the costs of keeping a severely brain-damaged person for 40 to 50 years, amongst the highest payments. In addition, although the usual time limit for bringing a civil action for compensation is usually three years from the date of the negligent incident or the knowledge of it or the harm suffered (see chapter 6), where there is mental disability, the time limits do not come into force until the disability ends (which usually is not till death). The result is that many cases may not come to court for many years after the events, as the case below shows.

Case 14.4   Midwife and health visitor mix-up[15]

When Sonja Taylor was born in 1974, both the midwife and the health visitor thought that the blood test for phenylketonuria had already been performed. The hospital records were not consulted. As a result, the child became seriously brain-damaged and the parents were not aware of the problem until it was too late to rectify it. Had the test been conducted, the child could have been placed on a diet and the harm prevented. In March 2000, £2.5 million was awarded in respect of this act of negligence.

Community midwife

Situation 14.3   Community midwifery

A very active community midwifery service existed in Roger Park District Health Authority. The midwives were proud of the fact that there was a much higher proportion of community confinements than in the rest of the country. In the community, medical support was provided by those general practitioners who had opted to care for obstetrical cases. Not all these GPs had received recent training in obstetrical practice. One such GP was Dr Marks, a 65-year-old doctor who had not attended a revision course in the last 30 years. He was a doctor of very fixed ideas. Grace Edwards had been practising midwifery for 18 years and had recently undertaken her statutory revision course at a large London hospital. She was called to Brenda Rice's home at 3.00 a.m. Grace realised that the birth was imminent. She phoned Dr Marks, advising him to come immediately and giving him details of the mother and fetal condition that were giving her cause for concern. On arrival, Dr Marks disagreed with Grace's view of the severity of the situation and refused to agree to an ambulance being called. He considered that a forceps delivery could be performed safely. Unfortunately, this proved not to be so and the baby was stillborn.

In a situation such as this, the midwife cannot avoid responsibility for her actions by saying that she obeyed the GP. If it is clear that his advice is mistaken and she fears for the health of the mother or baby, then she has a personal professional duty to them and would have to take further action. In extreme circumstances, this might mean summoning an ambulance or calling out an obstetrician from the hospital despite the objections of the GP. This example also illustrates the importance of ensuring that the community midwife should be experienced.

Medicines and the midwife

In Chapter 28 the law relating to medicines and administration and prescribing is considered. Here the specific powers of a midwife in relation to medicine are considered.

Under the Misuse of Drugs Regulations 1985, a registered midwife who has notified the local supervising authority of her intention to practise may possess and administer any controlled drug in so far as is necessary for the practice of midwifery, and may surrender to her appropriate medical officer any stocks no longer required. A midwife may lawfully possess only those drugs that she had obtained on a midwife's supply order signed by the medical officer (Misuse of Drugs Act Section 11985/2066 Regulation 11). The midwife's supply order must specify in writing:

1. name;

2. occupation of midwife;

3. purpose for which the drug is required;

4. total quantity required.

The Midwives Rules, Rule 41, makes further regulations on the administration of any medicines in respect of her training and the type and safety of any apparatus for the administration of inhalation analgesic. Rule 41 is shown in Box 14.3.

Box 14.3

Rule 41

1. A practising midwife shall only administer those medicines, including analgesics, in which she has been trained as to use, dosage and methods of administration.

2. A practising midwife shall only administer medicines including inhalational analgesics by means of apparatus if she is satisfied that the apparatus has been properly maintained and;
   a. it has a CE marking or, if it does not have such a marking,
   b. it is of a type for the time being approved by the UKCC as suitable for use by a midwife and in this paragraph, CE marking has the meaning assigned to it in the Medical Devices Regulations SI 1994 No 3017 (see Chapter 12 for Medical Devices regulations).

3. In a situation in which clinical trials involving new medicines including inhalation analgesics, or new apparatus, are taking place, a practising midwife may only participate under the direction of a registered medical practitioner.

Paragraphs 15 to 25 of the Midwives Code of Practice give further guidance on the supply, possession and use of controlled drugs, destruction and surrender of controlled drugs, controlled drugs and home births, prescription-only and other medicines, administration of homeopathic or herbal substances and the administration of controlled drugs.

Congenital Disabilities (Civil Liability) Act 1976

The Congenital Disabilities Act 1976 was enacted because, following the thalidomide tragedy, it was not clear in law whether the child, once born, had a claim in respect of pre-birth injuries. The Act enables a child who is born alive to sue any person (except the mother, apart from one situation – see below) who has caused him to be born disabled as a result of an act of negligence. In order for an action to succeed under the Act, it must be established that the harm that occurred was caused by the wrongful act. For example, a pregnant woman could be assaulted and subsequently go into premature labour. The child might suffer from some mental and physical handicaps. It must be established that these disabilities were caused by the assault. Causation in brain damage is particularly difficult to trace, as vaccination cases show. The law does not recognise the fetus as having a legal personality and it therefore cannot have legal rights of its own until it is born and has a separate existence from its mother. Once born, it does then have the right to sue under the Congenital Disabilities (Civil Liability) Act for pre-birth injuries. The 1976 Act was amended by the Human Fertilisation and Embryology Act 1990 by adding Section 1A to the Act. This is shown in Figure 14.4 and gives a right of action to a child who is born disabled as a result of fertility treatment. The Act can be seen in Appendix B on page 578.

In any case where

(a) a child carried by a woman as the result of the placing in her of an embryo or of sperm and eggs or her artificial insemination is born disabled,

(b) the disability results from an act or omission in the course of the selection, or the keeping or use outside the body, or the embryo carried by her or of the gametes used to bring about the creation of the embryo and

(c) a person is under this section answerable to the child in respect of the act or omission the child's disabilities are to be regarded as damage resulting from the wrongful act of that person and actionable accordingly at the suit of the child.

Figure 14.4 Congenital Disabilities (Civil Liability) Act 1976 Section 1A.

Liability of the midwife

If it can be shown that the midwife has failed without justification to follow the approved accepted practice, and as a consequence the fetus is harmed and the child is born disabled, then the mother has a right of action against her and also against the NHS Trust for the injury she has suffered. In addition, the mother can bring a claim in the name of the child for any harm suffered by the child. This latter action can be brought under the Congenital Disabilities (Civil Liability) Act 1976.

Professional standards

Section 1 (5) of the Act defines what is meant by professional standards and is set out in Figure 14.5.

> The defendant is not answerable to the child for anything he did or omitted to do when responsible in a professional capacity for treating or advising the parent, if he took reasonable care having due regard to then received professional opinion applicable to the particular class of case; but this does not mean that he is answerable only because he departed from received opinion.

Figure 14.5 Congenital Disabilities (Civil Liability) Act 1976 Section 1(5).

The working of the Act can be seen in another context. Imagine that another thalidomide-type situation were to occur. It might be possible that the mother had asked the midwife's advice in relation to a particular medicine/food during pregnancy. The midwife might reassure her that the particular product was fine. If, in fact, it then caused defects to the baby, would the midwife be liable to the baby under the Congenital Disabilities (Civil Liability) Act? The answer is that, if at the time her advice was reasonable in relation to what was known about the product and she was following the approved practice in recommending it, she would be unlikely to be found negligent. (The mother might, of course, have other remedies such as against the manufacturers (see chapter 12).)

Child's action is derivative

The child's right of action under the 1976 Act is derivative, i.e. only if the defendant would have been liable to one of the parents is the defendant then liable to the child. The father can be sued by the child. However, if the action concerns an occurrence that took place prior to conception, the defendant is not answerable to the child if at that time either or both of the parents knew of the risk of their child being born disabled. If, however, it is the child's father who is the defendant, the action can continue if he alone knew of the risk, but not the mother. To explain this provision, consider the following circumstance.

Situation 14.4   HIV

Bill was aware that he was suffering from AIDS. He was unwilling to allow the special clinic to inform his wife and he refused to give them his address. However, he continued to have sex with her and she became pregnant. She was not aware that she might become HIV positive. The baby was found to be HIV positive.

In this situation, it is possible that the child could maintain a successful action against the father under the provisions of the Act. Bill was in breach of the duty of care owed to the mother in that he failed to warn her that he was suffering from AIDS and as a consequence the baby was born HIV positive. It could be argued, however, that the father's negligence was in failing to prevent the baby from being born, not in actually causing harm to the child, and therefore the child would have no claim under the Act. This is discussed below in connection with the McKay case.

If both parents are aware of the possibility of the child being born disabled, no action can be commenced.

The mother's liability under the Act

The mother is liable to the child under the Act only if (Section 2) she is driving a motor vehicle when she knows (or ought reasonably to know) herself to be pregnant. Under this provision, she is to be regarded as being under the same duty to take care for the safety of her unborn child as the law imposes on her with respect to the safety of other people; and if, in consequence of her breach of that duty, her child is born with disabilities that would not otherwise have been present, those disabilities are to be regarded as damage resulting from her wrongful act and actionable accordingly at the suit of the child. In practice, of course, the child would be suing the company who insured the mother.

The rights of the child

An unborn child is not recognised in law as having a legal personality. At birth, however, he or she is able to bring an action in respect of any harm it has suffered.

The following case has made it clear that the courts have no power to make an unborn baby a ward of court.

Case 14.5   The rights of the unborn

The mother was aged 36 and had suffered from severe mental disturbance since 1977. Throughout 1982, she had led a nomadic existence, wandering around Europe. She had returned in 1983 and had been settled in a flat in south London. Her only means of support was supplementary benefit. The local authority was concerned about the baby expected towards the end of January. Early in January, the mother disappeared. The local authority instituted wardship proceedings.[16]

The Court of Appeal was of the opinion that if it had the power to institute wardship proceedings it would do so, but did it have the power? It concluded that it did not. There was no jurisdiction for the court to make a fetus a ward of court. The court pointed out the difficulties of enforcing such an order against the mother: 'If the law was to be extended so as to impose control over the expectant mother, where such control was necessary for the benefit of the unborn child then it was for Parliament to decide whether such controls could be imposed and, if so, subject to what limitations. In such a sensitive field affecting the liberty of the individual it was not for the judiciary to extend the law' (per Lord Justice Balcombe).

Action for wrongful life

> ### Case 14.6   German measles
>
> Mrs McKay was pregnant and suspected that she had contracted German measles in the early weeks of her pregnancy. Blood tests were arranged to see if she had been infected. Unfortunately, she was wrongly informed that she had not been infected. When the baby was born, it was found to be disabled as a result of the effect of German measles.[17]

The Court of Appeal held that the child's claim for wrongful life (i.e. if there had been no negligence, the child would have been aborted) could not be sustained. Although this child was born before the Congenital Disabilities Act 1976 was passed, the court still held that an action for wrongful life could not stand, even under the provisions of the Act. This decision does not, of course, affect the rights of the mother to sue for damages resulting from the negligence in informing her of the results of the tests and Mrs McKay brought her own action on that point. The former decision was concerned solely with the rights of the child.

Nurseries within midwifery departments

Problems can sometimes arise within the midwifery department over the responsibility for the nursery nurse staff and those who are caring for the babies. It is essential that clear lines of accountability and responsibility are laid down so that there is no confusion on this point: local practices might differ.

Special care baby units

These units may or may not be under the control of the midwifery department. Some may be under the paediatric department. The nature of the control should not affect the standard of care. The shortage of staff in these units has received much publicity and undoubtedly the pressure on resources has created difficulties for staff which have been considered in Chapter 4.

Care of the grossly handicapped

Those who work in special care baby units face the problem of determining the extent to which 'heroic' measures should be used to prolong the lives of grossly underweight or should be given to severely handicapped babies.

> *Case 14.7   Fetal accident inquiry in Glasgow*
>
> The parents of a girl born at 26 weeks' gestation, weighing 675 grams, requested an inquiry to discover why a paediatrician had made no attempt to resuscitate her. They alleged that the Royal Maternity Hospital operated a ban on resuscitating infants of less than 700 grams.

The sheriff ruled that the doctor had behaved in a correct professional manner by assessing the weight, gestation and general condition of the infant before deciding not to resuscitate[18].

It is illegal for the doctors to prescribe, either intentionally or recklessly, a substance to bring about the infant's death. The courts have, however, ruled that there is a legal distinction between killing and letting die and have applied this principle in several cases relating to severely disabled babies.

The Court of Appeal has made a declaration in the case of *Re C*[19] that an infant ward of court who was terminally ill, suffering irreversible and severe brain damage, was to be treated in accordance with the specialist's advice. The paragraph included by the trial judge relating to details of the treatment permitted, preventing the prescribing and administering of antibiotics, and preventing the setting up of intravenous fusions or nasal-gastric feeding regimes, was deleted by the Court of Appeal.

In the case of *Re J* (1990),[20] the baby suffered from severe disabilities and was likely to develop serious spastic quadriplegia and be both deaf and blind. He was not, however, on the point of death nor dying. In deciding whether he should be put back onto a mechanical ventilator, the Court of Appeal held that the test to be applied 'must be whether the child in question, if capable of exercising sound judgement, would consider the life tolerable'.

In the case of *Re J* (1992),[21] the baby suffered from a severe form of cerebral palsy with cortical blindness and severe epilepsy. The Court of Appeal held that the court will not exercise its inherent jurisdiction over minors by ordering a medical practitioner to treat the minor in a manner contrary to the practitioner's clinical judgement. In the practitioner's view, intensive therapeutic measures such as artificial ventilation were inappropriate. The Court of Appeal has declared that it would be lawful for doctors in their professional judgment to allow a severely disabled child to die. If a baby is born alive following an attempted abortion, then all reasonable care must be taken to ensure that the baby has a reasonable chance of surviving.

The Royal College of Paediatrics and Child Health has published guidelines on when it is appropriate to withhold or withdraw medical treatment.[22] The guidelines distinguish between the following clinical situations:

1. the brain dead child;
2. the permanent vegetative state;
3. the 'No Chance' situation;
4. the 'No Purpose' situation;
5. the 'Unbearable' situation.

In all these situations, the possibility of withholding or withdrawal of curative medical treatment might be considered. The guidance emphasises the importance of the fundamental principles of the duty of care and partnership of care and the respect for the rights of the child as set out in the United Nation's Convention on the Rights of the Child.[23] The guidelines of the Royal College of Paediatrics and Childhealth represent its interpretation of the law, but are not the law itself. Further advice has been published by the British Medical Association.[24]

Case 14.8   Death with dignity[25]

A child since birth had suffered from serious disabilities, in particular a severe, chronic, irreversible and worsening lung disease giving him a very short life expectation, coupled with heart failure, renal and liver dysfunction with a background of severe developmental delay. Doctors advised the NHS Trust that it was not in the child's best interests to be resuscitated and the Trust applied to court for a declaration. The child's parents opposed the application.

The court held that the paramount consideration was the welfare of the child; the high respect for the sanctity of human life imposed a strong presumption in favour of taking all steps capable of preserving it; there could be no question of the court directing treatment that was contrary to the clinical judgment of the doctor; the court held that full palliative treatment was in the child's best interests and would allow him to die with dignity. There was no breach of the European Convention on Human Rights of either the right to life (Article 2) or the right not to be subjected to inhuman or degrading treatment (Article 3).

A similar decision was taken in the case of a child born prematurely with problems including a chronic lung disease, where the parents disagreed with the medical view that ventilation would be distressing and risky and allow short-term improvement only. The court held that a declaration would be issued that medical treatment should be given as the clinicians saw best in the interests of the child.

Disputes over withdrawal of care

There are considerable advantages in seeking a declaration from the court before active treatment is withdrawn, especially where there are already allegations of negligence over what caused the disabilities. For example, parents accused a hospital of turning off their baby's life support to save care costs. The baby was born with considerable disabilities as a result of the alleged negligence of staff. However, the parents alleged that they were pressured into agreeing to the withdrawal of support treatment because the compensation for a dead baby was £7,500 whereas, had the baby been allowed to survive, compensation would be for the costs of care for the whole of his life.[26]

The Court of Appeal held it was lawful for doctors to carry out the operation to separate the twins. The crucial questions to be answered were:

1. Was it in J's best interests that she be separated from M?

2. Was it in M's best interests that she be separated from J?

3. If those interests were in conflict, was the court to balance the interests of one against the other and allow one to prevail against the other and how was that to be done?

4. If the prevailing interest favoured the operation, could it be lawfully performed?

The court concluded that the operation would give J the prospects of a normal expectation of relatively normal life. The operation would shorten M's life, but she remained marked for death. M was alive because she sucked the life blood out of J. She would survive only as long as J survived. The operation could be carried out under the doctrine of necessity. The essential elements of that doctrine were all satisfied:

1. the act was needed to avoid inevitable and irreparable evil;

2. no more should be done than was reasonably necessary for the purpose to be achieved; and

3. the evil inflicted must not be disproportionate to the evil avoided.

The court held that its decision was not in conflict with Article 2 of the European Convention on Human Rights (see Chapter 1).

The parents were given leave to appeal to the House of Lords, but decided not to do so. The operation was carried out: Mary died and at the time of writing, Jodie is off the ventilator and eating and breathing normally and has returned to Gozo. The extent of her disabilities is not known.

In recent years, concerns have been expressed over resources in special care baby units and the number of places available. An additional £6.5 million was made available in October 2000 to provide or replace essential equipment such as incubators, resuscitation trolleys, ventilators and life system monitors in neonatal intensive care units. £150 million was made available for critical care services in May 2000. In September 2000, £10.5 million was provided for additional nurse training in critical care, including neonatal intensive care.

Registration of births and stillbirths

Births

There is a duty on the doctor or midwife attending a woman in childbirth to notify the prescribed medical officer of the birth or stillbirth within 36 hours. This applies whether the birth is at home or in an institution.

Under the Births and Deaths Registration Act 1953, it is the duty of the father or mother to give information to the registrar within 42 days. If either of them cannot, then there is a duty to do so on the occupier of the house, or any person present at the birth, or any person having charge of the child. This provision might well involve the midwife. If there is a failure to register within 42 days, the Registrar can compel any qualified informant to attend to give information and sign the Register. The Registrar must give 7 days' notice in writing. There are additional powers if there is no registration after that date.

Stillbirths

A stillbirth is a child that is stillborn, which issued forth from its mother after the 24th week of pregnancy, and which did not at any time after being completely expelled from its mother breathe or show any signs of life (Section 41 of the Births and Deaths Registration Act 1953 as amended by the Stillbirth Definition Act 1992 Section 1). The stillbirth has to be registered and the informant has to deliver to the Registrar a written certificate that the child was not born alive. This would be signed by the registered medical practitioner or a certified midwife who was in attendance at the birth or who has examined the body.

A stillbirth should be disposed of by burial in a burial ground or churchyard or by cremation at an authorised crematorium.

What if the fetus is of less than 24 weeks' gestation?

If the fetus was delivered without any sign of life, then no registration is necessary. The fetus may be disposed of without formality in any way that does not constitute a nuisance or an affront to public decency. However, it is clear that even though the fetus is under 24 weeks, the bereaved parents should be given the sympathy and care that would be given if the baby was full term.

If the fetus is under 24 weeks' gestation and initially shows signs of life and breathing and then dies, it should be treated as a neo-natal death and be registered as a birth and death.

Use of fetal tissue

This has recently come into public debate with the news that transplanted fetal brain tissue has been used in operations for Parkinson's disease. There would appear to be no legal grounds to prevent such use, provided that the consent of the mother was given to the use and that the fetus was not aborted for the purposes of obtaining fetal tissue. The British Medical Association has issued guidelines that forbid the possibility of a human brain transplant, but that approve the controlled use of brain cell implants from aborted fetal tissue. These guidelines are in keeping with the recommendations made by the Peel Report (HMSO, 1972) which put forward a recommended code of practice for the use of fetal materials. These recommendations are summarised in the *Bulletin of the Institute of Medical Ethics* No. 35, February 1988. The Polkinghorne Committee has reviewed the guidance on the use of fetuses and fetal material and provided a Code of Practice[28] (see also the RCN Guidance Fetal Cell Transplantation[29]).

The announcement that eggs could be taken from dead fetuses and used to grow embryos for implantation has caused considerable concern and is currently before the Human Fertilisation Embryology Authority (for which see Chapter 22). Parliament subsequently approved secondary legislation permitting the use of stem cells from embryos for research under the control of the Human Fertilization and Embryology authority (see Chapter 22).

Disquiet was caused when it was learnt that the brains and other tissue had been kept from babies after post mortem examination at a hospital in Liverpool without parental consent or knowledge. Following an inquiry, the Chief Medical Officer has undertaken to produce robust guidelines by the end of 2000. It was learnt in November 2000 that a hospital in Birmingham had retained 400 fetuses (following abortion or stillbirth) without the knowledge or consent of the mothers. An inquiry was being sought by concerned parents. See discussion on the retention of organs on page 359.

National Guidelines on midwifery practice

'Changing Childbirth'

In April 1991, the House of Commons initiated an inquiry into maternity services because concerns had been expressed that the services did not meet the wishes of women. Its report was published in February 1992 (House of Commons Health Committee Session 1991–92 Maternity Services). It concluded that 'the policy of encouraging all women to give birth in hospitals cannot be justified on grounds of safety'. It made wide-ranging recommendations covering the development of midwife-managed units, involvement of midwives in junior doctors' training, and emphasis on the rights and involvement of the mother. A joint committee supported its recommendations. The government set up an expert committee chaired by Lady Cumberlege to review policy on NHS maternity care and this committee reported in 1993.[30] 'Changing Childbirth' identified three key principles that should underlie effective woman-centred maternity services: the woman must be the focus of maternity care; maternity services can be readily and easily accessible to all; services must be effective and efficient. Recommendations were made on action to implement these principles. An Implementation Committee was established and health authorities and NHS Trusts were required to implement the recommendations.[31]

Confidential Enquiry into Stillbirths and Deaths in Infancy (CESDI)

A confidential enquiry into still births and deaths in infancy (CESDI) is conducted each year and provides valuable insights into standards of care and areas for improved practice. The sixth annual report[32] highlighted many failures of practice in both antenatal, intrapartum and post natal care and care of the newborn. On 1 April 1999, the National Institute for Clinical Excellence (NICE) was established and the Confidential Enquiry was brought under its remit. The sixth annual report of CESDI states that:

> The remit of NICE includes the setting and implementation of national clinical guidelines, as part of clinical governance. NICE will be concerned to establish a balance between the autonomy and innovation of clinicians at a local level and the centralised direction of best practice.

Audit Commission Report in 1997

An Audit Commission Report in 1997[33] made significant recommendations for all aspects of maternity services, including the care of women in pregnancy, labour and birth and the care of women after childbirth and the care of the newborn babies. Amongst its many recommendations are:

For clinicians and managers

For the care of women in pregnancy:

1. advice on paying special attention to the needs of women with complicated pregnancies for good communication and support;

2. developing antenatal policies that are flexible, agreeing guidelines for antenatal assessment and protocols for referral with local GPs;

3. reviewing routine checks on low-risk women and reviewing routine attendance at consultant clinics and providing as much antenatal care as possible in the community;

4. ensuring women have access to specialist services and opinion;

5. avoiding duplication of doctors' and midwives' skills;

6. reviewing clinical procedures in antenatal clinics;

7. agreeing standards for information giving and counselling.

For the care of women in labour and birth:

1. involvement of women in decision making;

2. improved information giving and preparation for the woman and partner;

3. ensuring that training needs are met whilst protecting women's privacy and dignity;

4. providing professional support in labour with 1-to-1 midwifery support in established labour;

5. reviewing staffing levels and introducing more flexible methods of staff deployment; reducing numbers of different staff to the individual woman to the lowest possible number;

6. organising midwifery work to maximise continuity of care in labour;

7. documenting impact of maternal requests for procedures;

8. collecting and analysing data on women and interventions;

9. ensuring women receive accurate, unbiased and complete information about risks and benefits of intervention;

10. ensuring clinicians have access to training and education and keep up to date;

11. establishing multi-disciplinary clinical audit and peer review.

Postnatal care and care of sick babies in neo-natal units:

1. involvement of women in decisions;

2. clarifying objectives and setting standards for postnatal care;

3. reviewing staffing and skill mix;

4. promote breast-feeding;

5. developing guidelines to match home visiting to the needs of mothers and their families;

6. comparing lengths of stay with other trusts and investigating and following up differences;

7. reviewing activity levels and admission levels in neonatal units;

8. assessing links with neighbouring units.

Other major recommendations on staffing and organisational support are made to commissioners of maternity services and to the NHS Executive.

Record-keeping and midwifery

The Sixth Annual Report of CESDI made many recommendations on record-keeping. In particular, it noted that poor record-keeping occurred in a third of cases. The major problem was a failure to document events adequately and the report reiterated recommendations from earlier reports on record-keeping:

1. All professionals should make clear and adequate notes. The standard should be that which enables a colleague coming new to the case to be properly informed.

2. The quality of maternity records needs to be improved to enable clear identification of risk factors and documentation of management plans for those during both antepartum and intrapartum periods. These would be facilitated by a well-designed, universally used national maternity record.

There has been work on a national record for maternity services prepared by a National Group.[34] They have prepared a personal maternity record that would be looked after by the mother and covers the antenatal stages. Work is progressing on other stages. There is no evidence that the antenatal record has had an extended take up across the country.

AIDS and the midwife

The possibility of a midwife contracting AIDS from an HIV positive patient is a growing problem, and midwives are concerned at the possibility of protecting themselves by equipment, gloves, clothing, and screening of patients so that midwives are warned of the potential dangers. These anxieties are part of the general dilemmas in relation to AIDS and are considered in Chapter 26.

Future developments in midwifery

Midwives face a challenging time for the immediate future. On the one hand, litigation in obstetrics is increasing and leading to the highest payouts of compensation. There are major changes in standard setting taking place: the National Institute for Clinical Excellence (see Chapter 5) is investigating many midwifery and obstetric treatments and aids to diagnosis, such as electronic fetal monitoring, caesarean sections, and Anti-D, with a view to recommendations being made for national implementation. A National Service Framework for Midwifery and Childcare is also being prepared. On the other hand, the Royal College of Midwifery, in a press release on 29 November 2000, stated that midwifery was in a state of crisis in the UK: shortage of staff and unacceptable pressures had led to demoralisation of midwives; and increased the numbers of midwives leaving the NHS. Short-term measures to protect the standards of care for mothers and babies are being introduced by managers, sometimes leading to a curtailment of service, giving priorities to the essential services. Major changes will be required to resolve the crisis. In the light of these staffing pressures, the implementation of the full recommendations of 'Changing Childbirth' seem a lifetime away. It is hoped that the Midwifery Committee of the new Nursing and Midwifery Council to be set up in April 2002 will be prompt in making recommendations to the government on a midwifery strategy both for the short and long term.

Questions and exercises

1 What is the legal status of a birth plan? In what circumstances can a mother refuse to give consent to life saving treatment?

2 Analyse the principles set down by the Court of Appeal in the *Re MB* case (see Box 14.2) and consider the extent to which they have been incorporated into your practice.

3 What are the implications of the Congenital Disabilities (Civil Liability) Act 1976 for the midwife?

4 What statutory duties does a midwife have in relation to the registration of a birth or still birth?

5 Consider the recommendations of the Audit Commission A First Class Delivery and analyse the extent to which they are implemented in your own unit. What are the legal implications for any deficiencies?

6 What specific powers and rights does the midwife have in relation to drugs that are not possessed by the registered general nurse? (See Chapter 28.)

References

1 UKCC Midwives rules and code of practice 1998 UKCC
2 UKCC Registrar's letter 20/2000 Supporting women who wish to have a home birth UKCC June 2000 – a position statement
3 *In re S* (an adult) (refusal of medical treatment) 1992 4 All ER 671
4 *Tameside and Glossop Acute Services Trust* v. *CH* [1996] 1 FLR 762
5 *Norfolk and Norwich (NHS) Trust* v. *W* [1996] 2 FLR 613
6 *Rochdale NHS Trust* v. *C* [1997] 1 FCR 274
7 *Re MB* (An Adult: Medical Treatment) [1997] 2 FLR 426
8 Department of Health Circular EL (97)32 1997
9 *St George's Healthcare NHS Trust* v. *S* [1998] 3 All ER 673
10 *St George's Healthcare NHS Trust* v. *S* (Guidelines) (No 2) [1999] Fam 26
11 *In re T* (an adult) (refusal of medical treatment) 1992 4 All ER 649
12 *In re R* (A Child) (Care proceedings), *The Times Law Report* 19 July 2000 Family Division
13 *In re D (a minor)* v. *Berkshire County Council* and others 1987 1 All ER 20
14 Medical Defence Union Annual Report 1982, 30
15 Russell Jenkins, £2.5m payout for birth blunder after 26 years, *The Times* 9 March 2000
16 *In re F* (in utero) 1988 2 All ER 193
17 *McKay* v. *Essex AHA* 1982 2 All ER 771

[18] Quoted in the Bulletin of the Institute of Medical Ethics, February 1988, p. 3
[19] *In re C* (a minor) (wardship, medical treatment) 1989 2 All ER 782
[20] *In re J* (a minor) (wardship, medical treatment) 1990 3 All ER 930
[21] *In re J* (a minor) (wardship, medical treatment) 1992 4 All ER 614
[22] Royal College of Paediatrics and Child Health, Withholding or Withdrawing Life Saving Treatment in Children. September 1997 RCPCH
[23] United Nations' Convention on the Rights of the Child. 1989
[24] British Medical Association, Withholding and Withdrawing Life-prolonging Medical Treatment BMA 1999
[25] *A National Health Service Trust* v. *D*, *The Times Law Report* 19 July 2000
[26] Lois Rogers, Baby's Life Support cut off 'to save care costs', *Sunday Times* 30 July 2000 p. 6
[27] *In re A* (Minors) (Conjoined twins: medical treatment), *The Times Law Report* 10 October 2000
[28] The Polkinghorne Committee Review of the guidance on the research use of fetuses and fetal material HMSO Cmd 762 1989
[29] Royal College of Nursing, Fetal Cell Transplantation RCN 000120 March 1992
[30] Changing Childbirth: Report of the Expert Maternity Group, Department of Health, HMSO
[31] See Executive Letter (94)9, issued 24 January 1994 by the NHS Management Executive
[32] Confidential Enquiry into Stillbirths and Deaths in Infancy (CESDI), 6th Annual Report 1999, Maternal and Child Health Research Consortium, London
[33] Audit Commission, First Class Delivery: Improving Maternity Services in England and Wales 1997 Stationery Office
[34] National Maternity Record Group NMRP 6.97 V.P1 1997

15 The nurse on the gynaecology ward

Figure 15.1 sets out the areas of particular concern to the nurse who works in the gynaecology ward that will be considered in this chapter. For convenience, the chapter also includes the law relating to vasectomies within the topic of sterilisation.

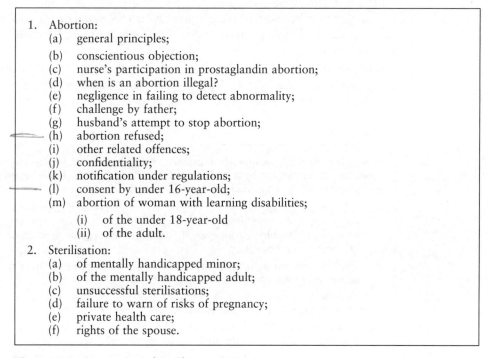

1. Abortion:
   (a) general principles;
   (b) conscientious objection;
   (c) nurse's participation in prostaglandin abortion;
   (d) when is an abortion illegal?
   (e) negligence in failing to detect abnormality;
   (f) challenge by father;
   (g) husband's attempt to stop abortion;
   (h) abortion refused;
   (i) other related offences;
   (j) confidentiality;
   (k) notification under regulations;
   (l) consent by under 16-year-old;
   (m) abortion of woman with learning disabilities;

   (i)   of the under 18-year-old
   (ii) of the adult.

2. Sterilisation:
   (a) of mentally handicapped minor;
   (b) of the mentally handicapped adult;
   (c) unsuccessful sterilisations;
   (d) failure to warn of risks of pregnancy;
   (e) private health care;
   (f) rights of the spouse.

Figure 15.1 Issues covered in Chapter 15.

Abortion laws

The general principles

Although the unborn child is not a legal personality and cannot sue or be sued until it is born (see chapter 14), its existence is protected in law by the Offences Against the Persons Act 1861, Section 58 of which makes it an offence to administer drugs or use instruments to procure a miscarriage and Section 59 prohibits other activities to procure a miscarriage. In addition, under the Infant Life Preservation Act 1929, it is an offence to destroy the life of a child capable of being born alive. The Infant Life Preservation Act 1929 provides that any person who, with intent to destroy the life of a child capable of being born alive, by any wilful act, causes a child to die before it has an existence independent of its mother, shall be guilty of felony, to wit, of child destruction. 28 weeks' gestation is prima facie evidence that the child is capable of being born alive. However, these Acts are subject to the Abortion Act 1967 as amended by the Human Fertilisation and Embryology Act 1990. An abortion that satisfies the legal requirements laid down in this Act is not an offence. Under Section 5(1) of the Abortion Act, no offence under the Infant Life (Preservation) Act 1929 takes place if the abortion is carried out by a registered medical practitioner who terminates a pregnancy in accordance with the provisions of the Act. If these legal requirements are not satisfied, then abortion is an offence which carries a maximum sentence of life imprisonment. The provisions of the Act as amended are set out in Figure 15.2.

Account may be taken of the pregnant woman's actual or reasonably foreseeable environment in deciding whether there is a risk of injury to health under paragraph (a) (Section 1(2)).

The abortion must be carried out in a NHS hospital or a place specifically approved by the Secretary of State or Minister of Health for the purposes of the Act. Emergency provisions are set out in Figure 15.3.

A person shall not be guilty of an offence under the law relating to abortion when a pregnancy is terminated by a registered medical practitioner if two registered medical practitioners are of the opinion, formed in good faith

(a) that the pregnancy has not exceeded its 24th week and that the continuance of the pregnancy would involve risk, greater than if the pregnancy were terminated, of injury to the physical or mental health of the pregnant woman or any existing children of her family; or

(b) that the termination is necessary to prevent grave permanent injury to the physical or mental health of the pregnant woman; or

(c) that the continuance of the pregnancy would involve risk to the life of the pregnant woman, greater than if the pregnancy were terminated; or

(d) that there is a substantial risk that if the child were born it would suffer from such physical or mental abnormalities as to be seriously handicapped.

Figure 15.2 Abortion Act 1967 Section 1(1) as amended by the Human Fertilisation and Embryology Act 1990.

The Provisions set out in Figure 15.2, including the requirement to have two registered medical practitioners, do not apply in an emergency when a registered medical practitioner is of the opinion, formed in good faith, that the termination is immediately necessary to save the life or to prevent grave permanent injury to the physical or mental health of the pregnant woman.

Figure 15.3 Emergency provisions of the Abortion Act.

Conscientious objection to participation in an abortion

The Abortion Act is one of the few examples where a professional can lawfully refuse to take part in an activity on the grounds of a conscientious objection. Thus Section 4 states that:

> no person shall be under any duty, whether by contract or by any statutory or other legal requirement, to participate in any treatment authorised by this Act to which he has a conscientious objection: Provided that in any legal proceedings the burden of proof of conscientious objection shall rest on the person claiming to rely on it.

This right is, however, subject to Section 4(2):

> Nothing in subsection (1) of this section shall affect any duty to participate in treatment which is necessary to save the life or to prevent grave permanent injury to the physical or mental health of a pregnant woman.

The extent of the protection from being involved in an abortion was considered by the Court of Appeal.

Case 15.1   The letter

Mrs Janaway, a medical secretary, refused to type a letter referring a patient from a general practitioner to a consultant with a view to a possible termination of pregnancy. She was a Roman Catholic who believed strongly that abortion was morally wrong. The genuineness of her belief was never in dispute. She was asked to type the letter and refused on the basis that she was protected by Section 4 of the Abortion Act. She was dismissed by the Health Authority and subsequently applied for judicial review of the Health Authority's decision. This was refused and she therefore appealed.[1]

The Court of Appeal held that she was not entitled to claim the protection of Section 4 of the Act. It could not be said that by typing the letter she was participating in any treatment authorised by the Act, nor could typing such a letter be regarded as a criminal offence prior to the Abortion Act so that it could be regarded as now being protected by the provisions of the Act.

Nurses' participation in prostaglandin abortions

In Case 15.2, overleaf, the House of Lords decided on a majority of three to two that the DHSS advice did not involve the performance of unlawful acts by members of the RCN. Lord Diplock's views are set out in Figure 15.4.

This decision has considerable significance for the scope of professional practice. It could be argued that even where a statute expressly places responsibilities upon a

In the context of the Act what was required was that a registered medical practitioner – a doctor – should accept responsibility for all stages of the treatment for the termination of the pregnancy. The particular method to be used should be decided by the doctor in charge of that treatment; he should carry out any physical acts, forming part of the treatment, that in accordance with accepted medical practice were done only by qualified medical practitioners, and should give specific instructions as to the carrying out of such parts of the treatment as in accordance with accepted medical practice were carried out by nurses or other hospital staff without medical qualifications. To each of them the doctor or his substitute should be available to be consulted or called in for assistance from beginning to end of the treatment. In other words, the doctor need not do everything with his own hands; the subsection's requirements were satisfied when the treatment was one prescribed by a registered medical practitioner carried out in accordance with his directions and of which he remained in charge throughout.

Figure 15.4 Lord Diplock's view in the case of *Royal College of Nursing* v. *The Department of Health and Social Security* 1981 1 All ER 545.

registered medical practitioner, the law is still followed when that activity is delegated to another health care professional acting under the aegis of the registered medical practitioner.

Case 15.2 Prostaglandin drip

The Royal College of Nursing brought a case on behalf of its members against the DHSS because members had complained that they were often left on wards to supervise (sometimes for several days) a patient who was having a prostaglandin-induced abortion. The doctor would set up the drip and then the nurse would undertake the care of the patient. The RCN queried the legality of this in the light of the wording of the Act that the pregnancy should be terminated by a registered medical practitioner. The RCN questioned, in particular, advice given in a DHSS letter and circular relating to the procedures that might be performed by an appropriately skilled nurse or midwife.[2]

When is an abortion illegal?

The simple answer is: under any circumstances other than those permitted under the 1967 Act as amended by the 1990 Act. It is specifically provided that no offence is committed under the Infant Life Preservation Act 1929 if the provisions of the 1967 Act are followed (Section 5 as amended by the 1990 Act) (see above).

The amendments to the 1967 Abortion Act limit termination to 24 weeks or less, but only for Section 1(1)(a). Sub-sections b, c and d give no time limit (see Figure 15.2).

Being born alive

Situation 15.1 *Birth or abortion*

Mavis Spencer was 15 and her pregnancy was discovered only at a late stage. From the information provided by her and from his own medical examination, the doctor judged her to be about 22 weeks pregnant. He agreed that a termination should proceed and he arranged for her to see a second doctor who agreed with him. Mavis was immediately admitted for a termination. However, because of unforeseeable delays on the ward, this was not commenced for another week. When the fetus was expelled it appeared to cry out and the nurse felt that it was breathing. She did not know what to do. The doctor told her to put the remains in the bucket for incineration. She was reluctant to do this, however, since she felt it to be a child capable of surviving. Where does the law stand?

If it is clear that there is a live birth, then all reasonable steps should be taken to preserve its life, otherwise there could be a prosecution for murder or manslaughter. A prosecution was brought against Dr Hamilton when an abortion produced a live fetus. However, the case did not proceed beyond the committal proceedings. In the above situation, if it is apparent that the aborted fetus is breathing and viable, then he or she should be transferred to a special care baby unit. Failure to do so could be grounds for a charge of attempted murder. In addition, of course, even if the child were to die shortly afterwards, it would still have to be registered as a live birth (see registration provisions in Chapter 14 on midwifery).

Negligence in failing to detect abnormality

In a case in 1991,[3] the plaintiff had an ultrasound scan when she was about 26 weeks pregnant. The radiographer queried a possible abnormality of the spine, but the consultant decided that there was no firm evidence of abnormality justifying further action. The baby was born and found to be suffering from spina bifida. The mother claimed that the defendants were negligent in not ascertaining the possibility of abnormality and thus enabling her to have an abortion. Her claim failed since (under the Abortion Act 1967, i.e. prior to the 1990 amendments) it would have been illegal to have carried out an abortion at that stage, since the baby would have been capable of being born alive within the meaning of the 1929 Act.

If similar facts were to occur now, compensation would be payable if the mother were able to establish negligence, since there is no longer any time limit for securing a termination if there is a substantial risk that if the child were born it would suffer from such physical or mental abnormalities as to be seriously handicapped.

Challenge by the putative father

> ### Case 15.3 *Father's intervention*
>
> An Oxford student whose girlfriend become pregnant sought to stop the abortion on the grounds that the fetus, of between 18 and 24 weeks, was viable and that the abortion would thus be an offence under the Infant Life Preservation Act 1929. In this case, the pregnant woman was given medication to terminate the pregnancy shortly after the time that conception must have occurred. It was assumed that the medication had been effective. She subsequently took anti-depressant drugs and underwent two chest X-rays, one of which was taken without any shielding to protect a fetus. Any of these treatments could have harmed the fetus. When she discovered that she was still pregnant, she obtained the two necessary signatures for abortion. The father brought the court action.[4]

The Court of Appeal decided that the fetus was not capable of being born alive and therefore the termination of the pregnancy would not constitute an offence under the 1929 Act. The medical evidence showed that the cardiac muscle would be contracting and that there would be signs of primitive movement. It was said that these were real discernible signs of life. But the fetus would never be capable of breathing, either naturally or with the aid of a ventilator. Since the amendment to the Abortion Act 1967, the viability of the fetus is no longer in issue. In a more recent Scottish case,[5] a father was refused an injunction to restrain his wife from having an abortion.

Husband's attempt to stop an abortion

> ### Case 15.4 *Husband's rights*
>
> In Case 15.3, the putative father was not married to the mother, but it might be asked whether, if he were married, it would give him any rights to prevent the abortion going ahead. This point came before the courts when Mr Paton asked the court to prevent his wife going ahead with a termination. Two doctors had signed that the termination should proceed. Mr Paton claimed that as the father of the child he had a right to apply to the court for the termination to be stopped.[6]

The court, however, disagreed. It held that, provided the requirements of the Act were met, then the husband did not have any right in law to prevent it proceeding. He had no *locus standi* before the court. Mr Paton took his case to the European Commission on Human Rights[7] arguing that the life of the fetus is protected under

Article 2 of the European Convention on Human Rights (right to life) and also the father's rights were protected under Article 8 (the right of respect for family life). He failed in both his arguments.

Right to an abortion

An abortion refused

Situation 15.2 *An enforced child*

After having two children, Beryl Edwards considered her family to be complete. They moved to a larger house with a huge mortgage and Beryl took a part-time job to help pay for the additional loan and the extras: meals out and holidays. She was horrified when she discovered that she might be pregnant. Beryl became severely depressed and visited her GP. He was very reassuring, stating that she could have an abortion, and within a few days she was referred to a consultant obstetrician. He listened to her case and then informed her that he did not consider that she satisfied the requirements of the Abortion Act and that he would therefore be unable to write a medical recommendation. Beryl's depression became worse and she was unable to work. Eventually, her husband suggested that she should seek another opinion. She was reluctant to do so, not believing that it would be of any value. Eventually, however, under pressure from her husband she paid privately to see another specialist, who informed her that in his opinion she did meet the Act's requirements. However, since she was now 23 weeks pregnant, he would be unwilling to propose an abortion since the pregnancy was too far advanced for an abortion to be performed safely and at this late stage he believed that it could constitute an offence under the Act. Beryl eventually had the child, but is seeking compensation against the first specialist. Is she likely to succeed?

Beryl does not have an absolute right to an abortion. To obtain compensation, she would have to prove that, in making his assessment of her present or foreseeable physical or mental health, the specialist was negligent in failing to take into account factors that approved medical practice would have expected him to have taken into account, and that his assessment had been made negligently. She may get some support from her GP but, of course, it was open to him to refer her to another doctor at an earlier stage. Indeed, the GP's failure to refer her to a second consultant might in itself give rise to a claim of negligence against the GP. However, if the first consultant's report had been adamant that there was no greater risk in proceeding with the pregnancy, then the GP could argue that there was no negligence on his part in accepting that view as the likely prevailing one and therefore a further referral was not justified.

Women may be dependent upon the personal views of the doctors when they seek a termination of pregnancy. However, to establish negligence by a GP, there must be clear evidence that the GP failed to follow a reasonable standard of care in advising about arrangements for termination. In one case,[8] a woman visited her GP to seek a termination of pregnancy. She did not know that the GP was opposed to abortion on ethical and religious grounds. The woman alleged that the GP, by stating that it was too late and that it would not be recommended, effectively prevented her from having an abortion and was therefore in breach of the duty of care owed to her. The GP referred her to an abortion counsellor who told her of a private clinic at which an abortion could be obtained. She continued with the pregnancy and following an antepartum haemorrhage gave birth to a brain-damaged child. Her claim against the GP was dismissed on the grounds that in the light of the contemporaneous records and what she and her boyfriend had said in other contexts, the evidence showed that she had changed her mind and gone on to arrange antenatal care.

There is concern that the availability of abortions varies according to where you live and therefore women who would satisfy the legal requirements of the Abortion Act 1967 may not receive a termination. A survey conducted by the Abortion Law Reform Association[9] in December 1999 showed that obtaining an abortion on the NHS depends upon criteria such as whether you have had one before, your age, finances and whether you have been using contraception. The Royal College of Obstetricians and Gynaecologists[10] has recommended a maximum waiting time of 21 days from first doctor consultation to the surgical procedure and 14 days should be the aim.

This is clearly an area where NICE could make recommendations for uniformity of NHS provision across the country (see Chapter 5 on the work of NICE).

Other related offences

The Offences Against the Person Act 1861 Section 58 makes it an offence to administer drugs or use instruments to procure an abortion. When a woman is charged, it must be shown that she is pregnant. This is not necessary when another person is charged with an offence. Section 59 of the 1861 Act makes it an offence to supply or procure any poison or any instrument or any other thing knowing that it is to be used with intent to cause a miscarriage whether or not the woman is with child. However, if the requirements of the Abortion Act are complied with, these provisions would not apply. Section 60 of the 1861 Act makes it an offence to conceal the birth of a child. Mr Reginald Dixon[11] was prosecuted under Section 58 of the Offences Against the Person Act 1861 when he continued carrying out a hysterectomy after discovering during the operation that the patient was pregnant. The patient subsequently said that had she known she would have wanted to keep the baby. He defended the charge on the grounds that he had acted in good faith to preserve the woman from grave permanent injury to her mental health within Section 1(1)(b) of the Act. He was acquitted by the jury.

Dr Bourne, a gynaecologist, was prosecuted under Section 58 of the 1861 Act after he had terminated the pregnancy of a 14-year-old girl who had been raped. He was found not guilty on the ground that his action was taken to preserve the life of the mother. This situation is now covered by the Abortion Act 1967.

Termination of one of multiple pregnancy

The Human Fertilisation and Embryology Act 1990 added a further amendment to the Abortion Act 1967 to cover the situation where one or more fetus(es) in a multiple pregnancy is terminated. The termination may be justified either to protect the health or life of the mother or where there is a substantial risk that if the child were born it would suffer from such physical or mental abnormalities as to be seriously handicapped (i.e. Section 1(1)(d)).

Confidentiality and illegal abortions

Situation 15.3   To tell or keep quiet

Pam Reynolds is admitted in an emergency to the accident and emergency department with severe bleeding. She is transferred to the gynaecology ward where it is clear to nursing and medical staff that she had probably tried to obtain an illegal abortion, though Pam herself is silent as to what happened. It is the third case this month that there has been such an admission and the gynaecologist suspects that one person may be responsible. Does he or the nursing staff have any duty in law to inform the police?

The simple answer is that there is no statute that places a duty on anyone to report a crime of causing a miscarriage or an offence under the Infant Life Preservation Act. If, of course, the police had heard of the illegal abortion and had begun to investigate, then they would be able to subpoena witnesses or obtain information for their enquiries under the procedures laid down under the Police and Criminal Evidence Act. What about notifying them before they are aware of the possible crime? Some would argue that the doctor has a public duty to inform the police in such circumstances; that it is in the public interest for him to disclose the information, but until the law is changed, this is not obligatory by law, but a nurse may have a professional duty to act in the public interest under UKCC guidance. For those offences which must be reported to the police, see Chapter 8.

Notification

The Abortion Regulations 1968 as amended by the 1976, 1980 and 1991 regulations place a duty on the practitioner to notify the chief medical officer on the appropriate forms, but restricts disclosure to anyone other than an authorised officer of the DHSS; the Registrar General; the Director of Public Prosecutions; the police; for the purposes of criminal proceedings; *bona fide* scientific research; to any practitioner with the consent of the woman; or at the request of the President of the General Medical Council for the purpose of investigating whether there has been serious professional misconduct. Regulation 3[12] requires a certificate of opinion to be given in writing by the registered medical practitioners.

Consent by a pregnant person under 16 years

If a young girl of 14 seeks an abortion, do her own parents have to consent on her behalf? The answer depends upon the competence of the girl and what is in her best interests. Assuming that the girl is not in the care of the local authority and is seeking an abortion, then provided that she has the capacity to make the decision, she could give a valid consent under the Gillick case principles discussed in Chapter 13 on children's nursing. What, however, if the girl's own parents wanted her to have the child and promised that they would care for it; could they refuse to allow the termination to proceed?

Case 15.5 *Whose choice?*

The mother was 15. She already had a son of 12 months and had been in care since she was 13 following a conviction for theft. She lived in a mother-and-child unit with schooling facilities and was then 12 weeks pregnant. Her own parents objected to the abortion (as they had done during the first pregnancy). Her father offered to take care of his grandson and leave the daughter with the new baby. On religious grounds, as a Seventh Day Adventist, he opposed the termination of life. He also thought that the girl would live to regret the decision she had taken. He was convinced that she was still a child and that she should not be allowed to take a decision that she could subsequently regret.[13]

The child was placed under the wardship jurisdiction of the court and Mrs Justice Butler-Sloss ordered that the termination of the pregnancy should proceed. The judge was clearly influenced by the wishes of the girl, who had set her mind on the termination and had not in fact contemplated that it might not proceed. She discussed the matter with the girl and formed the opinion that she was of a strong personality and mature views. The judge also held that, on the facts, the risks to the health of the mother and the interests of the existing child satisfied the requirements of the 1967 Act. The grandparents' objections were thus overruled and they were accorded no rights in the matter. In this case, of course, the child was already in the care of the local authority. Where this is not so, it may be the practice for the parents of the pregnant girl to sign the consent form for a termination. Probably, too, if there is a clash between the rights of the mother and the grandparents, the latter may put pressure on the girl to agree to an abortion since she may well be dependent on their help in bringing up the child.

Abortion and those with learning disabilities

Under 18 years old
The parents have the right to make decisions on behalf of the minor provided that they are acting in the interests of the child. The principles discussed in relation to the sterilisation of the minor by the House of Lords *In re B* which is considered below would thus apply. It is considered necessary to obtain the approval of the court.

The adult person with learning disabilities

> ### Case 15.6   The mother with learning disabilities
>
> The defendant was a woman aged 19 who was epileptic with severe learning disabilities. She was totally dependent upon others and was cared for by her mother. She became pregnant and termination of pregnancy was recommended by the medical advisers on the ground that there would be complications associated with that condition, and that she would be incapable of providing and caring for a child. The doctors also recommended that she should be protected from any further pregnancies by being sterilised. The doctors were, however, unwilling to carry out the abortion or sterilisation operation without authorisation. The mother thus applied to the court for a declaration that the procedures could be carried out lawfully.[14]

The court held that the situation was not covered by the Mental Health Act 1983 consent to treatment provisions (see Chapter 20), nor did a guardian under the Act have the power to give consent. The court was prepared to grant the declaration requested and declared the proposed treatment lawful and therefore a defence to any action for trespass to the person. The doctors would be carrying out the treatment in the interests of the patient as part of their duty of care to the patient. The court also held that it no longer had a power to act as *parens patriae* (a kind of wardship jurisdiction) and the court could therefore not give consent itself. (It held that this power had been repealed in 1959 and should be reinstated. A subsequent case,[15] however, has held that the courts did have the power to make decisions on the day-to-day care of mentally incapacitated adults. This case is considered in Chapter 19.)

Sterilisation

Sterilisation of a minor with learning disabilities

> ### Case 15.7   Sterilisation
>
> Jeanette was 17 years old, but was described as having a mental age of 5 or 6. Her mother and the local authority, who held a care order on her, advised by the social worker, the gynaecologist and a paediatrician, considered it vital that she should not become pregnant. She had been found in a compromising situation in her residential home. She could not be relied upon to take or accept oral contraceptives. Jeanette was likely to move to an adult training centre at the age of 19 and it would not be possible to provide her with the degree of supervision she had at present.[16]

The House of Lords decided that the paramount consideration was the interests of the girl and, taking account of all the medical evidence, decided that it was in her interests to be sterilised. They made no distinction between non-therapeutic and therapeutic care of the child and recommended that in future all such cases should come before the courts.

Sterilisation of an adult with learning disabilities

The House of Lords in the Jeanette case discussed above declared their decision before Jeanette reached 18, so they did not consider the law in relationship to the adult mentally handicapped person. This was considered in the case of *T* v. *T* considered above, but that decision was taken in the High Court. The view of the House of Lords on this situation was given in the case of *In re F* v. *West Berkshire Health Authority*.

In this case, the court had to decide whether the sterilisation of a mentally handicapped woman, F, aged 35 would be unlawful because of her lack of capacity to give her consent to the operation. Mr Justice Scott Baker in the Family Division granted a declaration that it was in the best interests of F to have the operation. He stated that there was a problem when, because of a mental condition, a patient was unable to give any meaningful consent to treatment for a physical condition. If he did nothing, a doctor could be said to be negligent; if he operated, he, *prima facie*, committed the tort of battery. The law's answer to this was that a professional was not liable if he acted in good faith and in the best interests of the patients. The Court of Appeal upheld this decision. The House of Lords confirmed the power at common law for a doctor to act in the best interests of the patient incapable of giving consent. The court also had an inherent jurisdiction to make declarations on the lawfulness of such treatment. Court involvement in cases of sterilisation was highly desirable as a matter of good practice.[17]

There can be disputes over what the best interests of a patient are and in a more recent case the Court of Appeal held that it was in the interests of a woman of 29 with severe learning disabilities to be fitted with an intra-uterine device rather than undergo a subtotal hysterectomy. The judge had failed to give proper weight to the unanimous medical evidence that supported the less invasive coil treatment.[18] In a case involving male sterilisation, the Court of Appeal held that it was not in the best interests of a man with learning disabilities to have a vasectomy, which his mother wanted to take place.[19] The Court of Appeal held that the best interests of the patient encompassed medical, emotional and all other welfare issues. In relation to sterilisation, the best interests of a man were not the equivalent of the best interests of a woman because of the obvious biological differences.

The Law Commission made recommendations on decision-making on behalf of the mentally incapacitated adult and recommended draft legislation.[20] Subsequently, the Lord Chancellor issued a consultation paper.[21] The Government's proposals were published in 1999[22] and legislation is expected shortly. The recommendations envisage a statutory power to act in the best interests of the mentally incapacitated adult, a continuing power of attorney which would cover treatments, and a reorganised court of protection to which applications for decisions on behalf of mentally incapacitated adults could be made. (This is discussed in Chapter 7.)

Unsuccessful sterilisations

> ### Case 15.8   Unwanted pregnancy
>
> Mrs Emeh, a mother of three children, underwent an operation for sterilisation in May 1976. In January 1977, she discovered that she was 20 weeks pregnant. She refused to have an abortion. She then gave birth to a child with congenital abnormalities who required constant medical and parental supervision. She claimed damages for the unwanted pregnancy and the birth and upkeep of the child. The trial judge held that the operation had been performed negligently and she could therefore recover damages for the time before she discovered the pregnancy, but since she refused to have an abortion, she was not entitled to the costs thereafter apart from the cost of undergoing the second sterilisation operation. Mrs Emeh appealed to the Court of Appeal and won.

The Court of Appeal held that since the avoidance of a further pregnancy was the object of the sterilisation operation, it was unreasonable after the period of pregnancy that had elapsed to expect the plaintiff to undergo an abortion. Her failure to do so was not unreasonable. She was therefore entitled to recover damages for her financial loss caused by the negligent performance of the sterilisation operation. She was awarded £7,000 loss of future earnings, £3,000 for pain and suffering up to the trial and £10,000 for future loss of amenity and pain and suffering that will occur during the life of the child.[23]

This decision is to be welcomed since it reverses an earlier decision.[24] The mother's refusal to have an abortion was not an unreasonable one and it could not be used as a reason to limit the damages payable. It has recently been confirmed in a decision of the House of Lords (see the McFarlane[25] case below) that arranging an adoption or abortion was not a requirement of the parents following the diagnosis of an unwanted child. 'There was no legal or moral duty to arrange an abortion or an adoption of an unplanned child.'

In a recent case,[26] a woman was sterilised when she was four weeks pregnant, a fact unknown to herself and the surgeon. The Health Authority accepted liability and damages of £96,631 were awarded which included the future cost of caring for and educating the child. A pregnancy test should have been carried out before the operation for sterilisation was performed. Subsequently, the issue as to whether there should be compensation for bearing a healthy (but unplanned child) has come before the House of Lords.

Unplanned healthy baby

The House of Lords has stated that compensation is not payable for the costs in bringing up a healthy child. In *McFarlane and another* v. *Tayside Health Board*,[27] (see Case 15.9 overleaf) the House of Lords laid down the principles that should apply to any assessment.

> ### Case 15.9 Unplanned pregnancy – compensation for healthy baby
>
> Mr and Mrs M had four children and Mr M agreed to have a vasectomy. Six months after the operation, he was advised that the sperm counts were negative and he could dispense with contraceptive precautions. Mrs M subsequently became pregnant and gave birth to a healthy daughter. They brought proceedings for damages for the cost of rearing the child and the pain and suffering by Mrs M in carrying and giving birth to her. Her claim was dismissed initially on the ground that such damages were irrecoverable in principle. The appeal succeeded and it was held that the couple should be given the opportunity to prove their loss and damage. The Health Board appealed to the House of Lords.

The House of Lords held that where medical negligence resulted in an unwanted pregnancy, and the birth of a healthy child, the parents were not entitled to recover damages for the costs of rearing that child, but the mother was entitled to recover damages for the pain and distress suffered during the pregnancy and in giving birth, and for the financial loss associated with the pregnancy. Damages for the cost of bringing up a healthy baby were irrecoverable since it was not fair, just or reasonable to impose liability for such economic losses on a doctor or his employer. Lord Steyn held that it was morally unacceptable to allow such a claim having regard to the principle of distributive justice which focused on the just distribution of burdens and losses among members of a society.

Unplanned baby with disabilities

In the McFarlane case, the House of Lords were considering the birth of an unplanned healthy baby. However, different considerations would arise if the unplanned baby were to be disabled. In the case of *Nunnerley and another v. Warrington Health Authority and another*[28] (held before the decision of the McFarlane case was known), the mother was given negligent advice that led to the unwanted birth of a disabled child. The High Court judge held that the claim for damages should not be limited to the costs of the care which they themselves had a legal duty to provide, but damages were payable for the cost of care beyond 18 years. The judge held that the normal principle of compensation should apply, i.e. the claimants were entitled to be put in the position that they would have been in but for the wrong done to them.

In another case,[29] M gave birth to a Down's syndrome baby. The doctor had failed to inform her of the results of a routine scan that indicated that she was likely to give birth to a child suffering from Down's syndrome. M said that had she been informed of the results of the scan, then she would have chosen a termination. Liability was admitted and she was awarded £118,746. The High Court judge held that the ruling in *McFarlane* v. *Tayside Health Authority* (see above) was confined to the birth of a healthy baby. This principle was followed in *Hardman* v. *Amin*[30] where a doctor misdiagnosed rubella as tonsilitis in a pregnant woman who therefore did not have a termination. The doctor subsequently admitted negligence. The mother successfully claimed the costs of the upbringing of a severely disabled baby.

Failure to warn of risks of pregnancy

There have been cases where no negligence in the performance of the operation has been proved, but compensation has been claimed on the grounds that the patient was not warned that there was a possibility of the operation being reversed and the patient becoming fertile or pregnant. This occurred in the following case:

Case 15.10   No warning

Mrs Gold, who had two children, decided when she became pregnant again that she would not have any more children. She was referred to the consultant obstetrician who suggested sterilisation, but did not discuss the possibility of the husband having a vasectomy which had a slightly lower failure rate, nor did he discuss the risk of failure with her. The sterilisation operation was performed the day after the birth of the child, but was not a success and Mrs Gold gave birth to a fourth child. She sued the Health Authority for negligence because she had not been warned of the risk of failure and the statement that the operation was irreversible was a negligent misrepresentation.

Initially Mrs Gold was awarded £19,000 damages on the grounds that, although the operation had not been negligently performed, the defendants had been negligent in failing to warn her of the possibility of failure of the operation. The defendants appealed and the Court of Appeal allowed the appeal for the following reasons:

1. The standard of care required of the medical practitioner was the same as that required of members of the profession, i.e. the ordinary skilled member of that profession who exercised and professed that special skill (see Chapter 3 for further details on this standard). Where medical advice had been given, the standard of care required did not depend on the context in which it was given, but on whether there was a substantial body of doctors who would have given the same advice. Since in 1979 a substantial body of responsible doctors would not have warned her of the risk of failure of the sterilisation operation, the Health Authority was not liable in negligence.

2. The statement that the operation was irreversible could not reasonably be constructed as a representation that the operation was bound to achieve its objectives. Mrs Gold therefore lost the case.[31]

The Court of Appeal made it clear that it did not accept any distinction between advice given for a therapeutic procedure and that for a non-therapeutic procedure. The same standard should be applied to both, i.e. the Bolam Test.

Advice has been provided at a conference of the Medical Defence Union (MDU) on Healthcare Risk Management which was quoted in the House of Lords in the Taylor case and this is shown in Box 15.1

Advice by Dr James to the MDU Conference on 22 Jan. 1991

'Claims arising from failed sterilisation procedures may be reduced if the following measures are taken. Counselling should be given by a doctor whose knowledge of the procedure is sufficient to describe the complications and failure rate accurately. It is helpful to provide the patient with an explanatory leaflet in the out-patient clinic which can be read at leisure and which will enable any additional points to be clarified on admission. A record of the counselling given should be made in the patient's case notes. . . . A specific consent form which warns of the risk of failure should be signed by the patient.'

Private health care

What if the case concerns an operation carried out in the private sector? Do any different principles apply? The significant difference between NHS care and private care is that there is a contract between patient and hospital in the provision of private care and failure to perform a satisfactory operation could lead to claims for breach of contract as well as a claim for negligence. In the case of *Thake* v. *Maurice*, the High Court awarded compensation for failure to warn the husband and the wife about the risks of the sterilisation failing. The Court of Appeal[32] decided that the standard of care required in the law of negligence would be the same as the standard to be given under a private contract for health care.

> 'The reasonable man would have expected the defendant to exercise all the special care and skill of a surgeon in that specialty; he would not in my view have expected the defendant to give a guarantee of 100% success.' (Neill LJ)

Similar arguments could not be used in an NHS context since there is no contractual relationship between an NHS patient and the health authority or doctor. The possibility of action arising from failed sterilisations has led to much more meticulous wording of the agreement and warnings in relation to the possibilities of failure (see Box 15.1).

The sterilisation of a child under 16 is considered in Chapter 13, which also considers the law relating to contraceptive advice for the under 16-year-old.

Rights of the spouse

There is no legal requirement that if a person wishes to be sterilised, the agreement of his or her spouse or partner must be obtained. Clearly, however, joint discussion with the couple of the implications is desirable.

Situation 15.4   The husband says 'no'

Audrey Rich was expecting her seventh child. Her eldest child was 10 years old and they lived with the husband in a four-bedroomed council house. She felt she could not cope with any further pregnancies and sought advice as to the possibility of being sterilised after the birth of the seventh. An appointment was arranged with the obstetrician for Audrey and Steve, but Steve refused to attend, claiming that he would never give his consent to Audrey being sterilised. Audrey went on her own to see the obstetrician who told her that he could not carry out the operation without her husband's consent.

There is no duty in law to obtain the consent of the spouse before sterilising the partner. In the past, there was a legal duty when the husband had a right of consortium and could sue any person who caused him to lose this right. However, this right to sue for loss of consortium was repealed by the Administration of Justice Act 1982 Section 2(a). The woman has never enjoyed such a right; the House of Lords refused to extend it to women in 1952.[33] There may be considerable advantages in obtaining a signature to say that the spouse knows of the intended operation, since if this is obtained the doctor is less likely to be summoned as a witness in divorce proceedings where one spouse is alleging that the operation was performed without his/her knowledge. However, a form signifying knowledge of the operation is very different from a form of consent.

In the situation outlined above, Audrey could obtain a solicitor's letter confirming the law, but this, of course, does not place any duty on the doctor to perform the operation. She could request referral to a doctor who would perform the operation or even apply to the health authority for assistance. Ultimately, she could seek a declaration from the court that such an operation could proceed without the husband's consent.

Questions and exercises

1. Obtain a set of the documentation that has to be completed when an abortion is performed and examine the legal requirements as shown in these forms.
2. What is the legal situation if an aborted fetus is found to be breathing?
3. What forms are completed in your hospital when an operation for sterilisation is performed? Can you see any significant differences in the form completed by the patient and the form completed by the spouse?
4. What information do you consider should be given to a patient before his or her consent is given to an operation for sterilisation? What are the legal requirements? (See also Chapters 7 and 22)

References

1 R. v. *Salford Health Authority ex parte Janaway*, *The Times* 2 December 1988
2 *Royal College of Nursing* v. *The Department of Health and Social Security* 1981 1 All ER 545
3 *Rance and another* v. *Mid Downs Health Authority and another* 1991 1 All ER 801
4 *C* v. *S* 1987 1 All ER 1230
5 *Kelly* v. *Kelly* 1997 SLT 896
6 *Paton* v. *Trustees of British Pregnancy Advisory Service* 1978 2 All ER 987
7 *Paton* v. *UK* (1980) 3 EHRR 408
8 *Barr* v. *Matthews* (2000)52 BMLR 217
9 Kathryn Godfrey, Abortion by Postcode, *Nursing Times* December 1 Volume 95 No 48 p. 30–1
10 The Royal College of Obstetricians and Gynaecologists, Report on Abortions 2000 RCOG London
11 *R v Dixon* (Reginald) 1995 (unreported)
12 Abortion Regulations 1991
13 *In re P* (a minor) 1981 80 LGR 301
14 *T* v. *T* 1988 1 All ER 613
15 *In Re F* (adult: Court's jurisdiction) *The Times Law Report* 25 July 2000
16 *In re B* (a minor) (wardship, sterilisation) 1987 2 All ER 206
17 *In re F* v. *West Berkshire Health Authority* [1989] 2 All ER 545
18 *Re S* (Sterilisation: patient's best interests) [2000] 2 FLR 389
19 *Re A* (Male sterilisation) [2000] 1 FLR 549
20 Law Commission Report no 231 Mental Incapacity 1995 Stationery Office
21 Lord Chancellor's Office, Who Decides? Lord Chancellor's Office December 1997
22 Lord Chancellor's Office, Making Decisions, Lord Chancellor's Office 1999
23 *Emeh* v. *Kensington and Chelsea and Westminster Health Authority* 1985 2 WLR 233
24 *Udale* v. *Bloomsbury AHA* 1983 2 All ER 522
25 *McFarlane and another* v. *Tayside Health Board* [1999] 4 All ER 961 HL
26 *Allen* v. *Bloomsbury Health Authority and another* 1993 1 All ER 651
27 *McFarlane and another* v. *Tayside Health Board* [1999] 4 All ER 961 HL
28 *Nunnerley and another* v. *Warrington Health Authority and another*, *The Times Law Report* 26 November 1999
29 *Rand* v. *East Dorset HA* [2000] Lloyd's Rep Med 181
30 *Hardman* v. *Amin* [2000] Lloyd's Rep Med 498
31 *Gold* v. *Haringey HA* 1987 2 All ER 888
32 *Thake* v. *Maurice* [1986] QB 644; [1984] 2 All ER 513
33 *Best* v. *Samuel Fox and Co.* 1952 2 All ER 394

16 Intensive care, transfusion and transplant surgery nursing

The areas considered in this chapter are set out in Figure 16.1. Definition of death is of such concern to the intensive care nurse in relation to requests for organs for transplantation that it was thought best to discuss it here. Further aspects relating to death are considered in Chapter 29. Other concerns for the transplant nurse are the decision not to resuscitate a patient and consent for the use of organs and tissues and in what circumstances machines can be switched off. A telephone survey was conducted by the RCN[1] that provided an analysis of the role of the nurse in intensive care and illustrated considerable differences in the functioning of nurses in ICUs and considerable flexibility of roles between doctors and nurses. These findings were confirmed by the report of the Audit Commission which is considered on page 360.

This chapter seeks to clarify the main principles that arise.

---

1. Definition of death: brain death.
2. Importance of exact time of death.
3. Cause of death.
4. Legality of switching machines off.
5. Not for resuscitation.
6. Relatives and the treatment of patient.
7. Refusal of treatment by patient.
8. Living wills.
9. Transfusions.
10. Organ transplantation.
11. Resource pressures.
12. Review of Critical Care Services.

Figure 16.1 Issues covered in Chapter 16.

Definition of death

The traditional method for the determination of whether life has ceased was to check whether breathing had stopped by checking the pulse, the heart beat, and placing a mirror in front of the mouth, i.e. the cessation of circulatory and respiratory functions as evidenced by an absence of heart beat, pulse, and respiration. For most cases this was satisfactory. However, if the patient was on a ventilator where breathing was maintained artificially, this traditional definition was inappropriate. In addition, the advance in medical technology, particularly in transplant surgery, meant that it was essential to use the organs as soon as possible after respiration had ceased, and if there was likely to be a delay, to keep the body ventilated, i.e. artificially breathing until such time as the organs required for transplant could be taken. In these cases, 'brain death' became the criterion for whether death had taken place. If the traditional definition of death was used, there was an 88 per cent incidence of post-operative renal failure in kidney transplants, whereas if the criterion of brain death was used on a patient maintained on a ventilator, the post-operative failure rate was 10–20 per cent. The same percentage occurs when kidneys from living donors are used.

What is brain death?

A conference of the Royal Colleges in 1976 set out the diagnostic tests to be used for the determination of brain death; these were circulated in 1978 and also included in the code of practice, 'The removal of cadaveric organs for transplantation', which was distributed to doctors in January 1980. A subsequent conference in 1981 made the recommendations set out in Figure 16.2.

The diagnosis of brain death should be made by two medical practitioners who have expertise in this field. One should be the consultant who is in charge of the case and one other doctor (or in the absence of the consultant, his deputy who should have been registered for 5 years or more with adequate previous experience in the care of such cases and one other doctor). The two doctors may carry out their tests separately or together. If the tests confirm brain death they should still be repeated. It is for the doctors to decide how long the interval between the tests should be. It may not be appropriate for the doctors to carry out all the recommended tests. The criteria are guidelines, not rigid rules.

These criteria are as follows:

1. All brain-stem reflexes are absent.
2. The pupils are fixed in diameter and do not respond to sharp changes in the intensity of incident light.
3. There is no corneal reflex.
4. The vestibular-ocular reflexes are absent.
5. No motor responses within the cranial nerve distribution can be elicited by adequate stimulation of any somatic area.
6. There is no gag reflex or reflex response to bronchial stimulation by a suction catheter passed down the trachea.
7. No respiratory movements occur when the patient is disconnected from the mechanical ventilator for long enough to ensure that the arterial carbon dioxide tension rises above the threshold for stimulation of respiration.

Additional recommendations are made as to how some of these tests should be undertaken.

Figure 16.2 Definition of brain death.

This same definition of brain stem death was adopted by the Department of Health in 1998,[2] which accepted that whilst there was no statutory definition of death, irreversible loss of the capacity for consciousness, combined with irreversible loss of the capacity to breathe should be regarded as the definition of death.

The possibility of brain death is recommended where the patient is deeply comatose (but where depressant drugs, primary hypothermia, and metabolic and endocrine disturbances can be excluded), or where the patient is being maintained on a ventilator because spontaneous respiration had previously been inadequate or had ceased (relaxants or other drugs should be ruled out as a cause of respiratory failure), or where there is no doubt that the patient's condition is due to irremediable structural brain damage.

Case 16.1   Definition of death

An infant of 19 months was placed on a ventilator following serious head injuries sustained at home. He showed no signs of recovery. The hospital followed the guidelines laid down by the Medical Research Council in carrying out various diagnostic tests and was satisfied that he was dead. It then applied to court for a declaration that the child could be removed from the ventilator. The Family Court judge, Judge Johnson, identified the results of the tests carried out by the doctors and stated that he had 'no hesitation at all in holding that A has been dead since Tuesday of last week, 21 January.' (It was then the 27 January.)[3]

The importance of the exact time of death

The actual timing of death can be a significant feature in a variety of court actions. A few examples are set out in Figure 16.3.

Civil Law:

A. Survivorship. The rules of inheritance depend upon the order in which people die. If, therefore, there are incidents leading to multiple deaths, which victim died first can be very significant for inheritance. There are certain presumptions in law relating to the order of deaths in such circumstances, i.e. the oldest died first. However, if one of the victims is supported on a life support machine and kept 'alive' longer the presumption would no longer operate.

B. Insurance policies often require that where death follows an accident it must be established that the death occurred within a fixed time limit in order to claim under the policy.

C. Where the machine is switched off this could lead to claims for compensation for negligence by professional staff especially where organs are used for transplantation.

(It used to be a requirement that to constitute the offence of murder, the victim had to die within a year and a day of the act leading to the death. This time limit was removed in 1996.)

Figure 16.3   Causes of action where the time of death has considerable significance.

Criminal law

In the past, to constitute murder the victim must have died within a year and a day of the act. In 1996, this time limit requirement was removed. However, issues of causation may still arise. If the victim is taken off the machine, is that the cause of death or is the cause of death the original assault on the victim? If he is kept on a machine for longer than that, is it murder? Several defendants have tried to argue that it was not.

> *Case 16.2   Causal link*
>
> Malcherek was convicted of the murder of a victim of assault who had been connected to a life support machine which had been disconnected by medical practitioners. He was sentenced to life imprisonment. In a similar case, Steel was also convicted and sentenced to life imprisonment. Malcherek appealed against this decision and Steel applied for leave to put in further medical evidence as to the sufficiency and adequacy of tests by the doctors to determine brain death. They were both effectively challenging that there was a causal link between the assaults and the deaths of the victims. The judge in each case had withdrawn the issue of causation from the jury.[4]

The Court of Appeal held that in each case it is clear that the initial assault was the cause of the grave head injuries in the one case and of the massive abdominal haemorrhage in the other. In each case, the initial assault was the reason for the medical treatment being necessary. In each case, the medical treatment given was normal and conventional. The court looked in detail at the tests carried out by the doctors and stated: 'It is not part of the task of this court to inquire whether the criteria, the royal colleges' confirmatory tests, are a satisfactory code of practice. It is not part of the task of this court to decide whether the doctors were, in either of these two cases, justified in omitting one or more of the so called "confirmatory tests". The doctors are not on trial: the applicant and the appellant were.' The Court of Appeal concluded that all the evidence suggested that at the time of death the original wound or injury was a continuing, operating and, indeed, substantial cause of death. The fact that the victim's life support treatment had been discontinued did not break the chain of causation between the initial injury and death. The issue of causation had therefore properly been withdrawn from the jury. The convictions were confirmed.

The legality of switching machines off

An article by Ian Kennedy[5] describes three different circumstances where a professional might be concerned about the legality of switching off a life support machine. These are set out in Figure 16.4. He also makes the point that there should be no difference in law between the legality of switching on the machine and of switching it off. The law does not expect a doctor to place every dying patient on a life support machine, only where there is a hope of recovery and the facilities exist.

A. *The unconscious dying patient*

1. The machine can be switched off if the patient is brain dead.

2. If the patient can breathe without it but weakly, then the decision to put the patient back on the machine depends on the medical prognosis. If treatment is futile then there is unlikely to be an obligation to put the patient back on again.

3. Where the patient can breathe on his own and the respirator is not needed, then the machine can be switched off. If the patient needs to have assistance again and the prognosis is hopeless, then there is unlikely to be a legal obligation to reconnect the respirator.

B. *The chronically dependent patient such as a polio victim*

1. If the patient requests discontinuation, as the law stands at present, it would be a criminal offence for anyone else to disconnect it. See the Suicide Act in Figure 16.5. Euthanasia is not recognised in English law.

2. If the machine is turned off against the wishes of the patient this would of course be murder.

C. *Temporarily dependent emergency patient*
If the ultimate prognosis is a recovery and improvement, then switching off the machine would be murder. However, if the ultimate prognosis is extremely poor and hopeless, then the considerations in A1 above would apply.

Figure 16.4 Switching off a life support machine.

Persistent vegetative state

Case 16.3 *Ending tube feeding*

Tony Bland was crushed in the Hillsborough football tragedy and for three and a half years was in a persistent vegetative state, being artificially fed but breathing unaided. He could not see, hear, taste, smell, speak or communicate in any way. The Trust, in agreement with the parents, applied for the withdrawal of nasal-gastric tube feeding. The House of Lords held that medical treatment, including artificial feeding, could be withdrawn from a patient in a persistent vegetative state, if this was in the patient's best interests and it did not amount to a criminal act.[6]

Another application to the courts in similar circumstances was made in January 1994 in respect of a patient in Bristol.[7] A court declaration is required in such circumstances, but the right to end treatment is still subject to controversy. Practical guidance has been issued by the Official Solicitor on the action to be taken when a patient is in a persistent vegetative state.[8] It emphasises the importance of the assessment and the time over which that must be conducted. Subsequently, the court[9] has issued a declaration that artificial feeding could be discontinued even though the criteria set out in the guidelines were not completely satisfied. In this case, D suffered serious head injuries in a road accident. There was expert evidence of nystagmus in response to ice water caloric testing, tracking of moving objects and a 'menace' response.

The court held that, notwithstanding the criteria were not wholly fulfilled, there was no evidence whatsoever of any meaningful life, so D was for all practical purposes in a permanent vegetative state and it was not in D's best interests to keep her body alive.

Not for resuscitation

Obviously, in intensive care units, it is usually the consultant who will decide if a ventilator is to be turned on or off. However, it is sometimes the practice for doctors to mark the patient's notes 'NFR' or DNAR (Do not Attempt Resuscitation) and the nurse is then in a quandary as to what she should do. She may feel that she is in an impossible, no-win situation: if she does not initiate resuscitation procedures following a collapse, then she could possibly be criticised by relatives or even face criminal charges; if, on the other hand, she ignores the letters 'NFR' and starts resuscitation procedures, then she could be criticised by the medical staff and face disciplinary proceedings. It is vital in these circumstances that the nurse is involved in the discussions over the patient's prognosis so that she can understand the likely outcome and the reasons for the doctor's decision. If she is in any doubt, she should seek expert advice and always err on the side of saving life. Unfortunately, the nurse is sometimes informed orally of the doctor's wishes, which are not written down, and this places the nurse in an even more vulnerable situation. A joint statement from the British Medical Association, Resuscitation Council (UK) and the Royal College of Nursing[10] provided revised guidance on decisions relating to cardiopulmonary resuscitation in 1999. This guidance was commended to NHS Trusts in September 2000 by the NHS Executive[11] in an NHS Circular. By this circular, Chief Executives of NHS Trusts are required to ensure that appropriate resuscitation policies that respect patients' rights are in place, understood by all relevant staff, and accessible to those who need them and that such policies are subject to appropriate audit and monitoring arrangements. The action required to be taken by NHS Trusts is shown in Box 16.1 The Commission for Health Improvement (CHI) has been asked by the Secretary of State to pay particular attention to resuscitation decision-making processes as part of its rolling programme of reviews of clinical governance arrangements put in place by NHS organisations. Guidance emphasises that there must be no blanket policies, each individual patient must be assessed personally and policy cannot depend solely on the age of the patient. The NHS Circular was the result of growing concern that there was evidence that old people were being deprived of intravenous foods and fluid drips. The police were investigating deaths of 60 elderly persons in such circumstances.[12] A Not for Resuscitation decision should only take place where:

1. the mentally competent patient has refused treatment;
2. a valid living will covering such circumstances has been made by the patient;
3. effective cardiopulmonary resuscitation (CPR) is unlikely to be successful;
4. where successful CPR is likely to be followed by a length and quality of life that would not be in the best interests of the patient to sustain.

Box 16.1

Resuscitation Policies: Action to be taken by NHS Trusts to ensure:

Patients' rights are central to decision-making on resuscitation

The Trust has an agreed resuscitation policy in place which respects patients' rights. The policy is published and readily available to those who may wish to consult it, including patients, families and carers.

Appropriate arrangements are in place for ensuring that all staff who may be involved in resuscitation decisions understand and implement the policy.

Appropriate supervision arrangements are in place to review the resuscitation decisions.

Induction and staff development programmes cover the resuscitation policy.

Clinical practice in this area is regularly audited.

Clinical audit outcomes are reported in the Trust's annual clinical governance report.

A non-executive Director of the Trust is given designated responsibility on behalf of the Trust Board to ensure that a resuscitation policy is agreed, implemented, and regularly reviewed within the clinical governance framework.

Relatives and the treatment of the patient

Situation 16.1   The relatives say 'no'

Katy Brown was 85 and just recovering from a particularly serious hiatus hernia operation. She was very weak and there was considerable likelihood that she would not survive. The relatives discussed her case with the doctors and asked that, in the possible event of a collapse, she should not be resuscitated since they did not want her to continue as an invalid and felt sure that this is what Katy would have wished. What is the doctor's position?

Ultimately, the relatives, even a spouse, have no right in law to refuse consent to any life-saving treatment required by the patient. Their motives can never be certain: perhaps they have designs on the patient's property. Where the patient is mentally incapacitated, the only criterion that can determine whether or not treatment should proceed is the ultimate prognosis of the patient, unless the patient has clearly expressed his views in advance (see below, living wills). Obviously, the relatives' views should be made known to the doctor, but they should not be the deciding factor in determining whether the patient is resuscitated.

Refusal of treatment by the patient

Since 1961, suicide has not been a crime (see Figure 16.5).

The position is clear for professional staff. Even though they sympathise with a patient's wish to die, they are prohibited by the criminal law in taking any steps or

Section 1 of the 1961 Suicide Act states that 'the rule of law whereby it is a crime for a person to commit suicide is hereby abrogated'. This, coupled with the right for a person to consent to treatment, means that it is possible for a seriously ill person to refuse consent to, say, antibiotics and staff have to accept that refusal. Only where there is a doubt over the person's mental competence to refuse treatment could the medication be given out of necessity to save the person's life (see the chapter in Part I on consent to treatment). While it is no longer a crime for a person to decide upon and bring about their own death, it is still, however, a crime for anyone to aid and abet in the suicide of another.

Section 2(1) states: 'A person who aids, abets, counsels or procures the suicide of another or an attempt by another to commit suicide, shall be liable on conviction on indictment to imprisonment.' (Up to 14 years.)

Figure 16.5   Suicide Act 1961.

giving any advice to the patient to help him carry out this wish. Where a patient is clearly refusing medication because of this desire, it is essential for staff to record detailed accounts of the patient's attitude, his level of competence, the advice given to him, and, preferably, where the patient takes his own discharge contrary to professional advice, to obtain the patient's signature to that effect.

Euthanasia is not recognised by law in this country. The courts recognised that in law there is a distinction between letting die and killing a person, even though this is not accepted by some philosophers. Decisions sometimes have to be made in special care baby units and in intensive care or renal dialysis units, or over transplants, on who is able to be treated. This effectively means that those not selected for treatment may eventually die. This is, however, a very different matter from taking an action that will bring about or assist in bringing about another person's death. The House of Lords Select Committee on Medical Ethics in 1994[13] did not make any proposals to change the law that makes euthanasia illegal. On 28 November 2000, the Netherlands became the first country in the world to legalise euthanasia.[14] The Dutch Parliament approved a bill guaranteeing doctors immunity from prosecution for mercy killing and assisted suicides provided that they observe a number of strict conditions. These include that the patient's request is voluntary, based on full information and carefully considered; that the patient's physical or psychological condition must be unbearable and untreatable. The doctor's opinion will have to be corroborated by a second physician. The doctor must have a long-standing relationship with the patient. It is unlikely that this legislation will be followed in this country.

Situation 16.2   To let go

Harry Judd, aged 84 years, had told his daughter that if he became ill and suffered a cardiac arrest, he did not want to be resuscitated. His wife had died two years before and he had become increasingly depressed and frail with failing eyesight caused by his diabetes. He was still managing to cope on his own with

Situation 16.2 *continued*

a home help, but it was becoming more and more of a struggle. One day, the home help found him in a coma and he was rushed into hospital. He remained seriously ill for several days and then slowly improved. His consultant physician, Dr Jones, discussed Harry's prognosis with his daughter and son-in-law. It appeared unlikely that he would be able to manage on his own. The daughter reported Harry's views about not being resuscitated. The next evening, Harry suffered a cardiac arrest. The staff nurse summoned Dr Jones, who was unwilling to use resuscitative machinery. Is he obliged to do so?

From the above discussion, it will be evident that it is essential to clarify two issues: first, the mental capacity of Harry when he stated that he would not want to be resuscitated, and secondly, the medical prognosis of Harry. If Harry were mentally competent when he asked not to be resuscitated, his views should be respected. If, however, his wishes were the result of extreme depression caused by his bereavement and illness, then it may be concluded that he was not mentally capable when he made that request. He must then be treated according to his best interests. If it is absolutely clear that Harry's prognosis is hopeless, then there is no legal duty to resuscitate. If, however, there is any chance that Harry could recover and would have a reasonable prognosis, then Dr Jones's duty would require him to resuscitate him.

The BMA have issued guidelines on withdrawing treatment.[15] Ann Winterton, MP, introduced the Medical Treatment (Prevention of Euthanasia) Bill to outlaw withdrawing or withholding food or medical treatment if the purpose is to hasten/cause a patient's death.[16] It received its second reading and reached Report stage, but was dropped when Parliament adjourned in July 2000.

Living wills

In this country, the legality of a 'living will', (also known as an advanced statement or an advance refusal), is recognised at common law (i.e. judge made law). There is no Act of Parliament setting out the law. This document, signed and witnessed, enables the patient to state what he wishes to happen to him in the event of his becoming incapacitated and requiring resuscitation or any other treatment or care. The doctor, if he believes this document to represent the wishes of the patient, can rely on its provisions as a defence if any action were to be brought for his failure to treat the patient. The Law Commission (Report 231, 1995)[17] recommended legislation covering advance directives. These recommendations were supported by the House of Lords Select Committee on Medical Ethics in 1994.[18] In its proposals for decision making on behalf of mentally incapacitated adults,[19] the government stated that it did not propose legislation at the present time, but considered that the situation at common law provided greater flexibility

Transfusions

Transfusion errors are still not unknown and, in an attempt to reduce errors, the British Committee for Standards in Haematology, Blood Transfusion Task Force, RCN and the Royal College of Surgeons of England[20] have produced the first clinical guidelines on blood transfusion. If hospitals implement them and provide the necessary resources and training, transfusion errors should be reduced. Those haemophiliac patients who were infected with HIV in the early 1980s would have been unable to succeed in obtaining compensation through the civil courts, since at that time AIDS/HIV was not recognised and blood for transfusions was not tested for it. The government paid compensation to them, but the agreement included a waiver to prevent them from taking action over other blood-borne viruses that they might contract in the future. This waiver is now being challenged by a haemophiliac who claims that he was infected with hepatitis C virus from a blood transfusion.[21] He has been granted legal aid to challenge the validity of the waiver. He is also seeking a public inquiry to find out where the contaminated blood came from and why patients were not told of the risk of acquiring the disease. There may also be a right faction under the Consumer Protection Act 1987 (see page 256 *A and Others* v. *National Blood Authority and Aother*, *The Times Law Report*, 4 April 2001).

Organ transplantation

The Human Tissue Act 1961 and the Corneal Tissue Act 1986 cover the use of organs of a deceased person, and the Human Organ Transplants Act 1989 covers the transplant of organs from a live donor and commercial dealings with organs from living or dead donors.

Human Tissue Act 1961 as amended by the Corneal Tissue Act 1986

This Act covers two separate situations:

1. where the donor, before death, has agreed in writing or by word of mouth, expressed during his last illness in the presence of two witnesses, a request that his body be used after his death. It would be necessary to check with relatives to ascertain whether there is evidence that the deceased withdrew this request.
2. where the deceased has made no request, but the person lawfully in possession of the body has no reason to believe:
   (a) that the deceased had expressed an objection to the donation;
   (b) or that the surviving spouse or any surviving relative objects to the body being so dealt with.

The patient must be certified dead and the removal of the organs or tissue must be by a registered medical practitioner. The removal of the eye or part of any eye can be done by an NHS employee who is not a doctor provided that it is carried out on the instructions of a registered medical practitioner.

A youth of 23 years is knocked down in a road traffic accident. He has no identification on him and appears to be unaccompanied. He is brought into hospital by the ambulance crew and is resuscitated. He is maintained on the ventilator, but the prognosis is poor. Transplant teams are anxious to remove his lungs, heart, kidneys and liver and an ophthalmologist would like to make use of his eyes. The police are asked to notify the relatives as soon as possible. They are advised by the surgeon that the organs should be removed within half an hour of death. The youth is kept on a positive pressure ventilator. Can his organs be used for transplant on diagnosis of death before the relatives are contacted? What difference would it make if he was found to be carrying a donor card?

The law covering these circumstances is the Human Tissue Act 1961 (see Figure 16.6). In addition, the case would automatically become a coroner's case because death occurred following an accident. The coroner's consent would therefore be required for any use of the organs (see Chapter 29). The present law is based on 'opting in' or the consent of the relatives.

There is no definition of what is considered to be 'such reasonable enquiry as may be practicable'. It could be argued that if after a day or so there is still no identification of the deceased, then the organs could be taken with the approval of the coroner. If, on the other hand, the deceased is identified and the parents, sister or indeed any relative expresses an objection to the organs being used, then this will effectively prevent their use. 'Any surviving relative' may in fact cover a very wide field.

What if the youth is carrying a donor card? (See Figure 16.7.) Where a card is present the relatives have no right of veto under the Act, unless of course they can prove that the deceased had changed his mind; not an easy task where he is still carrying the card. However, it would be rare in practice for the hospital management to give consent to the removal of the organs if the relatives objected. It would, of course, still be necessary for the coroner's consent to be obtained.

Other provisions of the Act require the parts of the body to be taken by a registered medical practitioner who must have satisfied himself by personal examination that life is extinct. The procedure requires death to be certified also by a doctor who is not involved with the transplant team.

Under Section 1(2) of the Human Tissue Act the person lawfully in charge of the body of a deceased person may authorise the removal of any part from the body for use for the said purposes (therapeutic, or medical education, or research) if having made such reasonable enquiry as may be practicable, he has no reason to believe: (a) that the deceased had expressed an objection to his body being so dealt with after his death, and had not withdrawn it: or (b) that the surviving spouse or any surviving relative of the deceased objects to the body being so dealt with.

Figure 16.6   Donation of organs where there is no consent.

Under Section 1(1) of the Human Tissue Act: If any person, either in writing at any time or orally in the presence of two or more witnesses during his last illness, had expressed a request that his body or any specified part of his body be used after his death for therapeutic purposes, or for the purposes of medical education, or research, the person lawfully in possession of his body after his death may, unless he has reason to believe that the request was subsequently withdrawn, authorise the removal from the body of any part or, as the case may be, the specified part, for use in accordance with the request.

The presence of the donor card will count as evidence that the deceased agreed to the use of his body. The card may constitute a general consent or it may be specific. Under this section the person lawfully in charge of the body does not have to carry out reasonable enquiries to ascertain if the deceased had changed his mind. All that is necessary is that he has no reason to believe that the request was withdrawn. In practice, the same reasonable enquiries will be made whether or not the donor was carrying a card.

Figure 16.7 Donation of organs where the deceased has consented.

There is no statutory definition of the person lawfully in possession of the body. This would normally be the next of kin or occupier where the relative died at home, and the hospital manager where the person died in hospital or was brought in dead. The Act specifically prohibits those entrusted with the body for the purposes of interment or cremation from giving authority for the removal of any parts.

There has been a recent debate over the need to increase the number of organs available for transplant. In October 2000, 6,000 persons were awaiting an organ transplant and many would die before one became available. One suggestion is that there should be an opting-out system, rather than an opting-in one, i.e. you carry a card if you do not want your body used for transplant purposes, and the absence of a card implies an agreement to the organs being transplanted. This suggestion has not met with wide acceptance. An alternative suggestion is that there should be a legal duty for the professionals to request an organ transplant from the relatives of the deceased or prospective deceased. This is described as the required request system. It has the advantage of removing some of the embarrassment that professionals feel when they have to broach the matter with relatives. They are able to say, 'I hate having to ask you this, but I have no option as it is my legal duty to do so; would you agree to the possibility of X's organs being used for transplant?' It is thought that such a statutory request would lead to more organs being forthcoming without the necessity for a change in the Human Tissue Act itself. The relatives would still have the freedom to refuse, but they would also have the opportunity to agree. A private member's Bill was put before Parliament (April 2000) recommending that there should be an 'opting out', i.e. there is a presumption that the deceased would consent to being a donor. This presumption could, however, be rebutted by evidence that the deceased would not wish to donate his organs. It was given its first reading, but did not proceed and the bill was never printed. An initiative supported by actors and actresses in the TV soap *Coronation Street* was designed to increase the number of organ donors. Information for potential donors is given on a DH website.[22] It was followed by a scheme whereby credit card companies will ask customers applying for a card to sign up on the organ donor register.[23]

The Human Organ Transplant Act 1989

The Human Organ Transplant Act 1989 regulates commercial dealings in organs and the use of human organs between living persons. Section 1 prohibits the buying, selling or advertising of human organs that have been or are to be removed from a dead or living donor. It came into force on 27 July 1989. The definition of organs (Section 7(2)) covers any part of the human body, which if wholly removed cannot be replicated by the body. Bone marrow transplants or blood donors are therefore excluded from the Act.

Section 2 places restrictions upon transplants from living persons who are not genetically related to the recipient. Section 2(2) defines what is meant by genetically related. The expression includes natural parents and children, brothers and sisters, and the natural children of the donor's brothers and sisters. Regulations have been passed under the Act.[24] Further guidance is provided in circular HC(90)7. Health authorities and Trusts can be liable for any offences on their premises (Section 4 of the 1989 Act).

An Unrelated Live Transplant Regulatory Authority (ULTRA) has been set up and all proposals for transplants between persons who are not genetically related must be referred to it. Central records are maintained by the UK Transplant Support Services Authority.[25] ULTRA must be satisfied that no payment is involved and that the donor (except in cases where the primary purpose is the medical treatment of the donor) has been given full information about the procedure, understands this information and has given a valid consent, knowing that it can be withdrawn at any time. The Act does not affect the validity of transplants from a live donor to natural parents and children, sisters, brothers, uncles, aunts, nephews and nieces and first cousins. The doctors have to check that this relationship exists. (A Statutory Instrument which came into force in August 1998[26] provides that the genetic relationship between the proposed living donor of an organ and the proposed recipient is to be established by means of genetic tests based on DNA.) The Act does not cover the donation of regenerative tissue such as bone marrow, hair, skin and blood. Failure to comply with the provisions of the 1989 Act can lead to prosecution.

Situation 16.4   Live Donation

A nurse cares for a renal patient aged 23 years. She has been on dialysis for a number of years, but has been advised that a kidney transplant is urgently required. Her mother has offered to be a donor and seeks the advice of the nurse over whether such an offer would be accepted

---

It is important that the nurse knows who the appropriate person is to give advice and information to the mother. It may be essential to involve an independent person to ensure that the mother has the mental capacity to make the decision and that she is not under any duress. It is also essential that all the necessary information be given to the mother about the risks involved. Regulations specify how the checking of the relationship between donor and recipient is to be carried out.[27] Otherwise there would be an offence under the Human Organs Transplants Act 1989.

Transplant and consent provisions

The principles of consent which are considered in Chapter 7 apply to the recipient of the transplant. If the person is mentally competent and over 18 years, then they can give consent or refuse. If the person is under 18 years, then the principles that are discussed in Chapter 13 on children apply. In the following case, the mother consented to the child's transplant, but the child refused.

Case 16.2   Child refusing a transplant[28]

A girl of 15 years old refused to consent to a transplant that was needed to save her life. She stated that she did not wish to have anyone else's heart and she did not wish to take medication for the rest of her life. The hospital, which had obtained her mother's consent to the transplant, sought leave from the court to carry out the transplant.

The court held that the hospital could give treatment according to the doctor's clinical judgment, including a heart transplant. The girl was an intelligent person whose wishes carried considerable weight, but she had been overwhelmed by her circumstances and the decision she was being asked to make. Her severe condition had developed only recently and she had had only a few days to consider her situation. While recognising the risk that for the rest of her life she would carry resentment about what had been done to her, the court weighed that risk against the certainty of death if the order were not made.

Transplants from mentally incompetent persons

Chapter 13 on children considered the rights of the parent to give consent to a donation of tissue from one child to another and the question of whether this would be lawful if one person was mentally incapacitated was considered. The sole question for the courts is what is in the interests of the donor where the donor lacks the mental capacity or capability in law to give consent in his own right. This situation arose in the American case of *Hart* v. *Brown* where the donor and recipient were identical twin girls. The court approved the parental request to transfer a kidney from one to the other. One of the main justifications was that, medically, such a graft was more likely to be successful, and another justification was that if they refused to allow the donation the donor might, in later life, feel guilty at not being allowed to be a donor.[29] In another American case (*Strunk* v. *Strunk*),[30] a kidney transplant was authorised to proceed from an institutionalised adult with the mental capacity of a 6-year-old to his brother who was terminally ill with kidney trouble. The court accepted the medical evidence that there was a strong emotional bond between the brothers and the mentally incompetent would suffer a severe traumatic experience if the brother died.

In England, the courts have discussed whether a mentally and physically impaired older sister could give bone marrow to her younger sister who was suffering from a serious blood condition[31] (*Re Y* 1996). The court held that it was in the older sister's best interest for her to give bone marrow to her younger sister and the risks to her were minimal. The important issue is that it is the interests of the donor that have to be considered, not the interests of the recipient. It can be a criminal offence for parents to fail to take appropriate action for the care of their children.

Liability arising from transplants

Situation 16.5 *Diseased organs*

A patient received a kidney transplant and was subsequently told that it was HIV infected. It was discovered that this was unknown to the doctors and family of the deceased patient. Does the patient who received the kidney have any rights of action?

In the above situation, there is a duty of care, according to the reasonable professional standard for the transplant team, to ensure that the kidney is reasonably safe for transplant. In determining whether this duty of care had been fulfilled, note would be taken of the time scale within which any tests would have to take place. The possibility of the patient being able to sue under the Consumer Protection Act 1987 depends upon whether the organ could be defined as 'goods' under that Act and whether the transaction could be seen as in the course of business. Since the Human Organs Transplants Act 1989 Act prohibits commercial dealings, it could be argued that organ transplantation is not in the course of business. However, the activities of hospitals and health organisations would be defined as in 'the course of business'.

The retention of organs

Considerable public concern was raised when it was learnt that human organs from children who had died had been retained at Bristol Royal Infirmary. New guidance was considered necessary when, during the inquiry into allegations of professional misconduct in carrying out paediatric heart surgery, it was learnt that more than 11,000 children who had died in the past 40 years had had their organs used for research in British hospitals without the explicit consent of their parents.

At the same time, concerns were raised about the retention of human brains and spinal cords at the Walton Centre, Liverpool and of children's organs at Alderhey Hospital. The Report of the Royal Liverpool's Children's Inquiry (chaired by Michael Redfern QC)[32] on the retention of organs and body parts was published on the 30 January 2001. Its publication coincided with three other publications:

1. A report of a Census of Organs and Tissues Retained by Pathology Services in England carried out by the Chief Medical Officer[33] and

2. The Removal, Retention and use of Human Organs and Tissue from Post-Mortem Examination Advice from the Chief Medical Officer[34] and

3. Consent to organ and tissue retention at post-mortem examination and disposal of human materials.[35]

The Inquiry found that thousands of children's body parts had been collected at the hospital, some going back to before 1973. Most, however, were retained after 1988 when Professor Richard Van Velzen was appointed to the Department of Pathology and there was a huge increase in the number of organs removed and retained.

In response to the Redfern Report, the Secretary of State has set up a Retained Organs Commission under the Chairmanship of Professor Margaret Brazier. It is a special health authority with the following functions:

1. Oversee the return of tissues and organs from collections around the country.
2. Ensure that collections are accurately catalogued.
3. Provide information on collections throughout the country.
4. Ensure that suitable counselling is available.
5. Act as an advocate for parents if problems arise.
6. Advise on good practice in this area.
7. Handle inquiries from families and the public.

The government's intention is to bring in legal changes to amend the Human Tissue Act, to make it an explicit requirement that the informed consent of the parents or relatives must be obtained for the post-mortem to be carried out, and for the removal and retention of organs or tissues. The possibility of creating a criminal offence for failure to obey the laws is also being considered.

In October 2000, the British Medical Association issued advice to its members that relatives should give informed consent to the retention of organs. It should also be made clear that relatives can refuse consent to a post-mortem examination, unless it has been ordered by a coroner.[36]

Resource pressures

There is national concern over the pressure placed upon intensive care beds, often highlighted during flu epidemics. Thus in the winter of 1999/2000 during a flu crisis, national figures showed very few spare ITU beds across the country.

An Audit Commission report[37] on intensive care units pointed out that 'it does not make sense to respond to pressures created in cheaper areas of the hospital by increasing the number of the most expensive beds.' The report found that critical care beds were not always used appropriately and 'critical care units can become the backstop of a poorly performing hospital'. It gave as an example of inappropriate use the fact that almost one third of hospitals place extra strain on critical care beds, and bear unnecessary extra costs, by nursing patients with epidurals for pain relief after major surgery within critical care units. The Audit Commission report found that there were great variations in the resources deployed. 'Some units employ twice as many nurses as others have in order to have, for example, five direct care "bedside" nurses on duty at any time. . . . Yet the cost of neither nurses nor doctors is related to mortality differences between units.' It suggests that there should be national research to record more scientifically the benefits offered by one-to-one nursing.

Situation 16.6   Inadequate staffing

During a flu epidemic, there was considerable pressure on ITU beds, and operations were being postponed because of the inability to offer patients follow-up in ITU. During this crisis, an extra bed was used in ITU, although the staffing numbers were not increased. Sarah Roberts was attempting to look after her own patient as well as cover for another patient, when the nurse was on break. Unfortunately, she administered the wrong dose of a drug and the patient died.

Sarah could face criminal proceedings for acting with a lack of professional care. If it can be shown that she is guilty of such gross professional recklessness and negligence that it amounts to a criminal offence, she could be found guilty of the manslaughter of the patient. Account would be taken of the pressure she had been placed under, and the extent to which she had fulfilled her professional duty to the UKCC under its Code of Professional Conduct by drawing the crisis situation to the notice of senior management and taking other appropriate action. The legal issues relating to resources are considered in Chapter 4.

Review of critical care services

Following the Audit Report, an Expert Group was set up to review Critical Care Services. Its report,[38] 'Comprehensive Critical Care' was published in 2000 along with a review of adult critical care nursing.[39] The Comprehensive Critical Care Report recommended a modernisation programme to develop consistent and comprehensive critical care services. Four levels of care were identified:

Level 0   normal acute ward care

Level 1   acute ward care, with additional advice and support from critical care team

Level 2   more detailed observation or interventions, e.g. patients with a single failing organ system

Level 3   advanced respiratory support alone or basic respiratory support together with support of at least two organ systems.

The Report highlighted the need for action in four areas:

1.   A hospital wide approach to critical care.

2.   A networked service.

3.   Workforce development.

4.   Better information with all critical care services, collecting reliable management information and participating in outcome-focussed clinical audit.

A health service circular[40] required the setting up of local plans to implement a modernisation programme. It also stated that any plans put in place by NHS Trusts for additional capacity or reconfiguration of services should include robust plans for the recruitment and education or training of nurses. Trusts should put in place high dependency training for ward staff as an early measure. An additional £145 million was made available for adult critical care, including £2.5 million to support local service redesign in 2000/1.

Other major concerns of relevance to the intensive care nurse include definition of the scope of her professional practice. For example, an ITU nurse may be placed in a situation where she is asked to undertake work that she has not been trained to do. This is considered in Chapter 24 and the same basic principles that are discussed there apply to the intensive care nurse. Other aspects relating to death are considered in Chapter 29.

Questions and exercises

1 What are the main provisions of our present laws relating to consent to donate organs? What are the advantages and disadvantages of retaining the present system?

2 What is meant by brain death? What problems arise from recognising this as opposed to the traditional definition of death?

3 Examine the role of the consultant nurse in ITU. What safeguards should exist to protect the patient?

4 Over a period of two weeks, list the legal problems that you have encountered in your work in an intensive care unit or transplant unit and refresh your memory of the basic principles of accountability.

5 Relatives often have very fixed views on the outcome they wish for the seriously ill patient. Prepare a short paper outlining the basic principles of consent that apply in order to clarify the situation for relatives.

6 A patient who is being ventilated asks you to switch off the machine. What is the legal position?

7 Look back over the records that you have made on a patient who was in hospital several weeks before. If you were now to be challenged on any aspect of your care in that case, how useful and comprehensive would your notes be? Are there any obvious gaps on which you should have kept a record and are there any faults in the record-keeping? (Refer to Chapter 9.)

References

[1] Royal College of Nursing, The Nature of Nursing Work in Intensive Care RCN 000 728 May 1997

[2] Department of Health, Code of Practice for the Diagnosis of Brain Stem Death March 1998 DoH

[3] *Re A* [1992] 3 Med LR 303

[4] *R v. Malcherek*; *R v. Steel* CA 1981 2 All ER 422

[5] Criminal Law Report, 1977, p. 443

6 *Airedale NHS Trust* v. *Bland* 1993 1 All ER 821

7 *Frenchay NHS Trust* v. *S.* TLR 19 January 1994 CA

8 Practice Note (Official Solicitor:Vegetative state) [1996] 2 FLR 375

9 *D* (Medical Treatment) [1998] 1 FLR 411 (see also *H* (a patient) [1998] 2 FLR 36)

10 British Medical Association, Resuscitation Council (UK) and the Royal College of Nursing, Decisions Relating to Cardiopulmonary Resuscitation BMA 1999; updated March 2001

11 NHS Executive, Resuscitation Policy HSC 2000/028 September 2000

12 Michael Horsnell, Doctors call for death inquiry, *The Times* 7 December 1999

13 House of Lords Select Committee on Medical Ethics HL Paper No 21 Vol 1 1994, London HMSO

14 Martin Fletcher, Dutch become first to legalise euthanasia, *The Times* 29 November, 2000

15 BMA Withdrawing Treatment guidelines 2000 BMA

16 News Item, *Nursing Times* May 11 2000 Vol 96 No 19 page 12

17 Law Commission Report 231 Mental Incapacity HMSO 1995

18 House of Lords Select Committee on Medical Ethics HL Paper No 21 Vol 1 1994, London HMSO

19 Lord Chancellor's Office, Making Decisions, Stationery Office 1999

20 British Committee for Standards in Haematology, Blood Transfusion Task Force, RCN and the Royal College of Surgeons of England, The Administration of Blood and Blood Components and the Management of Transfused Patients Transfusion Medicine 9.3 227–238 1999

21 Annie Flury, Man sues over blood infection, *The Times* 7 August 2000

22 www.nhs.uk/organdonor

23 Department of Health, Credit cards to promote organ donation 1 November 2000

24 Human Organ Transplant (Unrelated Persons) Regulation 1989/2840, Human Organ Transplants (Establishment of Relationship) Regulation 1989/2017 and the Human Organ Transplants (Supply of Information) Regulation 1989/2108.

25 UK Transplant Support Services Authority, Southmead Road, Bristol, BS10 5ND (Department HOT A)

26 Statutory Instrument, Human Organ Transplants (Establishment of Relationship) Regulations 1990 SI 1998 No 1428

27 Human Organ Transplants (Establishment of Relationship) Regulations 1989 SI 1989/2107

28 *Re M* (Medical Treatment: Consent) [1999] 2 FLR 1097

29 *Hart* v. *Brown* 289 A 2d 386 Conn. 1972

30 *Strunk* v. *Strunk* 445 SW 2d 145 (Ky App.) 1969

31 *Y* (Adult Patient) (Transplant: Bone Marrow), Re (1996) BMLR 111; (1996) 4 Med LR 204

32 Department of Health, The Royal Liverpool's Children's Inquiry Report 30 January 2001 London DoH

33 Chief Medical Officer, A report of a Census of Organs and Tissues Retained by Pathology Services in England January 2001 DoH

34 Department of Health, The Removal, Retention and Use of Human Organs and Tissue from Post-Mortem Examination Advice from the Chief Medical Officer January 2001 DoH

35 Department of Health consent to organ and tissue retention at post-mortem examination and disposal of human materials January 2001 DoH

36 British Medical Association Consent to organ retention October 2000

37 Audit Commission, Critical to Success: The place of efficient and effective critical care services within the acute hospital, Audit Commission 1999 London

38 Department of Health, Comprehensive Critical Care Report of an Expert Group DoH 2000

39 Department of Health, The Review of Adult Critical Care Nursing Report to the Chief Nursing Officer DoH 2000

40 NHS Executive, Modernising Critical Care Services HSC 2000/017 May 2000

17 Theatre and anaesthetic nursing and the recovery ward

Like the ward nurse, the theatre nurse is constantly concerned with the possibility of litigation and also with the problems of her role in relation to the surgeons and the anaesthetists. These areas and the others to be covered in this chapter are set out in Figure 17.1. Reference should also be made to Chapter 29 on the law relating to death and inquests and the need to report to the coroner if a patient dies on the operating table or shortly afterwards. Another concern for theatre staff when an aborted fetus shows signs of life is considered in Chapter 15.

Civil liability procedures and practices in theatre

Professional liability

Situation 17.1 Lost swab

Staff Nurse French was the scrub nurse for a hernia operation performed by a registrar. They were running late and still had two patients left on the morning list. The afternoon list was due to start in ten minutes. Just before the registrar sutured the patient's wound, he asked for a swab count. Staff Nurse French checked the thirty-four used swabs, which had been hung on the rack, and six unused swabs and two unopened packs with the operating department practitioner. She confirmed that those were the only ones in use and the patient was sewn up. A few days later, just before the patient would normally have been discharged, he reported violent pains and became seriously ill. It was decided to X-ray the patient prior to returning him to theatre. The X-ray showed up a swab. The relatives of the patient were told what had happened and they made it clear that they would seek compensation. An internal investigation was commenced to see if the cause of this error could be found. The conclusions were that there was an extra swab in one of the packs and this had not been spotted when the staff nurse opened and counted them. A dispute then ensued between the registrar and the staff nurse over liability for the incident. The staff nurse claimed that as she had checked the swabs in front of the registrar, he should accept responsibility for it; the registrar stated that as the staff nurse had clearly counted wrongly, it was entirely her responsibility and, in addition, the unscrubbed runner nurse had made a second check.

1. Civil liability procedures and practice
   (a) professional liability;
   (b) policies and practices.
2. Theatre nurse and the scope of professional practice.
3. Accidents in the theatre.
4. Consent in the theatre
   (a) after premedication;
   (b) consent refused.
5. Drugs and the operating department practitioner.
6. Recovery room nursing.

Figure 17.1   Issues covered in Chapter 17.

In a dispute like this, the patient would be able to argue that this is a case of *res ipsa loquitur* and the burden should pass to the NHS Trust to show that they were not negligent. (This is discussed in Chapter 6.) It will be recalled from the case of *Wilsher* v. *Essex Area Health Authority*[1] that the courts do not accept any concept of team liability (see page 56). The NHS Trust itself could be directly liable and, in addition, each individual professional could be liable for what he personally did or failed to do and would be judged according to the standards expected of them, but the employer would accept vicarious liability.

The actual proportion of responsibility in a case like the above would obviously depend on the actual facts of what went wrong. When the swabs were unpacked, were they properly checked to ensure that none was stuck together? What was the accepted approved practice that the doctor and the nurse should have followed? Were there any justifiable reasons why this need not have been followed? In addition, there might be some liability on the part of the manufacturer as well. Since 1 January 1990, health authorities have accepted responsibility for the negligence of doctors and dentists whilst acting in course of employment. This also applies to NHS Trusts. It is, therefore, less important how liability between nurse and doctor is shared, since the compensation will be paid to the patient by the employer. It is important, however, to allocate responsibilities through procedures and policies to ensure that similar harm does not occur again. It is essential that procedures are in place to prevent such incidents arising.

There have been some very rare cases where, although the scrub nurse points out that a swab is unaccounted for, the surgeon still proceeds with stitching up the patient. This may be justifiable in particular cases if the patient's condition is deteriorating and there is a greater risk in keeping him under the anaesthetic than in taking the risk of the swab still being inside him. It would be very different if the surgeon was simply ignoring the nurse's count without any justification.

The proportion of liability between nurse and surgeon thus depends entirely on the individual facts of the case.

Policies and practices

The situation illustrates the importance of having clear policies and codes of practice as to the responsibility of each person in theatre, so that there is no overlap. In

> Allergies not marked on notes.
> Units of blood not checked.
> Nerves over bony surfaces damaged.
> Eyes exposed to harm.
> Sharp and powered tools used dangerously.
> Faulty gauges on pneumatic cuffs, faulty monitors.
> Tourniquets left on too long and skin necrosis beneath tourniquet cuffs.
> Spirit solutions used with cautery.
> Hot instruments and hot water in tubing.
> Water mattresses overheating.
> Diathermy burns.
> Uninsulated electrodes.
> Misplaced footswitch.
> Faulty alarms and faulty equipment.

Figure 17.2   Potential hazards in the operating theatre.

a situation where the patient is unable to correct any wrong assumptions, it is essential that these codes cover every possible danger. The responsibility for the identification of the patient, the nature of the operation to be performed, including the identification of the part of the body or limb to be operated upon, must all be clearly allocated so that there can be no errors. Many of these procedures may be repeats of checks already made at ward level, but they cannot be omitted on that account in theatre. If any such cases came to court, the judge would expect evidence on what the procedure should have been and what in fact took place.

There are many implications for theatre nurses: they should clearly be familiar with the procedures and implement them, resisting any unjustifiable short cuts whatever the pressure. In addition, their records should be detailed and meaningful so that if there is a query about the care in the theatre, then they are able to refer to a comprehensive account of what took place. Booklets produced by the defence societies, the Royal College of Nursing and the National Association of Theatre Nurses on theatre safeguards cover procedures for admission, labelling and ward procedure, lost swabs and instruments, and other causes of potential hazards (see Figure 17.2). In 2000, the wrong kidney was removed from a patient in Prince Philip Hospital, Llanelly. In the subsequent report of the inquiry by the Commission for Health Improvement[2] into that incident, it was found that there were serious faults in the marking of X-rays and significant recommendations were made. At the time of writing, a police investigation is under way and the report on the investigation by the Trust has not been published.

The theatre nurse and the scope of professional practice

There is little uniformity in the tasks that nurses are expected to perform in theatre. The duties of a scrub nurse can depend upon the personal preferences of an individual surgeon and on whether the hospital is a teaching hospital. Anaesthetic nurses may also have a variety of duties: for example, in some theatres they may be expected to draw up the drugs in syringes for the anaesthetist to check; in others, the anaesthetist might do this himself. The nurse's role will also depend on the existence of and the duties performed by the operating department practitioner. Some of the tasks she performs will be regarded as expanded-role duties in which she might have been trained on a post-registration training course. In its report 'Anaesthesia under Examination',[3] the Audit Commission made significant recommendations on anaesthetic and pain management services and suggested that there was considerable scope for the role expansion of many of the different professional groups who work in theatres. The report illustrates how problems can arise when interdisciplinary teamworking breaks down. It puts forward practical suggestions on how Trusts can improve anaesthetic and pain relief services. (See Chapter 24 and page 483 on the scope of professional practice and the theatre nurse.)

Accidents in the theatre

An incident book should be kept to record accidents and other mishaps in theatre and the recovery room, and accidents and other untoward incidents should be reported to the Chief Executive or his/her assigned officer. There may be opposition from some medical staff over the necessity to record untoward incidents, but the nurse has a duty to ensure that records are maintained on incidents that cause harm: diathermy burns, an unintentional cut, and the more serious incidents such as operating on the wrong side of the patient or even on the wrong patient. A policy of disclosure to the patient should be encouraged. However, it is not for the nurse to notify the patient; this is the consultant's or manager's duty. The government has suggested a national reporting system of adverse health care incidents which is discussed in Chapter 5.

Consent in the theatre

Some particular problems arise in relation to consent in the theatre. One is the failure of ward staff to ensure that the appropriate forms have been filled in before the patient is sent to theatre. Consider Situation 17.2 on page 368.

Consent after premedication

In Chapter 7, it was pointed out that consent can be given in a variety of forms: in writing, by word of mouth, by implication. These are all equally valid in law. It could be argued, therefore, that the fact that Paula had given her consent to the registrar means that that can be relied upon and therefore the operation can proceed. However, consent in writing is infinitely superior as a form of evidence. Imagine that Paula's operation proceeded. When the biopsy was analysed, a malignancy was discovered and the surgeon therefore proceeded with a mastectomy. On recovery, however, Paula denied that she had any idea that this was a likely possibility and had she known she would have preferred to have had radiotherapy. This possibility cannot be discounted and in such a situation it would be far better for Paula to return to the ward and, when the premedication has worn off, to agree in writing that the operation can proceed. One can imagine certain circumstances where there would be such considerable risks in postponing the operation that on balance the advantages to the patient are in favour of proceeding rather than returning the patient to the ward. In such cases, there could be an action for negligence if harm were caused by this delay. However, these would be unusual circumstances. In general, it would be wiser to ensure that the patient has signed a consent form and has had all the risks and implications explained to her. Sending the patient back to the ward, although undoubtedly leading to a furious complaint from a rightly indignant patient, has several long-term advantages: the ward staff will be less likely to give the patient a premedication before checking whether the consent forms have been signed and the doctors will know that they cannot get by with a casual approach to patients' rights.

Situation 17.2   *Validity of consent*

Paula Green was admitted to hospital for a biopsy of the breast. It was intended that, should there be any malignancy, then a mastectomy would be carried out immediately. Paula was given the premedication by the ward staff and brought to theatre. When the theatre sister was checking through the records, she noticed that there was no consent form. The anaesthetist, who had begun to prepare Paula for the operation, said that he had seen Paula on the ward the previous day and knew there was no doubt that she wanted this to be carried out and that she might still be able to put her signature to a form. The theatre sister was very concerned about this. The surgical registrar then apologised and said that he had spoken to Paula about the operation and that she knew the implications of it. However, when he had visited the ward, he had run out of consent forms. He had intended returning to the ward to get Paula's signature but had been distracted and had completely forgotten about it. He saw no reason not to proceed with the operation and argued that Paula would be far more upset if the operation did not proceed and she returned to the ward without it than for the operation to go ahead without her signature. What should the theatre sister do?

A more difficult situation which occasionally occurs is where the patient himself, after premedication and prior to the general anaesthetic, asks the surgeon if something else could be 'sorted out', e.g. an ingrowing toe nail; a cyst, etc. What is the surgeon to do? It would seem churlish for him to say, 'No. I must have your consent in writing for that and since you have been premedicated you are incapable of giving a valid consent.' On the other hand, if he agrees to proceed and undertakes the additional task and there are some unforeseen or unmentioned side-effects, then litigation may result.

Consent refused

Situation 17.3   What the eyes don't see . . .

An adult Jehovah's Witness patient makes it clear that he will agree to a particular operation only on the understanding that he will not be given blood (see Figure 7.2). The surgeon agrees to operate on that basis, but does intend that, if blood is needed, the patient will be given it anyway and will be none the wiser. The operation proceeds. The patient begins to haemorrhage and the surgeon instructs that blood should be given. Somehow the patient discovers what has happened and sues the NHS Trust for trespass to the person.

In this case, it is clear that there has been a trespass to the person since the patient was given blood contrary to his express instructions and any deliberate intention to mislead the patient by the surgeon was a breach of professional conduct. The patient should therefore be entitled to substantial damages. Only if there was any doubt about the mental capacity of the patient and therefore the possibility that he was incapable of making a decision, could the judge consider that the actions were justified in the best interests of the patient. (See the case of *Re MB* which is considered in Chapter 7 and Chapter 14.) To avoid the possibility of court action, a surgeon could advise that he is not prepared to operate with restrictions upon his discretion and if the patient refused to give an unrestricted consent, then he would not be operated upon. (Note the case of *Malette* v. *Shulman* where blood was given to an unconscious card-carrying patient (see page 136, Case 7.5.)

Other restrictions that the patient may also wish to impose upon the surgeons are often refused; thus it should be made clear that the operation will not be performed by a particular surgeon or that there will be a specified anaesthetist or that any particular procedure will be followed.

Even though the patient has consented to a particular operation and is therefore prevented from bringing an action for trespass to the person, it might well be that if harm occurs, the patient will complain that he has not been informed of this possibility and side-effects and that, had he known, he would not have gone ahead with it. This possibility is discussed in connection with the Sidaway case (see Chapter 7).

One important point must be emphasised, however. The patient, in signing the consent form, is consenting to an action that without his consent would count as a trespass to his person. He is also consenting to undergo the risks of those unforeseen chances that, no matter how much care is taken, can still occur. He is not consenting to negligence nor to the possibility that harm could occur to him because a nurse or doctor is careless, or because the procedures are not followed correctly or inadequate precautions are taken to ensure that he will be safe.

Sometimes it might be pointed out to the patient that a particular operation is experimental, and he might expressly agree to undergo the additional risk of this unknown procedure, but he still does not consent to the possibility of a failure to follow approved accepted practice.

Other difficulties in relation to consent to treatment are considered in the chapters relating to children's nursing (Chapter 13), gynaecology (sterilisations) (Chapter 15), psychiatric nursing (Chapter 20), and accident and emergency departments (Chapter 21).

There have recently been successful claims by patients who have brought action on the grounds that whilst under the anaesthetic they were conscious of activities around them and suffered agonising pain, but were unable to move. A report in the journal of the Royal College of Anaesthetists[4] on a survey of doctors suggests that at least 7,750 patients are conscious during operations each year. Of these, about 250 feel their bodies being opened and internal organs manipulated by doctors. In 1985, £15,000 was awarded to Margaret Acters by Wigan. Clearly, nurses should be vigilant for any sign that the patient is not properly anaesthetised. The role of the operating department practitioner in relation to drugs is considered in Chapter 28.

Recovery room nursing

This is often under the control of the consultant anaesthetist. Recovery nurses would usually have post registration training in recovery nursing. The training would include developing the skills, expertise and knowledge to detect possible adverse side-effects resulting from the anaesthetic drugs. They must be trained to act speedily in an emergency and staffing ratios assume even greater importance than elsewhere in the hospital. It is essential that they are clear as to their competence in a wide area.

Another interesting facet of the law in this area is the fact that nurses may hear confidential information from the semi-conscious patient which would come under the principles discussed in Chapter 8. Similarly, it is essential that the nurses do not discuss the patient or any other patient in front of any of the semi-conscious patients in the recovery room since there are many accounts of patients who have overheard what staff have said and have been very upset by this. The nurse's duty of care obviously includes the duty of foreseeing what could harm a patient in this context and taking reasonable precautions to prevent that occurring.

Conclusions

This is an area that is central to any major success in the reduction of waiting lists and the decrease of litigation. It is highly likely that over the next few years, the work of theatre and related staff will be subject to inspection by the Commission for Health Improvement and to recommendations from the National Institute of Clinical Excellence. Significant changes are likely to result from changes in the scope of professional practice of the nurse.

Questions and exercises

1   How do the provisions of the Health and Safety at Work Act (see Chapter 12) affect the theatre manager?

2   Procedures do not provide the solution to every eventuality. In what circumstances do you consider a nurse would be justified in deviating from a specified procedure (see Chapter 3)?

3   How do the basic principles of consent to treatment affect the work of the theatre nurse (see Chapter 7)?

4   How do the principles relating to the scope of professional practice affect the theatre nurse (see Chapter 24)?

5   Obtain a copy of the incident book which is kept in the theatre in which you work and consider how some of these incidents could have been avoided.

References

1   *Wilsher* v. *Essex Area Health Authority* [1986] 3 All ER 801 CA
2   Commission for Health Improvement, Report on Prince Philip Hospital Llanelly 15 November, 2000
3   Audit Commission, Anaesthesia under Examination The Efficiency and Effectiveness of Anaesthesia and Pain Relief Services in England and Wales, Audit Commission 17 December 1997
4   *The Sunday Times*, 31 July 1994

18 Nurse educator and researcher

Law is relevant to the role of the nurse educator in several respects. Tutors have recently been involved in litigation in respect of what they have taught, how it was taught and when. In addition, the contract of employment for the learner is different from that of the ordinary employee and nurse lecturers should be familiar with the differences and implications. The legal issues arising from research are also relevant to the lecturer. They need also to be concerned with all the general aspects of the law covered in the first part of this book: not only in relation to their own position, but also because they might have to teach some of it! The topics to be considered in this chapter are set out in Figure 18.1.

Guidance on the standards for the preparation of teachers of nursing, midwifery and health visiting is provided by the UKCC.[1] In order to obtain registered status, students must not only pass the academic and practical requirements of the course,[2] there must also be a declaration by the head of the college (or department) of nursing that there is no reason why the student is not eligible to be placed on the UKCC register. This places a clear duty on the lecturers to ensure that any information that indicates that the person would be unsuitable should be brought to the attention of the head of the college or department of nursing . This requirement is particularly important in the light of the recommendations of the Clothier Inquiry into Beverly Allitt. The report[3] recommended that those with a history of personality disorder should not be taken into nursing (see Chapter 5).

---

1. Record-keeping by teachers.
2. Liability for instructing others.
3. Hearing about unsound practices.
4. Employment law
   (a) employees – yet students, fixed-term contracts;
   (b) dismissal on grounds of absenteeism and course failure;
   (c) clinical placements.
5. Legal aspects of research
   (a) control of a research programme;
   (b) confidentiality;
   (c) consent;
   (d) liability for volunteers in research;
   (e) fraud;
   (f) health and safety of the researcher.

Figure 18.1 Issues covered in Chapter 18.

Record-keeping by teachers

Record-keeping by teachers

Situation 18.1   Instruction in lifting – the evidence

Beryl Sharp, a nurse tutor, received a request from her hospital claims manager to provide her with the information she had given to a staff nurse on a lifting course. It appeared that this staff nurse had sustained a serious back injury at work and was suing the NHS Trust for a breach in its direct liability to take care of her safety. The claim was likely to amount to a considerable sum since the prognosis was poor and she was unlikely to be able to return to work in the foreseeable future. The NHS Trust was defending the claim on the grounds that the ward was adequately staffed and that the staff nurse had been given instruction in lifting. It now required evidence of that fact from Beryl. Fortunately, Beryl was a hoarder – a fact frequently greeted with derision by her colleagues. She never threw anything out and was able to go through her records and find the series of seminars that had been organised on lifting. She had both the dates and the names of participants, including the names of those who had failed to attend. She had not given the seminar herself: a physiotherapist had done the teaching. Beryl had simply organised it as part of her work as an organiser for continuing education. She checked her records and could find no record that the particular staff nurse had attended. In fact, she was able to see that she was included in the list of those who were supposed to attend, but was not present at a seminar and that 'sick' had been written against her name. There was no evidence that she had been invited to attend a subsequent seminar, although another three were held in the following months.

One can imagine that this information would disappoint the hospital claims manager in providing information to defend the staff nurse's claim. However, it is not completely fatal to any defence of the claim, since it might well be that the staff nurse had received appropriate training in lifting during her basic training. In addition, there may be some element of contributory negligence in that the staff nurse herself failed to ensure that she was included on another seminar once she had returned from sick leave.

Such a request gives rise to many further questions for the nurse lecturer. How long must the records be kept? What sort of detail is necessary? It will be recalled from the section in Chapter 6 dealing with the time limits for bringing a court action that in a case of negligence the action must be brought within three years of the negligent incident, unless the victim is under 18 years old, under a disability, or in cases where she was not aware of the fact of the negligence or the existence of harm, within the three years of such information becoming available. A period of retention of seven years is therefore likely to cover most eventualities apart from these exceptions. In addition, it could be argued that in those areas where regular retraining and revision study days are necessary, if several years have elapsed since the opportunity to go on to a course, then the authority is at fault in not providing a revision course. The information that should be retained is set out in Figure 18.2.

(a) the names of those who should have attended the sessions;

(b) the names of those who did attend;

(c) times and dates of the sessions;

(d) the content of the sessions and who did the teaching;

(e) the grades of achievement where there was any assessment.

Records are, of course, kept of the content, standard and timetable of learners, and it is not difficult to extend this to the post-basic courses.

Figure 18.2 Information that should be kept by the nurse tutor.

Liability for instructing others

In Chapter 3, there is an explanation of the duty of care owed by those who are instructing others so that if harm were to occur as a result of negligent instructions, the tutor can be sued by the person who has suffered the harm. This applies not just to the classroom situation, but to all those situations where advice is given in circumstances where the person receiving it can be expected to act upon it. If the advice has been given negligently, then an action in negligence for breach of a duty of care may follow.

Situation 18.2 Negligent instructions

Beryl Sharp acted as the course tutor on some of the post-basic courses. She ran one course, that of training nurses in the adding of drugs to IVs and failed to mention that the first dose of the drug to be added to the IV should always be given by a doctor. One of the staff nurses who had been at that session and had been deemed competent to give IV drugs returned to the ward and was instructed that a patient who was already on an intravenous drip had been written up for an IV drug. At the appropriate time, the staff nurse prepared the drug, checked it with another nurse, and added it to the drip according to the instructions she had been taught on the course. The patient reacted violently against the drug and a doctor was summoned urgently. An inquiry was then held to find out why the first dose of this drug had been administered by a nurse and not by a doctor. It was the local policy for the doctor to administer the first dose of a drug intravenously. It then emerged that Beryl Sharp had failed to point out this requirement in her teaching on the course.

In this situation, the victim is a patient. In other cases, the victim could be the person who received the negligent information or advice. Where a patient is the victim, the claim is relatively simple: he would show that he has suffered harm as a result of a negligent act of an employee acting in course of employment and therefore that the employer is vicariously liable for the harm. Alternatively, the individual employee could be sued as personally liable for the harm. In such a case, the employee may bring her own action against the tutor who was negligent in the instructions that she gave. In this type of action, the following facts would have to be shown:

1. A duty of care was owed by the instructor to the instructee.

2. There was a breach of this duty since the instructions were given negligently.

3. As a reasonable foreseeable consequence of this breach, the person has suffered harm (this might be personal injury, but it could also include financial loss or loss or damage to property).

It is essential that the person harmed can show that this harm was caused by the negligence of the tutor. If it was unreasonable for the person to rely upon the instruction by the tutor, then compensation would not be payable.

Hearing about unsound practices

If a lecturer in the college of nursing discovers from his/her learners about staff who are guilty of unacceptable practices or ill-treatment of patients, what action should the nurse lecturer take? Should she investigate the allegation and, if challenged, say why? Should she keep her source secret? Should she report her suspicions to nurse management? Obviously, there can be no single answer since much depends upon the circumstances. If, for example, the learner has witnessed ill-treatment of a patient by a member of staff on a ward, then the learner should be encouraged to write a statement setting out exactly what she has seen and the nurse lecturer should ensure that appropriate action is taken by nurse management, at the same time protecting the learner from any victimisation. (Refer to whistle-blowing and the Public Interest Disclosure Act 1998 considered in Chapter 4.) If the nurse witnesses a procedure being carried out on the wards that is not in line with present-day safe practices, the nurse lecturer could arrange appropriate revision courses with the in-service training officer colleagues.

Conflicts could also arise where the college has been teaching learners the basic principles of patients' rights, e.g. consent to treatment, and as a result the learner encounters difficulties with some medical staff. There could be criticism of the lecturers and of the college for its teachings. Such a situation indicates the importance of very close contact between the college and the NHS Trust. The college of nursing should not, however, be seen as a policing machine for the hospital. On the other hand, it has an essential part to play in maintaining the highest standards of nursing care in co-operation with the managers. Close integration of nurse clinical teaching and practice is essential.

Employment law

Students

Learners were once both employees and students. Following the introduction of Project 2000, learners are students, usually attached to a college of education. They are entitled to receive student bursaries, and the college negotiates an agreement with accredited hospitals for the clinical placements. In theory, students are supernumerary to the workforce, but inevitably, especially in the last years of training, the hospitals and community services may exploit their services. There is no right in the learning contract for the student to insist on employment once she is qualified.

Dismissal on grounds of absenteeism or course failure

Since the student is not an employee, if she should be dismissed during the course on the grounds of absenteeism or failing course assessments or examinations, then the student's remedy is an appeal through the appeal mechanisms of the college. These should have clear guidelines on the rules that operate in these circumstances and these procedures should be carefully followed. There is a contractual relationship between student and the college which is enforceable in law.

Clinical placements

There is normally a memorandum of agreement between colleges providing clinical training and the hospitals and community trusts providing clinical placements. This agreement should cover the issue of liability for the actions of the students if they cause harm to others through negligence. Since the students are not employees of the unit providing clinical placements, the latter can argue that they are not vicariously liable for the actions of students. In addition, the agreement should cover liability for harm to the student. Prior agreement between the college and the organisation providing the clinical placement can resolve such issues and also cover the topic of supervision of the student and clinical instruction.

Legal aspects of research

Research based practice is an essential requirement of professional care. The National Institute for Clinical Excellence (see Chapter 5) is seeking to identify and publish recommended clinically effective practice that has a strong research basis. Nurses are therefore increasingly likely to be involved in research: either conducting it herself or being involved in the care of patients who are the subjects of a research project. Often a research project is an integral part of a management course or post-registration qualification and she will be expected to prepare a dissertation or project that shows some original material and analysis. In addition, there may well be researchers coming into her department or ward: she should in either case be aware of the many legal issues that arise. Some of the basic problems relate to consent by the patient, confidentiality and disclosure of the findings, safety of the researcher, and liability for any volunteer in a drugs research programme. The conduct of research and the rights of the research subject are set out in the Declaration of Helsinki, which is reproduced as an appendix in the Department of Health's guidance for Local Research Ethics Committees.[4] In addition, a researcher would be required to observe the rights set out in the European Convention on Human Rights which since 2 October 2000 are actionable in this country (see Chapter 1 and appendix A). Where the nurse becomes aware that the rights of the patient are not being protected by the researchers, she would have a professional duty to raise this with senior management, and, if no action were taken, to make use of the whistle-blowing provisions of the Public Interest Disclosure Act 1998 (see Chapter 4). Reference can be made to the author's chapter exploring the legal implications of research.[5]

Control of a research programme

Situation 18.3   *Gagged*

Ann Jones, a ward sister, was on a management course that required her to complete a dissertation. She chose as her subject the consequences of the privatisation of cleaning services and studied one hospital where the services were contracted out to a private firm, and another hospital where direct labour ancillary staff were used. Her conclusions were that privatisation led to a lower standard of cleaning, a less hygienic environment for patients, and nursing staff undertaking more cleaning work because the private firm sent cleaners to the wards for only a short proportion of the day. Just before she was due to submit the dissertation for her diploma, her nursing director heard of it and asked to see it. She has now been told that her findings are politically unacceptable, that she cannot present it to the college, and that she must commence a totally different topic of research.

This situation gives rise to many legal issues. First, in this situation the researcher is also an employee. She therefore has responsibilities to her employer. Even if she were an independent researcher funded from outside the institution that is the subject of the research, she might well have had to agree to a clause that the research findings have to have the prior approval of the institution before the research results can be published. As an employee, she would be expected to obey the reasonable orders of the employer. Is it reasonable in these circumstances for the researcher to be silenced? The answer would depend on more detailed facts: for example, was it only because the results were unwelcome that they are being suppressed? Was the basis of her data collection and statistical analysis sound? If there is no criticism to be made of her method and findings other than that they are embarrassing, it could be argued that the same principles apply here as apply in the situation discussed in Chapter 7 relating to reporting on negligence by a colleague or some other form of unacceptable practice. Where management itself fails to take action, i.e. when all the internal procedures for improving the situation have been used to no avail, then it would not be considered unreasonable to take the matter to a higher authority, initially within the organisation and, if necessary, ultimately outside, but this obviously depends on the findings and the reasons for prohibiting publication. The Public Interest Disclosure Act 1998 can be used to ensure that any person properly reporting health and safety concerns or criminal matters is protected from victimisation (see Chapter 4).

Many difficulties can be avoided if the researcher receives the proper approval before beginning. In some cases, this might mean obtaining the approval of a local ethics committee. Where this authority is received, it would be more difficult to prohibit publication of the results purely on the grounds of embarrassment at the findings. The Department of Health issued advice on the establishment and operation of local research ethics committees, and any research involving NHS patients, access to their records or use of NHS premises or facilities must be referred to the LREC.[6]

Confidentiality

Where use is made of personal information, access to it and disclosure of it in such a form that the individuals can be identified is subject to the provisions of the Data Protection Act 1998 (see Chapter 8). This means that if the data is not exempt from any of the provisions of the Act, and if it is to be used in addition for research, then it must also be registered for research use. Even where the data is not automated, it would, in most health service cases, be subject to the rules of confidentiality. This means that it can be disclosed only in those exceptional circumstances outlined in Chapter 8. Difficulties can arise for the researcher where information is obtained that has nothing to do with the research, i.e. it is simply doing the research that has given the opportunity to gain this information. The General Medical Council states that information can be given by practitioners about their patients for the purpose of research, but the patient's consent should be sought or the information provided in an anonymous form.[7]

Situation 18.4   Silence or disclosure?

Sandra James, a staff nurse, was conducting a research project into the care of the post-operative surgical patient. She was interested in the rate of infection, length of stay, convalescent care and the nature of community care. Her research therefore required visits to the patients' homes. One of her patients, Glenda Mitchell, had been operated on for gallstones. She was in hospital for 7 days and was then discharged to her home. Her cohabitee had taken a few days off work to care for their 3-year-old daughter. While Sandra was visiting the home, she was surprised to see that the child was very frightened of her and was withdrawn and hostile. Sandra tried to talk to her and touch her and noticed severe bruising and pinch marks on the child's legs.

In a suspected case of non-accidental injury, there is a clear justification for disclosing confidential information in the interests of the child. In a case like this, Sandra might try to persuade the mother to explain the child's bruising and, if this were unsatis-factory, she should ensure that appropriate action is taken to protect the child, e.g. arranging for the health visitor to visit, initiating the non-accidental injury procedure or even bringing in the NSPCC. Whatever action she takes along these lines would be protected from any action for breach of confidentiality on the grounds that the public interest justified it. In one case,[8] the House of Lords stated that the NSPCC was entitled to maintain the secrecy of the names of its informants, even if they had been malicious. This decision is based on public policy because it is essential that people are prepared to report potential incidents of child abuse. If, however, the facts of this situation are changed slightly and instead of a potential NAI case a potential crime against property is suspected, e.g. stolen goods are seen in the house, many profes-sionals would feel that their professional duty of confidentiality must be maintained.

Consent

Unfortunately, not all research subjects are notified that they are to be included in a research project and their consent is not always obtained to the participation. Even in randomised controlled trials of drugs, patients should be informed that they have the right to refuse to take part. If the treatment is therapeutic rather than pure research, then in exceptional circumstances it could be argued that the doctor's right of therapeutic privilege (discussed by the House of Lords in the Sidaway case (see Chapter 7)) applied and there are special circumstances to justify not informing the patient of that fact. The right of therapeutic privilege could be relied upon only in exceptional circumstances and the presumption is that the patient's consent should be obtained.

The basic legal principles are as follows: consent to participate in research should be given freely by an adult, mentally competent person and should be preceded by sufficient relevant information about serious harmful side-effects, as approved practice would require the professional to give the patient. Where research is contemplated upon minors, those with learning disabilities, or others who lack the competence to give a valid consent, it should proceed only if it is in the subject's interests and the benefits substantially outweigh any potential harm. The question as to whether parents have the right to consent to non-therapeutic research on their children is discussed in Chapter 13. At present, no one can give consent to research on behalf of a mentally incapacitated adult. Where there are any risks to the adult, an application to court would probably have to be made. Where there are no risks, the Local Research Ethics Committee should be made aware of the lack of mental capacity of the research subjects. Failure to obtain consent to research or to give the necessary information could render the researcher liable to action. The Human Fertilisation and Embryology Act 1990 prevents research taking place on an embryo after the first 14 days from fertilisation, nor can a human embryo be placed in a non-human animal, nor the nucleus of a cell of an embryo be replaced. In 1999, the government announced that it was to issue new guidelines that would ban doctors from doing genetic research on human tissue unless they get the specific consent of the family of their donor first. The guidelines would be enforced by the Medical Research Council. New guidance was considered necessary as the result of the scandal at Bristol Royal Infirmary when, during an inquiry into allegations of professional misconduct in carrying out paediatric heart surgery, it was learnt that more than 11,000 children who had died in the past 40 years had had their organs used for research in British hospitals without the explicit consent of their parents. (See page 359)

Liability for volunteers in research

Situation 18.5 *Guinea-pig*

Benjamin Robinson was a medical student who was very short of money because he sent part of his grant home to his family each week. He heard of a research project being undertaken in the pharmaceutical department and offered his services. Because he was anxious to be accepted, he failed to tell the medical officer in charge of the research that he had suffered from glandular fever as a child. He subsequently took drugs to test out the toxicity of a drug for migraine. A few weeks later, he had a heart attack and died. Is there any liability for his death by the NHS Trust and/or the research team?

At present there is no law that the volunteer should automatically obtain compensation for harm that occurs as a result of the research participation. The Pearson Report of 1978[9] recommended that volunteers in medical research should be compensated on a no-fault basis, but this has not been implemented through legislation. At present, the Association of the British Pharmaceutical Industry (ABPI) has prepared guidelines for the provision of compensation to victims of research and supports through a written agreement with each research subject that any subjects who have been harmed as a result of participation in a drugs trial will be compensated on a strict liability basis without proof of negligence. This is a voluntary agreement, but would normally be a part of the protocol of the research project approved by the local research ethics committee. Apart from this scheme, as the law stands at present, the volunteer who is harmed as a result of participation in a research project can obtain compensation only on the basis of negligence, i.e. he must establish that a duty of care was owed to him; this has been broken and as a reasonably foreseeable result of this breach the subject has suffered some harm.

Applying these principles here, it is hoped that the pharmaceutical company undertaking the research would compensate Benjamin's family on a strict liability basis. If the pharmaceutical company failed to pay up, then the family would have to show that in one way or another the researchers were negligent. For example, the researchers failed to give Benjamin a proper medical examination or the design of the research was faulty and foreseeably dangerous to the volunteers. There is little evidence of that here and, in addition, Benjamin, by concealing his previous illness, would have been contributorily negligent and therefore considered to a certain extent to be responsible for what happened.

It is possible that if it can be established that Benjamin was harmed as the result of a defect in a product, then the Consumer Protection Act 1987 applies and Benjamin's family can obtain compensation under these provisions against the producer or supplier. This is considered at greater length in Chapter 12. Much of the debate on liability would hinge upon whether at the time of production the producer should have realised that there was a defect in the product.

Another possible defence against such a claim is the possibility of alleging that Benjamin, by volunteering willingly, assumed the risks of such an event occurring. This is known as the defence of *volenti non fit injuria* and is explained in more detail in Chapter 6. In order to rely on this as a defence, it would have to be shown not only that Benjamin knew of the risks, but also that he consented willingly to run them and agreed to waive all claim for compensation as a result.

Fraud in research

There is a danger that the pressure to undertake research and provide significant results could lead to fraudulent research practices. For example, it was discovered that a cancer specialist had fabricated the results of his research into the efficacy of a chemotherapy drug.[10] Failure by a practitioner registered with the UKCC to follow sound and honest research principles could be defined as professional misconduct and lead to her being struck off the register.

Health and safety of the researcher

Exactly the same principles of health and safety apply to the researcher as apply to other employees, i.e. the employer owes a duty of care at common law to ensure that they are provided with a safe environment, a safe system of work and competent staff. Where the researchers are not employees, the occupier of the premises on which they are working would still be expected to uphold the duty of care for their safety under the Occupiers' Liability Act 1957. It could be, however, that as specialists they would be expected to be aware of those risks which arise from their particular tasks, and the NHS Trust would not be liable for harm resulting from that. The provisions of the Health and Safety at Work Act 1974 would also apply (see Chapter 12).

Conclusions

Recent cases and the Human Rights Act 1998 suggest that the nurse tutor and the nurse involved in research is more likely to be facing legal scrutiny about her practice. There will be increasing pressure by the public for open and robust guidelines to protect the rights of the patient in the conduct of research. In addition, the NHS Plan and its recommendations for a substantial increase in the numbers of UKCC registered practitioners will increase the pressure on nurse lecturers to provide pre-registration training for nurses. PREP requirements dictate that to remain on the register, the nurse must have at least 5 days of training and development every three years and post registration tutors can therefore be expected to come under increasing pressure.

Questions and exercises

1 How could a nurse tutor defend herself if a nurse who is accused of causing harm to the patient blamed the teaching that she had received in the nurse training college?

2 What records do you currently keep on your teaching programmes? Review the period for which you keep them and their content in the light of this chapter.

3 What records do you keep in respect of external lecturers who are invited to teach in your department? How would you defend a case where an employee was suing for back injury and the manual handling training was carried out in your department?

4 In what ways does co-operation exist between the nurse training school and the wards and departments to ensure that the nurse's training meets the standards of approved accepted practice?

5 Prepare a procedure for initiating a research proposal, for obtaining the necessary approvals, for envisaging any possible difficulties in carrying it out, and for publishing the results.

References

[1] UKCC Standards for the preparation of teachers of nursing, midwifery and health visiting UKCC March 2000

[2] UKCC Requirements for pre-registration nursing programmes Registrar's letter 17/2000 UKCC May 2000

[3] Clothier Report, The Allitt Inquiry An independent inquiry relating to deaths and injuries on the children's ward at Grantham and Kesteven General Hospital during the period February to April 1991.HMSO 1994

[4] Department of Health, Guidance for Local Research Ethics Committees. DoH 1991 (HSG(91)5)

[5] B Dimond, Legal issues chapter 9 in Nursing Research an ethical and legal appraisal edited by Louise de Raeve Bailliere Tindall March 1996

[6] Department of Health, Guidance for Local Research Ethics Committees. DoH 1991 (HSG(91)5); Department of Health, Standards for Local Research Ethics Committees: A framework for ethical review. DoH 1994

[7] General Medical Council Confidentiality GMC London 1995

[8] *In re D* v. *NSPCC* 1977 1 All ER 589

[9] Report of the Royal Commission on Civil Liberty and Compensation for Personal Injury Cmnd 7054 London HMSO 1978

[10] Lois Rogers, Cancer 'cure' doctor admits bogus research, *The Sunday Times* 13 February 2000.

19 Legal aspects of the care of the elderly

It is a truism that every elderly person is different. The fact that a person is over 60 or 70 or 80 or 90 says absolutely nothing else about them. Standards of health, loneliness, housing, finance, mobility and capability are as varied as with any other age group. All that can be said of them as a group is that it is more likely than not that they will be faced with some problems – social, economic, health or others – and that these are more likely to be multiple problems, interrelated, with one triggering off another. For example, it might be that an old person living on his own has limited mobility, and therefore finds it difficult to get to the shops. He thus does not feed himself properly and comes under the hospital's care as a result of lack of proper nourishment. It is equally true that in itself there are no basic principles of law purely for elderly patients. All that has been said of the general principles of negligence and vicarious liability applies equally to the nurse who cares for the elderly. Discrimination issues may also arise in the care of the elderly from black and minority ethnic communities and these must also be addressed.[1] However, there are particular difficulties that the nurse who cares for the elderly is more likely to encounter than other nurses and it is to these that we now turn. In this section, particular attention will be paid to the issues illustrated in Figure 19.1.

There are, in addition, problems relating to the property and possessions of the elderly and these will be dealt with in Chapter 25. In Chapter 29, there is a discussion on the law relating to the making of wills and other aspects of dealing with death. Those nurses who care for the elderly in the community should refer to Chapter 23 for coverage of that topic. Those caring for elderly mentally infirm should refer to chapter 20.

1. Rights to care.
2. Consent to treatment.
3. Force, restraint and assault.
4. Medication and the confused elderly patient.
5. Multi-disciplinary care.
6. Standard of care.
7. Abuse of the elderly.
8. Long term funding of elderly care.
9. Filling the vacuum.

Figure 19.1 Issues covered in Chapter 19.

Rights to care

There are no laws that set a cut-off point at which interventions for the elderly are not justified. In the past, for example, there have been occasions where ambulances have been told to take patients over 65 to a ward for the elderly rather than to a coronary care unit; where a non-resuscitation policy has been based on the age of the patient rather than their physical condition and prognosis; where they have been refused surgical treatment because of their age. Such discrimination has no legal basis. There are in law no age limits for accessing treatment. The only criteria are the prognosis of the patient and the extent to which further investment in their health is justified in terms of the benefit that it would bring to that individual. Age Concern and other charities for the elderly are constantly bringing to the government's attention the need for an Age Discrimination Act that would give an elderly person a right not to be discriminated against on the basis of age. Whilst several private members have introduced Bills for Age Discrimination (one in 1996 and another in 1998), at the time of writing such legislation has not been enacted. An EU directive in December 2000 is expected to require all member states to introduce legislation prohibiting age discrimination.

In the absence of such legislation, if treatment were refused on the ground of age alone, then that patient could seek judicial review of the refusal. In addition, since 2 October 2000, the patient has the right to bring an action in the courts of this country and seek a ruling under the Human Rights Act 1998 as to whether such a refusal constituted a violation of his rights under Article 2 (right to life) or Article 3 (no torture or degrading or inhuman treatment or punishment) or Article 14 against discrimination (see Chapter 1 and Appendix A). The NHS Plan (see Chapter 5) stated that it is the government's intention to prevent age discrimination in health care. A National Service framework (NSF) that will set clear standards for the services that older people use, including those for stroke, falls, and mental health problems, is to be published at the end of 2000.

> The NSF will ensure that ageism is not tolerated in the NHS, with the elimination of any arbitrary policies based on age alone . . .
>
> All organisations will be required to establish and implement local resuscitation policies based on guidelines published by the BMA, RCN and Resuscitation Council (UK) and to include compliance with these policies in their clinical audit programme. The Commission for Health Improvement will assess progress with its clinical governance reviews.

(The NSF on the care of the elderly was published in March 2001, see Reference 25 on page 396.)
(See chapter 16 on the legal issues in resuscitation.)

Consent to treatment

In Situation 19.1 a relative, apart from the parent of a minor under 18, does not have the power in law to give consent on behalf of a patient. For example, what if

Gwen refused, not because she felt that it was not in Amy's best interest to have the operation, but because as the only child she would inherit Amy's possessions and she had built up considerable debts while caring for her son with learning disabilities? On the other hand, if the doctor goes ahead and operates without any consent and Amy does not survive the operation, is there any danger that the relatives would hold him responsible since a person of that age should not have been compelled to have an operation of this type?

Situation 19.1   An operation at 90?

Amy Ash was admitted to a long-stay geriatric hospital because she had reached the stage where she could not care for herself. Her daughter was unable to look after her as she was coping with her son who had learning disabilities. Amy was intermittently competent. There were days when she recognised Gwen, her daughter, and others where she did not, but instead abused Gwen when she came to visit her. She had been complaining increasingly of a pain in her chest. The ward sister arranged for the physician to see her and he diagnosed a hiatus hernia. There was considerable debate over the best method of treatment. Initially, a strict diet and medication were proposed, but there were signs that this was not working when Amy started bleeding internally. The physician asked Gwen to come in and see him to talk about Amy's future care. He said that possibly the only long-term course of treatment was an operation. However, at Amy's age there were considerable risks in undertaking this. Although she was in a reasonably good state of health, she might not withstand the operation. Gwen was in a dilemma, not knowing whether to sign the form of consent on Amy's behalf. She attempted to explain the position to Amy. Amy grasped the fact that she would have to have an operation. She made it clear to Gwen that she had had a good life and did not want to be cut open now. Gwen also spoke to the ward sister who explained that Amy was in very good health and would probably survive the operation, but, of course, one could not be 100 per cent sure. What should Gwen do?

The first question that arises is, of course, Amy's mental capability. It could well be that in her saner moments she is fully capable of understanding what is happening to her and of giving a valid consent or refusal. At other times, she may well be far removed from reality. If the doctor obtains her signature on a form consenting to the operation in one of these sane spells, can he rely on it when she becomes insane? The answer is probably yes. Supervening incapacity does not make a valid contract invalid provided the party had the capacity to contract at the time she agreed to the contract. While a consent form is not a contract, similar principles on capacity may prevail. It is essential, however, that only a reasonable time elapses between the signing of the form and the operation being carried out, and the operation must clearly be in the interests of the patient. What is reasonable? Certainly not as long as a year, but possibly up to three months. It depends upon the operation to be performed and whether the circumstances remain exactly as they were when the patient signed the form.

If Amy is incapable of signing the form at any time, it could be argued that although it would be wise to discuss all the various options with Gwen to ascertain where Amy's best interests lie, in the last resort it must be the doctor's decision to decide clinically if the operation should proceed. In reaching his decision, the doctor may well discuss Amy's standard of health and prognosis with the nurses. Ultimately, therefore, given this vacuum in the law and the inability of the relative to give a valid consent, the doctor can do only what he considers to be in her best interests. In a case such as Amy's, the relative would be consulted over what would be the best action, but in the ultimate resort the relative does not have the power of consent or of refusal to consent.

The government has put forward proposals for decision making on behalf of mentally incapacitated adults covering such circumstances as those of Amy.[2] At the time of writing, legislation is awaited. When these proposals are enacted, there will be clear decision-making powers given to persons for day-to-day decisions. More serious decisions would be referred to special courts. Had Amy, when mentally capacitated, made a living will or advance directive to cover such a situation, then that would have been binding on health professionals.

The Law Commission has recommended laws recognising advance directives for treatment (see Chapter 16, page 353).

Force, restraint and assault

Caring for confused elderly patients raises concerns about what action can be taken in fulfilment of the duty of care, when treatment is being refused contrary to the best interests of the patient or when they are at risk of harm and need to be restrained. Guidance is provided by the RCN on restraint and the care of the elderly.[3] Anyone using restraint of any sort must ensure that their actions are compatible with Article 3 of the Human Rights Convention which is discussed in Chapter 1 and can be found in Appendix A.

Restless patients

Situation 19.2   The wanderer

One further difficulty that the staff had with Amy (described in situation 19.1) was that she could never stay in one place. She always liked to be on the move. Her restlessness took her all round the hospital where she was well known and those with time on their hands would eventually bring her back to the ward. Unfortunately, building work started on site and the contractors were asked to take special care in crossing hospital roads. The nursing officer instructed Amy's ward sister to keep her on the ward because of the danger. The ward sister could not be sure that someone was always available to keep an eye on Amy and, rather than lock the ward door and imprison all the patients, she decided to use a restrainer on Amy so that every time Amy tried to get out of her chair a belt, which was fastened around Amy and to the chair, rang a bell and prevented Amy from leaving the chair. Gwen visited Amy and was distressed to see this form of restraint; Amy herself protested about it. What is the legal position?

To restrict a person's movement without lawful authority so that they have no way of escape is a form of false imprisonment. This effectively is what Amy is – imprisoned. Is there any legal justification? Temporary restraint, which was reasonable, could possibly be justified if it were on the grounds of preventing another person being injured by Amy or to prevent Amy harming herself. This is on the basis of the common law power to act in an emergency out of necessity in the best interests of a mentally incapable person.[4] However, the form of restraint used by the ward sister is clearly not temporary nor is it reasonable. What alternatives are available to the ward staff, given that they have a duty to care for Amy and to prevent her exposure to danger? Adequate staffing to keep an eye on each person is obviously one possibility, but given present-day economic constraints and nurse staffing levels it may not be a realistic option. Another possibility is the use of more volunteers to supervise certain patients. One suggestion is to change the locks so that it takes some ingenuity to open the door without the help of the ward staff, though this is not a happy compromise. Electronic tagging devices are also used, so that if a patient wearing such a device goes through an exit, then a bell warns the staff. Even if there are no contractors on site, there may be other dangers such as a main road nearby, a stream in the grounds, etc. The Royal College of Nursing has issued a booklet on the use of restraint in the care of older people. Reference should also be made to publications of the Social Services Inspectorate, such as 'No Longer Afraid'.[5] If unreasonable methods of restraint are used, this could be a violation of their Human Rights as set out in Article 3:

> No one shall be subjected to torture or to inhuman or degrading treatment or punishment.

Where staff consider that some form of restraint is necessary in order to control very aggressive elderly patients, they should obtain advice on whether detention under Mental Health legislation is appropriate, since powers of restraint could then be used lawfully and at the same time protection be given to the patient and also to the staff who would be working within their statutory powers (see chapter 20).

Control at night

At night, cot sides are often used to prevent patients climbing or falling out of bed. In one sense, where the elderly person is clearly struggling against them, these represent a form of restraint. On the other hand, they may in some circumstances be justified and indeed necessary where the patient is very confused and restless. Failure to use them might lead to action against the authority for failing in its duty of care for the patient. However, the potential danger of the patient trying to climb over the cot sides and causing himself harm must always be borne in mind. A risk assessment has to be carried out on whether the use of cot sides in each individual situation is justified. Records should be kept of this risk assessment.

Daily care

Situation 19.3 *Chiropody case*

One form of treatment that Amy could not tolerate was having her toenails cut. She was abusive to the pediatrist who found it very difficult to keep her nails in reasonable order. The pediatrist asked the ward sister if she would hold Amy down while she attempted to cut her nails. The ward sister was not happy with this suggestion and felt that they should first seek medical guidance as it might be preferable to cut the nails when Amy was mildly sedated. What is the legal position?

Chapter 7 discusses consent to treatment where it is stated that touching another person without their consent or some other lawful authority is a trespass to their person. Does the fact that Amy needs to have her toenails done constitute lawful authority? The answer to this is, in general, no. However, the fact that Amy lacks the capacity to give a valid consent may well justify the professionals taking some action to care for her. As has been seen earlier, professionals are justified in taking care of a patient in an emergency out of necessity to save his life. This is quite clear if the patient is unconscious. However, in considering chiropody, we are not talking of something that is, at least initially (though it may well be ultimately), a life-saving procedure. In addition, there are numerous nursing tasks and social tasks such as bathing, hairwashing and brushing to which patients like Amy may well object. In theory, of course, to brush Amy's hair without her consent is a trespass to her person. There may be occasions when Amy can be persuaded to have it done and will not struggle against it. However, inevitably, there may come a time when Amy needs to have something done despite her protests. In such cases, it is possible that reasonable force could be used provided it is justifiable in her interests. Under the Mental Health Act 1983, treatment can be imposed only for mental disorder on long-term detained patients. Proposals have been put forward for reform of the Mental Health Act 1983[6] and the Law Commission is considering the wider issue of decision making on behalf of mentally incapacitated adults. This is considered below. The House of Lords in *In re F*[7] (see Chapter 7) recognised the duty of a professional to care for an adult who was incapable of making decisions. It is not clear how far this would justify force and restraint. In extreme cases, some form of sedation may be justified in order to assist a patient to receive necessary care and treatment, though this must be closely monitored. Refer also to the following chapter on caring for the psychiatric patient and also Chapter 23 on the compulsory removal of patients from the community to a place of safety.

Medication and the confused elderly patient

The above principles apply equally to the administration of medication. The majority of patients in psychiatric hospitals are on some form of medication, but only a few of them are under a section (about 5 per cent). There are many occasions when, through a variety of reasons ranging from justifiable ones to pure cussedness or confusion, they reject the tablets, injections or liquid. What does the nurse do? Obviously, where the patient is capable of making that decision, his refusal should be respected. But this is rarely the case. Often the patient is in Amy's situation: intermittently or permanently confused and mentally infirm. It would be an abuse of the Mental Health Act to place all such patients under its compulsory provisions. Yet there is at present no interim legal stage between providing treatment under the Part 4 provisions of the Mental Health Act or providing life-saving treatment in an emergency and allowing the patient to make the decision. We have no system of guardianship where a guardian has the power of giving a proxy consent on behalf of the patient and, as explained above, the relative does not have this power for anyone of 18 or over. In this vacuum, the only advice that can be given to nursing staff is: ensure that the medication is essential and in the patient's interests; that the patient is incompetent to refuse; use all possible means to ensure that the patient will take it willingly, considering the use of force only in the most extreme cases and even then only after discussion with the psychiatrist, the social worker and the nearest relative as to whether detention under the Mental Health Act would be in the patient's best interests (see Chapter 20). The Law Commission's proposals are discussed below.

Medication may sometimes be used as a form of restraint. There are considerable dangers in so doing and the practice may be declared illegal under Article 3 of the Human Rights Convention (see Chapter 1 and Appendix A) on the grounds that it is degrading or inhuman treatment. A line has to be drawn between medication that is in the best interests of a mentally incompetent patient (and could therefore be given under the *Re F* principle[8] (see above)) and medication that is for other purposes. The latter would be unlawful.

Multi-disciplinary care and the elderly

Many health and social services professionals are involved in the care of the elderly and liaison across the organisational divide of health and social services is essential in order to ensure that a high standard of care is provided. The Audit Commission recommended innovative practice and close communication in preventing bed blocking and poor standards of care in its report 'The Coming of Age'[9] and in a recent report it has made strong recommendations on the care of the confused elderly.[10] In this latter report, it emphasises the range of services that those suffering from dementia require and the need for health and social services to work closely together to make the best use of available resources. The NHS Plan[11] (see Chapter 15 of the NHS Plan) has recommended closer co-operation between health and social services in order to ensure that patients are not blocking hospital beds because of a lack of funds held by social services. Its recommendations include: by April 2002, a single assessment process for health and social care, with protocols to be agreed locally between health and social services; each older patient and where appropriate their carers will be involved in agreeing a personal care plan; Care Direct will be established to provide a faster access to care, advice and support. This new service will provide information and advice about health, social care, housing, pensions and benefits by telephone, drop-in centres, on-line and through outreach services. Chapter 7 of the NHS Plan envisages the establishment of a new level of Primary Care Trusts which will provide for closer integration of health and social services. These bodies will be known as Care Trusts and will be able to commission and deliver primary and community health care as well as social care for older people and other client groups (see Chapter 23).

Standard of care

Situation 19.4 *An unknown break*

Fred, an elderly patient recovering from an orthopaedic operation, was occasionally restless in the night. On one such occasion, he fell out of bed. The night sister rushed to his aid and with the help of the other night nurses, she put him back in bed. Fred appeared none the worse, was happy to have a cup of tea, and then he settled down. The next morning, the night sister was about to mention to the day shift that Fred had had a disturbed night, but did not give them the details as they were distracted by a patient with a query. A few days later, Fred was seen to be avoiding putting any weight on his left leg. He was examined, sent for X-ray and a fracture diagnosed. His son asked how this had happened. However, no one could recall any incident in the day and the night staff had not entered the earlier incident in the records or reported an accident. An investigation was then initiated.

Even if the night nurse considered on reasonable grounds that there was no need to call the doctor out in the night, her failure to ensure that the incident was reported to the doctor on the following morning and her failure to arrange for a doctor to examine Fred was clearly not in accordance with approved practice. In addition, she failed to give to the day staff a full account of the night's events so that they were unable to ensure that the appropriate action was taken. The night sister compounded these omissions by failing to fill in an accident report. Unless there are any other mitigating factors in an incident like this, Fred would undoubtedly have a possible claim for compensation against the night nurse and therefore against the NHS Trust for its vicarious liability for their employee. Compensation is unlikely to amount to very much, since it would cover only the additional days of pain and suffering because the fracture had not been diagnosed earlier (unless, of course, the nurses were negligent in failing to put cot sides up and prevent the original fall). However, if it is discovered that those few days' delay have had considerable effects on the long-term prospects for Fred's recovery, then, clearly, compensation would be greater. The night sister would obviously face disciplinary proceedings and also professional conduct investigations.

Abuse of the elderly

Research suggests that abuse of elderly persons, or other vulnerable persons, is a significant issue. Claudine McCreadie of the Institute of Gerontology has published an extensive analysis of current research[12] on elder abuse that should be essential reading for every health professional caring for the elderly. She concludes that the term 'elder abuse' covers a diversity of situations; that the extent of the problems is still unknown, but sufficient to make the case for a service response; that research and training are essential; and she points to the danger that older people who are being abused will fall between existing service provisions and their needs will remain unaddressed unless action is taken.

More recently, information has come to light on the extent of financial abuse and exploitation. Ginny Jenkins, Director of Action on Elder Abuse, stated that it is estimated that one in ten of those granted powers under Enduring Powers of Attorney abuses the trust.[13]

Who is being abused?

A report by the Social Services Inspectorate of the Department of Health[14] in 1992 showed that in the two London boroughs that participated in the field work in 1990, most of the abused people were female and over half were aged 81 years or more. Frequently the abuse came from a close member of the family. In most cases, the abuser was the principal carer of the elderly person. Physical abuse was by far the most frequently mentioned form of abuse, but half the cases involved more than one type of abuse. Most of the abused people were already known to the social services department, and half the cases came to the attention of the social services departments through contact with social workers or other direct service providers. The rate of 'self-disclosure' of abuse was low. Requests for help were often 'masked' rather than direct. In a high proportion of cases, abuse was long standing. Policies for the management of elder abuse had not been developed. Field staff were working without departmental guidelines for the management of cases of elder abuse and they felt unsupported and indicated that they would appreciate a structure within which to work. They also said they would appreciate training in defining elder abuse, in skills to confront the abuse and in strategies for intervention.

Following the 1992 report on elder abuse, guidelines were issued in 1993 by the Social Services Inspectorate to local authorities to identify and take appropriate action.[15] 'No Longer Afraid: the safeguard of older people in domestic settings' gives practical guidelines where abuse of elderly people in domestic settings is suspected, alleged or confirmed. It recommended that local authorities should have a policy statement relating to older people which includes a policy on the management of abuse of older people including financial abuse. Social Services Departments, housing departments, legal departments, the police, the health authorities (both purchasers and providers), the voluntary and private sector should all cooperate in the formulation of policies and the development of a strategy for implementation.

Code of Practice

A steering group has been established by the Department of Health, under the chairmanship of Peter Dunn, to develop a Code of Practice for local authorities to use in protecting the elderly from abuse. The intention is that local authorities should have in place a procedure to be followed where there are concerns that an elderly person may be subject to abuse. Community nurses should obtain a copy of their local Code of Practice if they have reason to fear that one of their patients is subject to abuse, whether physical, sexual, emotional or financial.

'Action on Elder Abuse' has been established at the Age Concern headquarters in London and provides a confidential help line and information service. The help line is open to all: relatives, the victims, health and social services professionals, and others who have cause for concern. A community nurse, who has little support from her local authority in terms of guidance, would be able to secure practical help and advice from this organisation.[16] Box 19.1 sets out the steps that a community nurse should follow.

Box 19.1

Guidelines for action in elderly abuse.

1. Find out if the local authority has a procedure for the protection of vulnerable adults where abuse is suspected. If so, follow this procedure. Ensure you document your concerns and action.

2. In the absence of a procedure, seek the advice and guidance of senior management and the help line run by Action on Elder Abuse.

3. Keep clear records of the facts on which your suspicions are based.

4. Check if the circumstances set out in Section 47 of the National Assistance Act 1948 or Section 135(1) of the Mental Health Act 1983 (see Chapter 20) appear to be present.

5. Report your concerns to the appropriate social worker, suggesting, if appropriate, a community care assessment under Section 47 of the N.H.S. and Community Care Act 1990.

6. Ensure that the patient's general practitioner is also notified of your concerns.

Long term funding of care of the elderly

'With Respect to Old Age',[17] the Royal Commission Report on the elderly made radical recommendations for the future care of the elderly. It suggested that 'the costs of long-term care should be split between living costs, housing costs and personal care. Personal care should be available after assessment, according to need and paid for from general taxation; the rest should be subject to a co-payment according to means.' A minority of two members of the Royal Commission, in a note of dissent, stated that they could not support the majority view that personal care should be provided free of charge, paid for from general taxation, on the basis of need. The government did not accept the Royal Commission's recommendation that personal care should be met from public funds, although it made various recommendations to reduce the hardship of means tested payment of fees. In the NHS Plan,[18] it stated in paragraph 15.18:

- from April 2001: for the first three months from admission to residential and nursing home care, the value of a person's home will be disregarded from the means testing rules. This will give people a breathing space in which to consider their position and allow the possibility of a return home. This will benefit around 30,000 people each year.

- From October 2001 subject to a decision in Parliament, nursing care provided in nursing homes will be fully funded by the NHS. People should not be asked to contribute towards the costs of their nursing care.

It was estimated that this latter proposal will save up to £5,000 for a year's stay in a nursing home and benefit about 35,000 people at any one time. The government did not support the majority recommendation that personal care should also be free, pointing out (para.15.20) that personal care has never been free and has been means tested by social services since 1948. At the time of writing the government is revising its plans to fund nursing care costs.

The Royal Commission also recommended that a National Care Commission should be set up to monitor trends, including demography and spending, to ensure transparency and accountability in the system, to represent the interests of consumers, and set national benchmarks, now and in the future. The Care Standards Act 2000 sets out a new framework for regulation of the independent health care sector and most social care. A National Care Standards Commission is being established.

Court decisions concerning the assessment of means tested payments for nursing and residential care homes and community care are considered in Chapter 23.

In December 1997, the UKCC published a policy paper on the continuing care of older people.[19] Amongst its recommendations are that: the UKCC should recognise that the central features of the nursing role in continuing care are holistic assessment, health promotion and the ability to work in multi-professional partnership with clients, their carers and other agencies; that specialist practitioners, in particular community nurses and health visitors, be actively involved in all continuing care settings; and community nurses and health visitors have a key role in the assessment of older people for continuing care services and in ongoing assessment and review following placement.

Filling the vacuum on decision making for the mentally incapacitated adult

At present, there is a vacuum in law in that no relative or professional has a legal right to give consent to treatment on behalf of a mentally incompetent adult. The House of Lords decision on *In re F*[20] enables a professional to act in the best interests of the patients according to the approved accepted standard of care (i.e. the Bolam Test) in the absence of consent. However, where major surgery or treatment is contemplated (e.g. sterilisation), reference to the courts is required. The Law Commission in 1991 issued a Consultation Paper on Decision Making and the Mentally Incapacitated Adult.[21] Following feedback, three further papers were published covering private and public law issues and treatment decisions. The Commission recommended that legislation covering advance directives should be passed in order to clarify their validity, formation, revocation and status. It also recommended that there should be a statutory power to treat those who lack the mental capacity to make their own decisions. Its proposals were considered by the House of Lords Select Committee on Medical Ethics (1994). The Law Commission published in 1995 its final proposals for decision making on behalf of the mentally incapacitated adult.[22] Subsequently, the Lord Chancellor published a consultation paper[23] and proposals were put forward by the government.[24] These proposals envisage that there will be legislation to provide for a general authority to act reasonably in the best interests of the mentally incapacitated adult; to provide for a continuing power of attorney which can include the power to make decisions on treatment and care; and for a reorganised court of protection that will be able to appoint a manager to deal with personal welfare or health care issues on behalf of the mentally incapacitated adult. Draft legislation to bring these proposals into force is awaited at the time of writing.

The future

Major changes are likely to occur in the care of the elderly as the result of the government's proposals in the NHS Plan that social services and the NHS will come together with new agreements to pool resources, and the introduction of new care teams to commission health and social care in a single organisation; and as a result of the National Care Standards Commission. In November 2000, the government announced the appointment of a National Director of Older People's Services with a remit to stamp out any signs of ageism in the NHS as part of the overall plan to modernise services for older people. The appointee, Professor Ian Philip, stated that his three priorities were:

1. to make sure that everyone, regardless of age, has fair access to services and receives treatment on the basis of need;

2. to treat each older person as individual with their own specific and often complex needs; and

3. to ensure that there is an integrated approach where agencies work together rather than separately, to provide the highest levels of care.

Nurses caring for the elderly will without doubt share these principles and will benefit from the existence of a National Director with these responsibilities.

In March 2001, the Department of Health published its National Service Framework[25] for the care of older people, which will be supported by £120 million investment over the following three years. (This is in addition to the £1.4 billion by 2003 for health and social services for older people detailed in the NHS Plan.)

The NSF sets national standards to improve the quality of care for older people in the following areas:

1. rooting out age discrimination;
2. person centred care;
3. intermediate care;
4. general hospital care;
5. stroke;
6. falls;
7. mental health in older people;
8. promoting an active healthy life.

The implementation of the standards will be monitored by CHI, the Social Services Inspectorate and the National Care Standards Commission.

Reference should also be made to the Report by the Standing Nursing and Midwifery Advisory Committees: 'Caring for Older People: A Nursing Priority'.[26] This considers the role of the nurse in the care of older people in acute settings.

On 20 July 2001 the Department of Health announced publication of a guide on fair access to care services with the aim of securing consistency over the setting of eligibility criteria.[27] (See page 454)

Questions and exercises

1. A crucial factor in the care of the elderly is the extent to which the patient is mentally capable and able to make decisions. Look at the government's proposals on making decisions on behalf of mentally incapacitated adults and determine how the definition of capacity can be applied to your patients.

2. What particular precautions should you take when caring for disturbed elderly patients?

3. To what extent do you consider the nurse should be the advocate for the patient, and to what extent do you think that this role can be left to relatives?

4. Obtain a copy of your NHS Trust's summary of accidents to patients and analyse those relating to elderly patients. To what extent do you consider some of these accidents could have been prevented if different procedures had been adopted by the carers or by the NHS Trust itself?

5. Obtain a copy of the NHS Plan and look critically at the proposals relating to the elderly in Chapter 15. To what extent do you consider the proposals will raise standards for the elderly?

References

1 Royal College of Nursing, The Nursing care of older patients from black and minority ethnic communities RCN 000 860 April 1998
2 Lord Chancellor's Department, Making Decisions LCD 1999
3 Royal College of Nursing, Restraint revisited: rights, risk and responsibility RCN 000 998 October 1999
4 *Re F* (Mental Patient: Sterilisation) [1990] 2 AC 1
5 SSI No Longer Afraid HMSO, 1993
6 Reform of Mental Health Act 1983 Stationery Office 1983 Proposals for consultation Cm 4480 November 1999
7 *Re F* (Mental Patient: Sterilisation) [1990] 2 AC 1
8 *Re F* (Mental Patient: Sterilisation) [1990] 2 AC 1
9 Audit Commission, The Coming of Age Improving care services for elderly people Stationery Office 1997
10 Audit Commission, 'Forget Me Not' Mental Health services for older people Stationery office 2000
11 Department of Health, The NHS Plan: a plan for investment a plan for reform Cm 4818–1 Stationery Office July 2000
12 Claudine McCreadie, Elder Abuse: Update on Research Institute of Gerontology 1996
13 Speaking on Law In Action, BBC Radio 4, 22 October 1998
14 HMSO 1992
15 Social Services Inspectorate (1993), No Longer Afraid: the safeguard of older people in domestic settings. HMSO
16 0800 731 4141
17 Royal Commission, With Respect to Old Age, Stationery Office March 1999
18 Department of Health, NHS Plan CMND 4818–1 July 2000 HMSO
19 Abigail Masterson, UKCC policy paper No 1, The continuing care of older people UKCC London December 1997
20 *Re F* (Mental Patient: Sterilisation) [1990] 2 AC 1
21 The Law Commission Consultation Paper No. 119, 'Decision Making and the Mentally Incapacitated Adult' HMSO 1991
22 Law Commission, Mental Incapacity Report No 231 Stationery Office 1995
23 Lord Chancellor's Office, Who Decides? Stationery Office 1997
24 Lord Chancellor's Office, Making Decisions Stationery Office 1999
25 Department of Health Press release 2001/0151 27 March 2001
26 Standing Nursing and Midwifery Advisory Committees, Caring for Older People: A Nursing Priority, Department of Health March 2001
27 Department of Health Guidance on Fair Access to Care Services, DH 2001.

20 Nursing the mentally disordered

This chapter cannot cover all the law relevant to the nursing of the mentally ill and those with learning disabilities.[1] The intention is to deal with some of the more common dilemmas faced by these nurses through the case study approach, and to include in the diagrams a summary of some of the main points of the Mental Health Act 1983. This Act is the main legislation covering the detention of the mentally disordered and for the most part replaces the Act of 1959 which by the end of the 1970s was seen as failing to protect the rights of the mentally disordered. The Act is currently under review and the government has published proposals for reform. This chapter will cover the areas illustrated by Figure 20.1. Reference should be made to the Code of Practice of the Department of Health on the Mental Health Act which was revised in 1999[2]. The UKCC has provided guidelines for mental health and learning disabilities nursing[3] and also guidance for the nursing, midwifery and health visiting contribution to the continuing care of people with mental health problems.[4]

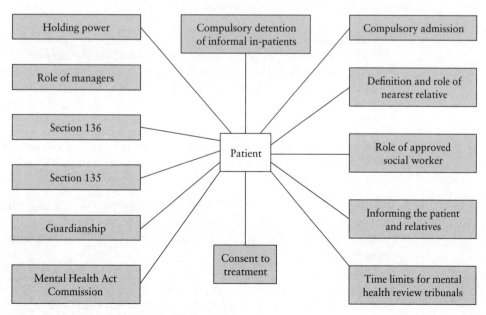

Figure 20.1 Issues covered in Chapter 20.

Informal patients

The vast majority (well over 90%) of patients who are cared for in psychiatric hospitals are not detained. They have either given consent to admission or, if they lack the mental capacity to consent to admission, they are being treated by common law powers recognised by the House of Lords in the *Re F* case[5] (see Chapter 7). The House of Lords in the Bournewood[6] case considered the question of whether a mentally incapacitated person, incapable of giving consent to admission, could be held at common law in a psychiatric hospital and not placed under the Mental Health Act 1983. It decided that Section 131 of the Mental Health Act 1983 did not require a mentally disordered person to have the capacity to consent to admission as an informal patient.

Case 20.1 Lack of capacity to consent to admission

L, an adult with learning disabilities, was informally admitted to a mental health unit. He was not detained under the Mental Health Act 1983. His carers asked for his discharge, but his psychiatrist considered that it was not in his best interests to be discharged and that he should remain in hospital. The carers challenged the legality of this decision. They lost in the High Court, but the Court of Appeal held that Section 131 of the Mental Health Act required a person to have the mental capacity to agree to admission; a person lacking the requisite capacity should be examined for compulsory admission under the Act. The House of Lords upheld the appeal of the NHS Trust, holding that an adult lacking mental capacity could be cared for and detained in a psychiatric hospital, using common law powers.

However, grave concern was expressed at the absence of statutory protection for such patients and the Department of Health stated that the legislative provisions were being reviewed. Such revision is necessary to ensure compliance with the Human Rights Act 1998 (see Chapter 1 and Appendix A). Article 5 of the European Convention of Human Rights which is set out in Schedule 1 in the Human Rights Act 1998 states:

> (1) Everyone has the right to liberty and security of person. No one shall be deprived of his liberty save in the following cases and in accordance with a procedure prescribed by law.

Included in the 'following cases' under (e) are 'persons of unsound mind'. However, the fact that mentally incapacitated adults can under the Bournewood ruling be detained without being placed under the Mental Health Act 1983 would suggest that this is not a procedure prescribed by law.

There is no doubt that to prevent patients leaving the ward when there is no justification in law could give rise to an action for false imprisonment. This is a civil action where the person bringing the action would simply have to show that they have been effectively detained against their will without any lawful justification. They would not be required to show that they had suffered any harm other than the loss of their liberty. In the example given in Situation 20.1, there would appear to be no justification for locking the ward and preventing everyone leaving simply to control Maud. It could therefore be argued that this is a false imprisonment of everyone in the ward. What about Maud? There may be justification in detaining Maud because she is a danger to herself were she to be allowed to wander away. It could perhaps be argued that this is lawful under the emergency provisions at common law discussed above. However, the situation is not clear, especially when what is involved is detention over a long period. The issue is the subject of a discussion document produced by the Mental Health Act Commission in which the Commission suggests that detention outside the powers of the Act should be used only in circumstances that would be justified at common law.

Situation 20.1   Resistance in the elderly (1)

Maud, a frail 85-year-old, was a 'wanderer' and occasionally resisted the efforts of the nursing staff to give her medication. She was an informal in-patient on a psychogeriatric ward. One day she attempted to wander off the ward and, because they were short staffed and could not keep an eye on her all the time, the ward door was locked. A visitor to another patient complained that it was illegal for the door to be locked when the patients were not under section. What is the legal position?

It is not unknown for some wards to cope with the problem of the confused elderly or other groups who need to be detained by arranging the door bolts and locks to be fixed in such a way that, while they are not technically locked, the degree of synchronisation required to open them is such that a confused person could not manage and is effectively locked-in in practice, though not in theory. Advice is given in the revised Code of Practice on the Mental Health Act (DH 1999) on what steps should be taken if informal patients are detained.

Situation 20.2   Resistance in the elderly (2)

On one occasion, Maud made it clear that she would not have her medication which was prescribed as a sedative and for her heart condition. As an informal patient, could she be forced to take the medication since it was for her benefit and she lacked the mental capacity to make a reasoned judgement over whether she should be taking it?

Unfortunately, this is not an uncommon problem for those working in hospitals for the mentally ill and mentally handicapped. Given the comparatively small number of patients who are actually detained and the reluctance to place patients under the detention provisions of the Act (even if they complied with the conditions for compulsory admission, which not all of them would), there are substantial problems for staff in caring for these patients, and ensuring they have the necessary medication and are kept in a place of safety. Many patients are intermittently confused and on occasions lack the mental competence to make rational decisions about their treatment. Can they be forced to have the treatment? The answer, as far as the common law is concerned, is yes, if the treatment is out of necessity and in the best interests of the patient. This is on the basis of the House of Lords decision in *Re F* (1989).[7]

Unfortunately, the problem is exacerbated by staffing difficulties, so that patients can sometimes be given medication that is not clinically indicated in order to control restlessness and aggression. There is certainly no legal justification for giving medication to patients compulsorily on the grounds of staff shortage. The RCN has provided guidance on managing aggression and violence[8] and has also reviewed the use of restraint on the elderly.[9]

It is clear that the present gap that exists in the law in relation to the informal patient and short-term admissions must be filled so that staff know where they stand in regard to the treatment of those who are incapable of making a rational choice but who are not under a detention order. Proposals have been made by the Law Commission and by the government which are discussed on pages 393–4.

Case 20.2   Care of incapable adults at risk of harm[10]

T, an 18-year-old girl with an intellectual age of 5 to 8 years, lacked the capacity to make decisions about her future. The local authority sought to invoke the inherent jurisdiction of the court under the doctrine of necessity to obtain directions as to where T should live and to supervise her contact with her natural family, principally her mother. The mother challenged the power of the court to make such a ruling, on the grounds that its former *parens patriae* jurisdiction had lapsed in 1959. The Court of Appeal held that in the present conflict, where serious questions hung over the future care of T if returned to her mother, there was no practicable alternative to intervention by the court. It was held that it was essential that T's best interests should be considered by the High Court and there was no impediment to the judge hearing the substantive issues involved in the case. Lord Justice Sedley specifically stated that this conclusion did not conflict with the European Convention for the Protection of Human Rights and Fundamental Freedoms[11] (see Appendix A).

Patients detained under mental health legislation

As stated above, only about 5–10% of psychiatric patients are at any one time detained under the Mental Health legislation. The next section gives an account of the main statutory provisions that apply to the detention and treatment of such patients. There are significant proposals for the reform of the Act and these are considered at the end of this chapter.

The holding power

> *Situation 20.3*   *To stop or let go*
>
> Bill Smith, an informal patient in a psychiatric hospital, admitted three weeks ago, wakes up at 3.00 a.m. and starts abusing nursing auxiliary Mavis Jones who is on her own, Staff Nurse Rachel Robinson having just gone for her break. Bill starts throwing furniture around and is threatening to leave the ward. Mavis contacts the night operator and asks for immediate help. What is her legal position in relation to Bill? Rachel Jones returns with a charge nurse. They telephone for the responsible medical officer and are informed that he will not be able to arrive until 9.30 a.m. What are their legal powers?

Figure 20.2 sets out the main points of the holding power of the nurse laid down by Section 5(4) of the Act. As a nursing auxiliary, Mavis is not a prescribed nurse for the purposes of using the holding power under the Mental Health Act. The only nurses designated as prescribed nurses under the Act are those who have been trained in mental illness or mental handicap. She does, however, have the health carer's duty to act in an emergency to save life. She also has the powers of the citizen to effect an arrest on the limited occasions set out in the Police and Criminal Evidence Act. If she feared for the life of Bill were he to be allowed to leave hospital immediately, or for the life of anyone else, she could legally prevent his leaving the ward in an emergency. Rachel Robinson would be regarded as a prescribed nurse if she is a registered nurse under Parts 3, 4, 5, 6, 13 or 14 of the UKCC register.[12] She can exercise the holding power set out under Section 5(4) of the Mental Health Act 1983 if the conditions set out in Figure 20.2 are present.

If all these requirements are present, then Rachel has the power to detain Bill for up to six hours. As soon as the appropriate medical practitioner arrives, however, the holding power will cease.

Rachel must fill in the appropriate forms and ensure that these are taken to the managers of the hospital immediately. Procedures vary: in some hospitals, it is the practice for the hospital manager to be on call for such purposes; in others, this duty is delegated to the nurse manager on duty at night and weekends. If the doctor arrives and decides that Bill should be detained under Section 5(2), then whatever part of

---

1. The patient is receiving treatment for mental disorder.
2. The patient is an in-patient.
3. It appears to the prescribed nurse that the patient is suffering from mental disorder to such a degree that it is necessary for his health or safety or for the protection of others for him to be immediately restrained from leaving the hospital.
4. It is not practicable to secure the immediate attendance of a practitioner who could exercise the powers under Section 5(2).

Figure 20.2   The holding power: Mental Health Act 1983 Section 5(4).

the holding power has elapsed before his arrival will become part of the 72 hours' detention.

From the situation described here, it is apparent that the appropriate doctor will not be able to arrive within the six hours. In this case, it is essential for the doctor to exercise his powers of nomination under Section 5(3) so that another medical practitioner can act as nominee and see Bill at the earliest possibility.

This situation gives rise to other questions. Must Rachel remain with Bill personally even though she is due off duty at 7.30 a.m.? There is no requirement in the Act that Rachel should stay. The fact that Bill is under a holding power should, of course, be made clear to the senior nurse on the shift that takes over from Rachel. In particular, she should be informed of the time of commencement of the holding power and, if a doctor fails to arrive, the time when the holding power is due to end.

What powers does Rachel have in relation to Bill? Could Bill, for example, forcibly be given some medication for which he has been written up? The Act gives Rachel the power to restrain Bill from leaving hospital. She does not have power under the Mental Health Act to compel Bill to have treatment. Informal patients or those who have been placed under short-term detention orders covered by Sections 5(2), 5(4) and Section 4 are specifically excluded from the compulsory treatment provisions of Part IV of the Act. Many feel that it is kinder to control Bill through medication than through physical restraint. There is no power to do this under the Act, however, and any such use of compulsory treatment can be lawfully justified only under the common law powers to act out of necessity. The legality of using them for this purpose is in doubt and practice varies.

What if Bill runs off during the period of the holding power – can he be brought back? Section 18(5), by implication, allows Bill to be brought back as long as the time limit for the holding power has not elapsed. Section 18(1) enables a patient who is absent without leave to be taken into custody and returned to the hospital by any approved social worker, by any officer on the staff of the hospital, by any constable, or by any person authorised in writing by the managers of the hospital.

Could the holding power be used if Bill was an in-patient in a general hospital? From the requirements listed above, it is clear that Bill must be receiving treatment for mental disorder. It is, of course, possible for Bill to be admitted for surgery while still under treatment for a mental disorder and in this case the holding power could be exercised, but only if the nurse had the appropriate registration.

Compulsory detention of an informal in-patient

What would happen in a general hospital if a patient became severely mentally disordered? Temporary emergency measures could be taken to save life: either the life of the patient or of others. In addition, it is possible for any registered medical practitioner in charge of the patient to exercise the powers under Section 5(2).

This section applies to an in-patient in a hospital. There is no requirement that he should be having treatment for mental disorder. The registered medical practitioner in charge of the patient's treatment must consider that an application ought to be made under the Act for the admission of the patient to hospital. He then furnishes the managers with a report to that effect and the patient may then be detained in the hospital for a period of 72 hours from the time the report is furnished. There is no requirement that the practitioner should be a psychiatrist, but the Mental Health Commission has recommended that advice should be sought from a psychiatrist before this power is exercised.

In such circumstances on a general ward, it would also be possible to make use of the powers under Section 4 (see Table 20.1). In this case, it would be necessary for the nearest relative or an approved social worker to make the appropriate application for admission.

Compulsory admission

Table 20.1 sets out the section numbers and requirements for each section that enable compulsory admission to take place and the length of detention. The requirements in relation to the two medical recommendations are set out in Figure 20.3.

---

1. Practitioners must have personally examined the patient either together or separately, but where they have examined the patient separately not more than 5 days must have elapsed between the days on which the separate examinations took place.

2. One of the medical recommendations must be from a practitioner approved by the Secretary of State for such purposes as having experience in the diagnosis or treatment of mental disorder and unless that practitioner has previous acquaintance with the patient, the other practitioner should have, if practicable.

3. One (but not more than one) of the medical recommendations should be given by a practitioner on the staff of the hospital to which the patient is to be admitted.

4. 3 above does not apply, i.e. both medical recommendations can be given by staff of the hospital in question, if
   (a) compliance with 3 above would result in delay involving serious risk to the health and safety of the patient; and
   (b) one of the practitioners works at the hospital for less than half of the time which he is bound by contract to devote to work in the health service; and
   (c) where one of the practitioners is a consultant, the other does not work in a grade in which he is under that consultant's directives.

5. A medical recommendation cannot be given by
   (a) the applicant;
   (b) a partner of the applicant or of a practitioner by whom another medical recommendation is given for admission;
   (c) a person employed as an assistant by the applicant or by any such practitioner;
   (d) a person who receives or has an interest in the receipt of any payments made on account of the maintenance of the patient;
   (e) except as set out in 3 and 4 above a practitioner on the staff of the hospital to which the patient is admitted or by specified relatives of the other practitioner giving the medical recommendation.

6. A general practitioner who is employed part-time in a hospital shall not be regarded as a practitioner on its staff.

These provisions also apply to the two medical recommendations for guardianship.

Figure 20.3 Requirements for the second medical recommendation.

Table 20.1 Compulsory admission provisions

Section	Duration (up to)	Applicant	Medical requirements	Other requirements
4 Emergency admission for assessment	72 hours	Approved social worker or nearest relative	1 recommendation only stating that patient is suffering from mental disorder and stating the provisions of Section 2 exist (see below)	Applicant must have personally seen patient within 24 hours before the application. Admission must be of urgent necessity
2 Admission for assessment	28 days	Approved social worker or nearest relative	2 medical recommendations (a) patient is suffering from mental disorder of a nature or degree which warrants detention in hospital for assessment and (b) he/she ought to be so detained in the interests of his/her own health or safety or with a view to the protection of others.	Applicant must personally have seen patient within the period of 14 days ending with the date of the application
3 Admission for treatment	6 months, renewable for a further 6 months, then for a period of 1 year	Approved social worker or nearest relative	2 medical requirements (a) patient is suffering from mental illness, (severe) mental impairment or psychopathic disorder and his/her mental disorder is of a nature or degree which makes it appropriate for him/her to receive medical treatment in hospital and (b) in the case of psychopathic disorder and mental impairment, such treatment is likely to alleviate or prevent a deterioration of his/her condition and (c) it is necessary for the health or safety of the patient or for the protection of others that he/she should receive such treatment and it cannot be provided unless he/she is detained under this section.	As above under Section 2. Approved social worker must consult with nearest relative before making an application unless this would not be reasonably practicable or would involve unreasonable delay. The application cannot be made if the nearest relative objects
37 Hospital order without restrictions	6 months, renewable for a further 6 months, then for a period of 1 year	Order can be made by Crown Court in case of person convicted of an offence punishable by imprisonment or by magistrates (a) if convicted of offence punishable on summary conviction with imprisonment or (b) if person is suffering from mental illness or severe mental impairment and magistrates are satisfied that he committed the crime	2 doctors required to give oral or written evidence that (a) offender is suffering from mental illness, psychopathic disorder or (severe) mental impairment of a nature or degree which makes it appropriate for him/her to be detained for medical treatment and (b) in the case of psychopathic disorder or mental impairment such treatment is likely to alleviate or prevent a deterioration of his/her condition and (c) the court is of the opinion, having regard to all the circumstances, that the most suitable method of disposing of the case is by means of a hospital order	
41 Restriction order (imposed in conjunction with hospital order Section 37)	For a specified period or without limit of time	Crown Court which has made a hospital order can impose a restriction order. Magistrates Court cannot make a restriction order but can send offender over 14 to Crown Court for a restriction to be made	As for Section 37; at least one of the 2 doctors must give evidence orally before the court.	

The role of the nearest relative

The nearest relative now has an important role to play and has to be given specific information; this task often falls on the nurse. The definition of nearest relative and the hierarchy is given in Figure 20.4. This diagram also illustrates the powers of the nearest relative.

Definition: the highest in the following hierarchy, Section 26(i)

    Relative who ordinarily resides with or cares for the patient
husband or wife
son or daughter
father or mother
brother or sister
grandparent
grandchild
uncle or aunt
nephew or niece

Preference is given in relatives of the same description to the whole blood relation over the half-blood relation and the elder or eldest regardless of sex.

    Husband and wife include a person who is living with the patient as the patient's husband or wife and has been so living for not less than six months. A person other than a relative with whom the patient ordinarily resides for a period of not less than 5 years shall be treated as if he were a relative. However such a person is at the bottom of the above hierarchy.

    Power of nearest relative

1. To apply for the admission of the patient for assessment, for assessment in an emergency, for treatment and for guardianship.

2. To be informed about the approved social worker's application to admit patient for assessment.

3. To be consulted about the approved social worker's proposed application for treatment and to object to it.

4. To be given information about the details of the patient's detention, consent to treatment, rights to apply for discharge, etc. (but subject to the patient's right to object to this information being given).

5. To discharge the patient after giving 72 hours' notice in writing to the managers.

6. To apply to a Mental Health Review Tribunal under Sections 16, 25 and 29.

Figure 20.4 Definition and powers of the nearest relative.

The role of the approved social worker

Table 20.2 sets out the main tasks of the approved social worker. Only social workers who have completed a specified training can be recognised as approved for the purposes of the Act. Whilst the Act allows the nearest relative to be an applicant for compulsory admission under Sections 2, 3, 4, and 7, in practice the applicant is usually the approved social worker and this is the preferred procedure.

Table 20.2 Role of the approved social worker and of any social worker

Duty	Details
Duties of the approved social worker	
Section 11(3) Inform nearest relative of admission of patient and of nearest relative's right to discharge	1. In admission for assessment (Sections 2 and 4) 2. Before or within a reasonable time after an application for admission for assessment is made 3. Such steps as are practicable to inform the person appearing to be the nearest relative
Section 11(4) Consult nearest relative on admission for treatment or guardianship and discontinue application if nearest relative notifies objection	1. Consultation with person appearing to be the nearest relative of the patient 2. Unless it appears that in the circumstances such consultation is not reasonably practicable or would involve unreasonable delay
Section 13(1) To apply for admission or guardianship order if satisfied application ought to be made and is of the opinion that it is necessary or proper for application to be made by him	1. In respect of patient within the area of local social services authority by whom he is appointed 2. Must have regard to wishes expressed by relatives of patient or any other relevant circumstances that are necessary or proper for application to be made by him
Section 13(2) To interview patient in suitable manner and satisfy himself that detention in a hospital is in all the circumstances of the case the most appropriate way of providing the care and medical treatment of which the patient stands in need	1. Before making application for admission to hospital
Section 13(4) To take patient's case into consideration with a view to making an application for admission. If decides *NOT* to make an application he will inform the nearest relative in writing of his reasons.	1. If nearest relative requires local social services authority of area in which patient resides, authority must direct approved social worker as soon as practicable
Duties of any social worker (approved social worker not specified)	
Section 14 To provide report on social circumstances	1. Where patient admitted to hospital an application by nearest relative other than Section 4 2. Managers must as soon as practicable give notice of that fact to local social services authority for area in which patient resided immediately before his admission
Duties of any social worker (approved social worker not specified)	
Section 117 Duty of district health authority and of local social services authority to provide after-care services	1. Applies to patients detained under Section 3 or admitted under hospital order (Section 37) or transferred under transfer direction (Sections 47 or 48) who cease to be detained and leave hospital 2. Authorities must cooperate with relevant voluntary agencies 3. After-care services to be provided until such time as the authorities are satisfied that the person concerned is no longer in need of such services (they shall not be so satisfied if the person is subject to after-care under supervision see page 413)

> The managers of the hospital in which a patient is detained under the Act must:
>
> 1. Take such steps as are practicable to ensure the patient understands:
>   (a) under which provisions of the Act he is for the time being detained and the effect of that provision; and
>   (b) what rights of applying to a Mental Health Review Tribunal are available to him in respect of his detention under that provision;
>   (c) the effect of certain provisions of the Mental Health Act including the Consent to treatment provisions, the role of the Mental Health Act Commission and other provisions relating to the protection of the patient.
> 2. The steps to inform the patient must be taken as soon as practicable after the commencement of the patient's detention under the provision in question.
> 3. The requisite information must be given to the patient in writing and also by word of mouth.

Figure 20.5   Informing the patient: Mental Health Act 1983 Section 132.

Informing the patient

The task of explaining his legal rights to the patient once a detention order has been imposed often falls on the nurse (see Figure 20.5).

Situation 20.4   Information

Edna Johns, an informal patient in a psychiatric hospital, became very disturbed and aggressive in the early hours of the morning, threatening to kill herself and wishing to leave hospital. Staff Nurse Thomas, an RMN, on learning that the responsible medical officer would take at least 30 minutes to arrive on the ward, decided to exercise the holding power under Section 5(4). When the appropriate doctor arrived, he decided to detain Edna under Section 5(2). Within the next 48 hours, the approved social worker applied for admission under Section 3 on the recommendation of Edna's doctor and a second recommendation. What duties exist in relation to informing Edna?

The duties set out under Section 132 are illustrated in Figure 20.5. Forms are available covering the information to be given under each section. Often the nursing staff have the task of giving out the forms and telling the patient about the provisions. It is vital that it is recorded that the patient has been informed since it is a statutory duty and there should be evidence that the statutory duty has been carried out.

In Edna's case, she will have been placed under three separate sections in less than 72 hours. She must be given the relevant information each time the section is imposed and will be given a different form each time. Section 132 requires the information to be given as soon as practicable after the commencement of the section. 'Practicable' must take into account the patient's physical and mental ability to take in what is said. To stand over a screaming, or even unconscious, patient reading him his rights would not seem to be a proper fulfilment of the statutory duty.

Informing the relatives

Where the patient is too disturbed to take in the information, the statutory duty to inform the nearest relative assumes even greater importance. Section 132(4) requires the managers to furnish the person appearing to them to be the patient's nearest relative with a copy of any information given to the patient, in writing, under the duty outlined above. The steps for this must be taken when the information is given to the patient or within a reasonable time thereafter. The patient has the right of veto and can request that this information is not given. Reasonable time here would seem to imply that it is not necessary to phone Edna's relative in the middle of the night to inform them of the exercise of the holding power, but this should be done as soon as possible the next day.

Consent to treatment provisions

See Figures 20.6 and 20.7.

Long-term detained patients

Under the provision of Part IV of the Mental Health Act 1983, those patients who are detained under long-term detention provisions (e.g. Sections 2, 3, 37 and 41) can in certain circumstances be given compulsory treatment. For these patients, the Act covers all possible treatments for mental disorder, both in emergency and non-emergency situations. The provisions are set out in Figure 20.6.

The role of the nurse

What is the role of the nurse in consent to treatment provisions? Under the provisions of Sections 57 and 58, the independent registered medical practitioner, in determining whether the treatment should proceed, must consult with a nurse and another professional who have been professionally concerned with the patient's medical treatment. The independent doctor must record the fact that he has consulted these two persons. Interestingly, however, there is no requirement on the form

---

1. Treatments involving brain surgery or hormonal implants can only be given with the patient's consent which must be certified and only after independent certification of the consent and of the fact that the treatment should proceed (Section 57).

2. Treatments involving electroconvulsive therapy, or medication where 3 months or more have elapsed since medication was first given during that period of detention can only be given either (a) with the consent of the patient and it is certified by the patient's own registered medical practitioner or another registered medical practitioner appointed specifically for that purpose that he is capable of understanding its nature, purpose and likely effects, or (b) the registered medical practitioner appointed specifically certifies that the patient has refused or is incapable of consenting but agrees that the treatment should proceed (Section 58).

3. All other treatments: these can be given without the consent of the patient provided they are for mental disorder and are given by or under the direction of the responsible medical officer (Section 63).

Figure 20.6 Consent to treatment: Mental Health Act 1983 Sections 57, 58 and 63.

These can be given according to the degree of urgency and whether they are irreversible or hazardous. The table below illustrates the provisions.

Any treatment	which is immediately necessary	to save the patient's life
Treatment which is not irreversible	if it is immediately necessary	to prevent serious deterioration
Treatment which is not irreversible or hazardous	if it is immediately necessary	to alleviate serious suffering
Treatment which is not irreversible or hazardous	if it is immediately necessary and represents the minimum interference necessary	to prevent the patient from behaving violently or being a danger to himself or others

Irreversible is defined as 'if it has unfavourable irreversible physical or psychological consequences' and hazardous is defined as 'if it entails significant physical hazard'.

Figure 20.7   Consent to treatment: urgent treatments.

that he should actually record their opinions, so it could well happen that both the nurse and the other professional counselled against, say, ECT, but that the doctor still recommended ECT. A disagreement is unusual, but it is advisable for the nurse, whether there is agreement or not with her views, to ensure that the advice she gave is recorded clearly and comprehensively.

Physical illness

These provisions on consent to treatment would thus appear to cover all eventualities concerning the long-term detained patient. However, there is a gap in relation to treatment for physical illness.

Situation 20.5   *Appendicitis*

Paul, a severely depressed patient, had been detained under Section 3 for two months. One morning, he complained of severe stomach pains. He was sick, with a high temperature. Paul was taken to the 'sick' ward for the treatment of physical illnesses within the mental hospital and was diagnosed as suffering from appendicitis. It was recommended that an operation be performed immediately. When Paul heard this, he immediately said there was no way in which he would agree to the operation. What is the legal position?

If Part IV of the Act is seen as applying only to the treatment of mental illness, then its provisions are irrelevant in these circumstances. Alternatively, it could be argued that if brain surgery can be undertaken under Section 62 to save the life of a patient (and this may cover informal patients, since they are covered by the provisions of Section 57), where the treatment is given for a mental disorder, then the words 'any treatment' in Section 62 can cover not only treatment for mental disorder, but also treatment for physical disorders. If the purpose is to save life, then Section 62(1)(a) covers the situation. This is a logical view, but it has not gained universal acceptance. The alternative is to say that the situation is not covered by Part IV of the Act and that the rules relating to acting in emergency under the common law to save life would apply. This would mean that treatment could be given without the patient's consent as part of the doctor's duty of care to the patient. *In re C 1994* (see page 133, Case 7.3) a Broadmoor patient's refusal to have an amputation was upheld by the court. In the case of *B* v. *Croydon Health Authority*, the Court of Appeal held that compulsory feeding by tube came under Section 63 (TLR 1 December 1994). There have also been several cases where a pregnant woman detained under the Mental Health Act 1983 has been compelled to undergo a caesarean section under Section 63 of the Act.[13] This has been disputed by the Court of Appeal in *Re MB*[14] (see Chapter 14 pages 305–6) It is clear that if a detained patient, suffering from mental disorder, has the mental capacity to understand the proposed treatment and the implications of his or her refusal, then the court would not order the treatment to proceed unless it could clearly be seen to be treatment for the mental disorder and therefore comes within Section 63. If, however, the patient lacks the mental capacity to refuse treatment in his or her best interests, treatment could lawfully be given under common law powers. There are considerable advantages in securing a declaration of the court that it is lawful to provide the treatment.

Short-term detained patients and informal patients

Short-term detained patients and informal patients are not covered by the Part IV treatment provisions of the Mental Health Act. There is only one exception to this: informal patients are specifically covered by the provisions of Section 57 relating to brain surgery and hormonal implants, and by the relevant provisions of Sections 59, 60 and 62. As far as Section 57 is concerned, this means that brain surgery for mental disorder or hormonal implants cannot be given without the safeguards set out above. The short-term detained patient is not explicitly covered, but there would appear to be no reason why he should not receive the same protection.

As far as all other treatments are concerned, one has to look outside the Act for the law relating to consent to treatment and this is set out in Chapter 7. Since only some 5 per cent of mentally ill and mentally handicapped patients are under the detention of the Mental Health Act 1983, the vast majority of patients are outside the basic provisions of the Act and the common law rules relating to trespass to the person and the duty of care to inform the patient, plus the emergency powers of acting in an emergency to save life, apply to them. Where a person is mentally incapacitated, then there is power at common law to act in their best interests (see above).

Community provisions

The philosophy behind the Mental Health Act 1983 is that a patient should be compulsorily detained in hospital only if informal admission is not an option and if alternative services in the community cannot be provided. There are very few community provisions in the 1983 Act except for Guardianship, Section 17 leave, Section 117 aftercare and aftercare under supervision. These will now be discussed.

Guardianship

> ### Situation 20.6   *How much control?*
>
> Paul has been under a guardianship order for three months. He lives with his mother, the guardian, and attends a day centre three times each week. He sees the community psychiatric nurse regularly, both at the centre and also at home, and is on substantial levels of medication. One day, he decides not to take the drugs. His mother pleads with him, but is unable to persuade him to take them. She informs the CPN who also attempts to persuade Paul, but is unsuccessful. His behaviour deteriorates and he becomes more aggressive. His mother asks if there is any way in which he could be compelled to take drugs as she fears that he will ultimately have to be readmitted. Is there a way?

The answer is that the Mental Health Act 1983 excludes from its provisions relating to consent to treatment those patients on guardianship orders. There are three statutory powers in relation to guardianship and these are set out in Figure 20.8.

There are no means of enforcing the guardianship powers over the patient other than the right of returning the patient to the specified place if he absconds. The ultimate sanction is possibly the knowledge that if the patient does not cope in the community, then he is likely to be admitted to hospital. It is not, however, good professional practice to use this as a threat. Apart from gentle professional persuasion, there is no way to force a patient to take drugs. Because of this dilemma, it had been the practice to use Section 3 and keep the patient on a long leash in the community by using the leave of absence provisions under Section 17. Thus, after a short initial admission under Section 3, the patient could be allowed back into the community on condition that he took his drugs, and if he failed to do this then he could be pulled back into hospital where he would remain under the section until he could be trusted to take his drugs in the community. This practice was declared illegal by the court in the Hallstrom case[15] and it was decided that there was no

---

(a)   the power to require the patient to reside at a place specified by the guardian;

(b)   the power to require the patient to attend at places and times specified for the purpose of medical treatment, occupation, education and training; and

(c)   the power to require access to the patient to be given at any place where the patient is residing to any registered medical practitioner, approved social worker or any person specified.

Figure 20.8   Statutory powers of the guardian.

power under Section 3 to do this since a requirement of Section 3 was that the patient was admitted as an in-patient. However the Court of Appeal has overruled the principle set in the Hallstrom case and held that detention can be renewed when the patient is on Section 17 leave, if the patient's treatment taken as a whole also requires an inpatient element. *R. v. Barking Havering and Brentwood Community Healthcare NHS Trust* [1999] 1 FLR 106 CA.

Section 17 leave

A detained patient can be given leave of absence by the responsible medical officer in charge of the patient. The leave does not have to be in writing, but good practice as recommended by the Code of Practice of the Department of Health[16] suggests that there should be a written record of the leave granted and the terms on which it is granted. Section 17 leave can be used as part of the care plan of the patient towards ultimate discharge from the section and from the hospital. Thus a patient on Section 17 leave can be required to stay in residential accommodation. (The patient cannot be charged for residential accommodation he is required to stay in as a condition of Section 17; see below). Section 17 leave can be withdrawn at any time on the written instructions of the RMO. Any nurse responsible for a patient would have to assess the patient prior to leave commencing so that there were no grounds for preventing the leave taking place.

Section 117 Aftercare services

A statutory duty is placed upon the health authority and local authority in conjunction with the voluntary sector to arrange for the provision of aftercare services for the patient. This duty continues until such time as the health and local authority consider that the patient is no longer in need of the services that they can provide. (The duty cannot end if the patient is in under supervised discharge; see below.) The section applies to patients who have been detained under Sections 3, 37, 47 and 48. However, the duty to provide a community care assessment under Section 47 of the National Health Service and Community Care Act 1990 applies to these patients and also to patients detained under other sections of the Act (e.g. Sections 2, 4, 5(2) and 5(4)) and also to informal patients.

The duties under Section 117 cannot be forced upon the patient who may refuse to accept the treatment plan or services provided. This therefore led to concerns that patients were being released from psychiatric care without adequate supervision in the community. The cases of Christopher Clunis and Ben Silcock reinforced these fears. Some local authorities had been charging patients on a means tested basis for residential accommodation provided under Section 117. The Court of Appeal[17] made it clear that where accommodation is provided under Section 117 for a patient, then a local authority may not provide it under Section 21 nor charge for it under Section 22 of the National Assistance Act 1948. Where patients are required to live in residential accommodation under Section 17, then they are entitled to this accommodation as an aftercare service under Section 117 when discharged from detention under the Act and cannot therefore be charged for it.

Aftercare under supervision (Supervised Discharge)

Concern has been expressed that many patients are being discharged prematurely and that there are inadequate powers to care for patients in the community. An earlier suggestion for a power for patients to be given compulsory treatment in the community was discussed in a report of the Royal College of Psychiatrists in 1987. In January 1993, the Royal College of Psychiatrists put forward proposals for a Community Supervision Order. In June 1993, the Health Committee of the House of Commons (session 1992–93) reported on Community Supervision Orders and considered that the RCP's proposals were fundamentally flawed. It recommended instead that the highest priority be given to making fully effective the present statutory and non-statutory provision for the care of people with a mental illness. In August 1993, an internal review, set up by the Department of Health, on legal powers for the care of mentally ill people in the community, recommended changes to the Mental Health Act, including amendments to extend guardianship, remove the time limit on Section 17, provide extended leave and set up supervised discharge arrangements for special categories of chronic patients. The Mental Health (Patients in the Community) Act 1995 saw the introduction of aftercare under supervision, or supervised discharge as it has become known.[18] The power to place patients under aftercare under supervision applies only to patients who are detained under Sections 3, 37 or 47 and 48. It must be applied for whilst the patient is still under section.

The grounds for aftercare under supervision are that:

1. the patient is suffering from a specified form of mental disorder, i.e. mental illness, severe mental impairment, psychopathic disorder, or mental impairment;
2. there would be a substantial risk of serious harm to:
   (a) the health of the patient; or
   (b) the safety of the patient; or
   (c) the safety of other persons; or
   (d) of the patient being seriously exploited if he were not to receive the aftercare services to be provided for him under Section 117 after he leaves hospital; and
3. his being so subject to aftercare under supervision is likely to help secure that he receives the aftercare services to be so provided.

The application is made by the responsible medical officer who must consult with the following:

1. the patient;
2. one or more persons who have been professionally concerned with the patient's medical treatment in hospital;
3. one or more persons who will be professionally concerned with the aftercare services to be provided for the patient under Section 117;
4. any person who, the RMO believes, will play a substantial part in the care of the patient after he leaves hospital, but will not be professionally concerned with any of the aftercare services to be so provided;
5. the person appearing to be the nearest relative.

Aftercare under supervision lasts for six months, but can be renewed if the specified conditions are present. The patient has the right of appeal to a Mental Health Review Tribunal against the imposition of aftercare under supervision. The purpose of the supervision is to ensure that the patient obtains the aftercare services specified under Section 117. Specific requirements can be laid down with which the patient must comply. However, failure to comply does not lead to automatic readmission to psychiatric hospital, but would lead to a review by the multi-disciplinary team over the appropriate action to be taken. A person is nominated as the supervisor of the patient, who together with the named community psychiatrist would be responsible for monitoring the care and compliance of the patient.

The provisions are currently under review as part of the preparation for a new Mental Health Act.

Removal to place of safety, Section 135(1)

Figure 20.9 sets out the basic provisions of this power of the approved social worker. The section has been amended by the Police and Criminal Evidence Act 1984, so it does not now have to be a named constable who accompanies the approved social worker to the house.

---

(1) If it appears to a justice of the peace, on information on oath laid by an approved social worker, that there is a reasonable cause to suspect that a person believed to be suffering from mental disorder
    (a)   has been, or is being, ill-treated, neglected or kept otherwise than under proper control, in any place within the jurisdiction of the justice; or
    (b)   being unable to care for himself, is living alone in any such place the justice may issue a warrant authorizing any constable to enter, if need be by force, any premises specified in the warrant in which that person is believed to be, and, if thought fit, to remove him to a place of safety with a view to the making of an application in respect of him under Part II of this Act, or of other arrangements for his treatment or care. Section 135(4) In the execution of a warrant issued under Section 135(1) a constable shall be accompanied by an approved social worker and by a registered medical practitioner (as amended by Police and Criminal Evidence Act 1984 Schedule 6 para 26).

Figure 20.9 Mental Health Act 1983 Section 135(1).

Removal from a public place by police, Section 136

The basic provisions of this section are set out in Figure 20.10. There has been considerable concern over the use of the section since the documentation has been inadequate; the police have not always recorded the details as to when they have used this section; and when the patient has been brought to hospital, the details have not always been recorded by the hospital staff and managers. Many hospitals have now designed their own forms for this purpose which record the date and time the patient arrives and the number and name of the constable who brings the patient in.

> (1) If a constable finds in a place to which the public have access a person who appears to him to be suffering from mental disorder and to be in immediate need of care or control, the constable may, if he thinks it necessary to do so in the interests of that person or for the protection of other persons, remove that person to a place of safety within the meaning of Section 135.
>
> (2) A person removed to a place of safety under this section may be detained there for a period not exceeding 72 hours for the purpose of enabling him to be examined by a registered medical practitioner and to be interviewed by an approved social worker and of making any necessary arrangements for his treatment or care.

Figure 20.10   Police Powers Section 136.

The Mental Health Review Tribunal

Table 20.3 illustrates the time limits for applying to the tribunal, the powers of the tribunal, and the applicants. A major innovation of the 1983 Act was that the managers must automatically refer a patient to the tribunal if he has failed to apply himself. There must be a tribunal hearing at least once every three years. Every child under 16 must be referred by the managers every year if he has not himself applied.

Table 20.3   Applications to Mental Health Review Tribunals

Section	Patient	Nearest relative	Manager
2 or 4	Applications by patients within first 14 days of detention	No application by nearest relative	No application by manager
3	Application by patient within first 6 months of detention, once within second 6 months, then annually	Yes, within 28 days of being informed that responsible medical officer has issued report barring discharge of patient When an order is made appointing a nearest relative under Section 29 On reclassification of patient under Section 16	Automatic referral if tribunal has not considered case within first 6 months of detention, thereafter if tribunal has not considered case within previous 3 years (1 year if patient is under 16)
37	Yes, once within second 6 months of detention, then annually	Yes, once within second 6 months of detention, then annually	Automatic if the case has not been considered by tribunal within previous 3 years (1 year if patient is under 16)
41	Yes, once within second 6 months of detention, then annually	No application by nearest relative	Automatic referral by Home Secretary if tribunal has not considered case within the preceding 3 years

The role of the managers

The managers are given certain statutory duties under the Act. These are set out in Figure 20.11. Of these, all can be delegated by the NHS Trust Board, except the

1. To accept a patient and record admission (Section 140).
2. To give information to detained patient (Section 132).
3. To give information to nearest relative (Section 132(4)) and inform him of discharge (Section 133(1)) or of detention (Section 25(2)).
4. To discharge patient (Section 23(2)(b)). Powers may be exercised by any three or more members of the authority (Section 23(4)).
5. To refer patient to Mental Health Review Tribunal (Section 63(1)(2)).
6. To transfer patient (Section 19(3), Section 19(1a) Reg. 7(2) and Reg. 7(3)).
7. To give notice to local social services authority specifying hospitals in which arrangements are made for reception in case of special urgency of patients requiring treatment for mental disorder (Section 140).

Definition of managers
District health authority or special health authority responsible for the administration of the hospital (Section 145).

All powers can be delegated by manager to the officers except for 4 above: discharging the patient.

Figure 20.11   Role of the managers.

duty to hear an application from a patient for discharge. In this case, the NHS Trust is empowered to appoint a subcommittee for hearing such applications.

The Mental Health Act Commission

Figure 20.12 illustrates the powers and constitution of the Mental Health Act Commission.

1. Composition: chairman and about 90 members (doctors, nurses, lawyers, social workers, academics, psychologists, other specialists and lay members).
2. Headquarters in Nottingham.
3. Ten National Standing Committees.
4. Duty to draft and monitor Code of Practice.
5. Prepare a biennial report to Parliament.
6. Review any decision at a special hospital to withhold a postal packet or its content.
7. Carry out on behalf of the Secretary of State duties in relation to the review of the exercise of powers and discharge of duties under the Act, visiting and interviewing detained patients, and hearing complaints from detained patients.
8. Exercise duties and appointment of second-opinion doctors in relation to Part IV. Consent to treatment provisions.

Figure 20.12   Powers and constitution of the Mental Health Act Commission.

Mentally ill patients and the European Convention on Human Rights

Several patients have won cases in Strasbourg for breach of their rights as set out in the European Convention on Human Rights. Thus in one case,[19] the European

Court of Human Rights held that the UK was in breach of Article 5 of the European Convention on Human Rights because for a considerable period of time the patient was not lawfully detained. Several Mental Health Review Tribunals had given the patient a deferred conditional discharge under Section 73 of the Act, but discharge had been delayed because the local authority had been unable to find suitable supervised hostel accommodation. After 2 October 2000, those who allege that their human rights have been infringed will be able to bring action in the courts of the UK, instead of going to Strasbourg (see Chapter 1 and Appendix A).

Reform of the Mental Health Act

An expert committee was set up by the government in 1998 under the chairmanship of Professor Richardson to review the Mental Health Act 1983. Its terms of reference included the degree to which the current legislation needs updating and to ensure that there is a proper balance between safety (both of individuals and the wider community) and the rights of individual patients. It was required to advise the government on how mental health legislation should be shaped to reflect contemporary patterns of care and treatment and to support its policy as set out in Modernising Health Services.[20] The Expert Committee presented its preliminary proposals, which set out the principles on which any future legislation should be based in April 1999, and its full report was published in November 1999.[21] The government presented its proposals for reform in 1999 with a final date for response by 31 March 2000.[22] The proposals include the reasons for proposed changes and cover the following topics:

1. Guiding principles for a new Mental Health Act.
2. Processes of applying compulsory powers.
3. Criteria for compulsory care and treatment.
4. The new Tribunal's remit.
5. Discharge and aftercare.
6. Interface with the criminal justice system.
7. Treatment.
8. Safeguards.

The guiding principles that the consultation paper suggests should be contained in a new Mental Health Act are set out in Figure 20.13. Other principles, recommended by the Review Committee and which the government considers should be included in a Code of Practice on the new Act, are shown below:

1. Non-discrimination.
2. Patient autonomy.
3. Consensual care.
4. Reciprocity.

> 1. Informal care and treatment should always be considered before recourse to compulsory powers.
> 2. Patients should be involved as far as possible in the process of developing and reviewing their own care and treatment plans.
> 3. The safety of both the individual patient and the public are of key importance in determining the question of whether compulsory powers should be imposed.
> 4. Where compulsory powers are used, care and treatment should be located in the least restrictive setting consistent with the patient's best interests and safety and the safety of the public.

Figure 20.13   Guiding principles to be included in a new Mental Health Act.

5. Respect for diversity.
6. Equality.
7. Respect for carers.
8. Effective communication.
9. Provision of information.
10. Evidence based practice.

Processes of applying compulsory powers

The government accepts the Review Committee recommendation that mental disorder should be defined as 'any disability or disorder of the mind or brain, whether permanent or temporary, which results in an impairment or disturbance of Mental Functioning.' This is consistent with the definition of mental incapacity adopted by the Law Commission in its report on mental incapacity.[23] Exceptions for disorders of sexual preference and misuse of alcohol and drugs should be recognised. It is seeking views on whether the applicant for admission should be a social worker or a mental health professional with specialist training. The application would be supported by two medical recommendations.

The Expert Committee suggested that a new assessment process should apply initially for up to 7 days. An application for a provisional order may then be made to an independent reviewer who would decide if a provision order for 21 days could be issued. Beyond the 28-day initial assessment and treatment phase, compulsory care and treatment must be authorised by a new mental disorder tribunal at a full hearing which the patient could attend. The tribunal would have powers to confer an order of detention for up to six months initially. The patient could challenge the detention during the initial 28-day period and in this case the tribunal hearing would be expedited. In emergency situations, there would be a 24-day detention period. The Committee also suggested that the common law powers to act out of necessity would continue to provide authority to detain and treat. Various models for the tribunal were put forward, including a single person panel, likely to be a specialist lawyer who could refer to a panel of doctors, and others with social care expertise. In relation to the statutory treatment provisions, the Committee recommended that special safeguards should apply to Electro Convulsive Therapy, polypharmacy and feeding contrary to the will of the patient. Statutory safeguards for the protection of the patient would include:

the Mental Health Act Commission;

hospital managers;

a nominated person (instead of the nearest relative);

advocacy; and

carers.

Other proposals related to long-term patients who lack mental capacity and who are at present outside the protection of the Mental Health Act 1983.[24] It is proposed that there should be a new statutory framework provided for them as recommended in the Lord Chancellor's proposals.[25]

At the time of writing, legislation is awaited on both the new Mental Health Act and also on the implementation of the proposals for decision making on behalf of the mentally incapacitated adult.

National Service Frameworks

As envisaged in the White Paper on the NHS,[26] the government has published National Service Frameworks for different specialties to ensure that there is a minimum standard of provision across the country. The National Service Frameworks for Mental Health were published in 1999 and set standards in five areas:

Standard one: Mental Health promotion.

Standards two and three: Primary care and access to services.

Standards four and five: Effective services for people with severe mental illness.

Standard six: Caring about carers.

Standard seven: Preventing suicide.

The Frameworks document describes the standards as 'realistic, challenging and measurable, and are based on the best evidence available. They will help to reduce variations in practice and deliver improvements for patients, service users and their carers, and for local health and social care communities – health authorities, local authorities, NHS trusts, primary care groups and trusts, and the independent sector.'

UKCC practitioners working in mental health services should ensure that they obtain a copy of these standards, and their updates, in order that they can ensure that the services they are providing are comparable with these National Standards.

Questions and exercises

1 Contrast the rights of the informal patient and compare these to the statutory rights of the patient detained under Mental Health legislation.

2 Study the restraint and seclusion policy in your hospital and consider the extent to which its implementation can remain within the law, in particular the Human Rights Act (see Appendix A).

3 Ask to see the latest report of the Mental Health Act Commission in your hospital.

4 In what ways would informal patients benefit from coming under the jurisdiction of the Mental Health Act Commission?

5 Analyse the provisions for giving compulsory treatment to those patients detained under the Act. Discuss the arguments for and against compulsory treatment in the community.

References

1 See B Dimond and F Barker, Mental Health Law for Nurses, Blackwell Scientific Publications 1996

2 Department of Health, Code of Practice on the Mental Health Act 1983 Third edition 1999 HMSO

3 UKCC Guidelines for mental health and learning disabilities nursing UKCC April 1998

4 UKCC The nursing, midwifery and health visiting contribution to the continuing care of people with mental health problems: a review and UKCC action plan UKCC 2000

5 *In re F* v. *West Berkshire Health Authority* [1989] 2 All ER 545

6 *R* v. *Bournewood Community and Mental Health NHS Trust ex p L* [1998] 3 All ER 289; [1999] AC 458

7 *In re F* v. *West Berkshire Health Authority* [1989] 2 All ER 545

8 Royal College of Nursing, The management of aggression and violence in places of care RCN 000 713 April 1997

9 Royal College of Nursing, Restraint revisited: rights, risk and responsibility RCN 000 998 October 1999

10 *In Re F* (Adult: Court's jurisdiction), *The Times Law Report* 25 July 2000

11 European Convention for the Protection of Human Rights and Fundamental Freedoms 1953 Cmd 8969

12 Mental Health (Nurses) Order 1998 Statutory Instrument 1998 No 2625

13 *Tameside and Glossop Acute Services Trust* v. *CH* [1996] 1 FLR 762; *Norfolk and Norwich (NHS) Trust* v. *W* [1996] 2 FLR 613

14 *Re MB* (An Adult: Medical Treatment) [1997] 2 FLR 426

15 *R* v. *Hallstrom and another ex parte W* (No. 2) 1986 2 All ER 306

16 Department of Health, Code of Practice of the Mental Health Act 1983 Stationery Office 1999 London

17 *R* v. *Richmond LBC ex parte Watson and other appeals* [2001] 1 All ER 436

18 B Dimond, The Mental Health (Patients in the Community) Act 1995, Quay Books Mark Allan Press 1996

19 *Stanley Johnson* v. *The United Kingdom* [1997] series A 1991 VII 2391

[20] Department of Health, Modernising Mental Health Services 1998
[21] Department of Health, Review of Expert Committee Review of the Mental Health Act 1983 November 1999
[22] Department of Health, Reform of the Mental Health Act 1983 Stationery Office 1999
[23] Law Commission Report No 231 Mental Incapacity Stationery Office 1995
[24] *R v Bournewood Community and Mental Health NHS Trust ex part L* [1998] 3 All ER 289
[25] Lord Chancellor, Making Decisions, Lord Chancellor's Office October 1999
[26] White Paper The New NHS Modern Dependable Stationery Office 1997

21 Accident and emergency, out-patients, genito-urinary departments and day surgery

Figure 21.1 sets out the main areas of concern to the nurse who works in these departments.

---

1. Accident and emergency department
   (a) pressure of work;
   (b) giving information to patients;
   (c) relationship between GP and the A & E dept;
   (d) extent of duty of care;
   (e) pressure to disclose confidential information.
2. Out-patients department
   (a) excessive waiting;
   (b) mistaken identity.
3. Genito-urinary medicine
   (a) confidentiality;
   (b) request for information by spouse;
   (c) tracing;
   (d) venereal disease regulations;
   (e) AIDS testing.
4. Day Surgery

Figure 21.1 Issues covered in Chapter 21.

The accident and emergency department

In recent years, the role of the nurse in the A and E department has undergone a fundamental change, not just as a result of the transfer of many activities formerly undertaken by medical staff to nurses, but as a result of the nurse taking on a wider sphere of responsibility and working within new parameters and developing a new specialty of A and E nursing. The new role of the nurse includes the provision of immediate care to patients and the determination of priorities for care (triage). The legal implications of the expanded role of the nurse are considered in Chapter 24. The RCN has provided a framework for the safe development of A and E nursing at specialist and advanced level.[1]

Pressure of work

Situation 21.1 *Priorities under pressure*

The accident and emergency department was unusually pressurised one weekend: staff shortages due to a flu epidemic and cut-backs because of an attempt to reduce overspending left only a skeleton staff. Unfortunately, there was a particularly horrific pile-up on the motorway in the fog. Twelve people were brought in with varying levels of seriousness. One of them, David Lewis, a boy of 10 years, appeared to be mainly suffering from shock and bruises. He complained of a sore wrist. His mother was advised to take him home and give him a few aspirin, a hot drink, and after a good night's sleep he would be fine. The next day, however, it was learnt that he had died during the night after inhaling vomit.

There is every possibility in this case that the mother will make an official complaint and possibly take legal action. Normally, it is not a successful defence to an action for negligence, that the staff were under pressure (see case 4.11 in Chapter 4), if it can be established that they failed to follow the approved accepted practice in relation to the care of the patient. Dealing with children is particularly difficult since they cannot always correctly identify the site of any pain and discomfort. The possibility of head injury does not appear to have been considered in this case and this would be subject to investigation. Was the mother told the correct way of caring for the boy? The legal position is as follows:

1. there is a duty to care for the boy;
2. it must be established by the parents that the staff failed to follow the accepted approved practice; and that
3. this failure reasonably foreseeably led to the death of the boy.

The workload in an accident and emergency department is extremely erratic. One moment there can be few demands, and then there may be a major incident or a sudden influx of patients and the pressure is on. What is the standard of care in such circumstances? Even though the nurses and doctors are under extreme pressure, each patient is still entitled to expect the appropriate standard of care. Thus it would still be actionable if a fracture remained undiagnosed or if a head injury were to be missed. However, the courts would take into account the pressure on the staff if priorities had to be set over who should be treated first. It would be open to the court to examine the basis of these priorities. In Chapter 4, the case of *Deacon* v. *McVicar*[2] is considered. In this case, a patient alleged that she should have been seen earlier, and the court was prepared to examine the records of other patients who were in the ward at the time to see if they were making demands on the staff at that time. The policy of triage has not yet been brought before the courts, but there is no reason to doubt that the above principles would apply, i.e. the professional staff have to take all due care in treating the patients and where priorities have to be decided upon, this must be according to approved accepted practice. There is no doubt that, in general, pressure of work does not justify a lower standard of care for the patient. It may, in addition, lead to a successful action against the NHS Trust itself if it can be established that the authority failed to provide adequate resources and training for the patients to be cared for safely. It may be necessary in emergencies for staff to undertake tasks that they are not properly trained to do. If so, it is a question of balancing one risk against another, i.e. the risk of not being treated at all against the risk of harm arising because the only available person to treat the patient has not had sufficient training. Inevitably, the only way of coping with wide variations in demand is either to bring in additional staff to meet peaks of demand or for patients with less severe conditions to wait till staff are available to assist. Even though successful legal action would probably not lie for a long wait, the complaints procedure might be used for those who consider that they have waited an unacceptable length of time. To prevent such claims, clear standards of communication with patients must be drawn up and implemented to ensure that patients are fully apprised of the situation.

Giving information to patients

Additional precautions must thus be taken to ensure that, where the patient is not detained overnight, he has sufficient information to recognise any signs and symptoms that suggest a return to the hospital or to the general practitioner for further consultation and examination. Most hospitals already have preprinted leaflets covering warnings in relation to head injuries, care of plaster, the need for anti-tetanus, and other potential dangers. There is a need to stress, by word of mouth also, the importance of a patient following these instructions. If a patient ignored the instructions, having had clear advice from the staff, there is unlikely to be any blame on the part of the staff and certainly there may be a large element of contributory negligence on the part of the patient. Where information is given by word of mouth to the patient, one frequent concern of the staff is, 'How can I prove what I said since it is only the patient's word against mine?' This is always a dilemma in negligence cases, since no matter how strong the defendant's case would appear to be on paper, it still has to be proved through witnesses to the satisfaction of the courts. It is here that good record-keeping can be very important. If the nurse notes that the patient was given the relevant information, this does not in itself prove that he was since the records do not necessarily reflect what actually took place, but it does indicate the existence of a system where the nurse is more likely than not to have given the requisite information. In addition, of course, any witness who can recall the events and substantiate what the nurse was saying will undoubtedly help her. An additional precaution where it is essential to emphasise the importance of following the correct advice is for the patient himself to be asked to sign that he has understood the importance of obeying the instructions and has received written instructions (see also Chapter 4).

Relationship between the duty of care owed by the GP and by the accident and emergency department

Another difficulty that arises in the accident and emergency department is the extent to which the department is used, inappropriately as far as the operational policy of the accident and emergency department is concerned, as a GP surgery or health centre.

Situation 21.2   Minor ailments

A patient came into the accident and emergency department complaining of a pain in his ear. He was registered by the admission clerk and seen by a nurse, who then told him to wait to see the doctor. The doctor asked him how long he had had the pain and the man said that he had had it for about three days. He was asked if he had been to see his GP and he said that he was not sure who his GP was. The house officer suggested that he should go to see his GP and that he should not have come to the accident and emergency department which was for emergency treatment of a serious kind. The man was very reluctant to go and very upset. It was subsequently learnt that he was admitted to the District General Hospital with mastoid meningitis and an enquiry was established to find out why he had not been diagnosed in the accident and emergency department.

The general principle would appear to be that once a patient comes through the doors, then a duty of care is owed and the patient should not be sent away without an adequate examination. The words 'through the doors' are important, since a duty of care is not owed in a vacuum. It is perfectly possible for a hospital to say 'we do not accept accident and emergency patients here' and refuse to treat a patient. However, once a hospital accepts a patient for attention, then a duty of care would arise to ensure that this patient receives the appropriate standard of care, even though it might mean arranging the transfer of the patient to another hospital.

Extent of duty of care

Situation 21.3   Referral for what?

A patient was referred to the accident and emergency department by the GP for X-ray because she had fallen and sustained a severe injury and considerable bruising to her leg. The house officer arranged for her to be X-rayed and it was found to be negative. The patient mentioned to the doctor that she was very short of breath and thirsty. However, only her leg was examined. She subsequently discovered that she was suffering from diabetes and claimed that the casualty officer should have diagnosed this.

This is another situation that raises the extent of the duty of care owed by the hospital staff to the patient. If the GP refers a patient for a very specific purpose, which is carried out, can it then be said that the patient should have been given a full examination so that other significant defects could have been detected? The answer must obviously depend upon the particular circumstances and what the reasonably accepted approved practice is.

The Clinical Nurse Specialist in the A&E Department

Increasingly, protocols are being developed for a nurse specialist to work within the A&E Department, seeing patients who are not examined by a doctor, prescribing on a limited scale and performing an expanded range of activities. The legal issues arising from this scope of professional practice are considered in Chapter 24.

Pressure to disclose confidential information

The basic principles relating to the disclosure of confidential information are discussed in Chapter 8. In that chapter, two examples are given of requests for information in accident and emergency departments. Staff are under particular pressure in this respect, since they are likely to be hounded by both the police and the press in order that sensitive and personal information can be disclosed. The professions owe a duty to society, i.e. to act in the public interest, which may take precedence over any duty of confidentiality owed to the patient. However, the codes of ethics are couched in general terms and do not cover specific examples. The advice is that, where in doubt as to where the individual's duty lies, advice should be taken from the professional associations and the UKCC. The statutory powers of the police under the Police and Criminal Evidence Act enable, in cases of serious arrestable offences, a special procedure to be followed to compel the production of personal information and human tissue which would otherwise be protected from disclosure. Some hospitals have different policies and procedures relating to disclosure in different circumstances and these vary in the degree of readiness with which this confidential information is disclosed. Whatever the policy, in the end it must be the individual professional's decision, since that individual may have to justify to the patient why confidentiality was not maintained.

Situation 21.4   Road traffic accidents

The police are entitled to know the names and addresses of those who have been involved in a road traffic accident. This does not mean, however, that the media are also entitled to know these names or to know the condition of the patient. If the patient gives consent (and possibly the relatives, though this is more doubtful), then the information can be disclosed. If, however, this consent is refused, the hospital spokesman must remain silent as far as the disclosure of any confidential information is concerned. Once again, practice varies and there is an absence of court cases to settle the issue. For example, some hospitals allow a condition report to be given to the press without obtaining the consent of the patient, e.g. 'Of the ten persons injured in the motorway pileup on Tuesday, one has since died, three have been discharged, four are comfortable, and two are on life support machines.' There are few who would see this as a breach of confidence. Anyone (and this includes medical staff) who is aware of information about people involved in a road accident where personal injuries occurred has a duty to ensure that the police are notified.[3]

Patients' records come under the provisions of the Data Protection Act 1998 and are, of course, subject to close controls over disclosure. NHS Trusts and Health Authorities should have appointed a Caldicott Guardian to oversee standards of confidentiality within the organisation (see Chapter 8). Any concerns could be raised with that person, normally a director of the organisation.

Aggression and violence in A&E

One major headache for accident and emergency staff is the increasing problem of dealing with aggressive drunken patients and the rights of the staff to claim compensation either from the criminal courts (if there is a successful prosecution of the assailant) or of claiming from the Criminal Injuries Compensation Authority. These topics are considered in Chapter 12.

Problems relating to the unconscious patient and the patient who has attempted to commit suicide have been considered in Chapter 7 on consent to treatment.

The out-patients department

Excessive waiting

Situation 21.5   *Waiting*

Bruce was self-employed and time was money. He had been suffering from a severe pain and his doctor had referred him to the consultant surgeon querying gallstones or cholecystitis. He was sent an appointment to see the surgeon at 9.30 a.m. in out-patients. Because he had an important meeting that afternoon, which could involve him in a lot of valuable work, he phoned the clerk who assured him that the clinic ended at lunch-time. When he got to the clinic, he discovered that 30 people had been booked in for 9.30, most of whom had arrived before him. As he sat chatting, he discovered that others who had been booked in for 12.00 a.m. had come early, since they were seen in the order of arrival and not according to appointments. He settled down for a long wait and then was told at 1.00 p.m. that the surgeon had had to rush off to theatre to cover for a colleague who had been taken ill, but that if Bruce waited, the doctor would see him when the operation was over. Bruce said that he could not wait as he had a very important meeting. The clerk replied that if he went away he would be treated as a 'did not attend' and would have to take his place in the queue being seen in out-patients. He would not be able to give him an appointment for at least another three months. Bruce insisted on seeing the sister in charge.

Oddly enough, there seems to be no grounds for bringing an action against an NHS Trust for causing excessive waiting in out-patients departments. At least, one has not yet been tried. If it was private practice and there was therefore a contract between professional and client, then it could be more clearly argued that there was a breach of contract when a client was kept waiting an unreasonable length of time. However, in NHS care, there is no contract between the patient and the NHS Trust or between the patient and the professional, and the patient who is aggrieved at having to wait an unreasonably long time would have to argue that there was a breach of the duty of care owed to the patient under the laws of negligence that has caused him some loss or harm – a loss or harm that is compensatable under the law. There have been actions when patients have waited excessively long periods of time for in-patient treatment. However, no action has been brought in relation to a long wait within the department itself. Such a complaint is more likely to be investigated by the hospital management and then, if the patient is not happy with the response, to end up on the desk of the Health Service Commissioner or ombudsman. He has investigated many complaints of unreasonable waiting times in accident and emergency, out-patients, and other departments. The procedure for handling complaints is considered in Chapter 27. The Patients' Charter and local charters set targets for maximum waiting times. Compliance with these targets cannot be enforced in a court of law, but complaints can be made through the hospital complaints procedure.

In the above situation, when the sister is confronted by a very disgruntled patient, she should ensure that the facts given by the clerk are accurate. It is unlikely, for example, that a patient who has been kept waiting in the way in which Bruce has, should be treated as a 'did not attend'. If so, the system is manifestly unjust. The sister should be able, with cooperation from the doctor, to arrange for Bruce to be seen much earlier. In addition, she may be able to arrange a compromise by arranging for Bruce to attend the meeting and to return that same day. Certainly, she should be able to take the heat out of the situation, explain the problems fully to Bruce, work out some acceptable solution, and, of course, apologise to him for what has happened. This is not law, but it is good practice. However, there are many such occasions where the patient may or may not have a right of action in law where skilled counselling and co-operation with the patient prevents a situation developing into a court action or Health Service Commissioner's inquiry.

Mistaken identity

Situation 21.6   The wrong notes

Sister Bailey was short-staffed in the out-patients department and the situation was made worse by a strike among the coordinators. However, the consultants were adamant that the clinics should continue. She called out for one patient, Handel Thomas, to come to the diabetic clinic. She checked that he was from The Marina, Fish Street, and he said he was. He was asked if he had brought any samples with him and he replied 'No, no one told me to'. He was then taken in to see the consultant. He was given a very full investigation and was asked how often he injected his insulin. He was a little surprised at this and replied that he had never been told to use insulin.

Situation 21.6 *continued*

After considerable confusion, during which time Handel was getting very disturbed, it emerged that there was another Handel Thomas in Fish Street. This Handel James Thomas lived at number 45 and was due to be seen in the eye clinic; the other Handel, Handel David Thomas from 2 Fish Street, should have been seen in the diabetic clinic.

In circumstances like this, there has been clear negligence by the sister in failing to check that she was taking the right patient to be seen and also by the doctor who also did not check. However, apart from causing distress to the patient and a breach of confidentiality of information about the other patient, no harm has been caused to either, so it is not a case that is likely to end up in the courts. However, the potential implications of this type of mistake are terrifying and the tightest control must be kept over patient identification. Unfortunately, one cannot always rely on patients to point out the error since they can become institutionalised and frightened at the prospect of challenging the professionals and stories abound as to what they are prepared to submit to by mistake.

Genito-urinary medicine

Confidentiality

In a genito-urinary department (formerly known as the VD clinic, or the special clinic), strict confidentiality must be maintained. This section looks at some of the problems and pitfalls that can arise over confidentiality in this context, and also at the statutory provisions.

Situation 21.7 *A reasonable request*

Mr Grey had just visited the GUM clinic and samples had been taken. He was told that the results would be available by the Thursday of the following week. He was naturally anxious and since he lived some 40 miles from the clinic, he phoned up late Thursday morning to find out the results. He gave his name and the nurse asked for his clinic number. She explained that it was on his card. He said that he had lost his card. She therefore told him that she would be unable to give him the result over the phone. He asked if that meant that the results were positive. She said not at all, but because of the principles of confidentiality, she could neither confirm that someone of the name had attended the clinic nor could she give any results over the phone without the clinic number. He became very angry, pointing out the inconvenience that he would suffer if he had to drive the 40 miles there and back, especially if the results were negative. She told him that she could not change the rules. He threatened to complain about her attitude and report her.

There is no doubt that the nurse is correct in not divulging information without being absolutely certain that she is talking to the patient. There are possible ways out of this dilemma. One would be for the nurse to phone a number that had already been given by the patient to the clinic for the notification of the results. The other would be to ensure that all patients are warned of the strict rules of confidentiality from the outset of their care so that they know the rules are firmly adhered to for their own protection, even in circumstances that cause them great inconvenience such as the one above.

A similar difficulty is the following situation.

Requests for information by a spouse

Situation 21.8 Spousely concern

A man phoned the GUM clinic saying that he was the husband of Mrs Robinson, a patient who had an appointment at the clinic that afternoon. He said that she had lost her appointment card and forgotten the time, and since he was giving her a lift, could they let him know the time of the appointment?

This is the sort of request that few staff in a general out-patients department would hesitate to respond to helpfully. Yet, if confidentiality is to be preserved, then it is essential that the person answering the phone does not admit to the fact (if this is indeed the case) that there is a patient of such a name attending the clinic.

Tracing

Obviously, it is essential that, as far as possible, any persons who have been in contact with someone who is infected should be traced and advised to have tests. It is important that this should be done without revealing the name of the contact. A form is completed to assist the clinic. Obviously, if original contacts can be persuaded to advise their contacts to have a check, this is preferable to their receiving a call out of the blue.

Venereal disease regulations

These regulations (National Health Service (Venereal Diseases) Regulations 1974 Section 1 No. 29 (as amended by SI 1982 No. 288)) ensure that any information about any sexually transmitted disease is kept confidential. They came into operation on 1 April 1974 and place a duty on every regional health authority and every district health authority to take all necessary steps to secure that any information capable of identifying an individual obtained by officers of the authority with respect to persons examined or treated for any sexually transmitted disease shall not be disclosed. The exceptions to this rule are disclosures: (a) for the purpose of communicating that information to a medical practitioner, or to a person employed under the direction of a medical practitioner in connection with the treatment of persons suffering from such disease or the prevention of the spread thereof; and (b) for the purpose of such treatment or prevention. It was suggested in the case of *X. v. Y and another* 1988[4] that AIDS came within the scope of these regulations. See Chapter 26 for a consideration of the legal issues in AIDS and infectious diseases.

AIDS testing

The question as to whether the patient's consent is needed for an AIDS test to be carried out and whether it is possible to test secretly without the patient being told the results are discussed in Chapter 26.

Day surgery

There has been considerable increase in the extent of day surgery in recent years enabling reductions in the numbers of beds to take place.

All those areas of law that are the concern of in-patient care also apply to those working in day surgery. However, there are additional problems that can arise from the speed of turnover, the fact that patients are seen for a very short time and that significant decisions have to be made urgently. For example, crucial decisions have to be made about whether an operation is to proceed following the necessary tests; should the patient be admitted after surgery or could he/she be allowed to go home; what information has to be given to the patient before the patient returns home. The pressure of work, the speed of patient throughput and the risk of harm arising means that clear protocols are necessary to ensure that patients receive a satisfactory standard of care, and that they and their carers are given essential information pre- and post-surgery. The following is only one of the situations where complaints and litigation can arise. Reference must be made to earlier chapters setting out basic principles of law.

Situation 21.9   Day surgery

Barbara was called for day surgery to have an operation for carpal tunnel syndrome. The operation was to be performed under a local anaesthetic. She was told to arrive by 9.00 a.m. even though she would be the last on the list. She waited for two hours before she was seen by a nurse, who then booked her in and told her that she should not have had any breakfast. Barbara queried this as a general anaesthetic was not planned. The nurse said it was a precaution in case the operation could not be performed under a local anaesthetic. At 2.30 p.m., she was taken down for surgery and told that she must stay in the ward until 6.00 p.m. She asked for and was given a cup of tea at 4.00 p.m. Apart from that, she had no food or drink. No instructions were given to her for post-operative care. She considers that she has been treated poorly. What rights does she have?

This situation is more likely to lead to a complaint than to litigation. There is the possibility of a claim under Article 3 of the Convention on Human Rights (see Chapter 1 and Appendix A) in that she may have been given degrading or inhuman treatment. She is unlikely to benefit from civil litigation for compensation, unless there is long-term harm as a result of the failure to give her post-operative and post-discharge instructions. For example, if she should have been advised not to drive a car after the operation and, as a result of this omission, she was involved in an accident, then there would appear to be a breach of the duty of care owed to her. However, these deplorable circumstances might well be the subject of a complaint and it is hoped that as a result of the complaint there would be significant and substantial review of the procedures in place.

Questions and exercises

1 Does the nurse (or doctor) who works in the accident and emergency department have a duty in law to assess the priority to be given to a patient, and could she be held liable in the civil courts for failures in making that assessment?

2 Can a patient be lawfully refused treatment in an accident and emergency department and be referred instead to his GP?

3 What remedy does a patient who has waited an excessive amount of time in the accident and emergency department or the out-patients department have?

4 What remedies does a member of staff have who has been injured by a drunken patient in the accident and emergency department? (See also Chapter 12.)

5 Do you consider that the spouse of a patient suffering from a sexually transmitted disease should have a right to be told of the spouse's medical condition? What is the law on this?

6 What precautions might be taken to preserve medical confidentiality in the accident and emergency department in relation to:
   (a) the press;
   (b) the police;
   (c) other staff?

7 In what way does the duty of staff in accident and emergency departments differ from those on the wards in relation to the care of the patient's property? (Refer also to Chapter 25.)

8 A patient is admitted into the accident and emergency department with severe bleeding. His clothes have to be cut from him and because they are badly soiled they are sent for incineration. He subsequently complains that there was £300 in the pockets of his jacket. What is the liability of the hospital or of the accident and emergency staff? (Refer to Chapter 25.)

9 A clinical nurse specialist who works in Day Surgery is asked if she would like to apply for a Nurse Consultant post in this speciality. What differences would she anticipate in these 2 roles? (Refer also to Chapter 24.)

References

[1] Royal College of Nursing, Accident and Emergency Challenging the Boundaries RCN 00 459 November 1994

[2] *Deacon v. McVicar and another* 7 January 1984 QBD

[3] *Hunter v. Mann* 1974 1 QB 767

[4] *X. v. Y and another* 1988 2 All ER 648

22 Human fertility and genetics

Nurses are increasingly likely to be caring for patients in clinics and on the wards who are receiving treatment in connection with problems of fertility. Medical technology has made vast strides in this field and now outpaces the law. This section provides guidance on the current legislation relating to artificial insemination by donor, embryo implantation, surrogacy and genetic engineering. The legal problems that arise from sterilisation and family planning are considered in Chapter 15. The areas to be covered are set out in Figure 22.1 The Human Fertilisation and Embryology Act 1990 introduced statutory controls in this field of medicine. Genetic research using human tissue is considered in Chapter 18.

---

1. Artificial insemination
   (a) by husband;
   (b) by donor.
2. Human Fertilisation and Embryology Act 1990.
3. *In vitro* fertilisation.
4. Human Fertilisation and Embryology Authority.
5. Consent provisions for retrieval, etc.
6. Surrogacy.
7. Conscientious objection.
8. Confidentiality.
9. Genetics.
10. Gene therapy.
11. Gender selection.
12. Genetic screening.
13. Cloning.

Figure 22.1 Issues covered in Chapter 22.

Artificial insemination

Artificial insemination by husband (AIH)

If a married couple require help in conception such that the husband's semen is artificially transferred to the wife, the law would see the outcome of this as being identical with natural conception. So as far as such aspects as inheritance, legal guardianship of the child, etc., are concerned, there is no difference between the artificially and the naturally conceived child. However, the involvement of a third person raises the possibility of other legal issues. For example, it is possible that if a pathology laboratory is involved, there could be a mix-up over the semen and the woman could be given semen from someone other than her husband. With genetic coding, it would now be possible to prove that the child is not the husband's, though, of course, it must be remembered that in order to succeed in a negligence action it must be established that there was a causal link between the negligent act and the harm caused (the woman could have had sex with a third person). Some have opposed AIH on moral grounds, since it is an unnatural form of conception, but the Warnock Committee[1] were of the view that it was an acceptable form of treatment except where a widow used semen that had been stored in a semen bank. They felt that insemination after the husband's death could lead to profound psychological problems for the child and the mother. (See Diana Blood case on page 438.) They felt that there was no need or even practical possibility of formal regulation of AIH, but recommended that it should be administered by or under the supervision of a medical practitioner.

No licence is required under the 1990 Act for artificial insemination by the husband. Nor is one required for AIP (artificial insemination of an unmarried woman with her partner's sperm). Neither AIH nor AIP requires the use of donated gametes. GIFT (gamete intrafallopian transfer) does not require a licence if the egg and sperm come from the woman and her partner/husband.

Artificial insemination by donor (AID)

Where the donor is not the husband, problems over legitimacy, rights to inheritance and the duties of the husband in relation to the child arise. A report from the Archbishop of Canterbury in 1948 recommended that AID should be made a criminal offence. The Feversham report set up by the government in 1960 recommended that AID should be discouraged. The opposite has happened. In 1973, a panel under the chairmanship of Sir John Peel recommended the setting up of accreditation centres for AID, but this has not taken place. In an early case[2] regarding the rights of the father, the father and mother had entered into an agreement that the girl would be artificially inseminated by him and then she would hand over the child on payment of £3,000. She refused to hand the child over and the trial judge gave the father limited rights of access. The Court of Appeal, however, gave him no rights of access.

Artificial insemination by donor is not unlawful, but in contrast to the child born from AIH, the child born as a result of AID is illegitimate and the husband of the mother has no parental rights and duties in relation to the child, unless he accepts the child as a child of the family. The donor could be held responsible for the maintenance of the child and could apply to the court for access or custody. A consultation paper was published by the government in 1986. As yet, only a few of these recommendations have been implemented in law, one of which is the treating of a child born to a woman as the result of artificial insemination by someone other than her husband as the child of the parties of that marriage. This is enacted by Section 27 of the Family Reform Act 1987. The main condition is that the marriage must be in existence at the time. Proof to the satisfaction of the court that the other party to the marriage did not consent to the insemination will prevent this provision arising. This means that the burden is placed on the husband to show that the insemination was performed without his consent. This provision came into force in April 1988 and applies only to children born subsequently.

Human Fertilisation and Embryology Act 1990

The Act was passed to implement the recommendations of the Warnock Committee.[3] A summary of the provisions of the 1990 Act is set out in Figure 22.2. It covers three main areas of activity:

---

1. Definition of terms 'embryo' and 'gamete'.
2. Specific activities prohibited:
   (a) bringing about the creation of an embryo or keeping or using an embryo EXCEPT in pursuance of a licence;
   (b) placing in a woman a live embryo other than a human embryo or any live gametes other than human gametes;
   (c) A licence cannot authorise:
      (i) keeping or using an embryo after the appearance of the primitive streak, not later than 14 days after the gametes are mixed;
      (ii) placing an embryo in any animal;
      (iii) keeping or using an embryo in any circumstances in which regulations prohibit its keeping or use; or
      (iv) replacing a nucleus of a cell of an embryo with a nucleus taken from a cell of any person or embryo or subsequent development of an embryo.
   (d) (i) No person can store gametes, provide treatment services for women (other than AID, AIP or GIFT), or mix gametes with live gametes of an animal, unless in pursuance of a licence.
      (ii) A licence cannot authorise storing or using gametes in any circumstances prohibited by regulations.
3. Human Fertilisation and Embryology Authority established with the function of:
   (a) reviewing information about embryos and advising Secretary of State;
   (b) publicising services provided to public by HFEA or in pursuance of licences;
   (c) providing advice and information;
   (d) other functions specified in regulations;
   (e) monitor committees to grant licences;
   (f) to give directions.
4. Licences for treatment, storage, research and conditions of holding licence.
5. Code of Practice to be issued by HFEA subject to Secretary of State's approval.
6. Definition of 'mother' and 'father'.
7. Register of information to be kept by HFEA with restriction on disclosure.
8. Amendments to Surrogacy Arrangements Act 1985 by providing that no surrogacy arrangement is enforceable by or against any of the persons making it.
9. Changes to Abortion Act 1967 (see Chapter 15).
10. Protection of those with conscientious objection.
11. Powers of enforcement given to HFEA including power to enter premises.
12. Offences established.

Figure 22.2 Provisions of the Human Fertilisation and Embryology Act 1990 (summary of contents).

1. licensed treatments, i.e. any fertility treatment that involves the use of donated eggs or sperm, or embryos created outside the body (i.e. IVF);
2. storage of eggs, sperm and embryos; and
3. research on human embryos.

In vitro fertilisation (IVF)

The external fertilisation of an egg, extracted from the ovary, with semen is a relatively new development and the Human Fertilisation and Embryology Act 1990 provides a framework for control, covering such issues as the disposal of unwanted embryos, their ownership, power to undertake research on these embryos, embryo donation to another woman, or genetic engineering to prevent hereditary disorders or to create a superhuman. Fertilisation outside the body coupled with transfer of the embryo into the uterus is, in its most simple form, a means of overcoming a fertility problem in a married couple. However, because of the possibility of egg and semen donation and subsequent transfer to a woman other than the provider of the egg, a complex situation can arise. In addition, it can be coupled with a surrogacy arrangement whereby a couple for whom the woman is unable to carry a child arrange for an embryo created from their egg and semen to be inserted into a host woman who will return the child to the genetic parents after birth. The surrogacy arrangements will be considered later. This part will deal with IVF and ET (embryo transfer to the uterus).

The majority of the Warnock Committee recommended a time limit of 14 days because, at about the 15th day after conception, the formation of the primitive streak can be identified. This is the first of several identifiable features that develop in and from the embryonic disc during the succeeding days.

Subsequently, a consultation paper and a white paper were produced in 1986. In a case in 1987,[4] the High Court refused an application for judicial review of decisions by consultants who decided that a woman should be refused IVF treatment, on the grounds of past convictions and her prostitution. In 1994, a 37-year-old woman was refused IVF treatment through the NHS on the grounds of her age.[5] Her application to the High Court to quash the health authority's decision failed on the grounds that, in the light of its limited resources, a health authority policy to set an age limit was not unreasonable.

A summary of the provisions of the Human Fertilisation and Embryology Act 1990 on IVF are set out in Figure 22.2. On 20 July 1994, the Human Fertilisation and Embryology Authority ruled that eggs from aborted fetuses could not be used in fertility treatment, but they could be used in research. The same ruling applies to the eggs of a dead woman, even though she is carrying a donor card.

Obtaining fertility treatment within the NHS has varied from health authority to health authority, with some couples having to pay as much as £3,000 to obtain each private fertility treatment, whilst others are able to obtain the treatment on the NHS. In November 2000, the Secretary of State for Health asked the National Institute for Clinical Excellence (NICE, see Chapter 5) to review the various fertility treatments with a view to ending the postcode lottery and to draw up national guidelines for the provision of fertility treatment within the NHS.

Human Fertilisation and Embryology Authority (HFEA)

The Human Fertilisation and Embryology Authority was established under the provisions of the 1990 Act. It has the power to issue licenses for centres to carry out IVF treatment and inspect them. It also issues a Code of Practice for the Centres and provides guidance to the government on new areas for litigation and control.[6] The Human Genetics Advisory Commission (HGAC) operated from December 1996 to December 1999, providing the government with independent advice on issues arising from developments in human genetics. It published papers on: insurance and genetic testing (December 1997); Cloning (December 1998); and Employment and genetic testing (July 1999). It was replaced by the Human Genetics Commission (HGC) in December 1999, which has the remit of advising on necessary changes to the advisory and regulatory framework, of providing information and guidance to the Minister on general issues in human genetics. Other non-statutory bodies advising in this area are: gene therapy advisory committee; genetics and insurance committee; and the Nuffield Council on Bioethics, an independent body established by the trustees of the Nuffield Foundation in 1991 to consider the ethical issues arising from developments in medicine and biology.

Consent provisions for retrieval, storage and use of human gametes under the Human Fertilisation and Embryology Act 1990

Diane Blood was refused permission by the Human Fertilisation and Embryology Authority to use the stored sperm from her dead husband on the grounds that the husband had not given written consent for this use as required by the 1990 Act. She brought a case seeking judicial review of the Authority's refusal to license the infertility treatment. The sperm had been taken from her husband as he lay in a coma as a result of meningitis. The Court of Appeal[7] held that, as a result of the restrictions under the 1990 Act, she could not be lawfully treated with the sperm in this country. However, she would be permitted to receive treatment in Belgium according to Article 59 of the EC treaty. She subsequently became pregnant and gave birth. Following this case, the Minister of Health appointed a committee under the Chairmanship of Professor Sheila McLean to review the consent provisions in the Human Fertilisation and Embryology Act 1990. The Committee sent out a questionnaire for public consultation and published its report in December 1998. In August 2000, the government published its response to the McLean Report.[8] It accepted all the recommendations of the report and went further, suggesting a retrospective effect:

1. The father's name should be allowed to appear on birth certificates where his sperm has been used after his death.

2. The legal position on consent and removal of gametes should remain unchanged: gametes can be taken from an incapacitated person who is likely to recover, if the removal of gametes is in their best interests.

3. The HFEA should have the power to permit the storage of gametes where consent has not been given, so long as the gametes have been lawfully removed. This will also benefit children who are about to undergo treatment that will affect their future fertility. (Legislation will be required to implement this.)

4. Families will be able to make these birth certificate changes retrospectively.

5. The best practice is for written consent to be obtained, since this most clearly constitutes effective consent. Where there is doubt over whether an effective consent has been obtained, this should be a matter for the courts.

The government has not recommended that there should be any legislative change over permitting the export of gametes that have been removed lawfully, since the Court of Appeal in the Diane Blood case held that sperm stored with consent can be the subject of export. The government intends to keep the position under review.

Surrogacy

This might be thought, like IVF, to be a result of the recent developments in medical technology. However, the Biblical story of Abraham resorting to the servant who could bear a child for him because Sarah was barren is an early example of one form of surrogacy. The possibility of embryo implantation has, however, increased the number of ways in which surrogacy can take place. The child that is born might have no genetic relationship with the ultimate parents, but be the natural child of the bearing mother or even an embryo from two donors. More likely, however, is the situation where the child is genetically related to the father as a result of artificial insemination, but not to the adopting mother. Prior to the Warnock Report, the only legislation that covered a surrogacy situation was the child care legislation and rules relating to adoption. Section 50, for example, of the Adoption Act 1958 prohibits any payment in connection with adoption. Such surrogate cases as Baby Cotton[9] revealed the gaps in the law and the uncertainties surrounding basic questions. Is a contract for surrogacy enforceable by either party, neither party, or only by the mother? What are the legal implications if the child is handicapped? What controls do the contracting couple have over the standard of life of the mother during the pregnancy, e.g. what if she smokes or drinks heavily? If she changes her mind and has an abortion, are damages then payable?

In Case 22.1 it was held that a payment to the mother in a surrogacy arrangement did not contravene the Act if payments made by those others to the natural mother did not include an element of profit or financial reward. Even if they were made for reward, the court had a discretion under the Act to authorise the payments retrospectively. The court granted the adoption order.

> ### Case 22.1 A surrogacy dispute
>
> Mr and Mrs A were unable to have children and because of their age had been refused as adoptive parents. They entered into a surrogacy arrangement with Mrs B who wished to help the childless couple. Under the arrangement, it was agreed that Mr and Mrs A would pay £10,000 to Mrs B who would give up her job to have the child. In due course, a child was conceived, but in the event Mrs B accepted only £5,000 and refused the balance. It was clear that the amount did not cover Mrs B's loss of earnings and expenses. After the birth, Mr and Mrs A applied to court for an adoption order. The question arose (a) whether the payment of money had been a payment of reward for adoption within the meaning of the Adoption Act Section 50(1) and (b) if there had been a contravention of the section, whether the court could make a retrospective authorisation in respect of the payment under Section 50(3) of the Act and grant an adoption order.[10]

The Surrogacy Arrangements Act 1985 prohibits the making of surrogacy arrangements on a commercial basis. Those companies that had come over from the United States and started to arrange surrogacy contracts were thus forced out of business in the United Kingdom. This approach had been recommended by the Warnock Committee, whose recommendations, however, went further and suggested that both profit- and non-profit-making organisations should be made illegal, and also that any professional who knowingly assisted in the establishment of a surrogacy pregnancy should be criminally liable. They recommended that all surrogacy arrangements should be held illegal and unenforceable in the courts. Section 36(i) of the Human Fertilisation and Embryology Act 1990 amends the 1985 Act to make a surrogacy arrangement unenforceable. It does not make it illegal.

The 1990 Act Section 30 enables a court to order a child to be treated as a child to the parties of the marriage where another woman has acted as surrogate, provided that certain conditions are met. In a case in 1996,[11] a couple applied under Section 30 for a parental order in respect of a child who was born following a surrogate arrangement. It was agreed that the unmarried woman would receive £8,280 to cover her expenses and loss of earnings. The High Court judge was satisfied that the requirements of Section 30 were met. In particular, the mother had given consent, although she admitted to it tearing her in half and the payments were reasonable and could be granted retrospectively. In this case, there was no man who was to be treated as the father and whose consent was required.

In 1997, Professor Margaret Brazier was appointed by the Department of Health to review the existing law relating to surrogacy arrangements. The terms of reference included whether payments for expenses should continue to be allowed; whether there was a case for the regulation of surrogacy arrangements through a recognised body and to advise on whether any changes were necessary to the 1985 Act and Section 30 of the Human Fertilisation and Embryology Act 1990. An extensive consultation exercise was undertaken and subsequently the Brazier Report recommended that the Surrogacy Arrangements Act 1985 and Section 30 of the 1990 Act (see above) should be replaced by new legislation and a Code of Practice on surrogacy should be drawn up by the Department of Health. At the time of writing, legislation and the Code of Practice are awaited.

Compensation amounts and surrogacy

In a recent case,[12] a woman claimed compensation as a result of medical negligence that led to a stillborn child and a subtotal hysterectomy. The defendant health authority accepted liability, but damages were disputed. She claimed in addition to damages for pain, suffering and loss of amenity, compensation for the post-traumatic stress disorder as a result of the stillbirth and hysterectomy, loss of earnings and the cost of surrogacy. The court held that she would be awarded £66,000 for the infertility and the accompanying psychological condition. It refused, however, to compensate her for loss of earnings, since it held that regardless of the stillbirth and hysterectomy, she would not have been able to start her training as a teacher earlier; the court also refused the cost of surrogacy, which the claimant was arranging in the USA. The judge held that under the present UK law surrogacy arrangements were unenforceable and, if commercial, illegal. It would therefore be wrong, and contrary to public policy, that damages should be awarded to enable an unenforceable and unlawful contract to be entered into. The judge did not conclude that it would always be wrong to award damages for the cost of surrogacy, but in the claimant's particular circumstances, she could not succeed.

Conscientious objection

The nurse's personal moral beliefs are taken into account by Section 38 of the Human Fertilisation and Embryology Act 1990, which provides a conscientious objection clause as follows:

1. No person who has a conscientious objection to participating in any activity governed by this Act shall be under any duty, however arising, to do so.

2. In any legal proceedings, the burden of proof of conscientious objection shall rest on the person claiming to rely on it.

3. In any proceedings, before a court in Scotland, a statement on oath by any person to the effect that he has a conscientious objection to participating in a particular activity governed by the Act shall be sufficient evidence of that fact for the purpose of discharging the burden of proof imposed by subsection (2) above.

Confidentiality

Section 33 of the 1990 Act places tight restrictions on the disclosure of information held by the HFEA or a licensing authority. The few exceptions to these restrictions were considered to be inadequate and the Human Fertilisation and Embryology (Disclosure of Information) Act 1992 was passed, amending Section 33 as follows: to enable the patient to give specific and general consent to disclosure; for information to be disclosed by a clinician to his legal adviser in relation to legal proceedings (the 1990 Act had permitted disclosures only in relation to action under the Consented Disabilities (Civil Liability) Act 1976); and for a couple to obtain information about the legal parentage of a child born to a surrogate mother. A Statutory Instrument[13] restricts the right of access to health records that would disclose information showing that an unidentifiable individual was or might have been born in consequence of treatment services under the Human Fertilisation and Embryology Act 1990. This does not affect the right given by Section 31(3), which enables a person of 18 or over to obtain information from HFEA if that person was born in consequence of treatment services, but an opportunity for proper counselling must be provided before disclosure.

Genetics

Considerable progress has been made in the science of gene identification. The Human Genome Project was an international collaboration by the United States Government and the Wellcome Trust that started in 1990. It aimed to identify every gene in the human body. At the same time, a private company, Celera Genomics Corp headed by Craig Venter, was pursuing the same object. The project was completed on 26 July 2000 when a dead heat was claimed between the two rival organisations. Genes linked with specific hereditary diseases have now been identified. One of the first genes to be linked with a specific disease was that of cystic fibrosis. Subsequently, there have been claims of genetic links with a wide range of medical conditions and human qualities and characteristics. For example, claims have been made for genetic links for sleeplessness,[14] for heart disease,[15] for dyslexia,[16] for hibernation,[17] for diseases of old age[18] and many other disorders and characteristics. These discoveries present many ethical and legal issues: to what extent should parents have the right to modify the genetic inheritance of their children? What controls should there be over individuals purchasing commercial testing kits? Should insurers have the right to compel those seeking insurance to be tested? Baroness Kennedy has been appointed by the government to head an inquiry into the implications of the mapping of the human genetic code.

Genetic testing for pregnant women

Which pregnant women should be offered genetic testing? The Human Genetics Commission[19] has issued guidance for consultation on behalf of the former Advisory Committee on Genetic Testing, whose work it has taken over. The guidance suggests that women should have access to prenatal genetic tests and the expertise she requires appropriate to her risk. There should be resources in primary care and hospitals for referral and subsequent care of the patient. Prenatal genetic testing for rare disorders should be arranged on a supra-regional or national level.

Gene therapy and genetic diagnosis

The Clothier Committee[20] recommended that research should continue for somatic cell gene therapy where treatment is given to an individual patient to alleviate disease (e.g. cystic fibrosis). However, germ line gene therapy, where future generations are affected, should not as yet be lawful. It recommended the establishment of a supervisory body, the Gene Therapy Advisory Committee, which was set up initially under the chairmanship of Professor Dame Jane Lloyd.

The Human Fertilisation and Embryology Authority and the Advisory Committee on Genetic Testing established in 1998 a joint working group to prepare a consultation paper on Pre-implantation Genetic Diagnosis (PGD). This paper was published in November 1999.[21] Pre-implantation refers to the two stage process in which IVF is used to create embryos that are then tested for a particular genetic disorder or to establish their sex (where the disorder is sex linked). Embryos that do not carry the genetic disorder or are not of the potentially affected sex can then be transferred to the uterus in the hope that a normal pregnancy will develop. Four centres in the UK are licensed to carry out PGD. Testing for CF is the most common reason for pre-implantation diagnosis for a single gene defect. However, there are concerns about the range of conditions for which PGD should be licensed, at the seriousness of the condition to be checked for, whether the late onset of a condition should be taken into account and what the nature of the regulation should be. Such issues are the subject of the consultation. At the time of writing, the results of this consultation exercise are awaited.

Gender selection

To what extent should parents be able to select the sex of their children? Certainly in some cultures, parental selection could lead to an oversupply of boys and very few girls, but there may be justification for it when hereditary diseases such as haemophilia are sex linked. A commercial organisation has been set up to assist couples in obtaining the gender of their choice for their child. Where this does not involve gametes of other persons, it does not come under the provision of the 1990 Act. Some consider, however, that there should be controls in this field. A public consultation paper was issued by the Human Fertilisation and Embryology Authority in January 1993.[22]

The present situation is that gender selection through the choice of embryos for implantation is permitted if there are sex linked medical conditions, but not for other purposes. This is currently being challenged in several cases. For example, parents who lost their only daughter in a fire, wish to have gender selection of embryos to ensure that they have another daughter.

Genetic screening and testing

Concern at the possibility that insurers and employers would require compulsory genetic screening led to the Nuffield Council on Bioethics reporting on the ethical issues involved in genetic screening. It recommended safeguards in relation to consent, confidentiality and monitoring of genetic screening programmes.[23,24]

Commercial screening kits

Do it yourself genetic screening test kits are now available and have raised considerable ethical concerns. 'A Code of Practice and Guidance of Human Genetic Testing' was published on 23 September 1997 by the Health Departments of the United Kingdom.[25] It was put forward by the Advisory Committee on Genetic Testing (ACGT) on the basis of proposals prepared by a subgroup (chaired by Professor Marcus Pembrey). It recommended that a voluntary system of compliance and monitoring should be established rather than a statutory scheme. The Code of Practice and Guidance is intended to be used by those who supply genetic testing services direct to the public. The Code itself covers the following areas: testing laboratories, equipment and reagents; confidentiality and storage of samples and records; proposed tests should be cleared with the ACGT and comply with the Code; tests should not be available to those under 16 years or to those unable to make a competent decision regarding testing; specified information should be provided to the customer; pre- and post-test genetic consultation should be available without additional charge; and finally the involvement of medical practitioners. Suggested forms for use by the suppliers are provided as well as addresses of the regional genetic centres and other relevant organisations. If the main users of the testing services are national organisations, and there is little private commerce, then there will be strong commercial reasons for the firms to comply with this guidance and quality standards, otherwise they stand to lose lucrative contracts. The attitudes of the suppliers and the purchasers will also influence the extent to which some of the guidelines become mere tokenism: The supplier is required to provide opportunities for pre- or post-testing genetic consultation, (which is widely defined). In practice, this may become a formality (a quick phone call) and after all, the purchaser might refuse to co-operate.

This voluntary Code may work, given suppliers who have goodwill and purchasers who are well informed, without the necessity of statutory controls and criminal sanctions. The Advisory Committee on Genetic Testing requires companies selling the kits to submit them for prior approval, but it has no statutory powers and its guidelines are not enforceable.

Code of Practice on genetic tests from the Insurers

The Association of British Insurers published a Code of Practice in 1997. It made further revisions to it in 1999.[26] It is a voluntary code for insurers over genetic tests and gives the following guidance.

1. It should not require a person to take a genetic test in order to obtain insurance cover.

2. If the results of a genetic test are in a person's medical records, they can be taken into account only if they apply to one of 7 conditions for which the tests are deemed reliable. (These conditions include breast cancer, Alzheimer's and Huntingdon's disease.)

3. If the test is later found to be unreliable, then the person is entitled to a refund of overpaid premiums and cheaper future payments.

4. A person is obliged to tell an insurance company if he has had a genetic test and disclose the results.

5. Anyone refused insurance cover or who wishes to complain can contact the ABI.[27]

Some evidence is emerging that contrary to the assertion of the ABI, some people are being refused insurance cover on the grounds that they have a genetic disorder.[28,29] It may be that either statutory intervention or some form of state insurance cover is necessary to protect those who are vulnerable. In October 2000, new guidelines were recommended by a Genetics and Insurance Committee established by the Department of Health.[30] The Committee recommended that the reliability and relevance of the genetic test for Huntingdon's Chorea is sufficient for insurance companies to use the result when assessing applications for life insurance. Insurers will not be able to require prospective clients to take the test, but they will be able to ask clients if they have taken tests for Huntingdon's Chorea, and to ask for the results to be given. The recommendations have been criticised, for example by the National Consumer Council, on the grounds that they will create a genetic underclass and will dissuade people from taking the tests.[31] In addition, scientists are fearful that potential volunteers for genetic tests will refuse to co-operate in this country. Thus many scientists would have no option but to work outside this country, where potential research subjects would not have to disclose results to insurance companies.[32] The Human Genetics Commission is, at the time of writing, formulating a public consultation exercise on the storage, protection and use of personal genetic information which will include the use of genetic data for insurance purposes.

Genetics and confidentiality

The identification of genes linked to disabilities has raised serious legal and ethical issues as the following situation illustrates.

Situation 22.1   Concealing information

Mavis undergoes a genetic test and discovers that she is carrying a gene that is linked with Huntingdon's Chorea. Her sister, Rachel, has just got married and Mavis knows her sister intends having children and that both her sister and any children could be at risk of suffering from that disease. Mavis decides that she will keep this information to herself.

In this situation, the ordinary laws of confidentiality (see Chapter 8) apply. There are no specific statutes that require the testers to disclose the results to any members of the family. If Rachel is unaware that there is a family risk of Huntingdon's Chorea, she would not have the grounds to have herself tested or to seek a disclosure of the results of the test on Mavis. By the time, Rachel has had her children and maybe finds that she is suffering from or is a carrier of the disease, it is too late to take preventative action. (Had she known of the risk, she could have opted for the testing of embryos before implantation – see above).

Cloning

Dolly the sheep in 1997 was the first vertebrate cloned from a cell of an adult animal. Because of the immense significance of this scientific development, the Human Genetics Advisory Commission set up a working group and held a consultation exercise on cloning. It issued a consultation paper in 1998.[33] Following this exercise, HFEA recommended that research should continue into creating cloned tissue that can be transplanted, but that cloning for reproductive purposes should continue to be illegal.[34]

Following the report of the Chief Medical Officer's Expert group on therapeutic cloning,[35] the government accepted its recommendations (press announcement, August 16 2000) and agreed that:

1. the currently permitted grounds for embryo research will include treatment for a range of human diseases and research on human embryonic stem cells should be permitted; (at present research on embryos is restricted to the first 14 days and is permitted for 5 specific purposes relating to infertility, congenital disease, gene or chromosomal abnormalities, miscarriage or contraception. Additional purposes can be added by Statutory Instrument.)

2. research involving cell nuclear replacement (so-called 'therapeutic cloning') should be allowed to help understand the biological mechanisms involved in the growth and development of human cells;

3. specific consent must be given before early embryos can be donated for stem cell research.

On 19 December 2000, the House of Commons passed secondary legislation legalising research on the stem cells of embryos and the House of Lords approved the changes in 2001. This means that it is now possible for stem cells to be used in the research for illnesses such a cancer, Parkinson's Disease, diabetes, osteoporosis, spinal cord injuries, Alzheimer's, leukaemia and multiple sclerosis. A licence is required from the Human Fertilisation and Embryology Authority and the cloning of human beings remains illegal.

The future

This area has seen and will see substantial and significant technological developments affecting health care. The completion of the Genome Project will have immense consequences for health care in terms of the detection of hereditary conditions and funding. The many legal issues arising include insurance and confidentiality. Genetic engineering is not covered in statutes and it is clear that a new statutory framework is now required.

Questions and exercises

1 Look at the daily papers and journals over the next month and collect details on the cases, debates and articles on the topics discussed in this chapter.

2 To what extent do you think that couples should have the right to obtain treatment for their infertility?

3 Where a child is born as the result of a surrogacy arrangement so that an embryo from a woman and her husband is transplanted into the uterus of another woman, what legal rights do you believe that the woman giving birth to the child should have over the genetic mother? What legal rights does she have at present?

4 Can experimentation on an embryo and its replacement in the uterus to develop as a human being be justified?

5 To what extent do you think the law is an appropriate machinery to determine the choices of parents and professionals in the topics discussed in this chapter?

References

[1] Committee of Inquiry into Human Fertilisation and Embryology chaired by Baroness Warnock 1984 Cmnd. 9314 HMSO London

[2] *A v. C* 1978 8 Fam Law 170

[3] Committee of Inquiry into Human Fertilisation and Embryology chaired by Baroness Warnock 1984 Cmnd. 9314 HMSO London

[4] *R v. Ethical Committee of St Mary's Hospital ex parte Harriot, The Times* 27 October 1987; [1988] 1 FLR 512

[5] *R v Sheffield HA ex parte Seale* [1994] 25 BMLR 1

[6] Human Fertilisation and Embryology Authority Code of Practice London HFEA 1995

[7] *R v. Human Fertilisation and Embryology Authority ex p. Blood* [1997] 2 WLR 806

[8] Department of Health Press announcement 25 August 2000 DoH

[9] *Re C(A minor)* (Wardship: Surrogacy) [1985] FLR 846 (the father was able to obtain a wardship summons in order to obtain custody of the baby)

[10] *In re an adoption* (surrogacy) 1987 2 All ER 826.

[11] *Re Q* (Parental Order) [1996] 1 FLR 369

[12] *Briody v. St Helen's and Knowsley HA* (2000), *The Times* 1 March 2000

[13] Statutory Instrument 1993 No. 746

[14] Nigel Hawkes, Uncontrollable sleepers find hope in gene clue, *The Times* 6 August 1999

[15] A correspondent, Heart gene discovered, *The Times* 8 November 1999

[16] Ian Murray, Genetic link to dyslexia is found, *The Times* 7 September 1999

[17] Roger Dobson, Found: the hibernating gene that could send man to the stars, *The Sunday Times* 6 February 2000

[18] Nigel Hawkes, Gene discovery may reduce diseases linked to old age, *The Times* 11 April 2000

[19] www.open.gov.uk/doh/genetics.htm

[20] Clothier Committee (HMSO, January 1992)

[21] Human Fertilisation and Embryology Authority and Advisory Committee on Genetic Testing Consultation document on Preimplantation Genetic Diagnosis. HFEA and ACGT 1999 London

[22] Human Fertilisation and Embryology Authority Public Consultation on Sex Selection January 1993 HFEA London

[23] A citizens' jury on the topic was being held in November 1997 at the University of Glamorgan. For further information on the report of the jury's recommendations contact Marcus Longley of the Welsh Institute of Health and Social Care University of Glamorgan 01443 483070

[24] Marcus Pembrey, The Progress Guide to Genetics, A Progress Educational Trust Publication 1996 for further information.

[25] Advisory Committee on Genetic Testing Code of Practice and Guidance on Human Genetic Testing 23 September 1997 Health Departments of the United Kingdom.

[26] Association of British Insurers Code of practice for genetic testing 1999

[27] Association of British Insurers 0207 600 3333

[28] News item, Insurers ignore genetics code, *The Sunday Times* 13 December 1998

[29] Robert Winnett, Medical underclass fears insurance blacklisting, *The Sunday Times* 26 March 2000

[30] Department of Health, Committee on Genetics and Insurance Report October, 2000

[31] Mark Henderson, Insurers to check for genetic illness, *The Times* 13 October, 2000

[32] Mark Henderson, Scientists attack gene test ruling, *The Times* 27 November 2000

[33] Human Genetics Advisory Commission (HGAC) and Human Fertilisation and Embryology Authority Consultation Document on Cloning Issues in Reproduction, Science and Medicine 1998 HGAC London

[34] Human Fertilisation and Embryology Authority and Human Genetic Advisory Commission, Cloning Issues in Reproduction, Science and Medicine, HFEA/HGAC December 1998

[35] Chief Medical Officer's Expert group on therapeutic cloning, Stem Cell research: Medical Progress with Responsibility, Department of Health August 2000

23 Community and primary care nursing

This chapter covers the law relating to nurses who work in the community and in primary care, including community/district nurses, health visitors, practice nurses and specialist nurses. Community psychiatric nurses will also find Chapter 20 on mental health care of relevance. The development of community care has meant that the focus for many health professionals has switched from the institution to the community and those who have always been community workers, such as the health visitor and the district nurse, are now feeling the increased pressure from the recent implications of the policy to transfer patients from the institution to the community. Recent developments have seen an increase in specialist posts in the community. Community nurses for the mentally handicapped and community psychiatric nurses are increasing in number and specialist posts for stoma care, incontinence and terminal illness are being established. Many liaison nurses are now seeking specialist training. There are increased appointments for occupational therapists, physiotherapists and community paediatricians. The organisational changes with the introduction of Primary Care Groups leading to Primary Care Trusts and Care Trusts has also brought about significant changes for these community nurses and also for practice nurses. These organisational changes are covered in this chapter and the overall organisation of the NHS is considered in Chapter 5. Figure 23.1 (overleaf) sets out the areas that will be discussed in this chapter and Figure 23.2 illustrates some of the particular difficulties with which these workers are faced.

NHS and Community Care Act 1990

The community provisions of this Act came into force on 1 April 1993 and are summarised below. They follow the recommendations of the Griffiths Report and the White Paper 'Caring for People'. The Act requires the following:

1. Community care plans. Under Section 46, local authorities in conjunction with health authorities and the voluntary and private sector must prepare plans for the provision of services in the community and revise them annually.

2. Assessment of needs for community care services. Section 47 requires local authorities to carry out an assessment of needs for community services on any individual in its catchment area who would appear to be in need of any services that it provides or for which it arranges the provision. Where appropriate, the health authority and/or the housing authority may be required to be involved

1. NHS and Community Care Act 1990.
2. Primary care groups, primary care trusts and care trusts.
3. NHS and social services provision.
4. NHS Plan and community care.
5. Carers.
6. Negligence and standard of care
   (a) key worker;
   (b) foreseeability and standard of care;
   (c) to whom is the nurse responsible?
   (d) giving advice;
   (e) vaccination.
7. Safety of the community professional
   (a) defective premises;
   (b) aggression.
8. Consent to treatment
   (a) mentally disordered;
   (b) forcible entry;
   (c) compulsory removal
       (i) Mental Health Act 1983;
       (ii) National Assistance Act 1948.
9. Protection of property.
10. Disclosure of information.
11. Criminal suspicion.
12. School nurse.
13. Clinic nurse.
14. Practice nurse.
15. Cervical screening.

Figure 23.1 Issues covered in Chapter 23.

1. Isolation.
2. Vulnerability.
3. Sole responsibility.
4. Pressure to go beyond job description.
5. Health and safety hazard and occupier's liability.
6. Variable facilities and resources.

Figure 23.2 Difficulties faced by the nurse in the community.

in the assessment. In urgent situations, community care services can be provided temporarily and an assessment should take place as soon as possible.

3. Financial arrangements for nursing and residential accommodation. The local authority has the responsibility for purchasing accommodation for clients from 1 April 1993. Those in residence on 31 March 1993 will continue to receive means-tested higher-level Income Support from the Department of Social Security.

For those residents who move in on or after 1 April 1993, the local authority, following an assessment, may purchase a place at a nursing home or residential home and recover the fees from residents, who can claim means-tested Income Support from the DSS, but only at the ordinary level.

4. Inspection and powers of the Secretary of State. Persons can be authorised by the Secretary of State under Section 48 to inspect premises used for the provision of community care services. Local authorities have inspection units. The Secretary of State can issue directions as to the exercise of social services functions (Section 50) and has required all local authorities to establish a procedure for considering any representations, including complaints about a failure to discharge local authority social services functions.

5. The Act also makes provision for the transfer of health service staff to local authorities (Section 49).

Considerable guidance has been issued by the Department of Health and Social Services Inspectorate on the implementation of these statutory duties. The Audit Commission, December 1993,[1] reported that cautious but steady progress has been made with the community care changes. Community health professionals are finding that they are caring for a more acutely ill population as the number of day cases increases and shorter lengths of stay for major surgery become the norm. The 'hospital at home' phenomenon places increasing pressure on community nurses who must ensure that their competence, skill and knowledge develop to meet their new roles. All community health professionals, whether caring for acute, chronically sick, mentally disordered, elderly or disabled patients, are finding that the demands upon them are increasing and there are greater pressures on resources. Waiting lists for occupational therapy services are increasing in length. Controversy has developed over the nature of assessment and the extent to which they should identify needs that cannot realistically be met. The practitioner who works in the community should ensure that she plays a full part in the preparation of community care plans and the identification of needs, and in upholding the professional duties to the patient set out in the Code of Professional Conduct.

Primary care services, groups, primary care trusts and care trusts

Family practitioner services are organised by the Health Authorities (replacing the Family Health Service Authorities in this function). Health Authorities contract with general practitioners, pharmacists and dentists to provide services in their areas. The practitioners do not usually become employees of the health authority, but provide services as independent contractors following terms and conditions of service that are nationally agreed. Under these terms of service, general practitioners are required to provide 24-hour care for the patients on their list. Whilst some partnerships still provide personal cover for their patients, in practice there have been recent changes in the provision of Out-Of-Hours services, including the formation of GP Co-operative and the use of deputising services. In October 2000, a review of Out-of-Hours care was published,[2] which proposed a flexible, national model of integrated out-of-hours provision with defined quality standards, ensuring that patient access should be based on a single telephone call and all professionals providing the service should work together. Major funding and organisational change are anticipated to implement the recommendations.

Following the White Paper on the NHS[3] and the Health Act 1999, Primary Care Groups (in Wales Local Health Groups) have been set up. These enable local health services to be provided and commissioned under the aegis of the health authority in accordance with identified needs. Often chaired by general practitioners, they have a strategic role in developing primary care. The functions of Primary Care Groups as envisaged in the NHS White Paper are shown in Box 23.1.

In England, many Primary Care Groups have taken on trust status under the provisions of the Health Act 1999. Ultimately, these Primary Care Trusts may become the employers of those providing community health services. The legislation permits considerable flexibility in the way in which Primary Care Trusts are organised and managed. Those involved in the provision of community nursing services may find that their contracts of employment are transferred to other organisations. Their functions and powers are set out in Chapter 5. The government stated in the NHS Plan[4] that it expected that by April 2004 all Primary Care Groups will have become Primary Care Trusts. The RCN has identified the knowledge and skills that nurses need to make Primary Care Groups a success.[5] Care Trusts which provide health and social services are being set up under the Health Act 1999 and Health and Social Care Act 2001 (see page 454).

Box 23.1

Functions of Primary Care Groups envisaged in the NHS White Paper

Be accountable to the Health Authority and

1. Be representative of all the GP practices in the Group.
2. Have a governing body that includes community nursing and social services, as well as GPs drawn from the area.
3. Take account of social services as well as HA boundaries to help promote integration in service planning and provision.
4. Abide by the local Health Improvement Programme.
5. Have clear arrangements for public involvement including open meetings.
6. Have efficient and effective arrangements for management and financial responsibility.

NHS and social services provision

Considerable problems have arisen in the provision of a seamless service between NHS and social services because NHS care is free at the point of delivery whereas most social services provision is means tested. Local criteria for the eligibility for NHS continuing care have been drawn up in each area and those who disagree with the decisions can use the complaints procedures established by the health authority and local authority.

Case 23.1   *NHS or Means Tested care?*[6]

Pamela Coughlan brought an action against the health authority in 1999 when she was told that she would have to leave the nursing home she was living in at NHS expense and move to another home that would be means tested. She had been grievously injured in a road traffic accident in 1971. She was tetraplegic, doubly incontinent and partially paralysed in the respiratory tract. She had been promised by the health authority that she would be able to stay in Mardon House for life, the costs of her care being met by the NHS.

The Court of Appeal held that nursing care for the chronically sick was not always the sole responsibility of the NHS, but could, in appropriate circumstances, be provided by a local authority as a social service and the patient could, depending on her means, be liable to meet the cost of that care. However, there was no over-riding public interest in the health authority breaking its promise to her that she could stay in that home for her life.

There was no appeal against the Court of Appeal's decision. Pamela Coughlan was able to continue to have NHS funding of her care, but the court had accepted the principle that nursing care did not always have to be funded by the NHS, so in that sense both parties won their case. However, the principle that nursing and other personal care should be funded by the NHS was put forward by the majority recommendations in the Royal Commission Report on the Long-Term Care of the Elderly,[7] which is discussed in Chapter 19, pages 392–3.

A dispute arose in relation to the provision of services to disabled people under the Chronic Sick and Disabled Persons Act 1970 and the extent to which the local authority could take into account its financial resources.

Case 23.2   *Assessment of disabled persons*[8]

A man of 79 with severe disabilities brought an action in Gloucester when the local authority informed him that it was going to withdraw his cleaning and laundry services. He obtained judicial review of the local authority's decision on the grounds that they had not reassessed his needs prior to withdrawing the services. The High Court judge refused to grant a declaration that, in carrying out the reassessment, the local authority was not entitled to take into account the resources available to it. The Court of Appeal allowed his appeal, on the grounds that the local authority was not entitled to take into account the resources available to it. The local authority appealed to the House of Lords.

The House of Lords allowed the appeal holding that, for the purposes of Section 2(1) of the 1970 Act, a chronically sick or disabled person's needs were to be assessed in the context of, and by reference to, the provision of certain types of assistance for promoting the welfare of disabled people using eligibility criteria. These criteria had to be set taking into account current acceptable standards of living, the nature and extent of the disability and the relative cost balanced against the relative benefit and the relative need for that benefit. Its impact on its resources had to be evaluated and therefore its financial position was relevant. The authority could not make the decision in a vacuum from which all considerations of costs were expelled.

In July 2001 the Department of Health published a consultation document 'Guidance on Fair Access to Care Services' to ensure greater consistency in the use of eligibility criteria for access to car services.

In 2000, the Audit Commission published its findings on the provision of equipment for older and disabled people.[9] It found that users were not asked basic questions about the sort of help they needed; they had to wait for long periods of time for their equipment; the equipment was not always suitable nor of a high quality; and the current organisation of equipment services is a recipe for inequality and inefficiency. Amongst its many significant recommendations are suggestions for involving users, restructuring of mobility services, the integration of health and social services provision for community equipment under the new powers of the Health Act 1999 and the introduction of policy reviews and dissemination of good practice.

NHS Plan[10] and community care

The NHS Plan has made some radical recommendations to improve joint working of health and social services. These are considered in Chapter 19 on the care of the elderly, but the proposals will affect other client groups. Chapter 7 of the NHS Plan envisages the establishment of Care Trusts which will commission and deliver primary and community health care as well as social care for older people and other client groups. Social services would be delivered under delegated authority from local councils. Nor is the government dependent upon local agreement for the establishment of Care Trusts since the NHS Plan states in paragraph 7.11:

> Where local health and social care organisations have failed to establish effective joint partnerships – or where inspection or joint reviews have shown that services are failing – the Government will take powers to establish integrated arrangements through the new Care Trusts.

Powers to effect this have been enacted in Sections 45–48 of the Health and Social Care Act 2001.

Carers

It has been estimated that Great Britain has an estimated number of 5.7 million carers, and one in six households contains a carer.[11] The Carers (Recognition and Services) Act 1995 required local authorities to carry out an assessment of the carer's ability to provide and to continue to provide care for the person receiving community care services, but it did not give local authorities the power to offer carers' services to support them in their caring role. In 1999, the government published a Carer's National Strategy Document[12] highlighting the need for legislation to enable local authorities to provide services direct to carers. A Carers and Disabled Children Act 2000 has four main purposes:

1. It gives local authorities the power to supply certain services direct to carers.

2. It enables local authorities to make direct payments to carers, including 16- and 17-year-olds, to persons with parental responsibility for disabled children and to the disabled children. These direct payments can then be used for a provider for those services chosen by the carer.

3. Local authorities can provide short-term break voucher schemes, which will give carers flexibility in the timing and choice of breaks.

4. The local authorities are given power to charge carers for the services they receive. In its assessment, the LA can take into account any assessment made under the 1995 Act. The 2000 Act does not apply if the carer is an employee or a volunteer for a voluntary organisation. The LA must consider the assessment and decide:
   (a) whether the carer has needs in relation to the care that he provides or intends to provide;
   (b) if so, whether they could be satisfied (wholly or partly) by services which the LA may provide; and
   (c) if they could be so satisfied, whether or not to provide services to the carer.

Negligence

The standard of care

Situation 23.1   Key worker

The Roger Park Community NHS Trust set up a series of location managers and teams of multi-disciplinary professionals for clients. Each client was assigned a key worker who would discuss with the team that particular client's difficulties and try to resolve them as far as possible on his own, thus preventing the client from being visited by a whole host of different professionals. This key worker could be any one of a variety of professionals, but as far as possible it was one whose training was most relevant to the client's needs.

Margaret Downs lived on her own and was recovering from a stroke. With the help of the physiotherapist she was making good progress and the community nurse, Angela Hide, was visiting her twice a week to dress a leg ulcer and also to give her a bath. The community nurse was Margaret's key worker. After a few weeks, Angela decided that Margaret would be able to manage to bath herself on her own if she had a bath rail and support. She got in touch with the local authority department that provided home aids and ordered the appropriate devices to

Situation 23.1 continued

be fitted. She told Margaret that once they were installed she would not need any assistance to bath, but that if she got into any difficulties she should let Angela know. A few days later Margaret, who had not been seen by neighbours for a few days, was found dead in the bath. A post mortem showed that she had slipped while trying to get out of the bath, that the hand rail was not in a suitable position and that she had probably died of exposure. The coroner held an inquest and Angela was asked to provide a statement, as was the occupational therapist in the team, since the task of assessment for bath aids was normally that of the occupational therapist.

In Situation 23.1 on page 455, at the inquest, it is possible that the relatives will be present and probably represented by a solicitor or barrister. The inquest might well be followed by a civil claim against the NHS Trust on the basis of its direct liability for the death of Margaret in failing to lay down an appropriate procedure for caring for patients in the community and also on the basis of its indirect or vicarious liability for Angela's negligence. Was Angela negligent? Obviously, there are very few facts given here on which the answer to such a question could be determined, but at the heart of the negligence action will be the question: did Angela follow the accepted approved practice in making those recommendations about the bath aids? Or if she did not follow the approved practice, was there justification for her not doing so and would that justification be supported by competent professional opinion? The question of whether such a decision was within her competence or whether she should have brought in the occupational therapist, whose training includes that type of assessment, will be crucial. It does not, of course, follow that the mere fact that Angela strayed outside her competence will automatically mean that she failed to follow a reasonable standard of care. In addition, the relatives will also have to establish that there was a causal link between the breach of duty by Angela and the harm caused to Margaret and that that harm was reasonably foreseeable.

The most important feature in any team approach and key worker system is that each should know the limits of their competence and the point at which the patient's safety demands that another person be brought in to advise. In the Wilsher case (considered in detail in Chapter 6), the court has held that there is no concept of team liability. It is a question of individual liability and/or the liability of the NHS Trust. (The legal issues arising from the Scope of Professional Practice are considered in Chapter 24.)

To whom is the nurse responsible?

Situation 23.2   A clash of duties

Community nurses in the Roger Park Unit had been given instructions that they should not carry drugs in their cars, nor should they personally arrange for drugs on prescriptions to be collected from the chemists. Ruth Green was caring for a terminally ill patient who was being nursed by her husband at home. The GP had left a prescription on his last visit and the husband asked her if she would be kind enough to bring the drugs back from the chemist. He said that he did not have any transport or any neighbours who could help and he did not want to leave his wife on her own. Ruth said that she was not allowed to collect drugs from the chemist for patients. He was clearly distressed and offered to come with her if she could provide the transport, but it would still mean leaving his wife on her own. She agreed to this and took him to the chemist and then home again – a round trip of about seven miles which took 20 minutes. The husband could not understand why he had to go with her, leaving his wife for such a long time and obviously in danger. Ruth herself felt that the rules were not appropriate to that situation and wondered whether there was any law that covered her duties.

Situation 23.2, where there is a clash between what the nurse is told to do and what she feels is her duty to the patient, is not unusual, nor is it confined to the community. Other situations, for example, where the nurse is told not to take patients in her car, or where she is given instructions about lifting that she cannot carry out because the facilities or staff are not available, place the nurse in a dilemma. Is she to fulfil what she believes to be her duty to the patient or should she obey the NHS Trust's or nurse manager's instructions? The clash can be seen as a conflict between the Code of Professional Conduct set down by the UKCC and her employer's orders. She has a contractual duty to obey the latter, since it is an implied term of her contract of employment that she obey the reasonable orders of her employer; on the other hand, she has a professional duty to follow the Code of Professional Conduct. If provisions of the Code are included in the contract of employment, then there should in theory be no clash between the two. Instructions by the employer must be reasonable and it can be argued that any instructions that clash with the professional obligations of the registered practitioner cannot be reasonable.

The first task for Ruth Green in a situation like this is for the nurse management to be given the full facts of any potential hardship suffered by the patient as a result of their instructions and procedures. Examples of the difficulties that have and will arise from following these instructions must be provided in detail. It may so happen that, when presented with this evidence, management might well feel that either the whole policy should be revised or that certain exceptions can be made in circumstances where the patient is likely to suffer harm. Alternatively, it may be possible for other arrangements to be made which will ensure the safety and well-being of the patient. For example, in rural areas, pharmacists sometimes provide a home delivery service for medicines and oxygen. If the management is adamant that the procedures must be followed without any exception, then the nurse has a duty to undertake those unless there is likely to be such harm to the patient that it is clearly contrary to her duty of care to the patient. In such a situation, her records would have to be very comprehensive to justify her action. In serious situations, the nurse should raise concerns with senior levels of management in accordance with the Public Interest Disclosure Act which is discussed in Chapter 4.

In the following case, the fact that a GP relied heavily upon the role of community nurses was the subject of disciplinary action.

Case 23.3   Medical treatment: reasonableness of doctor relying upon nurses[13]

A GP applied for judicial review of a finding by the Chief Executive of a Family Health Services Authority that he was in breach of his terms of service by relying upon district nurses who had visited the patient daily to treat a patient's bed sores. The patient suffered from senile dementia, incontinence and was bedridden. The doctor visited her, prescribed antibiotics for infected bedsores, leaving instructions with staff that he should be contacted if there was a deterioration. He was not contacted, but subsequently the patient was removed to hospital where criticism of her previous nursing care was made. The judge, in granting the application, held that the Chief Executive had failed to consider whether the doctor had behaved in accordance with his terms of service and had taken irrelevant considerations into account. There was also procedural unfairness in that the Chief Executive had not alerted the doctor to the importance he attached to these considerations so that the doctor could make relevant representations.

There are clear lessons for nursing staff from this case. If they are concerned about a patient's condition they should ensure that the doctor is called in to examine the patient.

Giving advice

One of the most important tasks of many registered practitioners, and in particular the health visitor, is giving advice to clients, young and old, on all aspects of their health and ways of keeping healthy. For example, one of the vexed questions these days is the extent to which the health visitor should encourage a mother to have her child vaccinated and the possibility of the health visitor herself being held liable for giving advice that turns out to cause harm. The topic of liability for communications was discussed in Chapter 4 where it was stated that exactly the same principles of liability apply in giving advice as apply in using skills. Thus if a health visitor, knowing that a child has a history of convulsions, fails to take this into account in advising the mother to have the child vaccinated, and also fails to ensure that the doctor is advised of this fact, then the health visitor may well share some responsibility for any harm that befalls the child as a result of undergoing the vaccination.

Vaccination

Compensation for vaccine damage can be obtained in two ways. First, there is a statutory scheme of compensation under the Vaccine Damage Payments Act 1979. Under this scheme £100,000[15] is now payable to a person who can establish that they have been severely disabled as a result of a vaccination against the specified diseases of diphtheria, tetanus, whooping cough, poliomyelitis, measles, rubella, tuberculosis, smallpox, and any other disease specified by the Secretary of State. The severe disability must be at least 80 per cent. Whether the disability has been caused by the vaccination shall be established on a balance of probabilities. The government announced on 27 June 2000[14] that it intended to lower the disability level from 80% to 60%. In addition, the six-year limit on making claims will be raised to any time up to the age of 18 years. This will enable more persons disabled by vaccines to claim the payment, including those who have already been turned down. They will be able to reapply under the new rules. Meningococcal Group C has been added to the diseases covered and the person need not be under 18 at the time of vaccination, nor need there be an outbreak of the disease. (Vaccine Damages Payments (Specific Diseases) Order 2001, SI 1652.)

This statutory scheme does not prevent a claim being made in the civil courts for negligence in relation to damage caused by vaccine. Clearly, if such a case could succeed, far more than £100,000 would be payable for severely disabled persons. However, civil action faces a further difficulty, as well as having to establish a causal link between the vaccine and the disability. The plaintiff must also show that the disability occurred as a result of negligence by the professional: for example, the professionals failed to take account of the person's present health condition or previous history and the vaccine was contra-indicated for that person. A claim could also be brought against the drug company if there were some defect in the vaccine, and this claim could now come under the Consumer Protection Act (considered in Chapter 12), under which it is no longer necessary to show negligence by a manufacturer, but simply that there was a defect in the product. This would be extremely difficult if the victim was the only one from a particular batch who suffered harm. The civil cases so far have not overcome the problems of proving causation apart from a case in Ireland (see below).

Case 23.4   Vaccine damage

Susan Loveday was vaccinated for whooping cough in 1970 and 1971, following which she suffered permanent brain damage. She claimed compensation from the Wellcome Foundation who made the vaccine and from the doctor who administered it.

The judge held that on a balance of probabilities the plaintiff had failed to show that pertussis vaccine could cause permanent brain damage in young children. The case therefore failed on this point of causation. The judge also said that even if he had found in favour of the plaintiff on this preliminary point, the plaintiff would still face insuperable difficulties in establishing negligence on the part of the doctor or nurse who administered the vaccine. Such a claim would have to be based on the ground that the vaccination had been given in spite of the presence of certain contra-indications.[16]

In a case in Ireland brought against the Wellcome Foundation,[17] £2.75 million was awarded in respect of brain damage following a vaccination. It was established that a particular batch of vaccine was below standard and should not have been released onto the market.

Safety of the community professional

Entering other people's homes can be dangerous. Unlike the NHS Trust, the occupiers have no obligations under the Health and Safety at Work Act 1974, but they do have obligations under the Occupiers' Liability Act 1957. This is discussed in detail in Chapter 12. The community worker faces problems in relation to both the standard of the structure and the fixtures and fittings. In addition, she might find difficulties caused by the client or the relatives.

Situation 23.3   Defective premises

Pam Hughes, a health visitor, had a large caseload in one of the poorer parts of the city. In one council house, conditions were very bad: the wallpaper was peeling off the walls and there were piles of empty milk bottles in the kitchen and a miscellaneous assortment of carpet pieces on the concrete floor. The local authority had been notified of certain defects to the roof and the fittings, but had said that because of the backlog of maintenance work and staff cuts, it would be several weeks before they could repair the property. The occupiers, Mr and Mrs James and their seven children, could not cope with the situation. Mr James was unemployed and attempted to rectify some of the defects, including putting a new piece of glass in the front door to replace the pane that had been broken when the door was slammed shut. The door had swollen owing to the guttering leaking onto it. Pam Hughes was well used to the family and had been visiting regularly because of her concern over the two youngest children. After one visit, she let herself out – as was her usual custom – and had to pull hard on the front door to open it. As she pulled, the new pane fell out onto her hand, cutting her severely across the wrist. After medical treatment and the advice of a specialist, it appeared that the tendons were severed and she would have very little movement in the four fingers of her right hand. It is certainly questionable whether she will be able to continue her work as a health visitor. Since she is unmarried, and the sole breadwinner, caring for her elderly mother, she is frightened at the prospect of losing her job. She is therefore anxious to recover financial compensation for the injuries.

This particular situation may be unique but it represents the many dangers with which a community worker is faced.

What are the practicalities of obtaining compensation? Is the NHS Trust liable? The answer is probably no, unless it can be shown that it was aware of the danger that an employee was in and failed to take reasonable precautions to safeguard her. There is no evidence that this was so in this case. However, the employers may be prepared to ensure that compensation is paid to her on an ex gratia basis since she was injured in the course of her employment. Mr and Mrs James are possibly liable. As occupiers, they failed to ensure that the premises were safe for the visitor. Mr James may well have repaired the door negligently. However, unless they are insured, the question is academic, since they are unlikely to be able to pay any compensation.

Since it is a council house, it may be that Pam could establish a case against the council in its capacity as landlord and therefore occupier of the building. However, to succeed it would be important to show that, from the obligations under the lease, the landlord had a duty to carry out repairs and his failure to do so had reasonably foreseeably caused the injury to Pam's arm. However, Mr James' repair work makes a break in this chain of causation. If Pam fails against all three potential defendants, then all she can do is fall back on her own insurance cover. Some household insurance schemes also cover for personal injuries or she may have her own personal accident cover. If not, she is unlikely to obtain any compensation other than the usual statutory sick pay scheme and the DSS injury benefits, which are considerably smaller than the level of compensation awarded in the civil courts.

The lesson is clear: because of the dangers of working in variable conditions, it is probably essential that community workers have some form of insurance cover for personal accidents. Some local authorities, professional associations and trade unions have negotiated group schemes of cover. It is, however, the policy of the NHS not to take out insurance cover. If the professional is working on NHS Trust premises all the time, then the authority as occupier has a duty to ensure that he is safe, and if it fails in this duty then it could be held liable under the Occupiers' Liability Act.

Case 23.5 Aggression in the community

Mrs Wyatt suffered from multiple sclerosis, could do nothing for herself and needed nursing assistance. The health authority had the duty to provide a home nursing service under Section 25 of the NHS Act 1946 (as amended by the 1973 Reorganisation Act). The husband, who was also an invalid, abused the nursing staff when they visited his wife and was aggressive and threatening. He was asked to give an assurance that he would cease to behave so, but he refused. The authority told Mrs Wyatt's solicitors that because of Mr Wyatt's behaviour they could not continue the nursing service.

The Court of Appeal held that the authority was doing all that could be reasonably expected of it and the application to compel the authority to provide the service would be dismissed.[18]

The principle established in the Wyatt case can be applied to other situations, including the dangerous nature of the premises. However, before any service can be justifiably withdrawn, the threat to the safety of the community worker must have reached a serious level and every possible precaution must have been taken. For example, it might be necessary for some nurses to be sent in pairs to clients where they face danger. One question that a community nurse sometimes asks is: Can I refuse to go if I consider that I am in personal danger? If the employer's instruction to go to a particular place is unreasonable with regard to the danger with which the worker is faced and the lack of precautions that the employer has taken for the employee's safety, then the employee can refuse to obey them. What is meant by unreasonable? This is a matter of balancing all the options available, including other precautions that it is reasonable for the employer to take against the risks involved and the needs of the client. Where the danger to the professional is the neighbourhood itself it might, for example, be reasonable for the employer to arrange for an alarm/warning system to be carried by the employee or to ensure that they visit homes in pairs. Where the danger comes from aggressive clients or their relatives, then it might be sufficient if a senior nursing officer accompanies the nurse to ensure her safety.

Situation 23.4   *Community dangers*

Albert was a man of 32 with learning disabilities who had been living in a community home for about six weeks. He had settled down well and, provided that he took his medication, he coped quite well, taking his share of the household chores. He was due for an injection, but to the surprise of the community nurse, he said that he was not going to take it. She pleaded with him, but to no avail. She said she would return that night, but he again refused the injection. She offered to provide it in tablet form, but he said that he would not take it in any form. The nurse tried to give the injection to him again, but he lost his temper, striking out and severely injuring her.

Several problems emerge from this: one is the issue of consent to treatment in the community, which we shall return to later; the other is the question of the safety of community nurses for the mentally ill and those with learning disabilities.

It is the employer's duty to take reasonable care of the health, safety and welfare of his employee. If it is known that a particular patient is a danger to nursing staff, then the employer has a duty to take reasonable precautions to see that they will be safe. These precautions might mean ensuring that a female nurse never visits the patient on her own. There is quite likely to be a need for refuge to be provided so that, if a client is particularly disturbed, he can leave the community or family house and make use of a respite bed, i.e. providing respite for the family. In the situation above, in deciding whether the NHS Trust is liable for the injuries suffered by the community nurse, account would have to be taken of whether it was known that the patient was aggressive and, if so, whether the appropriate precautions had been taken, whether the community nurse followed approved accepted practice in her dealings with the patient, or whether she provoked the patient by what she did and was therefore, to some extent, to blame for what happened.

Official advice on violence

The Health and Safety Commission has published guidance on the assessment and management of risks of violence and aggression to staff in health services.[19] This

Box 23.2	**Checklist for staff who make home visits: Have you:**

- had all the relevant training about violence to staff?
- a sound grasp of your unit's safety policy for visitors?
- a clear idea about the area into which you are going?
- carefully previewed today's cases? Any 'PVs'? (Potentially violent clients/patients)
- asked to double up, take an escort or use a taxi if unsure?
- made appointments?
- left your itinerary and expected departure/arrival times?
- told colleagues, manager about possible changes of plans?
- arranged for contact if your return is overdue?

Do you have:

- forms to record and report incidents?
- a personal alarm or radio? Does it work? Is it handy?
- a bag/briefcase, wear an outer uniform or car stickers that suggest you have money or drugs with you? Is this wise where you are going today/tonight?
- out of hours telephone numbers to summon help?

Can you:

- be certain your attitudes, body language, etc won't cause trouble?
- defuse potential problems and manage aggression?

includes in Appendix 3 a Home visiting checklist. The three Vs of visiting are 'Vet – Verify – Vigilance'. The checklist for staff is shown in Box 23.2. Another checklist is provided for managers.

Consent to treatment

Mental capacity

If a person is mentally capable, then they are entitled to make their own decisions.[20] A person, who has the necessary mental capacity, can refuse treatment for a good reason, a bad reason or no reason at all.[21,22] However, it is essential that the capacity of the individual to make decisions is assessed by the health professional since if the person lacks the mental capacity, then action has to be taken in their best interests.[23,24]

Mentally disordered

In Chapter 20, which deals with the psychiatric nurse, the problem of giving drugs in the community is discussed. The fact is that at present there are no means in law of giving a patient compulsory drugs unless it is under the common law powers to act in an emergency to save life. Proposals have been made to change the mental health legislation to permit treatment in the community, but at the time of writing legislation is awaited. In Albert's situation, described above, if he continues to refuse to take medication considered essential for the treatment of his mental disorder as defined in the Act, he would have to be admitted to a mental hospital as an in-patient in order to be treated compulsorily. This is not satisfactory for community workers or necessarily in the best interests of the patient, and the subject is currently under debate. Special difficulties arise in particular with those with learning disabilities over 18 years, since there is no system of decision making on their behalf by proxy. The Law Commission has made recommendations to provide such a system[25] and the government's proposals have been published.[26] Legislation is awaited at the time of writing.

Supervised discharge orders for specific mentally disordered persons and proposals for reforming the Mental Health Act 1983 are discussed on pages 413–14.

Forcible entry

Another point which often concerns the community nurse and the health visitor is whether they have any rights of entry. As far as the statutory law is concerned, the answer is no. There may be a power of entry at common law where it is feared that an old person is lying in need of help, but it exists only in an emergency to save life.

Situation 23.5   *A row of bottles*

Neighbours drew the attention of the community nurse to a row of bottles outside the house of an elderly recluse. They feared for her safety and suggested that they should break into the house to check that all was well. The community nurse was hesitant.

In a case like this, it is preferable from the practical, as well as the theoretical, point of view for the police to be summoned. Their entry would provide legal justification (under the Police and Criminal Evidence Act 1984 S17(e) as well as providing the most realistic means of entry. Social workers have statutory powers of entry under specific conditions, but the health workers do not.

Compulsory removal

Under the Mental Health Act 1983

Situation 23.6   *Refusal to leave*

Laura Thomas, a community nurse for the mentally ill, was notified that two sisters who were regarded as recluses had not been seen for several days. Neighbours

---

reported that a number of cats were howling around their home and that the curtains had not been drawn for three days. Laura was also informed that of the two sisters, Annie, the younger one, was considered to be mentally handicapped. Laura went to the house and the door was answered by Agnes. She was abrupt and unwelcoming. When asked about her sister, she said they did not want nosey-parkers and was quite happy. From the doorway, Laura could see that the house was in a dirty condition and Agnes herself was in a dishevelled state. She feared for the physical and mental well-being of Annie. What could she do?

As a community nurse, Laura has no power to enter the house. However, powers do exist: under Section 115 of the Mental Health Act 1983, an approved social worker employed by a local social services authority may at all reasonable times after producing, if asked to do so, some duly authenticated document showing that he is such a social worker, enter and inspect any premises (not being a hospital) in the area of that authority in which a mentally disordered patient is living, if he has reasonable cause to believe that the patient is not receiving care. This power enables the approved social worker to inspect premises other than hospitals, where a mentally disordered person is living. It does not, however, give the right to enforce entry, but refusal to permit the inspection could constitute an offence under Section 129 of the Mental Health Act 1983. Premises are not defined, but could include private premises, provided a mentally disordered person is living there, and provided there is reasonable cause to believe the patient is not under proper care. Laura would therefore have to arrange for an approved social worker to visit the home. If entry is obstructed under Section 115, the approved social worker would have to make use of her power to apply to the Justice of the Peace for a warrant to search and remove patients (see Chapter 20). The approved social worker would have to give information on oath that there is reasonable cause to suspect that a person believed to be suffering from mental disorder: (a) has been, or is being, ill-treated, neglected, or kept otherwise than under proper control, in any place within the jurisdiction of the justice; *or* (b) being unable to care for himself, is living alone in any such place. The justice may then issue a warrant authorising any constable to enter, if need be by force, any premises specified in the warrant in which that person is believed to be and if it is thought fit to remove him to a place of safety with a view to the making of an application for his care and treatment. An approved social worker must accompany a constable. If it is thought fit, Annie could be removed to a place of safety and kept there for up to 72 hours under Section 135 (3).

Removal under the National Assistance Act 1948

The provision of the Mental Health Act described in the last paragraph can be used only in the case of a person believed within the meaning of the Act to be suffering from mental disorder. There are occasionally cases where those powers are not appropriate. In the above situation, it may well be that, although Annie suffers from learning disabilities and may well come within the definition of suffering from mental disorder, Agnes might not, but she might equally be in need of help.

> The persons must be (a) suffering from grave chronic disease or being aged, infirm, or physically incapacitated, are living in insanitary conditions; AND (b) are unable to devote to themselves, and are not receiving from other persons, proper care and attention. In order to use this section there must be certification by the community specialist after thorough inquiry and consideration that in the interests of any such person or for preventing injury to the health of, or serious nuisance to other persons, it is necessary to remove any such person. An application is made to Court. Seven days' notice must be given of the application. If granted the person can be kept in a place of safety for a period not exceeding 3 months. This period can be extended.

Figure 23.3 National Assistance Act 1948 Section 47.

Section 47 of the 1948 Act authorises the removal to suitable premises of persons in need of care and control in order to secure the necessary care and attention. Its main provisions are set out in Figure 23.3.

Because of the dangers to the health of the person in delaying an application, an emergency application can be made under the provisions of the National Assistance Act 1951 (Amendment) under which the period of detention is three weeks. These provisions provide no power to treat the person compulsorily. The Law Commission has recommended changes to these provisions that are under discussion.[27]

Protection of property

If both Annie and Agnes were removed from the house, what happens to their home?

Under Section 48 of the National Assistance Act 1948, the council has a duty to provide temporary protection for the property of persons admitted to hospitals. The section gives the council power to enter the property at all reasonable times and to deal with any movable property in order to prevent or mitigate any loss or damage. The council can recover any reasonable expenses incurred in carrying out this duty from the person who is admitted or any person liable to maintain him.

These provisions cause considerable difficulty for community physicians who may be under considerable pressure from neighbours to make use of these statutory powers, but it is well known that such a removal can be fatal for the person concerned who may fail to thrive in institutional care. The dilemma between the rights of freedom of autonomy and the duty to act in the public interest and to safeguard the person's welfare is evident.

Disclosure of information

This topic is fully discussed in Chapter 8 where an example of the problems faced by community staff is considered. The health visitor is more likely to be required to give evidence in court than any other community worker and should refer to Chapter 9 on giving evidence in court. The policy that she should wait to be subpoenaed before giving evidence has changed because of her duty to the child under the Children Act 1989.

Criminal suspicion

Community nurses often work alone and if they are charged with theft, it is one professional's word against that of the client or relative. In a case like Situation 23.7, Kate could well have been accused of theft by the old lady herself if she was at all absent-minded and had forgotten what she had done. The safest rule is therefore never to accept gifts, even though this might distress the client. If the client is insistent and wishes to make a generous gift, then a health service manager could be called in to give advice, but the client should be represented, since if there is any evidence of undue influence the gift would be voidable.

Situation 23.7 *Suspected*

Kate Giles was a community nurse who had long been visiting an elderly widow who appeared to have no family apart from two grandchildren, who rarely visited, and a few other visitors. One of Kate's tasks was to dress the client's leg. On one occasion, the client was anxious to point out some of her treasures to Kate. They included some very fine pieces of bone china. It was suggested to Kate that she might like to have a tiny cat as a small gift. Kate protested that she was not allowed to receive gifts from clients. Her protests were ignored and the old lady wrapped the gift up in an old paper bag and gave it to Kate. Kate forgot to mention it to her nursing officer the next day and after that it seemed too small a matter to be of any concern. Shortly after this the old lady died. The grandchildren discovered that a piece of Spode was missing. They made some enquiries and Kate stated that she had been given it by the elderly lady, but that they would of course be entitled to have it back. Kate was severely reprimanded and the grandchildren said they did not believe her story, since the old lady had never been known to give anything away; they suggested that Kate had in fact stolen the china.

Nursing and residential homes

Formerly, the Registered Homes Act 1984 required mental nursing homes, nursing homes and residential care homes to be registered. The former were registered by the Health Authority in whose catchment area they are, and the residential care homes were registered by the local authority. Regulations specified the detailed requirements with which owners and managers of each category are expected to comply. Some homes were subject to dual registration, i.e. they have a number of specified places for residential care and a number of specified nursing places. Residential care homes do not employ registered nurse practitioners and their nursing services are provided by the community nurses. Nursing homes must provide the number of registered practitioners as set out in the registration provisions. Sometimes, community nurses find that residents are inappropriately admitted to a residential care home, thus increasing demands upon the community nursing services. Only homes that are registered to take detained patients can detain persons who are detained under the Mental Health Act 1983, unless the patient is admitted to the nursing or residential care home on leave of absence from the hospital under Section 17 of the 1983 Act (see Chapter 20). The White Paper on Social Services[28] envisaged a single independent system of regulation and inspection with Commissions for Care Standards. A new statutory body known as the General Social Care Council, which would register those involved in social care work together with a National Training Organisation, was recommended to improve standards in social care. National required standards for residential and nursing homes for older people were published in a consultation document by the Department of Health.[29] A Care Standards Act was passed in 2000 incorporating these recommendations and will, when implemented, lead to the repeal of the Registered Homes Act 1984.

Care Standards Act 2000

The main provisions of the Care Standards Act 2000 are given below.

Part 1 establishes that a new independent regulatory body for social care, and private and voluntary health care services, is to be established in England known as the National Care Standards Commission. In Wales, the National Assembly for Wales will set up a department or agency to be the regulatory body in Wales. These regulatory bodies will also be responsible for the regulation of nursing agencies.

Part II sets out provisions in relation to registration, right of appeals, and provisions for the regulation of establishments and standards and creates offences in respect of the regulations. National minimum standards will be issued for all homes. Local authority homes will have to comply with the same standards as those set for independent homes.

Part III provides for the inspection of local authority fostering and adoption by the National Care Standards Commission and the National Assembly for Wales.

Part IV of the Act makes provision for the registration of social care workers by a General Social Care Council for England and a Care Council for Wales. These Councils will regulate the training of social workers and raise standards in social care through codes of conduct and practice. The present Central Council for Education and Training in Social Work (CCETSW) will be abolished. The use of the title 'social worker' is also protected.

Part V of the Act, in response to the recommendations of the Report of Inquiry chaired by Sir Ronald Waterhouse,[30] establishes a Children's Commissioner for Wales.

Part VI makes arrangements for the regulation of childminding and day care provision, including checks on the suitability of persons working with children.

Part VII of the Act makes provision for the protection of children and vulnerable adults, including the duty of the Secretary of State to keep a list of persons considered unsuitable to work with children and vulnerable adults. There is a statutory duty on persons providing care for such individuals to refer potential individuals to the list holder.

Quality in Social Services

In August 2000, the government published a consultation document on improving quality of social care services in England.[31] It recommended the establishment of a new Social Care Institute for Excellence (SCIE) which will set out guidelines on effective social care practice and also set best practice guidelines 'to create a Lifelong Learning social care workforce culture'. Consultation will also take place on the introduction of a new quality framework for social services departments and on the reform of social work training, including the level and length of training, and a formal reregistration scheme for professional staff to be regulated by the General Social Care Council (see above). The JM Consulting Report, published at the same time, recommended significant upgrading of several aspects of qualifying training and proposed a national curriculum for social work training, the development of centres of excellence and a three year undergraduate qualification.

Consultations on these recommendations were to take place at the same time as consultation on the Quality Strategy consultation paper.

The school nurse

The role of the school nurse

The traditional role of one school nurse per school with a wide job description is dying out to be replaced by a nurse with responsibility for several schools, but having an advisory and teaching role rather than seeing children individually and with no direct involvement in first aid for pupils. She may be employed by the NHS, but works within an educational environment, which could cause tension as the following situation indicates.

Extent of duty

Situation 23.8   *An unexpected attack*

The deputy head teacher asked Audrey, the school nurse, if she would cover Form 9A for one lesson, since the school was having difficulty in providing sufficient staff to supervise and teach the children because of the teachers' industrial action and the cut-back on the provision of supply teachers. Audrey said that she was employed by the NHS Trust, not the education authority, and that her duty was to act as a school nurse, not a teacher or child minder. The deputy was adamant that she take the class and, protesting, Audrey did so. While she was supervising Form 9A, a child from Year 7, Justin Smith, had an epileptic fit. The form teacher, Kate Jay, sent a child to get the school nurse, but unfortunately Audrey could not

Situation 23.8 continued

be found. Kate had no experience in how to handle an epileptic patient and tried to lift Justin. His tongue slipped into his throat, he choked and went blue. Kate told another child to get the head teacher to call an ambulance. Unfortunately, by the time the ambulance arrived, Justin was dead and could not be resuscitated.

In this tragic situation, many different questions arise. What is the role of the school nurse? Is she on call for the whole time in school hours, waiting for such an emergency to arise? Many would say no, but it does, of course, depend on the individual employment contract and job description. The role she plays as far as teaching is concerned also varies from school to school. In some, she might take on the task of teaching such subjects as personal hygiene, health education, sex education, biology, etc. Where she is undertaking this role, it can hardly be expected that she will be fulfilling an emergency first aid role as well. In such circumstances, Audrey is not to blame for the death of Justin. A more likely action is possible against Kate and the education authority for failing to provide a basic first aid training for staff, especially when it would have been known that Justin was epileptic. Kate's action was the worst possible in the circumstances. An action is also possible against the local education authority for using the school nurse in another capacity so that she was not available.

Use of car

Like any community worker, a school nurse must ensure that she has the appropriate insurance policy to cover all the uses that she is likely to make of a car for work purposes.

Situation 23.9 Car insurance

A child, Mary Pugh, cut her head very badly in the gymnasium. The children had been told to trot around like ponies with their heads up high. Mary trotted straight into the teeth of another child. Blood gushed from the wound. Audrey, the school nurse, realised the importance of getting her to the accident and emergency department for stitches. She put the child in her own car and rushed to the local hospital. In her haste, she came out of a side road too quickly and crashed into a motor cyclist coming along the main road. She got out of the car to see what could be done and, seeing that other people had gathered around, she decided that it was her duty to get Mary to hospital. Subsequently, she was notified that the police were charging her with failing to report an accident, and having no adequate insurance cover. Relatives of the motor cyclist were also intending to sue her for causing the accident and failing to provide assistance, since the ambulance had taken 20 minutes to arrive and the cyclist had bled to death.

Any employee who does not usually use their car for work, other than going to and from work, would be well advised to ensure that insurance cover is provided for the exceptional circumstance when a car might be needed. Clinic nurses other than peripatetic nurses, school nurses, or out-patient nurses might all find that on very rare occasions they need to use their car for work purposes and then they are not covered. The effect is that, although the insurance company will pay out compensation to the victim, it has the right to claim this money back from the person whose insurance did not cover this use. If this exceptional use is foreseeable, it is wiser for the nurse to ensure that the company is notified of this possibility.

As far as the failure to report the accident is concerned, it is a duty under the Road Traffic Act 1972 to ensure that the police are notified of any accident in which personal injuries are caused. Audrey's failure to ensure that this was done could lead to a successful prosecution. Her failure to stop and help the cyclist is a difficult question. On the one hand, as was pointed out in Chapter 3, there is no obligation to volunteer help. However, in this case Audrey caused the harm and is under a legal obligation to mitigate it as far as possible. However, she also has a duty to Mary and it is a question of assessing who is in most need. From the facts given here, it would appear that the cyclist was in most danger and Audrey should have checked that there was nothing she could do before she went away.

The clinic nurse

Clinic nurses may spend their time in one clinic assisting at mother and baby clinics, or be attached to specialist clinics such as family planning clinics, or travel from school to school, assisting the school doctors in provision of medical, eye and other examinations for school children.

Obtaining consent

Situation 23.10   Consent to rubella vaccinations

Brenda West provided nursing assistance to the medical team that carried out the school medical examinations. One of their tasks was to offer the Year 8 girls a rubella vaccination. Letters were sent to the parents in advance, advising them of the service and asking for their consent. Unfortunately, Brenda failed to notice that the parents of Rachel Tyne had not signed the consent form and Rachel was given an injection by the school doctor. Shortly afterwards, Rachel came out in an all-over rash. Investigations were made and it appeared that Rachel had recently had a variety of drugs in anticipation of a holiday to Morocco and these had reacted with the rubella vaccination. The parents were threatening to sue since they did not want Rachel to have the vaccination as she had had German measles a few years before. They also felt that the doctor and nurse should have checked with them before they gave the vaccination to ensure that there were no contra-indications.

There are two separate issues here: the one is the consent of the parents; the other is the timing of the vaccination. As far as consent is concerned, the basic principles are that parents have the right to consent to treatment for their children. As far as school health is concerned, it could be argued that under the Education Acts the school can provide the care as long as the parents do not object. This may well cover medical examinations, but is unlikely to cover the giving of injections. Some schools rely upon a passive consent: We intend to examine and give your child X on . . . If you do not consent, please contact . . . The validity of such an arrangement has not been tested in court.

However, if the vaccination is to proceed, it is essential that actual consent should be obtained, that any potential contra-indications are identified, and that the parents advise the school of any recent events in the child's medical history that suggest that a vaccination would be inappropriate at that particular time or, indeed, at any time. Because of the importance of this, it is advisable for the parents to give positive consent to the vaccination and reassure the staff about the non-existence of any contra-indications.

As far as responsibility between the nurse and the doctor is concerned, much depends upon the local policy in relation to who has the duty of ensuring that the parents' consent has been obtained. In some authorities, this would fall upon the doctor. However, this does not necessarily mean that the nurse is free of all liability.

Minors

Situation 23.11 *Family planning and the under 16-year-old*

Maureen was working as a clinic nurse in the family planning clinic. She recognised one of the patients, Denise Wright, as a friend of her eldest daughter, aged 15 years. She completed the forms and the girl told her she was 17. Maureen knew that this was a lie. She was uncertain whether to tell the doctor and decided against this. The doctor prescribed the pill and asked Denise the name of her family doctor. Denise said she did not have one. She said she did not want any communication with her family, and the doctor said that would not be necessary if she was over 16.

Several issues arise here. One is the question of the nurse's personal knowledge and the extent to which she should inform the doctor of this. The other is the question of the law relating to an under 16-year-old in this context. This latter point is considered in some detail in the section dealing with children's nursing (Chapter 13).

From the House of Lords decision in the Gillick case, it can be seen that in exceptional circumstances treatment and advice can be given to a girl under 16 without the parents being involved. As far as the first issue is concerned, it could be argued that even though the nurse has acquired information about the patient from a different source, if this is relevant to the doctor's care and treatment of the patient, then it should be disclosed, i.e. her duty of care to the patient would require her to tell the doctor that the girl was 15. Similarly, if she knew that the girl suffered from epilepsy, even though the girl had not told the doctor this, the nurse should pass on the information. It could be argued that this principle applies only to information that is relevant to the care of the child. Thus, if she by chance knew that the girl had been charged by the police for shop-lifting, this need not be passed on.

The Children Act 1989 requires decisions relating to children to take into account the wishes of the child where the child has the capacity (see Chapter 13).

The practice nurse

The legal situation of the practice nurse can vary, especially as far as employment rights are concerned. Some practice nurses may be employed by single-handed or group general practitioners, others are employed by health authorities. Practice nurses employed by health authorities are more likely to be part of a nursing hierarchy and to receive guidance and policies from the employer. Recent years have seen a considerable growth in the educational and management support provided by health authorities to practice nurses. In many areas, a practice liaison nurse is appointed to provide assistance and professional advice across the health authority area.

Scope of professional practice and the practice nurse

Like other nurses, practice nurses are finding that their scope of professional practice is expanding as general practitioners require them to undertake a wider range of responsibilities. Whilst practice nurses were not identified in the first Crown report on nurse prescribing as one of the groups able to prescribe in the community, they were, together with nurses working in Walk-in Centres, added to the list of nurses who could prescribe in February 2000. The final Crown report envisages that many different health professionals will be recognised as dependent or independent prescribers. This is discussed further in Chapter 28. Legal issues relating to the scope of professional practice are considered in Chapter 24, see especially pages 482–3.

Cervical Screening

The practice nurse may be required to undertake cervical screening. It is essential that they have appropriate approved training. A practice nurse in Birmingham, who had been taught by her GP to undertake cervical screening, was discovered to be using the spatula by the wrong end and her failure to take the correct samples led to non-diagnosis of several women with cervical cancer.

The standard required in cervical screening came before the courts when East Kent Health Authority were alleged to have been liable for the negligent examination of cervical smears.

Case 23.6   Cervical screening[32]

The claimants brought an action on the grounds that their cervical smears were negligently examined and reported as negative between 1989 and 1992. As a consequence, they were deprived of the opportunity of obtaining early treatment which would have prevented the development of endocervical carcinoma. Screening was carried out by qualified biomedical scientists or by qualified cytology screeners. They were not qualified to diagnose; their only function was to report what, using their expertise, they were able to see. If the screener detected an abnormality in the smear or was in doubt whether what he saw was abnormal, he had to pass the smear on to a senior screener known as a checker. The trial judge decided that claimants should win.

He preferred the views of the claimant's experts as to whether, in the light of what the cytoscreeners saw, it was negligent to fail either to classify the smears as borderline or to refer the smears to the checker/and or to the pathologist.

The Bolam principle did not apply because Bolam concerned acceptable and unacceptable practice; whereas no question of acceptable practice arose in the instant case because the cytoscreeners were wrong in their classification of the smears.

Even if the Bolam principle were relevant, the defendant's experts' views did not stand up to logical analysis because the cytoscreeners did not have the ability to draw a distinction between benign and pre-cancerous cells and so should have classified the smears as borderline.

The Court of Appeal dismissed the appeal and upheld the finding that the Health Authority was liable. It held that the Bolam Test was appropriate where the exercise of skill and judgment of the screener was being questioned. In this case, however, the Bolam Test did not apply since the screeners were not expected to exercise judgment.

It was announced in 2000 that the government is to introduce a pilot study of a new form of cervical screening, liquid-based cytology (LBC), together with tests for the virus HPV which causes cervical cancer. The National Institute for Clinical Excellence has suggested that LBC could increase the sensitivity of the slides, reduce the number of badly taken smears and improve the speed and accuracy with which cytoscreeners can read the slides.[33]

Employment situation

The legal position of the practice nurse as an employee differs according to whether she is employed by a practice or single-handed general practitioner or if she is employed by the NHS Trust. In the former case, as an employee of someone who employs only a few people, she may not have all the statutory benefits to which the NHS Trust employee will be entitled. If she is employed by a single-handed general practitioner, she may find it more difficult to resist pressure for her to go outside her limits of competence and she lacks the back-up of a clear nursing hierarchy and nurse management support. Her professional standards should, however, be the same.

The future

Following the increasing amalgamation of community health services with primary care services within a Primary Care Trust, and the eventual establishment of Care Trusts, covering both social and health services, major changes are likely to be made in the traditional role of practice nurse, clinic nurse and community nurse. Whilst at present the majority of practice nurses are employed by a GP practice, in future they may well be employed by a Primary Care Trust or Care Trust and share the same employer with their community nurse colleagues. The potential for improvement and development in community health and primary care services as a result of the Health Act 1999 is at the time of writing only just being realised and will have major implications for the role of the nurse. In addition, the establishment of Care Trusts (combining primary health care and social service responsibilities) are envisaged in the Health and Social Care Act which will further assist in the integration of health and social care as envisaged in Chapter 7 of the NHS Plan.

Questions and exercises

1 As a community nurse, you visit a patient who appears to you to be incapable of caring for herself. What action would you take? Outline a procedure to cover the situation if the patient shows extreme reluctance to move from her home and there are no relatives to care for her.

2 You break an ornament while visiting a patient. The ornament is valued at £5,000. You are personally unable to meet the costs of replacing it. What remedies are available to the owner of the ornament? (See also Chapter 25.)

3 Obtain details of the procedures for assessment for community care as a result of the 1990 Act. What impact have these had on your practice? How are assessment procedures changed as a result of the NHS Plan?

4 What special concerns does the community professional have in relation to health and safety, and what specific precautions should be taken to protect her? (Refer also to Chapter 12.)

5 What difficulties, if any, arise from the fact that the school nurse is employed by the NHS Trust and works with education authority staff? Could the school nurse refuse to undertake tasks allocated by the head teacher? What are the likely implications?

6 What differences exist in law between the clinic nurse who spends all her time in a clinic and the nurse who visits patients in their own homes?

7 What possible differences may exist in law between the practice nurse who is employed by a general practitioner and the practice nurse who is employed by a Primary Care Trust?

8 Consider the expanded-role tasks which are sometimes undertaken by the practice nurse and outline the legal requirements. (See Chapter 24.)

9 What do you consider are the main benefits in the establishment of Primary Care Trusts or Care Trusts. In what way are they likely to affect your work and work relationships?

References

[1] The Audit Commission Taking Care: Progress with Care in the Community, December 1993 HMSO

[2] Department of Health Raising Standards for Patients New Partnerships in Out-of-Hours Care October 2000 DoH

[3] White Paper The New NHS: Modern – Dependable Stationery Office 1997 London

[4] Department of Health NHS Plan CMND 4818-1 July 2000 HMSO

[5] Royal College of Nursing The New Primary Care Groups RCN 000 924 October 1998

[6] R v. *North and East Devon Health Authority ex parte Coughlan* [2000] 3 All ER 850; [2000] 2WLR 622

[7] Royal Commission Report on the Long Term Care of the Elderly, with respect to old age Stationery Office 1999

[8] R v *Gloucester County Council and another ex parte Barry* HL [1997] 2 All ER 1

[9] Audit Commission Report, Fully Equipped. The provision of equipment to older or disabled people by the NHS and social services in England and Wales March 2000

[10] Department of Health, NHS Plan CMND 4818-1 July 2000 HMSO

[11] Explanatory notes to the Carers and Disabled Children Act 2000 (http://www.legislation. hmso.gov.uk/acts/en/2000en16.htm)

[12] Carer's National Strategy Document 'Caring about Carers' Stationery Office, 8 February 1999

[13] R v *Family Health Services Appeal Authority ex p Muralidhar* [1999] COD 80

[14] Alexandra Frean and Melissa Kite, Payments for vaccine damage to increase, *The Times* 28 June 2000 page 10

[15] The Vaccine Damage Payments Act 1979 Statutory sum order Statutory Instrument No 1983 2000

[16] *Loveday* v. *Renton and another, The Times* 31 March 1988

[17] *Best* v. *Wellcome Foundation, Dr O'Keefe, the Southern Health Board, the Minister for Health of Ireland and the Attorney General* 1994 5 Med LR 81

[18] R v. *Hillingdon Health Authority ex parte Wyatt CA, The Times* 20 December 1977

[19] Health and Safety Commission, Violence and aggression to staff in health services 1997 HSE Books

[20] *Re C* (adult: Refusal of Medical Treatment) [1994] 1 All ER 819

[21] *Re MB* (Adult Medical Treatment) [1997] 2 FLR 426

[22] *St George's Healthcare NHS Trust* v. *S* [1998] 3 All ER 673

[23] *Re T* [1992] 4 All ER 649

[24] *F* v. *Berkshire HA* [1989] 2 All ER 545

[25] Law Commission Report No 231 Mental Incapacity HMSO 1995

[26] Lord Chancellor's Office, Making Decisions, Lord Chancellor 1999

[27] Law Commission Report No 231 Mental Incapacity HMSO 1995

[28] Modernising Social Services CM 4169 Stationery Office 30 November 1998

[29] DoH 1999 Fit for the Future? National required standards for residential and nursing homes for older people (consultation document) London DoH

[30] Lost in care – the Report of the Tribunal of Inquiry (chaired by Sir Ronald Waterhouse) into the abuse of children in care in the former county council areas of Gwynedd and Clwyd since 1974 February 2000 Stationery Office HC 201

[31] Department of Health, A Quality Strategy for Social Care August 2000 DoH

[32] *Penney, Palmer and Cannon* v. *East Kent Health Authority* 2000 Lloyds Reports Medical 2000 page 41 CA

[33] Dr Thomas Stuttaford, New screening should cut smear errors, *The Times* 3 August 2000

24 The scope of professional practice, clinical nurse specialist and consultant nurse

The government's plans for the New NHS as shown in the White Paper[1] and in the document 'Making a Difference'[2] and in the NHS Plan[3] rely heavily upon a widened scope of practice for the nurse. NHS Direct and walk-in clinics are run by nurses and provide an increasingly extensive and popular service. As a consequence of these developments, the role of the nurse is changing radically and these changes have major legal implications. This chapter considers the background to the scope of professional practice and the UKCC advice, the role of the consultant nurse and clinical nurse specialist. One development in the scope of professional practice is the change in nurse prescribing and this is considered in Chapter 28. Topics covered in this chapter are shown in Figure 24.1

Scope of professional practice
Nurse Consultants
Clinical Nurse Specialists and Specialist nurses
Scope of professional practice and primary care
Scope of professional practice and theatre nursing
NHS Direct and walk-in clinics
Concerns on the scope:
    Cultural issues
    Training and education
    Resources
    Professional issues
    Management and insurance
Clinical Supervision
Agency Nurses

Figure 24.1 Issues covered in Chapter 24.

The scope of professional practice

In June 1992, the UKCC published the 'Scope of Professional Practice'. It marked a major development in the thinking underlying professional practice. Previously, the concept of the extended role highlighted the distinction between the basic training that the practitioner received in order to become a registered professional, and post-registration training. Under 'the extended role', professional development was seen as incremental, task orientated and often delegated from other professionals

The registered nurse, midwife or health visitor:

1. must be satisfied that each aspect of practice is directed to meeting the needs and serving the interests of the patient or client;

2. must endeavour always to achieve, maintain and develop knowledge, skill and competence to respond to those needs and interests;

3. must honestly acknowledge any limits of personal knowledge and skill and take steps to remedy any relevant deficits in order effectively and appropriately to meet the needs of patients and clients;

4. must ensure that any enlargement or adjustment of the scope of personal professional practice must be achieved without compromising or fragmenting existing aspects of professional practice and care and that requirements of the Council's Code of Professional Conduct are satisfied throughout the whole area of practice;

5. must recognize and honour the direct or indirect personal accountability borne for all aspects of professional practice; and

6. must, in serving the interests of patients and clients and the wider interests of society, avoid any inappropriate delegation to others which compromises those interests.

Figure 24.2 Principles for adjusting the scope of professional practice.

(usually medical). A circular in 1977 (CHC (77) 22) gave advice on extended role tasks. This advice has now been superceded by subsequent developments on the scope of professional practice.

In 1986, a working party was set up by the Standing Medical Advisory Committee and the Standing Nursing and Midwifery Committee to review the extended role of the nurse. Its report was circulated under cover as a DHSS letter from the Chief Nursing Officer, dated 26 September 1989, and it paved the way for the publication of the UKCC's 'Scope of Professional Practice'.

The UKCC emphasises that professional practice must be sensitive, relevant and responsive to the needs of individual patients and clients and have the capacity to adjust, where and when appropriate, to changing circumstances (paragraph 1). It sets out principles that should govern adjustment to the scope of professional practice (paragraph 9). These are laid out in Figure 24.2.

The 'Scope of Professional Practice' should be seen in the context of Post-Registration Education and Practice (PREP), which is the UKCC's framework for continuing education. It includes a duty on practitioners to have at least five refresher days every three years. Implementation commenced in April 1995. Undoubtedly, there are opportunities for nursing, midwifery and health visiting to develop safely beyond the original boundaries. It enables professional practice to develop naturally into areas that were once seen as delegated medical tasks; it moves development away from new tasks to a more holistic view of professional practice relevant to a nurse, midwife or health visitor.

The National Plan for the NHS,[4] published in July 2000, envisaged that within the reformed NHS there will be radical changes in the ways in which staff work. The new NHS Modernisation Agency (set up by the government to plan and implement the changes) will lead a major drive to ensure that protocol based care takes hold throughout the NHS.

The new approach will shatter old demarcations which have held back staff and slowed down care. NHS employers will be required to empower appropriately qualified nurses, midwives and therapists to undertake a wider range of clinical tasks including the right to make and receive referrals, admit and discharge patients, order investigations and diagnostic tests, run clinics and prescribe drugs.

The ten key roles identified for the nurse by the Chief Nursing Officer and set out in the NHS Plan are shown in Box 24.1.

Box 24.1

10 key roles for nurses in the NHS Plan

1. To order diagnostic investigations such as pathology tests and X-rays;

2. To make and receive referrals direct, say, to a therapist or pain consultant;

3. To admit and discharge patients for specified conditions and within agreed protocols;

4. To manage patient case loads, say for diabetes or rheumatology;

5. To run clinics, say for ophthalmology or dermatology;

6. To prescribe medicines and treatments;

7. To carry out a wide range of resuscitation procedures, including defibrilation;

8. To perform minor surgery and outpatient procedures;

9. To triage patients using the latest IT to the most appropriate health professional;

10. To take a lead in the way local health services are organised and in the way that they are run.

Nurse consultants

Clinical nurse specialists and consultant nurses are seen as having a major role to play in providing an improved service for patients. The NHS Plan envisaged that there will be 1000 nurse consultants and therapist consultants will also be appointed. The key features of the consultant nurse as envisaged in the Department of Health's 'Making a Difference',[5] are shown in Box 24.2.

Box 24.2

Key features of the Consultant nurse

1. Expert practice.
2. Professional leadership and consultancy.
3. Education and development.
4. Practice and service development linked to research and evaluation.

It is envisaged that at least 50% of their time will be spent on clinical work with career opportunities. NHS Trusts are required to agree the posts with regional offices of the DoH.

Clinical nurse specialists and specialist nurses

In addition, clinical nurse specialists have taken on a wide range of expanded duties often working within protocols agreed with medical staff. They may also have managerial responsibilities. Other specialist nurses may or may not come within the category of clinical nurse specialists, but are increasingly taking on expanded role functions. It would be impossible in a book of this type to explore the wide range of specialties covered by nurses, often functioning within a multi-disciplinary team, but making many decisions on their own. They include continence care, stoma care, pain management, diabetic and A&E nurse practitioners.

For example, nurses working in breast care in community, general practice and hospital settings are increasingly undertaking expanded roles. In the guidance for breast care nurses provided by the RCN,[6] a checklist is provided for extending roles, which is printed here, since it applies to all expanded role tasks:

Is this new skill/role consistent with nursing practice?

Is it consistent with my current job description?

Does it fit current priorities – nursing and organisational?

What changes will it entail?

Will I need to stop some parts of my current care?

Do I need accreditation?

How will I get it?

Do I need additional skills?

How will I get them?

Do I need a training period before I take on the new responsibility?

Do I have a mentor for this change?

How will I evaluate my performance in the new role?

Have I got clinical supervision?

Concerns about developments in the scope of professional practice

Practitioners have concerns, however, as a result of the move away from certified tasks and the rapid development in the scope of professional practice, which include the following:

1. How do I know if I am competent?
2. How does my employer know if I am competent?
3. What happens if I undertake an activity that is outside my field of competence?
4. Where do I stand if a doctor/senior manager/other professional ignores my refusal to undertake an activity because I have not sufficient competence or experience to undertake that activity?
5. How can I ensure that I receive the appropriate training for my expanded role?

Some situations will be considered that highlight these dilemmas.

Situation 24.1   Scope of professional practice 1

Mavis, a staff nurse, was asked by the registrar to do the intravenous infusions. The registrar rushed away before she had the chance to explain to him that she had not developed the skills, competence and knowledge to undertake that activity safely. However, she decided that she would carry out his instructions as best she could. Unfortunately, when she was adding a drug to Jimmy Price's intravenous infusion, she failed to set the speed of his drip correctly and as a result Jimmy became very ill. Where do Mavis and the registrar stand in relation to the responsibility for the harm to Jimmy?

As far as Mavis was concerned, she was at fault in failing to mention her lack of competence for that activity to the registrar. No nurse should work outside her range of competence and skill unless a dire emergency arises when the risks in failing to act are greater than the risks in acting. There is no suggestion that this was an emergency. The nurse ignored a fundamental principle of the Code of Professional Conduct (paragraph 4) to:

> 'acknowledge any limitations in your knowledge and competence and decline any duties or responsibilities unless able to perform them in a safe and skilled manner'.

The failure of Mavis to notify the doctor and the resulting mistake that caused harm to the patient could result in a civil action brought against her employer because of its vicarious liability for the negligent actions of an employee acting in course of employment (see pages 62–8).

Mavis herself may be subject to professional disciplinary proceedings before the UKCC Professional Conduct Committee. Were Jimmy to die, she might also face criminal proceedings. Her employer, of course, would commence its own disciplinary inquiry and proceedings.

What of the registrar? Is he also at fault? If the addition of drugs to intravenous transfusions is seen as a task delegated by a doctor to a nurse practitioner, then he would be liable as delegator in failing to ensure that he was delegating to a competent person. However, under the scope of professional practice, such activities are not seen as 'delegated tasks' and the duty was incumbent upon the individual nurse practitioner to ensure that, if she herself was not competent, another practitioner, whether medical or nursing, who was competent, performed the activity. The standard of care that the patient is entitled to expect does not depend upon which professional is undertaking a particular activity. The reasonable standard of care will be required of any professional carrying out an extended role: if that activity was formally carried out by a doctor, then a nurse undertaking that activity will be expected to provide the reasonable standard that a doctor would have provided. The Bolam Test, which is discussed in Chapter 3, will be used to define the reasonable standard. The managerial responsibilities in ensuring appropriate supervision and allocation of activities are discussed in Chapter 4.

Can a nurse refuse to undertake training in new areas of competency?

It was a principle under the concept of the 'extended role' that nurses could refuse to undertake a new task or activity. However, this approach is probably no longer appropriate in relation to the scope of professional practice. Clause 3 of the Code of Professional Conduct requires nurses to 'maintain and improve your professional knowledge and competence'.

It would be entirely inappropriate for a practitioner to refuse to develop her professional practice beyond the level she reached when she became registered. In addition, it is directly contrary to the principles of PREP. She would be contractually entitled to receive from her employer the necessary training to ensure that she was competent in the new range of activities. It is a contractual requirement of the employer to ensure that staff are competent to perform the work that they are asked to perform.

There are other contractual considerations. In an interview for a job, for example, a nurse might be told that a contractual requirement for that particular post is that the nurse is competent in a specified area. If the nurse agrees to this condition, then she is contractually bound to develop, with support from the employer, the appropriate skills, knowledge and competence. If she refuses the condition, she will probably not get the post.

The scope of professional practice in primary care

Situation 24.2 *Liability and the scope of professional practice 2*

Practice Nurse Jenny Brown was asked by the GP to make a primary visit to a child whose mother had reported him too ill to come to surgery. Jenny Brown visited the child, took his temperature and blood pressure, and examined him. She told the mother that she thought he was suffering from the flu that was going round at present, to keep him warm with lots of drinks and, if he worsened or failed to improve within a few days, to let the surgery know. She reported the results of the visit to the GP, who approved of her action. Unfortunately, that same night an emergency call was made by the mother to the out-of-hours service and the boy was rushed to hospital, where he was diagnosed as suffering from meningitis. He eventually died. The mother is now demanding that action be taken against both the nurse and the doctor. What is the responsibility of the nurse and the doctor?

If the nurse had acted outside her competence, been negligent and caused harm as a consequence, then she will be liable. The doctor will be vicariously liable for the actions of a negligent nurse employee. In this case, there would be an investigation to establish the tests undertaken by the nurse and the advice that she gave to the mother and whether her actions satisfied the standard of the reasonable medical practitioner. The competence of a nurse in making a primary visit will become of increasing importance with the expansion of nurse prescribing. In any case, where there is delegation of a task that is normally performed by a doctor, the doctor will remain liable in civil law for that task unless he has delegated it to a competent, trained person and provides the requisite supervision for the task to be done safely. Here one might question whether it was a suitable case for the practice nurse to undertake. Had she the necessary training and skills to detect whether the patient was suffering from mumps or another condition? Once she had visited the patient, should she not have arranged for the GP to attend or ensured that a closer eye was kept on him? Did she make all the appropriate tests and checks when she visited the boy? If these questions are answered in such a way that the nurse is shown to be at fault, then the GP could well be liable for any harm that has consequentially befallen the boy (there may in fact be no harm suffered, since the short delay in diagnosis may have had no effect) and the nurse would also be liable for undertaking a task that she was not competent to perform. In either event, the nurse would be held professionally accountable before the UKCC for her actions. Even if there has been no negligence on the part of the GP, he would be vicariously liable for the practice nurse's negligence as her employer.

Scope of professional practice and theatre nursing

Situation 24.3   The scope of professional practice and theatres

Myra Jones had worked in theatre for over 20 years and was an extremely experienced nurse. She had asked for training in acting as a first assistant, but the surgeons had stated that this was not a role that should be performed by nurses. One day, she was asked by the Registrar to assist in an appendectomy because there was a shortage of junior doctors. She knew that she could do the work competently, but was hesitant. What is the legal situation?

Should she refuse on the grounds that she has not been trained to fulfil this role? What if this request comes at night where there is only a registrar on his own and it is an emergency case? The basic principle is that, whatever duties she is called upon to perform, she should undertake no work that she is not competent to undertake. Reference should be made to the booklet prepared by the National Association of Theatre Nurses (see Recommended Further Reading).

In an emergency situation, when the harm to the patient of her acting is outweighed by the harm to the patient of her not acting, the balance might be in favour of her acting as assistant (but these occasions are likely to be rare). To refuse to perform certain tasks is not pleasant for the nurse, but it is her duty both in civil law and also as part of the rules of her profession. Only in this way can the safety of the patient be ensured. If such situations arise where the nurse is expected to undertake tasks for which she is not trained, this must ultimately be referred to nurse management. If this proves ineffective, then the nurse may need to take advantage of the whistle-blower's protection, which is discussed in Chapter 4.

In situation 24.3, it is hoped that the surgeons would ultimately recognise that this is an activity that is suitable for role expansion and ensure that they take part in the necessary training for the nurses selected to develop their practice in this way.

NHS Direct and walk-in clinics

Situation 24.4   Liability and the scope of professional practice 3

A nurse employed by NHS Direct received a phone call from a woman of 28 years who said she was suffering from severe indigestion and asked what was recommended. The nurse failed to clarify whether the woman was pregnant and suggested that she should take some indigestion pills. Subsequently, the woman was admitted in an emergency to hospital with hypertension. The family are now wishing to sue NHS Direct.

In this situation, there would probably be a protocol the nurse should have followed and ascertaining the possibility of pregnancy would have been an essential question to ask. There would appear to be prima facie evidence of negligence. Clearly, the safest advice to be given by any nurse answering calls on NHS Direct is for the patient to seek an appointment with his or her general practitioner. However, this might reduce the value of the service (see the criticisms discussed in Chapter 5).

Similar problems beset the nurse providing the services in walk-in clinics, since the majority are nurse-led. It is essential that the nurse practitioners have the appropriate training to run such clinics competently and to be aware of the limits of their knowledge and have the confidence to be firm on what they do not know. Minor injuries can probably be dealt with on a one off basis, such as suturing or bandaging a sprain. However, there may be a need to refer to X-Ray, to arrange for further diagnostic tests, or to seek specialist advice and the nurse needs to be confident when this is required, and when she needs to refer the patient on for medical advice. In February 2000, practice nurses and nurses who work in Walk-in Centres were given statutory powers to prescribe from a limited list, like community nurses and health visitors.[7] These powers increase the dangers of a nurse working outside her competence.

Concerns about the scope of professional practice

Nurses at a conference on the scope of professional practice were asked about their concerns about the development of their professional work. The reservations they had were grouped under the following headings: cultural; training and education; management and resource issues.[8]

Cultural issues

It was clear that to expand the scope of professional practice of the nurse is not simply of concern to the nursing profession alone: it will have an impact on the full multi-disciplinary team – patients, carers, managers and many others. Nurses are therefore concerned about potential opposition from some within these groups: open resistance, a reluctance to adjust their own particular ways of practice; being concerned with demarcation lines; undermining a nurse's attempt to undertake further professional activities. In a sense, what is required is almost a complete cultural change within the NHS: a major challenge and one that cannot be accomplished by one single discipline whatever the political pressure for change.

Training and education

The main concern of all participants about the safe development of their professional practice was the need to ensure that the appropriate training was given to them. This was not simply the instruction in a new activity, though this was clearly important. Their concerns were far wider and included the necessity of receiving supervised practice, of competent assessed teachers and having training and experience in a new role rather than just a new task.

Resources

There is a danger that, like care in the community, developing the scope of professional practice might be seen as a cheap alternative to employing more junior doctors. Care in the community has proved to be more expensive than running the large institutions that it replaced. Participants recognised that there were considerable resource issues in the development of the scope of professional practice that, if they were not resolved, could defeat any nurse development.

Professional issues

Obviously, many of the concerns related to the establishment of professional guidelines and agreeing procedures with other members of the multi-disciplinary team. One of the basic professional concerns was the need for more guidelines and protocols for determining standards within the expanded role. This is certainly the intention of the government whose NHS Plan published in July 2000 envisages that NICE will provide more appraisal and protocols to guide staff (see Chapter 5). However, as the discussion in that chapter shows, it cannot be assumed that following a protocol to the letter will always be a defence against any allegation of negligence, since in exceptional circumstances good practice might dictate a different course of action.

Management and insurance

The support given by management to the whole process is seen as vital to the success of the development. This included protecting nurses against legal liability, recognising that they would indemnify the nurse and uphold their actions. One of the crucial concerns of nurse practitioners was that they would not obtain support from management if things went wrong; they were concerned that they would be held personally liable and were also anxious about whether they should take out insurance cover. In Chapter 4, it was explained that an employer is vicariously liable for the negligent actions of an employee who is acting in the course of employment. Where, therefore, a practitioner is undertaking an extended role activity, that would normally be seen as in the course of employment. If, therefore, the practitioner is negligent, whilst she would be professionally accountable both to the UKCC and to her employer, she would probably not be held personally liable in the civil courts since her employer would pay compensation on the basis of its vicarious liability. Even when she has not obtained the approval of the employer for this extended activity, it would probably be held vicariously liable as long as she was acting in the interests of the employer's organisation. However, because of uncertainties on this latter point, the practitioner would always be well advised to obtain the agreement of the employer to developments in the scope of professional practice. As long as vicarious liability exists, the employee does not require her own personal insurance cover. If, however, she works on her own account, or she undertakes good Samaritan activities which are outside the scope of professional practice, then she needs to ensure that she has professional indemnity insurance. This is often provided by professional associations.

Clinical supervision

An important part of the support mechanism and professional development of the nurse is clinical supervision. Described by the UKCC in its position paper as 'Reflective Practice',[9] it provides an opportunity for nurses to discuss in confidence the issues that they have encountered in practice and how they can develop and learn from these experiences. Bond and Holland have provided guidance on the skills required.[10] Alec Grant raised issues about why clinical supervision is in practice falling short of the theory.[11]

Basic principles which apply to the scope of professional practice

1. Always work within the scope of your professional practice.
2. Identify any training or supervised practice needs and take steps to ensure that these are met.
3. Be aware that the law does not accept a principle of team liability: each individual practitioner is personally and professionally accountable for their own actions.
4. Do not obey orders, except in an extreme emergency, unless you are satisfied that they constitute reasonable professional practice.
5. Be prepared to refuse to undertake any activity unless it is within your competence.

6. Do not accept an undertaking that someone else will accept responsibility for what you do (I'll take responsibility!).

7. Ensure that any development in your professional practice takes place in the context of multi-disciplinary discussions, with full management support and an awareness of the need to educate the patient and others to the new situation.

Agency nurses

In recent years, the clear shortage in the number of nurses has led to the growth in the use of agencies for the provision of nurse staffing. Many nurses, too, find working for an agency suits their practical needs of combining family and work by giving them greater flexibility and control over their time. Nursing agencies were regulated under the Nurses Agencies Act 1957, but following the implementation of the Care Standards Act 2000, the National Care Standards Commission has taken over responsibility for their regulation. (In Wales, by a department or agency set up by the National Assembly for Wales.)

Nurses working for an agency should be clear over the legal implications of their status when they are allocated to a NHS Trust. Do they become employees of the Trust or are they employees of the agency or are they classified as self-employed practitioners? Their employment status has considerable repercussions for both their legal liability and also for their entitlements to statutory provisions for the employee (see Chapter 10). The RCN has provided a guide for good practice in nursing and care agencies[12] for the assistance of both those who wish to set up a nursing or care agency, and also those considering a career as a nursing and care agency manager. The guide will require updating in the light of the recent legislation and any rulings by the National Care Standards Commission.

Conclusions

Developing professional practice is not simply a question of teaching a nurse one more task or activity: it requires a total rethink of working practices of patient/staff education: in fact, a total change in the present culture within the NHS. A risk assessment and management exercise on the whole impact of the nurse undertaking responsibilities in a new area is required. There are, of course, specific training needs to be met, but, in addition, there are a wide range of management, resource, cultural, operational and strategic issues to be investigated which have far reaching implications for traditional ways of practice. The conclusion must be that appointing clinical nurse specialists and consultant nurses is no cheap quick easy fix for the NHS. A considerable number of risk management issues arise. If patients are to receive an enhanced service and effective use is to be made of all health care professionals and not just nursing staff, then these issues will have to be addressed head on and the appropriate resources made available.

Questions and exercises

1 Study a copy of your NHS Trust's policy on the scope of professional practice duties and the principles contained therein. In what ways do you consider that your professional practice could develop? What are the barriers to such development and how could these barriers be overcome?

2 You have been working as a clinical nurse specialist in the diabetic clinic and have now been asked if you would wish to seek a post of consultant nurse in the same department. What differences would you anticipate there would be between your present post and the post of consultant nurse? What legal implications would there be if you were to obtain the new post?

3 You are aware that your expanded scope of professional practice includes several activities that were originally performed by doctors. In what ways could you assure patients that you are competent to perform these activities?

4 You have been asked to undertake training to be able to act as a clinical supervisor. What are the legal implications of this role?

5 What documentation should be kept in respect of clinical supervision?

References

1 Department of Health, The New NHS – Modern Dependable, HMSO 1997
2 Department of Health, Making a Difference The new NHS Department of Health July 1999
3 Secretary of State for Health The NHS Plan Cm 4818–1 July 2000 Stationery Office
4 Secretary of State for Health The NHS Plan Cm 4818–1 July 2000 Stationery Office
5 Department of Health's Making a Difference: The new NHS July 1999
6 Royal College of Nursing, Developing roles: nurses working in breast care RCN 001957 May 1999
7 Statutory Instrument 2000 No 121 The National Health Service (Pharmaceutical Services) Amendment Regulations 2000
8 B. Dimond, The Scope of Professional Practice Healthcare Risk Report, March 2001 vol 7 Issue 4 pp. 16–17
9 UKCC Position Statement on Clinical Supervision London UKCC 1996
10 Bond M, Holland S, Skills of Clinical Supervision for Nurses, Bucks Open University Press 1998
11 Alec Grant, Why Clinical Supervision is not so super in reality, Nursing Times June 15 Vol 96 No 24 2000 page 42
12 Royal College of Nursing, Guide to Good Practice in Nursing and Care Agencies RCN 000 675 May 1998

Part III   General areas

25 The legal aspects of property

The nurse may have many concerns about property. She may wonder if she is liable if the patient's property is lost. This becomes of particular concern in those situations where the patient is incompetent to take care of his own possessions. What are the legal requirements? The nurse may also be concerned for her own property. Does the NHS Trust as an employer have any duty to make arrangements to care for the nurse's property? What happens if the nurse's car is damaged in the hospital car park? Does it make any difference to the liability of the employer if a patient damages the car? Figure 25.1 illustrates the topics to be covered in this chapter.

---

1. Principles of liability.
2. Administrative failures.
3. Exclusion of liability.
4. Property of mentally incompetent.
5. Day-to-day care of money.
6. Power of attorney.
7. Court of Protection.
8. Protecting patients from relatives.
9. Returning the patient's property.
10. Staff property.

Figure 25.1   Issues covered in Chapter 25.

Principles of liability

In Situation 25.1 on page 492 the first issue that arises is: can it be said that the NHS Trust is liable for the missing property and is Sister Thomas personally liable? In general, a person does not become liable for another person's property unless he or she can be shown to have assumed some responsibility for it. The person who undertakes to look after the property of another person is known as a bailee. The person whose property it is, is known as the bailor. Thus, if a patient were to give a gold watch to the ward sister, the sister on behalf of the NHS Trust acts as bailee of that property entrusted to it by the patient, the bailor. It is the duty of the bailee to carry out the instructions of the bailor and to surrender the property of the bailor when requested to do so or as previously agreed. In most circumstances,

Situation 25.1 *A Christmas casualty*

Dora Hardy, a widow of 72 years, was staying with her son James and his family over the Christmas holidays. On the Saturday night, the day before Christmas Eve, she complained of feeling very tired and retired to bed at 7.00 p.m. At 9.00 p.m. James suddenly heard his mother cry out and, rushing upstairs, he found her very pale, gasping for breath and clutching her heart. Ann, his wife, phoned for the ambulance and collected up her mother-in-law's handbag and toilet bag. Dora, still in her nightdress with an overcoat over her shoulders, was taken to Roger Park Hospital within 15 minutes. She was wheeled straight in, to the admission unit and a staff nurse asked James and Ann to wait in the waiting room. After five minutes, the staff nurse returned to ask them Dora's name, address and age. They then waited for over an hour without seeing any sign of anyone and then decided to find out what was happening. James walked into the admission unit and asked the sister on duty if he could see his mother. The sister explained that she had gone up to the medical ward about an hour before. She apologised, but said that, owing to the change of shift, she had not realised that Mrs Hardy had relatives with her and that anyone was waiting. To make up for her oversight, the sister phoned the medical ward and arranged for James and Ann to go straight up. James and Ann, who was still clutching Dora's possessions, were led to the medical ward. There were screens around Dora's bed and Dora seemed to be unconscious. Ann tiptoed to the head of the bed and placed Dora's handbag and toilet bag in the locker. Since it was clear that there was little that they could do, James and Ann left the bedside, calling in to the ward sister's office to make sure that the night nurse had their address and phone number.

Dora remained critically ill for three days, but on the fourth day she seemed to start pulling through. James visited her the day after Boxing Day and for the first time was able to chat with her. He asked if there was anything she needed and she said that she would like some Kleenex and orange squash. The next day, James and Ann took in the Kleenex and squash and £10 in cash to ensure that Dora could buy things from the ward trolley. Ann took the handbag from the locker and opened the purse to put the £10 inside. She noticed that there was already £60 in the purse. However, she added the £10 and replaced the purse in the handbag, which she put in the locker. Over the next few days, a number of relatives visited Dora, but on 3 January James had a phone call to say that she had taken a turn for the worse. James and Ann rushed to the hospital but Dora died later that night.

The next day, James returned to the hospital to collect the death certificate. The ward sister gave him a white plastic bag with 'Patient's Property' written over it. She handed him a checklist of its contents, which included 'handbag with purse containing 30 pence'. James glanced at the list and pointed out that the purse should have contained about £70. The ward sister stated that she had personally checked through the contents and that was all that there was. James explained that his wife had seen £60 there and had added £10. The ward sister advised him

Situation 25.1   *continued*

to see the unit manager since there was nothing more that she could do. The unit manager, on interviewing James, ascertained the following:

1. No warnings had been given at the time that Dora was admitted about the patient's property and hospital rules.

2. There was a notice in the ward about the hospital not being liable for patient's property unless it was handed in for safe custody, but this notice was not prominently displayed and James and Ann said that they had not seen it.

Sister Thomas was interviewed and said that she knew that there was a handbag in the locker, but had not looked inside it until after Dora's death when she was drawing up the checklist of contents.

the relationship of bailor/bailee is a voluntary one and one person cannot force another into being the bailee of one's property. When the person agrees to act as bailee (and there may be no reward for doing so), a transfer of possession takes place so that the bailee then becomes liable. In contrast with the usual principles of negligence, once the existence of the bailment is established, it is not for the bailor to establish negligence by the bailee, but for the bailee to show that he exercised all reasonable care for the goods and was not negligent. This is a reversal of the usual burdens of proof.

Applying this law to the above situation, it could be argued that at no time did the family or Dora ask the NHS Trust or its staff to become bailees of the property and take care of it. There was therefore no liability in law for the missing cash.

However, in the context of hospital care, another duty arises under the law of negligence. If an unconscious patient is brought into the accident and emergency department, the NHS Trust and the professionals have a duty to care for the patient and this would include caring for his property if he is unable to look after it. This is known as involuntary bailment. Looking at Dora's situation, were there any occasions when it could be said that the NHS Trust became an involuntary bailee of Dora's property and had a duty of care in relation to it? The answer is when she became unconscious and was unable to look after her property herself. However, we have Ann's evidence that the cash was still there after Dora had resumed consciousness, so it could be argued that the NHS Trust was no longer a bailee (whether or not it had ever been one). The next point at which an involuntary bailment may have arisen is Dora's death. At this point, the ward staff should assume control and ensure that a list of the property is drawn up and properly witnessed. If this is what Sister Thomas did and the cash was not there at that time, then it could be argued that the NHS Trust was not liable for the fact that it is missing.

This is the law in relation to bailment and would mean that in these circumstances the relatives would have difficulty in winning a case against the NHS Trust or Sister Thomas.

Administrative failures

However, what is more likely to occur is that there will be a complaint about the administrative procedures in relation to Dora's property, which would be based on failure of the staff to point out to the relatives procedures for dealing with the property or even checking whether they had brought any in for Dora. Complaints of this kind, though they may not lead to a court action, may, however, lead to the NHS Trust making an *ex gratia* payment to the patient or relatives. This is not an admission of liability, but an attempt to appease the relatives and make up for administrative shortcomings. Under the complaints scheme which was established in April 1996, any complaint of missing property would be investigated at a local level and an attempt made to resolve it. If the complainant is not satisfied with the outcome, then he/she can apply for an independent review hearing (see Chapter 27).

Situation 25.2   A lost engagement ring

Mavis was admitted for an appendectomy and was expecting to stay in hospital only for a few days. She took very little cash in with her, but did take her engagement ring. When she was using the wash hand basin in the toilets, she took off her ring, placing it on the side, and then forgot to put it back on. She had been back in the ward only a short time when she realised what she had done and rushed back to fetch it, but unfortunately it was gone. She knows that someone must have stolen it. Can she recover compensation from the Trust?

There is no legal right for Mavis to obtain compensation from the Trust. She did not entrust her property to the Trust employees, and at the time that it was lost she was responsible for it. However, she may be able to show that there were administrative failings. For example, it might not have been pointed out to her that she brings her property into the hospital at her own risk. Whilst, therefore, there may be no legal basis for a claim, she may be able to use the complaints procedure to raise concerns, and depending upon the results, the Trust may make an ex gratia payment to her. On the other hand, if the Trust explained the situation about patient's property and a notice (see below) pointing out that the Trust did not accept liability was shown to her, then she would probably be unable to obtain any compensation.

Exclusion of liability

What is the legal significance of the notice absolving the health authority of all responsibility for the patient's property? Under the Unfair Contract Terms Act 1977 (see Figure 6.6), such an exemption or exclusion notice is effective in relation to the loss or damage of property, provided that it is reasonable to exclude liability for the negligence that has led to such loss or damage. (Liability for negligence that leads to personal injury or death cannot be excluded.) How is reasonableness defined? The requirement of reasonableness is defined as:

> I acknowledge that the opportunity has been given to me to hand over my personal property to be placed in safekeeping, that I have been advised to do so and that I have declined the offer of safekeeping of my personal property.
>
> Signature of Patient
> Witnessed by
> (Member of Staff)
> Designation
> Date
> To be filed in Patient's case notes folder

Figure 25.2 Patients' property: form of notice disclaiming liability.

it should be fair and reasonable to allow reliance upon it, having regard to all the circumstances obtaining when the liability arose or [but for the Notice] would have arisen (Section 11(3)).

It is for the party claiming that a contract term or notice satisfies the requirement of reasonableness to show that it does (Section 11(5)).

In situation 25.1 where a notice was displayed on the wall, if it could be argued that the NHS Trust's employees had been negligent in relation to her property, then the NHS Trust might claim to rely upon the notice to avoid liability. It would then have to show that it was reasonable for them to rely upon it.

Patients should be advised not to bring valuable property into hospital. If they do, then it can be recommended to them that the property should be taken into safekeeping by the nursing staff. If they are unwilling to part with the property, then they can be asked to sign a form whereby they accept responsibility for the care of the property which has the added advantage of impressing upon the patient the dangers of having valuable property in hospital (see Figure 25.2).

The property of the mentally incompetent

What about the property of those who are unconscious or who have learning disabilities or who are mentally ill or the elderly infirm?

Temporary incapacity

Situation 25.3 *Lost teeth*

Arthur Brown was rushed into hospital one night with a cardiac arrest. He survived following a six-hour operation. When he recovered from the operation, he was told that it was touch and go as to whether he would pull through. A few days later, he discovered that his set of his teeth was missing. He told the staff nurse who said that a search would be started, but they were not found. What remedies does he have?

In this situation, it is clear that Arthur was incapable of taking care of his personal property on admission and it is likely that his teeth were removed pre-operatively. (There would have to be a check to see if they were removed pre-admission or by the ambulance crew.) If following investigations it appears that the hospital staff did remove them and failed to take reasonable care, then, the Trust would be seen as the bailee of the property and responsible for their loss. It would be advisable for the Trust to admit liability and make Arthur a speedy offer as an ex gratia payment. Some staff may feel that, in view of the fact that staff saved Arthur's life, it is unreasonable of Arthur to complain. However, if there is a justified complaint, the fact that a patient's life has been saved would not be a successful defence.

Permanent incapacity

In other situations of long term mental incapacity, there may be tensions between attempting to develop the autonomy of a person and the care of personal property as the following situation indicates.

Situation 25.4 Pocket money

The NHS Trust has the power to give patients with learning disabilities pocket money for sweets, cigarettes and other small personal purchases. Jimmy Jones, an adult of 24 with learning disabilities, rarely spent his money and since he was a hard worker and regularly earned himself substantial amounts, he accumulated over £100. The ward staff attempted to encourage Jimmy to put this in the bank. However, he could not be persuaded and there were rumours that he slept with it under his pillow at night. One morning, he screamed with distress and it appeared that all his money had been stolen from under his bed. A search revealed nothing and there was no hint as to where it had gone. Is the NHS Trust liable for the loss?

From the discussion about situation 25.1 on Dora, it will be apparent that in situation 25.4 there was no transfer of possession from Jimmy to the NHS Trust, so that the latter is not *prima facie* liable. However, much depends upon Jimmy's mental competence and whether sufficient effort was made to persuade him to allow it to be taken for safekeeping. A system of tokens can sometimes be devised to protect patients' property, though care must be taken not to limit their purchasing power and to ensure that the funds are available for them when they want them. In addition, in this case, it could be argued that the NHS Trust had a duty of care in relation to the security of the ward.

The Law Commission has made recommendations relating to decision-making on behalf of the mentally incapacitated adult. Its final recommendations were published in 1995.[1] It recommended that the present system, whereby appointees can collect DSS moneys on behalf of those incapacitated, should be subject to monitoring and regular review. The government's proposals,[2] following a consultation exercise, were published in 1999 and legislation is at present awaited.

Day-to-day care of money

Situation 25.5 *Shopping*

At the heart of the philosophy of community care of those with learning disabilities or severe mental health problems is the principle of autonomy. Clients are encouraged to shop and take part in community activities and realise as much of their potential as possible. In these circumstances, moneys might be entrusted to staff to guide patients in making small purchases. On one such shopping expedition, Gary White, the staff nurse at a community home for those with learning disabilities, took three residents to the shops. Two were able to manage their own purchases, but the third, Leonard, needed some guidance and Gary aided him in purchasing several small items – toiletries, sweets, etc. On their return, Leonard complained to another resident that Gary had spent all his money. This came to the attention of the home manager who asked Gary for an immediate explanation. Gary showed how the money had been spent, but was unable to produce any receipts or supporting evidence. Nor was he able to remember exactly where the money had gone.

In a situation like this, the member of staff is like a trustee for the resident's property and should be able to account for it in detail with supporting receipts. Of course, the receipts do not in themselves show that the money was spent on the patient but, together with evidence from other witnesses, it should be possible to record exactly how the money was spent and that it was spent in the interests of the resident. In a case like this, the home manager would discipline Gary for his failure to follow the correct procedure.

In the community, many residents may have considerable sums to spend and the staff are therefore vulnerable to an accusation that they have spent the money on themselves. One of the requirements under the Registered Homes Legislation (see Chapter 23) is that there should be accurate records kept of residents' property. It is essential that staff be trained in good practices of book-keeping and that there should be, as far as possible, witnesses to give evidence as to how the money has been spent. The ultimate aim is, of course, that the resident should be the watchdog for his own funds, but many residents/clients may never get beyond the stage of entrusting all such matters to others.

Power of attorney

Patients, who have the necessary mental capacity, can grant a power of attorney. This power is revoked (i.e. withdrawn) if the person granting it becomes mentally incapable. However, since this is often the very occasion when it would be useful to exercise the power on behalf of the patient, an Enduring Power of Attorney Act 1985 was passed which came into effect in 1986. This power comes into existence

1. Came into force 10 March 1986.

2. Enables a power of attorney to continue in force after the maker of the power (called 'the donor') becomes mentally incapable of handling his or her affairs.

3. After 1 July 1988 the enduring power of attorney must be in the exact form prescribed in the Enduring Powers of Attorney (Prescribed Form) Regulations 1987.

4. The Enduring Power of Attorney may give
   (a) a general power – which authorises the Attorney to carry out any transactions on behalf of the donor; or
   (b) a specific power – which authorises the Attorney to deal only with those aspects of the donor's affairs which are specified in the power.

5. The donor can revoke or cancel the Enduring Power at any time while she/he remains mentally capable, but the power cannot be cancelled or revoked once it has been registered unless the Court of Protection confirms the revocation.

6. When the donor becomes mentally incapable, the Attorney must apply to register the Enduring Power of Attorney with the Court of Protection before he/she can act under it.

7. Once registered, the Attorney has the power to act on behalf of the donor – either general or specific, but has no power over the person of the donor, and cannot make a will on behalf of the donor.

Figure 25.3 Enduring Power of Attorney Act 1985.

only if the person wishes the power to continue after the time at which he becomes incapable; he must sign to this effect and indicate that he is aware of the significance of the enduring element. Figure 25.3 sets out some of the requirements for and the characteristics of an enduring power of attorney. The enduring power of attorney applies only to financial and property matters and cannot be used for the delegation of treatment decisions to other persons. In its proposals for decision making on behalf of mentally incapacitated adults, the government has suggested that there should be in law a continuing power of attorney under which mentally incapacitated adults could delegate treatment decisions for others to make on their behalf.

Court of Protection

Where there is no enduring power of attorney in existence and the person is incapable of managing his affairs, an application can be made to the Court of Protection for the appointment of a receiver to manage the affairs. There is a short procedure that can be used where the assets are small. Otherwise a relative, or perhaps the authority, could apply for a receiver to be appointed to manage the patient's affairs and to allow money to be spent on the patient. The powers of the Court of Protection are considerable. The applicant will have to pay in to the court a sum of money as a recognisance. Notice of the application is given to the patient, who has the opportunity of opposing it. Medical evidence will also be required to show that the patient is incapable of handling his affairs by reason of mental disorder. This medical evidence can be challenged by the patient. The Court of Protection has the power of making a will in the name of the patient and can arrange for sums to be

95. (1) The judge may, with respect to the property and affairs of a patient, do or secure the doing of all such things as appear necessary or expedient:
    (a) for the maintenance or other benefit of the patient;
    (b) for the maintenance or other benefit of members of the patient's family;
    (c) for making provision for other persons or purposes for whom or which the patient might be expected to provide if he were not mentally disordered; or
    (d) otherwise for administering the patient's affairs.

    (2) In the exercise of the powers conferred by this section regard shall be had first of all to the requirements of the patient, and the rules of law which restricted the enforcement by a creditor of rights against property under the control of the judge in lunacy shall apply to property under the control of the judge; but, subject to the foregoing provisions of this subsection, the judge shall, in administering a patient's affairs, have regard to the interests of creditors and also to the desirability of making provision for obligations of the patient notwithstanding that they may not be legally enforceable.

96. (1) Without prejudice to the generality of Section 95 above, the judge shall have power to make such orders and give such directions and authorities as he thinks fit for the purposes of that section and in particular may for those purposes make orders or give directions or authorities for:
    (a) the control (with or without the transfer or vesting of property or the payment into or lodgement in the Supreme Court of money or securities) and management of any property of the patient;
    (b) the sale, exchange, charging or other disposition of or dealing with any property of the patient;
    (c) the acquisition of any property in the name or on behalf of the patient;
    (d) the settlement of any property of the patient, or the gift of any property of the patient to any such persons or for any such purposes as are mentioned in paragraphs (b) and (c) of Section 95(1) above;
    (e) the execution for the patient of a will making any provision (whether by way of disposing of property or exercising a power or otherwise) which could be made by a will executed by the patient if he were not mentally disordered;
    (f) the carrying on by a suitable person of any profession, trade or business of the patient;
    (g) the dissolution of a partnership of which the patient is a member;
    (h) the carrying out of any contract entered into by the patient;
    (i) the conduct of legal proceedings in the name of the patient or on his behalf;
    (j) the reimbursement out of the property of the patient, with or without interest, of money applied by any person either in payment of the patient's debts (whether legally enforceable or not) or for the maintenance or other benefit of the patient or members of his family or in making provision for other persons or purposes for whom or which he might be expected to provide if he were not mentally disordered;
    (k) the exercise of any power (including a power to consent) vested in the patient, whether beneficially, or as guardian or trustee, or otherwise.

Figure 25.4 Powers of the Court of Protection: Mental Health Act 1983.

paid to other persons who would have been dependent upon the patient or would have looked to him for help, even though these obligations would not have been legally enforceable. Obviously, there is a power to pay all debts. The details of the powers available are set out in Part 7 of the Mental Health Act 1983 and some of the most important ones are shown in Figure 25.4. At the time of writing, legislation to replace the Mental Health Act 1983 and to provide a statutory framework for decision making on behalf of mentally incapacitated adults is awaited.

Protecting patients from relatives

Situation 25.6 *Grasping relatives*

Mary Bennet was visited regularly by her daughter Jean and each week the ward sister noticed that Jean brought the pension book in for her mother to sign. However, it was noticeable that Mary never seemed to have any money for purchases from the ward trolley and if the ward had not supplied her with squash, tissues, and soap, she would not have had any of those items. Janice, the ward sister, mentioned it to Jean, who flushed a little and said that she did not have anything to do with her mother's money and by the time she had personally paid for the bus fare to the hospital, she did not have any funds for such purchases, and anyway the hospital provided that, did they not?

Many nurses would recognise this type of situation and the dilemma that arises for them is to what extent the nurse is a protector of the patient, even when she has to protect the patient from his own relatives. In one sense, this type of situation will not continue for very long since certain benefits are reduced and ultimately end after several weeks. However, the same issue can arise in other circumstances, for example, the signing of wills (considered in Chapter 29). In the above situation, there is little that the ward sister can do. In any event, she cannot be sure that the money is not being used to meet Mary's bills at home and the sum is, of course, far too small to consider taking out a Court of Protection Order. However, the fact that the relatives are aware of her concern might be of some small influence. The Law Commission[3] has recommended that the present system whereby the DSS recognises an authorised person to collect moneys on a person's behalf should be subject to monitoring and review.

The law relating to the care of a patient's property on the death of a patient and the making of wills is considered in Chapter 29.

Returning the patient's property

Situation 25.7 *Weekend property problems*

It was the accepted practice at Roger Park General Hospital for the money on any patients who were admitted in an emergency to be retained by the general office for safekeeping during their stay. On discharge, they were then able to obtain a cheque representing that amount of money from the general office. Most patients, except those with no bank accounts, accepted the system. Problems, however, arose at weekends when no general office staff were on duty or when discharge was sudden and the cheques could not be made available in time. On such occasions, patients complained that the actual cash that was taken from them was not returned and since not all banks were open on Saturday, they could not change the cheques and some had no cash with which to return home. What is the legal position?

The legal position depends to a certain extent on the circumstances of the money being taken by the NHS Trust. If the patient is fully conscious when the money is handed over, he should be told that he will be given a cheque for this amount on discharge. If he refuses to agree to this, then it is open to him to ask relatives to look after his money or to take the risk of keeping that sum on his person. If, however, the money has been taken from the unconscious patient after an emergency admission, then there is no chance of the terms of the bailment being agreed with him. In such circumstances, the hospital holds the money as part of its duty of care to look after the patient. It could be argued that this duty requires the hospital to return to the patient exactly the same coins and notes that were taken from him. Alternatively, it could be said that the hospital carries out its duty of care by giving the patient the equivalent of what was taken in the form of a cheque. Unfortunately, there is no decided case to clarify the position in law. As far as administrative practice is concerned, possibly the best solution is to discuss with the patient as soon as he is conscious and capable of handling his affairs what the patient would prefer and, if the patient is unhappy at receiving a cheque for the entire amount, to consider the possibility of providing part in cash for immediate needs. Where the discharge is contemplated for a weekend, then either the cheque should be prepared in advance or there should be an emergency scheme to provide the patient with a cash advance. Where the patient has no bank account, the hospital should be able to make special arrangements either for the cheque to be cleared at a local branch or for the cash to be made available.

Staff property

Situation 25.8   Lost handbag

Mavis Jarvis, a staff nurse, was going straight from work to a travel company to pay for her holiday to Greece. She was holidaying with a friend and had £500 in cash to pay for both of them. The money was contained in a wallet inside her handbag. At the hospital, all nursing staff were provided with a locker in a staff room in their ward or department. The lockers were fitted with a padlock and key. Mavis locked her locker and carried the key around for the whole shift. Several people knew that she was going to the travel agent after work. At the end of the shift, when she went to her locker, she found that it had been broken into: the small padlock had been forced open and the money was missing from the wallet. The police were summoned, but despite intensive questioning and search the money was never recovered or the thief discovered. Mavis feels that the NHS Trust should pay for the missing money since, she argued, the padlock was inadequate and a far tougher system should have been provided for taking care of staff property. Is she right in law?

Unfortunately for Mavis, it is highly unlikely that she would win in a court action against the NHS Trust. If we return to the terminology used in Dora's case in

Situation 25.1 above, the NHS Trust is not the bailee of Mavis's cash; she has not transferred it to its safekeeping. She has, so to speak, brought the property into the hospital at her own risk. If, of course, she had gone to the general office and said, 'Please take care of this for me since I have to go the travel agent straight after work,' and it had done so, the situation would have been very different. In that case, the NHS Trust would have become a bailee of her money and would be accountable to her for its return. What about the argument that the locker should have been stronger? The locker should be as strong as is compatible with the value of property that is reasonable to be kept in there. There must be few who would think that attempting to keep £500 is reasonable. Anyone who brings valuable goods to work and keeps them there cannot expect the NHS Trust to be held responsible for their loss, unless of course it is a requirement of the job that such items are brought to work, or unless the employer has assumed responsibility for them. The employer can, through the contract of employment, take on a wider responsibility for the property of employees, though this would be unusual. The courts are unlikely to imply a term that the employer has a duty to take care of the property of the employee. There would have to be an explicit undertaking to that effect.

Situation 25.9   Staff car park

Jean Jones, a staff nurse in the out-patients department, parked her car in the hospital car park, paying the daily fee of £3.00. When she came back, she found that her car had been broken into and the radio/cassette player taken. A pathology laboratory technician whose office overlooked the car park came up to her as she was looking at the damage and said that he had seen the whole incident. He had seen two youths break into the car who were then chased by the car park attendant. When car park charges were introduced, staff had been assured that there would be better protection for their cars. Could Jean Jones hold the security firm or the NHS Trust responsible for the damage?

There are two possible causes of action: one against the security firm and the other against the Trust. If it were the responsibility of the security firm to protect the cars in the park on a 24-hour basis, then they have failed to fulfil that responsibility. There may be a contractual right against them by the NHS trust, but it depends upon the terms of the contract. Although the Trust has a right of action in contract, Jean Jones does not have a right of action, unless she can make use of the recent Contracts (Rights of Third Parties) Act 1999, which enables a person not a party to the contract to sue for benefits under it. In addition, it may be argued that the security firm owed a duty of care in the law of negligence to each employee or user of the car park. This might be difficult to establish. Any liability of the Trust depends upon Jean's being able to establish that it owed Jean a duty of care in respect of her car and had not excluded any liability by an exemption notice. This would depend upon the actual facts. The likelihood is that Jean will be unable to obtain compensation from either the security firm or her employers and will be dependent upon any insurance cover she has for theft.

The future

The government has made significant proposals for decision making on behalf of mentally incompetent adults. These will include decisions over the care and responsibility for their property. At the time of writing, draft legislation is awaited.

Questions and exercises

1 How many disclaimer notices or exclusion notices do you see around the hospital? Consider the extent to which reliance on each notice would be reasonable to exclude liability for damage or loss of property caused by the negligence of the NHS Trust or its staff.

2 Consider the liability of the NHS Trust, if any, for the loss of a patient's pyjamas. It appears that they were removed when the patient was given a bath and probably placed with the sheets in the laundry bag. The laundry has denied any knowledge of them.

3 Examine the procedure followed in relation to property when patients are admitted to hospital.

4 You are working at a psychiatric hospital and one of the patients drags a nail along the side of your new car. Is the NHS Trust responsible? Would it make any difference if there were a notice by the car park exempting the NHS Trust from loss or damage to staff cars parked there?

5 The relative of a patient in your geriatric wards asks you if you would sign a power of attorney so that the relative can manage the patient's affairs on his behalf. You know that the patient is mentally disordered, but is reputed to be quite wealthy. What advice would you give to the relative?

6 The Court of Protection has been appointed to manage the property of one of the patients on your ward. What powers does it have and who will administer the property?

References

[1] Law Commission Mental Incapacity Report No 231 1995 HMSO
[2] Lord Chancellor's Office, Making Decisions, Stationery Office 1999
[3] See end note 1

26 Legal aspects of AIDS and other infectious diseases

All those general principles of law that have been discussed in relation to health and safety, consent, confidentiality and professional liability apply to the patient suffering from AIDS or who is HIV positive. There are very few specific laws and cases dealing with the AIDS patient. However, because AIDS is at present incurable, (although there has been recent progress in medications that delay the onset of AIDS from HIV), because a high proportion of HIV patients eventually suffer from AIDS itself, and because of the present hysteria that surrounds it (as can be seen from the way in which different professional groups have argued that the basic principles of law do not apply in relation to such sufferers), it is considered advisable to have a separate chapter on the law relating to AIDS and other infectious diseases, to discuss a few of the dilemmas that arise. The term 'AIDS patient' will be used to cover both the person who has AIDS itself and also the person who is HIV positive.

This chapter looks at those legal aspects of AIDS and infectious diseases that are shown in Figure 26.1.

---

1. Statutory regulations.
2. Characteristics of AIDS.
3. AIDS and employment
    (a) pre-employment medical examination;
    (b) tests for AIDS during employment;
    (c) AIDS and health and safety at work.
4. The AIDS patient.
5. Consent to screening.
6. Government policy on testing.
7. Blood donors.
8. Haemophiliacs and the recipients of blood.
9. Confidentiality.
10. AIDS Control Act 1987.
11. Notification of Infectious diseases.
12. Cross-infection.

Figure 26.1 Issues covered in Chapter 26.

Statutory regulations

The government has made regulations (Public Health (Infectious Diseases) Regulation 1985) which came into force on 22 March 1985 and which gave the powers that are illustrated in Figure 26.2. In addition, there is the AIDS Control Act 1987 which provides for periodic reports upon AIDS to enable the appropriate resources to be allocated and plans to be made. This Act is considered further below.

Apart from these rules and the existing public health laws that would cover AIDS, there has been minimal legislation. Codes of practice have been issued by the DH and by many professional associations, but these do not have the force of law. Although the guidance should usually be followed, failure to do so would not necessarily involve any illegality or give rise to a cause of action in law. Section 23 of the Health and Medicines Act 1988 enables the Secretary of State to make regulations on HIV testing kits and services.

---

1. Gives to local authorities the power to apply to a Justice of the Peace for the removal of an AIDS sufferer to hospital to be detained there.
2. Gives to the Justice of the Peace the power to make an order for a person believed to be suffering from AIDS to be medically examined. There are also powers in relation to the disposal of the body of an AIDS sufferer.

Figure 26.2   Public Health Act (Infectious Diseases) Regulations 1985.

Characteristics of AIDS

AIDS does, of course, appear to have some characteristics that, taken together, make the disease unique. These are shown in Figure 26.3.

The combination of these characteristics could possibly justify the judges making the law relating to AIDS an exception to the general principles of law and, until more cases are heard, the situation in law is uncertain.

It is incurable at present.
It is passed through body fluid contact.
It is of very puny strength outside body fluids.
A high proportion of those who are HIV positive are thought likely to suffer eventually from AIDS itself.
Screening for HIV positivity is beset with difficulties: there are false negatives and false positives. Early incubation over the first three months does not necessarily show up as HIV positive.
A person who is shown to be HIV negative could become exposed to and acquire the virus immediately after the test.

Figure 26.3   Characteristics of AIDS.

AIDS and employment

Some of the many questions which arise in employment are as follows:

Can I refuse to nurse an AIDS sufferer?

Can I be compelled to have a test for AIDS?

Can an employee insist that other employees are tested for AIDS?

Can I refuse to work with an employee whom I know is an AIDS sufferer or whom I suspect might be?

Can an employee who suffers from AIDS be fairly dismissed?

Pre-employment medical examination

Can an employer legally insist on a prospective employee being screened for AIDS prior to being taken on as an employee? The simple answer is yes. An employer's right to choose the most suitable, competent, capable person for the job, while not absolute, is extremely wide. He is constrained by the Sex Discrimination Act 1975, the Race Relations Act 1976 and the Disability Discrimination Act 1995 and cannot choose a particular sex or race or refuse to appoint a disabled person, unless the exceptions to those Acts apply. He is also prevented from compelling an employee to divulge a criminal offence if that conviction is spent for the purposes of the Rehabilitation of Offenders Act 1974 (however, most health service posts are excluded from the provisions of this Act. See Chapter 10). The requirement that a prospective employee has a medical examination can either be insisted upon before the contract of employment commences or it can result in the contract ending after it has commenced since the medical results are not satisfactory. Many occupational health departments carry out this examination for the NHS Trust and considerable hardship can arise if the employee commences the new post, having given in his notice in his previous employment, and only after starting work does the medical examination find him unfit and therefore he loses the new job. This could apply to a person suffering from AIDS or who is found to be HIV positive. Many of the codes of practice that exist advise that such tests should not be insisted upon. The Disability Discrimination Act 1995 may provide some protection, but the absence of an Act of Parliament that makes it illegal to test for AIDS in such circumstances makes the situation in law uncertain.

Tests for AIDS during employment

Once the employee's contract of employment has commenced, he has certain protection against unreasonable requests by the employer.

Situation 26.1   Compulsory testing

Eddie was a staff nurse in the operating theatre. It was well known that he was homosexual. His colleagues were concerned that he might be HIV positive and felt that he should not be allowed to act as a scrub nurse if there were any danger to the patients. They felt that he should be tested. A request was made to the Director of Nursing Services and she asked Eddie to undergo the test. Is this request unreasonable? Can Eddie refuse to comply?

Where the employee's physical or mental capability to do the job is in doubt, the employer can suggest that the employee submits to an independent medical examination, but there is no power to order this. If the employee has refused a medical examination and if subsequently, in consequence, the employee is dismissed on the grounds of the refusal, the employment tribunal will consider whether the employer acted reasonably in all the circumstances. Under the 1985 Regulations, the Justice of the Peace can make an order for a person believed to be suffering from AIDS to be medically examined by a registered medical practitioner (under the Public Health (Control of Disease) Act 1984 Section 34). This provision is for the purpose of preventing a danger to public health and could be used where a person suspected of being an AIDS sufferer is acting intentionally or recklessly in endangering public health. If the disease were confirmed, the powers of the local authority to apply to a Justice of the Peace for the removal of the sufferer and detention in hospital could then be used (Public Health Regulations 1985 and Public Health (Control of Disease) Act 1984 Sections 37 and 38). In extreme circumstances, it could be argued that these powers are available where the employer is concerned about a danger to public health. It is extremely unlikely, however, that their use could be justified in the circumstances described in Eddie's case. It could be argued that in Eddie's case the request to be tested for AIDS would be unreasonable for two reasons. If the test proves negative, it is of value only for the day of testing and it does not exclude the possibility that Eddie has recently been exposed to the virus which has not yet shown up in tests. Frequent tests would have to be carried out to cover this possibility. If the test proves positive, what is the significance of this? It shows that the individual has been exposed to the virus, but there is little indication to show the course of events: it could be many years before Eddie contracts the disease itself (if ever). It does reveal that he is a potential source of infection, but if good hygienic practices are followed, there should be no danger to other employees or patients. It could be argued that, being a theatre nurse, he is a greater danger to patients, but this does not follow if the proper procedures are complied with. In addition, it could be said that, since there is no obvious value to the employer in insisting upon such a test, such a request is unreasonable because of the harm it could cause the employee. As long as the disease is incurable and as long as it is impossible to tell which HIV positive patients will contract AIDS or ARC (AIDS-related complex) and when, the knowledge of an HIV positive result confers no benefit on the employee and, in fact, brings him considerable harm. It affects his eligibility for a mortgage and life insurance, and he may lose his job and be unable to obtain a new one. Tentative conclusions here are that at the present time such a request by an employer would be unreasonable, unless very exceptional circumstances existed. However, if Eddie has been in continuous employment for less than one year and is dismissed because he has refused to take the test, he is ineligible to bring an action for unfair dismissal before an employment tribunal and, provided he has been given the contractual period of notice to which he is entitled, he would probably have no remedy for wrongful dismissal. If he alleges that he is being discriminated against on grounds of disability, then he could bring an action under the Disability Discrimination Act 1995. If he is an NHS employee, he would be entitled to make an internal appeal against dismissal, but his only protection then is the overall policy of the NHS Trust and the rules of natural justice. The Department of Health has issued guidance on the management of infected health care workers and patient notification.[1] It recommends that infected health care workers should consult with the occupational health department. Whilst they have a duty of confidentiality to the employees, an exception to this duty may arise in the public interest (see Chapter 8).

In the case of *Bliss* v. *S.E. Thames RHA* 1985 1 RLR 308, the Court of Appeal held that an employee could not be required to submit to a medical examination unless there were reasonable grounds to believe that he might be suffering from physical or mental disability which might cause harm to the patients or adversely affect the quality of the treatment given to them.

Compensation for unfair dismissal

In one case,[2] a tribunal held that a cinema company had acted reasonably in dismissing a projectionist who was reported in the newspaper to have been importuning in a public toilet. The dismissal was not unfair. However, it does not follow that a dismissal on the grounds of homosexual conduct or being infected with AIDS/HIV will always be fair as the next case shows.

A gay supermarket manager was told to stay away from work after his bosses found out that he was HIV positive. He applied to the Employment Tribunal alleging sexual and disability discrimination and the employers agreed an out-of-court settlement thought to be in the region of about £250,000.[3]

Situation 26.2   The unwitting victim

Unknown to Mary Kemp, her husband was bisexual and was infected with the AIDS virus and eventually she was infected as well. She was not aware of this initially, but after being away from work for an intractable infection, it was discovered that she had AIDS. She was considered fit to return to work for the immediate future. She told her nursing officer of the diagnosis and it was suggested that she should return home and not consider working again. The nursing officer justified her decision on the basis that she was a risk to the staff and the patients and that she was unlikely to perform her job competently anyway.

This situation is likely to be very complex. It is not an established principle that the fact that an employee suffers from AIDS (or is HIV positive) is in itself justification for immediate dismissal. Nor can it be said that the employer's duty to safeguard the health of other employees would automatically require him to dismiss the sufferer or carrier. There may, of course, come a time when that employee is incapable, by reason of his physical or mental condition, of carrying out his duties and a dismissal in those circumstances may well be fair and not an infringement of the Disability Discrimination Act 1995. However, provided a safe system of work is followed and good hygienic practices are implemented, the AIDS sufferer should not be a danger to his fellow employees or the patients and should not be dismissed on those grounds alone. Similarly, a pregnant employee cannot be dismissed just because she is pregnant but, unlike the AIDS sufferer, the pregnant employee has the additional protection of a specific statutory right not to be dismissed solely on the grounds of pregnancy. A similar statutory provision might be required for the protection of AIDS sufferers or HIV positive persons.

If there were a clear danger to the health of patients or colleagues from infection, then dismissal, in the event of no suitable alternative work, may be fair. For example, the recent discovery that a surgeon had died of AIDS led to an extended public debate on the extent to which any health worker should be permitted to continue in work and possibly endanger the lives of his patients. In this particular case, death followed within a few weeks of the knowledge of the illness (the surgeon ceased working as soon as he was aware of the diagnosis) and the health authorities in which the doctor concerned worked made a vigorous effort to contact patients who had been operated upon by the surgeon and offer them AIDS tests. Interestingly, and perhaps not surprisingly, the take-up on the offer of tests was very low. The General Medical Council announced that doctors risked being struck off the medical register if they contract AIDS but ignore advice to stop practising. New guidelines were published for doctors that included the advice that doctors should inform the health authorities if they suspected that a colleague had the virus, but was not following advice. The General Medical Council announced that it was unethical for doctors who know or believe themselves to be infected with HIV to put patients at risk by failing to seek appropriate counselling or to act upon it when given. It could be added that if a doctor, knowing himself to be HIV positive, infected a patient as a result of his own carelessness, then it could be not only unethical, but also a civil wrong. This is discussed below on the duty of the AIDS patient. The Department of Health has issued guidelines to doctors and health authorities that make provision for the protection of patients in the case of HIV infection of health workers (April 1993).

The Midwives Rules, Rule 39, oblige a practising midwife to allow herself to be medically examined if necessary for the prevention of the spread of infection, when requested by the local supervising authority.

Reference should also be made to the UKCC Registrar's letter dated 6 April 1993 (12/1993), which sets out the Council's position on the routine HIV testing of health care professionals and the individual responsibility of the practitioner.

AIDS and health and safety at work

As explained in Chapter 12, the employer has a duty both under the common law and under the Health and Safety at Work Act 1974 to take care of the health and safety of his employees. Under the common law duty, he is required to ensure that the premises, plant and equipment are safe, that the staff are competent and that a safe system of work is implemented.

Situation 26.3   Caring for the AIDS patient

Ruth was a staff nurse in a ward that had been specially adapted for the care of AIDS patients. Unfortunately, because of the financial position of the health authority, it was necessary to reduce revenue costs. The recommended practice was that gloves should be worn at all times when dealing with the bodily fluids of the patients. However, the original type of glove that was provided was replaced by a cheaper alternative which tore easily. Since Ruth suffered from eczema, she was very nervous about working in the ward and asked if she could reasonably refuse to work there.

In carrying out its duty in relation to health and safety, an employer must ensure that all reasonable practical precautions are taken to safeguard the employee. A written statement of safety policy is a statutory obligation under the Health and Safety at Work Act 1974. In order to comply with its duties, each employer should ensure that the policy covers potential dangers from the AIDS virus. The employer has a duty to ensure that the equipment and protective clothing that are reasonably necessary to ensure the safety of the employee are provided. If a code of practice requires that, in the circumstances outlined above, gloves should be provided, then it would also be reasonable to provide gloves that met the needs of staff safety. If Ruth can show that the gloves provided are useless in protecting her and others could be purchased that would be effective at reasonable cost, then it could be argued that Ruth would be justified in requiring these reasonable precautions to be made for her safety. If she were to be dismissed in such circumstances, it could be argued that the employer was being unreasonable and that it was an unfair dismissal. The employee could not refuse to treat an AIDS patient simply because he had AIDS. There are no statutory grounds for refusing to take part in such care as is provided by the Abortion Act (see Chapter 15).

It is, however, unreasonable of the employer to endanger the safety of the employee when reasonable precautions could be taken but they are not. The employer's duty in this respect would include the laying down of safe codes of practice and ensuring that these were implemented, training of staff in safe systems of work, as well as the provision of reasonable equipment to ensure a safe environment. If, however, an employee failed to follow the safe practices and became infected, any claim for compensation against the employer might be reduced on the grounds of contributory negligence.

The guidelines of the UKCC have made it clear that it would regard the refusal by a registered nurse to treat an AIDS patient as professional misconduct. The UKCC has emphasised that the practitioner has no right to refuse to treat a patient suffering from AIDS or who is HIV positive.

If, in the above case, Ruth was provided with gloves that were considered suitable and yet she still refused to work on the AIDS ward, it is highly likely (depending of course on the details of the situation) that such conduct would be considered to be unreasonable. It would follow that the employers could use such conduct in refusing to care for the AIDS patient as a statutory reason for a fair dismissal. Ruth might also face disciplinary proceedings from the Professional Conduct Committee.

The Personal Protective Equipment (PPE) at Work Regulations 1999 require employers to carry out a risk assessment to avoid risks and, where this is not possible, to provide suitable PPE free of charge to employees exposed to these risks. Protection against dismissal in health and safety situations is given by employment legislation (see Chapter 10). Guidance has been issued for clinical health care workers on protection against infection with HIV and Hepatitis Viruses.[4] Recent advice from the NHS Executive[5] supplements previous guidance on hepatitis B infected health care workers and aims to reduce further the risk of transmission of infection to patients.[6]

The AIDS patient

Gradually, a clearer idea is emerging on the rights and duties of the AIDS sufferer. The issues are often concerned with the rights of consent to be tested and also the problems of confidentiality and to whom the information that X is suffering from AIDS be given. There are also some cases directly concerned with the AIDS patient in the criminal law. For example, a threat by an AIDS victim to harm another person can be a criminal offence.

Other countries have had AIDS related criminal offences: a man in Missouri, USA, injected his son with HIV to avoid paying child benefit support. The boy has survived. The father stole AIDS tainted blood from his job as a laboratory technician. He was sentenced to imprisonment and it was recommended that he serve life.[7] A doctor in Louisiana, USA, who injected his nurse lover with the AIDS virus was given a maximum penalty of 50 years' hard labour.[8]

It would seem that there is no reason why a person who knows that he is suffering from AIDS or is HIV positive and is therefore a potential source of infection should not owe a duty of care to any person whom he can reasonably foresee would be likely to be harmed by his actions. This is the same duty of care that is owed by anyone in the civil law of negligence to take such precautions as are reasonable to ensure that reasonably foreseeable harm does not occur as the result of their actions or omissions (see Chapter 3).

What is the nature of the duty of care owed by an AIDS sufferer to those who might be contaminated by him? Should he inform those with whom he is in contact that he has AIDS or is HIV positive? Take, for example, a situation where an AIDS sufferer is involved in a road traffic accident; should he tell the ambulance crew and those who are helping him as he lies bleeding in the road to take special precautions? If he fails to do so (and he might well fail to do so for fear that the volunteers might suddenly disappear) and some of the helpers become infected, would he then be liable to them? If the general principles of law are applied, there should be no reason why he is not under the duty to inform them, but the point still needs to be settled in the courts.

Consent to screening

There has been considerable debate in the press over whether people could be tested for AIDS without their knowledge and consent; for example, in epidemiological research when there is a need to establish the extent of the disease or the existence of HIV positivity in the country for the purposes of planning resources and future policies. Some have argued that if the tests are done on an anonymous basis and the individuals therefore not informed of the results, then such testing would be lawful. Others have stated that to take blood for such testing without obtaining the patient's consent is a trespass to their person.

One of the difficulties is that while the law requires the consent of an individual for any interference with his person, at present consent is given for blood to be taken and this seems to include consent to all the various tests that are to be carried out on the blood: few doctors or technicians would explain to a patient all the tests that are to be undertaken. For example, in pregnancy it is routine for a Wassermann test (for venereal disease) to be carried out on patients, but very few would be aware of the existence of the test or its purpose. It could be argued that consent to all these various tests is covered by the initial consent to the blood being taken. These tests are undertaken as part of the duty of care for the patient, to enable a proper diagnosis to be carried out and the appropriate treatment given. However, at present it is not clear that testing blood for AIDS or HIV is in the best interests of the patient. The knowledge that a person is HIV positive merely puts an uncertain burden over him with prognosis and timings remaining unknown. Insurance companies, for example, are refusing cover for persons who have received a test, not just for those who are HIV positive. However, a new scheme whereby insurance cover is not provided for AIDS-related illnesses might take away the need to make any declaration in relation to AIDS tests or to one's sexual preferences.

What are our conclusions? It has been pointed out that there is, under the public health legislation, power for a doctor to be authorised to examine a person suspected of having AIDS. Since this statutory power exists, no further powers that contradict the general principles of consent should be implied, i.e. if Parliament had wished to give wider powers it could have done so under this legislation. In all other cases, the principle that the patient should give consent to the testing should be applied and there should be no secret testing without the patient's knowledge or consent.

As the extent of the disease grows, there may well be specific laws changing this position. For example, there has been a strong plea in favour of anonymous screening for epidemiological reasons, and the government has supported the need. The Public Health Laboratory Service commenced a programme of anonymous HIV testing, using blood left over from other tests authorised by the patient. A UKCC Registrar's letter (12/93) dated 6 April 1993 sets guidelines for practitioners involved in such testing.

Government policy on testing

In December 1998, the government launched a campaign to encourage all pregnant women to have an HIV test. The press release stated that only 30% of women who are HIV positive are aware that they are infected. If a pregnant woman is known to be HIV positive, then the risk of passing on HIV to the fetus can be reduced by arranging for delivery to be by caesarean section. Avoiding breast feeding also removes the risk of passing on the virus through the milk. However, the law has not been changed and a test for HIV still requires the consent of the woman. The government set a national target to achieve an 80% reduction by December 2002 in the number of children who acquire HIV from their mothers.[9] In its HIV/AIDS Services 2000/2001 allocation and strategy, NHS organisations were instructed that part of the HIV prevention budget was to be used to support antenatal services in recommending an HIV test to all pregnant women. A research project to estimate the cost effectiveness of a universal, voluntary HIV screening programme has suggested that it is effective and should be implemented in the London area, with other areas being considered for screening.[10]

A GP who carried out secret HIV tests on five patients he suspected were indulging in risky sex was given a serious reprimand by the GMC. One of the patients had found out about the test when he applied for a life insurance policy and he notified the GMC. The disciplinary committee of the GMC noted that the GP believed that he was acting in the patients' best interests, but concluded that 'such a benevolent, paternalistic attitude has no place in modern medicine.'[11]

Case 26.1   Re C (HIV Test)[12]

The local authority applied for a specific issue order that a baby born to an HIV positive mother be tested for HIV. The mother was sceptical of the conventional treatment for HIV and AIDS, had refused medication during the pregnancy and intended to continue breast feeding until the child was about 2 years. The judge found that there was a 20–25% chance that the baby was infected with HIV; the risk had been increased with the breast feeding. The judge held that the views of the parents were important factors in the decision and any court invited to overrule parental wishes had to move extremely cautiously. He concluded that in the present circumstances the arguments for overruling the wishes of the parents and for testing the baby were overwhelming. The baby had rights of her own recognised in national and international law, the baby's welfare was paramount and in the baby's interests the test should take place. The parents appealed, but did not attend court on the date their application was due to be heard, having disappeared from their home, taking the child with them. The Court of Appeal refused permission to appeal: the question whether the child should or should not be tested was a matter relating to the welfare of the child, not the rights of the parents, and it was clearly not in the child's best interests for either the parents or the health professionals to remain ignorant of her state of health.

This field is of particular concern to midwives and operating theatre staff who wish to know whether it is possible to insist that all midwifery patients or all surgical patients be screened for AIDS. There is certainly no power to insist on such screening under the laws at present, though there is the power to order an AIDS test on an individual under the public health regulations discussed above. The difficult question is: if there were power to screen prospective surgical or midwifery patients and the tests were carried out and some were found to be positive, what happens then? Can the professional staff refuse to operate or to attend them in their confinements? Can additional precautions for the safety of the staff be taken? If the answer to the latter question is yes, then it gives the staff a false sense of security since, as was pointed out in the section on the characteristics of AIDS, there can be false negatives. It would be better practice for midwifery, operating theatre and other staff to maintain standards of practice that assumed that every patient was HIV positive.

In case 26.1 on page 513, an HIV positive mother refused to allow her baby to be tested for HIV.

Blood donors

The present practice is for blood donors to be asked to agree that their blood can be tested for AIDS and a leaflet is given to them to sign as to whether they are in any of the high-risk groups and which asks them not to give blood if they are. The donors should not, of course, run any risk of contracting AIDS as a result of giving blood.

Haemophiliacs and the recipients of blood

Before the disease of AIDS was recognised in this country as a possible killer, many haemophiliacs were given contaminated blood and have since contracted AIDS. In order to succeed in an action for compensation in respect of the harm caused by being given contaminated blood, they would need to be able to show that those professionals providing the blood should have tested it for AIDS and were in breach of their duty of care in failing to do so and that this failure was contrary to the standard accepted practices of the time. It is unlikely that those who were originally infected could show this and therefore they have been dependent upon government *ex gratia* payments and charity to assist them. Any person receiving contaminated blood now, however, which has not been properly tested, would have a *prima facie* case of negligence and might also be able to obtain compensation under the Consumer Protection Act (see Chapter 12).

Confidentiality

Situation 26.4   A justified disclosure?

Dr Jones, a general practitioner, was treating Ben James for an undiagnosed condition. He thought initially that it could be glandular fever. However, the blood tests revealed that he was suffering from AIDS. Dr Jones was uncertain as to whom he could inform about this result. Ben was anxious that no one should be told and that the information should be kept from his wife till much later on. Dr Jones wondered if the practice nurse and others working in the health centre who were likely to come into contact with Ben should be notified.

AIDS probably comes under the definition of venereal disease[13] and the Venereal Disease Regulations would therefore apply. AIDS was not a notifiable disease under the Public Health (Control of Disease) Act 1984. It was included in the list of diseases made notifiable under Regulation 3 of the Public Health (Infectious Diseases) Regulations 1988, to which only certain provisions apply. The AIDS Control Act 1987 regulates the reporting of cases and in 1988 this was extended to HIV positive persons. The powers set out in Figure 26.2 were given to local authorities and Justices of the Peace to prevent the spread of infection of AIDS (Public Health (Infectious Diseases) Regulations 1985). These were consolidated in the regulations made in 1988. In addition, in Chapter 8, the general exceptions to the principle of confidentiality were discussed and it will be recalled that one of the exceptions was where disclosure was justified on grounds of the public interest. This was one of the most difficult exceptions, since there is no clear judicial or statutory definition over what are the limits and extent of the term 'public interest' in this context. In Ben's situation (26.4), if Dr Jones also treats Ben's wife, it could be argued that he is not fulfilling his duty of care to her if he fails to inform her that she is at risk of contracting AIDS, and even if she is not his patient, he should inform her GP (unless, of course, he can persuade Ben to tell her). This breach in the duty of confidentiality owed to Ben is therefore justifiable on the grounds of the public interest. The same argument could be applied to informing any person in the health centre who is likely to be at risk from infection from Ben. Thus there may be justification in informing the practice nurse, but not the receptionist, since the latter is not likely to acquire the disease from Ben. The fact that the law is uncertain makes for considerable difficulties and ultimately it is up to individual practitioners to decide whether, in the specific circumstances of an individual case, there should be disclosure. The balance between an action for breach of confidentiality or an action for breach of a duty to care for the safety of a fellow employee is a very fine one.

In contrast to the case of *X* v. *Y*, the Court of Appeal recently allowed an order of disclosure of the person who had informed the press about an Ashworth patient. The case is further discussed in Chapter 8 page 150.

> *Case 26.2   X v. Y 1988*[14]
>
> The High Court held that public interest did not justify a newspaper publishing or using information disclosed by a health authority employee in breach of contract who admitted to a journalist that two identified doctors were being treated for AIDS at an identified hospital. The newspaper was fined £10,000 for contempt of a court order. However, the health authority was not able to obtain disclosure of the name of the informant employee, even though he/she was clearly in breach of the duty of employment, because this was not one of the occasions on which the press were obliged to disclose the source of their information under the Contempt of Court legislation.

AIDS Control Act 1987

This Act requires district health authorities to report to the regional health authorities (or Welsh Office) and for the regional authorities to report to the Secretary of State, giving information set out in the schedule and other such relevant information as the Secretary of State may direct. The schedule includes the following:

1. the number of persons known to be persons with AIDS and the timing of the diagnosis;
2. the particulars of facilities and services provided by each authority;
3. the numbers of persons employed by the authority in providing such facilities;
4. future provision over the next 12 months.

It also requires details of the action taken to educate members of the public in relation to AIDS and HIV, to provide training for testing for AIDS, and for the treatment, counselling and care of persons with AIDS or infected with HIV.

A subsequent statutory instrument has extended the information required to include HIV positive persons (Aids (Control) (Contents of Reports Order) 1988 SI 117). Nurses are likely to be involved in providing information to managers for the necessary returns to be made.

Notifiable Diseases

Diseases that are notifiable are shown in Figure 26.4.

Category A covers those notifiable diseases that come under the duties set by the Public Health (Control of Disease) Act 1984. These diseases must be reported to the local authority. Those diseases under category B are covered by Regulation 3 of the Public Health (Infectious Diseases) Regulations 1988[15] and the 1984 Act applies to a more limited extent.

> Category A. cholera, plague, relapsing fever, smallpox, typhus
>
> Category B. acquired immune deficiency syndrome (AIDS), acute encephalitis, acute poliomyelitis, meningitis, meningococcal septicaemia, anthrax, diphtheria, dysentery, paratyphoid fever, typhoid fever, viral hepatitis, leprosy, leptospirosis, measles, mumps, rubella, whooping cough, malaria, tetanus, yellow fever, ophthalmia neonatorum, scarlet fever, tuberculosis, rabies and viral haemorrhagic fever

Figure 26.4 Notifiable Diseases.

Procedure for notification

Under section 11 of the 1984 Act, a registered medical practitioner has a duty to notify the proper office of the local authority if he becomes aware, or suspects, that a patient whom he is attending within the district of a local authority is suffering from a notifiable disease or from food poisoning. The duty does not apply if he believes, and has reasonable grounds for believing, that some other registered medical practitioner has complied with the duty.

What information must be notified?

Figure 26.5 shows the information that must be notified.[16]

> 1. Name, age and sex of the patient and the address of the premises where the patient is;
>
> 2. the disease or, as the case may be, particulars of the poisoning from which the patient is, or is suspected to be, suffering and the date or approximate date of its onset; and
>
> 3. if the premises are a hospital, the day on which the patient was admitted, the address of the premises from which he came there and whether or not, in the opinion of the person giving the certificate, the disease or poisoning from which the patient is, or is suspected to be, suffering was contracted in hospital.
>
> (NB Section 11(4) imposes a criminal sanction on a person who fails to comply with an obligation imposed on him under the provisions set out above)

Figure 26.5 Information that must be notified.

Cross Infection Control

A recent report by the National Audit Office[17] has raised major concerns about the level of hospital acquired infection (HAI). The report suggested that HAI could be the main or a contributory cause in 20,000 or 4% of deaths a year in the UK and that there are at least about 100,000 cases of HAI with an estimated cost to the NHS of £1 billion. The NAO drew conclusions on the strategic management of HAI; surveillance, and the extent and cost of HAI; and the effectiveness of prevention, detection and control measures. Its recommendations include reviewing the following:

1. The value of using an Infection Control Manual should be considered.
2. The 1995 Guidance on Infection Control should be reviewed.
3. Cost effectiveness of screening patients and staff and isolation of patients together with standards and guidelines should be considered.
4. The policies on provision of education and training.
5. The arrangements for monitoring hospital hygiene and hospital practices.
6. Ensure advice on handwashing is implemented.
7. Review clinical audit arrangements to ensure infection control is covered.
8. Review isolation facilities.
9. Review guidance on management of HAI outbreaks.

Following this report, the government announced a multi-pronged initiative to tackle hospital-acquired infections. Amongst the initiatives planned are: an antimicrobial strategy, including a clampdown on inappropriate antibiotic use and better infection control measures.[18] In addition, there will be independent inspection of hospitals by the Audit Commission and Commission for Health Improvement. The government has stated that the Commission for Health Improvement and the Audit Commission would conduct ward inspections and be given the right to seek information on HAI and to publish it.[19] The report on the NHS commissioned by the government from Virgin Group reported that it found grubby wards, litter-strewn entrances and dirty casualty departments throughout the NHS. On 31 July 2000, the Health Minister, Lord Hunt, announced that NHS hospitals were to be given £150,000 each to clean up their wards and disinfect bathrooms as part of a £31 million campaign. The money could be used for extra cleaning staff, materials, equipment and new towels and linen. Patient Environment Action Teams would make unannounced inspections every six months and those hospitals who failed to meet standards would be 'named and shamed'. National Standards for cleanliness would form part of performance assessment guidelines for hospitals. In September 2000, 8 NHS hospitals were identified by the Department of Health as models for others. They were to assist in drawing up standards for a national action plan for cleanliness to be published in December 2000. The results of the National Audit Office were reinforced by a cross party report of the House of Commons which suggested that unhygienic hospitals were costing the NHS £1 billion a year by making patients worse. If hospital infection could be cut by just 10 per cent, the NHS could treat 50,000 more patients a year.[20]

In the light of this report the Secretary of State for Health admitted that Methicillin-resistant *Staphylococcus aureus* is endemic in England's hospitals.[21]

Another prong of the Government's campaign against cross infection is to make ward sisters responsible for ward cleaning and reintroduce the role of 'matron'. In a press release in January 2001,[22] the Department of Health announced a further £30 million to raise standards of cleanliness and that ward sisters will have the authority to agree with managers to withhold payments from contracted cleaning companies if standards are not reached. Managers will work closely with ward sisters to ensure that sufficient resources are being spent to provide high quality cleaning services. As a last resort, ward sisters will be able to request that alternative cleaning arrangements are made. In a press announcement on 4 April 2001,[23] the Secretary of State announced that each group of wards in the NHS were to have a matron, (male or female) in charge. Four of the ten key functions identified were the following.

1. Making sure the wards are clean.

2. Preventing and controlling hospital acquired infection.

3. Improving the wards for the patients.

4. Making sure nurses have more power.

Situation 26.5 *Cross infection nurse*

Joan was appointed as the hospital infection control nurse. Immediately on starting her new post, she undertook an audit of existing practices on infection control. She found that basic standards, including handwashing, were extremely lax, particularly amongst junior doctors. However, her attempts to raise standards appeared to be thwarted. What is the legal situation?

When Joan was appointed, she should have been notified of the organisational support which would be given to her post. This would include details as to whom she reported, who was her immediate line manager, and the strategy of the organisation in setting down and complying with the standards issued by the government. There should be in place a Committee for Infection Control. She would need to prepare a report on her findings, giving her conclusions in a clear unemotive report with constructive recommendations on the action that could be taken. If there is no follow up action from her report, then she may have justification in following the procedures set up under the Public Interest Disclosure Act 1998 (see Chapter 4) in order to ensure that action is taken.

Methicillin-resistant *Staphylococcus aureus* (MRSA)

One of the greatest challenges for all those working in health care is the control and eradication of methicillin-resistant Staphylococcus aureus (MRSA). At a conference in September 1999, George Duckworth of the Public Health Laboratory Service stated that the proportion of all S.aureus bloodstream infections caused by MRSA had increased from less than 3% before 1991 to 37%.[24] This poses a major problem for all hospital and community health professionals. It appears to be accepted that it is not a problem that will ever be completely eradicated. Robert Munro suggests that poor hygiene standards in hospitals are largely to blame for the increase in MRSA and other infections.[25] The Royal College of Nursing has provided guidance for nurses on MRSA.[26] As well as identifying the features of MRSA, it considers the revised guidelines for control, the standard infection control precautions, additional precautions for MRSA, treatment of patients with MRSA, and community and communication issues.

Tuberculosis (TB)

TB was once thought to have been eradicated. However, there is evidence that poor housing conditions, poverty and malnourishment are leading to an increase in TB levels, often particularly associated with the refugee population. The Department of Health has issued guidelines for the training of staff and the prevention of TB at a local level.[27]

The future

The situation in relation to AIDS and HIV is changing rapidly. It is essential, therefore, to refer to the current press and journals for the up-to-date position. For example, a sperm washing technique has recently enabled a father infected with HIV to become the father of a healthy baby.[28] There are likely to be more cases where the provisions of the Disability Discrimination Act 1995 are used to combat unfavourable treatment of those who are suffering from AIDS or are HIV positive. It therefore makes it less likely for the need of an AIDS Discrimination Act. Concerns over Hospital Acquired Infections are rising, and the nurse has a clear professional responsibility to ensure the highest standards of hygienic practice.

Questions and exercises

1 What is meant by 'reasonably practical precautions to safeguard the safety of other employees'? To what extent do you consider your present practice meets this requirement in relation to the dangers of infection from the AIDS virus? (See also Chapter 12.)

2 Obtain a copy of your authority's policy and guidelines on AIDS and discuss the extent to which these are fully implemented.

3 Do you consider that we require an AIDS Discrimination Act? What provisions do you think such an Act would contain?

4 What is meant by the duty of confidentiality in relation to AIDS? Are any exceptions to the duty justified? To what extent do you consider that the duty is carried out and what suggestions would you make for improvements for all staff to observe this duty? (See also Chapter 8.)

5 Many regard the hepatitis B virus as an even greater danger to health service staff than AIDS. What are the main differences in the law (if any) relating to AIDS and to hepatitis?

6 Look again at the laws relating to the notification of infectious diseases. To what extent do you consider they could impinge on your professional practice?

7 Study the figures of your organisation on the cross-infection of patients following admission. What improvements could be made in cross-infection control?

8 What role do you consider that the individual nurse should play in ensuring that hospitals and other health premises are clean and hygienic?

References

1. Department of Health, AIDS/HIV Infected Health Care Workers: Guidance on the Management of Infected Health Care Workers and Patient Notification DoH 1999
2. *Buck* v. *Letchworth Palace Ltd*. Reported in the Bulletin of the Institute of Medical Ethics, No. 28, July 1987, p. 5
3. Paul Wilkinson, Store boss banned over HIV wins cash, *The Times* 11 April 2000
4. UK Health Departments Guidance of Clinical Health Care Workers Recommendations of the Expert Advisory Group on AIDS January 1990 HMSO London
5. NHS Executive, Hepatitis B Infected Health Care Workers HSC 2000/020 DoH 2000
6. HSG (93)40 Protecting health care workers and patients from hepatitis B and its addendum EL(96)77
7. James Bone, Man injected his son with HIV to avoid payments, *The Times* 7 December 1998
8. News item, *The Times* 19 February 1999
9. HSC 1999/183
10. Postma MJ and others, Universal HIV screening of pregnant women in England: cost effectiveness analysis. BMJ Vol 318 pp. 1656–1660 19 June 1999
11. News item, HIV test reprimand, *The Times* 6 January 2000
12. *Re C* (HIV Test) [1999] 2 FLR 1004
13. See statement by judge in the case of *X* v. *Y and another* 1988 2 All ER 648
14. *X* v. *Y and another* 1988 2 All ER 648
15. Public Health (Infectious Diseases) Regulations 1988 (SI 1988 No 1546)
16. Public Health (Control of Disease) Act 1984 Section 11
17. National Audit Office, The Management and Control of Hospital Acquired Infection in Acute NHS Trusts in England 2000 Stationery Office London
18. http://www.doh.gov.uk/arbstrat.htm
19. DoH Press notice 12 June 2000; Jill Sherman, Infections caught in hospital to be exposed, *The Times* 13 June 2000
20. Helen Rumbelow, Hospitals that make us ill cost the NHS £1 billion a year, *The Times* 19 January 2001
21. David Charter, Milburn admits superbug is endemic, *The Times* 8 January 2001 p. 8
22. Department of Health, Ward sisters to have greater control over cleaning standards 17 January 2001
23. Department of Health press release, Health Secretary to bring back matron to the health service, 4 April 2001.
24. Esther Leach, Resistance Fighters, *Nursing Times* September 22 Volume 95 No 38 1999 p. 18
25. Robert Munro, Clean up your act, *Nursing Times* June 22 Vol 96 No 25 1999 pp. 26–7
26. Royal College of Nursing, Methicillin Resistant Staphylococcus Aureus 000 867 March 2000
27. Department of Health, The Interdepartmental Working Group on Tuberculosis: Prevention and Control of TB at Local Level DoH/PHLS 1996
28. Helen Rumbelow, Doctors protect baby from father's HIV, *The Times* 18 October 1999

27 Handling complaints

It is highly likely that at some time in her career a nurse will be involved in a complaint, either in relation to her own conduct, or in handling a complaint about someone else's. There is no doubt that there is an increase in the number of complaints made about the NHS. To some, this is a very bad sign and indicative of a growing discontent with the health services.

However, others see this as a positive and valuable sign: an opportunity to improve the service and at the same time a sign that patients are more prepared to raise their voices over their concerns. Certainly, the current emphasis on customer and consumer relations is encouraging patients, through consumer satisfaction surveys, to make their views known so that the service can be improved. Feedback from the patient is essential if the quality of care is to be improved. Unfortunately, as the reports of the Health Service Commissioner show only too frequently, whether or not a complaint is initially justified, the way in which the complaint is handled can itself be a cause for complaint. The Patients' Charter and local charters may also encourage patients to criticise the services they have received in comparison with the standards they were led to expect. This section will review the procedures for handling complaints and discuss the legal powers of those statutory bodies that can represent or investigate the grievances of the patient. Figure 27.1 sets out the topics covered in this chapter.

Methods of complaining
Handling complaints
Hospital Complaints Procedure Act 1985
New Complaints Procedure
Other Quality Assurance methods
Complaint or Claim?
Health Service Commissioner
Mental Health Act Commission
Community Health Council
Secretary of State Inquiries

Figure 27.1 Issues covered in Chapter 27.

Methods of complaining

Figure 27.2 shows the variety of ways of making a complaint about the NHS. Private hospitals have their own system for handling complaints and these tend to be on an individual hospital basis.

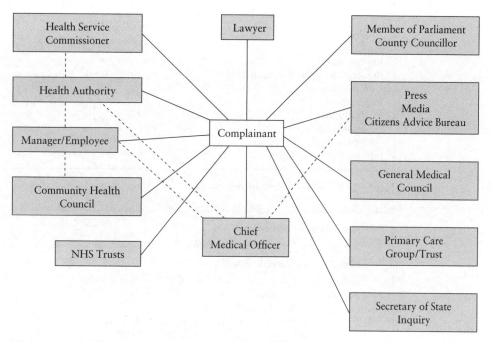

Figure 27.2 Various ways of making a complaint.

Many different motives exist behind a complaint. Some of the reasons why patients complain are shown in Figure 27.3, and the outcomes that they are seeking are shown in Figure 27.4. However, it should be appreciated that, for many people, to make a formal complaint requires considerable courage and there are many reasons why justifiable grievances are not brought to the attention of management (see Figure 27.5). It is very difficult for patients who are suffering from chronic conditions where they are dependent upon the continued support of a particular department to make a formal complaint.

A typical letter of complaint will be considered to illustrate how it should be handled and the role of the nurse.

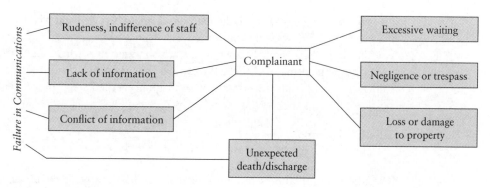

Figure 27.3 Why do people complain?

Apology.
Explanation.
Improvement.
Prevention of similar occurrences.
Compensation.
Punishment
    discipline;
    dismissal;
    striking off.
Criminal proceedings.

Figure 27.4 What do complainants seek?

1. No reason to complain.
2. No perceived reason to complain.
3. There is a perceived reason
   but
   A. Positive reasons
       (i)   sympathy with staff;
       (ii)   immediate apology/explanation offered;
       (iii) promise of rectification/improvement;
       (iv) immediate interview with consultant/senior manager.
   B. Negative reasons
       (i)   apathy/indifference;
       (ii)   ignorance of how to complain;
       (iii) acceptance that errors/inefficiency are inevitable;
       (iv) useless to complain – no point;
       (v)   fear of retribution.

Figure 27.5 Why do people not complain?

Handling a complaint

Situation 27.1   Dear Sir

Dear Sir

I was furious at the way my daughter was treated when we went to the diabetic clinic the other day. We waited two hours to be seen and then we saw a foreign doctor who could barely speak English and who changed her drugs. Since then she has had a diabetic coma and the GP has said that the dose should never have been changed. I think that that doctor should be prevented from practising again.

Yours sincerely

Valerie Machin

The above complaint is not untypical since, like many, it covers several different complaints, some of which relate to clinical matters and others to non-clinical matters, and often a lack of communication underlies the problem. This complaint is not directly concerned with nursing matters, but the nurses in the clinic may well be asked to provide a statement as to what took place in the clinic and whether the parents complained at the time and what was done.

The above complaint raises the following issues:

waiting time in an out-patients' department clinic;

communication between doctor and patient;

the clinical practice of the doctor; and

the patient's current clinical condition.

The normal procedure would be for a letter of this kind to be referred to the hospital complaints manager acting on behalf of the Chief Executive. Many complainants are not always aware of the procedure and the letter could be sent to anyone. Staff should be aware of a procedure that ensures the letter is received by the complaints manager, who can follow it up to ensure that the correct procedure is followed, and an acknowledgement, and later a report, are sent to the complainant by the Chief Executive.

The officer in charge of complaints would be responsible for ensuring that every point raised by the complainant is investigated and reported upon satisfactorily. The Chief Executive Officer would be expected to sign letters to a complainant personally (see below).

1. The first task would be to refer the last two points listed above urgently to the consultant in charge of the patient to assess: it may be necessary for the consultant to discuss her present condition urgently with the GP to ensure that she is now on the appropriate medication.

2. Once her present clinical condition is satisfactory, then the complaints relating to clinical matters would be investigated according to the appropriate procedure which is considered below.

3. An investigation into the waiting times would be initiated by asking the director of nursing services for a report and also asking for a report from the medical records officer or any administrative officer in charge of that department. It is an advantage if there is already a system for recording the times of the patients' arrival and departure and a system for pinpointing unreasonable delays. Some clinics do not operate an appointments system and block booking can often create unacceptable waiting times. Nursing staff will be required to provide information as to the usual way in which the diabetic clinic functioned, whether this could be improved and whether there were any extenuating circumstances on that occasion.

4. The consultant and director of nursing services would also be asked to report on the level of communication of the doctor in question, whether his English was at an acceptable level. It may be that that aspect of the complaint could be due to some form of racial prejudice, but it should never be assumed that the complaint is without foundation. A full inquiry must always be held.

The usual practice would be for the director of nursing services or his assistant to arrange for any individual nurse who was present at the time of the clinic visit to make a statement on what occurred. It is essential that the nurse receives guidance in preparing such a report and also checks with all the available documentation on the ward or department. Guidance is given in Chapter 9 on preparing statements. The nurse should never submit the statement unless she is 100 per cent satisfied with the contents and that she has, where possible, checked its accuracy. The report that is sent to the complainant will be based on what the nurse has said and if there are any inaccuracies in this which are not spotted by other hospital personnel, then the nurse could well be questioned by the independent review panel and, possibly even, the Health Service Commissioner, and criticism could be made of her (see below).

When the complaints manager has received all the relevant reports, including at this stage the report by the consultant on the clinical complaints, a response will be sent to the complainant. This might be just a letter or it might be an invitation to attend a meeting; or both. It is vital that every single point raised by the complainant is answered fully and honestly. This might at this stage mean apologising for some shortcoming that has been revealed in the service.

In serious cases, the NHS Trust might decide to set up an authority inquiry into the complaint. In future such inquiries will come under the recommendations set out in *Building a Safer NHS for Patients* (DoH 2001).

Hospital Complaints Procedure Act 1985 and Wilson Review

Under the Hospital Complaints Act 1985 each health authority must establish a complaints procedure. Guidance required authorities to establish a procedure in relation to community health services as well. Following a review chaired by Professor Alan Wilson into the handling of hospital complaints, a consultation document was published.[1] The Department of Health accepted the principal recommendations of the Wilson Report and published guidance and directions for its implementation by NHS Trusts and health service authorities.[2] Guidance was issued in 1999 for convenors.[3]

The Wilson Report found the system for dealing with complaints relating to health services to be confusing, bureaucratic, slow and inefficient. The report reviewed the current situation and set objectives for any effective complaints system. The principles it saw for any effective complaints system are set out in Figure 27.6

The report recommended that these principles should be incorporated into an NHS complaints system.

---

1. Responsiveness
2. Quality enhancement
3. Cost effectiveness
4. Accessibility
5. Impartiality
6. Simplicity
7. Speed
8. Confidentiality
9. Accountability

Figure 27.6 Key elements in a complaints procedure.

The areas covered by its recommendations are shown in Box 27.1

Box 27.1

Recommendations of the Wilson Report on the review of complaints procedures.

1.   There should be a common system for all NHS complaints.
2.   The complaints procedure should not be concerned with disciplining staff.
3.   Staff should be empowered to deal with complaints informally.
4.   There should be training of staff.
5.   Support should be provided for complainants and respondents.
6.   The degree of investigation should relate to the complainant's required degree of response.
7.   Conciliation should be made more widely available.
8.   Time limits should be set.
9.   Deadlines should be set for
     (a) the acknowledging of complaints (2 working days)
     (b) the response to the complaint (three weeks)
     (c) further action and response (two weeks).
10. Confidentiality should be preserved and complaints filed separately.
11. There should be a system for recording and monitoring.
12. Impartial lay people should take part in the system.
13. Key aspects of the system should be set by the Department of Health, but detailed implementation and operation should be left to individual organisations.
14. Threefold procedures:
     stage 1 immediate first line response;
     stage 2 investigation/conciliation;
     stage 3 action by chief executive officer for trusts.
     A panel should be set up to consider those complaints which cannot be resolved in the earlier stages.
15. There should be training in communication skills.
16. Oral and written complaints should be treated with the same sensitive treatment.
17. Community service staff should have particular training in responding to complaints.
18. Purchasers should specify complaints requirements in their contracts with non-NHS providers.
19. Complaints about policy decisions should be referred to the Health Service Commissioner if they cannot be resolved locally by the purchasers.
20. Where more than one organisation is involved it should be the organisation that receives the complaint that makes sure that a full response is sent.
21. Community care: there should be close liaison with local authorities and the government should consider further integration of NHS and local authority complaints procedures.
22. Stage 2 procedures: there should be a screening officer.
23. The jurisdiction of the HSC should be extended to GPs and the operation of the FHSA service committees.
24. Recommendations on implementation.

The new complaints procedure

This came into effect on 1 April 1996 and implements the majority of recommendations contained in the Wilson Report. Three stages are recognised.

A.   First stage: Local resolution

The complaint should be dealt with speedily and often an oral response will suffice. Where investigation or conciliation is required an initial response should be made within 2 working days and a final response within 4 weeks. Chief executives should personally approve and sign the response to all formal complaints. In family health services, practices will be expected and encouraged to set up their own practice based complaints procedure and use independent assistance where appropriate.

B.   Second stage: Independent review

i.   Consideration of an application for independent review

If the complainant remains dissatisfied after the first stage, he/she can apply for further consideration by an independent panel. This request will be considered by a non-executive director of the trust or health authority to whom the complaint was made. This non-executive director will be known as the convenor. He/she will have to decide whether the complaint should be referred to an independent review panel. The circumstances in which it is not recommended that there should be an independent review are shown in Box 27.2.

Box 27.2

Situations where there will be no independent review.

1. where legal proceedings have commenced or there is an explicit indication by the complainant of the intention to make a legal claim against a trust or health service authority or one of their employees or against a family health services practitioner; or

2. it is considered the trust/health authority has already taken all practicable action and therefore establishing a panel would add no further value to the process: consideration of the cost of instituting an Independent Review is not an appropriate reason for refusing to proceed; or

3. further action as part of Local Resolution is still believed to be appropriate and practicable – for example conciliation – so that referral back to the chief executive is considered preferable to instituting the Independent Review process.

Where the convenor refuses to refer the complaint for Independent Review, the complainant must be informed of his right to complain to the Ombudsman.

ii.   Independent Review Panel

All panels have an independent lay chairman. The non-executive director (known as the convenor) is also a member.

For non-clinical complaints, the panel comprises: a non-executive director of the relevant health authority, or where appropriate, a GP fundholder.

For family practitioner complaints, the panel is comprised of the convening health authority non-executive director and an independent lay person.

For clinical complaints, the panel is advised by 2 independent clinical assessors following advice from the relevant professional bodies.

The panel is established as a committee of the trust/health authority and the assessors are appointed by the trust/health authority to advise the panel.

C. Third stage: Health Service Commissioner (HSC) (Ombudsman)

The final option for unresolved complaints will be recourse to the ombudsman whose jurisdiction was extended in 1996 to cover complaints relating to the exercise of clinical judgement and those about family practitioners. Disciplinary matters will still not be included in his jurisdiction (see below). If a complainant is not satisfied with the response of the authority to a complaint or the refusal to hold an independent review, he can apply to the ombudsman for further investigation: the Health Service Commissioner in respect of complaints about the NHS and the Local Authority Commissioner in respect of complaints about local authority services. The HSC has a duty to prepare a report which is submitted to Parliament, under Section 14(4) of the Health Service Commissioners Act 1993. The Select Committee of the House of Commons has the power to investigate further any complaint reported by the HSC, if necessary summoning witnesses to London for questioning. The HSC is completely independent of the NHS and the government and has the jurisdiction to investigate complaints against any part of the NHS about:

1. a failure in service; or

2. a failure to purchase or provide a service one is entitled to receive; or

3. maladministration (administrative affairs).

Figure 27.7 shows the Jurisdiction of the Health Service Commissioner.

The following are excluded from his investigation.

(a) actions where there is already an existing remedy in law (but there is a discretion to hear such matters if the Commissioner is satisfied that it is not reasonable to expect the complainant to resort to this);

(b) personnel matters or contractual matters to do with the NHS;

(c) out of time complaints – there is a time limit of 12 months, though, again, there is discretion to extend this;

(d) complaints which have not yet been referred to the organisation for dealing through the complaints procedure.

Figure 27.7   Jurisdiction of the Health Service Commissioner.

Time limits

A time limit for making a complaint is six months from the event giving rise to the complaint; or six months from the complainant becoming aware of the cause for complaint up to a maximum of one year after the cause for complaint arose. There is a discretion to extend this time limit where it would be unreasonable in the circumstances of a particular case for the complaint to have been made earlier and where it is still possible to investigate the facts of the case.

Complaints within the family health services

As can be seen, they were brought within the common complaints system. Disciplinary procedures are kept separate from the complaints system.

A court challenge

The previous hospital complaints procedure was subject to judicial review in a case.[4] Complaints were made by eight families that a doctor employed by the first defendants and seconded to the second defendants diagnosed sexual abuse when it should not have been or delayed in telling the parents of the diagnosis. A legal aid certificate was obtained by one of the complainants. The doctor withdrew her co-operation in view of the possibility of legal proceedings. The defendants subsequently considered that an inquiry was inappropriate. The complainants applied for judicial review contending inter alia that there was a duty to review their complaints. The court held that the complaints procedure was not appropriate where litigation was likely because:

1. the purpose of the inquiry was either to obtain a second opinion and a change of diagnosis or to enable the health authority to change its procedures in the light of matters brought to its attention during the investigation;

2. the procedure depends on the co-operation of the doctor concerned which obviously would not be forthcoming if legal proceedings were likely.

Other quality assurance methods

Individuals who have complaints against the services provided in the NHS do not have any contractual right to bring an action before the court for breach of contract. If harm has been suffered as a result of a failure or omission, they may have a successful claim in the law of negligence (see Chapter 3) or, if a service has not been provided, they may be able to bring a case of breach of statutory duty for failure to provide that service (see Chapter 5). Otherwise they must rely upon the complaints procedure. They could apply for judicial review to the High Court if the principles of natural justice have not been followed, but they would be expected to exhaust appeals procedures within the NHS complaints system first. There are, however, many other mechanisms to ensure the maintenance of high standards of health care that cannot be directly utilised by the patient. The White Paper on the NHS put forward a strategy for improving quality assurance and its mechanisms which was implemented in the Health Act 1999. These mechanisms include a National Institute of Clinical Effectiveness (NICE), a Commission for Health Improvement (CHI) and a framework for national standards. The establishment of Clinical Governance whereby chief executives of trusts are held accountable for the clinical performance of their organisations provides more evidence to the patient about the standards of care locally. These innovations are discussed in Chapter 5. In addition, following the publication of the NHS Plan, a task force has been set up to ensure its implementation. It was required in August 2000 to visit those hospitals that had failed to decrease numbers on the waiting lists and set up strategies to improve the situation within 6 months.

Complaint or claim?

Difficulties arise where litigation is feared. This sometimes leads to an over-cautious defensive approach such that the complainant is forced into the hands of solicitors in order to obtain satisfaction. This is a difficult area, since initially it is not always known whether the complainant is seeking compensation. In theory, the complainant's objective should not affect the nature and comprehensiveness of the investigation. In practice, there is a natural reluctance to admit fault where a legal remedy exists. However, many complaints do not become legal claims, either because that is not the intention of the complainant, or because for that particular complaint there is no remedy in law. For example, in Situation 27.1 above, there could be a potential negligence case over the change in medication if that resulted in a diabetic coma; but there is no legal remedy for the waiting time and possibly not for the difficulties in communication between doctor and patient, though this might be significant evidence in a negligence action.

The House of Commons Select Committee

A final possibility in the complaints process, (and this can be very effective,) is for an inquiry to be set up by the Select Committee of the House of Commons, to whom the Health Service Commissioner reports. This committee has the power to investigate a matter further by summoning witnesses to appear before it and if in the report of the HSC it is clear that an authority has ignored its recommendations, the Committee can ask the authority to explain itself – an experience that few witnesses who have appeared before it will ever forget. There is no secrecy. All these cases are fully reported and the proceedings of the Select Committee are themselves published and may also be televised.

There is no doubt that the fact that eventually an authority might have to explain how it dealt with any complaint is an important factor in ensuring that the complaint is properly, speedily and effectively dealt with.

The Mental Health Act Commission

Under the 1983 Mental Health Act, there is a statutory duty placed on the Mental Health Act Commission to investigate complaints by detained patients. The jurisdiction could be extended to cover informal patients. The Mental Health Act Commission can also investigate complaints of a clinical nature and, in fact, a high proportion of the complaints that it has investigated are concerned with clinical matters such as medication, medical, and nursing care. The MHAC has no power to subpoena witnesses nor to take evidence on oath and is itself one of the bodies whose administrative function can be investigated by the HSC.[5] From the biennial reports of the MHAC, it is clear that the number and variety of the complaints that they are investigating are considerable. The Commission pointed out that it has complete discretion over how the complaints are to be investigated – methods range from a word to a ward sister to a full-scale investigation by Commissioners. It is also apparent that, while their terms of reference are so far only to cover the detained patient, many of their recommendations are wider and affect the care of the informal patient. For example, their procedure on the consent to treatment of the mentally disordered outside the provisions of Part IV of the 1983 Act has major implications for the care of the informal patient. In addition, the Code of Practice on the Mental Health Act provides advice about procedures and precautions to take if informal patients are detained in locked wards.

The Community Health Council (CHC)

Established in 1974, the CHC has the task of representing the interests of the patients. It has statutory powers of visiting health service premises and is entitled to information relevant to its functions. Increasingly, the CHC, and its Secretary in particular, has become 'the patient's friend' in relation to the handling of complaints. The new procedure on handling hospital complaints recommends that the hospital information booklet for patients should include the details of the local CHC so that any complainant can be advised as to the best method for dealing with the complaint. The CHC could, for example, advise a prospective complainant as to whether it would be better to refer the case to solicitors. The CHC has powers under the Community Health Councils (Access to Information) Act 1988 to obtain access to meetings and certain documents and information. The NHS Plan has recommended that the powers of the CHC should be transferred to local authorities, however, the government has since indicated its intention to retain CHCs.

Secretary of State inquiries

Statutory powers are given in the NHS legislation for the Secretary of State to set up an inquiry into any case 'where he deems it advisable to do so in connection with any matter arising under this Act'.[6] The powers of such an inquiry are extensive and include the power to summon witnesses and order the production of documents and the taking of evidence on oath. Any person who refuses to give evidence or attend or destroys documents is guilty of a criminal offence.

A public inquiry of this nature is kept for the most serious of complaints with very serious implications.

The Secretary of State also has statutory powers known as default powers: where he is satisfied after such inquiry as he thinks fit that a health authority has failed to carry out its statutory functions or is in breach of the regulations, then he can make an order declaring it to be in default. The effect of this is that the members of the authority in question must vacate their office and the Secretary of State can appoint new persons to undertake the functions. In addition, he has emergency powers to give appropriate directions to ensure that the functions are properly performed. This control enables the Secretary of State to force the health authorities to comply with policies (e.g. keeping within their budgets) set by the government or the DH which they might otherwise be unwilling to do. Just as the DH can give directions to the regional health authority, so can the latter give directions to the district health authority. The DH also has the power to give directions to NHS Trusts. The setting up of Inquiries and the role of CHI are considered in the D.H. *Building a Safer NHS for Patients* (DoH 2001).[7]

The future

The government has commissioned an investigation into the effectiveness of the new complaints procedure and is likely to report recommendations for change. The final report of the investigation undertaken by Public Attitude Surveys and the York Health Economics Consortium at the University of York is due to be submitted in 2001.

It is in the interests of all health professionals to ensure that any complaints by parents and children relating to the provision of health services are resolved as speedily as possible informally without requiring the complainant to make use of the formal procedure. Nurses should have the confidence to realise that complaints can be a useful way of monitoring and improving the services to patients, that it takes courage to make a complaint, especially where the patient suffers from a chronic condition and that improvements can be made if clients are prepared to discuss with the health professionals ways in which the services could be enhanced. The NHS[8] Plan envisages several new initiatives to support patients including a patient advocacy service and a new Citizen's Council to advise NICE.

Questions and exercises

1 Obtain a copy of the complaints procedure of your NHS Trust or employer and familiarise yourself with it.

2 What do you consider to be the most appropriate system for recording informal complaints?

3 Ask the designated complaints officer if you can see the complaints book which is kept centrally and if you can see how an individual complaint has been followed up. (Remember the duty of confidentiality.)

4 Complaints are one means of obtaining feedback from patients about their stay. Consider other means of a more positive nature to obtain information relating to patient satisfaction and consider the possibility of implementing them.

5 You are a staff nurse on a medical ward. A patient complains to you that he thinks that he is suffering from the side-effects of medication. How would you deal with this complaint?

6 In what ways do the power and jurisdiction of the Health Service Commissioner differ from those of the Mental Health Act Commission in the handling of complaints?

7 Consider the proposals in Chapter 10 of the NHS Plan and discuss how these would impact on the present complaints system.

References

[1] Being Heard, The Report of a review committee chaired by Professor Wilson on NHS complaints procedures, Department of Health 1994

[2] NHSE Guidance on the Implementation of the NHS Complaints Procedure London DoH March 1996; EL(96)19 Directions to NHS Trusts, health authorities and special health authorities for special hospitals on hospital complaints procedures; Directions to Health Authorities on dealing with Complaints about Family Health Services Practitioners; Miscellaneous Directions to Health Authorities for dealing with complaints March 1996 DoH

[3] NHS Executive, Good Practice for Convenors October 1999 DoH

[4] R. v. *Canterbury and Thanet District Health Authority and South East Thames Regional Health Authority ex parte F and W* QBD [1994] 5 Med L.R. 132

[5] See Health Service Commissioners Annual Report 1992/93

[6] NHS Act 1977 Section 84

[7] DoH Building a Safer NHS for Patients (DoH 2001)

[8] DoH NHS Plan Cm 4818, 1 July 2000 (Chapter 10)

28 Legal aspects of medicines

The main areas to be covered in this chapter are set out in Figure 28.1. Legislation has been passed to give nurses the power to prescribe in the community, but further legislation to implement the recommendations of the final Crown Report is contained in Section 63 of the Health and Social Care Act 2001 which is discussed below.

General Principles
Controlled Drugs
Drugs and the ODP
Problems in the administration of medicine
   (a)   conflict with the prescriber;
   (b)   sources of information;
   (c)   illegible writing;
PRN
Instructions by word of mouth
Supervision and administration
Self-administration
Nurse Prescribing
Community nurse prescribing
Group Protocols
Final Crown Report
Independent and Dependent Prescribers
Drug Addicts
Product liability and drugs

Figure 28.1   Issues covered in Chapter 28.

The main legislation controlling the supply, storage, and administration of medicines is the Medicines Act 1968 and the Misuse of Drugs Act 1971 and many subsequent statutory instruments. Of particular importance are the Misuse of Drugs Regulations 1985. The Medicines Act 1968 set up a comprehensive system of medicines controls, as can be seen in Figure 28.4 The main provisions of the Misuse of Drugs Act 1971 are seen in Figure 28.3 and the 1985 Regulations in Figure 28.6. The regulations relating to prescribing prescription only medicines were consolidated in the Prescription Only Medicines (Human Use) Order 1997.[1]

Figure 28.2 illustrates the main areas of control of drugs that are the concern of the nurse. The UKCC has published guidelines for the administration of medicines.[2] While this has no legal force in itself, it establishes principles for safe practice in the management and administration of medicines by registered nurses, midwives and health visitors. The 2000 booklet replaces the standards for administration of medicines that was published in 1992. The new guidelines also cover prescribing by nurses and the use of patient group directions (see below). Local policies may be drawn up that differ from the main guidelines and the advisory paper allows for this, but it sets out principles that should be taken into account in the setting up of these local policies. Any local policy must of course comply with the statutory framework.

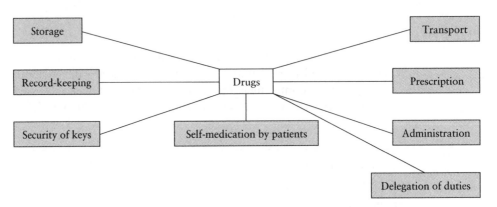

Figure 28.2 Areas that concern the nurse.

General principles

Under the Medicines Act, drugs are divided into categories for the purposes of supply to the public. The Part III regulations cover the following:

1. Pharmacy-only products, i.e. these can be sold or supplied retail only by someone conducting a retail pharmacy business when the product must be sold from a registered pharmacy by, or under the supervision of, a pharmacist.

2. General sales list, i.e. medicinal products that may be sold other than from a retail pharmacy so long as provisions relating to Section 53 of the Medicines Act are complied with, i.e. the place of sale must be the premises where the business is carried out; they must be capable of excluding the public; the medicines must have been made up elsewhere and the contents must not have been opened since make-up.

3. Prescription-only list, i.e. these medicines are available only on a practitioner's prescription. Schedule 1 of the subsequent regulations lists the prescription-only products and Part II of the schedule lists the prescription-only products that are covered by the Misuse of Drugs Act (see Figure 28.3). Hospitals are exempt from these prescription-only provisions (see Figure 28.4), as are midwives (see below).

The Misuse of Drugs Act and the 1985 Regulations make provision for the classification of controlled drugs and their possession, supply and manufacture. This is considered below.

> 1. Lists and classifies controlled drugs.
> 2. Creates criminal offences in relation to the manufacture, supply and possession of controlled drugs.
> 3. Gives Secretary of State power to make regulations, and directions to prevent misuse of controlled drugs.
> 4. Creates advisory council on misuse of drugs.
> 5. Gives powers of search, arrest and forfeiture.

Figure 28.3 Misuse of Drugs Act 1971.

> Sets up a comprehensive system of medicine controls covering:
> 1. Administrative system.
> 2. Licensing system.
> 3. Sale and supply of medicines to the public
>   (a) pharmacy only products;
>   (b) general sales list;
>   (c) prescription only list.
> 4. Retail pharmacies.
> 5. Packing and labelling of medicinal products.
> 6. British pharmacopoeia.
>
> N.B. Exception to Part III Regulations on sale and supply of medicines to the public. Midwives – see Chapter 13.
>   Hospitals: 'Prescription medicines may be sold or supplied by a hospital, provided they are in accordance with the written instructions of a doctor, although these instructions need not be contained in a formal prescription.'

Figure 28.4 Medicines Acts 1968 and 1971.

General principles in relation to the administration of drugs

Figure 28.5 shows a checklist that a nurse should go through before a drug is administered to a patient. There is no team liability for negligence, as was seen in the Wilsher case (page 53). Each professional must ensure that she fulfils her duties according to the approved standard of practice expected of her. If something goes wrong, she is accountable in the criminal courts, the civil courts, before her employer and before the Professional Conduct Committee of the UKCC for her activities and would have to show that she followed the approved accepted practice. Prescription only medicines can be administered without the direction of a doctor where the situation is an emergency for the purpose of saving a life. For example, a parent or teacher who needed to administer adrenalin when a child has suffered an anaphylactic shock are covered for such actions.

A. *The correct patient. Consent?*
   capacity to consent:
      child
      mentally ill or handicapped
   pre-existing disability or contra-indications.
   warnings about side-effects; drowsiness, etc.

B. *Correct drug*
   side-effects
   timing
   special precautions
   any contra-indications
   expiry date

C. *Correct dose*
   type of patient
   physique of patient
   allergy frequency

D. *Correct site and method of administration*
   injection: skin, muscular, vein, artery, site on body.

E. *Correct procedure*
   level of competence of nurse
   skill, training
   appropriate delegation
   safe equipment, sound sterile procedure
   correct gauge of needle, form of drug and transport

F. *Correct record-keeping of dose, time, drug and method.*

Figure 28.5   Checklist for the administration of drugs.

Controlled drugs

The classification of controlled drugs by the Misuse of Drugs Regulations 1985 is shown in Figure 28.6. Examples only are given here of the different schedules. The full list can be found in the *British National Formulary*. An example of the exemptions in relation to a nurse is shown in Figure 28.2. The nurse should be familiar with the procedure for access to the controlled drugs stock and the record-keeping and also the way in which any destruction of the drugs is recorded. This chapter is not concerned with drug abuse and addiction, but nurses should be aware of the case where two charity workers were jailed for knowingly permitting or suffering the supply of a Class A drug on the premises. Their concerns about breach of confidentiality are considered in Chapter 8.[3] Nurses who remove illegal drugs from patients on admission and who ensure that these drugs are immediately handed into the pharmacy department should be protected from charges of illegal possession of drugs.

Drugs and the operating department practitioner (ODP)

The profession of operating department practitioner, separate from the nursing profession, is still being developed. In 2001, it is planned that they should become

Drugs are divided into five schedules, each specifying the requirements governing the import, export, production, supply, possession, prescribing and record-keeping.

Schedule 1 e.g. cannabis, lysergide. Possession and supply prohibited except in accordance with Home Office authority.

Schedule 2 e.g. diamorphine, morphine, pethidine, glutethimide, amphetamine – subject to full controlled drug requirements relating to prescriptions, safe custody, the need to keep registers.

Schedule 3 e.g. barbiturates, diethylpropion, mazindol – subject to special prescription requirements but not safe custody requirements (except for diethylpropion) nor to the need to keep Registers.

Schedule 4 includes 33 benzodiazepines which are subject to minimal control. In particular, controlled drug prescription requirements do NOT apply and they are NOT subject to safe custody.

Schedule 5 preparations which because of their strength are exempt from most controlled drug requirements, other than retention of invoices for two years.

Makes provision for:

1. Certain exemptions from the Misuse of Drugs Act 1971 in relation to the production, importation, exportation, possession and supply of controlled drugs.

2. Prescriptions, records and furnishing of information concerning controlled drugs and for the supervision of the destruction of such drugs.

Examples of the Regulations

1. *Persons entitled* to have controlled drugs in their *possession* include under Paragraph 6(7)(f): a person engaged in conveying the drug to a person who may lawfully have that drug in his possession.

2. *Administration of drugs* in Schedules 2, 3 and 4, Paragraph 7(3): any person other than a doctor or dentist may administer to a patient, in accordance with the direction of a doctor or dentist, any drug specified in Schedule 2, 3 and 4.

Production and supply of drugs

Paragraph 8(2)(e)
In the case of Schedule 2 and 5 drugs supplied to her by a person responsible for the dispensing and supply of medicines at the hospital or nursing home, the sister or acting sister for the time being in charge of a ward, theatre or other department in such a hospital or nursing home as aforesaid . . . may, when acting in her capacity as such, supply, or offer to supply any drug specified in Schedule 2 or 5 to any person who may lawfully have that drug in his possession, provided that nothing in the paragraph authorises:

(a) . . .

(b) a sister or acting sister for the time being in charge of a ward, theatre, or other department to supply any drug otherwise than for the administration to a patient in that ward, theatre or department in accordance with the directions of a doctor or dentist.

Figure 28.6 Misuse of Drugs Regulations 1985 SI 1985/2066.

a state registered profession. There is a great diversity across the country over the role of the operating department practitioner *vis-à-vis* the nurse and the anaesthetist. One concern is whether the operating department practitioner is allowed by current law to hold the keys to the Controlled Drugs cupboard. Advice issued by the NHS Executive[4] advises employers to ensure that the employment of ODPs is limited to those whose names appear on the voluntary register held by the Association of ODPs.

Any practitioner not so registered should be appropriately supervised, and grandfathering arrangements should be set up to prepare for the assimilation of those into the profession. The guidance emphasises that ODPs are not one of the classes of health professionals authorised under the Misuse of Drugs Regulations 1985 to order, supply and possess controlled drugs. The responsibility rests with the sister in charge of the ward or department. An annex to the circular states that whilst the ODP is not permitted under the 1985 Regulations to order, supply, possess, prescribe or administer controlled drugs, he/she may lawfully convey a controlled drug. In addition, the sister could delegate to an ODP control of access. This access should be strictly controlled in practice and set out in locally agreed written guidelines. An ODP may also administer a controlled drug to a patient in accordance with the directions of a doctor. Amendments to the legislation may take place following the state registration of operating department practitioners and the implementation of the final Crown Report which is discussed below.

Problems in the administration of medication

Conflict with the prescriber

Situation 28.1   *Challenging the doctor*

Staff Nurse Johnson was a children's nurse with some two years' experience. One evening, a child was admitted with suspected meningitis. The house officer on call wrote the child up for antibiotics after having given an injection. Staff Nurse Johnson was surprised at the dosage and queried this with the house officer who was furious to find his treatment questioned by a nurse and confirmed that the nurse should administer that drug at the prescribed dose and at the intervals set out. Since Staff Nurse Johnson had not had many years' experience in paediatrics, she was uncertain what to do since she knew that the child was seriously ill and that a higher dose than usual might be justified in the circumstances. She also knew that it was imperative that there were no delays in administering the drug. She was in charge of the ward.

The nurse is personally accountable for her actions in administering any drug. Only in the most serious emergency where speed is of the essence could she rely on the fact that a doctor ordered her to give the drug and she did not have the opportunity to question the dosage because of the seriousness of the situation. In any case, where the nurse is not satisfied with some aspect of the drug she is instructed to administer, she must ensure the prescription is checked. She would have to do this despite considerable pressure brought by a junior doctor. The difficulties for Staff Nurse Johnson are that, at night, she may have to get someone in to check. She would inform her immediate nurse manager of her concern and would ask the registrar, and if necessary the consultant, to confirm that the medication, dosage, frequency and route are correct. If possible, she could obtain the advice of the pharmacist. In extreme circumstances, she is entitled to tell the doctor that she is refusing to administer the drug and the doctor then has the option of administering it himself or of rethinking the position. The nurse, of course, risks disciplinary action for her refusal, but if she has good grounds for her belief that the drug or dosage is inappropriate, she should have the support of her management.

Sources of information

The nurse should also be familiar with the *British National Formulary*. There should be an up-to-date copy on the ward and she should have easy access to it. There is some useful information at the beginning, giving guidance on prescribing.

Illegible writing

Nurses often complain that they are unable to read the doctors' writing on the drug charts. If they have any doubt about the drug prescribed, they should not administer it unless they have checked it with the doctor who wrote it, his superior or, in certain circumstances, the pharmacist. If the nurse fails to double-check illegible writing, she could herself become liable as the following case illustrates.

Case 28.1   Illegible writing

One of three items on a prescription was for 21 Amoxil tablets. The pharmacist misread this as Daonil. The patient suffered hypoglycaemia and sustained permanent brain damage. The pharmacist said that he had read the 'A' for a 'D' and the 'x' for an 'n'. There were other indications from which the pharmacist should have realised that his interpretation was for the wrong drug, i.e. the other drugs that were prescribed, the dosage and the fact that the patient paid for his prescription. (Daonil is a drug used by diabetic patients who do not have to pay prescription charges.) Both doctor and pharmacist were held liable for the harm that befell the patient. The doctor was held 25 per cent liable. Damages totalled £137,547.[5]

In a case where a woman was prescribed a top up epidural following a hysterectomy in a private hospital, the junior doctor mistook a dose of 3ml of diamorphine for 30 ml. The woman collapsed following its administration and the doctor was unable to use the resuscitation equipment as he had not had the necessary training. Although the consultant was able to revive her, she died a few days later.[6]

Bad Maths

The UKCC advised in 2000 that student nurses should be given more mathematics training following claims that drug calculation errors could be putting patients at risk. Professor Bryn Davis, a UKCC member, stated that the GCSE maths exam, which is a compulsory entry requirement for training, is failing to prepare nurses for complex drug calculations.[7] An example of the fatal effects of miswriting decimals was seen in October 2000 when it was alleged that a baby in a neo-natal unit died when a decimal point in a drug prescription was entered in the wrong place.[8] The death had been reported to the coroner.

Management of errors or incidents in the administration of medicines

The UKCC in its guidelines for the administration of medicines also gives guidance on the management of errors or incidents in the administration of medicines. It states that the UKCC will distinguish between those cases where the error was the result of reckless or incompetent practice or was concealed, and those cases that resulted from other causes, such as serious pressure of work, and where there was immediate honest disclosure in the patient's interests and it urges employers to consider each incident in its particular context and similarly to discriminate between these two categories.[9]

Shared Liability

It may happen that several different practitioners are involved in an incident that causes harm to a patient. The court has to determine the respective responsibility of each person and their employer (if any). Under the Civil Liability (Contribution) Act 1978, a successful claimant can obtain compensation from any one of several defendants, and that defendant can then claim from the others reimbursement according to their responsibility for the harm. An example of this is given below in Case 28.2. The case does not involve a nurse, but if the situation was in a hospital context rather than in the home, one can imagine a nurse being involved.

In Case 28.2 the trial judge decided that each defendant was liable: Dr Roderick was 45 per cent liable, Dr Jackson was 15 per cent liable and the pharmacists were 40 per cent liable. The Court of Appeal held by a majority that Dr Jackson was not negligent. It accepted his evidence that it was his usual practice to enquire what medication a patient was on. Liability was thus divided between Dr Roderick and the pharmacists. Mrs Dwyer received £92,000 compensation.

One of the very interesting aspects of this case was that the incident occurred in November 1973, but did not come to court until 1982. Thus the actual evidence of what happened was scanty and undoubtedly made Mrs Dwyer's case against Dr Jackson very difficult. The court commented adversely on the delay and suggested that the time might be ripe for changes designed to enable the court and the judiciary to play a greater part in encouraging the parties and their advisers to speed up the process of litigation. These changes have now taken place (known as the 'Woolf Reforms') and are discussed in Chapter 6. Cases may still commence only many years after an incident (see Chapter 6 on limitation of time) and therefore nurses must be aware of the importance of record-keeping (see Chapter 9). In any such incident, the nurse is likely to have very little personal recall, but will be heavily dependent on the clarity and comprehensiveness of the records.

Case 28.2   Overprescribing

It was alleged by Mrs Dwyer that Dr Roderick prescribed a particular drug (Migril) and was negligent in choosing the number and frequency with which the relevant tables should be taken, so that within a relatively short time she had received a dangerous overdose. The manufacturers had warned that not more than four tablets should be taken for any one attack of migraine and that no more than 12 tablets should be taken in the course of one week. Dr Roderick's prescription was for two tablets to be taken every four hours as necessary. He prescribed a total of 60 tablets. Dr Roderick admitted that this was utterly wrong: 'I have no satisfactory explanation. It was a mental aberration.' When the prescription was taken for dispensing, there were two qualified pharmacists in the shop, neither of whom noticed the error and simply repeated Dr Roderick's instructions on the label. They in turn accepted some liability. Over the next six days, Mrs Dwyer took 36 Migril tablets. As a result of this overdose, she suffered serious personal injuries, i.e. irreversible ergotamine poisoning which resulted in constriction of the blood vessels and gangrene of her toes and lower limbs. As well as suing the chemists and Dr Roderick, Mrs Dwyer sued as second defendant Dr Roderick's partner, Dr Jackson, who saw her three days after the prescription had been given and who failed to discover the fact that his partner had overprescribed the drug and failed to stop her taking it.[10]

PRN medication

PRN medication (*pro re nata* – 'as required, whenever necessary') enables a doctor to write the patient up for medication, but leaves to the nurse the discretion as to when, if at all, the drug should be administered, depending on the patient's condition.

The value of the system is that it allows the patient to have a drug when necessary, without calling the doctor for the specific purpose of prescribing the drug for it to be administered immediately. Thus pain relief drugs, sleeping tablets, and indigestion drugs can be prescribed in case the patient might need such help. Unfortunately, the doctor does not always ensure that sufficient information is given on the drugs sheet. Thus he might fail to give the maximum amount that can be given in any 24-hour period. He might also fail to specify the dose and the intervals at which it can be given. The hospital pharmacist should check the drugs sheets regularly to ensure that all the relevant information is present and the nurse should not administer these drugs without first checking the limitations. It is also essential that every drug that is administered PRN should be recorded when given, as overdoses could easily occur if a record is not kept. Each hospital should have a policy relating to PRN medication.

Instructions by telephone

The following situation is not uncommon.

Situation 28.2   Night orders

Ward Sister Dury was the night sister at a small geriatric hospital which was served by GPs. One night, she was very worried about the condition of a frail patient whose blood pressure and temperature were raised. She telephoned the duty GP and expressed her anxieties to him. He was of the opinion that she need not be concerned and suggested that the patient should be given paracetamol. She was reluctant to take instructions over the telephone, but decided that, since he would not visit, there was little else she could do for the patient. She gave the dose of paracetamol, but unfortunately the patient's condition deteriorated and she again telephoned the GP, who did not visit until 9.00 a.m., by which time the patient had died.

What is the position of the ward sister? Should she have taken instructions over the telephone? The UKCC guidelines[11] state:

'Instruction by telephone to a practitioner to administer a previously unprescribed substance is not acceptable. In exceptional circumstances, where the medication has been previously prescribed and the prescriber is unable to issue a new prescription, but where changes to the dose are considered necessary, the use of information technology (such as fax or e-mail) is the preferred method. This should be followed up by a new prescription confirming the changes within a given time period. The UKCC suggests a maximum of 24 hours. In any event, the changes must have been authorised before the new dosage is administered.'

It would now be possible for patient group directions to be drawn up so that, following appropriate training, the ward sister could prescribe and administer against an agreed protocol (see below).

Self-administration by patients

The involvement of the patient in his own medication is increasingly being adopted as a form of rehabilitation and as a move towards discharge and the assumption by the patient of responsibility for his own health and care. The UKCC welcomes this development in its guidance for the administration of medicines,[12] but stresses that the necessary safety, security and storage arrangements must be available and, where necessary, agreed procedures in place. The UKCC states that it is also important that if the nurse is delegating the responsibility for the administration of medicines, she must ensure that the patient or carer/care assistant is competent to carry out the task. This will require education, training and assessment of the patient or carer/care assistant and further support if necessary. The retention by the patient of medication in his bedside locker puts additional responsibilities upon the nurse who needs to ensure that there is a clear policy in relation to the safety of the medicines, especially from other patients and visitors and also in relation to the training and supervision of the patient himself, and that these policies are implemented.

The nurse as prescriber

There have been major developments in the scope of professional practice of the nurse which are considered in Chapter 24. Of these developments, one of the most significant ones is nurse prescribing. This section looks at the developments in prescribing in the community and then considers the recommendations and the implications of the Crown Reports. The prescribing powers of the midwife are considered in Chapter 14.

Community nurse prescribing

Legislation has been passed to give specified practitioners the power to prescribe specified medicines (Medicinal Products (Prescription by Nurses) Act 1992). The legislation followed the recommendations of the report of the advisory group on nurse prescribing (known as the first Crown Report) to the Department of Health in December 1989. Health visitors and community nurses who have had the requisite training can prescribe in the community from a nursing formulary. In February 2000, prescribing powers were given to nurses employed by a doctor on the medical list (i.e. GP) and also to nurses working in Walk-in Centres, defined in the regulations as 'A Centre at which information and treatment for minor conditions is provided to the public under arrangements made by or on behalf of the Secretary of State.'

Situation 28.3   Holding stocks in the community

Brenda was a community nurse who was eligible to prescribe medicines in the community. Often patients would, when the treatment had ended, offer her dressings and other medicines that they had been prescribed and were left over. She was happy to take them since to dispose of them would be a waste. She thus built up a considerable stock, which she kept in the boot of her car, and would issue to new patients before their prescriptions had been dispensed. She is now concerned to know the legality of what she is doing

---

There are considerable dangers in the practice followed by Brenda. In the first place, the medicinal products obtained on prescription for one patient should be used for that patient and not for others. Secondly, by supplying these medicinal products to others, she could be seen as the supplier under the Consumer Protection Act 1987 (see Chapter 12) and become liable for any defects. In addition, there is the security and safety aspect of keeping such products in the boot of her car. In order to ensure that a safe practice is followed, she should discuss with her manager and the pharmacist, the possibility of the pharmacist taking the unwanted goods back into stock.

Prescribing in hospital and primary care

The legal changes permitting nurse prescribing in the community brought into focus the situation in hospitals and family practitioner centres where nurse prescribing was taking place according to protocols or written instructions signed by the delegating doctor. The anomalies raised by this quasi-legal situation led the government to appoint Dr June Crown to review the position on prescribing, supply and administration of medicines and make recommendations.

Group Protocols or Patient Group Directions

The Crown Committee first considered the arrangements for and legality of group protocols and reported in March 1998 (see Figure 28.7) and recommended legislation

---

1. The majority of patients should continue to receive medicines on an individual basis. However there is likely to be a continuing need for supply and administration under group protocols in certain limited situations.
2. Current safe and effective practice using group protocols which are consistent with criteria defined in the Report should continue (see Figure 28.8).
3. The law should be clarified to ensure that health professionals who supply or administer medicines under group protocols are acting within the law.
4. All group protocols should comply with specified criteria.
5. Current protocols should be reviewed in the light of those criteria.
6. The Department of Health should disseminate widely the criteria.
7. An evaluation study should be undertaken on the use of the group protocols.
8. These recommendations should apply to all sectors of health care including the private and charitable sectors.

Figure 28.7 Crown Report on Group Protocols.

Criteria for group protocols

- should ensure that patient safety is not compromised or put at risk;
- should specify clear arrangements for professional responsibility and accountability;
- should contribute to the effective use of resources;
- should be consistent with the Summary of Product Characteristics which is part of the marketing authorisation granted for the product.
- The content of the protocol should state the clinical need which it is intended to address and the objectives of care which it will provide; the characteristics of staff authorised to take responsibility for the supply or administration of medicines under a group protocol;
- the description of treatment available; the management and monitoring of group protocols;
- the development of group protocols: by whom? approval; employer's final approval; date and signature and monitoring;
- implementation of group protocols.

Figure 28.8 Criteria for group protocols.

to ensure that their legal validity was clarified. The criteria against which any group protocol should be tested are shown in Figure 28.8 It recommended that certain products should be excluded from group protocols. These included:

1. new drugs under intensive monitoring and subject to special adverse reaction reporting requirements (the Black Triangle scheme);[13]

2. unlicensed medicines;

3. medicines used outside their licensed indications; and

4. medicines being used in clinical trials.

As a consequence of the Crown Report on group protocols, new regulations came into force on 9 August 2000.[14] These provide for Patient Group Directions to be drawn up to make provision for the sale or supply of a prescription only medicine in hospitals in accordance with the written direction of a doctor or dentist. To be lawful, the Patient Group Direction must cover the particulars that are set out in Part 1 of Schedule 7 of the Statutory Instrument. These particulars are shown in Box 28.1.

Box 28.1

Particulars for Patient Group Direction

a. the period during which the Direction shall have effect

b. the description or class of prescription only medicines to which the Direction relates

c. whether there are any restrictions on the quantity of medicine which may be supplied on any one occasion, and if so, what restrictions

d. the clinical situations which prescription only medicines of that description or class may be used to treat

e. the clinical criteria under which a person shall be eligible for treatment

f. whether any class of person is excluded from treatment under the Direction, and if so, what class of person

g. whether there are circumstances in which further advice should be sought from a doctor or dentist and, if so, what circumstances

h. the pharmaceutical form or forms in which prescription only medicines of that description or class are to be administered

i. the strength, or maximum strength, at which prescription only medicines of that description or class are to be administered

j. the applicable dosage or maximum dosage

k. the route of administration

l. the frequency of administration

m. any minimum or maximum period of administration applicable to prescription only medicines of that description or class

n. whether there are any relevant warnings to note, and if so, what warnings

o. whether there is any follow up action to be taken in any circumstances, and if so, what action and in what circumstances

p. arrangements for referral for medical advice

q. details of the records to be kept of the supply or the administration of medicines under the Direction.

The classes of individuals by whom supplies may be made are set out in Part III of Schedule 7 and include the following:

1. Ambulance paramedics (who are registered or hold a certificate of proficiency).
2. Pharmacists.
3. Registered health visitors.
4. Registered midwives.
5. Registered nurses.
6. Registered ophthalmic opticians.
7. State registered chiropodists.
8. State registered orthoptists.
9. State registered physiotherapists.
10. State registered radiographers.

The person who is to supply or administer the medicine must be designated in writing on behalf of the authorising person (see below) for the purpose of the Patient Group Direction. In addition to compliance with the particulars set out in Box 28.1, a patient group direction must be signed on behalf of the authorising person. This is defined as the Common Services Agency, the (Special) Health Authority, the NHS Trust or Primary Care Trust.

Final Crown Report (1999)

In March 1999, the Final Report was published.[15] Its recommendations are shown in Figure 28.9. and they cover the first three terms of reference:

1. to develop a consistent policy framework to guide judgements on the circumstances in which health professionals might undertake new responsibilities with regard to prescribing, supply and administration of medicines;
2. to advise on likely impact of any proposed changes . . . ;
3. to consider possible implications for legislation, professional training and standards.

Other recommendations are made to professional bodies on the criteria to be followed in making proposals for extensions to prescribing and the arrangements they should make for training; to the General Medical Council and postgraduate deans; and to employers to ensure that staff prescribing medicines have the right training and skills.

Independent and Dependent Prescribers

Perhaps the most significance recommendation of the Crown Report (1999) is that there should be two types of prescriber.

1. The legal authority in the UK to prescribe should be extended beyond currently authorised prescribers.

2. The legal authority to prescribe should be limited to medicines in specific therapeutic areas related to particular competence and expertise of the group.

3. Two types of prescribers should be recognised: the independent prescriber and the dependent prescriber.

4. A UK-wide advisory body, provisionally entitled the 'New Prescribers Advisory Committee' should be established under Section 4 of the Medicines Act to assess submissions from professional organisations seeking powers for suitably trained members to become independent or dependent prescribers.

5. Newly authorised groups of prescribers should not normally be allowed to prescribe specified categories of medicines including controlled drugs.

6. The current arrangements for the administration and self-administration of medicines should continue to apply. Newly authorised prescribers should have the power to administer those parenteral prescription only medicines which they are authorised to prescribe.

7. Repeatable prescriptions should be available on the NHS, with limits on the number of repeats and the duration of its validity.

8. There should be primary legislation which permits ministers through regulations to designate new categories of dependent and independent prescribers for the purpose of the Medicines Act, defining what classes of medicines they could prescribe.

9. The new arrangements should be subject to evaluation.

10. There should be an evaluation of likely costs and benefits to the NHS in specific areas before general adoption of the recommendations takes place.

Figure 28.9   Recommendations of Final Crown Report March 1999.

- The independent prescriber is defined as the person who is responsible for the assessment of patients with undiagnosed conditions and for decisions about the clinical management required including prescribing. This group would include doctors, dentists and certain nurses who are already legally authorised prescribers. Other health professionals may also become newly legally authorised independent prescribers.

- The dependent prescriber is defined as the person who is responsible for the continuing care of patients who have been clinically assessed by an independent practitioner. The continuing care can include prescribing that will be informed by clinical guidelines and will be consistent with individual treatment plans. Dependent prescribers may also be involved in continuing established treatments by issuing repeat prescriptions, with authority to adjust the dose or dosage form according to the patients' needs. There should be provision for regular clinical review by the assessing clinician.

Individual practitioners

The final recommendation of the Crown Report is to individual practitioners:

All legally authorised prescribers should take personal responsibility for maintaining and updating their knowledge and practice related to prescribing, including taking part in clinical audit, and should never prescribe in situations beyond their professional competence.

The situation following the Final Crown Report (1999)

Legislation implementing the Final Crown Report recommendations is contained in Section 63 of the Health and Social Care Act 2001, which amends the Medicines Act 1968 and enables the Secretary of State to draw up Regulations to lay down the conditions on which prescribing powers can be extended to specified health professionals. On 25 October 2000, the Department of Health issued a consultation paper to extend nurse prescribing. It proposed training about 10,000 nurses to prescribe treatment for a broader range of medical conditions including:

1. minor injuries and ailments such as cuts, burns and hayfever;
2. promoting healthier lifestyles such as help with giving up smoking;
3. chronic diseases including asthma and diabetes;
4. palliative care.

The NHS Act 1977 Regulations will be amended to permit an extension of nurse prescribing from September 2001 from an expanded Nurse Prescribers' Formulary. Instead of separate nurse prescribing formularies for different specialties, it was considered preferable to have one Nurse Prescribers' Formulary with individual nurses using their professional judgment to decide the items within it that they were competent to prescribe. Five options were put forward for consultation.

1. No change – all additional medicines could continue to be considered subject to individual application.
2. To expand the scope of the Nurse Prescribers' Formulary by adding all General Sales List (GSL) items and the Pharmacy medicine (P), except those listed in Schedules 10 and 11 of the NHS (General Medical Services) regulations.
3. To expand the scope of the Nurse Prescribers' Formulary by adding all General Sales List items and Pharmacy medicine, together with a specific range of POMs.
4. All GSL and P together with all licensed POMs with the exception of controlled drugs and a limited number of specified only POMs.
5. All drugs except for controlled drugs to be prescribable and dispensable as part of NHS pharmaceutical services by suitably trained nurses.

Consultation was also being sought on whether nurses should have power to prescribe 'off label' drugs (i.e. the use of a medicine for a clinical indication for which the medicine is not licensed) and which nurses should train to prescribe. Response to the consultation was required by 10 January 2001.

The implications of nurse prescribing for the scope of professional practice

The Crown Report has in a sense given its approval to a controlled development of professional competence in areas formerly the sole preserve of medical staff. However, clear checks are to be in place to ensure that these developments take place with well-defined precautions to secure patient safety and also to secure efficient use of resources. Whilst nurses are likely to be the most numerous group to develop pre-scribing skills, other professionals, such as physiotherapists, radiographers, orthoptists, dietitians, speech therapists and many others, will also find that the new legislation will facilitate professional development or at the minimum validate activities already taking place. The need to obtain a doctor's personal attendance on a patient in order that a specific drug could be prescribed has placed an unnecessary obstacle in the advancement of professional practice for many health professionals and this will now be lifted. (Issues relating to the scope of professional practice and the role of the clinical nurse specialist and the consultant nurse are discussed in Chapter 24.)

Drug addicts

Nurses may sometimes encounter patients in their work who are addicted to various substances. They should know the law relating to such persons and how it affects their own position. In the past, there was a requirement that doctors should send to the Home Office particulars of drug addicts. However, this requirement was revoked by the Misuse of Drugs (Supply to Addicts) Regulations 1997 in May 1997. Doctors are now expected to report on a standard form cases of drug misuse to their local Drug Misuse Database (DMD). Phone numbers are set out in the *British National Formulary* (BNF). The notification to the DMD should be made when a patient first presents with a drug problem or re-presents after a gap of six months or more. All types of problem drug misuse should be reported including opioid, benzodiazepine and CNS stimulant. The data held on the databases is anonymised, so it cannot be used to check on multiple prescribing. Under the Misuse of Drugs (Supply to Addicts) Regulations 1997, only medical practitioners who hold a special licence issued by the Home Secretary may prescribe, administer or supply diamorphine, Diconal or cocaine in the treatment of drug addiction, other practitioners must refer any addict who requires these drugs to a treatment centre.

Product liability and drugs

The case brought against the manufacturers of Opren has shown the difficulties and expense of suing a company for harm caused by medication. Initially, a judge decided that a class action could not be brought on behalf of all those who claimed to have suffered side-effects, but each person claiming compensation would have to sue individually and contribute his share to the total costs. This has led to a demand for changes in the procedure in respect of such actions involving thousands of litigants which are currently being considered. Class actions have now been initiated in respect of several drugs products.

Under the present laws of negligence it is in any case difficult to show that a firm failed to take all reasonable care in testing and manufacturing its products.

The victims of thalidomide did not establish negligence by the Distillers Company in this country, but agreed an *ex gratia* settlement. It is possible that the Consumer Protection Act 1987, Part I, which is applicable to damage suffered after the Act came into force, will make any action for liability by someone harmed by drugs easier on the basis that, provided the patient can prove that he has suffered injury as a result of a defect in a particular drug, it is then up to the manufacturer to show that one of the many defences open to him under the Act was present. This is further discussed in Chapter 12 and will not be considered further here.

Conclusions

At the time of writing, the full impact of the Final Crown Report and the development of nurse prescribing is unknown. The ability of nurses in hospitals and in primary care to issue prescriptions will have a major impact upon the development of their scope of professional practice. There are, however, considerable dangers, since the additional responsibilities, if not coupled with adequate resources and training, may lead to more litigation, complaints and professional conduct proceedings.

Questions and exercises

1 Review your practice in the administration of drugs. Are there any ways in which you consider that you might not be meeting the legal requirements?

2 A patient is concerned at the possibility of having suffered side-effects from medication. What is the relevant law?

3 In your hospital, when a patient is admitted, any drugs that he brings from home are immediately taken from him and destroyed. One patient complains about this practice because it is wasteful and because he paid the prescription price for those drugs. What do you consider should be the correct practice?

4 Design a policy for handling drugs to be learnt by a first-year learner.

5 What are the advantages and disadvantages of administering controlled drugs PRN?

6 What are the major problems that you envisage will follow from the expansion of nurse prescribing? What safeguards do you consider should be laid down to protect the patient?

References

[1] Prescription Only Medicines (Human Use) Order 1997 SI No 1830

[2] UKCC Guidelines for the administration of medicines October 2000

[3] Alan Simpson, What price confidentiality, *Nursing Times* March 2 2000 Vol 96 No 9 p. 35

[4] NHS Executive, The Employment of Operating Department Practitioners (ODPs) in the NHS

[5] *Prendergast* v. *Sam Dee Ltd and others, The Times* 14 March 1989

[6] Dominic Kennedy, Hospital blamed in report on overdose drug, *The Times* 3 July 2000 p. 4

[7] Rebecca Coombes, Nurses need a dose of maths, *Nursing Times* June 15 Vol 96 No 24 1999 pp. 4–5

[8] Greg Hurst, Baby dies after one decimal point drug dose error, *The Times* 11 October 2000

[9] UKCC Guidance for the administration of medicines UKCC 2000 p. 9

[10] *Dwyer* v. *Roderick* 20 June 1984 QBD

[11] UKCC Guidance for the administration of medicines UKCC 2000 p. 5

[12] UKCC Guidance for the administration of medicines UKCC 2000 p. 8.

[13] The Black Triangle scheme refers to newly introduced drugs, still subject to special monitoring for potential side-effects by the Medicine Control Agency (so called because they are identified by a black triangle symbol in the *British National Formulary*)

[14] Prescription only Medicines (Human Use) Amendment Order 2000 SI 2000 No 1917

[15] Department of Health, Review of Prescribing, Supply and Administration of Medicines Final Report (Crown Report) March 1999 Department of Health London

Legal aspects of death

Nurses inevitably encounter death in their work. It can be a distressing time and uncertainties surrounding legal issues and numerous questions from troubled relatives can add to the nurse's difficulties. It is important that the nurse should have confidence in her knowledge and be well acquainted with the procedures and the law so that she can answer questions or know from where further information is available. Figure 29.1 sets out the areas that will be considered in this chapter.

The certification and registration of death

Certification of death is a medical task. The complexities in dealing with brain death and organ transplants are considered in Chapter 16, which also deals with the definition of death and the importance of the exact time of death.

Here we consider the nurse's role and the procedures to be followed generally.

Situation 29.1   An expanded role?

Night porters at Roger Park Hospital had clear instructions that no body should be taken to the mortuary unless it had been certified dead. This resulted from an unfortunate incident some time before when a body was taken to the mortuary, but was seen to move and therefore quickly returned to the ward. An investigation revealed that the person had been certified dead by a nurse. The nurses were told always to call a doctor to certify death. However, house officers were not happy about being called out just to certify death and considerable pressure was put on the nursing staff. One night, it was clear that one patient was extremely ill. There were no immediate relatives, but a distant relative was notified of the situation. The patient died at 3 a.m. The nurse summoned the doctor, who said that he would not come down, but would see the patient in the mortuary and sign the certificate there in the morning. The nurse was asked by the Bed Bureau if she had a spare bed, as a GP had just phoned and was sending in an emergency case. The hospital had no spare beds at all, except the one occupied by the dead person. Could the nurse herself identify that death had occurred and arrange for the porters to remove the body?

> Certification and registration of death
> Disposal of the body
> Post Mortem
> Deaths to be reported to the coroner
> Inquest
> Property of the deceased
> Wills

Figure 29.1   Issues covered in Chapter 29.

The law requires a doctor to certify a death. The certification cannot be undertaken by nurses. However, a nurse may have had the training to be able to confirm that a patient has died, i.e. to verify a death. In certain parts of the country, the local medical committees have advised nursing homes and residential care homes that the nurse or manager in charge of the home should, where death is expected, confirm that death has taken place and the doctor would sign the certificate at a later time. If the nurse considers that she is unable to confirm that death has taken place, she should not give way to any pressure, however reasonable it might appear. In situation 29.1, the nurse may be able to obtain help from another nurse who is competent or from a doctor who is prepared to come to the ward.

Case 29.1   Fatal diagnosis[1]

The son of Mrs Maureen Jones summoned a GP when he found his mother collapsed in her bedroom. The GP said that she had died and advised the relatives to notify the police. The undertakers were summoned. A policeman called to the scene saw the woman's leg move and applied mouth to mouth resuscitation until the paramedics arrived. She then made a full recovery in hospital. She had been in a diabetic coma. A county court judge found the doctor negligent in making a diagnosis of death. Damages were agreed with the Medical Defence Union at £38,500. The Health Authority following an investigation agreed that the doctor could continue in practice, but was given an official reprimand, told to comply more closely with her terms of service and was required to undergo educational assessment and support.

The RCN has provided a paper on verification of death by registered nurses.[2] It states that experienced registered nurses will have the authority to verify death, notify the relatives, and arrange for last offices and the removal of the body to the mortuary. Education is necessary to ensure they have the confidence, competence, knowledge and skills to equip them for undertaking this role. Their records should document the action they have taken and contain information relating to the date, time and any other information required by hospital policy.

Issues relating to the scope of professional practice and the expanded role of the nurse are considered in Chapter 24.

The General Office of the hospital or the medical records department discusses with bereaved relatives the administrative details that must be dealt with. Sometimes

The medical certificate should be taken by the next of kin or, if not available, by any relatives living in the district or present at the death to the Registrar for Births, Marriages and Deaths within 5 days of the death. He will require the following information: the full name of the deceased; the last known address; date of birth; occupation; and whether the deceased was in receipt of a pension. The Registrar will give the person registering the death a certificate of disposal form which can be handed to the undertaker. If a cremation is intended, then certification by two doctors will be required. If the death has been referred to the coroner, then the relatives should be notified that they will not receive the certificate from the hospital. The coroner will issue his own disposal certificate.

The relatives will receive from the Registrar in addition to the certificate of disposal form a certificate of registration of death. This may be required by the DSS in order to claim any entitlements. (The death grant is no longer payable but other benefits are available to those who are eligible.) This certificate may also be required to obtain transfer of any bank accounts, etc., and further copies are available from the Registrar on payment of a fee.

Figure 29.2 Procedures for dealing with death.

there is a special office for dealing with the bereaved and during weekdays the relatives can be shown to this place. However, at night and during the weekends and bank holidays the nurse may have to deal with the administrative details. She should know the details relating to the registration of death and the disposal of the body. Figure 29.2 sets out the procedure to be followed.

Disposal of the body

Different arrangements exist according to the local hospital facilities. Some hospital mortuaries also double up as the public mortuary and it is possible for the body to remain there until collected by the undertakers for the funeral. Before the body is taken from the ward, the nurse must ensure that it is properly labelled and that a receipt is signed and that any property on the body, e.g. rings, are carefully noted and signed for. Similar procedures to check identification and property on the body and the giving of receipts must also be followed when the body is handed over by the porters, administrators or even nurses to the undertakers. Unfortunately, mix-up between bodies still occurs and the wrong body is released.

Post mortems

The coroner might require a post mortem to ascertain the cause of death and can direct a legally qualified medical practitioner to carry out the post mortem. A post mortem ordered by a coroner may or may not precede an inquest. If the coroner orders a post mortem, then the person in possession of the body has no choice but to agree. Sometimes, however, medical staff may request the relative's permission to confirm the cause of death or for research purposes. They require the consent of the person in possession of the body (Human Tissue Act 1961 Section 2 (2)). This can be a distressing request to make to relatives and the request should be put to them with sensitivity. Organs should not be retained by the hospital doctors without the consent of the relatives. (The issue of retention of organs and government advice is considered in Chapter 16.)

Deaths that have to be reported to the coroner

These are shown in Figure 29.3.

If it is likely to be a coroner's case, no unofficial post mortem should be undertaken without the coroner's approval. The coroner can order a post mortem examination to be carried out before deciding to hold an inquest.

(a) where there is reasonable cause to suspect a person has died a violent or unnatural death;

(b) where there is reasonable cause to suspect a person has died a sudden death of which the cause is unknown;

(c) the person has died in prison or in such place or under such circumstances as to require an inquest.

Those causes of death which should be reported to the coroner include: abortions; accidents and injuries; alcoholism; anaesthetics and operations; crime or suspected crime; drugs; ill-treatment; industrial diseases; infant deaths if in any way obscure; pensioners where death might be connected with a pensionable disability; persons in legal custody; poisoning; septicaemias if originating from an injury; and stillbirths where there may have been a possibility or suspicion that the child may have been born alive.

Figure 29.3 Deaths that have to be reported to the coroner.

Inquests

The Coroners Act 1988 covers the appointment of coroners, the holding of inquests, and post mortem examination.

Situation 29.2 *An unexpected death*

Bill Arthur was undergoing a stomach operation when the anaesthetist reported that his pulse was becoming very weak. Resuscitative procedures were undertaken, but unfortunately Bill died. The death was reported to the coroner who decided that an inquest should be held.

What is the purpose of the inquest?

The purpose is to ascertain the following:

1. the identity of the deceased;
2. how, where, and when the deceased came by his death;
3. the particulars, for the time being required by the Registration Acts, to be registered concerning the death.

Section 11(6) of the Coroners Act 1988 specifically states that the purpose of the proceedings shall not include the finding of any person guilty of murder, manslaughter, or infanticide.

Who should attend?

The coroner has a duty[3] to examine on oath all persons who tender evidence as to the facts of the death and all persons having knowledge of the facts whom he considers it expedient to examine. Under the Coroner's Rules,[4] the coroner has considerable discretion in deciding who should attend. He must notify the date, hour and place of an inquest to:

1. the spouse or a near relative or personal representative of the deceased whose name and address are known to the coroner; and
2. any other person who
   (i) in the opinion of the coroner is within Rule 20 (2), i.e. parent, child, spouse; any beneficiary under an insurance policy on the life of the deceased; any person whose act or omission or that of his servant or agent may have caused or contributed to the death of the deceased; any person appointed by a trade union to which the deceased belonged if the death may have been caused by an injury received at work or an industrial disease; an inspector appointed by an enforcing authority or government department to attend; the chief of police; any other person who in the opinion of the coroner is a properly interested person; and
   (ii) has asked the coroner to notify him of the particulars of the inquest; and
   (iii) has supplied the coroner with a telephone number or address for the purpose of so notifying him.

Examination of witnesses

Any of the persons listed under 2(i) above are entitled to examine the witnesses either in person or through a solicitor or barrister. The coroner has the power to disallow any question that in his opinion is not relevant or is otherwise not a proper question.

The procedure is for any witness to be examined first by the coroner and, if the witness is represented at the inquest, lastly by the representative. No witness is obliged to answer any question tending to incriminate himself. Where it appears to the coroner that a witness has been asked such a question, the coroner must inform the witness that he may refuse to answer.

Any person whose conduct is likely to be called in question shall, if he has not been summoned to give evidence at the inquest, be given reasonable notice of the date, hour and place at which the inquest shall be held. If any such person has not been summoned or notified, then the coroner must adjourn the hearing to enable him to be present. The inquest shall be adjourned by the coroner on notification by the clerk to the Magistrates Court that a person has been charged with an offence such as murder, manslaughter, infanticide, or causing death by dangerous driving or the offence of aiding and abetting a suicide under Section 2 (1) of the Suicide Act 1961. The Director of Public Prosecutions may also ask the coroner to adjourn the hearing. Where the coroner adjourns the hearing, he shall send to the registrar of deaths a certificate stating particulars required for registration.

Nature of the inquest

The coroner's inquest is very different from the hearings in the other courts of law in this country. It is an inquisitorial hearing as opposed to the civil and criminal courts which are accusatorial or adversarial. This means that in an inquest there are not two opposing parties with the coroner sitting back and hearing them argue out a case, intervening only to ensure fair play. At an inquest, the coroner takes the lead and is in control. It is up to him or her to obtain answers to the questions set out above. He/she calls the witnesses and decides the order in which they are to give evidence and generally controls the court and hearing. There is not always a jury, but where there is a point of public concern then the coroner will usually ensure that a jury is summoned.

Returning to Situation 29.2, the coroner's officer will have requested statements from relevant people who were present in theatre and who were concerned with Bill's treatment. It is helpful if those making a statement can keep a copy. (Refer to Chapter 9 for the making of statements.) The coroner will probably have requested a post mortem examination to ascertain the cause of death. He will decide which people he requires to summon as witnesses. Clearly, in Bill's case, there will have to be evidence of identity and also of what took place in theatre. The surgeon, anaesthetist and the nurse are all likely to be called to give evidence. If detailed pathology laboratory results are not yet available, there could well be an adjournment until they are ready. Bill's family will obviously wish to be present in order that they can ask for the relevant questions to be put to prepare for a possible case of negligence in the civil courts. The coroner has the power to prevent any question that he does not consider relevant to the inquest.

Preparation for the theatre nurse before attending the inquest

The theatre nurse has, one hopes, kept a copy of the statement that she made for the coroner. The statement should have followed those guidelines discussed in Chapter 9. She should be advised by a senior nursing officer who has had some experience in such matters on the sort of questions she can expect and how to cope. Preferably, she should be advised by the solicitor to the Trust. (For further information on this aspect see Chapter 9.) The importance of comprehensive, meaningful record-keeping cannot, once again, be overstressed. Prior to the hearing, the solicitor to the Trust should take her through her evidence and answer any concerns that she has.

Property of the deceased

When a patient has died, there is an obligation on the staff to ensure that the property is listed and accounted for. Usually the next of kin will arrange for clothes and small personal items to be taken away. However, any property that looks as though it might be of some value should be handed over to the executor or personal representative only on production of the grant of probate or letters of administration relating to the estate. A form of indemnity may be required to protect the NHS Trust. This is the only way in which the NHS Trust can defend itself if it is challenged for handing the property over to the wrong person. (See Chapter 25 on property.)

> ## Case 29.2 Property of the deceased[5]
>
> A patient was brought into hospital following a heart attack at a garden centre and was found to be dead on arrival. His widow realised that he was carrying the house keys in his pocket and asked for them so that she could return home. The sister stated that the keys had to be left in the safe until after the post mortem, even though the widow told her that she would not be able to get into her house without them. She returned to the house with her daughter, but was unable to get in and had to hire a locksmith the next day.

Even though the hospital was probably following the set procedure for handling property following an unexpected death which was reported to the coroner, there would appear to be reasonable grounds for permitting the widow to receive the keys, perhaps on receipt of an indemnity. There were no suspicious circumstances relating to the death and the hospital could have safeguarded its position by obtaining the consent of the coroner to the handing over of the keys.

Wills

The best advice to nursing staff in relation to the drawing up or signing of wills for patients is 'do not get involved'. Ideally, if a patient makes it known that he wishes to make his will (the person making a will is known as the testator), the unit manager should be advised and the patient's solicitor called. The nurse should not be involved. If there is likely to be any dispute as to the patient's competence to make a will, medical opinion should be obtained to confirm that the patient is mentally competent, since one of the grounds for challenging a will's validity is that the patient lacked the competence to sign it, since he was unaware of the implications of his act. Another ground on which its provisions can be challenged is that the patient was subjected to undue influence at the time of signing it so that its provisions do not represent his real intent. Nursing and medical evidence thus becomes crucial in any such legal dispute. If there is a statement in the medical records that the patient signed his will on such and such a day and that his state of mind was rational, clear and unconfused, while that is not in itself evidence of the truth of what is stated, it should at least contain sufficient information to assist professionals in the recall of events, should they be subjected to cross-examination on the patient's competence or independent state of mind.

Situation 29.2   *Execution at night*

Florence Evans was convinced that she was dying. She fretted that she had not made her will and asked the night sister if she would sign a piece of paper declaring how she would like her property disposed of. The night sister was very reluctant to become involved, although she knew that Florence was in fact very ill. Florence showed her the paper on which everything was written and asked her to sign it with the auxiliary as a witness. Just to settle Florence, the night sister agreed and she and the nursing auxiliary together watched Florence sign the piece of paper and then they signed their own names. Florence died that same week.

A few weeks later the sister was told that Florence's daughter was disputing the will which left everything to her two brothers and nothing to her. She said that the formalities were not complied with and that it was not a proper will.

This gives an example of one reason why nursing staff are advised not to become involved with will making. Hospitals should provide advice on what staff should do in this situation. In some hospitals, it would be possible for a sister in this situation to summon the on-call manager to take care of Florence's will. The actual signing and witnessing of the will is known as the execution of the will and strict rules are in force in relation to the validity of the process. These have been eased slightly since 1982, but the revised procedures must be strictly followed. Any irregularity in the execution of the will may lead to the will being declared invalid. There are no special forms to be used although these are available. The legal requirements are set out in Figure 29.4.

Any person who signs the will as a witness is prevented from being a beneficiary under the will and this applies to the spouse as well. (In one case where the solicitor allowed the beneficiary's spouse to sign the will, the solicitor was liable for the lost inheritance.) If the testator intends leaving a gift to the NHS Trust or its staff, then no one from the NHS Trust should be involved in the drawing up or signing of the will, otherwise the gift could be invalidated on the grounds of undue influence.

In the situation described above where the sister and the nursing auxiliary witnessed the will, it is unlikely that the will could be declared invalid on the grounds of its actual execution even though it might be challenged on other grounds (the lack of mental competence, undue influence, etc.). However, the possibility of involvement in litigation does illustrate the advantages of nursing staff ensuring that, where possible, the experts are involved.

Section 17 Administration of Justice Act 1982 amending Section 9 of the Wills Act 1837
No will shall be valid unless

(a) It is in writing and signed by the testator, or by some other person in his presence and by his direction; and

(b) it appears that the testator intended by his signature to give effect to the will; and

(c) the signature is made or acknowledged by the testator in the presence of two or more witnesses present at the same time; and

(d) each witness either
(i) attests and signs the will; or
(ii) acknowledges his signature,
in the presence of the testator (but not necessarily in the presence of any other witness), but no form of attestation shall be necessary.

Additional requirements:

(a) the testator must be over 18 (unless in the armed forces or the merchant navy);

(b) the testator must have the required mental competence at the time he signs the will.

Figure 29.4 Requirements for a valid will.

Questions and exercises

1 Obtain a copy of the local policy and guidelines on dealing with death and familiarise yourself with it.

2 Consider any patient whose death you have witnessed and whose relatives you have had to comfort and assist. Was there any information of which you were ignorant? Could you answer all their questions?

3 In what ways would an inquest differ from a hearing in the criminal or civil courts?

4 Draft a procedure for preparing a nurse who has been asked to give evidence at an inquest.

5 Obtain a copy of your NHS Trust's leaflet for the guidance of patients on the care of property. Does it consider the procedure to be followed at the death of a patient? What precautions would you as a ward sister take to ensure that the property of the deceased was cared for?

References

[1] Paul Wilkinson, £38,500 for woman given up for dead, *The Times* 27 September 2000
[2] Royal College of Nursing, Verification of death by registered nurses RCN 000 594 May 1996
[3] Section 11 (2) Coroners Act 1988
[4] Coroners Rules 1984 S.1 No. 552
[5] Oliver Wright, Widow forced to break in to home, *The Times* 28 August, 2000 p. 5

30 Complementary therapies

Background

A phenomenon in recent years has been the increase in the popularity of complementary or alternative therapies. An information pack for primary care on complementary medicine has been sponsored by the Department of Health.[1] The pack was initiated after a survey found that 1 in 4 adults would use alternative therapies at some point in their lives. Other evidence estimates that a third of the population has tried its remedies or visited its practitioners.[2] The Health Education Authority has published an A to Z guide which covers 60 therapies.[3] In addition, the House of Lords select committee on science and technology has reviewed the field of complementary and alternative medicines and made significant recommendations on their control and use within the NHS.[4] Much research needs to be done on the efficacy of these therapies and the Health Authority Council has approved a research project to be undertaken by the National Association of Health Authorities and Trusts into the prevalence of complementary therapies and their services for patients, purchasers and providers. The Health Authority Council has appointed a steering and working group to co-ordinate the project which will be undertaken by Blueprint Consultancy.[5] A Chair in Complementary Therapy has been provided at Exeter University. The Prince of Wales suggested the setting up of a group to consider the current positions of orthodox, complementary and alternative medicine in the UK and how far it would be appropriate and possible for them to work more closely together. Four working groups looking at (a) research and development; (b) education and training; (c) regulation; and (d) delivery mechanisms were established under a steering group chaired by Dr Manon Williams, Assistant Private Secretary to HRH the Prince of Wales. It reported in 1997 and made extensive recommendations.[6] These include encouraging more research and the dissemination of its results; emphasising the common elements in the core curriculum of all health care workers, orthodox and complementary and alternative medicine; establishing statutory self-regulatory bodies for those professions that could endanger patient safety; identify areas of conventional medicine and nursing that are not meeting patients' needs at present. It also recommended the establishment of an Independent Standards Commission for Complementary and Alternative Medicine. There is every likelihood that more and more pressure will be provided for various complementary therapies to be made available on the NHS. For example, the BMA at its conference in 2000 pressed the government to make acupuncture available on the NHS. Many GP practices are now providing complementary therapy services to their patients.

Background
Definitions of complementary and alternative therapy
UKCC Practitioner as a complementary therapist
Liability for using complementary therapies at work
Patients receiving complementary therapies
Conclusions

Figure 30.1   Issues covered in Chapter 30.

This chapter looks at the legal implications of complementary therapy practice for nurses, midwives and health visitors in two respects: one as a practitioner of a complementary therapy alongside the skills for which they are registered with the UKCC; the other as a carer of patients who may be receiving complementary therapies as well as care from traditional medicine. For more detailed information on the legal aspects of complementary therapies, see the author's work.[7] Reference should also be made to the many books written by nurses about individual complementary therapies.[8] The issues to be covered are shown in Figure 30.1.

Definition of complementary or alternative therapies

It is perhaps easier to define a complementary or alternative therapy negatively in the sense that it is treatment for which health giving or disease repelling properties are claimed that are not yet accepted by those who practice orthodox medicine. If this definition is used, it could be argued that chiropractic and osteopathy were once, but are no longer, complementary therapies, but by becoming state registered professions are now accepted as part of orthodox medicine and there are referrals funded by the NHS. If this definition is used, it would follow that homeopathy has long been part of orthodox medicine; since the Faculty of Homeopathy was established in 1848, five schools of homeopathy have been established and both the schools and the hospitals receive state support.

The term 'complementary or alternative therapy' covers a wide range of practices from the well established field of homeopathy to claims in respect of dowsing, radionics and astrology.

The UKCC practitioner as a complementary therapist

The UKCC has provided guidance in the use of complementary and alternative therapies in its recent guidelines for the administration of medicines.[9] It states that registered practitioners 'who practise the use of such therapies must have successfully undertaken training and be competent in this area. You must have considered the appropriateness of the therapy to both the condition of the patient and any co-existing treatments. It is essential that the patient is aware of the therapy and gives informed consent.'

A UKCC practitioner who has been trained in a complementary therapy may wish to use it for the benefit of her NHS patients. She may, for example, have acquired skills in aromatherapy, reflexology or acupuncture and believe that these may be more effective in reducing pain or relaxing the patient than medication. What restrictions would there be on her practising her additional skills?

The employer should have a policy covering the use of complementary or alternative therapies. This should include details about the information that should be given to the employer about qualifications and membership of the relevant associations. Unfortunately, there are considerable variations in the standards of training required and many therapies do not have a single overall professional body that sets standards. West Yorkshire has issued guidance on the information that should be retained by employers about the complementary therapies that staff may wish to practise.[10] The consent of the employer must be obtained as the following situation indicates.

Situation 30.1   Aromatherapy without consent

Brenda was an ITU nurse who had undertaken a course in aromatherapy. She knew that it would be relaxing and beneficial to the ventilated patients she was caring for and wished to use aromatherapy oils on them. Her employers were prepared to give consent to her using aromatherapy, but their policy on the use of complementary or alternative therapies required employees to obtain the consent of patients before initiating any treatment. Since most of Brenda's adult patients were unconscious and relatives could not give a valid consent on their behalf, she was thwarted in her plans. What is the law?

It is entirely reasonable for the employer to lay down instructions and protocols for the use of non-orthodox treatments. The requirement of the patient's consent is also consistent with the legal situation. Brenda, therefore, has to accept that until such time, if ever, aromatherapy becomes a recognised part of traditional nursing and medicine and could therefore be used in the best interests of a mentally incompetent patient, she would be unable to use it in ITU.

Liability for using complementary therapy at work

If consent is not obtained from the employer, and the nurse practices her complementary therapy skills during her work, there could be serious consequences for the nurse. On the one hand, she has disobeyed the reasonable instructions of the employer and she therefore faces disciplinary action, including dismissal. On the other hand, if she causes harm to the patient, she may face personal liability for the harm that she has caused, since the employer might deny that it is vicariously liable for an employee who is disobeying reasonable instructions and who is not therefore acting in the course of employment (see Chapter 4). Even if this argument by the employer did not succeed, since it could be held that the employee is still acting in the employer's interests, the employer might claim from the employee an indemnity for any compensation that it has to pay to the injured patient.

On the other hand, if the employee has obtained consent from the employer, not only would there be no justification for disciplinary action, but if harm were to occur to the patient as the result of negligence by the practitioner, the employer would be vicariously liable for that harm.

Different issues arise if the practitioner wishes to use her complementary therapy skills out of working hours, but on the employer's premises as the following case shows.

Case 30.1   Private practice in working hours.[11]

An occupational therapist was dismissed when he saw private patients for alternative therapy during working hours. His application for unfair dismissal failed. He had been warned by his employers not to conduct his private business during his working hours and lunch-times were for a break, not for private work.

It may be that as the clinical effectiveness of certain therapies is established, then employers will fund study leave for practitioners to develop these new skills as part of the scope of their professional practice (see Chapter 24). At this point, some of these therapies might be seen as part of the reasonable standard of care to be provided to a patient and could then be given to mentally incapacitated adults in their best interests.

Notifying the patients of risks of complementary therapy

There appears to be a common fallacy that complementary or alternative therapies, being natural, can do only good and not harm and there are no risks attached. However, this is not correct as some of the cases reported in the author's work show.[12] Any significant risks, which reasonable professional practice would suggest should be made known to the patient, must be explained to the patient before consent is obtained. Exactly the same principles apply in complementary therapies to the obtaining of consent and the information to be given to a patient as apply in orthodox medicine. These are discussed in Chapter 7. If, for example, a patient were to be given acupuncture and suffered harm, it would be a defence if the defendant could show that there was no negligence on the part of the practitioner, that the patient had given a valid consent and that information about significant risks of substantial harm had been notified by the practitioner to the patient. There are obviously advantages if this information could be conveyed both in writing as well as by word of mouth. The Bolam test[13] standard would apply to what information should be given. It may, however, be more difficult to establish this in non-orthodox medicine.

It might be asked if liability for harm in complementary therapies could be excluded by reference to a notice? The Unfair Contract Terms Act 1977 would prevent any exclusion of liability if negligence by the therapist caused personal injury or death (see Chapter 6).

The patient receiving complementary therapies

If it is found that the patient, in addition to being treated by orthodox medicine, is also in receipt of complementary or alternative therapies, then care must be taken to ensure that there are no contra-indications between the two treatments and as much information as possible is obtained about the other treatment. The patient may agree to giving the name of the complementary therapist who could be contacted for details of their treatment and treatment plan. It may be, for example, that the patient is given conflicting advice: in such a situation, good communication is essential between the orthodox practitioners and the complementary therapist. There are considerable advantages in UKCC practitioners obtaining a good understanding of the complementary therapies that their patients are most likely to be using, so that the practitioner can understand the implications for orthodox medicine and know where to obtain further advice and information.[14]

The consent of the client must be obtained as the following situation indicates.

Situation 30.2 Herbal medicine

Daphne asked a patient about various bottles that she saw on her bedside locker. The patient explained that she was receiving herbal medicine for her arthritis. Daphne asked for details about what she was taking, but the patient said it was nothing to do with Daphne or her stay in hospital because she was being treated for a heart condition. Where does Daphne stand in law?

There are clear dangers here, since it could be that the herbal preparations could react against any medication given for the patient's heart condition or could even exacerbate the condition. Daphne should ensure that the medical staff are aware of the situation and it might be advisable to arrange for the pharmacist to see the patient and try to persuade her to disclose sufficient details about the herbal preparations and the herbalist advising the patient so that any necessary action can be taken to ensure that the patient is safe.

Case 30.2 Standard of care of a complementary therapist[15]

S, who was suffering from a skin condition, consulted a practitioner of traditional Chinese herbal medicine. After taking 9 doses of the herbal remedy, S became ill and later died of acute liver failure, which was attributable to a rare and unpredictable reaction to the remedy. His widow brought proceedings against the practitioner, but failed. The High Court held that on the evidence before it the actions of the practitioner had been consistent with the standard of care appropriate to traditional Chinese herbal medicine in accordance with established requirements.

Conclusions

The RCN noted in its report on the views of nurses on the future[16] that there had been a burgeoning of interest in complementary therapies in recent years, and many nurses had undertaken some form of training in various therapies. However, they were encountering difficulties in integrating them into mainstream services. There was widespread misunderstanding of their use and effectiveness in nursing, too much variation in quality and content of courses available, and concerns that attaching these therapies to the old medical model would negate their potential as enhancers of holistic care. These concerns are probably still unresolved. It seems probable that there will continue to be further take up of complementary therapies and more and more state-registered practitioners will be acquiring skills in complementary therapies that they wish to practise alongside their traditional professional practice. There will be pressure from many of the different groups and associations to acquire state registration and there will be pressure upon them to ensure that their practice is research-based and standards are defined nationally. In addition, patients will be seeking for various therapies to be available within the NHS. Their likely success will depend considerably on the extent to which research can show that there is clear clinical evidence to establish their effectiveness over orthodox medicine alternatives.

In November 2000, the Scientific Committee of the House of Lords[17] reported that there should be regulations of complementary and alternative medicines (CAM) and there should be further research to evaluate their effectiveness. It divided such therapies into three groups:

1   Professionally organised therapies, where there is some scientific evidence of their success, though seldom of the highest quality and there are recognised systems for treatment and training of practitioners. This group includes acupuncture, chiropractic, herbal medicine, homoeopathy and osteopathy.

2   Complementary medicines where evidence that they work is generally lacking, but which are used as an adjunct rather than a replacement for conventional therapies, so that lack of evidence may not matter so much. Included in this group are Alexander Technique, aromatherapy, nutritional medicine, hypnotherapy and Bach and other flower remedies.

3   Techniques that offer diagnosis as well as treatment, but for which scientific evidence is almost completely lacking. This group cannot be supported and includes Naturopathy, crystal therapy, kinesiology, radionics, dowsing and iridology.

The Select Committee of the House of Lords considered that some remedies such as acupuncture and aromatherapy should be available on the NHS and NHS patients should have wider access to osteopathy and chiropractic. The implementation of these recommendations will lead to fundamental changes in how complementary and alternative therapies are viewed in relation to orthodox medicine and within the NHS.

Questions and exercises

1 You have decided that you would like to undertake a training in aromatherapy and eventually use it as part of your practice as a clinical nurse specialist in intensive care. What actions would you take to ensure that your plans are compatible with your role as a registered nurse?

2 Identify the ways in which the knowledge that a patient was receiving complementary therapy treatment could affect the care that you give that person.

3 Do you consider that those complementary therapists who so wished, should be permitted to have registered status under the Health Professions Council (Refer also to Chapter 11.) If not, what criteria would you lay down for a profession to receive registered status?

4 Do you consider that patients should be under an obligation to inform their NHS carers if they are receiving complementary therapies?

5 Obtain a copy of the House of Lords' Select Committee Report and consider the extent to which it could be implemented within the NHS and the likely consequences of its recommendations.

References

1 Complementary Medicine Information Pack for Primary Care www.doh.gov.uk

2 Jeremy Laurance, Alternative Health: An honest alternative or just magic? *The Times* 5 February 1996 p. 11

3 Health Education Authority, A-Z guide on complementary therapies. 1995

4 House of Lords Select Committee on Science and Technology 6th Report Complementary and Alternative Medicine 21 November 2000 Session 1999–2000

5 For further details contact Yvonne Mouncer Regional Development Manager NAHAT

6 Integrated Healthcare: A Way Forward for the Next Five Years, Foundation for Integrated Medicine 1997

7 B.C. Dimond, *Legal Aspects of Complementary Therapy Practice*, Churchill Livingstone 1998

8 See in particular Denise Rankin-Box (ed), *The Nurse's handbook of complementary therapies* Churchill Livingstone Edinburgh 1995

9 UKCC Guidelines for the administration of medicines 2000

10 News item, *Medical law monitor* Jan/Feb1996 6–8

11 Case of *Watling* v. *Gloucester County Council* Employment Tribunal EAT/868/94 17 March 1995, 23 November 1994, Lexis transcript.

12 B.C. Dimond, *Legal Aspects of Complementary Therapy Practice*, Churchill Livingstone 1998

13 *Bolam* v. *Friern Barnet* HMC [1957] 2 All ER 118

14 Royal Council for Complementary Medicine 0207 833 8897; Institute for Complementary Medicine 0207 237 5165; British Medical Association, *Complementary Medicine: New approaches to good practice* OUP/BMA Oxford 1993; links to alternative medicine sites: www.medic.org.uk/altmed

15 *Shakoor (Deceased)* v. *Situ* [2000] 4 All ER 181

16 Royal College of Nursing, Imagining the Future Nursing in the new Millennium RCN 000 912 August 1998

17 House of Lords Select Committee on Science and Technology 6th Report Complementary and Alternative Medicine 21 November 2000 Session 1999–2000

Articles of the European Convention on Human Rights

SCHEDULES

SCHEDULE 1

THE ARTICLES

PART I

THE CONVENTION

RIGHTS AND FREEDOMS

Article 2

Right to life

1. Everyone's right to life shall be protected by law. No one shall be deprived of his life intentionally save in the execution of a sentence of a court following his conviction of a crime for which this penalty is provided by law.

2. Deprivation of life shall not be regarded as inflicted in contravention of this Article when it results from the use of force which is no more than absolutely necessary:

    (a) in defence of any person from unlawful violence;

    (b) in order to effect a lawful arrest or to prevent the escape of a person lawfully detained;

    (c) in action lawfully taken for the purpose of quelling a riot or insurrection.

Article 3

Prohibition of torture

No one shall be subjected to torture or to inhuman or degrading treatment or punishment.

Article 4

Prohibition of slavery and forced labour

1. No one shall be held in slavery or servitude.

2. No one shall be required to perform forced or compulsory labour.

3. For the purpose of this Article the term 'forced or compulsory labour' shall not include:

(a) any work required to be done in the ordinary course of detention imposed according to the provisions of Article 5 of this Convention or during conditional release from such detention;

(b) any service of a military character or, in case of conscientious objectors in countries where they are recognised, service exacted instead of compulsory military service;

(c) any service exacted in case of an emergency or calamity threatening the life or well-being of the community;

(d) any work or service which forms part of normal civic obligations.

Article 5

Right to liberty and security

1. Everyone has the right to liberty and security of person. No one shall be deprived of his liberty save in the following cases and in accordance with a procedure prescribed by law:

(a) the lawful detention of a person after conviction by a competent court;

(b) the lawful arrest or detention of a person for non-compliance with the lawful order of a court or in order to secure the fulfilment of any obligation prescribed by law;

(c) the lawful arrest or detention of a person effected for the purpose of bringing him before the competent legal authority on reasonable suspicion of having committed an offence or when it is reasonably considered necessary to prevent his committing an offence or fleeing after having done so;

(d) the detention of a minor by lawful order for the purpose of educational supervision or his lawful detention for the purpose of bringing him before the competent legal authority;

(e) the lawful detention of persons for the prevention of the spreading of infectious diseases, of persons of unsound mind alcoholics or drug addicts or vagrants;

(f) the lawful arrest or detention of a person to prevent his effecting an unauthorised entry into the country or of a person against whom action is being taken with a view to deportation or extradition.

2. Everyone who is arrested shall be informed promptly, in a language which he understands, of the reasons for his arrest and of any charge against him.

3. Everyone arrested or detained in accordance with the provisions of paragraph 1(c) of this Article shall be brought promptly before a judge or other officer authorised by law to exercise judicial power and shall be entitled to trial within a reasonable time or to release pending trial. Release may be conditioned by guarantees to appear for trial.

4. Everyone who is deprived of his liberty by arrest or detention shall be entitled to take proceedings by which the lawfulness of his detention shall be decided speedily by a court and his release ordered if the detention is not lawful.

5. Everyone who has been the victim of arrest or detention in contravention of the provisions of this Article shall have an enforceable right to compensation.

Article 6

Right to a fair trial

1. In the determination of his civil rights and obligations or of any criminal charge against him, everyone is entitled to a fair and public hearing within a reasonable time by an independent and impartial tribunal established by law. Judgment shall be pronounced publicly but the press and public may be excluded from all or part of the trial in the interest of morals, public order or national security in a democratic society, where the interests of juveniles or the protection of the private life of the parties so require, or to the extent strictly necessary in the opinion of the court in special circumstances where publicity would prejudice the interests of justice.

2. Everyone charged with a criminal offence shall be presumed innocent until proved guilty according to law.

3. Everyone charged with a criminal offence has the following minimum rights:

    (a) to be informed promptly, in a language which he understands and in detail, of the nature and cause of the accusation against him;

    (b) to have adequate time and facilities for the preparation of his defence;

    (c) to defend himself in person or through legal assistance of his own choosing or, if he has not sufficient means to pay for legal assistance, to be given it free when the interests of justice so require;

    (d) to examine or have examined witnesses against him and to obtain the attendance and examination of witnesses on his behalf under the same conditions as witnesses against him;

    (c) to have the free assistance of an interpreter if he cannot understand or speak the language used in court.

Article 7

No punishment without law

1. No one shall be held guilty of any criminal offence on account of any act or omission which did not constitute a criminal offence under national or international law at the time when it was committed. Nor shall a heavier penalty be imposed than the one that was applicable at the time the criminal offence was committed.

2. This Article shall not prejudice the trial and punishment of any person for any act or omission which, at the time when it was committed, was criminal according to the general principles of law recognised by civilised nations.

Article 8

Right to respect for private and family life

1. Everyone has the right to respect for his private and family life, his home and his correspondence.

2. There shall be no interference by a public authority with the exercise of this right except such as is in accordance with the law and is necessary in a democratic society in the interests of national security, public safety or the economic wellbeing of the country, for the prevention of disorder or crime, for the protection of health or morals, or for the protection of the rights and freedoms of others.

Article 9

Freedom of thought, conscience and religion

1. Everyone has the right to freedom of thought, conscience and religion; this right includes freedom to change his religion or belief and freedom, either alone or in community with others and in public or private, to manifest his religion or belief, in worship, teaching, practice and observance.

2. Freedom to manifest one's religion or beliefs shall be subject only to such limitations as are prescribed by law and are necessary in a democratic society in the interests of public safety, for the protection of public order, health or morals, or for the protection of the rights and freedoms of others.

Article 10

Freedom of expression

1. Everyone has the right to freedom of expression. This right shall include freedom to hold opinions and to receive and impart information and ideas without interference by public authority and regardless of frontiers. This Article shall not prevent States from requiring the licensing of broadcasting, television or cinema enterprises.

2. The exercise of these freedoms, since it carries with it duties and responsibilities, may be subject to such formalities, conditions, restrictions or penalties as are

prescribed by law and are necessary in a democratic society, in the interests of national security, territorial integrity or public safety, for the prevention of disorder or crime, for the protection of health or morals, for the protection of the reputation or rights of others, for preventing the disclosure of information received in confidence, or for maintaining the authority and impartiality of the judiciary.

Article 11

Freedom of assembly and association

1. Everyone has the right to freedom of peaceful assembly and to freedom of association with others, including the right to form and to join trade unions for the protection of his interests.

2. No restrictions shall be placed on the exercise of these rights other than such as are prescribed by law and are necessary in a democratic society in the interests of national security or public safety, for the prevention of disorder or crime, for the protection of health or morals or for the protection of the rights and freedoms of others. This Article shall not prevent the imposition of lawful restrictions on the exercise of these rights by members of the armed forces, of the police or of the administration of the State.

Article 12

Right to marry

Men and women of marriageable age have the right to marry and to found a family, according to the national laws governing the exercise of this right.

Article 14

Prohibition of discrimination

The enjoyment of the rights and freedoms set forth in this Convention shall be secured without discrimination on any ground such as sex, race, colour, language, religion, political or other opinion, national or social origin, association with a national minority, property, birth or other status.

Article 16

Restrictions on political activity of aliens

Nothing in Articles 10, 11 and 14 shall be regarded as preventing the High Contracting Parties from imposing restrictions on the political activity of aliens.

Article 17

Prohibition of abuse of rights

Nothing in this Convention may be interpreted as implying for any State, group or person any right to engage in any activity or perform any act aimed at the destruction of any of the rights and freedoms set forth herein or at their limitation to a greater extent than is provided for in the Convention.

Article 18

Limitation on use of restrictions on rights

The restrictions permitted under this Convention to the said rights and freedoms shall not be applied for any purpose other than those for which they have been prescribed.

PART II

THE FIRST PROTOCOL

Article 1

Protection of property

Every natural or legal person is entitled to the peaceful enjoyment of his possessions. No one shall be deprived of his possessions except in the public interest and subject to the conditions provided for by law and by the general principles of international law.

The preceding provisions shall not, however, in any way impair the right of a State to enforce such laws as it deems necessary to control the use of property in accordance with the general interest or to secure the payment of taxes or other contributions or penalties.

Article 2

Right to education

No person shall be denied the right to education. In the exercise of any functions which it assumes in relation to education and to teaching, the State shall respect the right of parents to ensure such education and teaching in conformity with their own religious and philosophical convictions.

Article 3

Right to free elections

The High Contracting Parties undertake to hold free elections at reasonable intervals by secret ballot, under conditions which will ensure the free expression of the opinion of the people in the choice of the legislature.

PART III

THE SIXTH PROTOCOL

Article 1

Abolition of the death penalty

The death penalty shall be abolished. No one shall be condemned to such penalty or executed.

Article 2

Death penalty in time of war

A State may make provision in its law for the death penalty in respect of acts committed in time of war or of imminent threat of war; such penalty shall be applied only in the instances laid down in the law and in accordance with its provisions. The State shall communicate to the Secretary General of the Council of Europe the relevant provisions of that law.

Section 10

SCHEDULE 2

REMEDIAL ORDERS

Orders

1.—(1) A remedial order may—

    (a) contain such incidental, supplemental, consequential or transitional provision as the person making it considers appropriate;

    (b) be made so as to have effect from a date earlier than that on which it is made,

    (c) make provision for the delegation of specific functions;

    (d) make different provision for different cases.

(2) The power conferred by sub-paragraph (1)(a) includes—

    (a) power to amend primary legislation (including primary legislation other than that which contains the incompatible provision); and

    (b) power to amend or revoke subordinate legislation (including subordinate legislation other than that which contains the incompatible provision).

(3) A remedial order may be made so as to have the same extent as the legislation which it affects.

(4) No person is to be guilty of an offence solely as a result of the retrospective effect of a remedial order.

Procedure

2. No remedial order may be made unless—

    (a) a draft of the order has been approved by a resolution of each House of Parliament made after the end of the period of 60 days beginning with the day on which the draft was laid; or

    (b) it is declared in the order that it appears to the person making it that, because of the urgency of the matter, it is necessary to make the order without a draft being so approved.

Orders laid in draft

3.—(1) No draft may be laid under paragraph 2(a) unless—

    (a) the person proposing to make the order has laid before Parliament a document which contains a draft of the proposed order and the required information; and

(b) the period of 60 days, beginning with the day on which the document required by this sub-paragraph was laid, has ended.

(2) If representations have been made during that period, the draft laid under paragraph 2(a) must be accompanied by a statement containing—

(a) a summary of the representations; and

(b) if, as a result of the representations, the proposed order has been changed, details of the changes.

Appendix B

Congenital Disabilities (Civil Liability) Act 1976 (1976 c 28)

1 Civil liability to child born disabled

(1) If a child is born disabled as the result of such an occurrence before its birth as is mentioned in subsection (2) below, and a person (other than the child's own mother) is under this section answerable to the child in respect of the occurrence, the child's disabilities are to be regarded as damage resulting from the wrongful act of that person and actionable accordingly at the suit of the child.

(2) An occurrence to which this section applies is one which—
   (a) affected either parent of the child in his or her ability to have a normal, healthy child; or
   (b) affected the mother during her pregnancy, or affected her or the child in the course of its birth, so that the child is born with disabilities which would not otherwise have been present.

(3) Subject to the following subsections, a person (here referred to as 'the defendant') is answerable to the child if he was liable in tort to the parent or would, if sued in due time, have been so; and it is no answer that there could not have been such liability because the parent suffered no actionable injury, if there was a breach of legal duty which, accompanied by injury, would have given rise to the liability.

(4) In the case of an occurrence preceding the time of conception, the defendant is not answerable to the child if at that time either or both of the parents knew the risk of their child being born disabled (that is to say, the particular risk created by the occurrence); but should it be the child's father who is the defendant, this subsection does not apply if he knew of the risk and the mother did not.

(5) The defendant is not answerable to the child, for anything he did or omitted to do when responsible in a professional capacity for treating or advising the parent, if he took reasonable care having due regard to then received professional opinion applicable to the particular class of case; but this does not mean that he is answerable only because he departed from received opinion.

(6) Liability to the child under this section may be treated as having been excluded or limited by contract made with the parent affected, to the same extent and subject to the same restrictions as liability in the parent's own case; and a contract term which could have been set up by the defendant in an action by the parent, so as to exclude or limit his liability to him or her, operates in the defendant's favour to the same, but no greater, extent in an action under this section by the child.

(7) If in the child's action under this section it is shown that the parent affected shared the responsibility for the child being born disabled, the damages are to be reduced to such extent as the court thinks just and equitable having regard to the extent of the parent's responsibility.

[1A Extension of Section 1 to cover infertility treatments

(1) In any case where—

(a) a child carried by a woman as the result of the placing in her of an embryo or of sperm and eggs or her artificial insemination is born disabled,

(b) the disability results from an act or omission in the course of the selection, or the keeping or use outside the body, of the embryo carried by her or of the gametes used to bring about the creation of the embryo, and

(c) a person is under this section answerable to the child in respect of the act or omission,

the child's disabilities are to be regarded as damage resulting from the wrongful act of that person and actionable accordingly at the suit of the child.

(2) Subject to subsection (3) below and the applied provisions of Section 1 of this Act, a person (here referred to as 'the defendant') is answerable to the child if he was liable in tort to one or both of the parents (here referred to as 'the parent or parents concerned') or would, if sued in due time, have been so; and it is no answer that there could not have been such liability because the parent or parents concerned suffered no actionable injury, if there was a breach of legal duty which, accompanied by injury, would have given rise to the liability.

(3) The defendant is not under this section answerable to the child if at the time the embryo, or the sperm and eggs, are placed in the woman or the time of her insemination (as the case may be) either or both of the parents knew the risk of their child being born disabled (that is to say, the particular risk created by the act or omission).

(4) Subsections (5) to (7) of Section 1 of this Act apply for the purposes of this section as they apply for the purposes of that but as if references to the parent or the parent affected were references to the parent or parents concerned.]

2   Liability of woman driving when pregnant

A woman driving a motor vehicle when she knows (or ought reasonably to know) herself to be pregnant is to be regarded as being under the same duty to take care for the safety of her unborn child as the law imposes on her with respect to the safety of other people; and if in consequence of her breach of that duty her child is born with disabilities which would not otherwise have been present, those disabilities are to be regarded as damage resulting from her wrongful act and actionable accordingly at the suit of the child.

3   Disabled birth due to radiation

(1) Section 1 of this Act does not affect the operation of the Nuclear Installations Act 1965 as to liability for, and compensation in respect of, injury or damage caused by occurrences involving nuclear matter or the emission of ionising radiations.

(2) For the avoidance of doubt anything which—
    (a) affects a man in his ability to have a normal, healthy child; or
    (b) affects a woman in that ability, or so affects her when she is pregnant that her child is born with disabilities which would not otherwise have been present,
is an injury for the purposes of that Act.

(3) If a child is born disabled as the result of an injury to either of its parents caused in breach of a duty imposed by any of Sections 7 to 11 of that Act (nuclear site licensees and others to secure that nuclear incidents do not cause injury to persons, etc), the child's disabilities are to be regarded under the subsequent provisions of that Act (compensation and other matters) as injuries caused on the same occasion, and by the same breach of duty, as was the injury to the parent.

(4) As respects compensation to the child, Section 13(6) of that Act (contributory fault of person injured by radiation) is to be applied as if the reference there to fault were to the fault of the parent.

(5) Compensation is not payable in the child's case if the injury to the parent preceded the time of the child's conception and at that time either or both of the parents knew the risk of their child being born disabled (that is to say, the particular risk created by the injury).

4 Interpretation and other supplementary provisions

(1) References in this Act to a child being born disabled or with disabilities are to its being born with any deformity, disease or abnormality, including predisposition (whether or not susceptible of immediate prognosis) to physical or mental defect in the future.

(2) In this Act—
    (a) 'born' means born alive (the moment of a child's birth being when it first has a life separate from its mother), and 'birth' has a corresponding meaning; and
    (b) 'motor vehicle' means a mechanically propelled vehicle intended or adapted for use on roads
[and references to embryos shall be construed in accordance with Section 1 of the Human Fertilisation and Embryology Act 1990].

(3) Liability to a child under Section 1 [1A] or 2 of this Act is to be regarded—
    (a) as respects all its incidents and any matters arising or to arise out of it; and
    (b) subject to any contrary context or intention, for the purpose of construing references in enactments and documents to personal or bodily injuries and cognate matters,
as liability for personal injuries sustained by the child immediately after its birth.

(4) No damages shall be recoverable under [any] of those sections in respect of any loss of expectation of life, nor shall any such loss be taken into account in the compensation payable in respect of a child under the Nuclear Installations Act 1965 as extended by Section 3, unless (in either case) the child lives for at least 48 hours.

[(4A) In any case where a child carried by a woman as the result of the placing in her of an embryo or of sperm and eggs or her artificial insemination is born disabled, any reference in Section 1 of this Act to a parent includes a reference to a person who would be a parent but for Sections 27 to 29 of the Human Fertilisation and Embryology Act 1990.]

(5) This Act applies in respect of births after (but not before) its passing, and in respect of any such birth it replaces any law in force before its passing, whereby a person could be liable to a child in respect of disabilities with which it might be born; but in Section 1(3) of this Act the expression 'liable in tort' does not include any reference to liability by virtue of this Act, or to liability by virtue of any such law.

(6) References to the Nuclear Installations Act 1965 are to that Act as amended; and for the purposes of Section 28 of that Act (power by Order in Council to extend the Act to territories outside the United Kingdom) Section 3 of this Act is to be treated as if it were a provision of that Act.

5 Crown application

This Act binds the Crown.

6 Citation and extent

(1) This Act may be cited as the Congenital Disabilities (Civil Liability) Act 1976.

(2) This Act extends to Northern Ireland but not to Scotland.

Schedules 1 and 2 of Data Protection Act 1998

Data Protection Act 1998

(b) the contract requires the data processor to comply with obligations equivalent to those imposed on a data controller by the seventh principle.

The eighth principle

13. An adequate level of protection is one which is adequate in all the circumstances of the case, having regard in particular to—

(a) the nature of the personal data,

(b) the country or territory of origin of the information contained in the data,

(c) the country or territory of final destination of that information,

(d) the purposes for which and period during which the data are intended to be processed,

(e) the law in force in the country or territory in question,

(f) the international obligations of that country or territory,

(g) any relevant codes of conduct or other rules which are enforceable in that country or territory (whether generally or by arrangement in particular cases), and

(h) any security measures taken in respect of the data in that country or territory.

14. The eighth principle does not apply to a transfer falling within any paragraph of Schedule 4, except in such circumstances and to such extent as the Secretary of State may by order provide.

15.—(1) Where—

(a) in any proceedings under this Act any question arises as to whether the requirement of the eighth principle as to an adequate level of protection is met in relation to the transfer of any personal data to a country or territory outside the European Economic Area, and

(b) a Community finding has been made in relation to transfers of the kind in question, that question is to be determined in accordance with that finding.

(2) In sub-paragraph (1) 'Community finding' means a finding of the European Commission, under the procedure provided for in Article 31(2) of the Data Protection Directive, that a country or territory outside the European Economic Area does, or

does not, ensure an adequate level of protection within the meaning of Article 25(2) of the Directive.

Section 4(3)   SCHEDULE 2

Conditions Relevant for Purposes of the First Principle: Processing of any Personal Data

1. The data subject has given his consent to the processing.

2. The processing is necessary—

(a) for the performance of a contract to which the data subject is a party, or

(b) for the taking of steps at the request of the data subject with a view to entering into a contract.

3. The processing is necessary for compliance with any legal obligation to which the data controller is subject, other than an obligation imposed by contract.

4. The processing is necessary in order to protect the vital interests of the data subject.

5. The processing is necessary—

(a) for the administration of justice,

(b) for the exercise of any functions conferred on any person by or under any enactment,

(c) for the exercise of any functions of the Crown, a Minister of the Crown or a government department, or

(d) for the exercise of any other functions of a public nature exercised in the public interest by any person.

6.—(1) The processing is necessary for the purposes of legitimate interests pursued by the data controller or by the third party or parties to whom the data are disclosed, except where the processing is unwarranted in any particular case by reason of prejudice to the rights and freedoms or legitimate interests of the data subject.

(2) The Secretary of State may by order specify particular circumstances in which this condition is, or is not, to be taken to be satisfied.

Section 4(3)   SCHEDULE 3

Conditions Relevant for Purposes of the First Principle: Processing of Sensitive Personal Data

1. The data subject has given his explicit consent to the processing of the personal data.

2.—(1) The processing is necessary for the purposes of exercising or performing any right or obligation which is conferred or imposed by law on the data controller in connection with employment.

(2) The Secretary of State may by order—

(a) exclude the application of sub-paragraph (1) in such cases as may be specified, or

(b) provide that, in such cases as may be specified, the condition in subparagraph (1) is not to be regarded as satisfied unless such further conditions as may be specified in the order are also satisfied.

3. The processing is necessary—

(a) in order to protect the vital interests of the data subject or another person, in a case where—
(i) consent cannot be given by or on behalf of the data subject, or
(ii) the data controller cannot reasonably be expected to obtain the consent of the data subject, or

(b) in order to protect the vital interests of another person, in a case where consent by or on behalf of the data subject has been unreasonably withheld.

4. The processing—

(a) is carried out in the course of its legitimate activities by any body or association which—
(i) is not established or conducted for profit, and
(ii) exists for political, philosophical, religious or trade-union purposes,

(b) is carried out with appropriate safeguards for the rights and freedoms of data subjects,

(c) relates only to individuals who either are members of the body or association or have regular contact with it in connection with its purposes, and

(d) does not involve disclosure of the personal data to a third party without the consent of the data subject.

5. The information contained in the personal data has been made public as a result of steps deliberately taken by the data subject.

6. The processing—

(a) is necessary for the purpose of, or in connection with, any legal proceedings (including prospective legal proceedings),

(b) is necessary for the purpose of obtaining legal advice, or

(c) is otherwise necessary for the purposes of establishing, exercising or defending legal rights.

7.—(1) The processing is necessary—

(a) for the administration of justice,

(b) for the exercise of any functions conferred on any person by or under an enactment, or

(c) for the exercise of any functions of the Crown, a Minister of the Crown or a government department.

(2) The Secretary of State may by order—

(a) exclude the application of sub-paragraph (1) in such cases as may be specified, or

(b) provide that, in such cases as may be specified, the condition in subparagraph (1) is not to be regarded as satisfied unless such further conditions as may be specified in the order are also satisfied.

8.—(1) The processing is necessary for medical purposes and is undertaken by—

(a) a health professional, or

(b) a person who in the circumstances owes a duty of confidentiality which is equivalent to that which would arise if that person were a health professional.

(2) In this paragraph 'medical purposes' includes the purposes of preventative medicine, medical diagnosis, medical research, the provision of care and treatment and the management of healthcare services.

9.—(1) The processing—

(a) is of sensitive personal data consisting of information as to racial or ethnic origin,

(b) is necessary for the purpose of identifying or keeping under review the existence or absence of equality of opportunity or treatment between persons of different racial or ethnic origins, with a view to enabling such equality to be promoted or maintained, and

(c) is carried out with appropriate safeguards for the rights and freedoms of data subjects.

(2) The Secretary of State may by order specify circumstances in which processing falling within sub-paragraph (1)(a) and (b) is, or is not, to be taken for the purposes of sub-paragraph (1)(c) to be carried out with appropriate safeguards for the rights and freedoms of data subjects.

10. The personal data are processed in circumstances specified in an order made by the Secretary of State for the purposes of this paragraph.

Appendix D

Draft Order for the new Nursing and Midwifery Council

Draft legislation for the Nursing and Midwifery Council to be brought into force April 2002

The Government commissioned an independent review of the Nurses, Midwives and Health Visitors Act 1997 from JM Consulting Ltd. Its report was published in February 1999. The Government accepted its main recommendations that the UKCC and the 4 National Boards should be replaced by a smaller, more strategic Nursing and Midwifery Council with stronger lay input and ultimate ownership of the setting and monitoring of standards of training and conduct. The Health Act 1999 paved the way for the abolition of the United Kingdom Central Council for Nursing Midwifery and Health Visiting and its replacement by a new Nursing and Midwifery Council. Following a further consultation exercise draft Orders were published in April 2001. Following a consultation period they will be debated in Parliament and will, subject to any amendments, come into force in April 2002.

The significant changes to original proposals resulting from the consultation, are shown below.

A President of Council will be elected by Members. (The first was appointed following open competition.)

Members: each professional member is to have an alternate, entitled to attend and vote in his absence. To ensure the interests of the patients and public are genuinely represented, lay members cannot include current or former registrants.

The Midwifery Committee will have a professional majority and consultation rights on all matters affecting midwifery.

Fitness to Practise Committees: no one can serve on more than one committee at the same time; at least 3 panellists must hear each individual case; only the chair need be a Council member, there must be at least one professional from the same field as the respondent and one lay person. The Human Rights Act 1998 has been taken into account in the stipulation that statutory committees have membership independent from each other and in ensuring adequate professional input to hearings.

Functions and expenses. There are wider powers to pay fees and allowances to members of Council and its committees

Privy Council: the NMC is to be accountable to the Privy Council rather than the Secretary of State.

Inquiries: the Government is to have the power to set up inquiries into the Council's performance.

The appointments of the President, members and the Alternates were announced by the Department of Health in April 2001.

The following is a summary of the provisions of the draft Orders

Part I   General

Article 1 and 2 Citation commencement and interpretation

Part II   Nursing and Midwifery Council (NMC)

Article 3 The principle functions of the NMC shall be to establish from time to time standards of education, training, conduct and performance of nurses and midwives. Other functions may be conferred by this Order or by the Privy Council (after consultation with the Council)

In performing its functions, the Council shall:

(a)   Treat the health and well-being of persons using or needing the services of registrants as paramount;

(b)   Have proper regard to the interests of all registrants and prospective registrants and persons referred to in sub-paragraph (a) in each of the countries of the United Kingdom and to any differing considerations applying to the professions to which this Order applies and to groups within them;

(c)   Cooperate wherever reasonably practicable with:
     i.   employers and prospective employers of registrants,
     ii.   persons who provide, assess or fund education or training for registrants or prospective registrants, or who propose to do so,
     iii. persons who are responsible for regulating or coordinating the regulation of other health and social care professionals, or of those who carry out activities in connection with services provided by those professions or the professions regulated under this Order.

Four Committees, known as the statutory committees, of the Council shall be set up:

Investigating Committee

Conduct and Competence Committee

Health Committee

Midwifery Committee

(The Investigating Committee, the Conduct and Competence Committee and the Health Committee are also referred to as the 'Practice Committees'.)

The Council may establish other committees to discharge its functions and can delegate functions to them, other than any power to make rules.

The Council shall inform and educate registrants and the public about its work.

Before establishing any standards or giving guidance the Council shall consult representatives of any group of persons it considers appropriate including, as it sees fit:

(a) representatives of registrants or classes of registrants

(b) employers of registrants

(c) users of the services of registrants; and

(d) persons providing, assessing or funding education or training for registrants and potential registrants.

The Council shall publish any standards it establishes and any guidance it gives.

Part III   Registration

Article 4 The Council shall appoint a Registrar to hold office for such period and on such terms as the Council may determine and who shall have such functions as the Council may direct.

Article 5 The Council shall establish and maintain a register of qualified nurses and midwives. The Council shall from time to time establish the standards of proficiency necessary to be admitted to the different parts of the Register being standards it considers necessary for safe and effective practice under that part of the Register. The Register shall show, in relation to each registrant, such address and other details as the Council may prescribe.

Article 6 The Register may be divided into such parts as the Privy Council may by order determine, on a proposal by the Council or otherwise.

Each part shall have a designated title indicative of different qualifications and different kinds of education or training and a registered professional is entitled to use the title corresponding to the part of the register in which he is registered.

Powers of the Privy Council, after consultation with the Council, in relation to the Register are outlined.

Article 8 The Council shall make the register available for inspection by members of the public at all reasonable times and shall publish the register in such manner and at such times as it considers appropriate.

Article 9 A person seeking admission to a part of the register shall be entitled to be registered in that part if the application is made in the prescribed form and manner and the applicant:

(a) satisfies the Registrar that he holds an approved qualification awarded:
  (i) within such period not exceeding five years, ending with the date of the application, as may be prescribed; or
  (ii) before the prescribed period mentioned above and he has met such requirements as to additional education, training, and experience as the Council may specify under article 19(3)

(b) satisfies the Registrar that he meets the Council's prescribed requirements as to good health and good character; and

(c) has paid the prescribed fee.

Article 10 Provisions for renewal of registration and readmission require the applicant to satisfy the Registrar, in addition to other requirements, that he has met any prescribed requirements for continuing professional development within the prescribed time.

Article 11 Visiting EEA nurses and midwives are deemed to be registered.

Part IV   Education and Training

Article 15 The Council shall from time to time establish:

(a) the standards of education and training necessary to achieve the standards of proficiency it has established under Article 5(2)

(b) the requirements to be satisfied for admission to such education and training which may include requirements as to good health and good character.

These standards shall be set out in rules made by the Council and shall include such matters as the outcomes to be achieved by that education and training.

Article 16 The Council may appoint persons (Visitors) to visit any place at which any relevant education and training, examinations or test of competence is given or to be given.

Article 17 covers the information which the Council must give to any institution providing the education, training or test of competence.

Article 18 covers the refusal or withdrawal of approval of courses, qualifications and institutions.

Article 19 The Council may make rules requiring registered nurses and midwives to undertake such continuing professional development as it shall specify in standards. The rules may, in particular, make provision with respect to registrants who fail to comply with any requirements of the rules including provision for their registration to cease to have effect.

Article 20 The National Assembly for Wales may create or designate a body with which the Council may enter into any such arrangements as are referred to in relation to the approval of courses, qualifications and institutions.

Part V Fitness to Practise

Article 21

(1) The Council shall
   (a) establish and keep under review the standards of conduct, performance and ethics expected of registrants and prospective registrants and give them such guidance on these matters as it sees fit; and
   (b) establish and keep under review effective arrangements to protect the public from persons who are not fit to practise as nurses or midwives.

(2) The Council may also from time to time give guidance to registrants, employers and such other persons as it thinks appropriate in respect of standards for the education and training, supervision and performance of those providing services in connection with services provided by registrants.

(3) The Council shall, before establishing any standards mentioned in paragraph (1) consult the Conduct and Competence Committee in addition to the persons mentioned in Article 3(13).

Article 22 applies where any allegation is made against a registered person to the effect that:

(a) his fitness to practice is impaired by reason of:
   (i) misconduct
   (ii) lack of competence
   (iii) a conviction or caution in the UK for a criminal offence; or a conviction elsewhere for an offence, which if committed in England and Wales, would constitute a criminal offence,
   (iv) his physical or mental health, or
   (v) a determination by a body in the UK responsible under any enactment for the regulation of a health or social care profession to the effect that he is unfit to practise that profession, or a determination by a licensing body elsewhere to the same effect;
(b) an entry in the register relating to him has been fraudulently procured or incorrectly made.

A procedure is laid down for dealing with such allegations.

Articles 23 and 24 cover the appointment and function of screeners.

Article 25 The Investigating Committee shall investigate any allegation referred under Articles 22 and 24. The procedure to be followed is set out.

Article 26 The Conduct and Competence Committee, after consultation with the other Practice Committees, shall

(a) advise the Council on:
   (i)   the performance of the Council's functions in relation to standards of conduct, performance and ethics expected of registered professionals;
   (ii) requirements as to good character and good health to be met by registrants and prospective registrants, and
   (iii) the protection of the public from persons who are unfit to practise and

(b) consider:
   (i) any allegation referred to it by the Council, Screeners, the Investigating Committee or the Health Committee and
   (ii) any application for restoration referred to it by the Registrar.

Article 27 The Health Committee shall consider any allegation referred to it by the Council, Screeners, the Investigating Committee or the Conduct and Competence Committee and any application for restoration referred to it by the Registrar.

Article 28 sets out the procedure to be followed by the Health Committee and the Conduct and Competence Committee.

Article 29 covers interim orders which can be made by a Practice Committee to suspend a person's registration in specified circumstances.

Article 30 sets out the procedural rules for an investigation of allegations.

Article 31 covers the provisions for restoration to the register of persons who have been struck off.

Article 32 covers the appointment of legal assessors.

Article 33 covers the appointment of medical assessors.

Article 34 covers the appointment of registered professionals as registrant assessors with the function of giving advice on professional practice.

Part VI   Appeals

Articles 35–37 cover the appeal process to a Nursing and Midwifery Independent Appeals Tribunal.

Part VII   Visiting EEA Nurses and Midwives

Article 38 makes provision for the definition of EEA nurses and midwives and rules relating to their practice in the UK.

Part VIII   Midwifery

Article 39

(1) The role of the Midwifery Committee shall be to advise the Council, at the Council's request or otherwise, on any matters affecting midwifery.

(2) The Council shall consult the Midwifery Committee on the exercise of its functions in so far as it affects midwifery including any proposal to make rules under Article 40.

Article 40

(1) The Council shall by rules regulate the practice of midwifery and the rules may in particular:
    (a) determine the circumstances in which and the procedure by means of which a midwife may be suspended from practice;
    (b) require midwives to give notice of their intention to practise to the local supervising authority (LSA) for the area in which they intend to practise;
    (c) require midwives to attend courses of instruction in accordance with the rules.

Article 41 Each LSA shall:

    (a) exercise general supervision in accordance with the rules made under Article 40 over all midwives practising in its area;
    (b) where it appears to it that the fitness to practise of a midwife in its area is impaired, report it to the Council; and
    (c) have power in accordance with the Council's rules to suspend a midwife from practise.

(2) The Council may prescribe the qualifications of persons who may be appointed by the LSA to exercise supervision over midwives in its area, and no one shall be so appointed who is not qualified.

(3) The Council may by rules from time to time establish standards for the exercise by LSAs of their functions and may give guidance to LSAs on these matters.

Part IX   Offences

Article 42 Offence in respect of falsely claiming registration with intent to deceive, or falsely procuring registration.

Article 43

(1) A person other than a registered midwife or a registered medical practitioner shall not attend a woman in childbirth.

(2) Paragraph (1) does not apply:
  (a) where the attention is given in a case of sudden or urgent necessity; or
  (b) in the case of a person who, while undergoing training with a view to becoming a medical practitioner or to becoming a midwife, attends a woman in childbirth as part of a course of practical instruction in midwifery recognised by the Council or the General Medical Council.

Part X   Miscellaneous

Articles 44–50 cover powers of the Privy Council, and its approval of Rules and Orders, its exercise of powers and its default powers, annual reports to be provided by the Council and the finances and accounts of the Council.

Article 51 The Secretary of State may cause an inquiry to be held into any matter connected with the exercise by the Council of its functions.

Schedule 1 The Nursing and Midwifery Council and the Statutory Committees, their membership, tenure, the President (to be appointed by the members of the Council, after the first one appointed by the Secretary of State), Council rules on procedure, Powers of the Council, and the membership and procedures for the statutory committees.

Schedule 2 Transitional Provisions.

Schedule 3 Interpretation.

Glossary

accusatorial system of court proceedings where the two sides contest the issues (contrast with inquisitorial).

Act of Parliament, statute.

actionable per se a court action where the plaintiff does not have to show loss, damage or harm to obtain compensation, e.g. an action for trespass to the person.

actus reus the physical elements that make up the definition of a crime.

adversarial the approach adopted in an accusatorial system.

advocate a person who pleads for another: it could be paid and professional, such as a barrister or solicitor, or it could be a lay advocate either paid or unpaid.

affidavit a statement given under oath.

approved social worker a social worker who is qualified for the purposes of the Mental Health Act 1983.

arrestable offence an offence defined in section 24 of the Police and Criminal Evidence Act 1984 which gives to the citizen the power of arrest in certain circumstances without a warrant.

assault a threat of unlawful contact (trespass to the person).

bailee a person who undertakes to care for the property of another.

bailment the transfer of property from a bailor to a bailee.

bailor one who leaves property in the care of another.

balance of probabilities the standard of proof in civil proceedings.

barrister a lawyer qualified to take a case in court.

battery an unlawful touching (see trespass to the person).

bench the magistrates, Justice of the Peace.

Bolam Test the test laid down by Judge McNair in the case of *Bolam* v. *Friern HMC* on the standard of care expected of a professional in cases of alleged negligence.

burden of proof the duty of a party to litigation to establish the facts, or in criminal proceedings the duty of the prosecution to establish both the *actus reus* and the *mens rea*.

case citation the reference to an earlier reported case made possible because of the reference system, e.g. 1981 1 All ER 267 means the first volume of the All England Reports for 1981 at page 267, which is the reference for the case of *Whitehouse* v.

Jordan. Where Whitehouse is the claimant, Jordan the defendant and 'v' stands for versus, i.e. against. Other law reports include:

AC   Appeals Court
QB   Queens Bench Division
WLR   Weekly Law Reports.

cause of action the facts that entitle a person to sue.

certiorari an action taken to challenge an administrative or judicial decision (literally: to make more certain).

civil action proceedings brought in the civil courts. **Civil** refers to matters which are non-criminal, i.e. they pertain to the civil courts.

civil wrong an act or omission that can be pursued in the civil courts by the person who has suffered the wrong (see **torts**).

claimant a person who brings an action in the civil courts (term now used instead of plaintiff).

committal proceedings hearings before the magistrates to decide if a person should be committed to the crown court for trial.

common law law derived from the decisions of judges, case law, judge-made law.

conditional fee system a system whereby client and lawyer can agree that payment of fees is dependent upon the outcome of the court action; also known as 'no win, no fee'.

conditions terms of a contract (see **warranties**).

constructive knowledge knowledge that can be obtained from the circumstances.

continuous service the length of service that an employee must have served in order to be entitled to receive certain statutory or contractual rights.

contract an agreement enforceable in law.

contract for services an agreement, enforceable in law whereby one party provides services, not being employment, in return for payment or other consideration from the other.

contract of service a contract for employment.

coroner a person appointed to hold an inquiry (inquest) into a death in unexpected or unusual circumstances.

counter-offer a response to an offer that suggests different terms and is therefore counted as an offer not an acceptance.

criminal wrong an act or omission that can be pursued in the criminal courts.

committal proceedings the hearing that takes place in the Magistrates Court to determine if the case should go to the Crown Court for trial.

damage harm that has occurred.

damages compensation payable as the result of a tort or civil wrong.

declaration a ruling by the court, setting out the legal situation.

dissenting judgment a judge who disagrees with the decision of the majority of judges.

distinguished (of cases) the rules of precedent require judges to follow decisions of judges in previous cases, where these are binding upon them. However, in some circumstances, it is possible to come to a different decision because the facts of the earlier case are not comparable to the case now being heard, and therefore the earlier decision can be 'distinguished'.

ex gratia without admitting liability (usually refers to a payment by a prospective defendant).

expert witness evidence given by a person whose general opinion based on training or experience is relevant to some of the issues in dispute.

frustration (of contracts) the ending of a contract by operation of law, because of the existence of an event not contemplated by the parties when they made the contract, e.g. imprisonment, death, blindness.

Re F **ruling** a professional who acts in the best interests of an incompetent person who is incapable of giving consent, does not act unlawfully if he follows the accepted standard of care according to the Bolam Test.

guardian *ad litem* a person with a social work and child care background who is appointed to ensure that the court is fully informed of the relevant facts that relate to a child and that the wishes and feelings of the child are clearly established. The appointment is made from a panel set up by the local authority.

HSC Health Circular issued by Department of Health.

hearsay evidence that has been learnt from another person.

hierarchy the recognised status of courts that results in lower courts following the decisions of higher courts (see **precedent**). Thus decisions of the House of Lords must be followed by all lower courts unless they can be distinguished (see above).

indictable can be tried on an indictment.

indictment a written accusation against a person, charging him with a serious crime, triable by jury.

informal of a patient who has entered hospital without any statutory requirements.

injunction an order of the court restraining a person.

inquisitorial a system of justice whereby the truth is revealed by an inquiry into the facts conducted by the judge, e.g. coroner's court.

invitation to treat the early stages in negotiating a contract, e.g. an advertisement, or letter expressing interest. An invitation to treat will often precede an offer that, when accepted, leads to the formation of an agreement which, if there is consideration and an intention to create legal relations, will be binding.

judiciary judges.

judicial review an application to the High Court for a judicial or administrative decision to be reviewed and an appropriate order made, e.g. declaration.

justice of the peace (*JP*) a lay magistrate, i.e. not legally qualified, who hears summary (minor) offences and sometimes indictable (serious) offences in the magistrates court in a group of three (bench).

litigation civil proceedings.

magistrate a person (see **justice of the peace** and **stipendiary**) who hears summary (minor) offences or indictable offences that can be heard in the magistrates court.

mens rea the mental element required in most crimes. Crimes that do not require this mental element are known as crimes of strict liability.

next friend a person who brings a court action on behalf of a minor.

offer a proposal made by a party that, if accepted, can lead to a contract. It often follows an invitation to treat.

Ombudsman a commissioner (e.g. health, local government) appointed by the government to hear complaints.

plaintiff former term used for one who brings an action in the civil courts; **claimant** now used.

plea in mitigation a formal statement to the court aimed at reducing the sentence to be pronounced by the judge.

practice direction guidance issued by the head of the court to which they relate on the procedure to be followed.

precedent a decision that may have to be followed in a subsequent court hearing (see **hierarchy**).

prima facie at first sight, or sufficient evidence brought by one party to require the other party to provide a defence.

privilege in relation to evidence, being able to refuse to disclose it to the court.

privity the relationship that exists between parties as the result of a legal agreement.

professional misconduct conduct unworthy of a nurse, midwife or health visitor.

proof evidence that secures the establishment of a plaintiff's or prosecution's or defendant's case.

prosecution the pursuing of criminal offences in court.

quantum the amount of compensation, or the monetary value of a claim.

reasonable doubt to secure a conviction in criminal proceedings, the prosecution must establish beyond reasonable doubt the guilt of the accused.

res ipsa loquitur the thing speaks for itself.

rescission where a contract is ended by the order of a court, or by the cancellation of the contract by one party entitled in law to do so.

solicitor a lawyer who is qualified on the register held by the Law Society.

standard of proof the level that the party who has the burden of proof must satisfy, e.g. on a balance of probabilities or beyond all reasonable doubt.

statute law an Act of Parliament cited by year and chapter, e.g. Congenital Disabilities Act 1976 Ch.28.

stipendiary magistrate a legally qualified magistrate who is paid (i.e. has a stipend).

strict liability liability for a criminal act where the mental element does not have to be proved; in civil proceedings, liability without establishing negligence.

subpoena an order of the court requiring a person to appear as a witness (*subpoena ad testificandum*) or to bring records/documents (*subpoena duces tecum*).

summary offence a lesser offence that can be heard only by magistrates.

summary judgment a procedure whereby the claimant can obtain judgment without the defendant being permitted to defend the action.

tort a civil wrong excluding breach of contract. It includes: negligence, trespass (to the person, goods or land), nuisance, breach of statutory duty and defamation.

trespass to the person a wrongful direct interference with another person. Harm does not have to be proved.

trustee one who holds property in trust for another, e.g. has duties to care for it.

ultra vires outside the powers given by law (e.g. of a statutory body or company).

vicarious liability the liability of an employer for the wrongful acts of an employee committed whilst in the course of employment.

void is invalid or not legally binding.

voidable can be made void.

volenti non fit injuria to the willing there is no wrong; the voluntary assumption of risk.

ward of court a minor placed under the protection of the High Court, which assumes responsibility for him or her, and all decisions relating to his or her care must be made in accordance with the directions of the court.

warranties terms of a contract that are considered to be less important than the terms described as conditions: breach of a condition entitles the innocent party to see the contract as ended, i.e. repudiated by the other party; breach of warranties entitles the innocent party to claim damages.

Wednesbury principle the court will intervene to prevent or remedy abuses of power by public authorities if there is evidence of unreasonableness or perversity. Principle laid down by the Court of Appeal in the case of *Associated Provincial Picture House Ltd* v. *Wednesbury Corporation* [1948] 1 KB 233.

without prejudice without detracting from or without disadvantage to. The use of the phrase prevents the other party using the information to the prejudice of the one providing it.

writ formerly used to refer to a form of written command, e.g. the document that commences civil proceedings; term now used is **claim form**.

Recommended further reading

Appelbe, G.E. and Wingfield, J. (eds), *Dale and Appelbe's Pharmacy: Law and Ethics*, 5th edn, The Pharmaceutical Press, 1993

Beauchamp, T.L. and Childres, J.F., *Principles of Biomedical Ethics*, 3rd edn, Oxford University Press, 1989

Brazier, M., *Medicine, Patients and the Law*, Penguin, 1992

Brazier, M. (ed.), *Street on Torts*, Butterworth, 1993

Bristol Royal Infirmary Inquiry. *Learning from Bristol: The report of the public inquiry into children's heart surgery at the Bristol Royal Infirmary 1984–1995*. Command Paper CM5207, www.bristol-inquiry.org.uk

British Medical Association, *Medical Ethics Today*, BMJ Publishing, 1998

British Medical Association, *Consent, Rights and Choices in Health Care for Children and Young People*, BMA 2001

Campbell, A.V., *Moral Dilemmas in Medicine*, Churchill Livingstone, 1984

Card, R., *Card, Cross and Jones' Criminal Law*, 14th edn, Butterworths, 1998

Committee of Experts Advisory Group on AIDS, *Guidance for health care workers' protection against infection with HIV and Hepatitis*, HMSO, 1994

Department of Health, *AIDS/HIV Infected Health Care Workers*, April 1993

Denis, I.H., *The Law of Evidence*, Sweet and Maxwell, 1999

Dimond, B.C., *Accountability and the Nurse*, Distance Learning Pack, South Bank University, 1992

Dimond, B.C., *Patients' Rights, Responsibilities and the Nurse*, Central Health Studies, 2nd edn, Quay Publishing, 1999

Dimond, B.C., *Legal Aspects of Occupational Therapy*, Blackwell Scientific Publications, 1997

Dimond, B.C., *Legal Aspects of Child Health Care*, Mosby, 1996

Dimond, B.C., *Legal Aspects of Midwifery*, Books for Midwives Press, 1994

Dimond, B.C. and Barker, F., *Mental Health Law for Nurses*, Blackwell Science, 1996

Dimond, B.C., *Legal Aspects of Care in the Community*, Macmillan, 1997

Dimond, B.C., *Legal Aspects of Complementary Therapy Practice*, Churchill Livingstone, 1998

Dimond, B.C., *Legal Aspects of Physiotherapy*, Blackwell Science, 1999

Dimond, B.C., *Mental Health (Patients in the Community) Act 1995: An introductory text*, Mark Allen Publications, 1997

Ellis, N., *Employing Staff*, 5th edn, British Medical Journal, 1994

English National Board, *Preparation for Supervisors of Midwives*, Open Learning Programme, 1992

Faulder, C., *Whose Body Is It?*, Virago, 1985

Finch, John (ed.), *Speller's Law Relating to Hospitals*, 7th edn, Chapman and Hall Medical, 1994

Fletcher, N. and Holt, J., *Ethics law and nursing*

Gann, Robert, *The NHS A to Z*, 2nd edn, The Help for Health Trust, 1993

Glover, J., *Causing Death and Saving Lives*, Penguin, 1984

Glover, J., *What Sort of People Should There Be?*, Penguin, 1984

Ham, C., *The New National Health Service*, NAHAT, 1991

Harris, P., *An Introduction to Law*, 5th edn, Butterworths, 1997

Health and Safety Commission, *Management of Health and Safety at Work Regulations 1999 Approved Code of Practice and Guidance*, HMSO, 2000

Health and Safety Commission, *Manual Handling Regulations and Approved Code of Practice*, HMSO, 1992

Health and Safety Commission, *Guidelines on Manual Handling in the Health Services*, HMSO, 1992

Hepple, B.A. and Matthews, M.H., *Tort Cases and Materials*, 4th edn, Butterworths, 1991

Heywood Jones, I. (ed.), *The UKCC Code of Conduct: a critical guide*, Nursing Times Books, 1999

Hoggett, B., *Mental Health Law*, 3rd edn, Sweet and Maxwell, 1990

Howells, G. and Weatherill, S., *Consumer Protection Law*, Dartmouth Publishing, 1995

Hunt, G. and Wainwright, P. (eds), *Expanding the Role of the Nurse*, Blackwell Scientific Publications, 1994

Hurwitz, B., *Clinical Guidelines and the Law*, Radcliffe Medical Press, 1998

Ingman, T., *The English Legal Process*, 6th edn, Blackstone Publishing, 1996

Jones, M., *Medical Negligence*, Sweet and Maxwell, 1991

Jones, M. (ed. for *Nursing*) *Prescribing: Politics and Practice* Bailliere Tindal and RCN 1999.

Jones, R., *Mental Health Act Manual*, 6th edn, Sweet and Maxwell, 1999

Keenan, D., *Smith and Keenan's English Law*, 10th edn, Pitman Publishing, 1992

Kennedy, I. and Grubb, A., *Medical Law and Ethics*, 3rd edn, Butterworth, 2000

Kennedy, T., *Learning European Law*, Sweet and Maxwell, 1998

Kidner, R., *Blackstone's Statutes on Employment Law*, 3rd edn, Blackstone Press, 1993

Kloss, D., *Occupational Health Law*, 3rd edn, Blackwell Scientific Publications, 2000

Knight, B., *Legal Aspects of Medical Practice*, 5th edn, Churchill Livingstone, 1992

Mandelstam, M., *An A-Z of Community Care Law*, Jessica Kingsley Publishers, 1998

Markesinis, B.S. and Deakin, S.F., *Tort Law*, 4th edn, Clarendon Press, 1999

Mason, D. and Edwards, P., *Litigation: A Risk Management Guide for Midwives*, Royal College of Midwives, 1993

Mason, J.K. and McCall-Smith, A., *Law and Medical Ethics*, 4th edn, Butterworths, 1994

McHale, J., Fox, M., with Murphy, J., *Health Care Law*, Sweet and Maxwell, 1997

McHale, J., Tingle, J., and Peysner, J., *Law and Nursing*, Butterworth Heinemann, 1998

Miers, D. and Page, A., *Legislation*, 2nd edn, Sweet and Maxwell, 1990

Morgan, D. and Lee, R.G., *Human Fertilisation and Embryology Act 1990*, Blackstone Press, 1991

Montgomery, J., *Health Care Law*, Oxford University Press, 1997

National Association of Theatre Nurses, *The Role of the Nurse as First Assistant in the Operating Department*, 1993

Pearse, P. *et al.*, *Personal Data Protection in Health and Social Services*, Croom Helm, 1988

Pitt, G., *Employment Law*, 4th edn, Sweet and Maxwell, 2000

Pyne, R.H., *Professional Discipline in Nursing, Midwifery and Health Visiting*, 2nd edn, Blackwell Scientific Publications, 1991

Richards, P., *Law on Contract*, Financial Times and Pitman Publishing, 1999

Royal College of Midwives, *Examples of Effective Midwifery Management*, 1993

Royal College of Midwives, *The Midwife: Her Legal Status and Accountability*, 1993

Royal College of Nursing, *Focus on Restraint*, 2nd edn, 1992

Rowson, R., *An Introduction to Ethics for Nurses*, Scutari Press, 1990

Rumbold, G., *Ethics in Nursing Practice*, 2nd edn, Bailliere Tindall, 1993

Salvage, J., *Nurses at Risk: Guide to Health and Safety at Work*, Heinemann, 1988

Salvage, J. and Rogers, R., *Health and Safety and the Nurse*, Heinemann, 1988

Selwyn's *Law of Employment*, 8th edn, Butterworth, 1993

Selwyn's *Law of Safety at Work*, Butterworth, 1982

Sims, S., *Practical Approach to Civil Procedure*, 4th edn, Blackstone Press, 2000

Skegg, P.D.G., *Law, Ethics and Medicine*, 2nd edn, Oxford University Press, 1998

Smith, K. and Keenan, D., *English Law*, 10th edn, Pitman, 1992

Social Security Inspectorate, Department of Health, *No Longer Afraid: Safeguard of Older People in Domestic Settings*, HMSO, 1993

Speller's Law Relating to Hospitals, Finch, J. (ed.), 7th edn, Chapman and Hall Medical, 1994

Steiner, J., *Textbook on EC Law*, 3rd edn, Blackstone Press, 1992

Stone, J. and Matthews, J., *Complementary Medicine and the Law*, Oxford University Press, 1996

Thompson, R. and Thompson, B., *Dismissal: A basic introduction to your legal rights*, Robin Thompson and Partners and Brian Thompson and Partners, 1993

Thompson, R. and Thompson, B., *Equal Pay*, Robin Thompson and Partners and Brian Thompson and Partners, 1993

Thompson, R. and Thompson, B., *Health and Safety at Work*, Robin Thompson and Partners and Brian Thompson and Partners, 1993

Thompson, R. and Thompson, B., *Injuries at Work and Work-related Illnesses*, Robin Thompson and Partners and Brian Thompson and Partners, 1993

Thompson, R. and Thompson, B., *Women at Work*, Robin Thompson and Partners and Brian Thompson and Partners, 1993

Tingle, J. and Cribb, A. (eds), *Nursing Law and Ethics*, Blackwell Science, 1995

Tschudin, V. and Marks-Maran, D., *Ethics: A Primer for Nurses*, Bailliere Tindall, 1993

Vincent, C. *et al.*, *Medical Accidents*, Oxford University Press, 1993

Vincent, C. (ed.), *Clinical Risk Management*, BMJ, 1995

White, R., Carr, P., and Lowe, N., *A Guide to the Children Act 1989*, Butterworth, 1991

Wilkinson, R. and Caulfield, H., *The Human Rights Act a Practical Guide for Nurses*, Whurr Publishers, 2000

Young, Ann P., *Legal Problems in Nursing Practice*, Harper & Row, 1989

Young, Ann P., *Law and Professional Conduct in Nursing*, 2nd edn, Scutari Press, 1994

Zander, M., *Police and Criminal Evidence Act*, 3rd edn, Sweet and Maxwell, 1995

Reference should also be made to the many articles on different legal aspects of nursing, health visiting and midwifery practice that can be found in *Nursing Times, Nursing Standard, British Journal of Nursing, Senior Nurse, Professional Nurse, Practising Midwife, British Journal of Midwifery, Midwives Chronicle, Midwifery Matters, Midwife Community Care, Nursing the Elderly, Practice Nurse* and similar journals for registered practitioners in general. The *British Medical Journal*, the *Lancet* and the *Journal of Medical Ethics* and other medical journals also include articles on the legal and ethical issues that are of relevance to nurse practitioners. The Midwives Information and Resource Service (MIDIRS) provides an extremely useful guide to articles relevant to midwifery published in other journals (Institute of Child Health, Royal Hospital for Sick Children, St Michael's Hill, Bristol BS2 8BJ, Tel. 0272-251791).

A bibliography of general and specialist books on midwifery, nursing and medical books is available from Meditec, Nursing Book Service, York House, 26 Bourne Road, Colsterworth, Spalding, Lincs., NG33 5JE. Fax: 01775 571 1963

Index